Beginning VB.NET XML

Stewart Fraser
Steven Livingstone

wrox

Wrox Press Ltd. ®

Beginning VB.NET XML

Printing History
First published   November 2002

Published by Peer Information Inc.,
Arden House, 1102 Warwick Road, Acocks Green,
Birmingham, B27 6BH, UK
Printed in the United States
ISBN 1-86100-778-7

Trademark Acknowledgements

Wrox has endeavored to correctly render trademarks for all the companies and products mentioned in this book with the appropriate use of capitals. However, Wrox is unable to guarantee the accuracy of this information.

Credits

Authors
Stewart Fraser
Steven Livingstone

Additional Material
Brian Francis
Mark Horner
Chris Ullman

Commissioning Editor
Ian Blackham

Technical Editors
Catherine Alexander
Michelle Everitt
Alastair Ewins
Chris Hart
Robert FE Shaw

Managing Editors
Viv Emery
Jo Mason

Project Managers
Emma Batch
Darren Murphy

Author Agent
Emma Batch

Technical Reviewers
Kapil Apshankar
Adam Cartwright
Stuart Conway
Cristian Darie
Damien Foggon
Slavomir Furman
Jay Glynn
Mark Horner
Craig McQueen
Sean Medina
Matthew Milner
Robert Oliver
Larry Schoeneman

Production Project Coordinator
Sarah Hall

Illustrations
Sarah Hall

Cover
Natalie O'Donnell

Proof Readers
Dev Lunsford
Chris Smith

Index
John Collin

Series Editor
John Collin

About the Authors

Stewart Fraser

Stewart Fraser is a freelance web developer based in Glasgow, Scotland. His development efforts are currently focused on the provision of .NET solutions for a broad range of clients from large government organizations to small businesses. He can be reached at sf@g1tech.com.

This publication will always be dear to me, as while working on my chapters I gained both a fiancée, Debbie, and a wee Cocker Spaniel puppy called Max. Thanks Debs for your love, support and patience throughout the experience (and for accepting my proposal!) and thanks to Max for keeping me company through the long nights. Thanks also to my friends and family for all their support... I think I may owe some beers somewhere!

Steven Livingstone

Steven Livingstone is an IT Architect with IBM Global Services in Winnipeg, Canada. He has contributed to numerous Wrox books and magazine articles, on subjects ranging from XML to e-Commerce. Steven's current interests include e-Commerce, ebXML, .NET, and Enterprise Application Architectures.

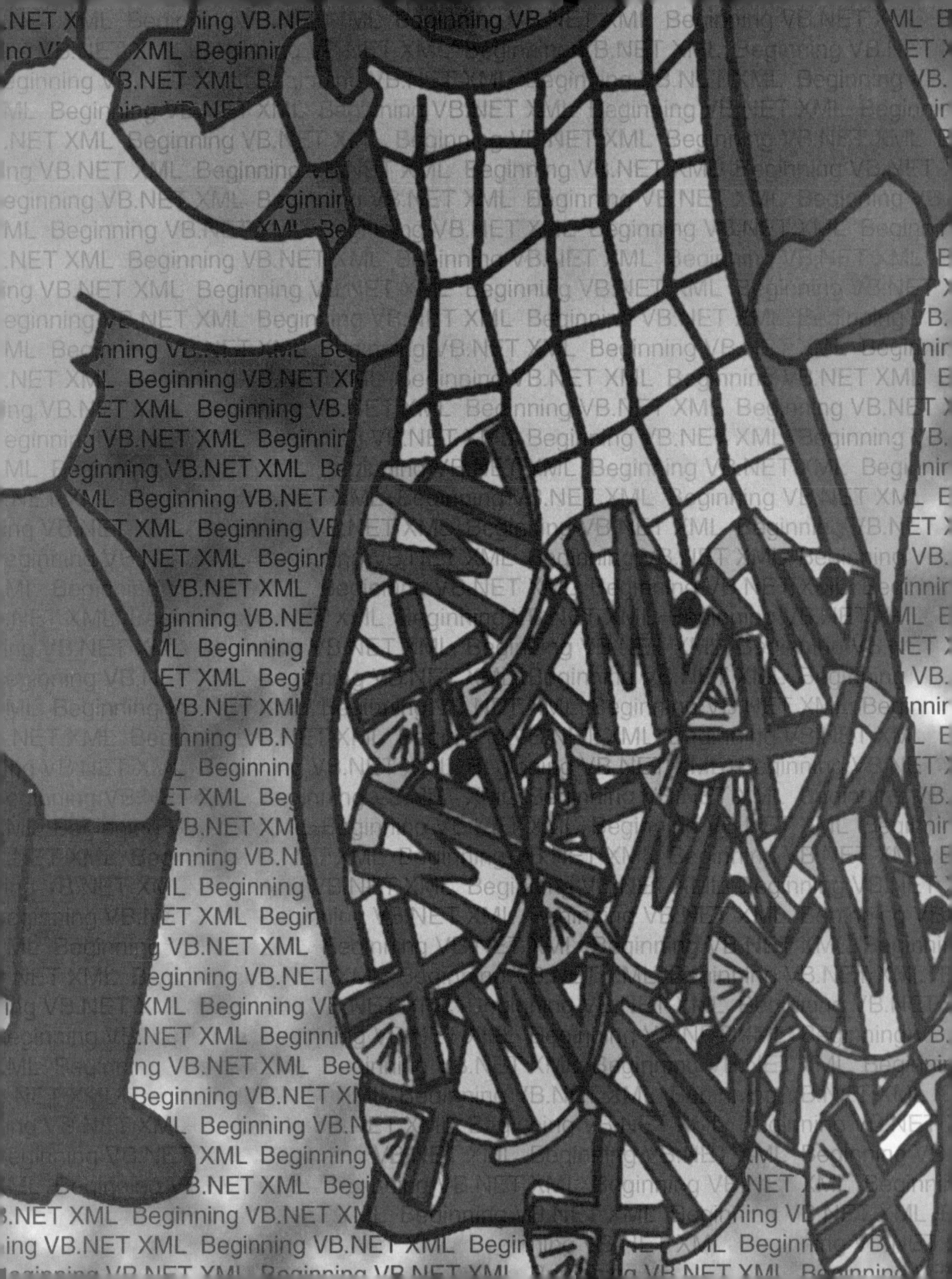
Beginning VB.NET XML

Table of Contents

Table of Contents

Table of Contents

Table of Contents

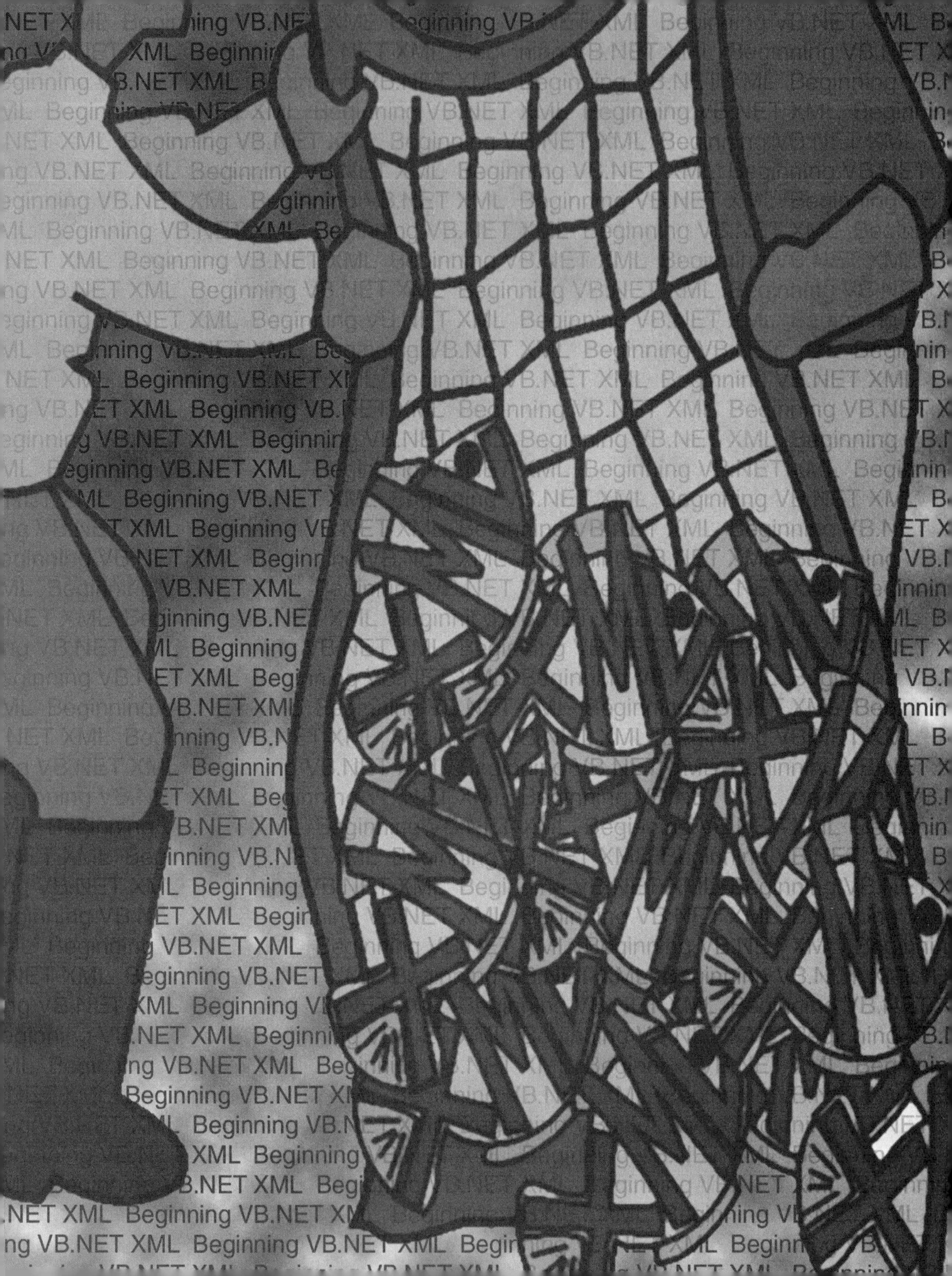
Beginning VB.NET XML

Introduction

Welcome to *Beginning VB.NET XML: Essential XML Skills for VB.NET Programmers.* Extensible Markup Language (XML) has been perhaps the biggest buzzword in application development for several years, and now Microsoft has built XML into the core of its .NET Framework. This book is aimed at teaching XML (and related technologies such as XPath, XSLT, and XML Schema) to developers who want to understand what XML can accomplish. To be able to deliver a targeted guide to the essential XML skills that you need, we assume that you have grasped some essential programming techniques, (in this case, a basic knowledge of programming in Visual Basic .NET,) and gained some experience using Visual Studio .NET, and that you can transfer these skills to a new technology.

Over the course of this book, readers will develop a good appreciation of not only what XML is, and how and when to use it in Visual Basic .NET, but also how to use XML to build applications to run on a single desktop, single web server or distributed, multi-platform web services, in ways that have been extremely difficult to achieve with previous technologies.

To reinforce the core concepts, this book makes use of numerous individual examples along with two case studies. Examples are carefully chosen to demonstrate the capabilities of XML and aid you in understanding the underlying concepts that you can apply when you begin to use this technology. First, there is an examination of how different XML-based approaches can be used in the development of an address book application. The complexity of the project develops as the reader's knowledge increases through the book. Second, we dedicate a full chapter to describing the use of XML and a SQL Server database in the implementation of a web-based news portal.

What Does This Book Cover?

- ❑ XML syntax and well-formed XML
- ❑ Using XML Namespaces
- ❑ Transforming XML using XSLT
- ❑ XML validation using DTDs and XML Schemas

❑   Using SOAP and Web Services

❑   Using ADO.NET to add database access to your applications

❑   Enabling XML support for SQL Server 2000 using SQLXML

Chapter 1: Why Use XML with VB.NET?

In this chapter, we will cover the basics. What is XML exactly? Why is it so important? Why is VB.NET such an ideal language to manipulate it with? Perhaps most importantly, what exactly can you do with XML? We'll be looking at all these things and seeing where XML fits in exactly with the .NET Framework and VB.NET, and why you should be learning about how to use it. We also look at our first, very simple, application.

Chapter 2: Overview of XML

The previous chapter gave a preview of XML. Now we start to look in more detail at what exactly XML is, how it is made up, and the rules and definitions that must be followed when creating an XML document.

Chapter 3: XML with .NET in Detail

Now that we understand the basic building blocks and concepts of XML, we look at how XML fits into the .NET Framework, and the support that .NET offers to XML development; then we will take a look at how the .NET Framework itself uses XML at the heart of its operation. Towards the end of this chapter, we are also going to start a phone book case study, using the understanding we have gained from the book thus far. We'll then continue to build on this in future chapters.

Chapter 4: Reading XML in .NET

We will look at how VB and XML are used in the .NET Framework and how we can use them together to create powerful applications. We will see how you read XML using .NET and VB and how to read different node types by working your way through the XML document. We will also consider how to read binary data and larger XML documents, as well as how to implement some validation in your XML documents.

Chapter 5: Writing XML in .NET with VB.NET

We're now going to look at programmatically writing XML data within our VB.NET code, using the functionality defined in some more .NET classes. Thankfully, as .NET developers, we have access to some very useful methods that handle writing elements, attributes, and so on, with a minimum of fuss, and this is what we'll be looking at in this chapter.

Chapter 6: Implementation of the DOM in .NET

This chapter is going to look at how the Document Object Model (DOM) is implemented in the .NET Framework. We looked at the theory of the DOM in Chapter 3; we are going to cover that material in more detail here. In this chapter, you will learn what the DOM is and how it differs from streaming models, how to use the `XmlNode` and `XmlDocument` class. We will then use the DOM with our ongoing case study.

Chapter 7: XPath and .NET

In this chapter we are going to extend our understanding of working with the DOM in .NET and discuss how `XPath` can be used in .NET to achieve complex navigation and filtering on our XML documents. We are also going to look at the basics of how serialization (and deserialization) of classes can be done directly in .NET using XML.

Chapter 8: XSLT

In this chapter we are going to look at the **XSL Transformation Language** (**XSLT**) and what support is available for it in the .NET Framework. XSLT is used to take an XML document and output it in another format such as an HTML page or another XML document (although we aren't limited to these formats). This transformation is based on the contents of the XML document, through matching elements and attributes (which can in turn be qualified within by namespaces) within the document.

Chapter 9: XSLT in .NET

In this chapter we apply our knowledge of XSLT from the previous chapter to see how it can be implemented using the .NET classes.

Chapter 10: XML Schema – Background, Language, and General Use

In this chapter we are going to start to look at the XML Schema Language, which is a more recent, but extremely important addition to the XML family that will essentially replace Document Type Definitions. It allows us to define the permitted structure and content of an XML document, and to validate that the XML document is of a given structure before it is transformed using XSLT. Schemas can be used in a wide variety of places, ranging from the simple validation of a document, the validating of XML documents for business applications, and web services.

Chapter 11: XML Schemas and .NET

In the last chapter we discussed the theoretical and practical aspects of the XML Schema language as defined by the W3C. In this chapter we are going to extend our knowledge of XML Schema to the world of .NET. We will look at the programmatic techniques of creating Schema documents as well as how to validate XML instances against these documents using .NET classes.

Chapter 12: XML in ADO.NET

ADO.NET is the new data access model for .NET applications, replacing and improving upon traditional ADO technology in many ways. The most significant improvement comes from its tight integration with XML, which will be our main focus throughout the chapter. We're going to briefly introduce the ADO.NET model and look at some examples to show how we can use it, and then we'll move on to look at how XML fits into the picture.

Chapter 13: Web Services and Remoting

In this chapter we will look at Web Services, again more of an application of the underlying technologies offered by the .NET Framework. We will look at: Web Services, the Global XML Architecture, Simple Object Access Protocol (SOAP), Web Service Description Language (WSDL), Microsoft's DISCO discovery XML document, the Universal Description, Discovery and Integration Service, and Remoting and XML configuration files. Clearly the scope of these topics is huge, but you should see how essential XML is to the entire underlying framework of these technologies. As they become better defined and utilized more within enterprises, the use of XML is going to become more essential and an understand of this usage will be very important.

Chapter 14: Case Study: A Simple News Portal

The case study demonstrates how many of the techniques shown throughout the book can be exploited to create a simple news portal. We use an editable `DataGrid` bound to a `DataSet` to facilitate the registration of content by remote content providers, and we show how we can query the `DataSet` using XPath when synchronized with an `XmlDataDocument`.

We demonstrate how an XSD schema can be used to validate the content to ensure the submitted XML/HTML file is structured appropriately for use in our system. Finally, we show how we can return XML directly from queries against a SQL Server 2000 database, which can be transformed directly to the browser using XSLT, allowing any browser type to be easily targeted, and the layout of the site easily changed.

Who Is This Book For?

Beginning VB.NET XML: Essential XML Skills for VB.NET Programmers is aimed at developers looking for a tutorial approach to build an awareness of what you can accomplish with skilled use of XML. However, this book isn't for novices and it's assumed that you have:

❑ Some knowledge of VB.NET – we don't use any particularly advanced features of VB.NET in this book, but you'll need to be comfortable with the basic syntax.

❑ Experience using Visual Studio .NET.

What You Need To Use This Book

The examples are designed to be run with Visual Studio .NET Professional or Standard Edition and SQL Server 2000, running on Windows 2000 or Windows XP Professional Edition.

The complete source code for all the samples is available for download from our web site, http://www.wrox.com/.

Style Conventions

We have used a number of different styles of text and layout in this book to help differentiate between the different kinds of information. Here are examples of the styles we used and an explanation of what they mean.

Code has several font styles. If it is a word that we are talking about in the text – for example, when discussing a `For...Next` loop – it is in `this font`. If it is a block of code that can be typed as a program and run, then it is in a gray box:

```
Private Sub Button1_Click(ByVal sender As System.Object, _
    ByVal e As System.EventArgs) Handles Button1.Click
End Sub
```

Sometimes, you will see code in a mixture of styles, like this:

```
Private Sub Button1_Click(ByVal sender As System.Object, _
    ByVal e As System.EventArgs) Handles Button1.Click

    MsgBox(TextBox1.Text)

End Sub
```

In cases like this, the code with a white background is code that we are already familiar with. The line highlighted in gray is a new addition to the code since we last looked at it. Code with a white background is also used for chunks of code which demonstrate a principle, but which cannot be typed in and run on their own.

Advice, hints, and background information comes in this type of font.

> **Important pieces of information come in boxes like this.**

Important Words are in a bold type font.

Words that appear on the screen, or in menus like the File or Window, are in a similar font to the one you would see on a Windows desktop.

Keys that you press on the keyboard like *Ctrl* and *Enter* are in italics.

Commands that you need to type in on the command line are shown with a > for the prompt, and the input in **bold**, like this:

```
>something to type on the command line
```

Customer Support and Feedback

We always value hearing from our readers, and we want to know what you think about this book; what you liked, what you didn't like, and what you think we can do better next time. You can send us your comments, either by returning the reply card in the back of the book, or by e-mail to feedback@wrox.com. Please be sure to mention the book ISBN and the title in your message.

Source Code and Updates

As you work through the examples in this book, you may decide that you prefer to type in all the code by hand. Many readers prefer this because it is a good way to get familiar with the coding techniques that are being used. However, whether you want to type the code in or not, we have made all the source code for this book available at the Wrox.com web site.

When you log on to the Wrox.com site at http://www.wrox.com/, simply locate the title through our Search facility or by using one of the title lists. Now click on the Download Code link on the book's detail page and you can obtain all the source code.

The files that are available for download from our site have been archived using WinZip. When you have saved the attachments to a folder on your hard drive, you need to extract the files using a de-compression program such as WinZip or PKUnzip. When you extract the files, the code is usually extracted into chapter folders. When you start the extraction process, ensure your software (WinZip, PKUnzip, and so on) has Use folder names under Extract to: (or the equivalent) checked.

Even if you like to type in the code, you can use our source files to check the results you should be getting – they should be your first stop if you think you might have typed in an error. If you don't like typing, then downloading the source code from our web site is a must! Either way, it will help you with updates and debugging.

Errata

We have made every effort to make sure that there are no errors in the text or in the code. However, no one is perfect and mistakes do occur. If you find an error in this book, like a spelling mistake or a faulty piece of code, we would be very grateful for feedback. By sending in errata, you may save another reader hours of frustration, and of course, you will be helping us provide even higher quality information. Simply e-mail the information to support@wrox.com. Your information will be checked and if correct, posted to the errata page for that title, or used in subsequent editions of the book.

To find errata on the web site, log on to http://www.wrox.com/, and simply locate the title through our Search facility or title list. Then, on the book details page, click on the Book Errata link. On this page you will be able to view all the errata that has been submitted and checked through by editorial. You will also be able to click the Submit Errata link to notify us of any errata that you may have found.

Technical Support

If you wish to directly query a problem in the book then e-mail support@wrox.com. A typical e-mail should include the following things:

- ❑ The **book name**, **last four digits of the ISBN** (7787 for this book), and **page number** of the problem in the Subject field.

- ❑ Your **name**, **contact information**, and the **problem** in the body of the message.

We *won't* send you junk mail. We need the details to save your time and ours. When you send an e-mail message, it will go through the following chain of support:

1. **Customer Support** – Your message is delivered to one of our customer support staff, who are the first people to read it. They have files on most frequently asked questions and will answer anything general about the book or the web site immediately.

2. **Editorial** – Deeper queries are forwarded to the technical editor responsible for that book. They have experience with the programming language or particular product, and are able to answer detailed technical questions on the subject. Once an issue has been resolved, the editor can post the errata to the web site.

3. **The Authors** – Finally, in the unlikely event that the editor cannot answer your problem, he or she will forward the request to the author. We do try to protect the author from any distractions to their writing; however, we are quite happy to forward specific requests to them. All Wrox authors help with the support on their books. They will mail the customer and the editor with their response, and again all readers should benefit.

> Note that the Wrox support process can only offer support to issues that are directly pertinent to the content of our published title. Support for questions that fall outside the scope of normal book support is provided via the community lists of our http://p2p.wrox.com/

p2p.wrox.com

For author and peer discussion join, the **P2P mailing lists**. Our unique system provides **programmer to programmer**™ contact on mailing lists, forums, and newsgroups, all *in addition* to our one-to-one e-mail support system. Be confident that your query is being examined by the many Wrox authors, and other industry experts, who are present on our mailing lists. At p2p.wrox.com you will find a number of different lists that will help you, not only while you read this book, but also as you develop your own applications.

To subscribe to a mailing list just follow this these steps:

1. Go to http://p2p.wrox.com/ and choose the appropriate category from the left menu bar.

2. Click on the mailing list you wish to join.

3. Follow the instructions to subscribe and fill in your e-mail address and password.

4. Reply to the confirmation e-mail you receive.

5. Use the subscription manager to join more lists and set your mail preferences.

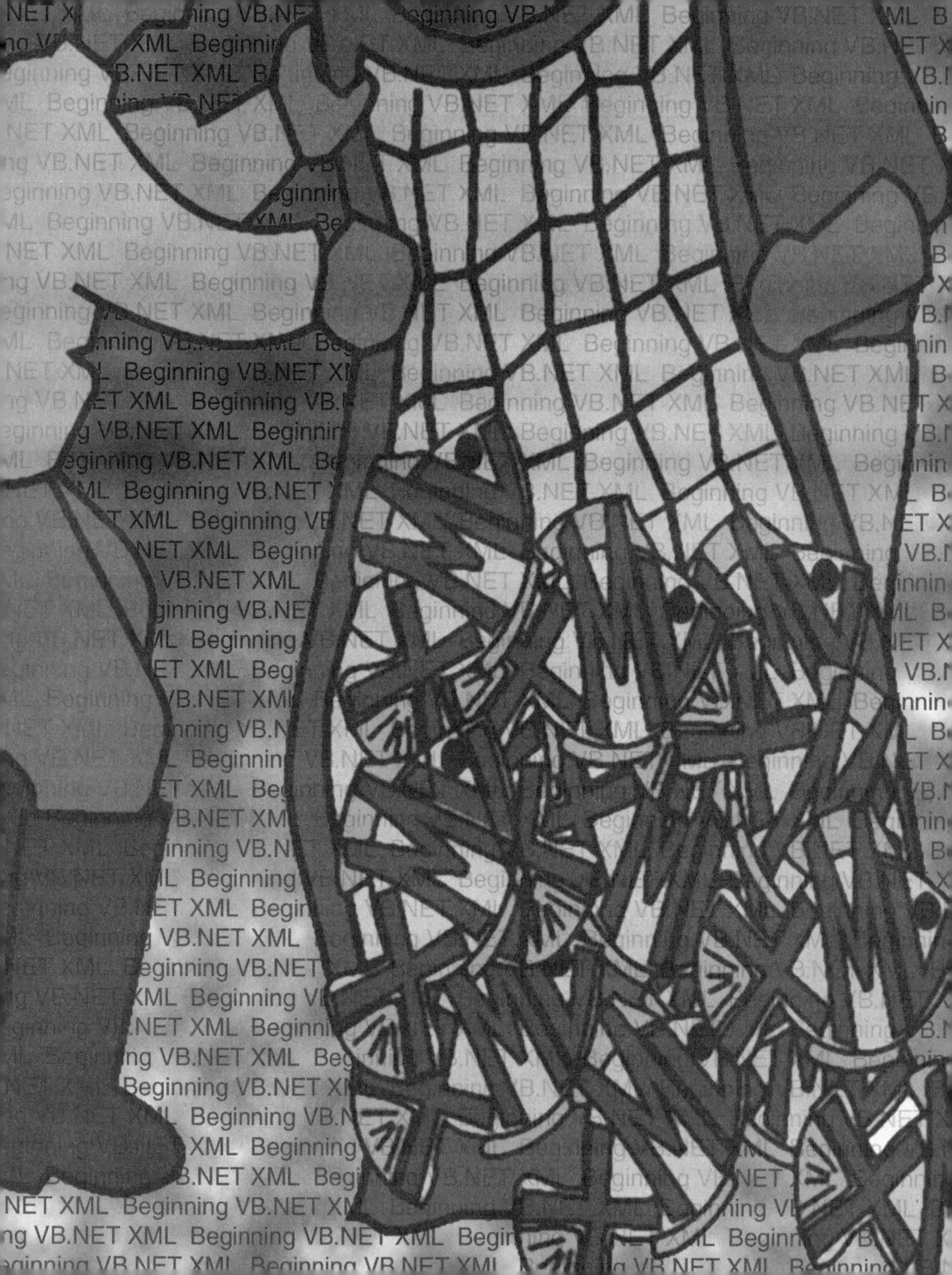
Beginning VB.NET XML

Why Use XML with VB.NET?

Since the earliest days of the Web, there have been several distinct phases to maturity. It was less than ten years ago that all a web page could display was static text and graphics. The first large step forwards was to integrate web pages with back-end databases, to display and allow manipulation of their contents via a web-based user interface. With the introduction of Internet Explorer 4, web services first emerged and started gaining notoriety. Although the first attempts at primitive push technologies, such as servers broadcasting "channels", left a lot to be desired, the underlying thrust of delivering only the information the client wanted rather than reams and reams of data has remained true. The latest, and perhaps most important phase, is the ability of client machines to discover their own web services when needed, instead of relying on push technologies, and integrate them, whether to download the latest updates to your software and service packs, or to check your own stock portfolio and broadcast alerts when the levels dip catastrophically.

Two separate, but key, technologies that have helped enable this latest phase are Microsoft's .NET Framework and the W3C standard Extensible Markup Language, more commonly known as XML. The .NET Framework was designed to help make code portable between platforms, and for applications with components written in different languages to fit together as smoothly as those written in the same language. It also blurs the line between writing applications to run locally on your own machine and writing applications that can be accessed over the Web. XML boasts a similar set of aims, as it is a text-based standard for representing data in a structured format. It too can be used on any platform, and by many different applications and components in numerous different languages. As it is written entirely in text, it is ideally suited to being used by web-based applications. It's not surprising that both play such a core part in Microsoft's plans for the future of the Web.

In this chapter, we're not going to pitch into the heavy areas. We'll try not to get bogged down in too many new buzzwords; we just want to get down to the basics. What is XML exactly? Why is it so important? Why is VB.NET such an ideal language to manipulate it with? Perhaps most importantly, what exactly can you do with XML? We'll be looking at all these things and seeing where XML fits in exactly with the .NET Framework and VB.NET, and why you should be learning about how to use it.

Why XML?

Presumably, as you're reading this book, you already have a good idea about why you're using VB.NET. VB.NET finally drags Visual Basic out of the realm of junior programming languages into the world of fully-fledged object-oriented ones. The great thing about the .NET Framework is that your choice of language doesn't affect what you can do underneath with it, so this could just as easily be a book about how C# or C++ works with XML, because underneath the Common Language Runtime ensures these languages are basically the same.

XML, however, probably needs a bit more demystification. You'll be aware that XML is a markup language like HTML, and we'll assume you're familiar with at least some basics of HTML (if not, I suggest picking up a basic HTML manual before you start reading this). While HTML is a language for displaying content and data that can be viewed on browsers, it says nothing about the data it displays. Consider the following example. Here we have an HTML document that describes the author of this book.

```
<html>
  <head>
    <title>Contacts</title>
  </head>
  <body>
    <b>Steven Livingstone</b> lives at 123 Anystreet, Anytown in WA. His postal
    code is 12345 and he lives in the USA.        <br>
    <br>
    <b>Address of Stewart Fraser: </b>
    <br>123 Anotherstreet
    <br>Anothertown
    <br>N.Y
    <br>90210
    <br>USA.
  </body>
</html>
```

The HTML tags describe to the browser how the document should be displayed, but there is no indication that:

❑   The data consists of two distinct parts, name and address

❑   There are two people's details listed

❑   One record is stored on one line, while the other is stored on six separate lines

In fact HTML isn't meant to do any of this; it does its own job just fine. All it should do is format your data in such a way that Internet Explorer or Netscape Navigator can display it:

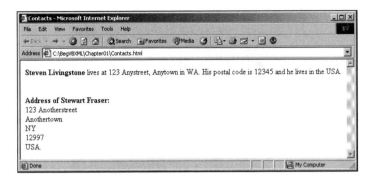

As such, HTML has no facilities for displaying just one section of a web page, or filtering out particular irrelevant information on the page, or even grouping sections of similar information together. It displays the entire web page every time.

XML, on the other hand, doesn't contain anything that a browser can use to display it with, so if you view an XML page, you'll just get to see the tags and the data held in them. It won't be displayed with graphics or tables or frames. XML takes a much more explicit approach to the data, stating exactly what the data signifies. The example below, which we will name `Contacts.xml`, is the equivalent document in XML:

```
<?xml version="1.0"?>

<contacts>
  <contact>
    <firstname>Steven</firstname>
    <lastname>Livingstone</lastname>
    <address>123 Anystreet</address>
    <city>Anytown</city>
    <state>WA</state>
    <postalcode>12345</postalcode>
    <country>USA</country>
  </contact>
  <contact>
    <firstname>Stewart</firstname>
    <lastname>Fraser</lastname>
    <address>123 Anotherstreet</address>
    <city>Anothertown</city>
    <state>NY</state>
    <postalcode>12997</postalcode>
    <country>USA</country>
  </contact>
</contacts>
```

What it does do, though, is give a good way of structuring your data. When viewed in a browser you will see the following, in which the structure is maintained:

There are some significant differences in the way that the data is represented, but it makes it a lot easier for a consuming application to work out if the addresses are the same or, for example, to arrange last names into alphabetical order.

As the content of our XML document is entirely down to us, we can describe our data in whatever way we want. So, for example, if we wished to describe the `<postalcode>` data as `<zipcode>12345</zipcode>`, or anything else, we can do this. We define the tags for our application, so we are free to structure and name the same data in different ways to suit the requirements of an application or category of applications. This is where the 'extensible' in Extensible Markup Language comes from.

So, XML allows the user to specify the format of the data, as it allows the user to specify the tags themselves, but what advantages does this confer? Well, importantly, data can then be easily transmitted across the Internet and particular parts of the data could be filtered out or sorted at the other end by another application. If you sent an HTML page, then all you'd have is a jumble of text, and returning anything useful to a browser would be difficult. Browsers don't distinguish between the different bits of text they receive.

With XML, it's probably not even a browser you're intending as the recipient of the data. This is where VB.NET (or any programming language) comes in. A VB.NET application can sort the data depending on the tags you used to specify it with. It can filter out information of no interest to the user, for example records older than a year, or it can group records of data that have something in common, such as all addresses in Massachusetts. Let's take a look at some more specific advantages that XML enjoys as a data format.

Openness

The major common thread between the world of VB.NET and the .NET Framework and the XML technologies (and a major reason for the success of XML) is their **openness** via specifications and standards. The .NET Framework defines open language specifications such as the Common Language Runtime (CLR) and Common Type System (CTS) that allow other languages that conform to these specifications to interoperate with applications written in any other language conforming to these standards. In theory that also means .NET can run on any other platform and any language can be a .NET language (even Java is now a .NET-compliant language in the form of J#).

> **Have a look at** http://www.go-mono.com **to see an open source working implementation of the .NET Framework on Unix/Linux. It supports VB.NET and C#, and you can even create Windows Forms and ASP.NET pages!**

Yet, when we talk of openness and cross-platform development, the most enabling technology over recent years has undoubtedly been XML, and the technologies related to XML. XML technologies allow data to be read and processed on any platform according to standard specifications. More ambitiously, XML technologies are at the forefront of enabling distributed web services, allowing the exchange of XML data across HTTP and other transport protocols. As the .NET Framework is a new development environment, XML support has been built directly into the Framework itself (rather than on top). You will come to appreciate the power of this as you read through this book.

This new wave of programming offered by the combination of .NET and XML allows any language of choice running on any platform to work with any other language on any other platform, communicating via open data standards. This is a big move away from the idea of everyone learning a single language for multiple platforms and having to use proprietary communications protocols.

Simplicity

As we've already hinted, XML documents are just plain text. There can't be anything much simpler in computing terms (that a human could understand anyway – arguably binary data would be simpler). If you need to exchange data between two different systems, then the simplest format for a human to use will almost always be text.

Self-Describing

The fact that XML can be used to explicitly indicate the meaning of individual parts of a data model is termed **self-describing**. It has this term because you can (generally) tell by looking at the tags around a given data item within an XML document what that data is. So, whereas the text "12345" may mean nothing (without using some kind of technique to determine where the text that describes the significances of the integer is), the text `<postalcode>12345</postalcode>` immediately tells you that the number is a postcode.

Interoperability

Once again, as XML documents are plain text, it makes them easily transferable between systems. This is not just because of the human element of "simplicity", but also because XML documents can move between applications and across barriers more easily. Different environments or operating systems can communicate with each other, and this is particularly useful for businesses with a mixture of legacy and modern systems.

Structure

XML has the ability to describe simple one-line data structures, such as 'the car is red', more complex text-based data, such as books (for example the entire works of Shakespeare), and much more complex data structures like arrays or collections. XML documents are sent with a set of rules for creating them. These rules normally take the form of a schema, which gives the receiving application everything it needs to know to validate the document.

Dividing Structure and Content

In complex applications XML has an even more significant advantage than in simple demonstrations such as this; when working with HTML we deal with both presentation and data with no distinction, whereas, with XML there is a distinct separation of the data from its presentation. In HTML the content is often muddled with presentational features.

Extensibility

Using XML we can specify our own languages customized to our own needs. There are many custom languages such as MathML (a mathematics markup language), CML (Chemical Markup Language), and TecML (a technical data markup language) all derived from XML, each for its own specific environment. XML creates a framework for the representation of your own data. All languages you create to represent your own data are languages in their own right that are simply extensions to XML.

As you can now start to appreciate, the power of combining these two technologies (.NET and XML) is going to vastly improve the interoperability of our applications, which, more than ever, require us to operate with disparate systems that are often located in different geographic locations. We will look in detail at how XML is used with VB.NET and the .NET Framework later in the chapter. However, to understand why XML has been affecting almost every area of Microsoft application development, it is necessary to understand exactly what XML is and what it can and cannot be used for. So, let's make sure we fully understand the Extensible Markup Language (XML).

What is XML?

To recap quickly, the Extensible Markup Language of XML is a text-based format that uses HTML-like tags to structure data. It isn't proprietary, so anybody can use it for no extra cost, and it is governed by a set of standards, which is presided over by the W3C consortium, so there aren't millions of different variations of it. It's easily customizable as it can be used to create hundreds of HTML-like languages, which act as extensions to the language.

XML is Not Just One Language, But Many

When we talk of XML we often refer to it as though it is some single specification, when in fact we generally mean a family of technologies, such as XML Stylesheet Language (XSL), XSL Transformations (XSLT), the XML Path Language (XPath), and the XML Schema Language (XSDL), based on the XML 1.0 World Wide Web Consortium (W3C) Recommendation. It's probably groups of acronyms like this all beginning with the letter X that put people off in the first place. However, while we will eventually within the course of this book consider all of these, in this chapter we will concentrate almost solely on the language of XML, rather than the surrounding technologies.

An XML Document

Let's go back to our XML document for a moment. We're actually going to dig deeper into the different parts of XML documents in the next chapter, but for the time being just consider it as a whole.

One of the main focuses of XML is its ability to describe information in a way that can be read and understood by a parser. So, while HTML can display some text in a browser about a user's name and address, as we were saying earlier, XML can actually be used to specify which parts of the document are the first name, last name, and address, for example:

```xml
<?xml version="1.0"?>

<contacts>
  <contact>
    <firstname>Steven</firstname>
    <lastname>Livingstone</lastname>
    <address>123 Anystreet</address>
    <city>Anytown</city>
    <state>WA</state>
    <postalcode>12345</postalcode>
    <country>USA</country>
  </contact>
  <contact>
    <firstname>Stewart</firstname>
    <lastname>Fraser</lastname>
    <address>123 Anotherstreet</address>
    <city>Anothertown</city>
    <state>NY</state>
    <postalcode>12997</postalcode>
    <country>USA</country>
  </contact>
</contacts>
```

It is probably pretty clear to the reader that we are describing two different instances of the same type of information; both contain first and last names and comparable address details. However, to an application that doesn't understand that these are comparable, things can get pretty difficult if you want to do anything with the data (and remember this is only a very simple example). XML has given structure to our data and there's nothing difficult to understand about it.

This document is just a text document that is saved with a `.xml` suffix to identify it. You could open it up and read it in any text editor you care to name. In fact, it's so simple, that's all we want to say about it for the time being.

Who uses XML?

Let's now look at some areas where XML is used.

Content Presentation

HTML has long been the preferred technology for marking up documents that are to be displayed on a browser, and in the near future it is unlikely this is going to change – especially for simple content. The advent of XML hasn't made a huge impact on the presentation layer, at least from a browser point of view, due to the lack of support for styling techniques, like XSL (Extensible Stylesheet Language – see the section on XSL later in this chapter for more details), to determine how the XML document should be displayed. Applications that do use XML in creating the presentation output will generally use server-side techniques to generate simple HTML that is then sent to the client.

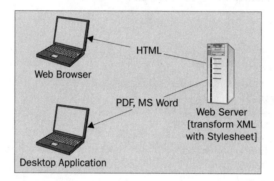

However, as XML technologies have become better supported on browsers, much of this processing is now done on the client, with almost no effect on the server. In fact, a specification known as XHTML is attempting to move the web-publishing world from flat HTML (which is not XML and would generally fail when passed through an XML parser) to an XML-compliant form of HTML called XHTML that could be manipulated as XML. For more information on XHTML see the specification at http://www.w3.org/TR/xhtml1/.

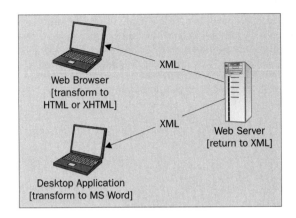

One of the main advantages of this is that you don't need to save your documents in multiple formats – you can transform your XML data structure to the output format you desire, whether that is HTML, PDF, or MS Word, although working with proprietary document formats, such as PDF or MS Word, is more work than simply outputting HTML. Transforming to MS Word, for example, uses fairly complex HTML markup, which involves using Word-specific namespaces. If you intend to use this method, I suggest creating a simple Word template that you can model your XSLT document on, rather than attempting to output the exact format that Microsoft Word outputs.

A further advantage is that you can reorganize the view of an XML document without having to change the XML itself – you simply alter the stylesheet that renders the XML and the new document is displayed.

Business-to-Business Commerce

Perhaps the largest development area and driver for XML at the moment is its use in Business-to-Business commerce, which involves many disparate applications on multiple environments, distributed throughout different geographical locations. Businesses are typically spread over many different areas, with many different types of application and software often purchased over a number of years. I've worked in offices with mainframes sat in the corner churning data, while the support staff worked on PCs running Windows and the sales staff worked on dumb terminals hooked up to distant UNIX servers. The question of how to get your data across from a member of the sales staff to the support staff caused enough problems, let alone having to worry about how to interface with the other 30 departments in the organization, and then the outside world!

XML is text, and this is very easily transported over Internet protocols, and on to any kind of storage media. It has very quickly become an extremely popular option in the business-to-business environment, enabling everything from the exchange of catalogs and product information to purchase orders and invoices. Many XML-based schemas, principally from RosettaNet (such as the purchase order schemas), but also from xCBL and BizTalk, have emerged and some have become globally popular. Many of these have even been integrated within products such as Microsoft's BizTalk server, which has its own library of schemas, as well as supporting transformation to and from RosettaNet schemas. (For general information on Schemas, see the section entitled *XML Related Standards* later in this chapter, or go to Chapters 10 and 11 for a detailed look at this subject).

In contrast to the presentation scenario for XML usage, the B2B example rarely displays anything to users. To XML and related technologies, a business application is just another consumer of the data, and in the same way as output to end users, styling sheets can be used to transform the original data format to the format required by the consuming application. This is illustrated in the following diagram:

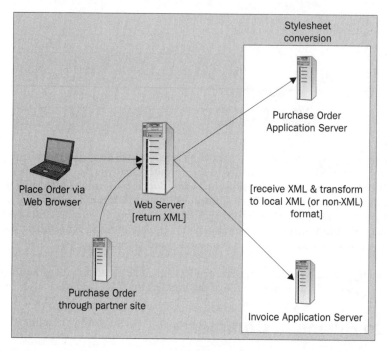

As you can see, XML forms the hub of an information exchange. A great advantage that it has over previous techniques is that anyone can interact with these systems at very low cost, due to the low overhead of XML, as there is no complex development or software required to cope with a proprietary format. Although business-to-business commerce has been used for years, this is an area that is going to continue to grow in popularity, and we are still in the early days of B2B.

Remote Procedure Calls

The idea of being able to call services on a remote server has been one that has enjoyed a lot of popularity.

The most immediately obvious communications protocol to provide this functionality has been HTTP, as this is the protocol that Internet communication is based upon (on top of the TCP/IP transport-level protocol); it is universally supported, and is generally allowed through firewalls. However, to intelligently mark up the information to pass to other servers so that they understand exactly what they are to do and what information has to be returned, technologies have had to be developed on top of HTTP. The earliest was XML-RPC, which allowed an application to call services on some remote server, and this is still very popular.

The fastest growing technology for distributed computing now has to be the Simple Object Access Protocol (SOAP), which is a technology based on XML, to be used over HTTP, and has development environments available from companies such as Microsoft and IBM. The idea (and again, we are still in relatively early days) is that you can call methods on objects distributed around the Internet without having to worry about whether they are on your local network or on some server on the other side of the world, what platform they are on, or even what language they have been written in.

All of this has now been termed "**Web Services**", which generally refers to the idea that an application can be built up of distributed parts, or services, throughout the Internet. Web services are an area that is subject to intense development at the moment, and there are already many useful web services distributed throughout the Internet. The diagram below illustrates how web services can be used to realize a simple e-commerce web site:

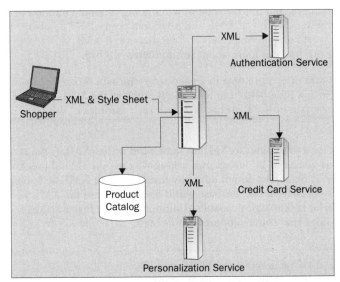

You can make any .NET component accessible as a web service on many transport protocols such as HTTP, SMTP, and transport protocols such as TCP and UDP. The term "**Web Services Anywhere**" is used in .NET because the idea is that you can call a service from any application over any transport (such as TCP/IP) using any payload encoding (such as XML).

Although web services are fairly new, many have the potential to become immediately popular, for tasks such as credit card authorization and authentication. Even within an enterprise, the ability to seamlessly use web services within applications is very important because it readily allows component reuse in the increasingly complex infrastructure of the enterprise (which typically involves internal firewalls and distributed server clusters).

Data Storage and Access

Of course, XML is not just useful for passing data around the Web; it is also a popular format for storing data. In fact, perhaps its most obvious advantage is that it stores information about the data as well. If you store information in a relational database in different fields, it doesn't hold any detail about the structure. XML stores its data within clear structures:

```
<contact>
  <firstname>Steven</firstname>
  <lastname>Livingstone</lastname>
  <address>123 Anystreet</address>
  <city>Anytown</city>
  <state>WA</state>
  <postalcode>12345</postalcode>
  <country>USA</country>
</contact>
```

So, it has become increasingly popular to use databases to directly store XML. Many databases support the transformation from XML with their proprietary database formats. There are even XML databases that are optimized for storing only XML data, such as Tamino (http://www.softwareag.com) and TextML (http://www.ixiasoft.com). Most common databases such as Oracle and SQL Server now support XML technologies, and there is a lot of work going on that continues to look specifically at this area, and how the different worlds of XML and relational (and other) databases will work in harmony. As an example, the world of querying relational databases and XML structures is being looked at in XQuery, which you can find out more about at http://www.w3.org.

Although relational databases store data in a proprietary format, this relational data can be represented in an XML format, with a little help from technology, such as the XML schemas. You can almost always describe the relational data in XML format. You will see examples of this later in the book when we look at ADO.NET.

An important point for a newcomer to XML to remember is that XML is **not a replacement** for databases (I often see questions in newsgroups asking why people should use XML rather than databases) and equally, databases do not do many things that the XML technologies do. In fact, what we are seeing is the best ideas from the database world and the best of the XML world being combined to produce more powerful technologies capable of supporting both formats. Again XQuery is a good example of a technology that could support both formats.

> **You can see and try an online demo of XQuery at:**
> http://131.107.228.20/xquerydemo/demo.aspx.

When Not to Use XML

A common mistake is the belief that XML does everything. It does a lot, but it has to be used properly. The following list is a general list of when not to use XML:

❑ Don't expect to solve all of your presentation requirements in XML; even when browsers come to support all of the major XML technologies, there are still going to be other pervasive devices, such as small handheld digital assistants or mobile phones, that won't support the full set of XML technologies and so will require some work to be done (although often that work may be done by some application of XML).

❑ As discussed above, don't try to replace database functionality with XML; use the appropriate technology to satisfy the requirements. There may be valid cases for describing database structures in XML format, such as when working with disconnected database structures or serializing tables for transport in a distributed environment. We will see examples of this when we come to look at ADO.NET (see Chapter 12) and serialization.

❏ Don't exclusively use XML between components – ideally offer an interface that returns natively typed objects (such as Booleans, Integers, and so on) and another that returns an XML result so that a client can get type safe interfaces while allowing simple XML calls where desired (often an alternative to reflection techniques).

XML Standards

One of the main reasons why XML and its technologies are being so successful and making a huge impact in all areas of application development is due to heavy standardization on these technologies, which makes them interoperable with other developer's implementations and products on multiple platforms. Obviously, however, someone has to take responsibility for creating and managing these standards, as well as the typical iteration in versions as people want more and more from the technologies. This work is done, as we have already mentioned, by a standards organization called the World Wide Web Consortium or W3C.

What is the World Wide Web Consortium?

The World Wide Web Consortium (W3C) started in 1994, and according to its web site, it has the following goals:

❏ Universal Access – provide access to web resources for all users despite disabilities or client device

❏ Semantic Web – describe the resources on the web so that they can be meaningfully linked together to provide information for users

❏ Trust – allow resources (human or automated) to be able to know and verify who they are interacting with as well as be verified themselves

❏ Interoperability – that software components can integrate together through open standards

❏ Evolvability – allow the web to improve and evolve via the principles of simplicity, modularity, and extensibility

❏ Decentralization – that the number of centralized systems can be reduced and pushed to a more distributed model to limit bottlenecks and reduce vulnerability

❏ Improved Multimedia – to make the web more interactive and rich via multimedia and improved graphical quality, such as 3D and animation

Although we won't touch on how XML impacts on all of these areas, if you visit the web site at http://www.w3.org you will find many technologies that impact on one or more of these areas and use XML as their technology basis.

The W3C is not a body on its own – it has many members consisting of some of the largest and most important companies in the technology world (such as Microsoft, IBM, Sun, and so on) who work together to produce these standards – which is why such a good level of interoperability is possible. When some technology is to be standardized, the W3C produces **Recommendations**, which detail how the technology should be implemented by vendors and developers. Perhaps its most famous recommendation was the HTML Recommendation, which helps ensure that web browsers following this recommendation display your information correctly (pity there was never a specific DHTML Recommendation).

However, HTML was only just the start of the Internet evolution – the family of XML technologies is the main focus of the W3C and it is likely to have a much bigger impact than even HTML has had up to the present time. Let's discuss in a little more detail the XML technologies that we will touch upon within this book and those that are currently impacting software development.

The XML Standard

In case you have never heard of it, the **XML 1.0 Recommendation** is the basis of the entire family of XML technologies and became a W3C Recommendation in February 1998. It discusses the syntax and rules that XML documents have to follow and what implementing parsers have to validate in XML documents. More information is available at http://www.w3.org/XML/.

XML-Related Standards

Other XML-related technologies W3C looks after include:

❑ **Namespaces** – Namespaces allow XML vocabularies and documents (consisting of XML elements and attributes) to be differentiated from each other; this is particularly important where there are two elements or attributes with the same name that mean different things. More details can be found at http://www.w3.org/TR/REC-xml-names/.

❑ **DOM** and **SAX** – The Document Object Model (DOM) provides an API that allows applications to work with an in-memory tree view of an XML document. The Simple API for XML, or SAX, is **not** a W3C Recommendation, but it is still a very important specification. It works in the opposite way to the DOM. While the DOM loads the entire XML document into memory and creates a tree view, SAX simply iterates through the nodes within the XML document and sends notifications when specific elements or attributes are found. More information on DOM is available at http://www.w3.org/DOM/ and more details on SAX are available at http://www.saxproject.org/.

❑ **XHTML** – XHTML is a well-formed version of HTML. This means that it can be read by XML parsers, and requires only a little more effort to ensure it meets the requirements of XML. More details on XHTML can be found at http://www.w3.org/TR/xhtml1/.

❑ **XPath** – XPath is the query language for XML documents allowing you to ask for specific parts of a document. More information about XPath can be found at http://www.w3.org/TR/xpath.

❑ **XPointer** and **XLink** – The XML Pointer Language (XPointer) became a W3C Recommendation in September 2001 and uses XPath expressions to address specific parts of XML documents. The XML Linking Language (XLink) became a W3C Recommendation in June 2001 and is designed to allow you to link together XML web resources and improve on the referencing used in HTML hyperlinks. It allows you to describe the links between the resources, and the links can even be described without the resources being linked. More information about XPointer can be found at http://www.w3.org/TR/xpath. More information about XLink can be found at http://www.w3.org/TR/xlink/.

❑ **XInclude** – The XML Include specification became a W3C Recommendation in February 2002 and is an extremely useful technology in that it allows you to separate your XML documents into modules and exclude them from any other XML document. More information about XInclude can be found at http://www.w3.org/TR/xinclude/.

❑ **XSL** – The full specification actually consists of **XSLT** for transforming XML documents from one format to another and **XSL Formatting Objects** (**XSL-FO**) that deal with the display of the document. There is currently no direct support for XSL-FO in Microsoft XML products, but XSLT is well supported in Internet Explorer and the Microsoft XML parsers. XSL-FO is supported by products such as XML Spy and Epic Editor from ArborText. Further details on XSLT can be found at http://www.w3.org/TR/xslt.

❑ **DTDs** and **XML Schemas** – Document Type Definitions (DTD) and the XML Schema language both deal with the validation of XML documents, in terms of structure and content. In fact, the DTD is the only validation language that must be supported by validating parsers, as it was built as part of the XML 1.0 specification. DTDs are covered in detail in Chapter 2; for more depth on XML Schemas, see Chapters 10 and 11. The XML Schema specification allows the reuse of documents, validation of the structure of the content, and validation of the content of documents against built-in data types as well as custom types. Information on DTDs can be found at http://www.w3.org/TR/REC-xml#dt-doctype.

❑ **SOAP** and **Web Services** – Simple Object Access Protocol (SOAP) and web services in general are relatively new additions to the range of XML-related technologies, but are different from many of the technologies discussed above in that they use XML to enable application operability rather than to build applications. These technologies enable applications to use objects distributed across networks and the globe, and enable easier interoperation with other distributed and non-distributed applications. Web services are a rapidly changing technology and the latest activity from the W3C can be found at http://www.w3.org/2002/ws/.

Why Standards Matter

In other words, the W3C looks after pretty much everything related to XML, but why exactly is it important to make sure someone is looking after the standards? Unfortunately a quick look back at the browser wars of Internet Explorer versus Netscape Navigator shows why you can't just let the companies get on with doing the "innovating" themselves. In 1996, both Microsoft and Netscape raced to be the first to create Dynamic HTML, which enabled users in the new versions of browsers to be able to drag and drop bits of the page, and to interact more richly with the Web than they had before. The trouble is, they came up with exclusive solutions both "masquerading" under the name Dynamic HTML. Netscape's version was based on a `<layer>` tag, while Microsoft's relied on the properties and methods of a `Document` object. It wasn't possible to write a truly dynamic page that worked in both browsers without producing two exclusive sets of code, one tailored for each browser. As a result, the whole "dynamic" revolution just didn't take off with web users, until the introduction of server-side technologies that couldn't be hampered by an individual's particular browser.

There are a variety of technologies related to XML, and if XML is to fulfil its design aim of being a platform-neutral yet simple data format, it is essential that the related standards be maintained by an independent body such as the W3C.

How Does XML Fit in with .NET?

So we've seen how XML is regulated by the standards body W3C to ensure it has a uniform implementation across different platforms, but where does it fit in with .NET, which is of course a Microsoft technology? The answer is, practically everywhere.

The .NET Framework has been developed from the ground up to take full advantage of XML and even the Framework itself makes significant use of XML when creating applications, with features such as application configuration, documentation, and many other aspects using XML directly. Visual Basic has been revamped into what is almost a new language to take advantage of many of the offerings of XML. The key tools that support development of the main .NET languages, such as Visual Studio and Web Matrix, also have extensive support for XML, allowing web service creation, object serialization, configuration, and many other features all based on XML. Throughout this book you will learn many of the areas that XML has been applied to and how you can make use of it in your own developments.

To support this change, the way applications are developed has also had to change. XML was the first major step towards language- and platform-independent application integration. XML has been so successful that it has found its way into almost everything relating to application development; so much so that many products and product development tools have had a whole host of add-ons to allow for integration between old and new technologies. A prime example is the SOAP Toolkit release, which integrates with Visual Studio.NET and allows web services to be built on top of existing COM applications and ASP pages. There have also been add-ons to SQL Server, and XML now features in many areas of web development.

Using XML Within the .NET Framework

ADO.NET

Arguably the single most important place XML fits in as a data format is with ADO.NET. ADO started life as a wrapper for Microsoft's OLEDB technology, which was a way of guaranteeing that any application could access the contents of a data store, whether that data store was an Access, SQL Server, or Oracle database, an Excel spreadsheet, the contents of an e-mail archive, or even a text file. ADO became ADO.NET in the .NET Framework and offers much better integration with XML.

ADO.NET offers facilities for manipulating XML files in the same way you'd use other data stores, in that it allows you to add new records, delete old ones, filter the records, and group them in particular ways. The advantage is that the files can be read on any system.

Let's take a look at a very quick example that uses ADO.NET to interface with our contacts XML file, replacing the first record in the file with another record and saving it as a separate file. We're not going to explain the code; we just want to show that ADO.NET offers strong facilities for manipulating XML. You can either create this example yourself, or you can run it from the code available for download at www.wrox.com.

Try It Out: Adding a Record to an XML File with ADO.NET

1. Open Visual Studio. NET and open a new project. Choose a Visual Basic Project with a Windows Application template. Name the application AddXML. Add a DataGrid and two buttons to the form. Keep the default names for these buttons, but set the Text property of Button1 to Display and the Text property of Button2 to Update.

2. Add the following code to the form:

```
Public Class Form1

Inherits System.Windows.Forms.Form

Private Sub Button1_Click(ByVal sender As Object, ByVal e As System.EventArgs) _
    Handles Button1.Click

Dim XmlFilename As String
XmlFilename = "C:\AddXML\contacts.xml"
Dim objDataSet As New DataSet()
objDataSet.ReadXml(XmlFilename)
DataGrid1.DataSource = objDataSet.Tables(0).DefaultView
End Sub

Private Sub Button2_Click(ByVal sender As Object, ByVal e As System.EventArgs) _
    Handles Button2.Click

Dim objDataSet As New DataSet()
' read in the XML file
objDataSet.ReadXml("C:\AddXML\Contacts.xml")
' show it in a grid
DataGrid1.DataSource = objDataSet.Tables(0).DefaultView
' modify a row

objDataSet.Tables("Contact").Rows(0).Item("firstname") = "Vervain"
objDataSet.Tables("Contact").Rows(0).Item("lastname") = "Delaware"
objDataSet.Tables("Contact").Rows(0).Item("address") = "142 Chelscote Gardens"
objDataSet.Tables("Contact").Rows(0).Item("city") = "Pleasantville"
objDataSet.Tables("Contact").Rows(0).Item("state") = "Greater London"
objDataSet.Tables("Contact").Rows(0).Item("postalcode") = "E12 Y34"
objDataSet.Tables("Contact").Rows(0).Item("country") = "UK"

' add a new row to the table
Dim objTable As DataTable

Dim objNewRow As DataRow
' save it to a new file

objDataSet.WriteXml("C:\AddXML\Contacts2.xml")
' read in the new file

Dim objDataSet2 As New DataSet()
objDataSet2.ReadXml("C:\AddXML\Contacts2.xml")
' show it in another grid
DataGrid1.DataSource = objDataSet2.Tables(0).DefaultView
End Sub

End Class
```

3. Right-click on the application name, and select Add | Add New Item. Select XML File, name it Contacts.xml, and click Open. Add the code for Contacts.xml that we saw earlier in the chapter.

4. Run the project. Click the **Display** button to view the information currently in `Contacts.xml`:

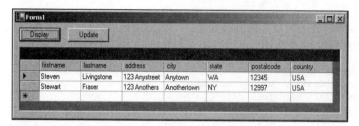

5. Click the **Update** button to view our new contact information:

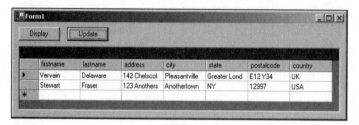

6. If you open up `Contacts2.xml`, you'll be able to see the XML as well.

```xml
<?xml version="1.0" standalone="yes"?>
<contacts>
  <contact>
    <firstname>Vervain</firstname>
    <lastname>Delaware</lastname>
    <address>142 Chelscote Gardens</address>
    <city>Pleasantville</city>
    <state>Greater London</state>
    <postalcode>E12 Y34</postalcode>
    <country>UK</country>
  </contact>
  <contact>
    <firstname>Stewart</firstname>
    <lastname>Fraser</lastname>
    <address>123 Anotherstreet</address>
    <city>Anothertown</city>
    <state>NY</state>
    <postalcode>12997</postalcode>
    <country>USA</country>
  </contact>
</contacts>
```

How It Works

We'll be studying in detail in Chapter 12 how you can use ADO.NET with VB.NET to manipulate XML files. All we wished to demonstrate here is that ADO.NET allows you to use XML files in pretty much the same way as all other types of data store.

Config Files

The area of web server administration is being constantly changed in the Microsoft web server IIS, and rather than having to change settings such as script timeouts, buffering, and permissions manually, it is now possible to specify them within configuration files. There are two main configuration files, `machine.config`, which specifies machine-wide settings, and `web.config`, which specifies settings local to your application. These files are, you guessed it, XML documents. A typical web configuration file might look like this:

```
<configuration>
  <system.web>
    <customErrors mode="Off"/>
      <compilation debug="true"/>
  </system.web>
</configuration>
```

This file is just making it clear that the compiler is set to debug mode, and the custom error handling is switched off, so that the application it deals with displays full details of any errors caused in a browser. This setting is ideal if you're working remotely and testing VB.NET applications on a web server. The whole idea behind using XML documents as configuration files is so that they are easy to read and use.

Web Services

Web services are one of the key parts of the .NET Framework. The technical definition of a web service is a component of programmable application logic that can be accessed using standard web protocols. In the .NET Framework, XML Web Services take center stage. Web services do not have to be XML, but XML Web Services have great potential as they only contain text.

The following diagram illustrates a typical web services scenario:

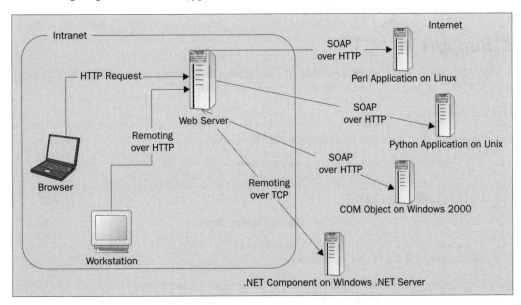

The diagram illustrates an internal network where a browser can make an HTTP request to a web server or a workstation can establish a Remoting connection over HTTP. In turn, the server interacts with a variety of operating systems and languages using SOAP and Remoting. XML features in many aspects of this, from the advertising and discovery of the services to their configuration and payload encoding over the transport.

SOAP

SOAP originally stood for Simple Object Access Protocol and allowed developers to manipulate objects remotely. As it's evolved it has left behind its original meaning, and SOAP is no longer considered an acronym. SOAP is a method for exchanging XML data. The goal of SOAP is to eventually create a standard way for exchanging text between all clients and applications on the Internet.

It's a very lightweight and easy-to-learn protocol. It works by packaging XML data up within further XML in the form of a header and footer. The header forms a list of instructions that a web service must act on and give a response to. The body contains the data to exchange, and if something goes wrong during the exchange it also contains information about the fault.

One great advantage about SOAP is that it doesn't require a specific transport protocol such as HTTP; it could be sent via e-mail, or floppy disk, or over a network. The .NET Framework uses SOAP to call lots of different sorts of remote functions.

Remoting

Web services allow us to call services across a network. They can be used as a communication link with many different technologies, such as getting a Java client to talk to web services developed with ASP.NET. However, there are drawbacks with web services – they are not fast and flexible enough for some business requirements in intranet solutions. With .NET Remoting, the term **Web Services Anywhere** is used, which means that it is possible to run web services in every application type. By this we mean that web services can not only be used in any application, but any application can offer web services. So you can use console apps or web forms applications with web services, you're not just restricted to using them with IIS.

XML Support in .NET

The .NET Framework also offers a number of namespaces for creating and reading XML documents within VB.NET or whichever language you choose to use with .NET.

These namespaces are:

- ❑ System.XML – overall namespace for XML support
- ❑ System.XML.Schema – offers support for the W3C and Microsoft schemas
- ❑ System.XML.Serialization – offers support for the serialization of objects to and deserialization from XML
- ❑ System.XML.XPath – supports parsing and evaluation
- ❑ System.XML.XSL – this supports transformations within XML (that is, the transformation of documents via styles and stylesheets)

Again, we're going to steer clear of the latter four (they're all namespaces we will come across later in this book) and just dig a little into the System.XML namespace. This is composed of four classes. These classes are:

- ❑ `XMLTextReader` – checks documents for "well-formedness" but doesn't validate them

- ❑ `XMLValidatingReader` – allows the checking and validation of documents against an XML schema

- ❑ `XMLTextWriter` – fast forward-only way to write to XML files

- ❑ `XMLDocument` – implements an in-memory representation of the XML document according to the W3C Document Object Model

It is these classes that will enable you to read from and write to XML documents within your own VB.NET applications.

Reading and Writing XML

What does this mean in practical terms? Well, we've already used an example with ADO.NET where we used the following line to read in an XML file to our application:

```
objDataSet.ReadXML("C:\Contacts.xml")
```

Go back to our `Contacts.xml` file and remove a closing `</contact>` tag, and then rerun the application to see what happens:

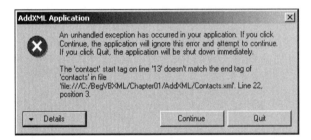

You'll see it generates an error in our program, not because the program itself was wrong, but because we broke the rules of how an XML document should be laid out. The `ReadXML` method is derived ultimately from `System.XML`'s `XML TextReader` class, and this method is what checks to see if the document is well-formed. We have strayed a little outside our limits, as it's not until the next chapter that we examine in depth the structure of an XML document and what "well-formed" XML documents are, and what they aren't. Basically testing whether a document is "well-formed" means testing it to see whether the structure of an XML document is syntactically correct. However, we have demonstrated that the .NET Framework offers a simple set of classes with properties and methods for being able to check XML documents and write to XML documents within your own applications. This is just the starting place for using XML within your own VB.NET applications.

Summary

This chapter gave you the big picture and an introduction to what XML is, why it came about, and what standards there are within the XML family. It discussed how these standards are supported and realized within the .NET Framework and some of the architectures and technologies available.

We initially discussed what XML is – a text-based format for structuring data, and its similarities to, and more importantly differences from, HTML. We discussed some very strong reasons why it is being used, and its advantages as a method for representing data.

We went on to discuss the importance of standards in HTML and looked at the role of the W3C, what it is and what it does, as well as the key role it has in the development of the XML family of technologies. We discussed what these technologies were.

Lastly, we looked at how XML fits in with the .NET Framework and the typical tasks it is most commonly used to perform. Now let's move on and look at XML in the .NET Framework in detail: its syntax, structure, and rules.

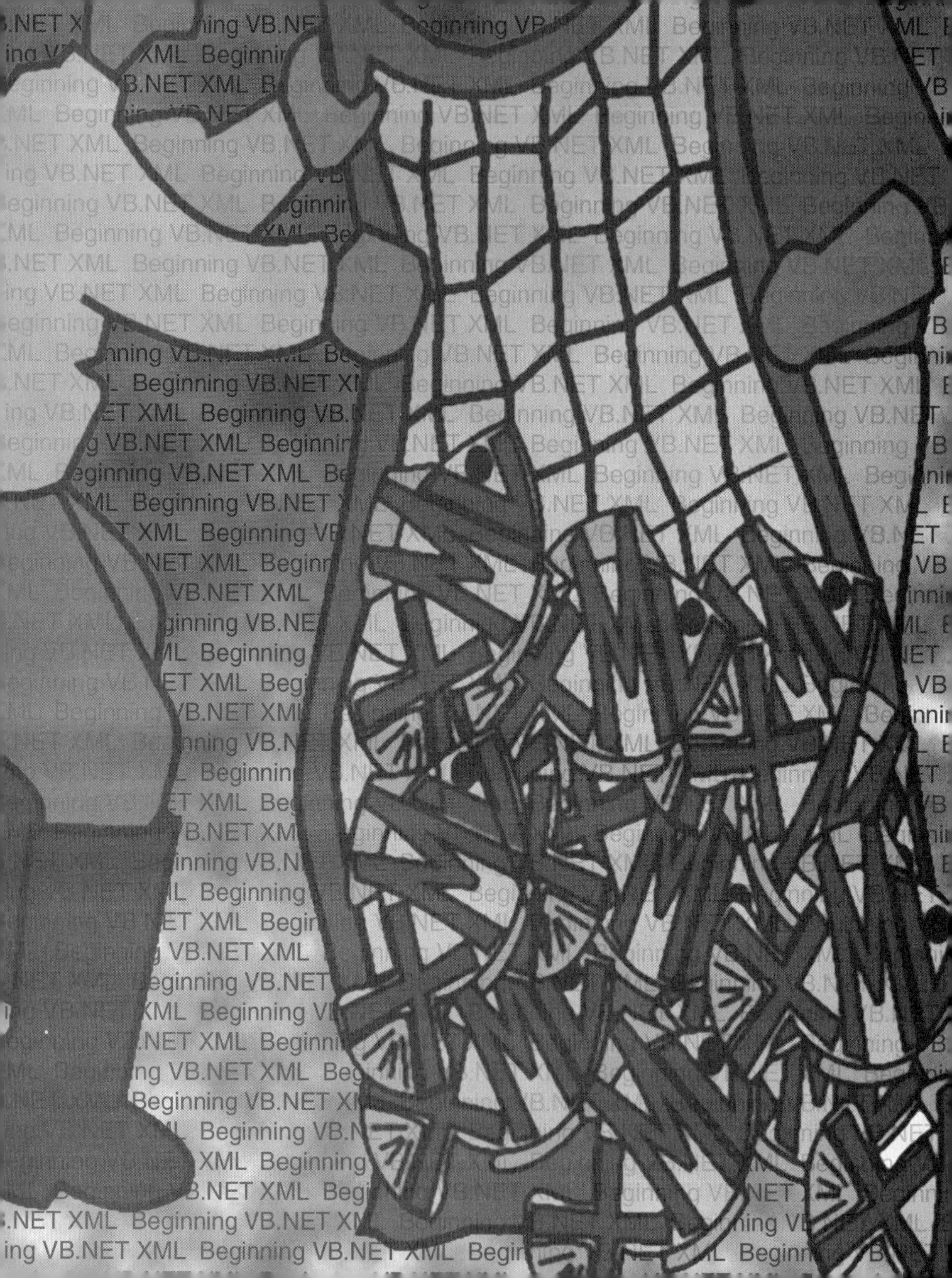
Beginning VB.NET XML

Overview of XML

The previous chapter gave a high-level overview of how the Extensible Markup Language (XML) has made a huge impact not only on the .NET Framework, but on application architectures in general. However, now it's time to start looking in more detail at what exactly XML is, how it is made up, and the rules and definitions that must be followed when creating an XML document. Because XML is so flexible, it's easy to represent the same data in many different ways using different names for elements, different attributes, and so on. The power and potential of XML is only really unleashed if we follow rules that help us to structure our XML documents in a specific way, ensuring that they adhere to a logical structure so that they can be understood by consuming applications.

In this chapter, we'll be concentrating on two aspects of XML – creating XML that is well formed, and validating XML using DTDs (which is the first validation method we'll look at in this book).

This chapter aims to teach you:

- ❏   What XML is and what it can be used for
- ❏   What elements and attributes are in XML and how they are used to produce well-formed XML documents
- ❏   How to validate our XML documents using Document Type Definitions (DTDs)
- ❏   The importance of understanding encoding in XML

Along the way, we'll also introduce schemas, which are another validation method that we'll encounter again later in the book. Let's start from ground level and look at the concepts that we'll encounter when working with XML.

What is XML?

XML clearly defines a way to structure, describe, and interchange data. XML isn't about formatting data, unlike HTML. With HTML, you have access to a limited set of descriptive tags, such as `<title>`, which can give you some clues as to the type of information they contain, but you're restricted to using only the limited HTML vocabulary (the HTML element set). Most tags represent generic structures such as `<p>` for paragraph, or `<body>` for the main content. HTML tags define how to display data, but do not define what the contents of each element actually represent, so when we get data as HTML we can display it, but it is very difficult or practically impossible to do anything else with this data (transform it to another format, save it to a database, search within it).

However, imagine being able to describe your data using an unlimited number of tags, structured according to your own requirements, such as `<title>`, `<firstname>`, `<surname>` and so on; you can immediately identify what the data represents and, more importantly, you can use the various XML technologies to do something with this data. Let's look at some more of the basics of XML.

XML Elements

The core of an XML document is the elements contained within it. Elements are not a new concept and if you worked with HTML, or even viewed the source of a web page, you will have come across them.

In XML, an element is a similar concept. As far as naming of elements is concerned, the rules are looser than when working with HTML, but the loose structure of HTML elements (the ability to code up a page without closing all the HTML tags) isn't acceptable in XML. All opening occurrences of XML elements must have a closing equivalent, and the case of each opening tag must match its corresponding closing tag because XML is **case-sensitive**.

> **When we talk of valid XML, we mean XML that conforms to the rules specified in the W3C XML 1.0 Recommendation.**

This means that although the following HTML fragment would be valid HTML, it would be invalid in XML.

```
<html>
  <Title><head>Contacts</head></title>
  <body>
  <h2>Contact List</h2>
  <hr>
  Steven Livingstone
</html>
```

There are a couple of problems with this as an XML document. The `<body>` element is opened but never closed (there is no `</body>` closing tag), as is the `<hr>` element. Also, the opening `<Title>` element is a different case from the closing `</title>` element. In order to make this a valid XML document you would have to close the open elements and change the case of either the opening or closing `<title>` element so that they match. A rewritten version of this document that is a valid XML document is shown below.

```
<html>
  <title><head>Contacts</head></title>
  <body>
  <h2>Contact List</h2>
  <hr/>
  Steven Livingstone
  </body>
</html>
```

As you can see with the `<body>` element, to close the tag you simply have the same element name, preceded by a slash, encapsulating the data that is to be within that element. In this case, all elements between the opening `<body>` and closing `</body>` elements are called the **child nodes**. Notice that the `<hr>` element is slightly different. When the element in question contains no data, it is known as an **empty element**. The `<hr>` element and the `<br>` element are empty elements, they will never contain any data, and so instead of having a corresponding `</hr>` tag, we can close the tag by adding a slash to the end of the element: `<hr/>`.

XML Attributes

Again, similar to HTML, XML elements can have attributes attached to them which are generally used to add some information on the element or data contained within the element. Looking back to the HTML example above, we can add the `bgcolor` attribute to the `<body>` element as follows.

```
<html>
  <title><head>Contacts</head></title>
  <body bgcolor=red>
  <h2>Contact List</h2>
  <hr>
  Steven Livingstone
</html>
```

This specifies to an HTML browser that the background color on a page will be red. However, this syntax will cause the previously valid XML document to be invalid. This is because the XML specification states that attribute values must be enclosed in quotes (either single or double quotes, ensuring that the opening and closing quote mark are the same type). To ensure that the above is valid XML, the structure would be updated as follows:

```
<html>
  <title><head>Contacts</head></title>
  <body bgcolor="red">
  <h2>Contact List</h2>
  <hr/>
  Steven Livingstone
  </body>
</html>
```

Now the attribute value `"red"` is enclosed in quotes and so will ensure that the document is valid XML again.

35

> **The condition where a given document is valid according to the XML 1.0 specification is known as well-formedness.**

There are ways to check that an XML document is well formed, and that's using what's known as an XML Parser. Let's look at what these are next.

An XML-compliant version of HTML exists, and is known as XHTML. The XHTML specification was created with the aim of removing the browser barriers that have plagued developers for so long. A page viewable on an older version of Internet Explorer would rarely work correctly when viewed on an older version of Netscape, and so on. The modern versions of most browsers are much better at displaying the same output as intended based on the same HTML source, but there are still inconsistencies. If all developers adhere to the XHTML standard, and as long as browsers support it, there should be fewer and fewer banners proudly stating that "In order to view this page, you need to download a different web browser". For more information on XHTML, you can refer to Beginning XHTML, Wrox Press, ISBN: 1-86100-343-9.

XML Parsers

In the same way that a web browser knows how to interpret and display documents marked up using HTML elements, XML also requires a processor, or parser, that will allow a consuming application to read the XML. A parser is a software component that implements the rules of the XML 1.0 Recommendation and all XML parsers have the basic requirement that they check for well-formedness. Well-formedness means that all rules in the XML specification are adhered to, for example, for every opening element in XML there is an equivalent closing element, attribute values are surrounded by quotes, and so on.

There are two types of parsers – **non-validating** and **validating** parsers. Non-validating parsers only check that a document is well-formed, which means it conforms to the basic rules outlined in the XML 1.0 Recommendation.

Validating parsers, however, have the added ability to check that an XML document is valid against another document that defines the rules for the structure and content of the XML document. The XML 1.0 Recommendation defines a feature known as Document Type Declarations (DTDs) which allows you to specify structural rules that the XML file must conform to in order to be valid. We'll look at DTDs in detail later in this chapter. Later in the book we look at schemas, which are another type of validation mechanism that works quite differently from DTDs.

For the first part of this chapter, let's concentrate on well-formed XML. We'll also encounter a simple non-validating parser that's built into Internet Explorer for working with XML files.

Building XML

Let's look at an example where we can use the concepts presented in the last few sections to build an XML document from an HTML document.

Take, for example, the HTML file below (`CapitalCities.htm`):

```
<html>
  <head><title>Global Capital Cities</title></head>
  <body>
    <p>
      <b>Scotland</b><br>
      Edinburgh
    </p>
    <p>
      <b>Chile</b><br>
      Santiago
    </p>
    <p>
      <b>Italy</b><br>
      Rome
    </p>
  </body>
</html>
```

A possible XML representation for this file is shown below:

```
<?xml version="1.0"?>
<capitals>
  <country name="Scotland">Edinburgh</country>
  <country name="Chile">Santiago</country>
  <country name="Italy">Rome</country>
</capitals>
```

It is very important at this point to understand there was no "formula" involved in deciding how the XML structure was designed. This is only one possible representation of this data. An alternative XML representation could take the form shown below:

```
<?xml version="1.0"?>
<data>
  <Scotland CapitalCity="Edinburgh" />
  <Chile CapitalCity="Santiago" />
  <Italy CapitalCity="Rome" />
</data>
```

This data can be structured in many different ways. Remember that the data shown is only data and does not contain any layout information.

Let's now look at creating our own XML file.

Try It Out: Creating and Viewing an XML File

Internet Explorer 5 (and above) allows you to directly view an XML file within the browser. Let's create and view the XML we discussed previously.

> *Note that all the sample code for this chapter is available for download from http://www.wrox.com. We will be storing sample code for this chapter within the following folder:* `C:\BegVBXML\Chapter02`. *You may, of course, use a different folder depending on what you prefer.*

1. Open up a text editor, for example Notepad, and enter the following code, which will form our XML document:

```
<?xml version="1.0"?>
<capitals>
  <country name="Scotland">Edinburgh</country>
  <country name="Chile">Santiago</country>
  <country name="Italy">Rome</country>
</capitals>
```

2. Save the file as `MyCapitalCities.xml` in your `BegVBXML\Chapter02` directory.

3. Using Windows Explorer, navigate to the location you saved the file and open the `MyCapitalCities.xml` file in Internet Explorer. You will see something like the screenshot below:

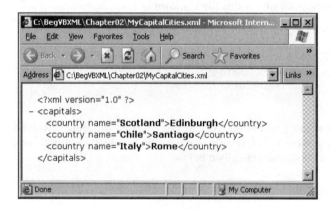

How It Works

Internet Explorer has a built-in stylesheet for displaying XML documents that adds the coloring and defines the layout for our XML documents when displayed in IE. The data in the XML file is unchanged, and no actual formatting has been saved to the XML document itself. Note that the rendered XML file includes the "-" character next to the `<capitals>` node, which we can use to collapse and expand this section. In larger XML files we'll see more of these marks which we can use to collapse all nodes except those which we wish to view at any one time. We'll meet stylesheets again later in this book when we discuss XSL and stylesheets in Chapter 8.

Note also that Netscape Navigator 6.0 (and above) has built in support for displaying XML along with some basic styling capability using Cascading Style Sheets (CSS), so there is more scope for sending XML directly to the browser (with styling of course to make it look like a normal HTML page to the user). The same page viewed on Netscape 7 (with default settings applied) looks as follows:

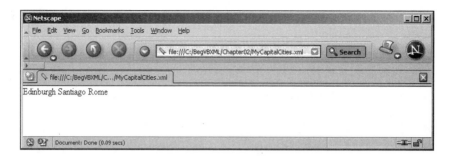

For the purposes of this book, we'll be sticking to Internet Explorer as our browser because of the view it provides of XML documents. For more information on Netscape 7 and its support of XML, you can check out http://www.netscape.com.

The Sections of an XML Document

An XML document can be made of up to four parts (three of the four parts are actually optional), which must, if they appear in the document, be presented in the following order:

❑ The Prolog (Optional)

❑ The DTD (Optional)

❑ The Document Root

❑ The Epilog (Optional)

The Prolog

The Prolog section of an XML document typically contains information that appears prior to the start tag of the document or root element. This includes information that applies to the document as a whole, such as character encoding, document structure, and stylesheet references. It also includes the XML declaration, comments, and processing instructions (for the parser), although all of these are actually optional.

The **XML declaration** itself is the most important of these, and although optional, many systems and parsers will not accept an XML document without a proper declaration. The declaration identifies the document as an XML document to a parser and allows you to specify information such as:

❑ The version of the XML syntax, currently version 1.0.

❑ The encoding of the content of the document. This is optional, and if the document is saved as UTF-8 or UTF-16 the encoding can be determined by the parser. Other encodings need to be specified in the declaration (we talk about encoding later in this chapter).

❑ Whether the document is standalone (defaults to no), indicating that the document relies on external files, such as a Document Type Definition (which we'll look at next).

So, in its most basic format, the XML declaration itself looks something like the following:

```
<?xml version="1.0"?>
```

Another declaration may look like this:

```
<?xml version="1.0" encoding="ISO-8859-1"?>
```

We'll look at all the various encoding options later in this chapter. The declaration, if inserted, must be at the very start of the file with no line breaks or whitespace before it.

The Document Type Definition (DTD)

The Document Type Definition describes the content of an XML document. It defines the valid structure and content that the XML document it is applied to must adhere to in order for it to be described as a valid document. The DTD will ensure that the XML document is correctly structured (elements and attributes appear in the correct order) and it gives us some basic validation of the data values that are within the elements and attributes. For example, you can specify that the value of a given element must be one of a short set of possible values.

This is where the concept of **validating** and **non-validating parsers** comes in. Non-validating parsers do not care about any DTD information within the XML document and do no validation against the document, so the document can have an invalid structure or invalid data and no warning will be given. Validating parsers, as their name implies, validate the XML document against a specified DTD, so the application can be informed if there is a problem with the XML source. Any XML document that is successfully parsed by a validating parser is known to be **valid**. Internet Explorer has a validating parser built in as of version 5.0, but by default validation has been turned off. This allows you to use programmatic techniques to validate your XML documents in the browser. We'll learn more about DTDs later in the chapter.

The Document Root

The document root is required and is the first element within the document after the prolog and DTD sections. It can contain attributes, sub-elements, comments, character data and even processing instructions (instructions to the parser, but are very rarely used). The document root of the sample XML we have been working with is `<capitals>` and must have a closing `</capitals>` element. Between the opening and closing root tags will be the bulk of our XML file.

The Epilog

The epilog is similar to the prolog in that it is where processing instructions are placed, but it comes at the end of the document, typically to perform some clean-up work, it can also contain comments. Again the epilog is an optional section of an XML file and is rarely used.

Creating Well-Formed XML Documents

The core behavior of XML documents is that they are **well-formed**. A well-formed XML document is one that conforms to the syntax rules specified in the XML 1.0 specification. As this specification, available at http://www.w3.org/TR/REC-xml, can get fairly detailed, let's examine some of the core concepts this document states.

Elements in XML

The basic rule which we encountered briefly earlier is that when working in XML, all tags must be closed. What this means is actually two things; the first is that for every opening XML tag such as `<tag>`, there must be a closing XML tag such as `</tag>`. This was evident in our capitals example we saw before.

```
<?xml version="1.0"?>
<capitals>
  <country name="Scotland">Edinburgh</country>
  <country name="Chile">Santiago</country>
  <country name="Italy">Rome</country>
</capitals>
```

Alternatively, if the element contains no sub-elements or data within it, we can directly close it using the empty element syntax we saw earlier, as follows:

```
<?xml version="1.0"?>
<capitals>
  <country name="Scotland" />
  <country name="Chile" />
  <country name="Italy" />
</capitals>
```

All elements must be closed – they can contain hierarchies of elements and other XML data, but each hierarchy must be closed at the same level it was opened. So the following XML document is invalid.

```
<?xml version="1.0"?>
<capitals>
  <country name="Scotland"><city>Edinburgh</country></city>
  ...
</capitals>
```

This is invalid because the highlighted line does not properly close, that is, it overlaps the `<city>` element and `<country>` elements. We opened the `<city>` element, but then closed the `<country>` element before the `<city>` element was closed.

Beyond simply ensuring that open elements are closed, there are a series of other rules that must be applied to XML documents to ensure that they are well-formed.

One Document Root

The document **must** have only **one** document root element. The root element contains the rest of the document data. The rest of the document is a child of the root element – in other words, the following XML document is not well-formed:

```
<?xml version="1.0"?>
<capitals>
  <country name="Scotland">Edinburgh</country>
  <country name="Chile">Santiago</country>
```

```
    <country name="Italy">Rome</country>
  </capitals>
  <continents>
    <continent>Africa</continent>
    <continent>South America</continent>
  </continents>
```

There are two "document root elements" here – <capitals> and <continents>, so this is not a well-formed document. To make it well-formed, the two main elements, <capitals> and <continents>, would have to be wrapped in a document root element, for example:

```
<?xml version="1.0"?>
<worldInfo>
  <capitals>
    <country name="Scotland">Edinburgh</country>
    <country name="Chile">Santiago</country>
    <country name="Italy">Rome</country>
  </capitals>
  <continents>
    <continent>Africa</continent>
    <continent>South America</continent>
  </continents>
</worldInfo>
```

Legal and Illegal Names

Secondly, there are some naming conventions used when working with elements in XML; they are **case-sensitive** and there are some other naming restrictions. Hence, the following element names are ALL different and "mean" completely different things:

```
<capital>
<CAPITAL>
<Capital>
<CapitaL>
```

The following table illustrates other rules and gives a sample invalid and valid element name.

Rules	Invalid Example	Valid Examples
There cannot be a space after the "<" character	<Capital List>	<CapitalList>
Names can start with letters or the underscore character, but not numbers or other punctuation characters	<1stList>	<_1stList>
After the first character, "." and "-" are also allowed.	<-city>	<city-name>
	<.city>	<city.name>

Rules	Invalid Example	Valid Examples
Never use a colon ":" character; although it is allowed, there are very good reasons to never use it as an element name (it is used in namespaces which are discussed in detail in the next chapter)	`<city:name>`	`<city-name>`
You cannot start an element with the text "xml" in any combination of upper or lower case characters (although Internet Explorer does not enforce this rule; other parsers do)	`<Xml_Char>`	`<_Xml_Char>`

Illegal Characters

The text that comes between opening and closing elements is called **Parsed Character Data or PCDATA**, and you are free to use whatever characters you want for this data, except for two XML reserved characters, notably "<" and "&". Using one of these in your XML document will give you something like the result in the screenshot below (Look at `CapitalCitiesErr.xml` from the code download).

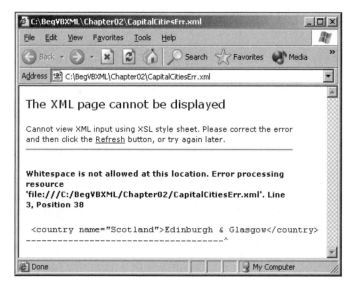

In this case, the "&" character has been used and is an illegal XML PCDATA character.

Thankfully, there is a way around this problem through the use of entity references.

Entity References

Entity references allow you to use the two reserved XML characters as well as use some other commonly used XML characters. These are listed in the table below and allow a character to be entered within the PCDATA and keep the XML document well-formed. This list is similar to HTML encoded characters.

Character	XML Entity reference	Example	Output
&	&	Steven & Loreto	Steven & Loreto
<	<	<6	<6
>	>	>6	>6
'	'	'Hello'	'Hello'
"	"	"World"	"World"

Furthermore, other characters can be escaped using character references and these can be inserted as &#xxx; where "xxx" would be replaced by the Unicode number of the character you want to insert (or &#xXX, where XX is the hexadecimal number representation of the Unicode character). You would do this if your editor does not support Unicode/UTF-8 encoding or you aren't saving your documents as Unicode or UTF-8. So, for example, you can include the character "¥" with the character reference ¥. We look more at encoding later in the chapter.

You can also create your own entity references (called General Entities) for characters or strings that are repeated within the XML document. Within the DTD (internal or external), you define the entity as follows:

```
<!ENTITY copyright "This document is copyright Wrox Press">
```

If the text you want to associate with this entity is large you may prefer to put it in a separate file, for example copyright.txt. This way you could create the entity as follows:

```
<!ENTITY copyright SYSTEM "copyright.txt">
```

You could then include this within an XML file as follows:

```
<document>
   <para>blah blah</para>
   <copyright>&copyright;</copyright>
</document>
```

CDATA Sections

In large documents, you might not want to look through every character that may be invalid and replace it with its appropriate entity or character reference. In these situations, we can escape a block of characters in bulk, simply by wrapping them in a CDATA section. So consider the following invalid XML fragment:

```
<syntax>You cannot use "<" or "&" characters in XML.</syntax>
```

This will fail because of the use of "<" and "&" directly as PCDATA characters. However, we can escape the entire sentence as follows:

```
<syntax><![CDATA[You cannot use "<" or "&" characters in XML.]]></syntax>
```

This will now parse and you will have no problems in leaving the sentence as it is. Typically you will use CDATA to escape larger section of text in the XML document that's likely to contain illegal characters – particularly when the process is managed by an application. Additionally, you can specify that certain elements will contain CDATA and not PCDATA by adding this rule to a DTD or XML Schema, rather than embedding the !CDATA directive in the XML document itself.

We've covered a lot of ground in ensuring that XML documents are well-formed. Let's now see how much you have learned and if you can recognize how to ensure a document is well-formed.

Try It Out: Ensuring XML is Well-Formed

1. Enter the following code and save the file as `CapitalCitiesCopy.xml`:

```
<?xml version="1.0"?>
<capitals>
  <country name="Scotland">Edinburgh</country>
  <country name="Chile">Santiago</country>
  <country name="Italy">Rome</country>
  <copyright>
    The content of this <xml> file is © NoCompanyAtAll Limited
  </copyright>
  <footer>
    This is just a section that contains a whole load of "characters" that
    maybe could cause some problems when working with XML files. We know that <
    and & characters cause problems, but what about $ and %?? Well, by the time
    you read this you will know.
  </footer>
</capitals>
```

2. Open the file in Internet Explorer and you should see the following:

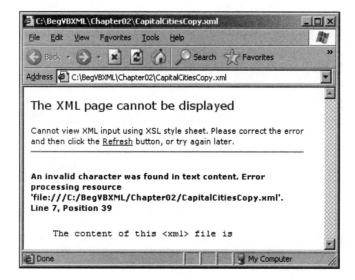

There are quite a few problems with this document, and the first one encountered by the parser is displayed in our browser window.

3. Open the file in Notepad and make the following changes to fix our XML:

```
<?xml version="1.0"?>
<capitals>
  <country name="Scotland">Edinburgh</country>
  <country name="Chile">Santiago</country>
  <country name="Italy">Rome</country>
  <copyright>
      The content of this &lt;xml&gt; file is &#xA9; NoCompanyAtAll Limited
  </copyright>
  <footer>
<![CDATA[This is just section that contains a whole load of "characters" that
maybe could cause some problems when working with XML files. We know that < and &
characters cause problems, but what about $ and %?? Well, by the time you read
this you will know.]]>
  </footer>
</capitals>
```

4. Save the file and again open it up in Internet Explorer and you will see something like the screenshot below – the document is now well-formed.

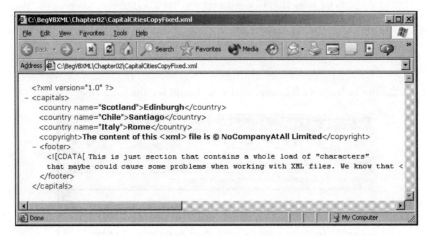

How It Works

Our original XML file had several invalid items in it which meant that we saw error messages when viewing the file in Internet Explorer. In order to fix these errors we had to do the following:

```
The content of this &lt;xml&gt; file is &#xA9; NoCompanyAtAll Limited
```

In the `<copyright>` element, we changed the < character before the letters xml to its entity reference `&lt;` and changed the > character to its entity reference `&gt;` so that the **<xml>** piece of text wasn't interpreted as an element by the parser. We also changed the © character to its character reference `&#xA9;` so that it could also be correctly parsed.

The other fix we had to make was to wrap the PCDATA of the `<footer>` element in a CDATA node, to escape all the illegal characters in that last paragraph:

```
<![CDATA[This is just section that contains a whole load of "characters" that
maybe could cause some problems when working with XML files. We know that < and &
characters cause problems, but what about $ and %?? Well, by the time you read
this you will know.]]>
```

All of the illegal characters and the legal ones are gathered together into one character data section, and are therefore displayed verbatim when the file is viewed in the browser. There's no longer any need to escape the known illegal characters separately.

Let's move on now and look at some more important rules of XML.

Whitespace is Significant

One of the most confusing areas in XML is something you don't actually see – whitespace. When developing web pages with HTML, we have all got used to spacing and tabbing things into a particular place, either to lay it out or just to make it easier to work with. It is almost always in vain, however, because as soon as it is rendered in the browser, all whitespace is collapsed into a single space. To get around this we use `<br>` and `<p>` tags to separate our paragraphs, along with the ` ` entity, which we can use to insert a non-breaking space.

In XML this is not the case. The family of XML technologies, and XML itself, have various methods of handling whitespace and it is all very controllable. There are differences between how whitespace is handled as data within an element, and how whitespace is handled between two element tags.

When whitespace is within the text of the element (PCDATA), for example:

```
<a><b>I am   whitespace</b></a>
```

There are three spaces between the word am and the word `whitespace` in this code. This will be read as:

```
I am   whitespace
```

However, if the whitespace occurs between tags, it is treated differently, for example:

```
<a>   <b>I am   whitespace</b>   </a>
```

We now have three spaces between each element, and three spaces, as before, within the text of the `<b>` element. This code will be read as follows:

```
I am   whitespace
```

The whitespace that existed between the two element tags has been collapsed. This means we can use whitespace outside of elements to indent and arrange our code to make it easier to work with when designing our XML files.

According to the XML parser, whitespace is considered significant when it is within PCDATA. However, some applications (such as an HTML parser) may not care about the whitespace and collapse it anyway, so we need a way of specifying whether the whitespace of PCDATA is significant or not. This can be done with the xml:space attribute, which can have the value default or preserve. If it's set to default, the whitespace can be removed from the text if desired, but preserve indicates that whitespace **must** be preserved at all times. In the following example, we could preserve whitespace so that the following list of names appear on separate lines:

```
<a><b xml:space="preserve">
    Steven Livingstone
    Loreto Perez
</b></a>
```

The output would be something like:

```
    Steven Livingstone
    Loreto Perez
```

With four spaces before each name.

> **Unfortunately, the default style sheet for Internet Explorer removes the spaces when it displays in the browser because the XML source is converted to HTML that can be displayed on the browser, and HTML rendering on IE doesn't preserve spaces!**

Element Nesting

The last issue that we need to discuss when working with elements is that the meaning of a document changes as its structure changes. Element names are not always interpreted as being the same no matter the location – their location is important. Consider the following structure:

```
<register>
  <person>
    <name>Steven</name>
  </person>
  <homeCity>
    <name>Glasgow</name>
  </homeCity>
</register>
```

Notice that, although we re-use the <name> element within this document, it means two completely different things each time. The first represents a person's name and the second represents the name of a city – they are qualified by what the tag they are wrapped in, or their parent element, defines. The first <name> element has the <person> element as its parent and the second <name> element has <homeCity> as its parent.

When developing XML documents one of the key points is that you can create your own tags where desired and as you create the tags, you are responsible for defining some of the meaning surrounding the content of that tag. While it's fairly obvious to us what each <name> tag represents in the above example, it could cause confusion for applications consuming the data, and in larger documents (which you're more likely to meet in the real world) the potential for confusion is increased. There are ways of avoiding this potential problem, though. In the next chapter we will look at XML Namespaces, which help in ensuring that we don't get confused when working with elements with the same names.

Let's move on now and take a look at attributes, and look at some comparisons between using attributes and elements.

Attributes in XML

Attributes are name/value pairs associated with an element. We have already used attributes to specify the name of the country in the capitals example that we saw earlier:

```
<?xml version="1.0"?>
<capitals>
   <country name="Scotland">Edinburgh</country>
   <country name="Chile">Santiago</country>
   <country name="Italy">Rome</country>
</capitals>
```

Attributes must always have some value and some of the naming rules we discussed when talking about elements also apply to attributes:

❑   Never use a colon ":" character, although it is allowed, in an attribute name as this characters is used in namespaces (discussed in the next chapter) which will make a huge impact on almost all of your XML documents.

❑   You cannot start an attribute with the text "xml" in any combination of upper or lower case characters (although Internet Explorer does not enforce this rule; other parsers do).

Additionally, you cannot have two attributes on one element that have the same name, although, remember that attributes are also case-sensitive and so name and Name are different.

When Do We Use Attributes?

One of the biggest topics of debate in the world of XML is the use of attributes versus the use of elements. Much of the time they are quite interchangeable, but sometimes it is better to choose one over the other.

Attributes as Metadata

Attributes can be useful when we want to specify some metadata about the item you are describing within the element. Consider the situation where you want to specify some data about a person.

```
<person>
  <name>Graham Livingstone</name>
  <age>25</age>
</person>
```

The core information here is the person's name, and we could consider the age of this person as metadata on this. There is no magic formula on what you can consider as metadata – it is up to you. We can use elements to store the data, and attributes to describe that data, so we could instead write our XML as follows:

```
<person age="25">Graham Livingstone</person>
```

It is up to you while creating your XML to decide on what can be regarded as a kind of metadata and what cannot, but sometimes it makes the concepts more readable.

Attributes are Easier to Work With

Often attributes are easier to work with than elements, as using elements all over the place can make the XML look more complex than it actually is and less readable to humans. Consider the following for example:

```
<country>Chile is in South America<capital>Santiago</capital></country>
```

Now, this line gives us all the information we need and can easily be parsed, but it is not as easily readable as it might be because elements are embedded within the PCDATA information, which breaks up what is quite a simple sentence.

We can clean up such a structure as follows.

```
<country capital="Santiago">Chile is in South America</country>
```

This is much more readable and still tells us the exact same information , using slightly fewer characters. In fact we can even describe this fully using only attributes without losing any information as follows.

```
<country capital="Santiago" text="Chile is in South America" />
```

Now, because there is no content within the <country> element, it has become an empty element, so we can end the country element with a slash.

Elements can be More Complex

Elements have the ability to deal with complex structures and can easily be extended in the future if required. Consider the following structure:

```
<person>
  <name>Graham Livingstone</name>
  <age>25</age>
  <address street="72 Gettison Avenue, Yoker" City="Glasgow" />
</person>
```

What if, for some reason, you wanted to further categorize or extend the address element? Using attributes, you are limited to a single value, or you would have to create new attributes, which becomes more problematic if there are multiple addresses (for example, home address, work address, and so on). With elements you can easily create a hierarchical structure to represent your data, such as the following:

```
<person>
  <name>Graham Livingstone</name>
  <age>25</age>
  <address>
    <streetNumber>72</streetNumber>
    <streetName>Gettison Avenue</streetName>
    <area>Yoker</area>
    <city>Glasgow</city>
  </address>
</person>
```

DTDs Can Validate Attributes

One advantage that attributes have historically had over elements is stronger data typing when working with DTDs, which was for a long time the only validation mechanism within XML. Elements can only contain either PCDATA (any text string) or sub-elements, so there's not too much need for validation here.

However, attributes can be declared to be either CDATA types (character data), an ID type, an Entity, an option from an enumerated list, or other types. Although this is not regarded as powerful when we look at what the XML Schema language now gives us, relative to what was available for elements, this was quite an improvement in validation. We'll look at this topic in more detail later in the chapter.

Sometimes Attributes Just Won't Work

There are cases where you really just can't use attributes in any sensible way. Typically, when you have a situation where the attributes are repeated you have to look at using elements (because you cannot have the same named attributes on an element). This happens often when you have multi-value nodes.

As an example, imagine a SELECT statement against a relational database that you want to serialize (convert) to XML (a feature that now comes with SQL Server). If you asked for all cities of a given country to be represented using attributes, you may be unable to directly persist the results as XML, for example:

```
<cities>
  <country name="scotland" city="glasgow" city="edinburgh" city="aberdeen" />
</cities>
```

This syntax is invalid, and we would be unable to persist this as XML. We have repeated the city attribute several times within the same element, so it would fail on any XML parser. To fix this, we would have to use elements, for example:

```
<cities>
  <country name="scotland">
    <city>glasgow</city>
    <city>edinburgh</city>
    <city>aberdeen</city>
  </country>
</cities>
```

Alternatively, we could use another format that uses attributes:

```
<cities>
  <country name="scotland">
    <city name="glasgow" />
    <city name="edinburgh" />
    <city name="aberdeen" />
  </country>
</cities>
```

Attributes Can Save Space

This is a fairly obvious difference between using elements and attributes; an element generally requires an opening tag and a closing tag, whereas an attribute uses only a single name, meaning we use less characters when using attributes compared to elements. While this may sound fairly innocuous, in a large document, this may have a significant effect on the total file size of the document. For example, consider this fragment:

```
<?xml version="1.0"?>
<capitals>
  <country name="Scotland">
    <population>5,500,000</population>
    <capital>Edinburgh</capital>
    <continent>Europe</continent>
  </country>
  <country name="Chile">
    <population>24,000,000</population>
    <capital>Santiago</capital>
    <continent>South America</continent>
  </country>
  <country name="Italy">
    <population>56,000,000</population>
    <capital>Rome</capital>
    <continent>Europe</continent>
  </country>
</capitals>
```

Imagine a case where we represent every country in the world – the file size would be substantially affected by the use of elements to describe the population, capital and continent of the country. Using attributes, we can dramatically affect the size of the document.

```
<?xml version="1.0"?>
<capitals>
  <country name="Scotland" population="5,500,000" capital="Edinburgh"
    continent="Europe"/>
  <country name="Chile" population="24,000,000" capital="Santiago"
    continent="South America" />
  <country name="Italy" population="56,000,000" capital="Rome"
    continent="Europe">
</capitals>
```

To illustrate what we have been discussing above, let's look at the effect of using elements versus using attributes. In the code download folder are two files (CapitalCitiesElements.xml and CapitalCitiesAttributes.xml) based on the simple XML fragments we just looked at.

By looking at the sizes of these two files we see that `CapitalCitiesElements.xml` is approximately 475 bytes in size and that the `CapitalCitiesAttributes.xml` file is approximately 328 bytes.

The file size is affected even with these simple fragments. Now, of course these kinds of file sizes won't have any real effect on performance, but consider where we want to represent another 200 countries of the world. Extrapolating these figures by 200 gives us 95,000 (or 95k) for the majority elements file and 65,600 (65.6k) for the majority attributes file. This gives a ratio of almost 2 to 3. So the file with elements is already one-third bigger (approx 35k) than the one with attributes.

There's one last topic that we need to discuss that relates to the basic structure of XML documents, and that's the use of comments.

Comments in XML

We can add comments to our XML documents that add some description about the contents of our document as and when required, in a similar way to adding comments to HTML documents, or C# or VB.NET code. Comments in XML documents are structured the same way as HTML documents, a sample of which is as follows:

```
<!-- I am an XML comment -->
```

Comments can appear anywhere in an XML document after the XML declaration.

So, we've looked at the basic structure of XML files, including elements, attributes, and comments. Knowing how these are all formed and structured is essential if we want to create well-formed XML documents. We now need to consider how we can ensure that our XML files are valid, in that they follow a specific structure to ensure consistency and aid collaboration.

Validating XML Documents

As you now know, XML is highly flexible and allows you to create many variations of elements and attributes that go to make up a given document instance, as long as you stick to the rules of the XML 1.0 Recommendation. This flexibility comes at a price – the format of an XML document representing the same data can vary dramatically depending on the author (whether it be a person or automated).

Consider two such representations of the capitals XML document we have been working with. The first is the form we are familiar with:

```
<capitals>
  <country name="Scotland">Edinburgh</country>
  <country name="Chile">Santiago</country>
  <country name="Italy">Rome</country>
</capitals>
```

The second is an alternative representation of the same information.

```
<capitals>
  <Scotland>Edinburgh</Scotland>
  <Chile>Santiago</Chile>
  <Italy>Rome</Italy>
</capitals>
```

One way of validating an XML document we create is by using Document Type Definitions, another method is to use Schemas. We will concentrate on DTDs in this section and give only an overview of schemas here since we will be covering them in more detail in later chapters.

Document Type Definitions

> This covers a subset of DTDs and you should have a look at Beginning XML 2e (ISBN 1-86100-559-8) or Professional XML (ISBN 1-86100-505-9) from Wrox Press for further information.

So how do we define the structure that our XML files will follow? How do we ensure that the values entered by the creator of the document are actually valid? One answer is something we talked about briefly earlier in the chapter, Document Type Definitions (DTDs). DTDs contain a set of rules that XML documents must follow to be considered valid. So when there are DTDs along with an XML document, all involved parties can be sure that a given document follows a structure similar to that defined by the DTD, which helps ensure consistency, accuracy and validity of the data. In fact, DTDs are the only validation mechanism built directly into the XML 1.0 Recommendation and hence are still fairly popular compared to the new Schemas.

Let's take a look at a simple example of a DTD.

Try It Out: Using Embedded DTD Information

In this example, we'll add DTD information to the XML document we looked at earlier (MyCapitalCities.xml). We'll look at how to add DTD information to the XML document itself. We'll look at how DTDs are structured in detail after this example.

1. Open up MyCapitalCities.xml in your editor, and add the following highlighted lines of code:

```
<?xml version="1.0"?>
<!DOCTYPE capitals [
  <!ELEMENT capitals (country)*>
  <!ELEMENT country (#PCDATA)>
  <!ATTLIST country name CDATA #IMPLIED>
]>
<capitals>
  <country name="Scotland">Edinburgh</country>
  <country name="Chile">Santiago</country>
  <country name="Italy">Rome</country>
</capitals>
```

2. Save the file and view it in your browser:

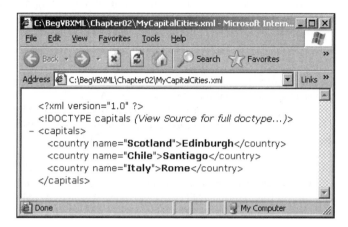

As the text implies, we can view the whole DTD information by viewing the source of our page, and all we see then is the original code once more.

How It Works

We've added DTD information, and we know that our document is still well-formed (or else we would have had an error when we tried to view the page). Our document now includes information that can be used to validate our document. By default, we've not actually validated our XML file. In order to validate our XML, we need to install a plug-in for Internet Explorer, which we'll look at later in this section.

Let's take a quick look at our code:

```
<!DOCTYPE capitals [
  <!ELEMENT capitals (country)*>
  <!ELEMENT country (#PCDATA)>
  <!ATTLIST country name CDATA #IMPLIED>
]>
```

The syntax here is quite different from the XML syntax we've seen so far. This syntax – known as Extended Backus-Naur Form (EBNF) – takes some explanation, as it's not as intuitive as basic XML syntax. Let's start our tour of how to create DTDs and explain these lines of code as we go along.

Document Type Declaration

The Document Type Declaration is the DOCTYPE that you see at the start of a DTD.

> *Take care not to confuse the Document Type **Declaration** with the Document Type **Definition** (which is abbreviated to DTD). For clarity, we only ever contract the Document Type Definition to DTD, and talk about the declaration in full.*

The syntax of a document type declaration can occur in one of three ways. The first is:

```
<!DOCTYPE name [...]>
```

This is used where you embed DTD information within a XML document, as we saw in the previous example, and the *name* attribute must be the same as the name of the root element of the XML document that it is to validate.

```
<!DOCTYPE name SYSTEM uri [...]>
```

The second syntax is used where you want to use an external DTD, stored in a separate DTD file that resides on the same physical system, to validate the document. Again, the *name* attribute must match the name of the root element of the XML document you want to validate, which must be followed by the capitalized string SYSTEM (separated by a single space), followed by the URI to the DTD document. This URI can be a file URL ("file:///C:\mydtd.dtd"), an HTTP URL ("http://www.somesite.com/mydtd.dtd") or, if in the same directory as the source XML document, the name of the file itself ("mydtd.dtd"). In this situation you could also embed DTD information within the declaration, if desired – any information that appears within the declaration is called the **internal subset**, whereas declarations in the external DTD are referred to as the **external subset**.

```
<!DOCTYPE name PUBLIC identifier>
```

The final syntax relates to public DTDs, which are effectively catalogs that are usually registered and well known. For example, there is a DTD available for validating HTML, which can be referenced as follows (depending on the HTML version):

```
<!DOCTYPE HTML PUBLIC "-//W3C//DTD HTML 4.01//EN"
    "http://www.w3.org/TR/html4/strict.dtd">
```

Notice we now use the PUBLIC identifier, followed by the URL to the DTD we require. Another example DTD, defined by IBM, is a DTD that can be used to validate XHTML documents. This DTD can be referenced as follows:

```
<!DOCTYPE html SYSTEM "http://www.ibm.com/data/dtd/v11/ibmxhtml1-
    transitional.dtd">
```

Element Declarations

Element declarations allow us to specify the elements that may occur in a document, and the structure they may appear in. The declaration of an element is as follows:

```
<!ELEMENT name (...)>
```

The *name* attribute is actually the name of the element and within the parenthesis there are a number of options to determine constraints on this element. Equally, as DTDs are not namespace-aware, you have to actually insert the namespace prefix exactly as it will appear in the document (we'll meet namespaces in the next chapter).

The **content model** appears after the name of the element, and defines what may appear (or not) within the element. It can be one of the following:

❑ **Empty** – the element may have an empty content model; for example, `<country/>` can be specified as

```
<!ELEMENT country EMPTY>
```

❑ **Element** – Used to specify that an element may contain other elements; for example, `<capitals><country>...</country></capitals>` can be specified as:

```
<!ELEMENT capitals (country)>
```

This is similar to one of the lines in the example we looked at earlier.

❑ **Mixed** – This content model states that a mixture of text and elements may appear within this element; for example, `<country>Scotland</country>` can be specified as:

```
<!ELEMENT capitals (#PCDATA)>
```

This is similar to another of the lines in the example we looked at earlier.

❑ **Any** – The ANY keyword indicates that any of the elements declared within the DTD can be used as children of this element; this is defined as:

```
<!ELEMENT capitals ANY>
```

We've started to unravel our brief example from the beginning of this section, but there's more to learn before we can completely explain the code.

Sequences and Choices

In addition to content models, there are **sequences** and **choices**, which we can use to further refine the content of an element.

Sequences are separated by a comma and indicate that the elements must be used in the order they are defined. Consider the following DTD fragment:

```
<!ELEMENT country (name, capital, continent)>
```

This states that the country element can contain the name, capital, and continent elements in that order. A valid example fragment of a conforming XML document is shown below:

```
<country>
  <name>Chile</name>
  <capital>Santiago</capital>
  <continent>South America</continent>
</country>
```

Choices state that any of the elements defined within the definition may appear. Again, consider the following DTD fragment:

```
<!ELEMENT GeographicArea (city | country | continent)>
```

57

This states that the `GeographicArea` element can contain the `city`, `country`, or `continent` element. A valid example fragment of a conforming XML document is shown below:

```
<GeographicArea>
  <continent>South America</continent>
</GeographicArea>
```

Finally, we can combine the two to produce a more complex content model:

```
<!ELEMENT atlas ((city | country | continent), population, language)>
```

This states that the `atlas` element can contain the `city`, `country`, or `continent` element, followed by the population and language elements. A valid example fragment of a conforming XML document is shown below:

```
<atlas>
  <country>United States</country>
  <population>240 Million</population>
  <language>English</language>
</atlas>
```

Cardinality

In our *Try It Out* example, we had the following line of code:

```
<!ELEMENT capitals (country)*>
```

While we've explained what the majority of this code means, we've not explained why there's an asterisk at the end of the line. This asterisk is a cardinality indicator, which indicates how many times an element may appear in a document. There are four types of cardinality indicator:

Cardinality	Description
[none]	When no indicator exists, the element must appear once and only once.
?	The element can appear once or not at all.
+	The element must appear one or more times.
*	The element can appear zero or more times.

So our line of code actually means "the `capitals` node may contain zero or more `country` elements".

For a more involved example, we could extend the `atlas` example and have the following definition:

```
<!ELEMENT atlas ((city | country | continent), population?, language+)>
```

A valid XML fragment that follows this definition could appear as follows:

```
<atlas>
  <country>United States</country>
  <language>English</language>
  <language>Spanish</language>
</atlas>
```

In the DTD we stated that the population is optional and that the language element may appear at least once, but with many occurrences.

Attribute Declarations

Attribute declarations are slightly more powerful than elements from a typing perspective because you can apply limited restrictions on the value that may be contained within an attribute.

Attributes are declared in an ATTLIST which is associated with an element and has three main parts:

- ❑ The attribute name – simply the name of the attribute
- ❑ The attribute type – can limit the type of the value of the attribute
- ❑ The attribute value declaration – can be used to specify further information on the attribute

In our *Try It Out* example, we had one attribute declaration:

```
<!ATTLIST country name CDATA #IMPLIED>
```

In this line of code, we associated the name attribute with the country element, specified that it contained character data, and that it is implied, which means it is optional, with no default or fixed value. Let's look at each of these options in more detail.

The attribute name must be declared along with any namespace prefix that may appear within the XML document. The type of the attribute can be defined as one of the following:

Data type	Description
CDATA	The attribute value is character data
ID	The value of this attribute uniquely identifies the containing element
IDREF	The value of this attribute is a reference to an element uniquely identified by an ID
IDREFS	The attribute value is a whitespace-separated list of IDREF attributes
ENTITY	The value of the attribute is a reference to an external unparsed entity such as an image or other binary file
ENTITIES	The value is a whitespace-separated list of ENTITY references
NMTOKEN	The value of the attribute is a token (string of character data comprised of standard name characters)
NMTOKENS	The attribute value is a whitespace-separated list of NMTOKEN values
Enumeration	You can define an enumerated list of possible value attributes

Attribute Value Declarations

Finally, the attribute value declarations allow us to specify the following details about an attribute

❑   The attribute has a default value

❑   The attribute has a fixed value

❑   The attribute is required

❑   The attribute is implied

So let's take a look at some examples incorporating all of these.

An attribute can be assigned a **default value**, which means the instance will have the specified value, even if it's not included in the instance document. This can be defined as follows:

```
<!ATTLIST country capital (Glasgow | Santiago | Milan) "Glasgow">
```

This fragment specifies that the `capital` attribute of the `country` element will have either the value `Glasgow`, `Santiago`, or `Milan`, and defaults to the string `Glasgow`. The following examples are valid fragments according to this definition:

```
<country capital="Glasgow"/>
```

Which is equivalent to:

```
<country />
```

Also, an attribute can have a **fixed value**, which means that the specified value of an attribute cannot be changed. Such an attribute may be defined as follows:

```
<!ATTLIST country capital CDATA #FIXED "Glasgow">
```

And a valid instance of this could be:

```
<country capital="Glasgow"/>
```

An invalid instance would be:

```
<country capital="Santiago"/>
```

You can say that an attribute is **required**, so that if the attribute is not within the document instance then the validation will fail. This can be done as follows:

```
<!ATTLIST country capital (Glasgow | Santiago | Milan) #REQUIRED>
```

A valid instance that follows this definition would be:

```
<country capital="Milan"/>
```

An invalid instance would be:

```
<country />
```

Finally, when an attribute is none of the above, that is, it is optional, doesn't have a default or fixed value, then it must be declared to be **implied**. This is the most common attribute declaration and is specified as follows:

```
<!ATTLIST country capital (Glasgow | Santiago | Milan) #IMPLIED>
```

So a valid instance following this definition would be:

```
<country capital="Santiago"/>
```

Equally, another valid instance would be:

```
<country />
```

Declaring Multiple Attributes

Up until this point, we have looked at declaring single attributes, but we can declare multiple attributes as follows:

```
<!ATTLIST country capital (Glasgow | Santiago | Milan) #REQUIRED
                  population CDATA #IMPLIED
                  planet CDATA #FIXED "Earth">
```

Each attribute declaration is simply separated by whitespace, so a valid instance is shown below.

```
<country capital="Santiago" population="5,000,000"/>
```

Entity Declarations

Entity declarations are references to characters that have no direct meaning in XML. We looked at the built-in entities (<, > and so on) earlier, but we can also include references to other special characters via **character entities**.

So, to reference the special character "å" we can use the character reference å or, using the hex equivalent, å. The actual value of the character is either the Unicode decimal or hexadecimal value and you can reference pretty much every character in the world using this mechanism.

We also have general entities, which are effectively definitions of constants within your DTD, meaning you have a central place to make changes. For example, you can define a copyright notice as a general entity as follows:

```
<!ENTITY copyright "Copyright, S Livingstone, 2002.">
```

You can then reference this within your XML instance as `&copyright;`. Once the XML document has been parsed and all entities replaced by their values, you cannot get back to the entity that created the value. Hence there is no way of knowing what entity may have created a given value.

Notation Declarations

A **Notation declaration** allows us to refer to external resources that cannot be processed by an XML parser and hence associate them with some external handler.

For example, you can use the NOTATION declaration to associate JPG files with Internet Explorer as follows:

```
<!NOTATION jpg SYSTEM "iexplore.exe">
```

All of the declarations we've looked at in this section can be embedded into an XML document, but you can also keep your DTD information within a separate file and simply point to it, thus enabling better reuse and centralization. Let's look at an example of this so we can see it in action.

Try It Out: External DTD Validation

Let's look at how to use external DTDs that can be referenced within XML documents to ensure they are valid.

> As the XML parser that ships with Internet Explorer is not a validating parser (that is, it doesn't validate that the document being loaded is valid, only that it is well-formed), we need to take an extra step before we can complete this Try It Out.
>
> Download the "IE XML/XSL Viewer Tools" at http://msdn.microsoft.com/msdn-files/027/000/543/iexmltls.exe, which allows you to validate that a document is valid according to its DTD. Once installed, you need to follow the instructions in the **Readme.txt** file (located within the folder created during the installation) to enable the context menu options for validating XML.

1. Re-open our `MyCapitalCities.xml` file from the previous example (which contained the internal DTD information) in Internet Explorer.

2. When Internet Explorer launches, you will see the XML document in the browser. However, to ensure that the file is actually valid, we use the IE XML/XSL Viewer tools we have downloaded. Right-click somewhere in the browser and select the Validate XML option from the context menu. The XML document will then be validated and you should get a pop-up as shown below:

As expected, our document is validated successfully. Let's now draw that DTD information into an external file.

3. Now, open up `MyCapitalCities.xml` in your text editor and amend your code as shown:

```
<?xml version="1.0"?>
<!DOCTYPE capitals SYSTEM "CapitalCities.dtd">
<capitals>
   <country name="Scotland">Edinburgh</country>
   <country name="Chile">Santiago</country>
   <country name="Italy">Rome</country>
</capitals>
```

4. Save this as `CapitalCities_ExternalDTD.xml`. Now we need to create the external DTD. Open up a blank file and enter the following code:

```
<?xml version="1.0"?>
<!ELEMENT capitals (country)*>
<!ELEMENT country (#PCDATA)>
<!ATTLIST country name CDATA #IMPLIED>
```

Save this as `CapitalCities.dtd` in the same location as your XML files. Now view `CapitalCities_ExternalDTD.xml` in your browser, right-click in the code and select **Validate XML** from the menu:

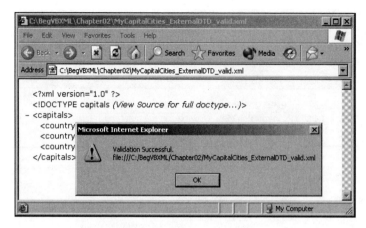

5. Again our XML is validated correctly. Now try adding the following line to your `MyCapitalCities_ExternalDTD_Valid.xml` file:

```
<?xml version="1.0"?>
<!DOCTYPE capitals SYSTEM "CapitalCities.dtd">
<capitals>
  <username>Steven</username>
  <country name="Scotland">Edinburgh</country>
  <country name="Chile">Santiago</country>
  <country name="Italy">Rome</country>
</capitals>
```

6. Save the file as `MyCapitalCities_ExternalDTD_Valid.xml` and open the file in Internet Explorer.

7. Again, right-click on the document and choose Validate XML. This time you will get something like the screen below:

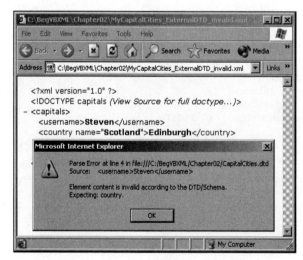

How It Works

In the first part of the example, we validated the XML document that contained the embedded DTD information that we'd met in the previous exercise. We then set about extracting the DTD information from this file into a separate DTD, and we checked to make sure the new document was being validated correctly against the new external DTD.

In order to split out the DTD information, we firstly added a simple reference to the external DTD in the XML document, replacing the DTD definitions that were there previously:

```
<!DOCTYPE capitals SYSTEM "CapitalCities.dtd">
```

This declaration references an external DTD that resides on the local system, and is called `CapitalCities.dtd`. We don't need to include a path to the DTD because it resides within the same physical directory as the XML file. Next we placed the declarations in the `.dtd` file:

```
<?xml version="1.0"?>
<!ELEMENT capitals (country)*>
<!ELEMENT country (#PCDATA)>
<!ATTLIST country name CDATA #IMPLIED>
```

Notice that we've also included an optional XML declaration at the top of the file. However, there was no DOCTYPE declaration in the DTD; we directly defined the elements and attributes instead.

We then tried out an invalid XML document, one that would break the rules of this DTD. Upon opening the document, nothing seemed wrong until we tried to validate the file, which is when we got the message that the username element was an invalid child of the capitals element.

From our discussions, we now know that our DTD defines the following:

❑ Our capitals element can only contain zero or more country elements.

❑ The country element contains PCDATA.

❑ The country element can have only a name attribute, if required. If this attribute is included, it contains character data.

So we've seen what DTDs can offer us; however, they don't solve everything, and there are a few problems with DTDs – let's examine these in detail.

Problems with DTDs

DTDs have had a series of problems that have made them gradually less popular and have caused the adoption of a new validation language (although DTD will remain popular for a very long time).

❑ **Non-XML syntax:** DTDs use a syntax called Extended Backus-Naur Form (EBNF), which is not an XML syntax, and so you can't use all of the XML tools and techniques to work with DTDs. Writing tools for creating DTDs is difficult and has never really become popular.

❑ **DTDs aren't easily extended:** although you can use entities and files to include declarations from other sources, there can be many interdependencies and so the DTD can get difficult to understand and follow, particularly when it is are changed.

❑ **One DTD per XML document:** an XML file may only have a single DTD per document and it is pretty much impossible to validate against multiple definitions. You can use a technique with external parameters to modularize your DTDs but they must share a single namespace, so extension and reuse is extremely difficult.

❑ **There are namespace limitations:** we can use namespaces (discussed in the next chapter) to prevent the collision of elements and attributes that have the same name but different meanings; these have become very popular in XML. In DTDs you must include all elements that derive from that namespace, and you cannot define two elements with the same name in a single document.

❑ **Basic data typing:** as you may have noticed there are a limited number of data types that you can use to validate values in DTDs. Furthermore, these are pretty much limited to attributes. We cannot validate against common data types such as Booleans, integers, and so on, and you cannot create your own custom data types.

All of these reasons and a few more meant that creators of XML documents and developers of XML applications were asking for more powerful validation techniques. These techniques have been realized in the powerful XML Schema Definition Language (XSDL) from the W3C.

XML Schema

The XML Schema Language is the W3C's recommended replacement for DTDs and is the future language for defining and constraining XML documents. We'll not be looking at schemas in depth in this chapter, but you can find the full discussion in Chapter 10. Let's just take a moment to introduce the concept of schemas so we can understand how they differ from DTDs.

Why XML Schemas?

XML Schemas have several advantages over DTDs:

❑ **Written in XML:** XML Schemas are written entirely in XML and can be parsed like any XML document. This means that the complete family of XML technologies can be used with XML Schema, such as the Document Object Model and Extensible Stylesheet Language, all of which are discussed later. XML Schemas can also be read and edited using common XML tools and editors.

❑ **Namespace support:** XML Schemas support namespaces and allow you to validate parts of XML in a document against a separate schema from other XML areas in another namespace. It is also fully namespace-aware; namespaces are discussed in detail in the next chapter.

❑ **Extensive data type support:** XSD offers huge improvements on the data type support given by DTDs, providing a host of primitive data types supported (such as string, Boolean, date, and so on), derived data types (nonNegativeInteger, language, and so on) and the ability to create your own custom simple and complex data types and structures. Furthermore it supports regular expressions, allowing powerful pattern-matching validation capabilities.

❑ **XSDL is self-documenting:** XSDL has documentation elements built into the syntax and so you can use the DOM to dynamically create documentation about a given schema.

❑ **It is fully extensible:** you can use parts of other Schemas, define complex structures to reuse in other Schemas and derive new types based on existing types, as well as referencing multiple Schemas within a single Schema document.

The creation of XML Schema documents is quite a bit different from DTD creation and we will be exploring this in detail later on in Chapters 10 and 11.

XML Encoding

Character encoding is one of the most common problem areas, not only for beginners using XML, but also for experienced users. The world of encoding is a book in itself, so we don't intend to cover all possible areas and definitions of all the standards and specifications, but at least the next few pages will help you to understand, right from the start, that encoding DOES make a difference when working with XML. Ignore it at your peril!

Encoding isn't only a concern for users who work with international documents in which encoding of documents can vary quite widely. As the desire grows to store more and more data in XML, either as a transport payload or persisting as a document (as a file or in a database) increases, the limitations imposed by simple character encoding schemas will start to show. For example, even working with SQL Server 2000 gives you options of storing data as ASCII or Unicode, and as more products move to Unicode you will have to have an understanding of that encoding schema. Also, when working with web services, you may find various services use different encoding mechanisms.

Encoding Basics

At the core of all computers, data is stored in a binary format. Each character is stored, at the core of every computer system, as a binary number. An encoding defines the mapping from these numbers (which can be easily represented as decimal or hexadecimal numbers as desired) to actual characters; for example, the French character ç is mapped to the decimal value 231, the hexadecimal equivalent being 0xE7.

On Windows operating systems, the ASCII character set has been popular for many years. There are two versions, one using 7-bit encoding (that is, 7 bits are required to encode each character) which is standard across many systems. This limits us to only 128 different characters though; a-z, A-Z, 0-9 and punctuation. This proves to be a problem when you move outside Western languages, and so an 8-bit version of ASCII is far more popular, allowing encoding on Latin-based language character sets, such as the characters •, ñ, , and so on. Encoding 8-bit characters is called single byte encoding (which derives from the fact that there are 8 bits to the byte on computer systems).

When working in Windows, things aren't this simple, however. The Notepad application, for example, uses ANSI coding as the default encoding – a version of extended ASCII encoding. However, the actual name for this encoding is Windows-1252. Another character encoding format is ISO-8859-1, which is also based on 8-bit ASCII encoding and therefore very similar to the Windows-1252 character set.

This last point is actually an important one. Because XML is in a format that can be passed around any system and in theory interpreted by ANY parser, the Windows-1252 encoding is rarely used (unless you know you're only working with parsers that understand this encoding). Alternatively, you may save documents as Windows-1252, and due to the similarity of the two encoding formats, you can in fact use ISO-8859-1 encoding to identify the encoded format. This is a much wider standard and supported by almost all XML parsers.

When you save with "no encoding" in Windows (that is, you haven't explicitly specified one yourself), you are most probably saving in the default Windows-1252 format. When working with XML, this is best interpreted by specifying that the encoding is ISO-8859-1 encoding at the top of the XML file (or programmatically) – we look at how we do this shortly.

The above encodings work fine for Latin character sets, but they don't include characters from Japanese, Chinese, or other non-Latin character-based languages. So how do we work with these? Well, there are even more encoding standards for these languages. Japanese, for example, has three major standards, Shift-JIS, ISO-2022-JP, and J-EUC, all different from each other. Furthermore, encoding text in these character sets requires two (and sometimes even three) bytes per character. These character sets are also known as a **double-byte** character sets.

Unicode

The problems with all of these different character sets were recognized, and in 1996, version 2.0 of the Unicode (http://www.unicode.org/) standard was released, backed by many large companies. Unicode is built into many common applications such as Internet Explorer 4.x and Netscape Navigator 4.x (to name just a couple) and is fully supported by Windows NT, Windows 2000, and Windows .NET Server. It has been described as the future of encoding. Indeed, Unicode has sometimes been termed "the last character set".

Unicode provides a single character set that covers all the characters of the languages of the world and so we don't have to jump from character set to character set when implementing applications that span the globe, or even use unusual characters. Sounds great, doesn't it? So, where's the catch? Well, if we can encode Latin characters using 7 or 8 bits, but it takes 3 bytes to encode an Asian character, then how do you determine how to encode a given character? The answer is that Unicode offers three types of encoding (but STILL using the same character set). This poses no problem because a parser that understands Unicode will understand how the characters are encoded.

Unicode is a multi-byte character set (MBCS) and so can use a given number of bytes to encode a character depending on the encoding as follows:

❑ UTF-32, which uses single 32-bit units to encode each character

❑ UTF-16, which uses one or two 16-bit units to encode each character

❑ UTF-8, which uses one to four 8-bit units to encode each character

UTF-32 is not generally supported by software applications as it uses far too much space to store a single character, however, UTF-16 and UTF-8 are generally supported and in fact are required to be supported by XML parsers. Also, because Unicode is a MBCS, even files with a minimal amount of content can at least double in size; this can sometimes become an issue, more so when transferring across a network rather than in storage, however the benefit of interoperability across the world makes it a definite advantage.

Now, that leaves us with UTF-8 and UTF-16 to encode files that we will work with. Obviously if there are many characters that require more than two bytes for encoding it starts to be more efficient to use UTF-16. So to read a single Asian character taking two bytes, you would read one 16-byte unit of code. However, in the same situation, using UTF-8 you have variable length encoded characters to read and so it can be quite difficult to code against as you don't know up front whether the character requires the next byte (or more) to be correctly interpreted.

Consider the opposite, however, if you are using many Latin characters. These are encoded within one byte and so you can encode the character in one single 8-bit unit, rather than in UTF-16, which would leave 8 bits free per Latin character. So what should you use? Well, if you are working primarily with Latin languages, then you are better off encoding in UTF-8; it also saves on space. However, if you are going to work with languages or characters requiring two or more bytes to encode, then you are far better with UTF-16. The recommended encoding is in fact UTF-16 and is perhaps the best option as a beginner to start using.

Finally, there is the issue of 'little-endian' or 'big-endian' encoding. Little-endian means that the least significant byte comes first and big-endian means that the most significant byte comes first and when you save a file as Unicode, you will generally have the option of saving in one of these (although you should check which your editor uses by default). Big-endian is the recommended method to save your files. These have importance when dealing with character sets where a character is written as a stream of bytes. When using 16-bit encoding, for example, we are using 2 bytes per character. Both little-endian and big-endian govern the order in which these two bytes are stored. So, how do we know what order the character data is stored in, the first part of the character in the first byte and the second part of the character in the second byte or vice-versa?

By this point you will no doubt want to see how this works with XML and why it is so crucial, so let's look at encoding and XML.

Encoding and XML Parsers

Thus far we have discussed how to save documents with a specified encoding, the various types of encoding we can use, and the advantages and disadvantages of both. However, when an XML parser (or any other kind of parser reading the document) has to read the document, how does it know what format it has been saved in and therefore how it should interpret the characters?

Well, luckily there's a neat feature that helps with this problem. When a file is saved, a Byte Order Mark (BOM) may be inserted at the beginning of the file to indicate the encoding it was saved in. When using Windows, the default is Windows-1252 (where all Latin characters are supported), so when you save a file using the default encoding in Windows, there will be no BOM. If you save a file as Unicode, a BOM **is** inserted at the start of the file.

> **You won't see these BOM characters in most editors, because they understand Unicode and so strip out header information that the viewer is not supposed to see.**

So, how does an XML parser read these documents and then ensure that it parses and outputs the correct character interpretations?

When an XML parser reads an XML file, the W3C defines the following three rules to decide how the document should be read:

❑   If there is a BOM, this defines the file encoding

❑   If there is no BOM, then look at the encoding attribute in the XML declaration

❑   If there are neither of these, then assume the XML document is UTF-8 encoded

Of course, if the BOM is for some reason wrong, then it is likely that the XML file won't be correctly parsed and will throw an error. Equally, if there is no BOM or encoding declared and the default UTF-8 is used, but the document is not UTF-8 encoded, then equally an error will be thrown. These should really not be a surprise – how can it decode characters when its definition is completely wrong? In fact, because the first 128 characters of Unicode are the same as that of ASCII, then if your file consisted only of these characters you would be fine – however, if you included ASCII characters beyond 128, such as ü, é or à then it will fail.

This is really all we need to know about how the XML parser itself knows how to parse an XML document. We now understand how the first and third points illustrated above are determined. However, we've not yet looked at the XML declaration, which also has an impact on encoding. Let's have a look at what happens when we create XML documents and save them using differing document encoding.

Try It Out: Under the Hood of Encoding

This Try It Out uses a utility called `CharacterReader.exe` which is included in the code download for this chapter. It is used to write the decimal value of each byte of a file to the console.

1. Open up a text editor and enter the text below into the document.(you can enter the ñ character by holding the Alt button while typing 0241 using the number keypad)

   An ñ

2. Save using the default ANSI encoding as the file `encode.txt`.

3. Open a console window (choose **Start | Run** and type **cmd** and press **OK**) and change to `C:\BegVBXML\Chapter02\` and type "**CharacterReader** *path*" (where path is the full path to the file `encode.txt`, for example, "`C:\encode.txt`") and hit the *Enter* key.

4. You will see something like the following:

5. Now, return to the text editor and choose **Save As** and this time change the **Encoding** drop-down to UTF-8. Again run the **CharacterReader** utility from the console window. You will now get the following:

```
Visual Studio .NET Command Prompt
C:\BegVBXML\Chapter02>CharacterReader C:\BegVBXML\Chapter02\encode.txt
239
187
191
65
110
32
195
177

C:\BegVBXML\Chapter02>_
```

6. Finally, return to the text editor and choose Save As and save the file as Unicode (that is, UTF-16) and run the CharacterReader utility to give you the following:

```
Visual Studio .NET Command Prompt
C:\BegVBXML\Chapter02>CharacterReader C:\BegVBXML\Chapter02\encode.txt
255
254
65
0
110
0
32
0
241
0

C:\BegVBXML\Chapter02>_
```

How It Works

The ñ character is a special character and not covered by the first 128 ASCII characters, but it IS covered by the Windows-1252 and ISO-8859-1 encodings, so saving as ANSI works fine as it saves in the Windows-1252 encoding format. This stores each character as a single byte and has no BOM, so you simply see a listing of the decimal value of each byte in the string.

We then looked at UTF-8 and can see the BOM at the start of the file as the decimal values 239 187 191. However, UTF-8 is the same as the first 128 characters, but differs after this in that it will use a variable number of 8-bit units to encode a special character. Notice that it uses the decimal values 195 and 177 in combination to specify our special character. Hence the encoding of this character will only make sense in UTF-8 when these two values occur next to each other.

We then looked at UTF-16 and can see the BOM at the start of the file 255 254 (the file was saved as little-endian). UTF-16 uses two 16-bit units to encode the character and so because only the first 16 bits are required to encode the characters we are working with, the second 16-bit is zero. This is the same for each character and so you can see why it can take up so much space; however, it is very easily extended (and efficient) to support more complex languages and character sets, such as Asian characters. Note that the UTF-16 decimal for our special ñ character is 241, like the Windows-1252 encoding.

Encoding and XML Documents

XML itself has a way of specifying the encoding of a document and the use of this can be very confusing to beginners – this is why we have gone through the above discussions. One of the most common problems is where developers of XML documents get the impression you can just specify a different encoding within the XML to change the way the parser reads that document. Of course by now you understand that it is how the document was encoded when it was created that is the key – you cannot just change this without resaving the document using a new encoding.

The encoding attribute is part of the xml declaration as shown below.

```
<?xml version="1.0" encoding="xxx"?>
```

So, to specify that an XML file is encoding in UTF-8 format, you would do one of the following.

```
<?xml version="1.0" encoding="UTF-8"?>
```

Alternatively, you could simply type:

```
<?xml version="1.0"?>
```

Remember that the encoding attribute is optional and will default to UTF-8 when not present.

To indicate that the file is encoded using the default Windows encoding, you could do this.

```
<?xml version="1.0" encoding="windows-1252"?>
```

Or, as they are so similar, you may do the following and provide access to a wider range of XML parsers.

```
<?xml version="1.0" encoding="ISO-8859-1"?>
```

As specifying the encoding is usually a manual process there are often quite a few problems that can occur, so let's look at the most common of these.

Try It Out: Valid Character Encoding

Let's look at how we can work with valid character encoding and demonstrate a situation where you will have no problems with encoding.

1. Open up your text editor and enter the XML below into the document:

```
<?xml version="1.0"?>
<root>n</root>
```

2. Save the file using the default ANSI (that is, Windows-1252/ISO-8859-1) encoding and call the file char1.xml.

3. Open char1.xml in Internet Explorer and you will see something like the figure below:

4. Open char1.xml in Notepad again and add the encoding attribute as follows and save the file using the default ANSI encoding again.

```
<?xml version="1.0" encoding="UTF-8"?>
<root>n</root>
```

5. Open char1.xml in Internet Explorer and you will see something like the screenshot below:

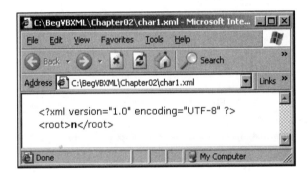

How It Works

When we started this Try It Out, the document was saved as ANSI which is the default Windows encoding, that is, windows-1252 (which, as discussed, is pretty much the same as ISO-8859-1). So no BOM is added to the start of the document and no encoding was specified, and so the parser assumed the document was UTF-8 encoded.

Now, we know that it wasn't UTF-8 encoded (we saved it as ANSI), but the first 128 characters of windows-1252 and Unicode (UTF-8, and so on) are the same and so when each character byte is read by the XML parser, it makes sense in Unicode and so no exception is thrown.

Equally, if we explicitly specify the encoding as UTF-8 then the same process and result occurs.

Try It Out: Invalid Character Encoding

This time, let's look at a slightly more complex situation where the character we are using is not from the low numbered ASCII character range; the Spanish character Eñe (ñ).

1. Open up your text editor, create a new document, and enter the XML below into the document. Note that if your keyboard doesn't directly support the ñ character you can enter it by holding the Alt button while typing 0241 using the number keypad (it won't work with the numbers at the top of the keyboard!). Alternatively you can use the character map by going into the Command Window (type charmap in the Start | Run textbox and hit OK), looking for the character you are interested in and copying it to the XML file.

```
<?xml version="1.0"?>
<root>ñ</root>
```

2. Save the file using the default ANSI encoding and call the file char2.xml.

3. Open char2.xml in Internet Explorer and you will see something like the screenshot below.

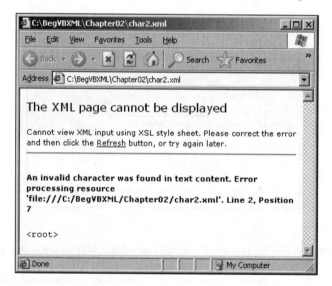

4. Open up char2.xml again and add the encoding attribute as follows.

```
<?xml version="1.0" encoding="windows-1252"?>
<root>ñ</root>
```

5. Save this and open char2.xml in Internet Explorer and you will get something like the screenshot below:

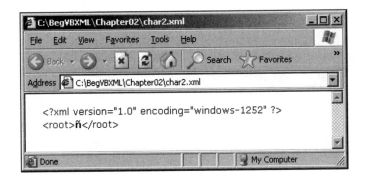

6. Repeat this for the encoding ISO-8859-1 and you will get the same result, with only the value of the encoding attribute differing in the output.

7. Again, open up `char2.xml`, and this time select File | Save As... from the menu. Change the Encoding drop-down to UTF-8 and save the document.

8. Open the document in Internet Explorer and you will get the following:

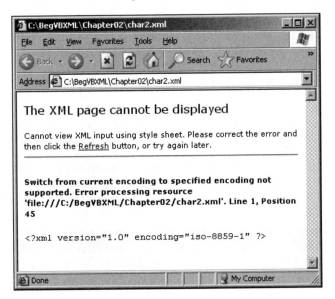

9. Finally, open `char2.xml` again and remove the encoding attribute entirely and save the file (it will save as UTF-8 as this was the last format you used). Opening it in Internet Explorer will give you the following:

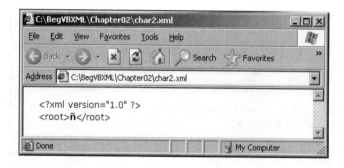

How It Works

In the previous Try It Out, we used the character "ñ" which worked fine for all encodings because it was within the first 128 characters of Unicode. However, the ñ character is beyond ASCII character 128 so Unicode encodes such characters differently. Unicode uses MBCS to encode this and so the ñ character is actually encoded by the decimal numbers 195 and 177 (0xC3 and 0xB1). Hence, when the byte is read and gives decimal 241 with no next byte to make this a valid UTF-8 Unicode character, it causes an exception and says it's an invalid character.

When we changed the encoding to `windows-1252` because we had specified an encoding and there was no BOM at the start of the file (ANSI does use a BOM) ,the XML parser understood that it wasn't to use the default UTF-8 encoding, but the one specified. The parser then reads the byte directly as decimal 241 and maps this to the Windows-1252 character set where it found that it is a valid character; bizarrely enough, the ñ character! Additionally, because the Windows-1252 and ISO-8859-1 character sets are so alike, the exact same thing happened when you changed the encoding.

When we kept the new encoding attribute, but saved the document as UTF-8, the inverse of what happened earlier occurred. It saved characters over the decimal value 128 in multiple bytes, but the encoding attribute read them in as single byte values and hence an invalid character is again read (or *not* read).

Finally, we removed the XML encoding attribute entirely, staying with the UTF-8 Unicode document encoding format, and when the file was viewed there was no problem. This is because the file was saved in UTF-8 MBCS and the default value of the encoding attribute of the XML declaration is UTF-8 and so the XML parser read using the MBCS of UTF-8 and so read the ñ character correctly.

Try It Out: Difference in Unicode Formats

This example will look at what happens when we change from UTF-8 to UTF-16.

1. Open up `char2.xml`, which we worked with in the last Try It Out. When we last saved it, it had no encoding attribute and was saved as UTF-8 – this is where we continue.

2. This time, add the encoding attribute to the document, specify the encoding as UTF-16 and save the document. Opening this up in Internet Explorer will give you another error page.

3. Go back to `char2.xml` and this time save the document encoding as Unicode. Open the document again in Internet Explorer and you will see the following:

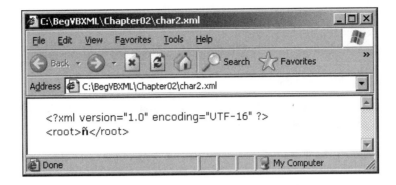

How It Works

This highlighted an interesting difference within Unicode itself. If the document is not signed with a BOM then you can run into problems (hence it is probably better to ensure that your XML docs are saved with a BOM). The document was first saved using UTF-8, and so used multiple units of single byte encoding for the character, whereas UTF-16 reads in units of two bytes, which meant that the ñ character again made no sense.

When we changed the encoding to specify that two-byte units should be read, as per UTF-16, then the XML parser understood the decimal representations and was able to make mappings to valid characters.

Character Entities

What happens when we want to continue to use some kind of encoding (for example, windows-1252) but use a character that is only available in Unicode? This is where character entities can be used to individually reference Unicode characters by their decimal or hex value and they are parsed independently of the character set. So, ñ can be represented by the Unicode decimal value 241 as `&#241;` or in hex `&#F1;`. Let's look at an example.

Try It Out: Character Entities

Let's look at how we can still use the ñ character within a file not encoded in Unicode, and where you want the reference to a Unicode character to be independent of the character set.

1. Again, open up `char2.xml` and this time next to the ñ character add its Unicode decimal equivalent, 241, encoded in XML as `&#241`:

```
<?xml version="1.0" encoding="UTF-16"?>
<root>ñ&#241;</root>
```

2. Save the file – it will still be in UTF-16 Unicode format. View this file in Internet Explorer and you will see two ñ characters displayed next to each other.

3. Now, remove the encoding attribute from the XML file and save the file in ANSI document encoding. View the file in Internet Explorer and you will see another error page.

77

4. Add the encoding attribute to the `char2.xml` document and set its value to Windows-1252 (or ISO-8859-1).

```
<?xml version="1.0" encoding="windows-1252"?>
<root>ñ&#241;</root>
```

5. Save the document in its current ANSI encoding and view the document in Internet Explorer. You will get the ñ character displayed twice.

6. Finally, remove the ñ character from the file, and remove the encoding attribute from the XML declaration as follows:

```
<?xml version="1.0"?>
<root>&#241;</root>
```

7. Save in the current ANSI encoding. View the document in Internet Explorer and you will see the following:

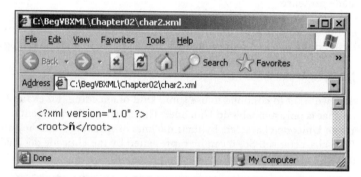

How It Works

When we initially saved the document in UTF-16 format, the encoding was already specified to be UTF-16 and so the characters were correctly read. The character entity was already correctly read as the same Unicode character and so we got two instances of the same ñ character.

However, when we removed the encoding and saved as the default ANSI document encoding, we ran into an error because the ñ character was read in as the default UTF-8 format, so we encountered the MBCS problem we saw earlier.

However, removing the ñ character and changing the XML declaration encoding attribute to any encoding value, there was no problem, because the `&#241;` character entity was correctly and independently parsed as the Unicode character ñ.

Summary

In this chapter we looked at the different parts of an XML document. By now, you should be familiar and comfortable with XML syntax to the extent that you know how to create valid and well-formed XML documents. We've learned how to add rules that govern how our XML files are structured, and we've learned how XML file encoding can have a significant impact on the results when the XML file is consumed.

Having worked through this chapter, you should be familiar with the following:

- ❑ An XML document is comprised of a prolog, a DTD, a document root, and the epilog.

- ❑ How elements and attributes are used in XML as well as legal and illegal XML syntax and the issues of escaping characters using CDATA sections.

- ❑ Validation, and how to create and use DTDs that allow us to define how an XML document can be structured and limit the values and types of the element and attributes it defines.

- ❑ How DTDs are created and what problems are inherent in DTDs. We also introduced XML Schemas and gave the reasons as to why this is the preferred way of validating an XML document.

- ❑ The often-overlooked importance of understanding encoding in XML. We saw that there is a variation of how documents can be encoded and what effects this can have on managing your XML documents.

- ❑ That UTF-8 is the default for XML parsers and how UTF-16 is the recommended encoding mechanism.

Now that we've got an understanding of the fundamental principles of XML documents, let's look at some more advanced XML topics, including Namespaces (which we've encountered a couple of times in passing in this chapter), and the DOM (Document Object Model).

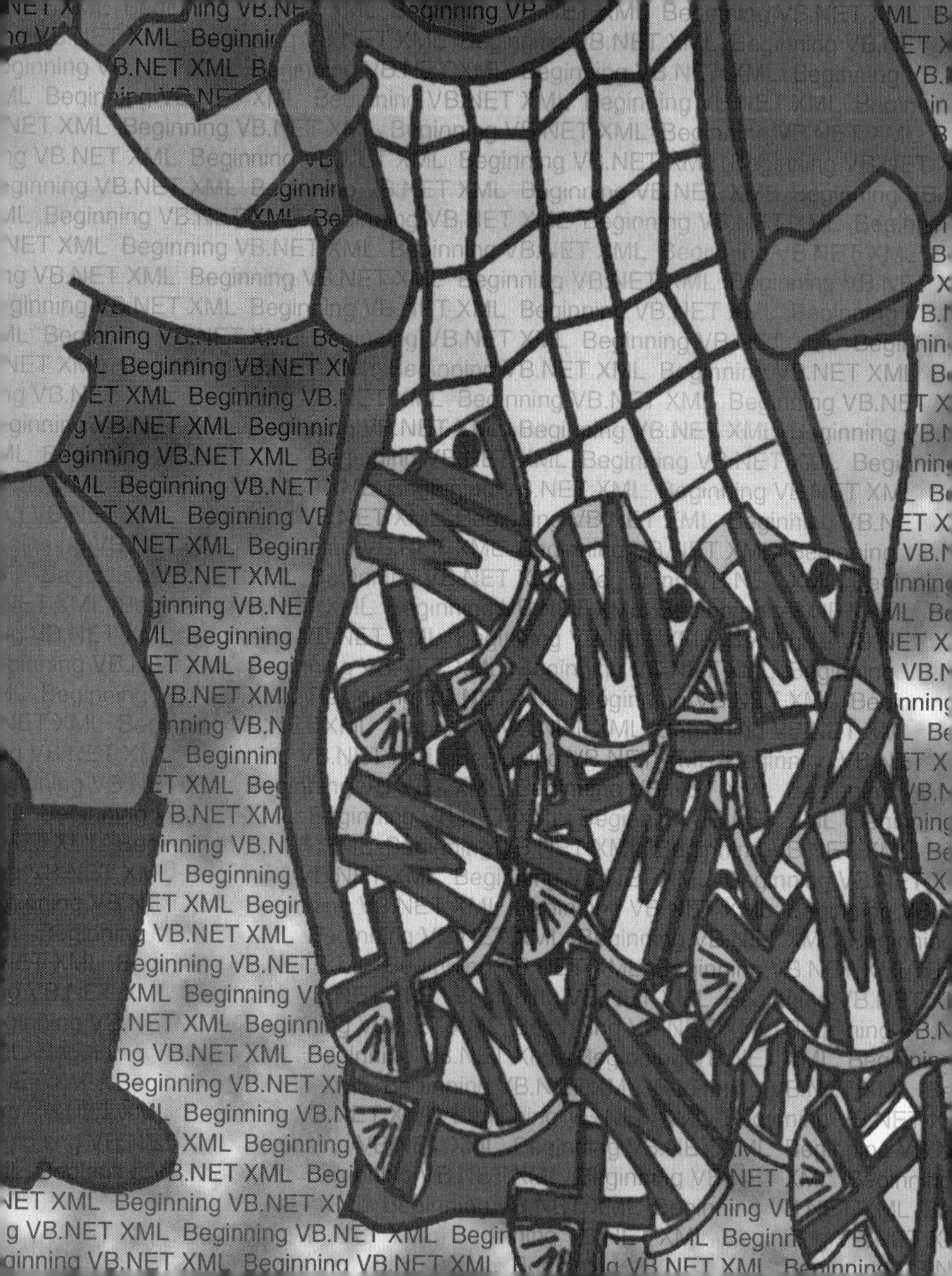
Beginning VB.NET XML

XML with .NET in Detail

In the last chapter we covered a lot of ground – by now, those of you who had never really looked at XML should now understand some of the basic building blocks and concepts of XML, and those of you who had been using XML have hopefully learned a few new things. We also explored the definition of well-formed XML and the standards and recommendations that govern this. We are going to extend that discussion in this chapter by first looking closely at how XML fits into the .NET Framework, among these standards, and the support that .NET offers to XML development; then we will take a look at how the .NET Framework itself uses XML at the heart of its operation.

As we work through the relationship between XML and the .NET Framework in this chapter, we will focus on the following areas:

❑ Defining Namespaces, how they are constructed and why we use them

❑ What the Document Object Model is and how it works

❑ XPath, including syntax, patterns and operators, Location Paths, Axes, Node Tests and the Data Model

Towards the end of this chapter, we are also going to start a phone book case study, using the understanding we have gained from the book thus far. We'll then continue to build on this in future chapters.

Again, for detailed information about XML we recommended you look at *Professional XML 2nd Edition*, from Wrox Press (ISBN 1-86100-505-9) or a similar XML-specific title.

How Does XML Fit in with .NET

We have now had an overview of some of the most important XML technologies. This chapter is dedicated to filling in the gaps of technologies we haven't examined fully yet by looking closely at each and, as this book has is committed to showing you how to actually use these technologies with VB.NET, we should now look at what they are and how they are supported in the .NET Framework.

XML

The .NET Framework supports the processing of XML Documents and Document fragments through a series of classes contained in the `System.Xml` namespace. These are made available to the VB.NET application through the use of an `Imports System.Xml` statement at the beginning of the application. The following diagram shows some of the classes dedicated to working with XML:

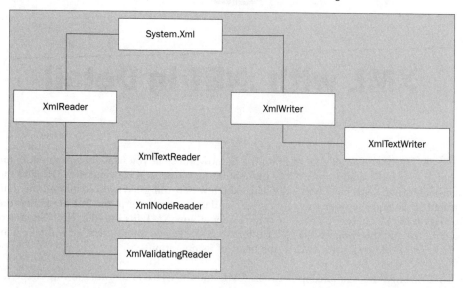

The two main classes are the `XmlReader` (see Chapter 4 for more details) and `XmlWriter` (see Chapter 5 for more details). The `XmlTextReader` class allows you to read an XML document without any validation and only checks that the XML is well-formed. This means that it ensures that the XML document conforms to the rules outlined in the W3C XML 1.0 Recommendation, such as having a closing element for every element that is opened. It is read-only and very fast and will probably be your most common class for just reading XML documents.

The `XmlNodeReader` class allows you to pass in DOM fragments, so a sub-tree or a single node of an existing XML DOM document can be passed in. This class only checks that the fragment is well-formed and doesn't perform any validation.

Finally, the `XmlValidatingReader` is a very powerful class that allows you to validate an XML instance document or fragment against a DTD or XML Schema. Rather than being a class separate from the `XmlTextReader` and `XmlNodeReader` classes, the `XmlValidatingReader` class in fact uses either of these classes to actually read in the document and then performs the validation on top of this. This validation involves ensuring that the XML structure conforms to the rules defined in the DTD or schema associated with that document.

The other main class is the `XmlWriter` class, which provides the functionality to write out XML documents to either streams or files. A stream is a generic sequence of bytes, but the `Stream` class in the .NET Framework is abstract so it is implemented as one of several different types of `Stream`s, such as a `MemoryStream` (allowing you to store the stream in memory), a `FileStream` (allowing you to send the `Stream` to a physical file) and a `NetworkStream` (allowing you to send the `Stream` across the network using sockets).

The `XmlReader` uses a pull model to tell the parser which nodes it is interested in, as opposed to the transitional SAX (see below) push model, which raises every node that is found to be handled by some content handler.

The pull model removes the need to manage complex state in the application because it removes the need for content handlers that have to know where they are in the document. The pull model can work through events in a procedural manner always knowing where it is in the document. None of the details are cached, however, so if you want to get back to an element you have to reread the XML document and wait until the element you are interested in is read. If we wish to use be able to not only access our information but to make changes and additions to it, we need a method of working with XML documents through the use of code, and a way to interface with that code in the programs we write. For this we could use the Document Object Model.

The Document Object Model (DOM)

In itself, an XML document is simply a useful way to represent data in a way that is platform agnostic – that is, the data can be passed around through many platforms and mean the same thing to them all. It is useful to be able to store data in such ways, but to be able to actually use that data we need ways of reading what is in that document. XML provides two primary methods of doing this.

The first method is to load the entire document into memory and build a tree structure from it, based on the elements and attributes defined in the document. This tree structure is termed the Document Object Model, as it models the data you have in the XML document. The DOM is a powerful structure as it provides read/write capabilities and uses other technologies such as XPath to navigate to selected parts of the document. If you need random access to parts of the XML document, or you must be able to modify the document, then you should use this. An obvious disadvantage, however, is that to first load the document into memory and then create a tree structure from it means that you are potentially using a large amount of memory and it is generally less efficient. Unless, however, your documents start to get fairly large (for example, over 1MB), you are unlikely to notice the time this takes relative to the alternative method.

The alternative method is to use SAX (defined with the DOM in Chapter 1). This is the method we will look at in future chapters, and it involves iterating through the documents, accessing each item within the document one by one. This is similar to how you may iterate line-by-line through a text file, when the data you are interested in is separated by new lines. The power in using such an approach is that no matter how large your XML document gets, you are only ever loading the next item into memory; unlike the DOM there is no tree creation. This is very fast for larger documents, but because the parser cannot ensure that any content you add to the document is valid (because it cannot read ahead to check what is expected at that part of the document), this method is read-only. In order to modify the document, you would have to start reading the document and perform the writing, with any updates, separately (or run in parallel). As mentioned above, however, unless your documents start to get quite large, you are not going to notice too much of a difference. It is, therefore, best to use the reading method most appropriate to the situation. In other words, if you don't need random access to the document and you don't need to modify it directly, use the SAX technique.

How the DOM Interacts

The DOM is usually added as a layer between the XML parser and the application that needs the information in the document, meaning that the parser reads the data from the XML document and then feeds that data into a DOM. The DOM is then used by a higher-level application. The application can do whatever it wants with this information, including putting it into another proprietary object model if so desired. Therefore, in order to write an application that will be accessing an XML document through the DOM, you need to have an XML parser and a DOM implementation installed on your machine.

The following diagram illustrates the position of the DOM in this process:

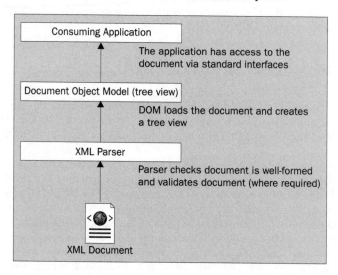

The XML document is read in by the parser which checks it is well-formed and, if applicable, that the document is validated against any schemas (these are discussed in detail in Chapters 10 and 11). An in-memory hierarchical tree view of the document is then created via the Document Object Model processor, and then the consuming application has access to this tree via the DOM API (discussed below) to locate and modify the document.

DOM Interfaces

With any technology these days, there are almost always programmatic ways of working with the technology via interfaces, and XML is no different. The Document Object Model (DOM) is both a specification in itself (it defines a hierarchical object model known as a tree) as well as defining a specification of interfaces for accessing the elements within the XML document. These interfaces allow the creation of a standard Application Programming Interface (API) that allows you to programmatically read and modify an XML document. To get an idea of what interfaces are involved in the DOM, let's take a very simple XML document such as the one below:

```
<parent>
  <child id="123">text goes here</child>
</parent>
```

When represented by the DOM, this would be viewed as this:

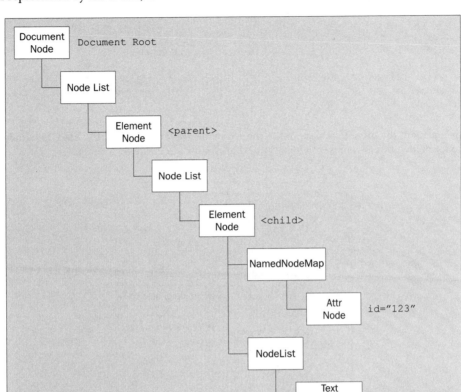

Each box represents an object that will be created; the names in the boxes are the interfaces that will be implemented by each object. For example, we have an object to represent the whole document, the Document Node, and objects to represent each of the elements. Each object implements a number of appropriate interfaces, such as Text, CharacterData, and Node for the object, representing the "text goes here" character data. In the DOM, all elements and attributes, and in fact all other constituents of an XML document, are called nodes.

How the DOM Views a Document

As we have mentioned, the DOM represents an instance of an XML document as a hierarchical tree. This hierarchy is made up of a root element that may contain child elements. Let's take an XML example that is based on one we looked at in the last chapter.

```
<?xml version="1.0"?>
<person age="25">
  <name>
    <firstname>Graham</firstname>
    <middlename>Mark</middlename>
```

```
      <lastname>Livingstone</lastname>
   </name>
   <address type="home">
      <streetNumber>72</streetNumber>
      <streetName>Gettison &amp; Loots Avenue</streetName>
      <area>Yoker</area>
      <city>Glasgow</city>
   </address>
</person>
```

We can represent the hierarchical model of the elements and attributes in this XML document as the tree model below (boxes represent elements and attributes are in the oval shapes).

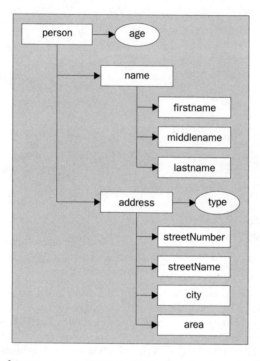

The hierarchy defined in this structure is very similar to the structure used by the XML DOM to process XML documents. The first element that you can see in the diagram (Person) is also called the **Document Element**. Beneath this, the Document Element can have any number of Child Nodes, such as name, which may have Child Nodes themselves (like firstname) or attributes, like age.

Support for the DOM – the .NET Framework

The .NET Framework has some excellent support for both techniques with the System.Xml namespace. The core class for working with the DOM is the XmlDocument class, which represents XML document nodes (that is, elements, attributes, namespaces, and so on) and is the base class for a host of classes that allow you to manipulate the XML document. This is derived from the XmlNode class, which represents individual XML nodes. The figure below illustrates the hierarchical position of XmlDocument and other key derived classes of the XmlNode class.

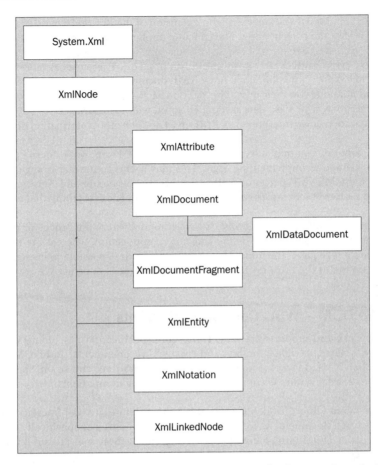

The XmlAttribute class extends the XmlNode class and provides functionality relating to XML Attributes. The XmlDocument class also extends the XmlNode class and is a representation of the entire XML document, implementing the W3C DOM Level 1 and Level 2 standards, which are discussed in detail below. This class allows you to load an XML document as well as to navigate and edit the XML. The XmlDocument class is extended by the XmlDataDocument class that allows storage of selected data from a relational database or an XML document. The data is stored in the DataSet (a relational view of the data) and feeds into the XmlDataDocument class which then allows the data to be manipulated using the methods of the XML DOM discussed as part of the XmlDocument class above.

The XmlDocumentFragment class represents a fragment of an XML document and is generally useful for creating sections of XML that you are going to edit and insert into larger documents. The XmlEntity class represents an entity node. An entity node is the definition of some string literal that was defined in the DTD associated with the XML document, such as using &logo; for the string "What do you want to .NET today?", saving you from having to rewrite the entire string each time it is used in the document. There are also a number of XML entity references that are defined as part of the XML specification: & for the & character, < for the < character; > for the > character; ' for the ' character and " for the " character. (For more information on this, see Chapter 2). The XmlNotation class represents a notation declaration in a DTD.

Finally, the XmlLinkedNode abstract class is an extension of the XmlNode class and provides access to the node before or after the current node. The concrete implementations of the XmlLinkedNode class are XmlCharacterData, XmlDeclaration, XmlDocumentType, XmlElement, XmlEntityReference, and XmlProcessingInstruction. These classes represent all the kinds of nodes that can come before any other node in an XML document. Attribute nodes are part of an element node and not nodes on their own. The XmlCharacterData class allows you to work with various **CDATA** sections, which is a data section, enclosed with the characters <![CDATA[and]]>. Data within a CDATA section is *not* interpreted as XML markup (For more information on this, see Chapter 2).

In terms of SAX support, you may have noticed that the .NET Framework doesn't actually have any classes explicitly defined as implementing SAX. This may seems somewhat strange bearing in mind the success of SAX in the MSXML parser and other parsers such as Saxon and Xerces, however with the XmlReader and XmlWriter classes you can actually implement everything that is offered by SAX.

The models are slightly different in that SAX is a push model where the processor pushed each element to the surface and it has to be handled by the consuming application, whereas the XmlReader takes a pull approach where it requests the nodes that are of interest. It is possible to create a SAX implementation on top of the XmlReader class, but the reverse is not true. We cover this in much greater depth in chapter 4.

Support for the DOM – W3C Core Specifications

The .NET Framework also supports the W3C DOM core specifications, including W3C DOM Level 1 (this defines how to parse, navigate, modify, and create XML documents) and DOM level 2 (events, different views of an XML document, setting stylesheet declarations, and so on) specifications. The W3C DOM Level 2 specification is comprised of the following components:

❑ The Document Object Model (Core) – this section defines a set of interfaces that can access any structured document, as well as defining a set of interfaces specifically for accessing XML documents. A DOM implementation must implement these interfaces if it is to be regarded as compliant.

❑ The Document Object Model (HTML) – this section describes HTML-specific extensions to the DOM, many of which you may have used if you have had previous experience with DHTML. This is outside the scope of this book, however.

The Level 2 specification also defines some features that are not part of the core and also not implemented by the .NET Framework. These are:

❑ The Views section, which provides a way to distinguish between different views of an XML document.

❑ Providing programmatic support for specifying declarations of stylesheets that are to be used.

❑ Supporting traversal and ranges, the first defining mechanisms for traversing an XML document and the latter defining how ranges can be manipulated in an XML document.

❑ The Events section, which adds an event system designed to know when parts of the document are modified as well as a UI-style events system providing event information such as telling you when a given node receives focus.

> **The W3C DOM Level 2 core specification can be found at**
> http://www.w2.org/TR/DOM-Level-2/core.html.

The W3C activity standards are broken into specification levels: Level 1, Level 2, and at the time of writing Level 3 is currently in draft format. The Level 2 core specification, which is at Recommendation level (that is, it will not change) is of most interest to us as that is what is implemented in the .NET Framework. It builds upon what was offered in the Level 1 specification and as we said, the Level 3 specification has not yet been promoted to Recommendation (so the specification is still subject to change).

Namespaces

Namespace support is provided through all of the .NET Framework for XML. The main class for managing these is the XmlNamespaceManager class that manages the binding of prefixes to namespaces. This class enables you to be able to set and check for namespaces within XML documents, allowing you to prevent the duplication of element and attribute names.

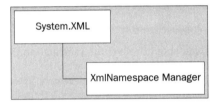

As anyone can easily create XML documents and vast numbers of new documents are being written all the time, it is likely that common names for elements and attributes within XML documents are going to be the same. When we talk about a duplication of names, consider the following example:

```xml
<?xml version="1.0" encoding="utf-8" ?>
<Purchases>
  <person>
    <title>Mr.</title>
    <name>Steven Livingstone</name>
  </person>
  <book>
    <title>Application development with MSXML 4.0</title>
  </book>
  <book>
    <title>Professional XML 2nd Edition</title>
  </book>
</Purchases>
```

Notice that there is a <title> element for both <person> and <book> in this example. There is the possibility that although one refers to a person's title and the other is a book title, a consuming application would not know the difference.

Consider the following revised document:

```
<?xml version="1.0" encoding="utf-8" ?>
<pur:Purchases xmlns:pur="urn:purchases" xmlns:per="urn:person"
    xmlns:bk="urn:book">
  <per:person>
    <per:title>Mr.</per:title>
    <per:name>Steven Livingstone</per:name>
  </per:person>
  <bk:book>
    <bk:title>Application development with MSXML 4.0</bk:title>
  </bk:book>
  <bk:book>
    <bk:title>Professional XML 2ⁿᵈ Edition</bk:title>
  </bk:book>
</pur:Purchases>
```

Here we have set prefixes, `pur`, `per`, and `bk`, for our `purchases`, `person` and `book` elements. The `xmlns:` attribute is included as this is the syntax for declaring namespaces.

```
<pur:Purchases xmlns:pur="urn:purchases" xmlns:per="urn:person"
    xmlns:bk="urn:book">
```

The actual prefixes are up to us and should reflect the information they represent, which is why we chose `per` for person and `bk` for book. These prefixes are then associated with the namespaces, `urn:purchases`, `urn:person` and `urn:books` respectively. Now, when we refer to each of the two `<title>` elements, they are preceded by their respective prefixes and so are uniquely identified by different namespaces.

It's great that now we have identified each of the elements uniquely within this document using prefixes, but how could this be managed across multiple documents intending to use the same vocabularies? There would need to be some way of administering and ensuring the uniqueness of the prefixes themselves, and that could end up being a bigger headache than we had in the first place. The way this is resolved is by using URIs.

Universal Resource Identifier

XML namespaces actually use an association between the prefixes in a given document and a Universal Resource Identifier (URI). A URI could be a URL used by the web, and in fact these work well because the purpose of the URI is to ensure that our namespaces are not duplicated. If we are using an XML document over the Internet, for example, where they might be any number of other XML documents, the chance of finding a duplicate namespace name is quite high. In associating our prefix with, say, the Wrox.com website, we can be fairly sure that no other company is going to have the same namespace because that domain name belongs to Wrox. As the only purpose of the URI is to lend uniqueness to a namespace name, they don't have to represent anything. Most of the time you will find that they point to an HTTP address, even though there may be nothing at that URL but some documentation on the namespace. The advantages of using this method are that globally unique domain names can be used to ensure exclusivity.

Let's modify the previous sample XML document to demonstrate.

Try It Out: Associating Prefixes with URIs

We're going to create an XML document that associates URIs with the namespaces used in our document.

Note that all the sample code for this chapter is available for download from http://www.wrox.com. We will be storing sample code for this chapter within the following folder: C:\BegVBXML\Chapter03. You may, of course, use a different folder depending on what you prefer.

1. Open up your text editor and type in the following XML document:

```
<?xml version="1.0" encoding="utf-8" ?>
<pur:Purchases xmlns:pur="http://deltabis.com/purchase"
      xmlns:per="http://deltabis.com/person"
      xmlns:bk="http://deltabis.com/book">
  <per:person>
    <per:title>Mr.</per:title>
    <per:name>Steven Livingstone</per:name>
  </per:person>
  <bk:book>
    <bk:title>Application development with MSXML 4.0</bk:title>
  </bk:book>
  <bk:book>
    <bk:title>Professional XML 2ⁿᵈ Edition</bk:title>
  </bk:book>
</pur:Purchases>
```

2. Save the document as `namespace.xml` and open it in Internet Explorer to see the XML document displayed as below.

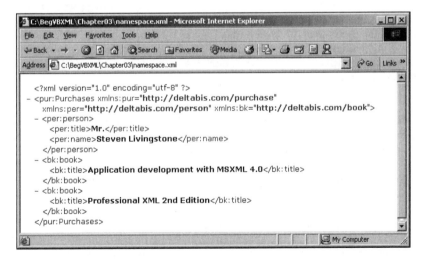

How It Works

In the document above we have associated three prefixes with three separate namespaces, `pur` for purchase, `per` for person and `bk` for book, and put these at the root of the XML document. This means they have scope over the entire document and we can therefore append the appropriate prefixes to the element names to qualify them. However, to make our namespaces more unique still, we have linked them with a URI. Now, any XML parser will not see the expressions `<per:title>` and `<bk:title>`, but rather the URI equivalents of the prefixes; in other words, `http://deltabis.com/person:title` and `http://deltabis.com/book:title`, respectively.

Beyond name duplication, the concept of namespaces is also prevalent in the .NET Framework as a way to group similar classes into a single namespace. As you will learn later in the book, XML documents are validated against schema documents, which define the grammar governing the structure and content of the XML file. The set of elements within a document that fall under a given namespace can be validated against a schema associated with that namespace independent of any other nodes within the document.

And Attributes?

So far we have only been considering elements, but attributes are the same, right? Wrong. Attributes typically don't have any explicit namespace definition at all and are generally associated with the element they are an attribute of.

Consider the following case.

```
<?xml version="1.0" encoding="utf-8" ?>
<person xmlns="http://deltabis.com/person">
  <name firstname="Steven" surname="Livingstone" />
</person>
```

In this case all elements are part of the default `http://deltabis.com/person` namespace. As the `firstname` and `surname` attributes are part of the qualified name attribute (also known as the QName, which is the prefix plus the local name, such as `p:person` where the `p` is bound to a namespace by some namespace declaration), these are also part of this namespace. Hence the two attributes are effectively `http://deltabis.com/person:firstname` and `http://deltabis.com/person:surname`.

However, say we wanted to add a new attribute that fell under a different namespace. This would be useful if we want to extend an existing document, but not interfere with the definitions in that document (this is particularly important as Schemas use namespaces to validate documents and adding new elements and attributes randomly can cause validation to fail).

How do we do that? Well, you can just explicitly associate it with the respective namespace, as follows.

```
<?xml version="1.0" encoding="utf-8" ?>
<person xmlns="http://deltabis.com/person"
        xmlns:jobs="http://deltabis.com/jobs">
  <name firstname="Steven" surname="Livingstone" jobs:position="author"/>
</person>
```

Alternatively, you could have written it as follows, with the namespace definition locally scoped.

```
<?xml version="1.0" encoding="utf-8" ?>
<person xmlns="http://deltabis.com/person">
  <name xmlns:jobs="http://deltabis.com/jobs" firstname="Steven"
        surname="Livingstone" jobs:position="author"/>
</person>
```

The parser will throw an exception if you try to use a prefix that has not been associated with a namespace as in the example below:

```
<?xml version="1.0" encoding="utf-8" ?>
<person xmlns="http://deltabis.com/person">
  <ns:name xmlns:jobs="http://deltabis.com/jobs" firstname="Steven"
           surname="Livingstone" jobs:position="author"/>
</person>
```

Or, if you try to use a namespace that is not yet in scope as in the following example:

```
<?xml version="1.0" encoding="utf-8" ?>
<person xmlns="http://deltabis.com/person" jobs:position="author">
   <name xmlns:jobs="http://deltabis.com/jobs" firstname="Steven"
         surname="Livingstone" />
</person>
```

In these two cases the exception will say that you tried to reference an undeclared namespace. If a namespace is not in scope for a given element, it is regarded as if it were never declared at all.

DTDs and XML Schemas

There are limited programmatic facilities for manipulating DTDs themselves as they are complex to create. However, the .NET Framework provides extensive support for the XML Schema specifications within the System.Xml.Schema namespace, with the ability to cache, query, create, and update XML Schemas. We won't show all of the classes available as there are a great deal, but the diagram below shows the main classes.

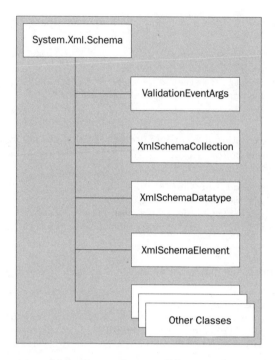

The `ValidationEventArgs` class returns schema validation information to an event handler when an XML instance does not conform to the validation information within the XSD (XML Schema Definition). The XSD is a recommendation of the W3C that establishes how to describe the elements within an XML document. The Schemas that are used to validate the XML document are typically stored in the `XmlSchemaCollection` class (although they can be explicitly referenced within the XML document itself), which is a cache of XSD and XDR (XML Data Reduced, which is a very early schema representation of XML) documents for specified namespaces. The `XmlSchemaDatatype` class provides the facility of mapping XSD datatypes to .NET Framework datatypes – for example, you can map an XSD string datatype to a .NET `String` datatype. Finally, the `XmlSchemaElement` class models an XSD `Element` datatype and allows you to get or set values of an element. At the end of the diagram there are a series of empty boxes to illustrate the fact that there are many more classes to represent working with different parts of an XML Schema document (including reading and manipulating the structure and content of the Schema). For more information on Document Type Definitions, see Chapter 2, and for Schemas, look at Chapters 10 and 11.

XPath

The XML Path Language, XPath, is a technology of the XML family that allows you to filter an XML document so that it returns only the parts of the document you are interested in. It acts like a query language for XML documents. Although it is a separate specification, XPath is almost always used with another XML technology such as the XML DOM (discussed previously), XSLT, the XML Pointer Language (XPointer), the XML Query Language (XQuery), and potentially many others.

> The latest XPath specification, currently version 1.0, was made a W3C
> recommendation on 16 November 1999 and can be found at
> http://www.w3.org/TR/xpath.

What is XPath?

XPath enables the addressing of, or navigation to, chosen parts of an XML document, and additionally specifies a number of functions to allow for string, number, Boolean, and node-set manipulation. XPath expressions are incorporated into your VB.NET application in a very similar way to SQL queries. The following syntax:

```
Dim selectExpr as string  = String.Empty
selectExpr = "person/name"
```

should return "Christopher Williams" from the XML file shown below. It has navigated to the starting point of the document, which is the `<person>` element, and set the next destination as the name element.

```
<?xml version='1.0'?>
<person>
  <name="Christopher Williams">
    <title>Mr</title>
    <age>27</age>
  </name>
</person>
```

When addressing an XML document, using XPath, a starting point is specified which is known as the **context node**. The context node is an extremely important concept when working with XPath; in fact many of the problems encountered when working with technologies employing XPath are due to not knowing the context node you are currently on. You arrive at a destination node (a node that you arrive at as the result of an XPath expression) via a series of **location steps**. A location step selects the next set of nodes to be evaluated at each point in the XPath expression. A **location path** is a particular expression that selects a set of nodes relative to the context node and consists of a series of location steps. Each location step has a direction (forward or reverse) known as an **axis** and additionally, a location step may contain a **node test** which specifies the type of node selected and its expanded name, where applicable. Finally, a location step may have one or more **predicates,** which are arbitrary expressions used to further refine and filter the set of nodes selected by the location step.

To illustrate the concept, consider that you are driving in a city looking for a bookstore to get the latest copy of Professional XML (ignore that you would get a taxi to get the book as soon as possible!). You start at point A and have a map, which you will use to arrive at one (or more if it has already sold out) of the potential bookstores.

The starting point, A, is where you start the journey and can be considered equivalent to the XPath context node. As you don't know exactly the direction you are going in, you will choose to go to go via a series of intermediate points and at each point evaluate all of the possible options that will get you to the end point. Each intermediary can be regarded as equivalent to a location step, as you will determine the direction to walk in (axis), whether it's a one-way street (like a node test) and even if the distance to the closest bookstore to determine if it is too far away (like a predicate). The series of steps that got you from your starting point to this end point can be regarded as equivalent to a location path in XPath.

95

Location Paths

A location path is a particular type of XPath expression that is used to select a set of nodes relative to the context node. It consists of a series of location steps composed of the following:

❑ An axis, of which there are thirteen.

❑ A node test specifying the type of node selected and if applicable, its expanded name.

❑ Zero or more optional predicates, which are arbitrary expressions used to further filter and refine the set of nodes selected by the location step.

It is important, when working with XPath, to be familiar with the concept of the **document root**, which is not the root element. As there can be other things at the beginning or end of an XML document before or after the root element, XPath needs a virtual document root to act as the root of the document's hierarchy. In XPath, the document root is specified by a single "/".

Consider the following XML document once more:

```
<?xml version="1.0" encoding="utf-8" ?>
<Purchases>
  <person>
    <title>Mr.</title>
    <name>Steven Livingstone</name>
  </person>
  <book>
    <title>Application development with MSXML 4.0</title>
  </book>
  <book>
    <title>Professional XML 2nd Edition</title>
  </book>
</Purchases>
```

If we only wanted to match against the <person> element, instead of the entire document, we could write the XPath expression "/person". XPath reads expressions from left to right, so in this case it would read, "start at the document root node, and return the <person> element, which is a child of that node". Remember, the location path specifies where you are going in the document, and the context node is the section of the document that you're starting at. So in this example, our context node is the document root.

Let's now look at the thirteen axes of XPath.

The Thirteen Axes

An XPath axis is either a **forward axis** or a **reverse axis**. A forward axis only contains the context node, or nodes that are after the context node in document order. The reverse axis contains the context node with nodes that are before it in document order, or just the nodes before the context node. The value of the position() function is interpreted **differently** depending on the axis in use. For a forward axis it is the relative position within the node-set from the context node; for a reverse axis it is the position from the end of the node-set.

Example – XPath Axes

As a practical exercise, let's define the relevant axis for nodes within an XML document.

Consider the following XML document where the context element is the first Company element node.

```xml
<?xml version="1.0" encoding="utf-8" ?>
<Catalog xmlns="http://www.deltabis.com/ns">
  <Company email="loreto@deltabis.net">Loreto Productions Int</Company>
  <Company email="steven@deltabis.net">Steven Productions Ltd</Company>
  <Company email="eileen@deltabis.net">Eileen Productions Inc</Company>
</Catalog>
```

The following table defines each different type of axis and associates it with the relevant node from the example above:

Axes	Definition of Axes	Nodes within axis
child	This axis contains the children of the context node. However, remember that attribute and namespace nodes are *not* children of element nodes and so the child axis never returns attributes or namespaces in the returned node-set. To access these attributes or namespaces you can use the child axis in combination with the relevant axis (for example, the namespace axis and the attribute axis).	The child axis will contain the "Loreto Productions Int" text node.
parent	This axis contains the node that is the parent of the context node (that is, the containing node). The document root node has no parent.	The parent axis will be the <Catalog> element node.
descendant	This axis will contain the descendants of the context node, such as the context nodes children, grandchildren, and so on. Like the child axis, this axis never contains attribute or namespace nodes.	The descendant axis will contain only the "Loreto Productions Int" text node.
descendant-or-self	This axis contains all the nodes of the descendant axis as well as the context node.	The descendant-or-self axis will contain the <Company> context element node and the "Loreto Productions Int" text node.

Table continued on following page

Axes	Definition of Axes	Nodes within axis
Following-sibling	This contains all of the following sibling nodes of the context node and is always empty if the context node is an attribute or namespace node.	The `following-sibling` axis contains two `<Company>` element nodes.
Following	This axis contains all of the nodes following the context node in document order after the context node, excluding any descendants, attribute nodes, or namespace nodes.	The `following` axis will contain the two `<Company>` element nodes and their two respective text nodes.
Attribute	This axis contains the attributes of the context node and will be empty unless the context node is an element.	The `attribute` axes will contain the single `email` attribute node.
namespace	This axis will contain any namespace nodes of the context node and will be empty unless the context node is an element.	The single default namespace, because this is in scope from the parent.
self	This axis will contain only the context node.	The first `<Company>` element node itself.
ancestor	This axis is the opposite of the `descendant` axis and contains the ancestor nodes of the context node. That is, the parent and grandparent and so on of the context node. This will always contain the document root unless the context node *is* the document root.	`<Catalog>` document element node and the document root node.
ancestor-or-self	This axis will return all of the nodes of the `ancestor` axis as well as the context node.	`<Catalog>` document element node and the document root node and the first `<Company>` element node itself.
preceding-sibling	This axis will contain all of the preceding sibling nodes of the context node and is the opposite of the `following-sibling` axis. However, when the context node is an attribute node or a namespace node, the axis will also be empty.	Will be empty.
preceding	This axis contains all the nodes before the context node in document order and so includes all the nodes that appear before the context node.	`<Catalog>` document element and the document root node.

The following diagram shows a graphical representation of all of these axes – note that a given node can be part of many axes as illustrated.

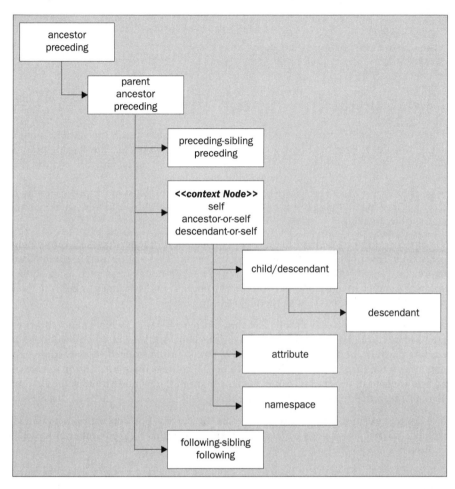

Context in XPath

The context in XPath is the starting node for any queries that are to be evaluated, so it is important that you understand how the context node is determined. There are six parts to the definition of context and we will use the following XML file, from an earlier illustration, to aid our understanding.

```xml
<?xml version="1.0"?>
<person age="25">
  <name>
    <firstname>Graham</firstname>
    <middlename>Mark</middlename>
    <lastname>Livingstone</lastname>
  </name>
  <name>
```

```
        <firstname>Steven</firstname>
        <lastname>Livingstone</lastname>
    </name>
    <name>
        <firstname>Cathy</firstname>
        <lastname>Livingstone</lastname>
    </name>
</person>
```

Context nodes are made up of:

❑ The context node is arrived at via some XPath expression and is the starting point for further expressions. It is similar to how you may navigate to a web site. The starting point will be the domain name www.wrox.com, which is like the context node, and you can use the relative path /images/logo.gif to arrive at the absolute location www.wrox.com/images/logo.gif. So, in our example, some expression may determine that the first <name> element is our context node (we will look at how we create these expressions shortly).

❑ The context node-set defines a node-set (a collection of nodes) that is currently being processed. This node-set is determined as the result of a location step in some XPath expression, which we discussed earlier. When a set of nodes is selected using some expression you will iterate through them. As you do, the context node changes to become the current node in that collection – that is, the node at each index.

Again this is similar to a web site. The root of the web site may have many directories and you may iterate through each child directory off the root, and as you do you will be at a new starting position for any subsequent relative paths. In the example above, some expression may return the three <name> elements to be the context node-set. As you iterate through each <name> element, the context node changes to be that new node (that is, the first <name> element, then the second and finally the third).

❑ The context position and context size define the current position within the context node-set, which is always less than or equal to the context size (that is, the number of nodes in the context node-set).

Looking at the node-set with the <name> elements in it, the context size if the number of nodes in the collection and so that would be three. As you iterate through each node, you change the context position, from one (the first <name> element), to two (the second) and finally to three (the last <name> element)

❑ Variable bindings allow you to map some variable value to a variable name within XPath. Variables can be node-sets, strings, numbers and Booleans, which may be evaluated at execution time rather than at design time. Variables are popular when working with the Extensible Stylesheet Language that we look at later in the book.

❑ A set of functions names that are mapped to defined functions, some of which are defined by the XPath specification. XPath defines functions such as string-length() to calculate the length of the text value of the context node, or last() to return the value of the context size. There are many other functions defined by the XPath specification. You also have the ability to create your own functions that may perform some functionality not available in the XPath functions (such as ConvertFirstCharToUpper(), and so on).

Node Tests

A node test is used on an axis to filter the node-set along the axis on which we are working. The node test specifies the node type and expanded name on which to filter the axis node-set. There are two types of node test; the first is a **name test** and the second is a **node type test**.

Name Tests

A name test is the most common type you will see when working with XPath expressions and can be based on all nodes of the principal node type (the axis you are working on), the QName of the node (qualified name) such as `p:person` (where the p is bound to a namespace by some namespace declaration) or the NCName of the node (an XML name that does not contain a colon) such as `person`. The principal node type test is based on the axis that is being evaluated and so for the `attribute` axis, it is `attribute`; for the `namespace` axis it is `namespace` and for all other it is `element`. An asterisk (*) is used to select all nodes of a given type based on the principal node type.

The second type of XPath name test is based on the QName or Qualified Name and in this case, when a node is qualified by a namespace, this namespace must be part of the XPath expression to evaluate the match to `True`. Any prefixes are first expanded to the full namespace URI before evaluation based on the definitions in the context document and so prefixes have no meaning as they are *always* expanded. Although your XPath expression may match the *name* of an element, for example, within the document, if you do not also qualify this with the relevant namespace you will not get that element returned in the node-set.

The final type of XPath name test is based on the NCName where the prefix is expanded in the same way as a QName, but the nodes are selected according to the principal node type. The matching of nodes is based on the same expanded namespace URI and the local name is irrelevant.

When given some axis, you filter using a double colon followed by the name test. So the following example selects the child `company` elements of the context node.

```
child::company
```

Similarly, the following XPath expression will return the attribute named `name` in the context element.

```
attribute::name
```

We look in detail at XPath expressions later.

Node Type Tests

XPath expressions can also have node type tests that allow you to override the principal node type and select from other axes. There are four such tests.

- ❑ `comment()` – this can be used to select comment node types from a document.
- ❑ `node()` – this can select any node type from the source document.
- ❑ `processing-instruction()` – this can select processing-instructions nodes from the source document.
- ❑ `text()` – this returns text nodes in the document

Example – XPath Node Tests

We have looked at the different node tests we can do, so let's now see some practical examples of this.

Consider our previous XML document example. Again the context element is the first `<Company>` element node.

```
<?xml version="1.0" encoding="utf-8" ?>
<Catalog xmlns="http://www.deltabis.com/ns">
  <Company email="loreto@deltabis.net">Loreto Productions Int</Company>
  <Company email="steven@deltabis.net">Steven Productions Ltd</Company>
  <Company email="eileen@deltabis.net">Eileen Productions Inc</Company>
</Catalog>
```

XPath expression	Node-set returned
`attribute::*`	This will be the `email` attribute as well as any other attributes that are added to this element node (or that are part of new child element nodes).
`following-sibling::*`	This will be the two following `<Company>` element nodes.
`child::text()`	This will be the text "Loreto Productions Int", which in this case would be the same as the expression `child::node()` because there is only one child node. Note that the attribute node (`email="..."`) is not part of the returned node-set.

Up to this point we have looked at accessing a particular axis and returning a node-set based on a particular principal axis (or even from some other axis), but we can use predicates to further filter the node-set. Let's continue with a look at predicates.

Predicates

Predicates can be used on an XPath expression to further filter a node-set on a given axis to produce a new node-set, in a similar way to the `Where` clause used in a SQL statement to filter the rows selected. The predicate is enclosed within square brackets after the node test and returns either a number or a Boolean value. When a number is returned it is evaluated based on the context position of the node. If the context position and the number evaluated are equal, then the expression is evaluated to a Boolean `True` and it is included in the result node-set; otherwise it is excluded.

So, the following expression selects the first child `company` element of the context node.

```
child::company[position()=1]
```

Similarly, to get the last `company` child element of the context node, you would use the following expression.

```
child::company[position()=last()]
```

This example will return any `company` child elements that have a child `title` element with the text "XPath Services".

```
child::company[title = 'XPath Services']
```

You can even use other axes within the predicate to filter the node-set. The following example will return a node-set where the child `company` element also has a `size` attribute.

```
child::company[attribute::size]
```

In contrast to the `title` example above, this example will return any `company` child elements that have a `title` attribute with the text "XPath Services".

```
child::company[@title = 'XPath Services']
```

This example uses abbreviated syntax for attribute. This technique it discussed in the section entitled *Unabbreviated and Abbreviated Syntax*, later in the chapter.

There can also be multiple predicates to filter a node set and so the following example will select the second `company` child element that has a `size` attribute.

```
child::company[position()=2][attribute::size]
```

You can see that this is like the AND keyword of a SQL statement and you can list as many predicates in this way as you wish. Again, we look at examples of these kinds of expressions later in this chapter.

Data Model

The XPath data model is very similar to the Document Object Model, which we will looked at earlier in this chapter. It also represents the XML document as a tree and everything is defined as one of 7 node types as part of its data model:

- ❑ Root Node
- ❑ Element Nodes
- ❑ Attribute Nodes
- ❑ Namespace Nodes
- ❑ Processing Instruction Nodes
- ❑ Comment Nodes
- ❑ Text Nodes

For more information on this specific model, you could look at the following web page: www.w3.org/TR/xpath#data-model.

Every node has exactly one parent element node, except the root node, which has no parent. The node descendants of a node are its children and their children are grandchildren, and so on. Consider this XML document:

```
<?xml version="1.0"?>
<person age="25">
  <name>
    <firstname>Graham</firstname>
    <middlename>Mark</middlename>
    <lastname>Livingstone</lastname>
  </name>
  <address type="home">
    <streetNumber>72</streetNumber>
    <streetName>Gettison &amp; Loots Avenue</streetName>
    <area>Yoker</area>
    <city>Glasgow</city>
  </address>
</person>
```

The <person> element is the document's element node (distinct from the document's root node). The age attribute node is the first (and only) attribute node of the element node. The <name> element node is the first child node of the element node and the <address>element node is the second child element node of the document's element node; additionally, the <name> and <address> elements are sibling nodes. The <firstname> element node is the first child node of the <name> element and the first grandchild node of the <person> document element. From this information the other nodes follow a similar pattern.

So, let's look at each of the XPath node types.

Root Node

Every XML document has an implicit root node, which sits at the top of the XPath tree, and therefore never has a parent. This should not be confused with the <person> element in the above example, which is the document's element node. The root node is the implicit node that is the parent of this node.

Element Nodes

Every XML document must have at least one element node – the document element, but it will typically contain many element nodes. Every well-formed XML document consists of a single document element, which contains any number of descendant elements. The children of a given element node are the Element nodes, Comment nodes, Processing Instruction nodes and Text nodes of its content. Attribute nodes are **not** regarded as child nodes in XPath.

Attribute Nodes

An attribute node is associated with an element node, which may have zero or many attribute nodes. An element node is the parent of an attribute node, but an attribute node is *not* the child of an element node. Although this may seem strange, it allows elements and attributes to be selected using different XPath axes, which we will look at shortly. An attribute node also has an expanded name and value, the first being similar to an element expanded name and the value conforming to the normal rules of XML (an empty string is also permitted).

Namespace Nodes

Each distinct namespace node is associated with the element in which it is declared. The XML 1.0 Recommendation also declares an implicit namespace for XML itself – you don't have to declare it, however, as it is also part of any document that is valid XML. This namespace is accessed using a prefix of "xml:" and allows you to use the xml:lang (specifies the human language used in the element it is attached to), xml:space (determines how whitespace should be handled) and xml:base (specifies a base URL for any relative URLs specified in child nodes) attributes without having to worry about declaring namespaces.

Similar to attributes, the element node is the parent of the namespace node(s), but namespace nodes are *not* children of the element node. Elements also never share namespace nodes.

An element will have a namespace node for the following conditions:

❑   For every attribute on the element whose name starts with xmlns:

❑   For every attribute on an ancestor element whose name starts with xmlns: (unless the element or some closer ancestor choose to re-declare the prefix)

❑   For an xmlns: attribute, if the element or some ancestor has an xmlns attribute and the value of this attribute for the nearest such element is non-empty

To actually declare the namespace, you use the syntax xmlns:prefix="URI". The xmlns actually tells the parser we are declaring a namespace and the *prefix* defines the shorthand that is used to associate nodes with this namespace. Finally, the value between the quotes is the full namespace which is unique in the document and can be associated with nodes (via the prefix) to uniquely identify them in the document. Below are some examples:

```
xmlns:xsd = "http://www.w3.org/2001/XMLSchema"
xmlns:ns = "http://www.wrox.com/bks"
xmlns:ns = "urn:myNs"
```

You can declare a default namespace by not using the prefix (for example, xmlns="http://w3.org/ns") and any unprefixed descendant elements are taken to be members of it.

> It is important to remember that a namespace does not have to point to any real document. It is simply a unique identifier for that document. However, as these XML documents may be used on a global scale, the domain name of the company creating the document is often used. We discuss namespaces and prefixes in much greater detail later in the chapter.

Processing Instruction Nodes

Processing Instruction nodes are distinguished by the <? and ?> delimiters, although the XML declaration itself is not actually a processing instruction. An often confusing point is that the string value of the processing instruction is in fact the part following the target, excluding the "?>" at the end. When the ?> is reached at the end any processing stops. The string value often contains multiple attributes, but they are not treated in the same way as an attribute node and are in fact treated as a single string value.

As an example, consider the following processing instruction:

```
<?xml-stylesheet href="someURI.xsl" type="text/xsl"?>
```

This text defines the XSL stylesheet. The value of this processing instruction is the string `href="someURI.xsl" type="text/xsl"` and you cannot access the `href` or `type` attributes individually as they are treated as a single string.

Comment Nodes

There is a comment node for every comment in an XML document (except the DTD) and they do not have an expanded name. The value of a comment node is the text between the `<!--` and `-->` characters.

So in the following example, the value of the comment node is `"I am a comment."`.

```
<!--I am a comment. -->
```

Text Nodes

Text nodes are groups of character data. You can never have two immediately adjacent sibling text nodes. Text nodes must always have at least one character of data and each text node will contain as much character data as possible. So in the following example, there is a single text node between the opening and closing `<first>` element:

```
<first>Steven</first>
```

Equally, the following element contains a single text node as well:

```
<name>
   Steven Livingstone
</name>
```

The new lines and all text are treated as a single text node – rather than separate nodes for each.

The actual value of a text node, which must contain at least one character, is simply the character data. Each character within a CDATA section is treated as though the `<![CDATA[` and `]]>` characters were removed and the special XML characters are escaped. In other words, in the following fragment:

```
<note>Steven <![CDATA[earns < $100 per year]]></note>
```

The actual text that the DOM would see for this CDATA section is:

```
earns &lt; $100 per year
```

Therefore the text node within the `<note>` element would be the combination of the first text node `"Steven"` and the second text node (which is the CDATA text) and thus the value of the text node is `"Steven earns &lt; $100 per year"`.

Characters inside comments, processing instructions and attribute nodes do not produce text nodes. Furthermore, computer files typically organize files with combinations of end of line characters such as carriage return characters (#xD) and line-feed characters (#xA). In order to make it easier for consuming applications, an XML parser must convert all line-feed (#xA) characters and combinations of carriage-return/line-feed characters (#xD#xA) into a single line-feed character (#xA). This helps prevent confusion of random end of line characters in XML documents.

XPath Syntax

Up to this point we have been discussing how XPath expressions are built up, but beyond some simple examples, we haven't really looked at what these expressions finally look like. This is because there are a few different ways in that XPath expressions are created. They can use relative and absolute location paths as well as an unabbreviated and abbreviated syntax.

Absolute and Relative Location Paths

XPath expressions are based on either a relative location path or an absolute location path. This path determines the route you need to take in order to get to the node you are aiming for within the document. The following example XML document will be used to illustrate these points.

```xml
<?xml version="1.0" encoding="utf-8" ?>
<section>
  <para>
    <sentence>abc</sentence>
    <sentence>def</sentence>
    <sentence>ghi</sentence>
  </para>
  <para>
    <sentence>123</sentence>
    <sentence>456...</sentence>
  </para>
</section>
```

For an **Absolute Location Path**, the root element, which in our example is the `<section>` element, is represented by a single forward slash character (/). The following steps are then separated by further "/" characters. The code example below is the **Absolute Location Path** of the second `<sentence>` element that is the child of the first `<para>` element.

```
/child::para[position()=1]/child::sentence[position()=2]
```

There are two location steps here; the first selects the first `<para>` child element of the root element. In this case, as we have explicitly started at the root element, which is, therefore, the context element. This differs from the **Relative Location Path** as we will discuss below. This location step sets the context node for the next location step, so the context step for the following location step is set to the first `<para>` child element. The second location step now selects the second `<sentence>` child element of the first `<para>` element.

The way that the Absolute Location Path differs from the Relative Location Path is that the Absolute Location Path sets an absolute course through the document. Every location step is explicitly laid out, including the starting point of the root element. However, the Relative Location Path for the same example as above would be as follows:

```
child::para[position()=1]/child::sentence[position()=2]
```

The only difference between the two, in these examples, is that there is no initial forward slash. This is because the Relative Location Path charts its course through the document based on the position of the context node. It is does not have to begin at the root node, but in this example, as the root node is the parent of the <para> element, they are the same. In fact, the Absolute Location Path is made up of Relative Location Paths after its initial orientation at the beginning of the expression because, as we have already stated, each location step becomes the context node for the next step.

Unabbreviated and Abbreviated Syntax

The examples you have seen so far have all been using the unabbreviated XPath syntax where you specify the full name of the axes you want to use and separate the node test with a double colon. Some of the more complex XPath expressions can get quite complex and hard to follow if they are written in this unabbreviated syntax. However, XPath supports an abbreviated syntax, which is normally interchangeable with the unabbreviated syntax. You will probably use the abbreviated syntax almost all the time unless you have to use the unabbreviated syntax for something you can't do, such as selecting nodes along the ancestor axis.

Consider the following unabbreviated XPath expression, from our example above.

```
child::para[position()=1]/child::sentence[position()=2]
```

This can be rewritten in the following abbreviated format.

```
para[1]/sentence[2]
```

You can see that this is much shorter and should be easier to follow. Leaving out the child axis is possible because, where no axis is declared, it is assumed that we are talking about a child axis. There are other ways to shorten to the abbreviated syntax; for example, the attribute axis can be replaced by an ampersand so the unabbreviated expression shown below:

```
attribute::name
```

can be rewritten as:

```
@name
```

Also, the expression:

```
descendant-or-self::section
```

can be rewritten as the following syntax, when started from the root:

```
//section
```

Let's look now at a series of abbreviations that are available by looking at XPath Patterns.

XPath Patterns

An XPath Pattern's role is to provide a series of conditions, each of which must be met before moving onto the next condition, working in an almost identical way to a location path. For example, the following syntax:

```
/name/first
```

would aim to match *any* `<first>` element which is a child of a `<name>` element, which is a child of the document root. The difference between an XPath pattern and expression is that the expression lays down a path to a particular node, whereas the pattern is seeking a *type* to select. When using patterns, as opposed to expressions, without an absolute path being laid down (which can be done in the same way as for location paths, by including a slash at the beginning of the pattern) any element in the document that matches the pattern could be selected.

Operator	Function
//	This operator is the abbreviated syntax and equivalent to the unabbreviated `descendant-or-self` expression when started from the root. This expression always starts from the root and selects all descendant nodes and therefore can be very resource expensive in larger documents. For example, `//person` will select all `person` elements in the entire XML document.
/	This operator is the abbreviated syntax and equivalent to the unabbreviated `child` axis. It selects the immediate children of the element node on the left of the operator. If used at the document root then it selects all nodes. As an example, the expression `//person/name` will return all `name` elements that are children of any `person` elements in the XML document (note that they have to be child nodes of `person`).
.	This is the abbreviated syntax for the context node and equivalent to the unabbreviated `self` axis. So, if the context node is a `name` element, then the expression `.` will return this node. This is useful when working with XPath functions and you want to pass the current node in as the argument to a function.
*	This is a wildcard operator and selects all elements regardless of their name and it can be used in both abbreviated and unabbreviated syntax. For example, the expression `name/*` will select all child element nodes of the `name` child element of the context node.
@	This selects the attribute of a given node and is the abbreviated expression equivalent of the `attribute` axis. To illustrate, the expression `//person[@age]` will return any `person` elements in the document that have an `age` attribute.
@*	This abbreviated syntax is similar to the above operator, but selects all attributes of the context node regardless of their name. The equivalent unabbreviated syntax is `attribute::*`. Therefore, the expression `//person/@*` will return a node-set containing all of the attributes of each `person` element that is found in the document, regardless of their name.

Operator	Function
:	This is a namespace separator and is equivalent in both abbreviated and unabbreviated syntax. The expressions `child:ns:section` and `ns:section` are equivalent if `ns` represents the same namespace. Therefore, say we have created a namespace declaration in the document that states `xmlns:per="http://www.someperson.com/person"` and so binds the `per` prefix to this namespace and the `name` element is qualified in this namespace, as `per:name`. The expression `//per:name` will return all `name` elements that are qualified by the prefix binding (but ignore all other `name` elements that are not associated with this prefix – such as `name` elements related to a city name).
[]	These characters are used to enclose filtered expressions or predicates. We can extend the example we looked at above for the @ definition. The expression `//person[@age='25']` will return any `person` elements that have an `age` attribute whose value is "25".

Try It Out: XPath Patterns

The following example is an opportunity to play with some XPath queries, using a front-end form that we have provided for you. We are not going to look at the code behind the form in this chapter as our focus is on the XPath syntax here. If you would like to examine the code issues involved with XPath at this stage, please see Chapter 7.

The XML file (sample.xml) used for this example is shown below.

```xml
<?xml version="1.0" encoding="utf-8" ?>
<Catalog>
  <Company email="loreto@deltabis.net" name="Loreto Productions International">
    <ProductFamily familyID="pftops" LastUpdate="2001-08-26T18:39:09"
        buyersURI="http://www.deltabis.com/buyers/tops">
      <Product ProductID="CFC3" items="34">
        <colour>green</colour>
        <size>M</size>
        <price>31.99</price>
        <colour>green</colour>
        <size>L</size>
        <price>45.99</price>
      </Product>
      <Product ProductID="CFC4">
        <colour>black</colour>
        <size>L</size>
        <price>32.99</price>
      </Product>
    </ProductFamily>
  </Company>
</Catalog>
```

1. Go to the XPathExamples1 download and double-click on the XPathExamples.exe file.

2. You will get a Windows Form appearing that looks like the screenshot below.

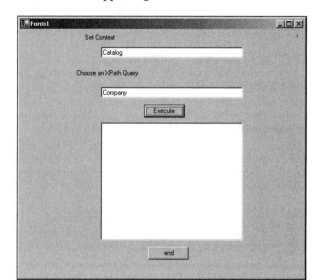

3. The Set Context field is where you set the element that is to be the context node. The second box is for the XPath query. The default context node will be the Catalog element, which is also the root element of the document. The XPath Query field is abbreviated syntax to select the Company child node, of which there is just one. The result of executing this procedure is to get the name of the selected node (Company), followed by a colon separator and then the concatenation of the text nodes that are descendants of the selected node. So, click the Execute button, then click OK when prompted and you should get the following.

4. The equivalent unabbreviated syntax for the above query can be demonstrated by changing the XPath query to child::Company and clicking the **Execute** button. You will get the same results as the above example.

5. Now, without changing the context, change the XPath query to //Product. Executing this will cause all Product elements in the document to be returned and so you will get two Product entries in the display box with differing values.

6. The unabbreviated equivalent of the above query is descendant-or-self::Product and will return the same result.

7. Finally, change the context expression to //Product[1] and change the XPath expression to be @* and click **Execute**. The ProductID and items attributes with their respective values will be returned.

8. The equivalent unabbreviated syntax for the above expression is to change the context setting expression to descendant-or-self::Product[position()=1] and the XPath expression to attribute::* and you will get the same result.

XPath Operators

Additionally, there are some operators that are associated with more numeric/arithmetic type operations.

Operator	Function
[]	This is used to hold an index to an item within a collection and so like in the example above, we can have the syntax //Product[1] to select the first Product node.
+	This performs addition and so the unabbreviated expression child::Product[position()+1] would select the next child Product element node. The equivalent abbreviated syntax is Product[position()+1].
-	This performs subtraction and so the unabbreviated expression child::Product[last()-1] returns the penultimate Product element node.
div	This performs a floating point division. You can use this in the form [x div y]; we will see an example below in the next Try It Out.
*	This performs multiplication. You can use this in the form [x * y]; we will see an example in the next Try It Out.
mod	This returns the integer remainder from a truncating division and is used in the form [x mod y]. So we could get every second element by the following predicate [position() mod 2 = 0].

Note also that parentheses, ( ), are used to establish precedence.

XML with .NET in Detail

Try It Out: XPath Operators

This Try It Out uses the same example as for the XPath Patterns Try It Out, so run the `XPathExamples1` application. We are working with the same XML document as in the previous example.

1. Set the context node to the `ProductFamily` element with the following XPath expression: `Catalog/Company/ProductFamily`. Now enter the XPath query `Product[position()=last()-1]/@ProductID`, click the Execute button and you will be returned the `ProductID` attribute with the value CFC3.

2. Now alter the XPath query to `Product[(last() div 2)+1]/@ProductID`, click the Execute button and you will be returned the `ProductID` attribute with the value CFC4.

3. Finally, enter the XPath query `Product[position() mod 2 = 1]/@ProductID`, click the Execute button and you will be returned the `ProductID` attribute with the value CFC3.

How It Works

In the first example, we selected the child `<Product>` element node that was second to last – this was achieved by the `position()=last()-1` predicate. This would position you back at the first `<Product>` child node because there are only two `<Product>` child nodes. We then asked for the value of the `ProductID` attribute, which is CFC3.

The second example was similar, but instead we used the precedence of brackets to first get the predicate to get the index of the last `<Product>` child node (using the `last()` function) and then divide this by two. As there are two child `<Product>` elements, the result of `last()` is two and so dividing this by two (using the `div` operator) will give 1; back to the first `<Product>` element again. Finally we added 1 to this and we got two, and then the second `<Product>` element node was returned.

The last example used the `mod` function to divide the `position()` of the selected `<Product>` nodes by two and return only those that have a remainder of 1. This will therefore return all odd-numbered nodes, which in this case will be the first `<Product>` element node.

XPath Comparison and Union

In addition to the operators we have looked at above, XPath also provide Boolean and comparison operators that can be used in unabbreviated and abbreviated expressions.

Operator	Function
and	This operator performs logical AND operations. So the expression `child::MyElement[attribute::name and child::MySubElement]` would return all child nodes of the context node that are called `MyElement` and have an attribute called `name` and at least one `MySubElement` child element. The equivalent abbreviated syntax would be `MyElement[@name and MySubElement]`. In comparison, the expression `child::MyElement[attribute::name][child::MySubElement]` first selects all child elements called `MyElement` with a name attribute and then selects those from that node-set that also have a `MySubElement` child element.

Table continued on following page

113

Operator	Function
`or`	This performs logical OR operations. Hence the previous example could be modified to be `child::MyElement[attribute::name or child::MySubElement]` which will return all child `MyElement` nodes that have a name attribute or have a `MySubElement` child element node. This can be abbreviated as `MyElement[@name or MySubElement]`.
`not()`	This operator provides the negation of the value of an expression. Again, we could modify the above examples to be `child::MyElement[attribute::name and not(child::MySubElement)]` which will return all `MyElement` child nodes which have a `name` attribute and have no `MySubElement` child nodes.
`=`	This is an equality operator and has been used often in the previous examples.
`!=`	This is an inequality operator and returns `True` if two expressions are *not* equal. So we could return all the `MyElement` child nodes of a context node except the last one with the following expression: `child::MyElement[position()!=last()]`.
`&lt;`	This is a less-than operator. So to get all of the `MyElement` child elements except for the last one, we could do the following; `child::MyElement[position() &lt; last()]`.
`&lt;=`	This is a less-than or equal to operator. So to get the first four of the `MyElement` child elements, we could do the following `child::MyElement[position() &lt;= 4]`.
`&gt;`	This is a greater-than operator. So to get all of the `MyElement` child elements except for the first, we could do the following `child::MyElement[position() &gt; 1]`.
`&gt;=`	This is a greater-than or equal to operator. So to get all of the `MyElement` child elements except for the first, we could also do the following `child::MyElement[position() &gt;= 2]`.
`|`	This is a set operator and will return the union of two sets of node selections and can be useful for joining two diverse node-sets into a single node-set. This may be useful when you want to return a node-set containing all `<name>` elements that are children of the `<business>` element and combine these with all `<name>` elements that are children of `<friends>` elements. In this case you may use the expression `business/child::name	friends/child::name` to accomplish this.

Note that you **only** have to escape `&gt;`, `&gt;=`, `&lt;`, and `&lt;=` in an XML document. Otherwise their normal equivalent characters can be used: >, >=, <, and <=. (For more information on escaping characters, see Chapter 2).

Try It Out: XPath Comparison Operators

This Try It Out uses the same XML document as before, so run the `XPathExamples1` application.

1. Set the context to the `Catalog` element (using the following XPath expression `Catalog`). Now enter the XPath expression `//Product[not(@items)]/@ProductID`, click the **Execute** button and the `ProductID` attribute will be returned to you with the value **CFC4**.

2. Set the context to the `Catalog` element with an XPath expression of `Catalog`. Now enter the XPath expression `//Product/colour[position() > 1]`, click the **Execute** button and the `colour` element will be returned to you with the value **green**.

3. Finally, set the context to the `Catalog` element and enter the XPath expression `//Product[1]/price[2] | //Product[2]/price[1]`. Click the **Execute** button and you will be returned two `price` element nodes with the value **45.99** and **32.99** respectively.

How It Works

In the first example, we selected the child `Product` element nodes that do *not* have the `items` attribute and returned the `ProductID` attribute value. In this case the second `Product` element node is selected and its `ProductID` attribute value is `CFC4`.

In the second example, we selected all `colour` element nodes that were not the first child of the `Product` element node. In this case only one will be returned from the first `Product` element node as this is the only one that has multiple `colour` child element nodes.

The final example selected the second `price` element node from the first `Product` element node and added this to a node-set with the first `price` element node of the second `Product` element node. This returns a two node node-set containing the values **45.99** (first node selection) and **32.99** (second node selection).

XPath and Namespaces

When working with namespaces it is very important to know what namespaces you want to use to qualify the nodes you want to select. However, as important as this is, it doesn't actually drastically effect the creation of the expressions. In fact, as long as you remember that elements should be qualified in appropriate namespaces, the rest of the expression remains the same.

Consider the following XML document:

```
<?xml version="1.0" encoding="utf-8" ?>
<person xmlns="http://deltabis.com/person">
  <name firstname="Steven" surname="Livingstone"/>
</person>
```

If you executed the XPath query `//name` you would get no result returned. This is because you didn't explicitly qualify the `name` element in the `http://deltabis.com/person` namespace and so it only looked for a `name` element with a null namespace. To correctly implement this kind of expression, you must use programmatic techniques provided by the XML parser to associate a prefix with an appropriate namespace. This can then be included in your expression (for example `//per:person` to select all `person` elements in the namespace associated with the `per` prefix).

> We are not going to look at the details of this implementation quite yet. It uses the
> `System.Xml` **namespace discussed in the next chapter and the** `System.Xml.XPath`
> **namespace discussed in Chapter 7.**

So, due to the similarities of the XPath expressions with or without namespaces, we are going to launch straight into examples. The XML file we were working with above has now changed to use namespaces. It is shown in the listing below (`sample.xml` in the `XPathExamples2` folder).

```xml
<?xml version="1.0" encoding="utf-8" ?>
<Catalog xmlns:co="http://www.deltabis.com/catalog"
         xmlns:pb="http://www.deltabis.com/productsBought"
         xmlns:ps="http://www.deltabis.com/productsSold">
  <Company email="loreto@deltabis.net" name="Loreto Productions International">
    <ProductFamily familyID="pftops" LastUpdate="2001-08-26T18:39:09"
        buyersURI="http://www.deltabis.com/buyers/tops">
      <pb:Product ProductID="CFC3" items="34">
        <colour>green</colour>
        <size>M</size>
        <price>31.99</price>
        <colour>green</colour>
        <size>L</size>
        <price>45.99</price>
      </pb:Product>
      <pb:Product ProductID="CFC4">
        <colour>black</colour>
        <size>L</size>
        <price>32.99</price>
      </pb:Product>
      <ps:Product ProductID="TT79">
        <colour>red</colour>
        <size>S</size>
        <price>12.99</price>
      </ps:Product>
      <ps:Product ProductID="PP09">
        <colour>red</colour>
        <size>L</size>
        <price>35.99</price>
      </ps:Product>
    </ProductFamily>
  </Company>
</Catalog>
```

There are now three namespaces in the document. The first, `http://www.deltabis.com/catalog` is the default namespace and applies to the `Catalog`, `Company`, and `ProductFamily` element nodes. There are another two namespaces then defined. The first, `http://www.deltabis.com/productsBought`, is associated with the prefix `pb` and identifies products that the company buys. It is unique from the `http://www.deltabis.com/productsSold` namespace associated with the prefix `ps`, which represents products that the company sells. These last two namespaces are needed so that product information between what the company buys and sells doesn't get confused.

Let's now launch into some examples on using this document.

Try It Out: XPath Namespace Examples

We are now going to work through some examples of XPath queries using all of the techniques we have been discussing above. We will use the sample application in the `XPathExamples2` folder, called `XPathExamples2.exe`.

Enter the Context and XPath expressions and hit the **Execute** button to test each sample.

1. Leave the **Set Namespaces** section as it is.

Context: `/`

Abbreviated XPath expression: `./*`

Unabbreviated XPath expression: `child::*`

The result is shown below:

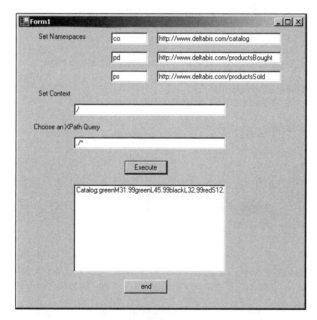

2. At the **Set Namespaces** section, change the "ps" prefix to "ab"

Context: `/co:Catalog/co:Company/co:ProductFamily`

Abbreviated XPath expression: `ab:Product/@ProductID`

Unabbreviated XPath expression: `child::ab:Product/attribute::ProductID`

The result is shown below.

3. Change the ab prefix back to ps.

Context: `/co:Catalog/co:Company/co:ProductFamily`

Abbreviated XPath expression:
`ps:Product/@ProductID | pb:Product/@ProductID`

Unabbreviated XPath expression:
`child::ps:Product/attribute::ProductID |`
`child::pb:Product/attribute::ProductID`

The result is shown below:

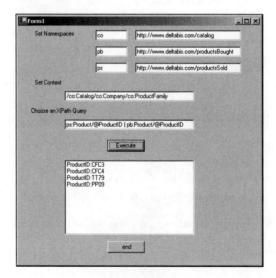

4. Context: `/co:Catalog/co:Company/co:ProductFamily`

Abbreviated XPath expression:
`pb:Product/pb:colour[not(.=preceding::pb:colour)] |`
`ps:Product/ps:colour[not(.=preceding::ps:colour)]`

Unabbreviated XPath expression:
`child::pb:Product/child::pb:colour[not(self::*=preceding::pb:colour)`
`] |`
`child::ps:Product/child::ps:colour[not(self::*=preceding::ps:colour)`
`]`

The result is shown below:

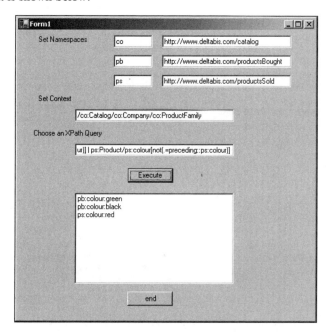

How It Works

The first expression selects the child node of the document root, which is the `Catalog` element. It does this independently of the namespace because `*` asks for all elements in any namespace.

The second example selects the `Product` element nodes, which are children of the `ProductFamily` element node and are qualified in the `http://www.deltabis.com/productsSold` namespace. Notice that the namespace was changed from "ps" to "ab" to illustrate that the actual prefix has no effect as it is *always* converted to its namespace equivalent prior to evaluation.

The third example selects all `ProductID` attribute nodes from both the `http://www.deltabis.com/productsBought` and `http://www.deltabis.com/productsSold` namespaces and unions these together to produce a single output node-set.

Finally, the fourth expression returns a node set with the repeating `colour` elements removed from each namespace. So, as the first namespace has "green" as a `colour` twice, this is removed from the result, as is the `colour` "red" for the second node-set. It does this by using the `not` operator in combination with the context node to determine whether its value is the same as any of the preceding nodes of the same name that were selected. In other words, if the context node is the same as any previous `colour` node, it is ignored and not added to the output node-set.

In addition to the array of syntax available to XPath, there are also a considerable number of functions.

Support for XPath

The W3C XPath version 1.0 standard is fully supported by the .NET Framework within the `System.Xml.XPath` namespace that allows you to perform read-only iteration and selection of an XML document. Within this namespace, there are five classes that allow XPath specific functionality, as shown by the figure below.

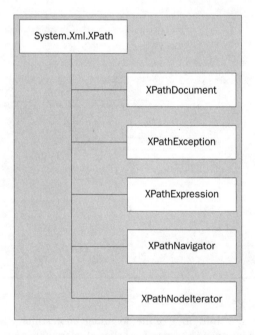

The `XPathDocument` class provides a read-only view of the XML document that allows you to cache an XML document. The `XPathException` class is the exception that is thrown when an XPath query encounters a problem and contains properties of getting details on the exception.

The powerful `XPathExpression` class encapsulates a compiled XPath expression, which is an XPath expression that was compiled using the `Compile()` method of the `XPathNavigator` class. Expressions need only be compiled once into a binary format optimized for the document the XPath expression is working on and can then be executed many times. As they are compiled, they give a big performance improvement over non-compiled queries, which are stored as normal XPath text expressions and compiled and evaluated each time.

The `XPathNavigator` class is created by calling the `CreateNavigator()` method on the `XPathDocument` you want to execute XPath expressions against. This class provides the ability to perform read-only, random XPath queries on a data store and provides the navigation facilities for working with the XML document created in the `XPathDocument` class. Finally, the `XPathNodeIterator` class is created from an XPath expression execution, which selected a set of nodes that match the XPath expression criterion. This class provides capabilities to iterate over a node set (a collection of selected XML nodes).

XSLT

The .NET Framework includes support for the XSL Transformations (XSLT) 1.0 W3C standard via the `System.Xml.Xsl` namespace. This allows you to perform actions such as transforming XML documents and working with XSLT functions, as well as implementing your own custom functions that can be your own .NET classes. There are five classes within this namespace, as shown below:

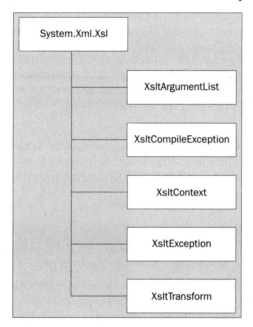

The `XsltArgumentList` class provides the ability to add parameters to the XSLT document as well as binding any extension objects used within the XSLT. Extension objects allow you to create custom .NET classes that can be used within your XSLT, for example to allow you to communicate with an external database or access some external web service during the processing of the stylesheet. Any exceptions thrown by the XSLT document when it is loaded are available in the `XsltCompileException` class and the `XsltException` class will contain any error created when the actual transformation is invoked. The `XsltContext` class allows functions, parameters, and namespaces within the current context of the XSLT processor to be resolved within XPath expressions. The `XslTransform` class actually causes the transformation of a source XML document using a provided XSLT stylesheet.

What we have been discussing is how to work with XML using various classes in .NET. However, the .NET Framework also uses XML internally, in its configuration, in some of the functionality it provides for web services and when working with databases.

The Framework Makes Use of XML

We have discussed how developers using VB.NET can make use of the extensive support of many of the XML technologies when building their applications but the impact of XML was not only intended to be realized by application developers. The creators of the .NET Framework itself saw some obvious benefits that could be had by using XML in the fundamental operation of the Framework.

We will now look at how the .NET Framework itself uses XML at its core to manage the environment and applications running on it.

Config Files

Configuration files play a large part in the .NET Framework as they enable developers and administrators to set machine, application, and security policies, as well as allowing access for other users. These configuration files are in fact XML files that are read by the environment or applications.

There are three types of configuration files. The first, called `machine.config` and located in %SystemRoot%\Microsoft.NET\Framework\v1.0.3705\CONFIG\machine.config, specifies configuration settings for machine-wide assembly-binding, Remoting and ASP.NET. When an application is run the system will first check the `machine.config` file to determine any application configuration details.

The second type of configuration file is an application configuration file and it contains settings specific to a given application. An application configuration file is named in the format of *ApplicationName*.config.exe and an ASP.NET configuration is called `web.config`.

There is a common schema shared among the configuration files. The settings that can be controlled by them are:

❑ Environment startup settings – specifies detail such as the runtime to be used. This will be found in the machine and/or application configuration files.

❑ Runtime language settings – this gives details on how garbage collection should be managed in the CLR (Common Language Runtime) and details on the assemblies to be used during run time. These settings can be found in the `machine.config` and/or application configuration files.

❑ Settings on Remoting – there are a number of settings available for Remoting (discussed later in this chapter and in detail in Chapter 13). Details such as the remote objects and channels to be used (HTTP, TCP, and so on) are specified here. These are typically specified in the application configuration file, although you can specify details in the machine configuration file.

❑ Encryption mappings – this defines the cryptography settings to authenticate and secure your application. These settings map friendly names that can be used in your applications to classes implementing cryptographic functionality. This is typically found in the `machine.config` file, but can also be in the application configuration file.

❑ Network Settings – this specifies details on how the ASP.NET runtime will connect to the Internet, with details such as the maximum number of requests and proxy server details. Typically this information is found in the `machine.config` file.

❑ Custom settings – you are also able to add your own application configuration information to the machine or application configuration files. This is very useful for things like start up paths to resources or database connection strings.

❑ Trace and debug settings – this can specify listeners, which are Trace and Debug objects collate the output from a Trace statement. This enables you to trace an application's execution and store and route messages to give you further information on the execution of your application. This is commonly used in ASP.NET applications. You will typically create these settings in the application configuration file, although you can do it in the machine configuration file where desired.

❑ Settings for ASP.NET – you can specify a whole host of ASP.NET configuration details in the application configuration file. Examples are things like the authentication methods to be used, browser capabilities filters and web service settings.

❑ Security Configuration – The security configuration files, `Security.config` and `EnterpriseSec.config`, control system-wide security and permissions. The Enterprise file can be found in %SystemRoot%\Microsoft.NET\Framework\v1.0.3705\CONFIG\Enterprisesec.config, the Machine file is in %SystemRoot%\Microsoft.NET\Framework\v1.0.3705\CONFIG\Security.config or the User level file in %USERPROFILE%\Application Data\Microsoft\CLR Security Config\ v1.0.3705\Security.config.

Documentation

Unlike C#, VB.NET has no direct method of generating XML-based documentation based on the comments in the code. However, using the Tools | Build Comment Web Pages, developers still have the option of generating HTML help pages.

> There is a utility called the **XML Documentation Tool** available from www.gotdotnet.com/team/vb/ that allows VB.NET developers to generate XML documentation for their classes. The advantage of this is that when some other assembly makes use of this class they get useful details on what the classes and members do in the IntelliSense.

ADO.NET

ADO.NET is the way in which developers work with data from relational databases in the .NET Framework and it has also been tightly integrated with the XML classes. This allows a unified method of accessing structured data, whether the data comes from a database or an XML document. In fact, the `XmlDataDocument` class, which was discussed earlier as being derived from the `XmlDocument` class, is the main class that joins the two worlds, in that it allows relational data to be to be represented as XML and vice versa. In fact, using XSD (which stands for XML Software Description) you can fully describe the structure and relationships of a table or set of tables that can be passed with an XML instance to provide string checking on any data that is appended to the XML instance. Equally, an XSD can be engineered via the `XmlDataDocument` into a relational model, via an intermediary DataSet, which, in theory, could be used to also create a set of database tables.

Furthermore, SQL Server 2000 now has a SQLXML add-on component, which comes with additional .NET classes. This also addresses the relationship between XML and relational data and there is a demonstration of this in the case study at the end of the book.

SOAP & Web Services

It's not surprising that with web services and related technologies being the biggest thing to hit the Web since HTML, that the .NET Framework is offering a lot of functionality around building and exposing web services. Although in some of these services the actual use of XML is hidden within the SOAP communication protocol, there are other cases, such as configuration and description of the services, sending/receiving XML documents, and when you want greater control over the serialization/deserialization of an object (for example to encrypt/decrypt the serialized object before it is sent across the network), where you are exposed to working with XML – at least to some extent. So, it's important that you understand what web services are and how XML is used within these web services.

The following diagrams show how to consume web services in the .NET Framework.

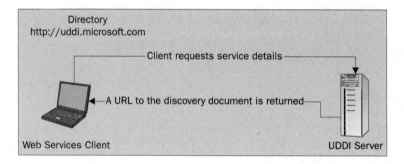

The first step is to access the Universal Description, Discovery, and Integration (UDDI) Service that allows you to discover web services via a simple XML interface. The query is made against a UDDI service database in which available services are registered – there are currently databases maintained by Microsoft, Ariba, and IBM but future servers from Microsoft are going to support the internal creation of UDDI directories that can be updated and searched within the enterprise. This will return a URL to a Discovery document.

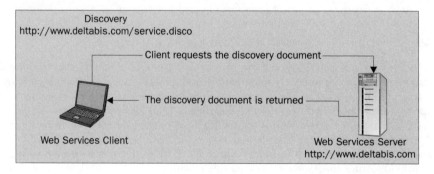

The Discovery document is an XML document and the client can use this document to dynamically discover information on the service it is looking to consume, such as schema information or a detailed description of the web service (such as how to programmatically interact with it). The document that details how to work with the web service is a Web Services Description Language (WSDL) document, which is also in an XML format.

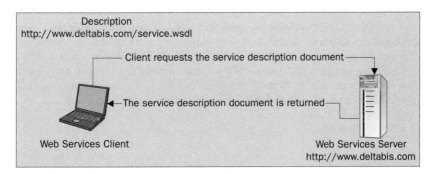

The WSDL document describes the methods available from the web services and information for calling these services. It also describes the bindings associated with the various ways the services can be called, such as via SOAP, HTTP, SMTP, and many other protocols. In fact, the XML Schema Language is used to describe the format for exchange, the elements used, and the relationships between them.

The WSDL document tells the client about the web services available and their location, allowing them to be invoked.

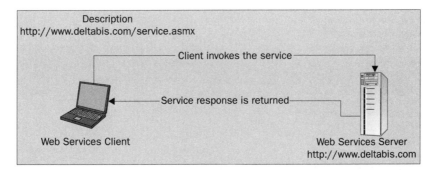

The web services can actually be invoked in many different ways – HTTP is but one of the protocols that is supported, although it is the most popular. The .NET Framework enables you to invoke a web service directly using an HTTP GET command or using SOAP to call the service. Both rely on XML as their underlying structure.

This method of working with web services is great for geographically distributed applications or applications in separate environments, such as other operating systems, development languages, or platforms. However, for intranet scenarios where there is more control over these elements, the overhead associated with SOAP can be unnecessarily high. Previously, the solution was DCOM, but with the .NET Framework, Microsoft has replaced DCOM with **Remoting**, enabling web services performance to be improved within the enterprise.

125

Case Study – A Phone Book-Style Application

At this point you should have a fairly good understanding of the various XML technologies and be ready to apply .NET and VB.NET to this knowledge. To get us underway we are going to start with a case study that will run throughout the book. This will be based on a Phone Book.

The purpose of this phone book-style application is to store names, home addresses, work addresses, and general notes about a contact in the same way you may do in Outlook or some other application. To start the case study we are simply going to create a simple XML document template describing the most common fields we would wish to store. We will use some of the markup language techniques you have learned as well as namespaces in this example. The idea is that we can start to apply our knowledge of the XML technologies and VB.NET as we work though the book.

The XML template is shown below.

```
<?xml version="1.0"?>
<ct:ContactDetails xmlns:ct="http://www.deltabis.com/Contact"
                   updateDate="">
  <name title="">
     <first> </first>
     <middle></middle>
     <last> </last>
  </name>

  <homeAddress>
     <name> </name>
     <street> </street>
     <city> </city>
     <postcode> </postcode>
  </homeAddress>

  <workAddress>
     <name> </name>
     <street> </street>
     <city> </city>
     <state> </state>
     <zip></zip>
  </workAddress>

  <ct:notes> </ct:notes>
</ct:ContactDetails>
```

Following is an example instance document as displayed in Internet Explorer.

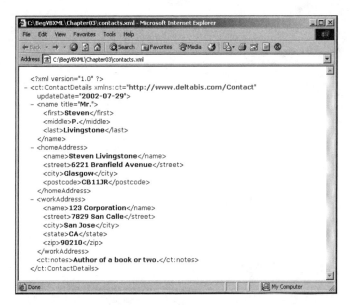

That's all there is to it just now. Only the ContactDetails and notes elements are qualified in the http://www.deltabis.com/Contact namespace. This is because of the way that these elements are defined when working with the XML Schema Language, which sets definitions for validating the document. You will see why this is important when we come to the section on XML Schema in Chapters 9 and 10.

Summary

In this chapter we have looked at the following:

- ❑ The base classes for XML in .NET

- ❑ Defining the DOM, DOM interfaces and .NET support

- ❑ Why we use Prefixes and Namespaces in XML documents and using URLs for uniqueness

- ❑ Defining XPath and examining its syntax, Location Paths, Axes and Node Tests. syntax such as location steps, location paths and predicates

- ❑ XPath patterns and operators

- ❑ The way that the Framework uses XML within its functionality

- ❑ Started the case study application, demonstrating creating an XML document and using namespaces

We examined XML Document Object Model, the XML Path Language and Namespaces, defining these technologies and giving specific examples of how they are used. We also discussed the support and integration allowed to these and other XML technologies by .NET. We ended the chapter by setting up an XML template as an initial step towards setting up our Case Study Application.

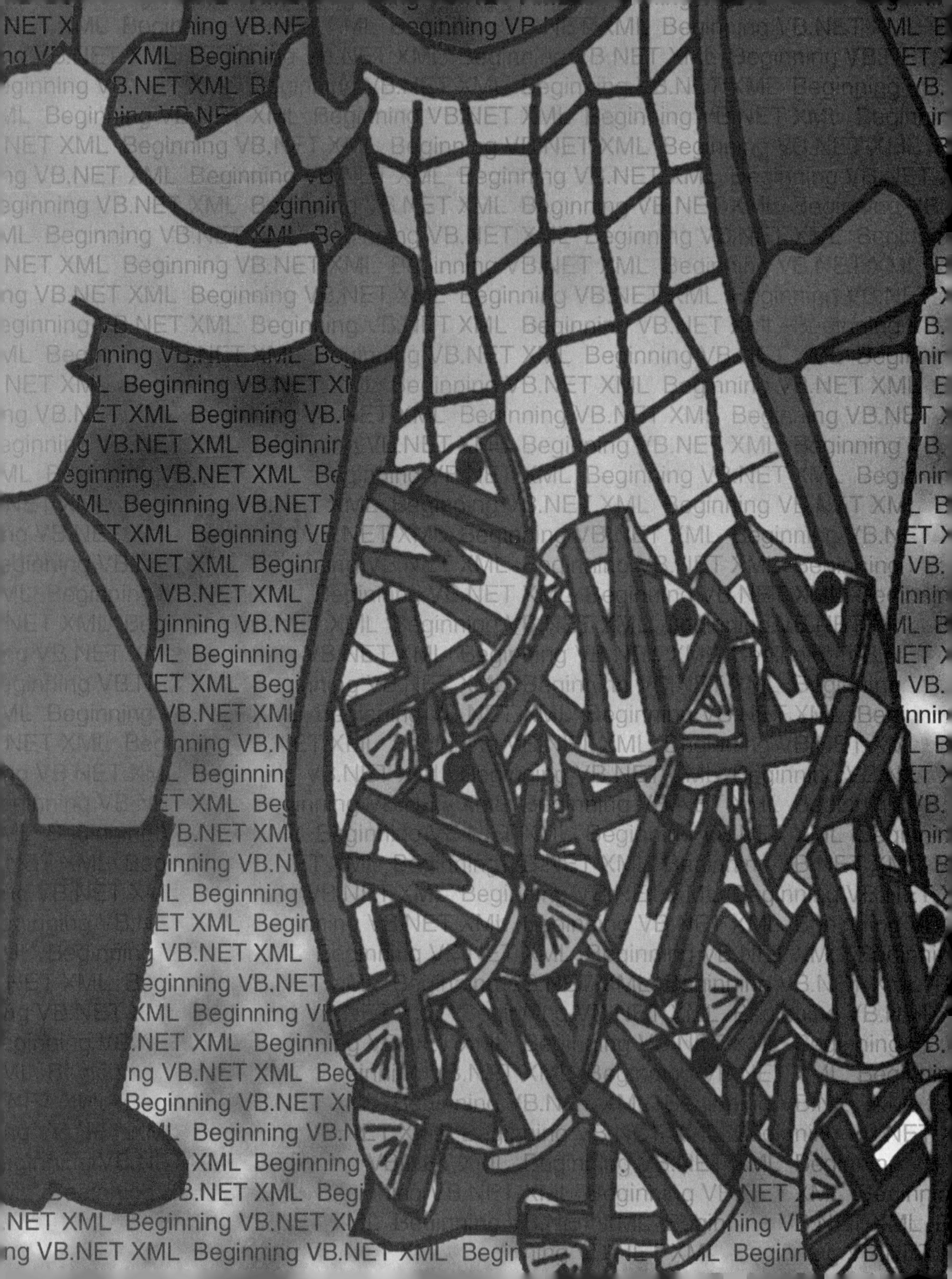
Beginning VB.NET XML

Reading XML in .NET

In the previous chapters, we have covered the basics of XML to ensure that we have a good foundation to our understanding. We have also looked briefly at how XML is used in the .NET Framework. It is now time to start applying some of the knowledge we have gained and to build on it. In this chapter, we will look at how VB.NET and XML are used together in the .NET Framework and how they can be combined to create powerful applications.

The focus of this chapter is to look at how you read XML using .NET and VB. We'll examine how to read different node types by working your way through the XML document, consider how to read binary data and larger XML documents, and also look at how to implement some validation in your XML documents.

Specifically, we will cover:

- ❑ What Streaming is and its advantages
- ❑ The .NET `XmlReader` class and its application
- ❑ Using .NET classes to read large quantities of data
- ❑ The `XmlNodeReader` and `XmlValidatingReader` class

Let's start by looking at how various streaming models work with XML documents and how streaming is implemented in the .NET Framework.

The Streaming Model

We discussed the Document Object Model in detail in the previous chapter and although it is a very useful part of XML and has many advantages, it does have one distinct disadvantage. **The XML document must be parsed into memory as a tree before you can start to work with the document**. In cases where the XML documents are not too large or there are not too many to be processed, there is no issue.

To illustrate this, consider the following two cases; in the first case, we have a phone book application in which we want to be able to allow a user to retrieve the document, search for contacts and possibly modify the details for that contact. The number of contacts is likely to be less than 100 and so the document is not likely to be large. We also require random access to any contact with the ability to change records as required. In this example, working with the DOM is an advantage. For the second scenario, imagine that your company has an archive of all hits on its web site over the last month and wants to create a report containing the details on who hit the site, what time of day they visited the site and what they looked at. You get a lot of visitors to your site, so you generate a lot of data, making the files very large. You also don't have any requirement to modify the data, so it can be read-only. This case will be a clear winner for working with a streaming model.

Streaming versus DOM

Streaming models were created to combat the resource problems caused by large XML files. When working within certain scenarios with larger XML documents you can gain huge performance improvements using a streaming model because, while the DOM requires the whole XML file to be in-memory and creates a hierarchical tree of the nodes, a streaming model only has the current node it is processing in-memory at any point in time.

The advantages of the DOM are as follows:

❑ It has a simple programming model, consisting of calling methods and properties

❑ It allows editing and updating of the XML document

❑ You can randomly access the data in the document (that is, you can use XPath to get to particular document fragments)

❑ It is better integrated with XPath

❑ It is a better choice for complex queries

❑ It is supported by many browsers such as Internet Explorer and the latest version of the Mozilla browsers (streaming models are not natively supported by any browsers)

Alternatively, a streaming model is a better choice with the following conditions:

❑ You have a very large XML document to process

❑ You do not need to edit the document, as it is read-only

❑ You do not require to navigate backwards in the document as it is forward-only

❑ You do not need to randomly access the data in the document

❑ You need to abort the parsing at any time

❑ You want to retrieve small sections of data from the document

❑ You want to serialize the document rather than having it built in memory

❑ You want to start processing data within the document immediately

So now we understand the distinguishing features between working with Document Object Model and a streaming model. However, even the implementation of the streaming models varies between two implementations, so let's look at this next.

Variations in Streaming Models

We know that streaming models iterate through each node in an XML document one at a time and are very useful for processing large documents, with low memory overhead. However, even in the implementation of these streaming parsers there are two popular variations – a "push" model and a "pull" model.

The first, based on a "push model", is called the Simple API for XML, or SAX, and has been popular for a few years. The second, based on a "pull model", is the style used by the .NET Framework's `XmlReader` class, which is a relatively new but innovative implementation of a streaming parser. We discuss the .NET method of streaming in detail in the next section, so let's look at the SAX model, which, prior to .NET, has been the traditional way of implementing streaming models for XML.

SAX is in fact based on a streaming model and is similar to the DOM in that it defines an abstracted API for working with XML documents. It is different from the DOM in that SAX is not W3C standard and not maintained by W3C. It is public domain standard developed (originally for Java) by David Megginson and several others from the XML-DEV mailing list hosted at http://www.xml.org. You can learn more about SAX on http://www.saxproject.org/.

SAX is an event-driven push model and is slightly more difficult to use than the DOM. Rather than parse the document into the DOM and then use the DOM to navigate around the document, we tell the parser to raise events whenever it finds something. SAX pushes events to a consuming application and the application itself has to determine what to do with those events. This means that a series of interfaces must be implemented in the consuming application and registered with the SAX parser.

Streaming in .NET is implemented a little differently. The streaming model has been improved upon, but with all the advantages and disadvantages between streaming and DOM remaining the same. Although MSXML 3.0 and later supports SAX version 2.0, the .NET Framework itself doesn't in fact provide an implementation for SAX. The reason for this is that .NET implements its own version of a streaming model. This implementation is via an abstract base class called `XmlReader` and three concrete classes called `XmlNodeReader`, `XmlTextReader`, and `XmlValidatingReader`. The `XmlReader` class itself provides a fast, forward-only, read-only parser for consuming document streams and in this sense, it is the same as the SAX processor, but there are some key differences.

First, while SAX uses a push model for raising events where every node found is pushed out to the consuming application, which has to then decide how to handle the node, the `XmlReader` implementation actually pulls out nodes that it is interested in from the reader as it works through the document.

SAX requires that content handler interfaces must be written and registered with the SAX processor. These interfaces will have to handle and process every node that is pushed to the application as well as manage complex state on the relative location of the processor as it works through the document (for example, it is currently positioned at attribute A of element B, which is a child of element C and so on). In contrast, the `XmlReader` implementation defines a standard set of methods that can be called to access the parts of the document of interest – this makes it similar to the DOM implementation, which also defines a standard set of interfaces. The figure below shows the implementation of the `XmlReader` abstract class.

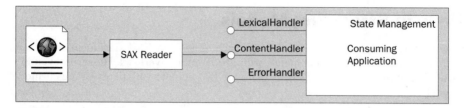

The pull model removes the need to manage complex state in the application because it removes the need for content handlers that have to know where they are in the document. The pull model can work through events in a procedural manner always knowing where it is in the document. Additionally, with the pull model you can put together multiple input streams, which is a technique that is difficult in push model architecture – this would allow you to work with content from multiple documents at the same time, for example if you wanted to combine the results of more than one document, or use the value of a node found by one reader to influence the second reader.

The push model can actually be layered on top of the pull model, whereas the reverse is not true; hence you can use a SAX-based model if you prefer. The diagram below illustrates the architecture behind this combined pull/push model.

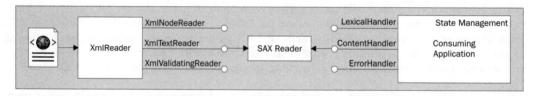

In this case, an XmlReader instance continues to read the XML document. The difference is that for each node that is read by the XmlReader, a content hander class is invoked to determine how that node is to be handled. This allows the combination of the pull reader model, whilst pushing these nodes to a SAX processor.

This kind of combined model is particularly useful where you have code that currently works using a SAX model with say, MSXML 4.0 (or other processors such as SAXON) and you want to upgrade your code to use .NET.

> **A good example of creating a SAX parser using the** XmlTextReader **class can be found at** http://www.xmlforasp.net/codeSection.aspx?csID=36.

As a last note on performance, when using the SAX model every node that is found causes the client to be notified, whereas the XmlReader's pull model can selectively process nodes, increasing the overall efficiency of the application.

To fully understand how .NET reads XML documents we need to look more closely at the classes that implement the XmlReader abstract class. Let's begin by looking at the XmlTextReader class.

The XmlTextReader Class

The `XmlTextReader` class is one of three classes that implement `XmlReader`. `XmlTextReader` is a fast way to parse XML efficiently as it checks that a document is well-formed, but it doesn't support validation of the documents against DTDs or schemas. Furthermore, only the current XML data node that is being read is cached in memory. Previous elements that are already parsed no longer exist in memory and as a result they cannot be accessed again unless the XML data is read again from the beginning.

Let's look at the `XmlTextReader` in detail now by examining some examples of its usage.

Try It Out: Iterating through a Document

Note that all the sample code for this chapter is available for download from http://www.wrox.com. We will be storing sample code for this chapter within the following folder: `C:\BegVBXML\Chapter04`. You may, of course, use a different folder depending on what you prefer.

In this example, we will iterate through an XML document, displaying the value of every kind of node that is found.

1. Create a new Windows Application project. Name the project `XMLReading` and click the OK button.

2. Next, from the **Toolbox**, drag on a **ListBox** and a **Button** control to look like the screenshot below. Change the **Text** property of the **Button** control to **Example1**.

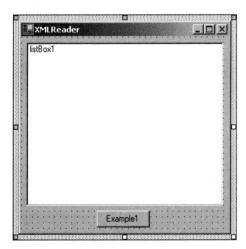

3. Double-click the **Example1** button and in the event handler for this button, enter the code as shown below.

```
Private Sub Button1_Click(ByVal sender As System.Object, _
    ByVal e As System.EventArgs) Handles Button1.Click
  'Reads an XML document and populates the listbox with node names
  Dim strFilePath As String = "..\sample.xml"

  Dim objTxtRd As XmlTextReader

  'Clear existing items
  Dim errmsg As String = ""
  ListBox1.Items.Clear()

  Try
    'create new text reader from xml file
    objTxtRd = New XmlTextReader(strFilePath)

    'iterate through document nodes
    While (objTxtRd.Read())
      'add the Value property of each node
      ListBox1.Items.Add(objTxtRd.Value)
    End While
  Catch err As Exception
    errmsg = errmsg + "Error Occurred While Reading" & strFilePath & " " _
              & err.ToString()
    ListBox1.Items.Add(errmsg)
  Finally
    If Not objTxtRd Is Nothing Then
      'close reader
      objTxtRd.Close()
    End If
  End Try
End Sub
```

4. Don't forget that we need to add the import statement to the top of the file:

```
Imports System.Xml
```

5. Go to the **Solution Explorer** window and right-click on the **XMLReading** project root and select **Add | Add Existing Item** and in the dialog box that appears, navigate to the `C:\BegVBXML\Chapter04` folder, select to display files of all types and select the `sample.xml` file and click the **OK** button.

6. In the top menu, select the **Debug | Start** option, or press *F5* to start the application. When the application has started, click the **Example1** button to run the sample.

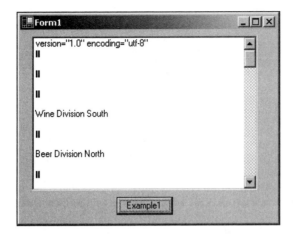

How It Works

The output of this example, as you will see if you scroll up and down the form we have created, is every node that is found in the XML document, `sample.xml`, as shown below:

```xml
<?xml version="1.0" encoding="utf-8" ?>
<Invoices date="28/11/2001" xmlns:cat="uri:Business-Categories">
  <customers custname="Chile Wines Inc" phone="0141 952 56223"
             email="cw@deltabis.com" custid="192398" delivery="international"
             offerID="27">
    <cat:busInfo>Wine Division South</cat:busInfo>
    <cat:busInfo>Beer Division North</cat:busInfo>
    <order orderID="OID921" batchid="123">
      <details>
        <items cat:num="2">
          <item>Rancagua White</item>
          <item>Rancagua Red</item>
        </items>
      </details>
    </order>
    <order orderID="OID927">
      <details>
        <items num="5">
        <item>Chillan Red</item>
        <item>Rancagua White</item>
        <item>Santiago Red</item>
        <item>Rancagua White</item>
        <item>Rancagua Red</item>
        </items>
      </details>
    </order>
    <order orderID="OID931" batchid="123">
      <details>
        <items num="6">
        <item>Southern Fruity Red</item>
        <item>Rancagua White</item>
```

```
            <item>Rancagua Red</item>
            <item>Rancagua White</item>
            <item>Chillan Red</item>
            <item>Northern Sweet White</item>
              </items>
            </details>
          </order>
        </customers>
      </Invoices>
```

At the top of our outputted form, you can see the XML declaration. This is the first thing in the XML document and so it is probably no surprise that it is the first node that is output – notice that its value is the full text of the declaration. After this you see some strange characters, which are caused by linefeed and carriage return characters in our XML editor. This is a significant point. Often you find in XML documents that there are stray whitespace characters that come from the various editors, and in fact you can control this with the WhitespaceHandling property of the XmlTextReader. You also see blank lines quite often, but this is because there are no text nodes and the other nodes themselves don't actually have values (that is, an Element node type doesn't specifically have a value, but it may have a child text node that does have a value – this distinction is an important one).

After this, you see the contents of the various elements that were in the XML documents, listed in the order that they appear in the document (that is, in document order).

So how does the code work? The first thing we do is to specify the path to the sample XML document we are going to use.

```
Dim strFilePath As String = "..\sample.xml"
```

Next, an instance of the XmlTextReader class is created with the filename passed in the constructor. Constructors are classes that can enable methods, which will always be invoked as objects are created. These are excellent for code that performs initialization processes as the methods are run before any other methods are invoked.

The passing in of the filename causes the sample XML document to be parsed and loaded (but only checked to be well-formed, and not validated).

```
objTxtRd = New XmlTextReader(strFilePath)
```

Finally, the Read() method is called and will return True while nodes exist (that is, while you are not at the end of the XML document). For each node that is found, the Value property returns the text content of the node, which is then inserted into the Listbox control.

```
While (objTxtRd.Read())
   'Add the Value property of each node
   ListBox1.Items.Add(objTxtRd.Value)
End While
```

The `Read()` method is the key to working with the `XmlReader` class. It moves to the first, or next, node in the stream returning `True` while nodes exist and `False` when you are at the end of the stream (that is, no more nodes exist). This method must always be called prior to actually doing anything with the `XmlReader` because until it is called there is no information available to the client. It is common to loop through the document using the `Read()` method, which will terminate when the end of the document is reached.

XmlTextReader Properties

Extracting and displaying the content of nodes in an XML document is just one way of using the information held there. As you iterate through a document you may want to perform some kind of functionality based on the type, name or other properties of the nodes found. `XmlTextReader` provides properties to allow you to do exactly this.

The NodeType Property

The `NodeType` property could be used, for example, if you have a method that handles and processes all element nodes, or another that processes all attribute nodes. In our example above, you might also want to do some specific processing when you find element nodes called `item` or the attribute node called `batchid`.

Using the following XML example, let's look at the various node types that we can identify and work with.

```
<?xml version="1.0"?>
<?xml-stylesheet type="text/xsl" href="somestyle.xsl" ?>
<ct:ContactDetails xmlns:ct="http://www.deltabis.com/Contact"
                   updateDate="">
<!--Contains contact information about colleagues.-->
  <name title="Mr.">
    <first>Steven</first>
    <last>Livingstone</last>
  </name>

  <homeAddress>
    <name>162</name>
    <street>North &amp; East Drive</street>
    <city>Sydney</city>
    <postcode>67287</postcode>
  </homeAddress>

  <ct:notes>Lived in <city>Milan</city> <country>Italy</country>.<![CDATA[Works
          for SG&R Inc.]]></ct:notes>
</ct:ContactDetails>
```

The list below contains all of the `NodeType` members that are illustrated in our example:

❑   `Attribute` – an XML attribute. The `updateDate` and `title` nodes are both of this type.

❑   `CDATA` – a CDATA section. The `<![CDATA[Works for SG&R Inc.]]>` within the `<ct:notes>` element is this type of node.

- ❏ Comment – an XML comment. The line `<!--Contains contact information about colleagues.-->` is this `NodeType`.

- ❏ Document – a document object representing the document root of the tree. This node is invisible, but is the parent of the `<ct:ContactDetails>` element node.

- ❏ DocumentFragment – associates a node with a node or sub-tree of the XML document without actually being part of the XML document.

- ❏ DocumentType – the document type declaration in any DOCTYPE tag.

- ❏ Element – an opening element in the XML document. The `<ct:ContactDetails>` element is of this `NodeType`.

- ❏ EndElement – a closing element tag. The closing `</ct:ContactDetails>` element is of this `NodeType`.

- ❏ Entity – an entity declaration.

- ❏ EndEntity – returned when the entity replacement has actually been made in the XML document via a call to the `ResolveEntity()` method (see below).

- ❏ EntityReference – a reference to an entity. The `&amp;` within the `<street>` element is an example of this `NodeType`.

- ❏ None – returned if the `Read()` method has not yet been called (see below).

- ❏ Notation – a notation node in the DTD.

- ❏ ProcessingInstruction – a processing instruction node. The `<?xml-stylesheet....?>` is a processing instruction of this node type.

- ❏ SignificantWhitespace – The whitespace between elements (mixed content) or when the XML attribute `xml:space="preserve"` has been defined. The whitespace between the closing `</city>` and opening `<country>` element in the text `<city>Milan</city><country>Italy</country>` is this kind of `NodeType` (otherwise it would read "MilanItaly").

- ❏ Text – the content of a text node. The text `Lived in` is a child text node of the `<ct:Notes>` element.

- ❏ Whitespace – the whitespace nodes between elements. The new line between the closing `</name>` element and the opening `<first>` element is of this `NodeType`.

- ❏ XmlDeclaration – the XML declaration at the top of an XML document. This is the `<?xml version="1.0"?>` node at the top of the XML file.

The Value Property

This property will return the text value of the current node, depending on the `NodeType` that the current node actually is. It returns the actual value of the node the reader is positioned on – not the inner text value. This may lead to some confusion, but it is best to remember the following points. When the reader is positioned on an element node, the `Value` property will be null because there is no text value to an element `NodeType`. There may be child `NodeType` of type `Text` and it is this node, which will have the textual content of this element. Similarly, while an `Attribute` may have a textual value, an `EndElement` node will have no value.

In fact, all node types other than the ones below return the value `String.Empty`, which is a string of no value.

❑   `Attribute` will have the value of the attribute returned

❑   `CDATA` returns the value of the CDATA section

❑   `Comment` returns the content on the comment

❑   `DocumentType` will have the internal subset of the DOCTYPE returned

❑   `ProcessingInstruction` returns the value of the PI, excluding the target value

❑   `SignificantWhitespace` returns the whitespace between elements (in mixed content)

❑   `Text` will return the value of the text node

❑   `Whitespace` will return the whitespace within elements

❑   `XmlDeclaration` will have the content of the XML declaration

The Name, LocalName, and NamespaceURI Properties

When it comes to getting the name and namespace values for a node, there are three ways of accessing this information, depending on what exactly you want. The `Name` property actually returns the fully qualified name of the current node, therefore including any prefix.

So, in the following XML document, the value of the `Name` property for the `title` element would be `per:title`.

```
<?xml version="1.0" encoding="utf-8" ?>
<Info xmlns:per="http://deltabis.com/person">
  <per:person>
    <per:title>Mr.</per:title>
    <per:name>Steven Livingstone</per:name>
  </per:person>
</Info>
```

Notably, not every node will have a name and so the value of the `Name` property is dependent on the value of the `NodeType` property. This `Name` property will return `String.Empty` for all nodes, except for the following `NodeType`'s.

❑   `Attribute` will return the name of the attribute.

❑   `DocumentType` will return the name of the DOCTYPE.

❑   `Element` will return the name of the tag.

❑   `EntityReference` will return the name of the entity that has been referenced.

❑   `ProcessingInstruction` will return the target of the PI.

❑   `XmlDeclaration` will return the string `xml`.

The same logic follows for the `LocalName` property, which will return the local name of the current node This is the `Name` without any prefix. Hence, for our previous example, the `LocalName` property would return `title` for the XML element node `per:title`.

Finally, the NamespaceURI property also follows the above rules and allows you to get the URI of the node. Where there is a prefix, this will be the namespace associated with the prefix, and where there is not, it will be the namespace that is in scope for the given node. So, for our example element node, the NamespaceURI property would return the value http://deltabis.com/person.

Note that if you wish to get the text of the prefix, you can use the Prefix property, which in our case would return the text per.

Other Properties

There are several other abstract properties that are part of the XmlReader class and these are defined in the table below for convenience.

Property	Description
AttributeCount	Returns the number of attributes on the current node and applies only to the NodeType members Element, DocumentType, and XmlDeclaration.
BaseURI	This returns the base URI of the current node, which is particularly important when an XML document is included in another. A common scenario would be the inclusion of external entities from one URI within XML documents in another URI.
CanResolveEntity	This property returns True when the reader supports schema or DTD information and determines whether the reader can parse and resolve entities. Its default value, however, is False.
Depth	This property will return the depth of the current node in the document
EOF	This returns True when the reader is positioned at the end of the stream; otherwise False. This will happen when the return value of the ReadState property is EndOfFile, signifying the reader is at the end of the stream.
HasAttributes	This property returns True if the current node has any attributes; otherwise False.
HasValue	This will return True if the current node can have a value; otherwise it is False. The same rules apply here as to the Value property discussed above and so it is limited to specific members of XmlNodeType.
IsDefault	This property will return True if the current node is an attribute that was generated from the default value defined in the DTD or schema. If the value was entered explicitly in the XML document this property will return False.

Setting default values is a way to ensure that an attribute has a value even if the creator of the XML instance has not entered one. We look at schemas in chapters 9 and 10. |

Property	Description
IsEmptyElement	This will return True if the current node is an empty element. Otherwise it will return False.
Item	The Item property allows you to get the value of an attribute that is in an array of attributes of a given element. You can get the value by specifying the attribute in one of three ways: First, by using the index of the attribute, starting from zero. Second, by using the name of the attribute or, third, by using the local name of the attribute and the namespace it is in.
NameTable	This property will return the XmlNameTable used by the current instance to store and lookup element and attribute names, prefixes and namespaces. The purpose of this name table is to improve efficiency by allowing object comparisons rather than string comparisons. It does this by returning a single String object for all occurrences of the same name in an XML document (that is, a given element name is only stored once in the name table), so you can do object comparisons rather than string comparisons (which are much more expensive).
QuoteChar	This will returns the character used to enclose the value of an **attribute node**, which will be either " or '.
ReadState	This property returns the read state of the reader and is one of the members of the ReadState enumeration. These are: Initial when the reader has been instantiated. Interactive when the Read() method has been called. Error if an error occurs during the read operation. EndOfFile when the end of the XML data file is reached. Closed when the Close() method has been called.
XmlLang	This property is read-only and will return a String of the value of the xml:lang that is currently in scope. In the case where we have xml:lang="en-GB", the return value of this property would be "en-GB" (the -GB is the sub-scope).
XmlSpace	This will return the scope of the xml:space attribute, which is used in an XML document to specify whether whitespace should be preserved (xml:space="preserve") or use the default (xml:space="default"). The value returned is one of the XmlSpace enumeration values, which are Preserve, Default, or None.

Now we know a little more about `XmlReader` properties, let's take another look at our example where we outputted the value of the nodes, but this time, using the `NodeType` property discussed above, we'll output the type of each node.

Try It Out: Discovering Node Types

1. First, add a new button to the form we were working with above and change its **Text** property to **Example2**.

2. Double-click the new button and enter the following code into the event handler for this button.

```
Private Sub Button2_Click(ByVal sender As System.Object, _
                          ByVal e As System.EventArgs) Handles Button2.Click
    'Reads an XML document and populates the listbox with node names
    Dim strFilePath As String = "..\sample.xml"

    Dim objTxtRd As XmlTextReader

    'Clear existing items
    Dim errmsg As String = ""
    ListBox1.Items.Clear()

    Try
        'create new text reader from xml file
        objTxtRd = New XmlTextReader(strFilePath)

        'iterate through document nodes
        While (objTxtRd.Read())
            'add the value of the NodeType property of each node
            ListBox1.Items.Add(objTxtRd.NodeType)
        End While
    Catch err As Exception
        errmsg = errmsg + "Error Occurred While Reading" & strFilePath & " " _
                    & err.ToString()
        ListBox1.Items.Add(errmsg)
    Finally
        If Not objTxtRd Is Nothing Then
            'close reader
            objTxtRd.Close()
        End If
    End Try
End Sub
```

3. Next, run the application (press *F5*) and click the **Example2** button. You will get an output like the following screenshot.

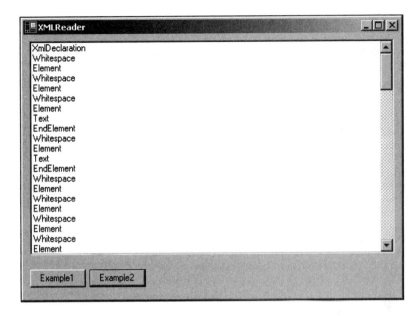

How It Works

In this example, you can see the node types that are detected by the parser and if you were to compare the lines of output from this example with the output from the previous example, you would in fact see a one to one mapping between the node type and the value output. In fact, the first Text node output is on the 8th line and corresponds with the "Wine Division South" output on the 8th line in the previous example.

You may have noticed that there are no attribute nodes in these listings. This is expected, because attribute nodes are children of element nodes and not strictly speaking part of the structure of the document. Hence, to access the values of the attributes, we must separately step through the attributes axis – we look at this further below.

The code itself is almost identical to the previous example, except for the following line:

```
ListBox1.Items.Add(objTxtRd.NodeType)
```

This time we used the NodeType property to output one of the NodeType enumeration strings we looked at earlier.

We can extend this example further still by now filtering the type of node we output and displaying some information based on that output.

Try It Out: Filtering Node Types

1. First, add a new button to the form we have been working with and change its Text property to **Example3**.

2. Double-click the new button and enter the following code into the event handler for this button:

```
Private Sub Button3_Click(ByVal sender As System.Object, _
    ByVal e As System.EventArgs) Handles Button3.Click
    'Reads an XML document and populates the listbox with node names
    Dim strFilePath As String = "..\sample.xml"

    Dim objTxtRd As XmlTextReader

    'Clear existing items
    Dim errmsg As String = ""
    ListBox1.Items.Clear()

    Try
        'create new text reader from xml file
        objTxtRd = New XmlTextReader(strFilePath)

        'iterate through document nodes
        While (objTxtRd.Read())
          'check node type and write out message
          If ((objTxtRd.NodeType = XmlNodeType.Element) Or _
            (objTxtRd.NodeType = XmlNodeType.EndElement) Or _
            (objTxtRd.NodeType = XmlNodeType.XmlDeclaration)) Then

              ListBox1.Items.Add(objTxtRd.Name & " is type " _
                & objTxtRd.NodeType.ToString())
          End If
        End While
    Catch err As Exception
      errmsg = errmsg + "Error Occurred While Reading" & strFilePath & " " _
        & err.ToString()
      ListBox1.Items.Add(errmsg)
    Finally
      If Not objTxtRd Is Nothing Then
        'close reader
        objTxtRd.Close()
      End If
    End Try
End Sub
```

3. Run the application and click the **Example3** button. You will see something like the following:

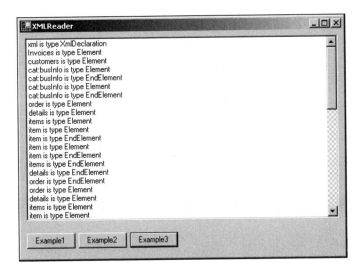

How It Works

Here we can see how the `XmlTextReader` walks through the document in order, through each element node and its descendants and so on. We are searching here for `Element`, `EndElement` and `XmlDeclaration` node types. Furthermore, you can see how an element starts and sub-elements are opened and closed when walking through the children, prior to closing the parent element nodes (with the `EndElement` node type). This in fact is a very important point in this style of reading XML documents' document state. When you come to write your own custom readers (which we look at in the next chapter), you have to know in which order elements may be opened and closed in the document, and the above example highlights this.

The changes that have been made to the code from the previous examples are in how we find the type of the node for each iteration. The `XmlNodeType` enumeration is the best way to do this and has an entry for every type of node you will find in an XML document.

```
While (objTxtRd.Read())
    'check node type and write out message
    If ((objTxtRd.NodeType = XmlNodeType.Element) Or _
       (objTxtRd.NodeType = XmlNodeType.EndElement) Or _
       (objTxtRd.NodeType = XmlNodeType.XmlDeclaration)) Then

        ListBox1.Items.Add(objTxtRd.Name & " is type " _
                                      & objTxtRd.NodeType.ToString())

    End If
End While
```

Currently we only output information for three core node types, but there is no reason to limit this depending on the intentions of an application. In fact, you could very feasibly perform different types of processing depending on the type of node – for example, finding an `Element` node may determine that you then check its attributes, whereas an `EndElement` may cause something else to happen.

As a simple example, the pseudocode below could be used to convert each attribute of an element to a child element of the same name.

```
While (objTxtRd.Read())
  If (objTxtRd.NodeType = XmlNodeType.Element) Then
     'iterate through each attribute of this element
     'get the name of the attribute
     'write out an element with this name
     'write text of the attribute as the inner text of the new element
     'close element
  End If
End While
```

We look at reading attributes following our next example, which looks at how to extract information from Text nodes within our elements.

Try It Out: Reading Text Values

1. First, add a new button to the form we were working with above and change its Text property to Example4.

2. Double-click the new button and enter the following code into the event handler for this button.

```
Private Sub Button4_Click(ByVal sender As System.Object, _
    ByVal e As System.EventArgs) Handles Button4.Click
  Dim strFilePath As String = "..\sample.xml"

  Dim objTxtRd As XmlTextReader

  'Clear existing items
  Dim errmsg As String = ""
  ListBox1.Items.Clear()

  Try
     'Create new text reader from xml file
     objTxtRd = New XmlTextReader(strFilePath)
     'Iterate through document nodes
     While (objTxtRd.Read())
       'Check for text nodes & write value
       If (objTxtRd.NodeType = XmlNodeType.Text) Then
         ListBox1.Items.Add(objTxtRd.Value)
       End If
     End While
  Catch err As Exception
     errmsg = errmsg + "Error Occurred While Reading" & strFilePath & " " _
       & err.ToString()
     ListBox1.Items.Add(errmsg)
  Finally
     If Not objTxtRd Is Nothing Then
        'Close reader
        objTxtRd.Close()
     End If
  End Try
End Sub
```

3. Next, run the application and click the **Example4** button and you will get the following output:

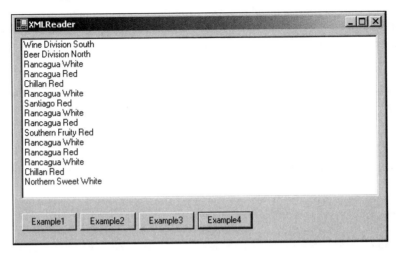

How It Works

This example is very similar to the last one, except we are checking for text nodes using the `XmlNodeType.Text` enumeration value.

```
If (objTxtRd.NodeType = XmlNodeType.Text) Then
  ListBox1.Items.Add(objTxtRd.Value)
End If
```

Remember that text nodes themselves may contain other child nodes such as `Entity` nodes that may have to be resolved prior to returning the text value, so you may have to iterate through these child nodes first.

Reading Attributes

When an element node type is found, it is common to look at the attributes present on that element and do some processing with them. However, attributes are not part of the XML documents flow – to access an attribute you have to be on an element and explicitly ask for attributes on that element. This means that if you iterate through all of the nodes of a document you will not find any attribute nodes, because you have to explicitly access the attribute axis to get to these. So to access the attributes, you must use a specific set of properties and methods that can return you the appropriate values. The important properties are:

❑ `HasAttributes` – this property will returns `True` if the element node has attributes; otherwise `False`.

❑ `AttributeCount` – this property will return the number of attribute nodes on the current element node.

The most common methods are:

The MoveToAttribute() Method

The `MoveToAttribute()` method will move to the attribute specified in the argument list and return `True` if the move was successful; else `False`. There are three overloads for this method, as shown below.

```
MoveToAttribute(1)
```

The first method takes a zero-based integer specifying the index of the attribute on the containing element – this example moves to the second attribute on the containing element.

```
MoveToAttribute("title")
```

The second method actually takes the qualified name of the `title` attribute and will move to the `title` attribute on the current element.

```
MoveToAttribute("title","http://www.deltabis.com/ns")
```

The final method moves to the attribute defined in the first parameter within the namespace specified in the second parameter – so in this case, we move to the attribute `http://www.deltabis.com/ns:title` on the containing element.

The MoveToFirstAttribute() Method

This moves the position of the reader to the first attribute node of the current node and returns `True` if it finds an attribute. If there are no attributes on the current node it returns `False`.

The MoveToNextAttribute() Method

The `MoveToNextAttribute()` complements the above method in that it moves to the next attribute and returns `True` while there is another attribute, otherwise it will return `False` and the reader's position doesn't change. If the current node happens to be an element node, a call to this method will move to the first attribute.

Try It Out: Reading Attributes

In this example, we will iterate through an XML document, displaying the value of *every* kind of node that is found.

1. Open the example XMLReading project we were working with earlier and add a new button to it, with the display text Example5.

2. Double-click the Example5 button and in the event handler for this button, enter the code as shown below.

```
Private Sub Button5_Click(ByVal sender As System.Object, _
    ByVal e As System.EventArgs) Handles Button5.Click
    Dim strFilePath As String = "..\sample.xml"

    Dim objTxtRd As XmlTextReader
```

```
'Clear existing items
Dim errmsg As String = ""
ListBox1.Items.Clear()

Try
    'Create new text reader from xml file
    objTxtRd = New XmlTextReader(strFilePath)

    'Iterate through document nodes
    While (objTxtRd.Read())
        'Get element nodes
        If (objTxtRd.NodeType = XmlNodeType.Element) Then
            'Does this element have any attributes?
            If (objTxtRd.HasAttributes) Then
                'It does, how many?
                ListBox1.Items.Add("The element " _
                    & objTxtRd.Name.ToString() & " has " _
                    & objTxtRd.AttributeCount.ToString() _
                    & " attributes.")
                ListBox1.Items.Add("The attributes are : ")
                'Iterate through each attribute & write value
                While (objTxtRd.MoveToNextAttribute())
                    ListBox1.Items.Add(objTxtRd.Name & " = " & objTxtRd.Value)
                End While
            Else
                'No attributes on this element
                ListBox1.Items.Add("The Element " & objTxtRd.Name _
                    & " has no attributes.")
            End If

            ListBox1.Items.Add("")
        End If
    End While
Catch err As Exception
    errmsg = errmsg + "Error Occurred While Reading" & strFilePath & " " _
        & err.ToString()
    ListBox1.Items.Add(errmsg)
Finally
    If Not objTxtRd Is Nothing Then
        'Close reader
        objTxtRd.Close()
    End If
End Try
End Sub
```

3. Press *F5* to run the application and click the **Example5** button and the output should be like the screenshot below.

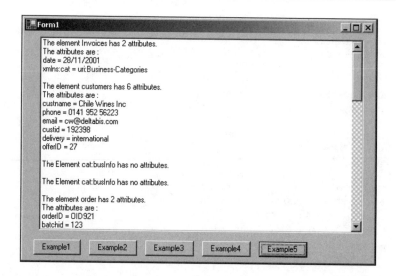

How It Works

This example shows how we can access the attributes on an element node. Once we have determined that the current node is an `Element` node, we enter an `If Else` branch. The `HasAttributes` property of the `XmlTextReader` will tell us if the current node has attributes, and in this example, if there are not, we write out an appropriate message saying the element name has no attributes.

```
If (objTxtRd.NodeType = XmlNodeType.Element) Then
  'Does this element have any attributes?
  If (objTxtRd.HasAttributes) Then
    ...
Else
  'No attributes on this element
  ListBox1.Items.Add("The Element " & objTxtRd.Name & " has no attributes.")
```

However, where there *are* attributes (`HasAttributes` returns `True`) we add an entry to the listbox with the name of the element node and use the `AttributeCount` property, which will tell us the number of attributes on the node.

```
ListBox1.Items.Add("The element " & objTxtRd.Name.ToString() & " has " _
  & objTxtRd.AttributeCount.ToString() & " attributes.")
```

Finally, we write out the attribute's `Name` and `Value`. To do this we can use the `MoveToNextAttribute()` method which acts like the `Read()` method in that it will return `False`, and hence terminate the `While` loop when there are no more attributes on the element.

```
ListBox1.Items.Add("The attributes are : ")
'Iterate through each attribute & write value
While (objTxtRd.MoveToNextAttribute())
  ListBox1.Items.Add(objTxtRd.Name & " = " & objTxtRd.Value)
End While
Else
```

```
          'No attributes on this element
          ListBox1.Items.Add("The Element " & objTxtRd.Name & " has no attributes.")
        End If

        ListBox1.Items.Add("")
      End If
    End While
```

This next example is designed to illustrate the usefulness of XmlTextReader in the fairly common scenario, where you need to know that a given node is in a particular namespace, or in the case where namespace information is unimportant, you may just want to get the local name of the element. Let's look at how to do this.

Try It Out: Reading with Namespaces

1. First, add a new button to the form we have been working with and change its Text property to Example6.

2. Enter the following code into the event handler for this button:

```
Private Sub Button6_Click(ByVal sender As System.Object, _
    ByVal e As System.EventArgs) Handles Button6.Click
  Dim strFilePath As String = "..\sample.xml"

  Dim objTxtRd As XmlTextReader

  'Clear existing items
  Dim errmsg As String = ""
  ListBox1.Items.Clear()

  Try
    'Create new text reader from xml file
    objTxtRd = New XmlTextReader(strFilePath)

    'Iterate through document nodes
    While (objTxtRd.Read())
      'check for elements with a prefix
      If ((objTxtRd.NodeType = XmlNodeType.Element) And _
        objTxtRd.Prefix <> "") Then
        'Write prefix and namespace association
        ListBox1.Items.Add("The prefix " & objTxtRd.Prefix _
            & " is associated with the namespace " & objTxtRd.NamespaceURI)
        'Write equiv element and namespace
        ListBox1.Items.Add("The Element with the local name " _
            & objTxtRd.LocalName & " is associated with " _
            & "the namespace " & objTxtRd.NamespaceURI)
      End If
    End While
  Catch err As Exception
    errmsg = errmsg + "Error Occurred While Reading" & strFilePath & " " _
          & err.ToString()
    ListBox1.Items.Add(errmsg)
```

```
      Finally
        If Not objTxtRd Is Nothing Then
          'Close reader
          objTxtRd.Close()
        End If
      End Try
    End Sub
```

3. Run the application and click the **Example6** button.

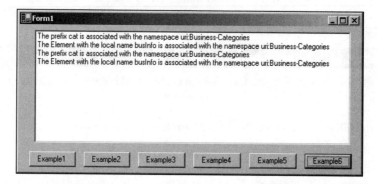

How It Works

In this example, we iterate through each node, first determining if the current node is an element node and whether that node has a prefix – that is, isn't in the default null namespace (for more information on namespaces, see Chapter 3). To do this we can use the `Prefix` property of the `XmlReader` class in combination with the `NodeType` property.

```
        If ((objTxtRd.NodeType = XmlNodeType.Element) _
        And objTxtRd.Prefix <> "") Then
```

Next, the actual prefix is added to the listbox, along with the namespace that this element, and hence the prefix, is associated with using the `NamespaceURI` property.

```
        ListBox1.Items.Add("The prefix " & objTxtRd.Prefix _
              & " is associated with the namespace " & objTxtRd.NamespaceURI)
```

Finally, we can use the `LocalName` property to return the name of the element, without the prefix or namespace URI, although we mention the associated namespace in the listbox entry.

```
        ListBox1.Items.Add("The Element with the local name " _
          & objTxtRd.LocalName & " is associated with the namespace " _
          & objTxtRd.NamespaceURI)
      End If
```

Reading Large Chunks of Data

The `XmlTextReader` is not only powerful in the way that it can handle smaller sized textual data, but it can also work with larger more complex data structures such as large character streams, BinHex-encoded data (a common Macintosh format) and base64-encoded data.

BinHex-encoding encodes a file from its 8-bit binary representation into a 7-bit ASCII set of text characters (none of these encoded characters is a special XML character) and has been popular for encoding Macintosh documents. Base64-encoding (also known as Multipurpose Internet Mail Extensions or MIME) uses the 64-character subset of "A-Za-z0-9+/" (notice that none of these encoded characters is a special XML character either, and so it can be safely put in an XML document) to represent binary data and "=" for padding. Both encoding formats are useful for encoding binary images to put in XML documents, such as `JPEGs` or `GIFs`, but can support encoding of any binary document.

The ReadChars() Method

The `ReadChars()` method is the best way to read large sections of character data encoded as US-ASCII within an XML document and works only on element nodes. It is so much more powerful as it returns buffers of character data rather than potentially huge strings of data. This is better than trying to read a huge stream in one go into inefficient text strings – much like the difference between using the DOM and a streaming model. If the document you are reading is very large it may take a long time before you can start doing anything with it and it could consume a large amount of memory. Using this buffered approach means that only a limited number of characters and therefore limited amount of memory resource is required at any one time.

```
Public Function ReadChars(ByVal buffer() As Char, _
                    ByVal index As Integer, _
                    ByVal count As Integer) As Integer
```

The method's first parameter is a character array to which the characters that are read in are written. The second parameter is the integer position within the buffer from which to start writing and the final parameter is the number of characters to write to the buffer. The value returned is the number of characters that were read, being zero when you are not on an element node (or it is empty).

Everything within the element is returned with no resolution of character entities and any XML that is not well-formed is also ignored and returns zero when positioned after the end tag.

As an example, imagine some archived file containing text from a daily web blog – a blog is typically a personal diary of anything you want to share with the world.

> **You can find this example in the `ReadChars` project, in the code download.**

My world isn't as exciting as most but an extract is shown below (in some cases the size of these blogs can be hundreds of lines long) as the XML file, `archive.xml`.

```
<BlogArchive>
  <day number="1">
    Today I typed stuff over and over again.
```

```
        Today I typed stuff over and over again.
        Today I typed stuff over and over again.
        Today I typed stuff over and over again.
        ...another 100 lines
    </day>
</BlogArchive>
```

It would be inefficient to read the contents of the <day> element in one go because as the data gets larger, copying into the string variable, where you would store the data, becomes very inefficient.

The ReadChars() method could be used as shown below to improve the efficiency of handling the large amounts of text data.

```
Imports System.IO
Imports System.Xml

Module Module1

    Private Const filename As String = "..\archive.xml"

    Sub Main()

      Dim reader As XmlTextReader
      Try
        'Declare variables used by ReadChars
        Dim XmlBuffer() As Char
        Dim charCount As Integer = 0
        Dim buffSize As Integer

        'Load in some large archive file with a lot of data
        reader = New XmlTextReader(filename)
        reader.WhitespaceHandling = WhitespaceHandling.None

        'Character variables
        buffSize = 5
        XmlBuffer = New Char(buffSize) {}

        'Read file
        reader.MoveToContent()
        While (reader.Read())
          If (reader.Name = "day") Then
            charCount = reader.ReadChars(XmlBuffer, 0, buffSize)
            While (charCount > 0)
              Console.Write(New String(XmlBuffer, 0, charCount))

              'Clear the buffer
              Array.Clear(XmlBuffer, 0, buffSize)
              charCount = reader.ReadChars(XmlBuffer, 0, buffSize)
            End While
            Console.ReadLine()
          End If
        End While
```

```
      Catch
      Finally
         If Not reader Is Nothing Then
            reader.Close()
         End If
      End Try
   End Sub

End Module
```

The key to this code is where we create a new buffer array to hold the content strings as we iterate through the document. In our case, the array will be of size 5 as we will be reading the characters in 5-character increments.

```
'Declare variables used by ReadChars
Dim XmlBuffer() As Char
Dim charCount As Integer = 0
Dim buffSize As Integer
```

Next the iteration through the file is done – the `MoveToContent()` method is called to get to the document root element and then the reader is iterated through until the <day> element is found.

```
'read file
   reader.MoveToContent()
   While (reader.Read())
      If (reader.Name = "day") Then
```

The `MoveToContent()` method will check whether the current node is a content node (that is, an `Element`, `CDATA`, `EndElement`, `EntityReference`, or `EndEntity` node – for more information on node types, see the `NodeType` property section earlier in the chapter) and if not moves the reader to the next content node. The return value will be the `XmlNode` type of the current node or `None` if you reach the end of the stream without getting a content node. Note that if the current node is an attribute node, this method will move the reader back to the containing element node. This is useful when you are unsure what node you are on (or don't care) and simply want to get to a content node. It is also often used when you have significant whitespace (such as new lines between nodes) in the document that you want to skip.

When a <day> element is found, another loop is started which uses the `ReadChars()` method to fill the buffer by reading up to the next 5 characters – if there are less than five characters, it will fill the buffer with as many as it has. The string of characters represented in the buffer is then written to the screen and the buffer cleared. So at any point in time, only 5 characters are in memory. This is repeated until the end of the content is reached.

```
charCount = reader.ReadChars(XmlBuffer, 0, buffSize)
While (charCount > 0)
   Console.Write(New String(XmlBuffer, 0, charCount))

   'Clear the buffer
   Array.Clear(XmlBuffer, 0, buffSize)
```

```
            charCount = reader.ReadChars(XmlBuffer, 0, buffSize)
        End While
        Console.ReadLine()
      End If
    End While
```

This will give the following output.

```
Today I typed stuff over and over again.
Today I typed stuff over and over again.
Today I typed stuff over and over again.
Today I typed stuff over and over again.
Today I typed stuff over and over again.
...
another 100 lines
```

Notice that whitespace is also preserved, hence why you have indenting for the text in the output.

The ReadBinHex() Method

This method will decode a BinHex-encoded file and returns the decoded bytes:

```
Public Function ReadBinHex(ByVal array() As Byte, _
                      ByVal offset As Integer, _
                      ByVal len As Integer) As Integer
```

The method's first parameter is a byte array, to which the characters that are read in are written. The second parameter is the integer position in the array from which the method can start writing to the buffer and the final parameter is the number of bytes to be sent to the buffer. The value returned is the number of bytes that were written to the buffer.

Similar to the ReadChars() method above, it can read large amounts of data by successively reading the data into the buffer.

The ReadBase64() Method

This method will decode a base64-encoded file and returns the decoded bytes.

```
Public Function ReadBase64(ByVal array() As Byte, _
                      ByVal offset As Integer, _
                      ByVal len As Integer) As Integer
```

The method's first parameter is a byte array to which the bytes that are read in are written. The second parameter is the integer position that determines from where to start writing and the final parameter is the number of bytes to write to the buffer. The value returned is the number of bytes that were written to the buffer.

Similar to the methods above, it can read large amounts of data by successively reading the data into the buffer.

Now let's consider the example we looked at for the ReadChars() method. If, rather than the <day> element, we were looking for a <picture> element that was a base64-encoding binary representation of a JPEG, then the following modifications to the code we presented earlier would support this case and write the result to the output.

```
Dim XmlBuffer() As Byte
Dim charCount As Integer = 0
Dim buffSize As Integer

'Load in some large archive file with a lot of data
reader = New XmlTextReader(filename)
reader.WhitespaceHandling = WhitespaceHandling.None

'Character variables
buffSize = 100
XmlBuffer = New Byte(buffSize) {}

'Read file
reader.MoveToContent()
While (reader.Read())
  If (reader.Name = "picture") Then
    charCount = reader.ReadBase64(XmlBuffer, 0, buffSize)
    While (charCount > 0)
      'Console.Write(New String(XmlBuffer, 0, charCount))
      Dim i As Integer
      For i = 0 To buffSize
        Console.Write(XmlBuffer(i))
      Next
      'Clear the buffer
      Array.Clear(XmlBuffer, 0, buffSize)
      charCount = reader.ReadBase64(XmlBuffer, 0, buffSize)
```

The array is changed to now contain an array of bytes, rather than an array of characters as was required earlier.

The ReadBase64() method will then repetitively fill the buffer with the next buffSize number of decoded characters (they are decoded back to their binary representation) and the decoded binary representation will be written out using the XmlBuffer(i) code.

This completes our look at the XmlTextReader class – it is probably the XmlReader class you will use most often and can be very powerful. Let's now look at the XmlNodeReader class, which is another class responsible for implementing the XmlReader abstract class.

The XmlNodeReader Class

The XmlNodeReader class works with an XmlNode object that has been passed in and can be used to navigate through a tree of such nodes that have been placed in memory, such as a DOM tree. Like the XmlTextReader, it doesn't perform any validation against DTDs or schemas. When you use the XmlNodeReader everything is read in as an XmlNode class, which is every part of an XML document anyway – we look in detail at the XmlNode class in Chapters 6 and 7. You can then use methods and properties get information on the nodes within this given fragment.

So when would you find this useful? One good example is where you have a node list and want to find out more information on each node. The `XmlNode` class itself has some properties and methods that can be used to find out the name, namespace, and so on, of the given node, but more generally you will want to view the XML node as if it were an XML fragment. To illustrate, consider the following XML document:

```
<?xml version="1.0" ?>
<messages>
  <message id="7836733" target="Loreto" status="sent">
    <sender>Steven</sender>
    <body>...</body>
  </message>
  <message id="7836712" target="Eileen" status="sent">
    <sender>Loreto</sender>
    <body>...</body>
  </message>
  <message id="7836735" target="Steven" status="pending">
    <sender>Eileen</sender>
    <body>...</body>
  </message>
</messages>
```

This XML document represents a random set of messages sent out between users and, in a real scenario, the list could be substantially bigger. Furthermore, it may contain a lot more information that you actually need, so you may want to filter it to produce a list of nodes based on an XPath expression. (For more information on XPath, see Chapter 3). So, the XPath expression `//*[@status='sent']` would return a node list of length two (the first and second child nodes on the `messages` element, as these match the attribute criteria). Each node of the resultant node set could then be passed into an instance of an `XmlNodeReader` class and so you could access the element node, attributes nodes, child nodes and other properties and methods available on this class. In fact this gives you a lot more power than if you were to try the same thing with just the `XmlNode()` method and properties themselves.

Let's take a look at an example of this in action.

Try It Out: Reading a Node using the XmlNodeReader

In this example, we will iterate through an XML document, displaying the value of every kind of node that is found.

1. Create a new Visual Basic Windows Application project in Visual Studio .NET with the project name `XMLNodeRead`. Add a new XML document called `sample.xml` and enter the following XML into the editor:

```
<?xml version="1.0" ?>
<messages>
  <message id="7836733" target="Loreto" status="sent">
  <sender>Steven</sender>
  <body>...</body>
  </message>
  <message id="7836712" target="Eileen" status="sent">
    <sender>Loreto</sender>
```

```
      <body>...</body>
    </message>
    <message id="7836735" target="Steven" status="pending">
      <sender>Eileen</sender>
      <body>...</body>
    </message>
</messages>
```

2. Add a Listbox and a Button to the form and change the Text property of the button to Execute.

3. Double-click on the button and add the following code to the event handler:

```vbnet
Imports System.Xml

Private Sub Button1_Click(ByVal sender As System.Object, _
    ByVal e As System.EventArgs) Handles Button1.Click

    'Reads an XML document and populates the listbox with node names
    Dim strFilePath As String = "..\sample.xml"
    ListBox1.Items.Clear()

    'Create XML DOM instance
    Dim document As XmlDocument = New XmlDocument()
    document.Load(strFilePath)

    'Select all message elements with a status attribute
    Dim objXList As XmlNodeList = document.SelectNodes("//message[@status]")

    'iterate through each node
    Dim objNode As XmlNode
    For Each objNode In objXList
        'read each node
        Dim objNdRd As XmlNodeReader = New XmlNodeReader(objNode)
        'read through all child nodes of this node

        While (objNdRd.Read())
            'get element nodes
            If (objNdRd.NodeType = XmlNodeType.Element) Then
                'find <message> elements
                If (objNdRd.Name = "message") Then
                    'add the message details to the list
                    ListBox1.Items.Add("The message with id " _
                        & objNdRd.GetAttribute("id") _
                        & " was sent to " & objNdRd.GetAttribute("target") _
                        & " and is currently " _
                        & objNdRd.GetAttribute("status") & ".")
                ElseIf (objNdRd.Name = "sender") Then
                    'else if <sender> element, then add these details
                    ListBox1.Items.Add("The message was sent by " _
                        & objNdRd.ReadString() & ".")
                    'delimit message
                    ListBox1.Items.Add("=========================")
```

```
          End If
        End If
      End While
   Next

End Sub
```

4. Running this application and clicking the **Execute** button will give the following result:

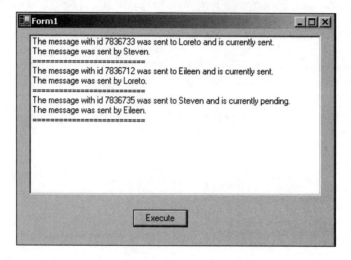

How It Works

Don't worry about the parts of this example that you are not familiar with – the key to this example is to illustrate the `XmlNodeReader` class.

To create a proper illustration we used the `XmlDocument` class, which we are going to look at in detail in Chapters 6 and 7, to load an instance of the sample XML document. When this document was loaded, we used the `SelectNodes()` method of the `XmlDocument` class to return a list of nodes that matched the XPath expression `//message[@status]` – in other words, return all message element nodes that have a `status` attribute (which in fact is all of them in this example).

```
Dim document As XmlDocument = New XmlDocument()
document.Load(strFilePath)

Dim objXList As XmlNodeList = document.SelectNodes("//message[@status]")
```

Next, we iterate through each of the nodes in the node list and load each node, in turn, into an `XmlNodeReader` instance – so each iteration will load a new message node into a new `XmlNodeReader` class.

```
For Each objNode In objXList
  'Read each node
  Dim objNdRd As XmlNodeReader = New XmlNodeReader(objNode)
```

Then we iterate through all the nodes (and child nodes of the node) and match those that are `Element` nodes.

```
While (objNdRd.Read())
  'get element nodes
  If (objNdRd.NodeType = XmlNodeType.Element) Then
```

When there is a match, we check whether the current element is a message element or `sender` child element. If it is a `message` element, we add some information to the listbox, using the `GetAttribute()` method of the `XmlNodeReader` specifying the name of the attribute we want to retrieve the value of.

```
If (objNdRd.Name = "message") Then
  'add the message details to the list
  ListBox1.Items.Add("The message with id " _
    & objNdRd.GetAttribute("id") _
    & " was sent to " & objNdRd.GetAttribute("target") _
    & " and is currently " & objNdRd.GetAttribute("status") _
    & ".")
```

When a `sender` element is found, the string contents of the element are displayed.

```
    ElseIf (objNdRd.Name = "sender") Then
      'else if <sender> element, then add these details
      ListBox1.Items.Add("The message was sent by " _
        & objNdRd.ReadString() & ".")
    End If
  End If
End While
Next

'Delimit message
ListBox1.Items.Add("===========================")
```

This was a fairly brief look at the `XmlNodeReader` class and we will look at it more in the upcoming chapters, but now let us also cover the `XmlValidatingReader`, which is the third implementation of the `XmlReader` class. Again we will leave more detailed coverage of this until the chapters on Schemas, particularly Chapter 11, later in the book.

The XmlValidatingReader Class

The `XmlValidatingReader` class is important because it allows you to validate the XML document against a DTD or a schema. It is effectively a layer on top of the `XmlTextReader` class providing the validation functionality that `XmlTextReader` does not. It is slower than the `XmlTextReader` because the entities it expands or files it uses to validate may be external to the file and so have to be loaded and parsed prior to being used by this class. This has the largest effect when the external files are at remote locations and so may have to be loaded over the web. The class is very efficient, however, and the relative performance (compared to the `XmlTextReader`) will depend on a number of factors such as the number and location of the entities and schema documents that will be used for validation.

This class has a `ValidationType` property, `Schema` property, and a `SchemaType` property. The `ValidationType` property is used to specify the type of schema that will be validated against, which is one of "auto" (determined by reader itself), "DTD", "XDR", "None", or "Schema". The `Schemas` property is very powerful and allows you to create a cache of Schemas associated with namespaces, which can then be used to validate your XML document, which could be extremely useful, for example for an application to verify that purchase orders posted to the system are in a valid format. It is too early to look at how this is done, but it is covered in detail in Chapters 9 and 10 on Schemas and validation. Finally, the `SchemaType` property can be used to provide information on the type of validation that is being performed on the current node. So, when validating using a Schema, you can use a query to find the type of validation (for example, `datatype`, `simpleType`, or `complexType`) and when validating using DTD's this property returns null.

Try It Out: Reading Attributes – Revisited!

This example is going to demonstrate how DTDs can be used with .NET to validate an XML document. Refer to Chapters 9 and 10 for more detail.

1. Create a new Visual Basic Windows Application project in Visual Studio .NET with the project name **XMLValidate**.

2. Add a **TextBox** and a **Button** to the form. Ensure the `Text` property of the **TextBox** is blank, the `Multiline` property value is set to `True`, and enter the **Button's** `Text` property as **Validate**. Now create a new XML file called `sample.xml` in the root of the project and enter the following XML into it:

```
<?xml version="1.0" ?>
<!DOCTYPE message SYSTEM "..\sample.dtd">
<message>
   <sender>Steven</sender>
   <recipient>Loreto</recipient>
   <title>Remember!</title>
   <body>Feed my poor cat.</body>
</message>
```

3. Similarly, create a new file called `sample.dtd` in the root of the folder and enter the following into this file (or copy the contents of `sample.dtd` from the code downloads folder).

```
<!ELEMENT message (sender, recipient, title, body)>
<!ELEMENT sender (#PCDATA)>
<!ELEMENT recipient (#PCDATA)>
<!ELEMENT title (#PCDATA)>
<!ELEMENT body (#PCDATA)>
```

4. Double-click the **Validate** button and in the event handler for this button and enter the code as shown below.

```
Private Sub Button1_Click(ByVal sender As System.Object, _
    ByVal e As System.EventArgs) Handles Button1.Click
  'Create a new instance of a textreader using the fragment
  'from the text box - it is a Document
```

```
    Dim objXTRead As XmlTextReader = _
       New XmlTextReader(TextBox1.Text, XmlNodeType.Document, Nothing)

    'Layer validation on top of this
    Dim objXValRead As XmlValidatingReader = New XmlValidatingReader(objXTRead)

    'Set the validation type to a DTD
    objXValRead.ValidationType = ValidationType.DTD

    Try
       'Perform validation
       While (objXValRead.Read())

       End While

       MessageBox.Show("Validation Completed")
    Catch exception As Exception
       MessageBox.Show(exception.Message)
    Finally
       If Not objXValRead Is Nothing Then
          objXValRead.Close()
       End If
    End Try
 End Sub
```

Don't forget to add the following code to the top of the file:

```
Imports System.Xml
```

5. Press *F5* to run the application, enter the contents of sample.xml file into the **TextBox** and click the **Validate** button. The output should be something like the figure below:

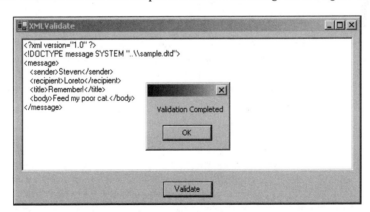

6. Edit the contents of the XML in the TextBox and change the <recipient> element to be <recepient> and again click the **Validate** button. This time you will get a different result, illustrated below:

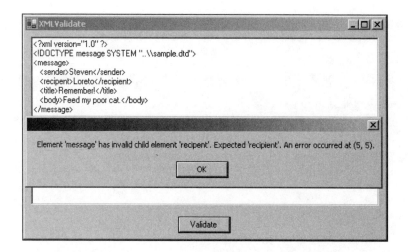

How It Works

This example showed how we could very simply perform validation, even using the older DTD language, using .NET. Let's look briefly at the DTD.

```
<!ELEMENT message (sender, recipient, title, body)>
```

A root element called message is specified to have four child elements called sender, recipient, title and body. Each of these is defined to take only character data as content using the PCDATA attribute.

```
<!ELEMENT sender (#PCDATA)>
<!ELEMENT recipient (#PCDATA)>
<!ELEMENT title (#PCDATA)>
<!ELEMENT body (#PCDATA)>
```

In our Button_Click event, the first thing we did was to create an instance of an XmlTextReader. We set our reader to read the text entered into the **TextBox**, then specified that it was a full XML document that we were passing in and that the parser context was Nothing (this is simply additional information used by the parser such as encoding, namespace scope, and information to resolve entities).

```
Dim objXTRead As XmlTextReader = _
    New XmlTextReader(TextBox1.Text, XmlNodeType.Document, Nothing)
```

When this has been set up, an instance of an XmlValidatingReader is created, passing in the XmlTextReader object in the constructor. Additionally, because we want to validate using a DTD we should specify that the ValidationType property is equal to the ValidationType.DTD enumeration value. It defaults to ValidationType.Auto where the parser tries to determine the validation type you want to perform (but always better to be explicit!).

```
'Layer validation on top of this
Dim objXValRead As XmlValidatingReader = _
  New XmlValidatingReader(objXTRead)

'Set the validation type to a DTD
objXValRead.ValidationType = ValidationType.DTD
```

Finally, we wrap the `Read()` in a `Try...Catch` statement, because this `Read()` causes validation to occur. We also include our error routines in this part of the code.

```
Try
  'Perform validation
  While (objXValRead.Read())

  End While

  MessageBox.Show("Validation Completed")
Catch exception As Exception
  MessageBox.Show(exception.Message)
Finally
  If Not objXValRead Is Nothing Then
    objXValRead.Close()
  End If
End Try
```

After we had initially tested our application, we deliberately caused a single error to be raised by specifying an element that wasn't a valid member of the document type definition. In our case we just raise errors, but typically an error handler is specified which has the advantage in that you can collect all of the errors of the instance and present them to the user (to all be fixed at the same time), rather than repetitive validation errors each time the document is re-validated – we will see examples of that in Chapters 9 and 10.

Summary

In this chapter we worked through our first real coding examples and saw some of the basics of what can be done when XML and .NET are combined. We covered the following:

- ❑ Differences between the DOM and the streaming model; we also covered when one may be preferable over the other.

- ❑ SAX and how SAX itself is quite different from the XmlReader abstract class, which is a pull implementation rather than a push implementation.

- ❑ The XmlReader class in detail, working through a series of examples that use this class and examining some of the useful properties and methods which form the foundation of much of the manipulation that is done with XML in .NET.

- ❑ How the XmlReader implementations can support large chunks of data.

❑   The other implementations of the `XmlReader` abstract class, namely the `XmlNodeReader` for working with individual nodes and the `XmlValidatingReader`, used in conjunction with XML schemas to validate XML documents. We will look at these again in the coming chapters.

For now, let's continue our understanding by looking at how to write out XML now that we now how to read it.

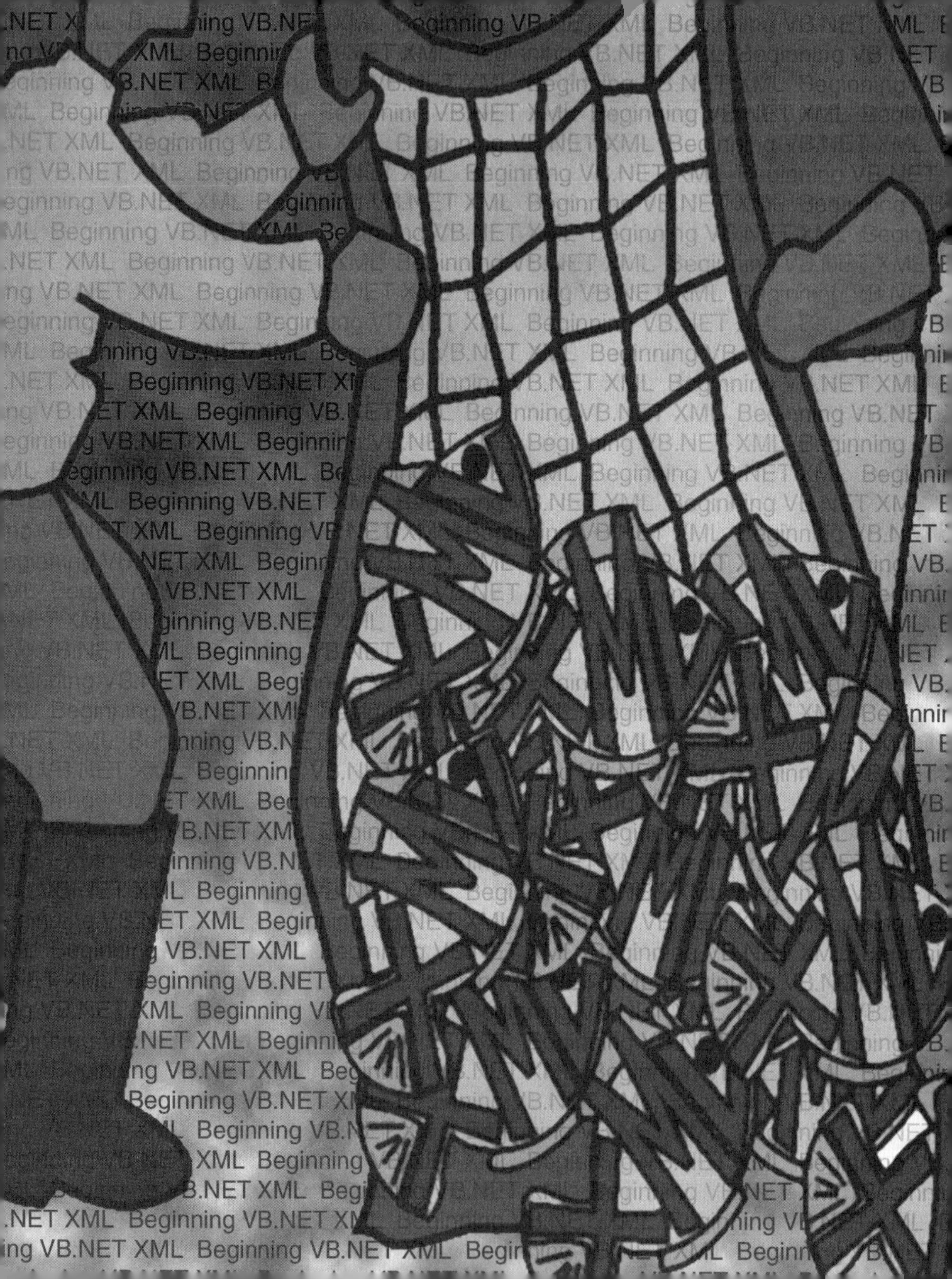
Beginning VB.NET XML

Writing XML in .NET

At this point in the book we have covered the fundamental concepts of XML, and we've created programs that read XML code using classes provided for us by the .NET Framework. We're now going to look at programmatically writing XML data within our VB.NET code, using functionality defined in some more .NET classes.

We've seen how we can write XML documents by hand, so why would we need to write XML out programmatically? Well, imagine you're creating an application that receives requests for information – the format or content of that information may vary according to the request. We can code up our application to take a request for information, and to write out a specific XML document and stream it back to the calling application. We could also code up a different type of application that relies on XML-formatted configuration files that will vary in content depending on the options selected during installation, or post installation. We can therefore generate the appropriate XML configuration file depending on the data we require. We could do all this by manually writing "less-than symbol", text, "greater-than symbol", and so on, until we finally create an XML file. However this process would be extremely lengthy, and error-prone. Thankfully, as .NET developers, we have access to some very useful methods that handle writing elements, attributes, and so on, with a minimum of fuss, and this is what we'll be looking at in this chapter.

In the previous chapter, we introduced the concept of streaming. In this chapter we'll see how we use streaming when we write XML documents, which is a similar concept to reading our XML documents as we discussed in Chapter 4. Using the tools available for programmatically writing XML information, we are able to not only output XML documents, but we're also able to output streams that can be used by other classes. We're even able to write out large data chunks, such as creating base64-encoded fragments of JPEG images (and other binary formats) that can be safely embedded in an XML document.

In this chapter, we'll learn:

❑ How to write XML documents programmatically using the .NET classes

❑ How the members of the XmlWriter abstract class provide basic functionality

❑ How this functionality is implemented in the XmlTextWriter class

We'll also look at:

❑ Building a practical example of writing XML using the `XmlTextWriter` class

❑ Working with binary data, such as JPEG images

The basic functionality that defines how we can write XML data is defined within the `XmlWriter` class. Let's start this chapter by taking a look at what this class provides, and how we can use this functionality in our applications.

Writing XML Using .NET Classes

Like the `XmlReader` class, `XmlWriter` is also an abstract base class within the .NET Framework. It is part of the `System.Xml` namespace and provides a fast, non-cached, and forward-only method of writing XML data to a file or a stream. This means it writes data *sequentially* to a stream that is sent to a buffer, which can be either a file or a memory location. We can't go back and change data that we've already written – for example to add attributes to an element that we've already written.

Because the `XmlWriter` is an abstract class, we don't actually use the members defined in this class directly, but we can use these members from any class that derives from the `XmlWriter` class. The only class supplied with the .NET Framework that derives from the `XmlWriter` class is the `XmlTextWriter` class. When we look at examples in this chapter, we'll be using the methods available in the `XmlTextWriter` class.

The XmlWriter Class

As we mentioned previously, this class is the abstract class that defines the basic methods and properties available when writing XML. It doesn't have the overhead associated with an object model, such as the DOM, and it only performs validation checks to ensure that the document is well-formed and that namespaces are used correctly according to the Namespaces Specification. All XML data that is written out using methods and properties from this class will conform to the W3C XML 1.0 Recommendation and W3C Namespaces Recommendation, which means that our elements and attributes will be created correctly as long as we understand how to use the methods and properties. Ensuring that our documents are well-formed is one half of the problem, and the fact that these methods help with the simple matters of creating well-formed elements and attributes leaves us to concentrate on ordering these correctly, to make sure we end up with a correctly-structured document.

By using the methods and properties defined in the `XmlWriter` class, we are able to:

❑ Ensure that the XML document is well-formed

❑ Decide whether the XML document will have namespaces

❑ Encode the document as `base64`, `BinHex`, or even your own custom encoding

❑ Write a document or multiple documents to a single stream, such as a file or the console

❑ Flush and Close the output, at which point the XML we've defined so far is actually streamed to the required destination

- ❏ Specify the `xml:lang` and `xml:space` scope
- ❏ Define the prefix of an element
- ❏ Write all of the node types that we discussed in the last chapter

In this section, we'll start by looking at the `XmlWriter` class, with some examples using the implemented functionality via the `XmlTextWriter` class. Then, in the next section, we'll look at the functionality specific to the `XmlTextWriter`.

Let's start by looking at some of the methods we can use to write XML, and then we'll take a look at some practical examples of these methods in action.

XmlWriter Methods

Let's look at how we can write basic XML documents using a selection of methods that are part of the `XmlWriter` abstract class. Some of these methods are self-describing by name (for example, `WriteStartElement()`) while others are less clear, but we'll look at each in turn and see how they can be used.

In this section, we'll look at:

- ❏ The `WriteStartDocument()` and `WriteEndDocument()` methods
- ❏ The `WriteStartElement()` and `WriteEndElement()` methods
- ❏ The `WriteStartAttribute()` and `WriteEndAttribute()` methods
- ❏ The `WriteElementString()` and `WriteAttributeString()` methods
- ❏ The `WriteString()` method
- ❏ The `WriteNode()` method

We'll also mention some other `XmlWriter` methods you may encounter when writing your own XML documents, which we'll not cover in quite so much detail. We're concentrating on the methods you are more likely to use day to day, and as such, this section isn't intended to be comprehensive – for a full list of all available methods, you may want to refer to the MSDN documentation.

The WriteStartDocument() and WriteEndDocument() Methods

When we write the start of an XML document, as we discussed in Chapter 2, we can include the following information:

- ❏ The version number of the XML standard we're using
- ❏ Whether the document is standalone
- ❏ The encoding of the document

The `WriteStartDocument()` method is used to write the XML declaration, and includes the ability to control two of these options: the version number of the XML and whether the document is standalone.

If we call this method on a derived class that outputs XML, such as `XmlTextWriter`, without any arguments, the following XML code is generated:

```
<?xml version="1.0"?>
```

By default, this method doesn't add the `standalone` attribute to the declaration, but you can use an overload which takes a `Boolean` `True` as an argument to write the standalone attribute with the value "yes" (using an argument of `False` means that the standalone attribute is added to the declaration with the value "no").

So, if we'd modified our code to read `WriteStartDocument(True)`, the output would change our declaration to the following:

```
<?xml version="1.0" standalone="yes"?>
```

We mentioned that this method only adds two parts of the declaration, and it isn't used to specify the encoding of our document. The encoding is actually determined by the derived `XmlWriter` (`XmlTextWriter` lets us specify an encoding through its constructor) and from this the value of the encoding attribute can be determined. We'll see this in action in an example in just a moment. Of course, the XML rule of the default UTF-8 encoding will apply when there has been no encoding explicitly specified.

A side-effect of calling the `WriteStartDocument()` method is that by including this in our document, the writer assumes that the subsequent XML will be a complete well-formed document. If this method is not called on the writer, then it assumes that you are in fact writing an XML fragment and so no checks are made.

You can't call `WriteStartDocument()` more than once. If you try, an exception will be thrown. This is because the writer keeps track of the state of the document we're writing out (we can discover its current state through the `WriterState` property of the writer, which we'll meet shortly). We can only call `WriteStartDocument()` if the state is `Start`. Once we've called it, it changes the state to `Prolog`. By keeping track of this state, and only allowing us to call certain methods in each state, the writer is able to enforce the creation of a well-formed document.

The `WriteEndDocument()` method makes sure that we have closed all elements and attributes (that is, closing quotes and closing elements are written to the document), and sets the `WriterState` property of the writer back to `Start`. If the document that has been created is not valid XML, then calling this method will cause an exception to be thrown stating that the document is invalid XML.

The WriteStartElement() and WriteEndElement() Methods

The `WriteStartElement()` and `WriteEndElement()` methods are used to write specified start and end tags. Let's take a look at how we use these methods.

The `WriteStartElement()` method has three overloads:

```
WriteStartElement(localname As String)

WriteStartElement(localname As String, namespace As String)

WriteStartElement(prefix As String, localname As String, namespace As String)
```

The first overload will write out the start element with the local name equal to the string passed to the method. For example, if we wanted to write a simple element, we could use the following code:

```
WriteStartElement("para")
```

This code would produce the following:

```
<para>
```

The second overload available to us will write out a start tag with the local name specified in the first parameter of the method, and in the namespace specified in the second parameter of the method. If the namespace in the second argument is already in scope and has some prefix association, then this prefix will also be appended to the new element. Take, for example, the following code:

```
WriteStartElement("para", "http://www.deltabis.com/ns/")
```

This will write out the following XML element:

```
<para xmlns="http://www.deltabis.com/ns/">
```

The third overload will write out a start element, with the local name specified in the second parameter, and the namespace specified in the third parameter. The prefix specified in the first parameter is passed to the method. So, if we were to write the following code:

```
WriteStartElement("db", "para", "http://www.deltabis.com/ns/")
```

This will write out the following XML element:

```
<db:para xmlns:db="http://www.deltabis.com/ns/">
```

In the third example, even if the namespace you defined in the third parameter is already in scope, you will get another prefix bound to this namespace. Let's look at an example:

```
WriteStartElement("db", "para", "http://www.deltabis.com/ns/")
WriteStartElement("ns", "sentence", "http://www.deltabis.com/ns/")
WriteEndElement()
WriteEndElement()
```

The XML fragment that will be written by this code is as follows:

```
<db:para xmlns:db="http://www.deltabis.com/ns/">
  <ns:sentence xmlns:ns="http://www.deltabis.com/ns/" />
</db:para>
```

Once you have called `WriteStartElement()`, you have opened a new element node. As such, you are now able to write attribute nodes, comments with `WriteComment()`, strings with `WriteString()`, or more child element nodes with `WriteStartElement()`.

Once an element is finished, and all appropriate content added, the element node opened by the call to `WriteStartElement()` is closed by a call to `WriteEndElement()`, which closes the element in one of two ways. If the element contains no content then the opened element node is closed with a `"/>"` empty element, otherwise it is closed by an end tag. Also, any namespace scope opened by the element created in the `WriteStartElement()` call is also closed.

> *Note that there is also a `WriteFullEndElement()` method that we could use, which will close any opened element node writing the full closing element tag regardless of whether it contains content or not. Hence, for an empty para element, where the `WriteEndElement()` method would write `<para/>` when there is no content, the `WriteFullEndElement()` method will always write `<para></para>`. This is mainly useful when working with HTML (for example, HEAD, SCRIPT, and so on) that expects there to be full closing tags.*

Let's look at these methods in action when implemented in the `XmlTextWriter` class by starting to build up an example. In this example we are going to look at these methods in practice by creating an XML document and adding a root element to the document. Because we can't directly use methods contained within the `XmlWriter` class, we need to use the implementation of these methods available in the `XmlTextWriter` class.

Try It Out: Creating the XML Declaration and Root Element

The first thing we have to do is create the XML Declaration that should be at the top of any XML document. However, if you remember that an XML document is only valid if it at least has the root element, then we must add this as well if we intend to save the document. After we have created this, we will look at our newly-created XML file in Internet Explorer. Over the course of this chapter we'll be adding to this example to build up a larger XML file.

1. First create a new VB Windows Application project and call it `WritingXMLExample`.

2. On the form that appears, change the Text property of the form to **Examples of Writing XML Documents**. Now, add a multi-line `TextBox`. Delete the `Text` property of the Textbox, then add a `Button` control to the form, setting its text property to **Example 1** as shown below:

3. Next, double-click the **Example1** button and enter the following code into the event handler.

```
Private Sub button1_Click(ByVal sender As System.Object, _
    ByVal e As System.EventArgs) Handles button1.Click

    textBox1.Text = ""

    'Creates document outline
    Const strFileName As String = "WriteXMLExample.xml"
    Dim objXmlTW As XmlTextWriter = New XmlTextWriter(strFileName, Encoding.UTF8)

    'Write XML Declaration
    objXmlTW.WriteStartDocument()

    'Write root element
    objXmlTW.WriteStartElement("ct","ContactDetails", _
                              "http://www.deltabis.com/Contact")

    objXmlTW.WriteEndElement()

    'End the XML Document
    objXmlTW.WriteEndDocument()

    'Write to the file and close
    objXmlTW.Flush()
    objXmlTW.Close()
End Sub
```

4. Add the following code to the start of the file before any other code:

```
Imports System.Xml
Imports System.Text
```

5. Save this file and click the start button (or press the *F5* button). When the application has started, click the **Example1** button.

6. Open Windows Explorer and navigate to the directory where you saved the Visual Studio .NET project (for example, `C:\BegVBXML\Chapter05\WritingXMLExample\`) and go to the `bin` directory.

7. Open `WriteXMLExample.xml` in Internet Explorer and you will see the following:

How It Works

We started by creating a new instance of the `XmlTextWriter` class by passing the filename `WriteXMLExample.xml` and the encoding to be `UTF-8` (the default in XML) to the constructor of the `XmlTextWriter`.

```
Const strFileName As String = "WriteXMLExample.xml"
Dim objXmlTR As XmlTextWriter = New XmlTextWriter(strFileName, Encoding.UTF8)
```

An XML declaration was then written. This must be the first thing that is written to the document or an exception will be raised. The `WriteStartDocument()` method is used to do this.

```
'Write XML Declaration
objXmlTR.WriteStartDocument()
```

We then proceeded to write our root element, `ContactDetails`. In our case, we added a prefix called `ct` to be associated with the namespace `http://www.deltabis.com/Contact` and the `ContactDetails` element node to be qualified in this namespace (that is, prefixed by `ct`). We then called the `WriteEndElement()` method to close the element.

```
'Write root element
objXmlTW.WriteStartElement("ct","ContactDetails", _
                                   "http://www.deltabis.com/Contact")

objXmlTW.WriteEndElement()
```

Notice that the document element currently has no child nodes, so the XML element is written using the empty element syntax. For simple elements, we can also use the `WriteElementString()` method, instead of the `WriteStartElement()` method. We'll look at how we can do this in an upcoming section, and highlight the pros and cons of using `WriteStartElement()` over `WriteElementString()`.

Finally, you must state that you have finished with the document by calling in the
WriteEndDocument() method.

```
'End the XML Document
objXmlTW.WriteEndDocument()
```

When this is complete, you need to call the Flush() method to write the data to the underlying
stream, and the Close() method to save the new XML file. We'll look at these methods in a bit more
detail shortly.

```
'Write to the file and close
objXmlTW.Flush()
objXmlTW.Close()
```

Let's continue with our examination of the methods defined in the XmlWriter class to learn how we
can add attributes and other features to our XML document.

The WriteStartAttribute() and WriteEndAttribute() Methods

The WriteStartAttribute() method, as its name suggests, writes the start of an attribute. It has
two overloads:

```
WriteStartAttribute(localname As String, namespace As String)

WriteStartAttribute(prefix As String, localname As String, namespace As String);
```

The first of these overloads writes the start of an attribute with the local name from the first parameter
qualified in the namespace specified in the second parameter. The second overload works in a similar
manner, but also appends a prefix to the attribute associated with the specified namespace in the
method. We'll see an example of this method in action in just a moment.

The WriteEndAttribute() method will close the attribute created in previous call to
WriteStartAttribute(). A call to either the WriteStartAttribute(),
WriteAttributeString(), or WriteEndElement() methods also closes any attribute created by
the WriteStartAttribute() method call.

The WriteElementString() and WriteAttributeString() Methods

The techniques we have looked at so far for creating elements and attributes using the XmlWriter class
are very flexible and allow us to create fairly complex elements and attributes. These methods may
require other methods to be called to determine the content.

However, quite often you want to create an element or attribute that takes a well-defined string value,
and the content is not complex. There are two methods available for doing this –
WriteElementString() for elements and WriteAttributeString() for attributes. These
methods automatically close the element or attribute after the string value has been written.

The WriteElementString() method writes an element containing a string value and has two overloads.

```
WriteElementString(localname As String, value As String);

WriteElementString(localname As String, namespace As String, value As String);
```

The first overload takes the name of the element to create and the text value it will contain. So the code:

```
WriteElementString("para", "Some paragraph text!")
```

Will produce the output:

```
<para>Some paragraph text!</para>
```

The second overload additionally takes the namespace as a parameter and so qualifies the element that is output. So the code:

```
WriteElementString("para", "http://www.deltabis.com/ns/", "Some paragraph text!")
```

will produce the output:

```
<para xmlns="http://www.deltabis.com/ns/">Some paragraph text!</para>
```

If the namespace that is added is already associated with some prefix in the document, then this prefix is used.

The WriteAttributeString() method is very similar, but has an extra overload. The overloads are:

```
WriteAttributeString(localname As String, value As String)

WriteAttributeString(localname As String, namespace As String, value As String)

WriteAttributeString(prefix As String, localname As String, namespace As String, _
    value As String)
```

The first overload will create a new attribute with the name localname and its contents will be the second string, called value.

The second overload will perform the same function, but the attribute will now be qualified in the namespace given in the second argument.

The final overload will again create the attribute, but this time it will append the prefix in the method and associate this with the namespace also passed in the method.

When the value of an attribute is set, it will replace any occurrences of double quotes with the " entity and any occurrences of single quotes with the entity '. Also, if you are setting the xml:space attribute on an element it will check that the value you give it is either default or preserve, but it will *not* do any validation for the xml:lang attribute value.

So, with the code:

```
WriteAttributeString("ch", "reviewer", "http://www.deltabis.com/bk/", "Ian")
```

The following would be the output if this were applied to a `<para>` element node:

```
<para ch:reviewer="Ian" xmlns:ch="http://www.deltabis.com/bk/">
```

So now you see there are two ways to write the content of elements and two ways to write the content of attributes. What's the advantage of one over the other?

The WriteStartElement() Method versus the WriteElementString() Method

The `WriteStartElement()` and `WriteEndElement()` methods are more useful in slightly more complex scenarios where you want to write additional node rather than just a string as per `WriteElementString()`. So you may want to write a `para` element which is to contain multiple sentence child elements. To do this you would need to use the `WriteStartElement()` to open the element, create the `sentence` elements (using either `WriteStartElement()` or `WriteElementString()`) and then use `WriteEndElement()` to close the original `para` element. For example:

```
WriteStartElement("para")
WriteElementString("sentence", "My first sentence.")
WriteElementString("sentence", "My second sentence.")
WriteEndElement()
```

This would write out the following XML:

```
<para>
  <sentence>My first sentence</sentence>
  <sentence>My second sentence</sentence>
</para>
```

This is the method you would also use to create entities or qualified names within the element. When using the `WriteElementString()` method, as shown above, you only have the option of writing text nodes, which is a simple and quick way of writing elements to the output.

The WriteStartAttribute() Method versus the WriteAttributeString() Method

A similar situation exists for the `WriteStartAttribute()` and `WriteEndAttribute()` methods in relation to the `WriteAttributeString()` method we have just discussed. As an example, consider the situation where you want to write out a special character (for example, the ñ character we discussed in Chapter 2) within the value of an attribute called `author` on the `para` element discussed above to name the person who last updated that paragraph (let's imagine it's a collaborative document). The following code could be used:

```
WriteStartElement("para")
WriteStartAttribute("author", null)
WriteString("Do")
WriteCharEntity("ñ")
WriteString("a")
WriteCharEntity("&")
WriteString("L. Perez")
WriteEndAttribute(
WriteEndElement()
```

179

This will write out the following XML fragment:

```
<para author="Do&0241;a&amp;L. Perez" />
```

Now, in the `author` attribute you have the Unicode equivalents for the ñ (within the string Doña which means Mrs) and & characters – ensuring that your document will not fail to parse when loaded by other encoding schemes.

Let's add some attribute information to our previous example.

Try It Out: Adding an Attribute

We are now going to look at how we can add an attribute to the root element node and give it some value.

1. Add a new button to the form and change the `Text` property value to `Example 2`.

2. Double-click the button and add the following code to the event handler.

```
Private Sub button2_Click(ByVal sender As System.Object, _
    ByVal e As System.EventArgs) Handles button2.Click
```

```
    textBox1.Text = ""

    'Creates document outline
    Const strFileName As String = "WriteXMLExample.xml"
    Dim objXmlTW As XmlTextWriter = New XmlTextWriter(strFileName, Encoding.UTF8)

    'Write XML Declaration
    objXmlTW.WriteStartDocument()

    'Write root element
    objXmlTW.WriteStartElement("ct", "ContactDetails", _
                               "http://www.deltabis.com/Contact")

    'Write attribute to the root element
    objXmlTW.WriteAttributeString("updateDate", "20021201T14:00")

    objXmlTW.WriteEndElement()

    'End the XML Document
    objXmlTW.WriteEndDocument()

    'Write to the file and close
    objXmlTW.Flush()
    objXmlTW.Close()

    textBox1.Text = textbox1.text + ReadDocument(strFileName)
End Sub
```

3. Next, add the following private method after the event handler. This will make use of our textbox by displaying the generated XML in the window:

```
Private Function ReadDocument(ByVal strFileName As String) As String

    'Read the XML into a Text Box
    Dim objXmlTR As XmlTextReader = New XmlTextReader(strFileName)
    'Move to the first content node
    objXmlTR.MoveToContent()

    Dim XmlString As String = objXmlTR.ReadOuterXml() 'read outer XML

    objXmlTR.Close() 'close the reader

    Return XmlString
End Function
```

4. Save the file and run the application by pressing *F5*. When the application has started, click the **Example2** button and you will get the following output:

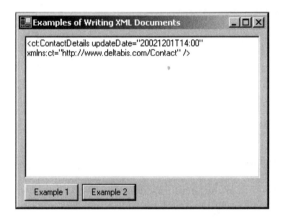

How It Works

The code in the first part of this example is quite similar to the code we looked at in the previous example. However, we have added one new line to the code after the `WriteStartElement()` method creates the root element.

```
    'Write root element
    objXmlTW.WriteStartElement("ct", "ContactDetails", _
                                "http://www.deltabis.com/Contact")

    'Write attribute to the root element
    objXmlTW.WriteAttributeString("updateDate", "20021201T14:00")

    objXmlTW.WriteEndElement()
```

As the `WriteAttributeString()` method is called immediately after the root element is created, it will apply to the root element and so an attribute called `updateDate` with the specified value will be created on the `ContactDetails` element node.

Like the `WriteElementString()` method, when this method is used to create attributes you can't call any more methods to create the attribute value, such as calling methods to create character entities within the attribute (such as Unicode characters as we discussed earlier in the chapter) . We will see how to do this later, however.

In the second part of this example, the `ReadDocument()` method is defined which will load a document given by filename and return the XML of this file as a string. An instance of the `XmlTextReader` class is created, passing the name of the file we created with the `XmlTextWriter` to the constructor. The `MoveToContent()` method is called which will take us to the document element, and from there the `ReadOuterXml()` method is called which will return the document element including all child nodes (although we've not created any in our example just yet – this is a task for a later example). This is written to the textbox on the form and the text reader is closed.

```
Private Function ReadDocument(ByVal strFileName As String) As String

    'Read the XML into a Text Box
    Dim objXmlTR As XmlTextReader = New XmlTextReader(strFileName)
    objXmlTR.MoveToContent() 'Move to the first content node - these are....

    Dim XmlString As String = objXmlTR.ReadOuterXml() 'read outer XML

    objXmlTR.Close() 'close the reader

    Return XmlString
End Function
```

We'll be using this function in the other examples in this chapter.

Let's continue our discussion of useful methods defined in the `XmlWriter` class with two more methods; the `WriteString()` method and the `WriteNode()` method.

The WriteString() Method

The `WriteString()` method writes the text content specified in the parameter which is passed as a `string`. This can be useful when writing the content of an element node or an attribute node.

As it creates well-formed XML, the special characters are escaped by character entity equivalents and so &, < and > are replaced by &, <, and > respectively. Furthermore, the characters between 0x and 0x1F are replaced by their equivalent character entities &x0; to &#0x1F; (control characters), except for the 0x9 (tab), 0xA (newline), and 0xB (carriage return).

Furthermore, if this is called in the content of an attribute node, when the value of an attribute is set, it will replace any occurrences of double quotes with the " entity and any occurrences of single quotes with the entity '.

So if we are writing the value of some attribute node called `keypoint`, which is an attribute of a `para` element node, then with the code:

```
WriteString("He was reported to have said <quote>'Of course VB is better" _
    & " than Java!'</quote>")
```

we would get the following output:

```
<para keypoint="He was reported to have said &lt;quote&gt;&quot;Of course VB" _
    & " is better than Java!&quot;&lt;/quote&gt;">
```

The WriteNode() Method

The `WriteNode()` method is used to copy nodes from an `XmlReader` instance and write them out to an `XmlWriter` stream – useful when you basically want to copy exact fragments from the input reader and write them out unchanged to the `XmlWriter` stream.

The first parameter to the `WriteNode()` method is an `XmlReader` instance (or instance of a derived class) which will be positioned at a node (for example, an element or attribute). The second `Boolean` parameter to the `WriteNode()` method will tell the writer whether it should copy the default attributes from the reader (`True`) or not (`False`). Default attributes are specified by an XML Schema document to be appearing on an element if no attribute by that name is specified.

It then copies everything from the current node in the `XmlReader` object and moves to the start of the next sibling node. In fact, it always copies the current node except for the `Attribute`, `EndElement`, and `EndEntity` nodes. In the case of an `Attribute` node you should use `WriteStartAttribute()` or `WriteAttributeString()` instead. Note also that in the case of `Element` nodes, any attribute nodes on the element are also copied across.

As an example, consider the following XML fragment:

```
<para>
  <sentence>
    The <b>XmlWriter</b> class writes XML content to a Stream.
  </sentence>
</para>
```

The following code fragment demonstrates how you might use this method, with the variable `reader` representing an `XmlTextReader` for the above XML document.

```
While (reader.Read())
  If (reader.Name = "sentence" AND reader.NodeType = XmlNodeType.Element)
    writer.WriteNode(reader,True)
  End If
End While
```

The `WriteNode()` method in this example will output the XML below and move straight to the next node (that is, the reader will not walk through any child nodes such as the `<b>` element) – the `para` `EndElement` node in this case.

```
<sentence>
   The <b>XmlWriter</b> class writes XML content to a Stream.
</sentence>
```

Other XmlWriter Methods

There are several other abstract methods that are part of the XmlWriter class, some of which we'll see in examples in this chapter, others that you will find useful when working on your own projects. Let's take a quick look at some of these methods:

❑   The Close() method: closes any open elements or attributes and finally closes the writer and any underlying streams, setting the WriteState property (which we'll look at in more detail in a moment) to Closed.

❑   The Flush() method: used to write any data in the buffer to the underlying stream and then clears the buffer. You should use this when you want to output what is in the buffer without closing the stream itself. You may do this if you want some component to do some processing on the stream – for example, a purchase order component may append a unique PO ID as an attribute on an element within the XML in the stream and write the updated XML back to the original stream to continue processing.

❑   The WriteComment() method: used to write an XML comment containing the text that is passed as a parameter to the method. If we wrote the following code:

```
WriteComment("Updated Today.")
```

The resultant XML output would be:

```
<!--Updated Today.-->
```

❑   The WriteDocType() method and the WriteEntityRef() method: the WriteDocType() method writes out a DOCTYPE declaration based on the string four parameters. The first parameter is required and defines the name of the DOCTYPE. The others are optional, the second writing the PUBLIC attribute, the third writing the SYSTEM attribute and the final argument being the contents of the DOCTYPE.

As an example, consider the case where we add a formatted version of today's date multiple times in our XML documents. The following code fragment would allow us to define this once:

```
'Write the XML delcaration
writer.WriteStartDocument()

'Write the DocumentType node
writer.WriteDocType("today", Nothing, _
  Nothing,"<!ENTITY today 'Aug 07 2002'>")
writer.WriteStartElement("para")

'write modified attribute
writer.WriteStartAttribute("modified", Nothing)
writer.WriteEntityRef("today")
writer.WriteEndAttribute()
```

```
'add todays data
writer.WriteString("Today's date is ")
writer.WriteEntityRef("today")

'Write the close tag for the root element
writer.WriteEndElement()
writer.WriteEndDocument()
```

This will output the following XML document:

```
<?xml version="1.0"?>
<!DOCTYPE today[<!ENTITY today 'August 07 2002'>]>
<para modified="&today;">
   Today's date is &today;
</para>
```

Notice that we can now define the today entity at the top if the XML document and reference it multiple times within the document using the WriteEntityRef() method.

❑ The WriteProcessingInstruction() method: This method will take the parameter to define the name or the processing instruction and the second parameter defines the text of that processing instruction, for example:

```
WriteProcessingInstruction("xml-stylesheet","type='text/xsl' href='somefile.xsl'")
```

This will generate the output:

```
<?xml-stylesheet type="text/xsl" href="somefile.xsl " ?>
```

❑ The LookupPrefix() method: use this method to return the prefix for the namespace passed as an argument to the function. If the namespace is the default namespace then you will be returned String.Empty, and if there is no corresponding namespace, then null will be returned.

❑ The WriteChars() method: used to write larger amounts of text to a buffer at a time. This method takes a char array containing the text to be output in the first parameter, the second parameter is an integer specifying the index to start in the array, and the final parameter is an integer of the number of characters to write out.

❑ The WriteWhitespace() method: takes a single string parameter of whitespace characters that will be written to the output in order to format the document. The valid whitespace characters that you will commonly use are the tab character (0x9), the new line character (0x10), the carriage return (0x13) and the space character (0x20). An exception will be thrown if you try to use non-whitespace characters in this method.

XmlWriter Properties

In addition to the methods of the XmlWriter class which we've just looked at, there are three properties we'll find useful when writing XML documents that we will look at now. These properties are:

- ❑   The WriteState property
- ❑   The XmlLang property
- ❑   The XmlSpace property

Let's look at what each of these properties is used for, and how we can use them in our code.

The WriteState Property

This read-only property is used to return the state of the writer as the nodes are being written. For example, when the writer has written the XML declaration, the WriterState will be Prolog and so your application know that it has to next write a comment, processing instruction, or document element node. It is commonly used with the WriteXXX methods that we've just looked at. For example, the WriteStartElement() method writes the opening element of an XML document – at this point the WriteState property is set to Element, so your application knows it can then write attribute values. In a simple example this may not be a concern, but when you have many methods creating different parts of the document it is useful to know what state it was left in by the last method call.

Changing the state of the writer will return one of the following values of the WriteState enumeration:

- ❑   Attribute: an attribute value is being written.
- ❑   Closed: the Close() method of the writer has been called.
- ❑   Content: the content of the element is being written.
- ❑   Element: an element start tag is being written.
- ❑   Prolog: the XML declaration is being written.
- ❑   Start: the writer has been instantiated, but a writer method has not yet been called. The WriteEndDocument() method resets the state of the writer to Start, allowing the creation of a new XML document.

The XmlLang Property

This property is a read-only property and will return the xml:lang scope for a node, which determines the language that the content of the node will be written in. The value of the xml:lang is either defined on the node itself, or inherited from a parent node. The XmlLang property will return nothing if no language has been defined.

An example of the xml:lang attribute is shown below:

```
<doc>
  <chapter>
    <para xml:lang="en-us">
      Some <b>exciting</b> text.
    </para>
    <para xml:lang="es">
      Algun texto excitante.
    </para>
  </chapter>
</doc>
```

If the writer is positioned on the first <para> element node, the value of the XmlLang property would be "en-us" and if on the second <para> element node, it will be "es". Similarly, the XmlLang property for the <b> element node will also return "en-us" as the xml:lang attribute value would default to the value of the nearest ancestor.

As an example of this in action, consider a reporting application that generates graphs along with textual descriptions in multiple languages that describe what the graphs represent. One component may generate the graph, and we could use an XML fragment to contain the text. We could then call our XmlWriter component to write the actual text description. Using the xml:lang attribute and the XmlLang property of the XmlWriter, we can determine the language the first component wants us to write the text in, and generate the appropriate description.

The XmlSpace Property

The XmlSpace property will return the value specified by any xml:space attribute on the current element or the nearest ancestor element, determining how whitespace within that element is to be handled – that is, should line breaks and spaces be kept, or should the whitespace be removed (affecting space between elements, not the actual text node strings). The xml:space property works in a similar way to the xml:lang attribute in that it defaults to the nearest ancestor to determine its value.

The xml:space attribute can take the value default or preserve – the System.Xml.XmlSpace enumeration allows you to set this property to Preserve, Default, or None. When the value is set to xml:space="preserve", all whitespace within that element node and all descendant nodes is significant (unless some descendant node resets the value of xml:space). When the value is set to xml:space="default", then the default processing is required, which means that the whitespace is handled as defined by the consuming application.

Consider the following XML document as an example.

```
<doc>
  <chapter>
    <para xml:space="default">
      Some <b>exciting</b> text.
    </para>
    <para xml:space="preserve">
      Algun texto excitante.
    </para>
  </chapter>
</doc>
```

When the writer is positioned on the first <para> element node, then the value of the XmlSpace property will be "default". When positioned on the second <para> element node, the value of the XmlSpace property will be "preserve". Finally, when the writer is positioned in the <b> element node, the value of the XmlSpace property will be "default".

Let's consider two examples to see how this is used. In the first case, imagine you are presenting a monthly web statistics report to be read by your IT manager. In this situation, you will probably want the line breaks and spaces within the document to be preserved as they will generally have a significant impact on how the paragraphs and sentences in the report are structured.

However, in the second example, you could be sending a document across the network to be processed by an application. In this case, you may want to have all whitespace removed from the document to make the size of the document as small as possible – since the information is to be processed by a machine, the visual presentation of the data is unimportant, and removing whitespace will reduce the file size.

So, we've looked at some of the core functionality that's defined within the XmlWriter class, all of which is implemented in the derived XmlTextWriter class. Let's move on now and build on these foundations, and take a look at the functionality specific to the XmlTextWriter class.

The XmlTextWriter Class

As we mentioned, the XmlTextWriter is derived from the XmlWriter abstract class. It adds some additional properties to these in the abstract XmlWriter class, which we'll look at in a moment.

We're going to start by looking at the constructors available to the XmlTextWriter which we've met in passing in the previous two examples, and explain a bit more about how they work.

XmlTextWriter Constructors

There are three ways to construct an instance of an XmlTextWriter class. The first is by passing an existing TextWriter instance to the constructor, which is the TextWriter you are going to write to. The System.IO.TextWriter class is simple a stream of sequential characters and has no XML validation applied to it, but the XmlTextWriter class assumes that the encoding set on the TextWriter instance is correct.

The second constructor takes as its first parameter the stream to which you are going to write, and as the second, the encoding (from the System.Text.Encoding class) that we'll use for our XML document (although if set to null it defaults to UTF-8).

The final constructor takes the name of the file you want to write to as a string (overwrites if one already exists) and the second parameter is the encoding as defined in the previous paragraph.

All of these constructors set the following default properties:

- ❑ The Formatting property to None
- ❑ The Indentation property to 2
- ❑ The IndentChar property to &#20; (space character)
- ❑ The Namespaces property to True
- ❑ The QuoteChar property to " (double quotes)
- ❑ The WriteState property to Start

Out of this list, we've only met the WriteState property in our discussions so far when we were looking at the properties in the XmlWriter class. The other properties are unique to the XmlTextWriter class, so let's find out more about each of these now.

XmlTextWriter Properties

The following are the additional properties added by the `XmlTextWriter` concrete implementation.

The Formatting Property

This read/write property allows you to state how you want the writer to format the XML that it creates. Its value is one of the `System.Xml.Formatting` enumeration values:

❑ `Indented` – this will cause child elements to be indented based on the `Indentation` and `IndentChar` properties discussed below. It does not affect how mixed content is output.

❑ `None` – this means that no formatting will be applied to the output.

The Indentation Property

The `Indentation` property will set the integer number of characters that the nodes are to be indented and defaults to two. This will only be applied when the `Formatting` property is set to `Indented`.

The following `XmlNodeType` members are affected by this setting:

❑ `DocumentType`

❑ `Element`

❑ `Comment`

❑ `ProcessingInstruction`

❑ `CDATA`

All other `XmlNodeType` members are not affected by this setting.

The IndentChar Property

The `IndentChar` property is used to specify the character that will be used to make the indenting when the formatting property is set to `Indented` and defaults to the space character (0x20). Hence, the default setting for all indentation is two space characters (indentation is set to two).

So, how an XML file is indented is defined according to a combination of the `Indentation` and `IndentChar` properties. The `Indentation` property will tell the writer how many characters to indent by and the `IndentChar` property will define the actual characters that will be used for the indentation.

Although you can actually specify any character to perform the indentation, it is best to stick with one of the following whitespace characters to ensure the XML output is valid.

❑ A tab character: 0x9

❑ A new line character: 0x10

❑ A carriage return: 0x13

❑ A space character: 0x20

The Namespaces Property

This read/write property can be used to determine whether the writer should have namespace support and defaults to `True`. Set it to `False` to have no namespace support. Setting it to `False` will improve performance slightly as no mapping is required between nodes and namespaces; however, it loses all the power offered by namespaces and so is recommended against.

The QuoteChar Property

This read/write property determines the quote character used for attributes and defaults to a double quote (`0x34`).

Alternatively it can be set to a single quote character (`0x39`).

The BaseStream Property

This is a read-only property and will return the `Stream` object that is being used by the `XmlWriter` (or `null` when there is no underlying `Stream` object).

If the writer was constructed using a `Stream`, then this property will return the `Stream` that was used in the constructor to the writer. So if a file stream was used (that is, a stream that writes bytes to a file) then the Stream representing the file will be returned. However, if a `TextWriter` instance that inherits from the `StreamWriter` class is used in the constructor then the `BaseStream` will be the same as `StreamWriter.BaseStream`. If the `TextWriter` was not constructed from a `StreamWriter` (such as a `StringWriter` instance), then the `BaseStream` property will return null.

As an example, consider the following code, which is a .NET command-line application:

```
Imports System.Xml
Imports System.IO
Imports System.Text

Module StreamWrite

  Sub Main()
    'Write XML to memory
    Dim ms As MemoryStream = New MemoryStream()

    'Create a new TextWriter
    Dim tr As TextWriter = New StreamWriter(ms)

    'Create an XmlTextWriter from this
    Dim xw As XmlTextWriter = new XmlTextWriter(tr)
    xw.WriteElementString("root","The root element")

    Console.WriteLine(xw.BaseStream.Position)

    xw.Flush()
```

```
        Console.WriteLine(xw.BaseStream.Position)
        xw.BaseStream.Seek(0,SeekOrigin.Begin)
        Console.WriteLine(xw.BaseStream.Position)
    End Sub

End Module
```

The output from this is shown below:

```
0
29
0
```

The first stream that was created was a `MemoryStream` instance which stores the data in memory. Following this a `TextWriter` can be created via the concrete `StreamWriter` instance – the `MemoryStream` instance is passed to the constructor which means anything written to the `TextWriter` can be written directly to the underlying `MemoryStream` instance.

An `XmlTextWriter` instance can then be created from the `TextWriter` instance which is passed to the constructor. Now, with an `XmlTextWriter` instance we can write XML – the goal we are ultimately after (well, in this book anyway!). We don't write anything interesting – just a root element and some text, but immediately after this we use the `BaseStream` property to return a reference to the `MemoryStream` (after all, this is the stream that everything was originally created from). The `Position` property of this stream will then return where we are currently positioned within this stream.

This is zero just now and for good reason. Although we have written to the top level `XmlTextWriter`, we haven't told it to write to the underlying streams. To do this you call the `Flush()` method and this will ensure that data in the `XmlTextWriter` is written to the underlying streams. So, now if we once again check the `Position` of the `BaseStream` property it will be set to 29 – the number of characters in the stream "`<root>The root element</root>`". However, it is set to the end of the stream now, so if we wanted to read the data in the `MemoryStream` we have to set the pointer back to the start of the stream. To do this we can again use the `BaseStream` property to get us a reference to the `MemoryStream` and then use the `Seek()` method to set the new position within this stream. The `Seek()` method takes the first parameter telling us how many bytes to move relative to the position specified by the second parameter – in this case we move 0 characters from the beginning of the `MemoryStream`.

Working with the XmlTextWriter

Now that we have looked in quite a bit of detail at the members of the `XmlWriter` abstract class and `XmlTextWriter` derived class, we're going to extend the brief examples we looked at earlier in the chapter to use more of the new methods and properties we've discussed.

We're going to continue the examples we started looking at in Chapter 3. The structure of the XML document that we are intending to create, the XML document template, is shown below:

```
<?xml version="1.0"?>
<ct:ContactDetails xmlns:ct="http://www.deltabis.com/Contact" updateDate="">
  <contact>
```

```
<name title="">
  <first> </first>
  <middle></middle>
  <last> </last>
</name>

<homeAddress>
    <name> </name>
    <street> </street>
    <city> </city>
    <postcode> </postcode>
</homeAddress>

<workAddress>
    <name> </name>
    <street> </street>
    <city> </city>
    <state> </state>
    <zip></zip>
</workAddress>

    <ct:notes> </ct:notes>
  </contact>
</ct:ContactDetails>
```

We'll continue to use the XmlReader functionality to display our results in the main textbox so we can check our progress.

Try It Out: Creating Child Elements with Nesting

We will typically have to add child nodes to the root element, so let's look at how we can do this, with appropriate formatting.

1. Again, add a new button to the form and change the Text property value to Example 3.

2. Double-click on the button and add the following code to the event handler:

```
Private Sub button3_Click(ByVal sender As System.Object, ByVal e As _
    System.EventArgs) Handles button3.Click

    textBox1.Text = ""

    'Creates document outline
    Const strFileName As String = "WriteXMLExample.xml"
    Dim objXmlTW As XmlTextWriter = New XmlTextWriter(strFileName, Encoding.UTF8)
    'Sets the indentation for the XML file
    objXmlTW.Formatting = Formatting.Indented
    objXmlTW.Indentation = 4

    'Write XML Declaration
    objXmlTW.WriteStartDocument()
```

```
    'Write root element
    objXmlTW.WriteStartElement("ct", "ContactDetails", _
                            "http://www.deltabis.com/Contact")

    'Write attribute to the root element
    objXmlTW.WriteAttributeString("updateDate", "20021201T14:00")

    'Write a comment describing the document
    objXmlTW.WriteComment("This document contains contact information.")

    'Write contact child element node
    objXmlTW.WriteStartElement("contact")

    'Write empty title attribute
    objXmlTW.WriteAttributeString("title", String.Empty)

    'Write <name> element node
    objXmlTW.WriteStartElement("name")

    'Write <first> element node
    objXmlTW.WriteElementString("first", "Steven")

    'Write <middle> element node
    objXmlTW.WriteElementString("middle", String.Empty)

    'Write <last> element node
    objXmlTW.WriteElementString("last", "Livingstone-Perez")

    'Write Full end of <name> element node
    objXmlTW.WriteFullEndElement()

    'Write Full end of <contact> element node
    objXmlTW.WriteFullEndElement()

    objXmlTW.WriteEndElement()

    'End the XML Document
    objXmlTW.WriteEndDocument()

    'Write to the file and close
    objXmlTW.Flush()
    objXmlTW.Close()

    textBox1.Text = textBox1.Text + ReadDocument(strFileName)
End Sub
```

3. Save the file and run the application by pressing *F5*. When the application has started, click the Example3 button and you will get the following output.

```
Examples of Writing XML Documents                    _ □ X

<ct:ContactDetails updateDate="20021201T14:00"
xmlns:ct="http://www.deltabis.com/Contact">
    <!--This document contains contact information.-->
    <contact title="">
        <name>
            <first>Steven</first>
            <middle />
            <last>Livingstone-Perez</last>
        </name>
    </contact>
</ct:ContactDetails>


        Example 1      Example 2      Example 3
```

How It Works

After the root element has been created, and after its attribute have been created, we call the
`WriteComment()` method, passing in the string that we want to create as our comment.

```
objXmlTW.WriteComment("This document contains contact information.")
```

This inserted the following comment into the document:

```
<!--This document contains contact information.-->
```

In this example, as we want to create child elements, it is likely that we also want them to be formatted
in the traditional way that XML documents are formatted with indentation for child element nodes. To
do this, we set the `Formatting` property of the `XmlTextWriter` instance to `Indented` and set the
`Indentation` property to four characters (the default character is a space in this case as this is the
default value of the Indentation property).

```
objXmlTW.Formatting = Formatting.Indented
objXmlTW.Indentation = 4
```

Following this, and after the root element has been opened and its attribute created, the contact child
element node is opened using the `WriteStartElement()` method. Also, an attribute called `title` is
created with the `WriteAttributeString()` method and is currently set to be empty using the
`String.Empty` property (we will see this being populated later in the examples).

```
'Write contact child element node
objXmlTW.WriteStartElement("contact")

'Write empty title attribute
objXmlTW.WriteAttributeString("title",String.Empty)
```

Next, to create child nodes of the contact element, just call the `WriteStartElement()` method
before calling any method to close the contact element. So we open a new element node called `name`
and write three child elements called `first`, `middle`, and `last` using the `WriteElementString()`
method because these elements only have text child nodes.

```
'Write <first> element node
objXmlTW.WriteStartElement("name")

'Write <first> element node
objXmlTW.WriteElementString("first","Steven")

'Write <middle> element node
objXmlTW.WriteElementString("middle",String.Empty)

'Write <last> element node
objXmlTW.WriteElementString("last","Livingstone-Perez")
```

When these elements have been added we close the name element with the `WriteFullEndElement()` method call to close both the `name` element and `contact` element nodes. We just use this here to illustrate its use – you could equally have used `WriteEndElement()` in this case:

```
'Write Full end of <name> element node
objXmlTW.WriteFullEndElement()

'Write Full end of <contact> element node
objXmlTW.WriteFullEndElement()
```

Sometimes we may want the values of our attributes to be more complex than a simple string, such as including character entities (for example, an Asian character representation in Unicode) or general entities (such as an `&copy;` entity to reference a string defined in the DTD and is used throughout the document) as we discussed earlier.

We looked at creating the `title` attribute of the contact element and deliberately left it empty. Let's look at how we can populate this value now.

Try It Out: Adding Qualified Attribute Values

1. Add a new button to the form and call it `Example 4`.

2. Double-click the button and copy over the code from the `button3_click` event handler into the `button4_click` event handler. Within the code, we're going to make one small change. In the previous example, we had the following code:

```
'Write empty title attribute
objXmlTW.WriteAttributeString("title", String.Empty)
```

Change these lines as shown in the highlighted lines below:

```
Private Sub button4_Click(ByVal sender As System.Object, ByVal e As _
   System.EventArgs) Handles button4.Click

   '... Same code as above

   'Write contact child element node
   objXmlTW.WriteStartElement("contact")
```

```
    'Add in Qualified Title Attribute
    objXmlTW.WriteStartAttribute("title", Nothing)
    objXmlTW.WriteQualifiedName("Mr.","http://www.deltabis.com/ns/titles/")
    objXmlTW.WriteEndAttribute()


    'Write <name> element node
    objXmlTW.WriteStartElement("name")


    '... Same code as above
End Sub
```

3. Save the file and run the application by pressing *F5*. When the application has started, click the **Example 4** button and you will get the following output:

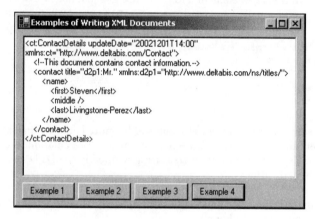

How It Works

This time, after we have created the contact element, the `WriteStartAttribute()` method is called to open an attribute. The `title` is specified as the name in the first parameter and the second namespace parameter is set to null so the attribute won't be explicitly associated with any namespace.

```
    'Add in Qualified Title Attribute
    objXmlTW.WriteStartAttribute("title",Nothing)
```

Next, with the attribute not yet closed, we can call methods that create the value of the attribute. In our case we want to create a value that itself is actually qualified in a namespace defining the titles people can have, such as Mr., Miss, Mrs., and so on. To do this the `WriteQualifiedName()` method is called passing in the value of the attribute, `"Mr."`, in the first parameter and in the second parameter the namespace that this value is to be associated with, that is, `http://www.deltabis.com/ns/titles/`.

```
    objXmlTW.WriteQualifiedName("Mr.","http://www.deltabis.com/ns/titles/")
```

The output from this call is as follows:

```
<contact title="d2p1:Mr." xmlns:d2p1=" http://www.deltabis.com/ns/titles/"/>
```

This may be a little confusing as a namespace definition and attribute has magically appeared on the `contact` element and the prefix is also used in the value of the `title` attribute – and we didn't do that, did we?

Well, when you created the new qualified attribute, the writer doesn't just add the value appended by the namespace, it actually first checks to see if the namespace has been previously defined and some prefix associated with it. If this is true, this prefix is reused to qualify the value of the attribute. However, in our case the namespace had never been declared before, so the writer creates a new prefix for us, appends it to the value of the attribute and also creates a new namespace definition on the element bound to this prefix.

This raises an important point. No matter what prefix you use, always, but *always* work with the namespace that a node is qualified in. Prefixes are *always* expanded to their namespace associated and so the parser will always see `http://www.deltabis.com/ns/titles/` rather than d2p1. So avoid comparing prefixes or expecting prefixes when creating your code.

After all this has been done, the `WriteEndAttribute()` method is called to close the attribute.

```
objXmlTW.WriteEndAttribute()
```

Try It Out: Adding a CDATA Section and Creating Valid XML

Often you have to add data to your XML document that can be potentially not well-formed or invalid in XML. For example if you use the < character in some data and don't escape it, the XML will be invalid. Let's look at how a CDATA section, which can contain any character data (including the XML special characters such as & and <) and this data is not interpreted by the XML parser, can be used to ensure that this doesn't happen. We will also look at some more general cases where you want to ensure your XML stays valid.

1. Add a new button to the form and call in `Example 5`.

2. Double-click the button, copy over the code from the previous event handler, and add the following highlighted lines:

```
Private Sub button5_Click(ByVal sender As System.Object, ByVal e As _
    System.EventArgs) Handles button5.Click

    '... Same code as above

    'Write Full end of <name> element node
    objXmlTW.WriteFullEndElement()

    'Write notes element
    objXmlTW.WriteStartElement("notes","http://www.deltabis.com/Contact")
    objXmlTW.WriteRaw("CEO of NTA Limited, producer of the ProPortal")
    objXmlTW.WriteCharEntity("©")
```

```
objXmlTW.WriteRaw(" system at http://www.deltabis.net. Security token is: ")

objXmlTW.WriteCData("<securityAlgorithm>88hhdhddhs8*&W^H¥@HKJW)~~d" _
         & "<ssssowowo>>sswooowsw&(*&&^£&DJnxxj</securityAlgorithm>")

objXmlTW.WriteEndElement()

    'Write Full end of <contact> element node
    objXmlTW.WriteFullEndElement()

    '... Same code as above
End Sub
```

3. Save the file and run the application by pressing *F5*. When the application has started, click the Example 5 button and you will get the following output:

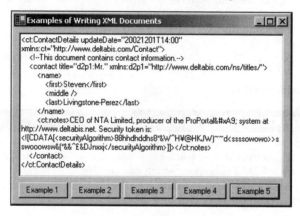

How It Works

The last element node of each contact node is used to create additional general purpose notes about the contact you have created. In the template this element is actually qualified by the namespace the ct prefix is bound to (we will see the effect of this later in the book when we cover the schemas chapters).

So the first thing we do is open an element called notes, qualified in the http://www.deltavis.com/Contact namespace.

```
objXmlTW.WriteStartElement("notes","http://www.deltabis.com/Contact")
```

The result is that the notes element is created, appended by the ct prefix as the writer checks the document to see if this namespace has already been declared and is in scope, and uses the prefix previously assigned to it, in this case ct.

Following this, some text is written as a child of this element using the WriteRaw() method which will directly write the string specified without escaping any characters in it, so beware of creating invalid XML as you won't get an exception until you try to read the document. Hence the following works:

```
objXmlTW.WriteRaw("CEO of NTA Limited, producer of the ProPortal")
```

However, it we had written something like the following, it would have rendered the XML invalid and when you tried to read this with the `XmlTextReader` you would get an exception.

```
objXmlTW.WriteRaw("CEO of NTA Limited & ABC Corp, producer of the ProPortal")
```

To write the above example so that it would be valid, you'd have to use the & character entity `&amp;`.

Next we wish to write out the copyright character, ©. Now although entering this character directly into the document may be fine in most encodings, if you, for example, enter this character directly in Notepad and save in ANSI format, then the file will fail when read by an XML parser that thinks it is UTF-8 encoded. So a document that was perfectly valid when you created it may end up being invalid because its encoding is not understood or is misinterpreted by the parser. If the character was some unusual character or one from an Eastern language, its pretty certain it would fail in most Western systems that don't have language support for those characters. To ensure that it doesn't fail, we can go back to Unicode which helps us ensure that no matter what encoding may be specified in the XML document, we can escape the output using the `WriteCharEntity()` method which will write the Unicode character reference for the given character. Hence the call:

```
objXmlTW.WriteCharEntity("©")
```

will write out `&#xA9;` instead of the copyright symbol which makes it a lot safer when working with the XML document. Next, after another call to `WriteRaw()`, we create a new CDATA section using the `WriteCData()` method:

```
objXmlTW.WriteRaw(" system at http://www.deltabis.net. Security token is: ")
objXmlTW.WriteCData("<securityAlgorithm>88hhdhddhs8*&W^H¥@HKJW)~~d<ssssowowo>>" _
& "sswooowsw&(*&&^£&DJnxxj</securityAlgorithm>")
```

The reason we want to do this, in this case, is because the contact has given us some kind of security public key that can be used to encrypt any messages you may want to send to him (this algorithm is completely random as an illustrative example, but expect to see more and more of this kind of thing as digital signatures become more popular!). If you look at the text within this method, you will see that there are a few characters that may cause our XML parser some problems if not escaped. So, by calling the `WriteCData()` method and wrapping the text in a CDATA section, we ensure that the text will cause the XML to be invalid.

Finally, the `notes` element is closed with a call to `WriteEndElement()`.

```
objXmlTW.WriteEndElement()
```

In this example we used the `WriteRaw()` method, the `WriteCharEntity()` method, and the `WriteCData()` method. These methods are all defined in the `XmlWriter` class, and implemented in the `XmlTextWriter` class.

Try It Out: Creating the Full XML Document

In this example we are going to create the full sample application XML document by adding the last few parts to our example.

1. Add a new button to the form and call it `Example 6`.

2. Double-click the button, and again copy in the code from the previous event handler. Then, add the following highlighted code:

```
Private Sub button6_Click(ByVal sender As System.Object, ByVal e As _
    System.EventArgs) Handles button6.Click
    '... Same code as above

    'Write Full end of <name> element node
    objXmlTW.WriteFullEndElement()

    'Write <homeAddress> element node
    objXmlTW.WriteStartElement("homeAddress")

    'Write <name> element node
    objXmlTW.WriteElementString("name", "Steven Livingstone")

    'Write <street> element node
    objXmlTW.WriteElementString("street", "61 Bralan Road")

    'Write <city> element node
    objXmlTW.WriteElementString("city", "Glasgow")

    'Write <postcode> element node
    objXmlTW.WriteElementString("postcode", "CB11JR")

    'Write Full end of <workAddress> element node
    objXmlTW.WriteFullEndElement()

    'Write <homeAddress> element node
    objXmlTW.WriteStartElement("workAddress")

    'Write <name> element node
    objXmlTW.WriteElementString("name", "NTA Limited")

    'Write <street> element node
    objXmlTW.WriteElementString("street", "7283 San Calle")
    'Write <city> element node
    objXmlTW.WriteElementString("city", "San Jose")

    'Write Notes element
    objXmlTW.WriteStartElement("notes","http://www.deltabis.com/Contact")

    '... Same code as above
End Sub
```

3. Save the file and run the application by pressing *F5*. When the application has started, click the **Example 6** button and you will get the following output:

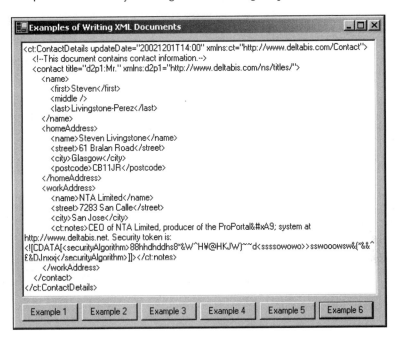

How It Works

This time, after the first name element node and its child nodes have been created, there are two sibling nodes created before the notes element. This uses a combination of `WriteStartElement()`, `WriteElementString()`, and `WriteEndElement()` to create the document structure.

While we've not introduced any new functionality by adding these last few nodes, we have now finished our document, and it does indeed follow the format we described earlier. If we had a DTD or schema against which we could validate our XML data, we would have produced a document that would pass validation.

Writing Large Chunks of Data

We discussed the methods that are available in the .NET Framework for working with binary data and larger chunks of data earlier in the chapter. A piece of functionality that has often been missing when working with XML has been the easy ability to include images within the XML document itself, rather than as a separate file or set of files that can get easily separated. However, you also have to be careful because although there are methods provided to accomplish this, you want to limit it to circumstances where there is a significant binding between the text data and the binary data. Binary data is more efficient and faster when read directly (rather than decoded first as would be required when it is embedded in an XML file) and XML tools (that is, parsers) themselves are optimized to work with text content and not binary data. However, there may be a time where you want to send someone your résumé and include with it an encoded image of yourself – this is where writing binary data within XML files can be very powerful.

You can use the `WriteBase64()` and `ReadBase64()` methods to encode an image within an XML file and then read it back out when you want to display it.

The `WriteBase64()` method encodes binary bytes as base64 and writes the resulting text. This method takes a byte array of the entity to be encoded as the first parameter. The second parameter is an integer specifying the start position for the encoder within this array (it is common to iterate through the through a large byte array and stream out sections on the array) and the final parameter is an integer of the number of bytes to encode.

The advantages of encoding images are that you can be sure that no invalid XML characters are being used in the file that would cause a document with the binary image within it to fail on parsing. The fact that you can then store the encoded image with the XML file ensures that all documents are kept together (rather than pointing at some location which may change).

Base64 encoding is defined at http://www.ietf.org/rfc/rfc2045) and uses the characters A-Z, a-z, 0-9 as well as +, / and = to encode a binary stream.

You could encode a file as base64 as follows:

```
'Read in the file Image.jpg to a BinaryReader
Dim binRead As BinaryReader = New BinaryReader("image.jpg")

'Loop through the reader reading len number of bytes until we have read them all
Do
   'get len bytes into base64Buffer byte array
   readByte = binRead.Read(base64Buffer, 0, len)

    'write readByte number of bytes encoded in base64 to writer
   xw.WriteBase64(base64Buffer, 0, readByte)
Loop While (len <= readByte)
```

With a binary reader you can read an image and then you iterate though this `BinaryReader` object and use the `WriteBase64()` method to write the encoding format to the output stream.

Similarly you can read the data using the following code:

```
'read binary data into array
Dim readByte As Integer = 0
Dim bytesToRead As Integer = 100

'Create a buffer to hold the binary data
Dim base64Buffer(100) As Byte

'Read 50 bytes from the reader to the base64Buffer byte array
len = reader.ReadBase64(base64Buffer, 0, 50)

'loop while there are still bytes left in the file; that is, len not zero
Do
   readByte = binRead.Read(base64Buffer, 0, bytesToRead)
   objXmlTW.WriteBase64(base64Buffer, 0, readByte)
```

```
    'loop through buffer and write each byte to the output
    Dim i as Integer = 0
    For i=0 To base64len-1
      Console.Write(base64Buffer(i))
    Next
  Loop While (bytesToRead <= readByte)
```

In this case, a buffer is created up front and the data is read into the buffer. The buffer can then be iterated through and the file written to an output stream.

Try It Out: Encoding an Image

In this first example we are going to look at how to encode a message so that it can be embedded within an XML document. To simplify things we will encode only the root element and a single child element containing the image.

1. Firstly, we need the image file for our example. Download `image.gif` from the code download for this chapter, and save it within our project folder. The image in its normal state looks as follows:

2. To continue with our example, add a new button to the form and call it `Example 7`.

3. In the event handler for our button, enter the following highlighted lines of code:

```
Private Sub button7_Click(ByVal sender As System.Object, ByVal e As _
    System.EventArgs) Handles button7.Click

    'Read the image into a FileStream
    Dim fs As FileStream = New FileStream("..\\image.gif", _
                                    System.IO.FileMode.Open)

    'Pass the file stream to a BinaryReader
    Dim binRead As BinaryReader = New BinaryReader(fs)

    'create the text writer to insert data to
    Dim objXmlTW As XmlTextWriter = _
         New XmlTextWriter("..\\contactsWithImage.xml", System.Text.Encoding.UTF8)

    'Write XML Declaration
    objXmlTW.WriteStartDocument()

    'Write root element
    objXmlTW.WriteStartElement("ct", "ContactDetails", _
                        "http://www.deltabis.com/Contact")
```

```
'Write image element with encoded data
objXmlTW.WriteStartElement("image")
objXmlTW.WriteAttributeString("companyLogo", "image.gif")

'read binary data into array
Dim readByte As Integer = 0
Dim bytesToRead As Integer = 100

'Create a buffer to hold the binary data
Dim base64Buffer(bytesToRead) As Byte

'do this while there are still characters
Do
    readByte = binRead.Read(base64Buffer, 0, bytesToRead)
    objXmlTW.WriteBase64(base64Buffer, 0, readByte)
Loop While (bytesToRead <= readByte)

'close image element
objXmlTW.WriteEndElement()

'close root
objXmlTW.WriteEndElement()

'Write XML Declaration
objXmlTW.WriteEndDocument()

objXmlTW.Flush()
objXmlTW.Close()

textBox1.Text = textBox1.Text + ReadDocument("..\\contactsWithImage.xml")
End Sub
```

4. Add another line at the top of your code next to the other `Imports` declarations:

```
Imports System.IO
```

5. Save the file and run the application by pressing *F5*. When the application has started, click the **Example7** button and you will get the following output.

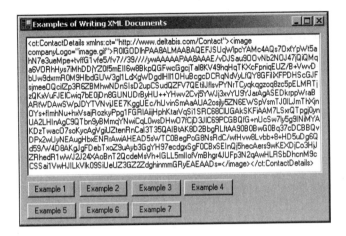

How It Works

We first load the image into a `FileStream` instance, so that we can actually access the data.

```
System.IO.FileStream fs = _
    new System.IO.FileStream("..\\..\\image.gif",System.IO.FileMode.Open)
```

We next want to read the binary data of this image, so the `FileStream` is passed into the constructor of a `BinaryReader` instance.

```
System.IO.BinaryReader binRead = new System.IO.BinaryReader(fs)
```

Now we are in a position to start reading the data, but we have nowhere to write it to. So we next create an `XmlTextWriter` instance so that we can create our XML document and send it to the file `contactsWithImage.xml`.

```
XmlTextWriter objXmlTW = _
    new XmlTextWriter("..\\contactsWithImage.xml",System.Text.Encoding.UTF8)
```

We then open the document and write the XML declaration, write out a root `ContactDetails` element and then a child `image` element.

```
objXmlTW.WriteStartDocument()
objXmlTW.WriteStartElement("ct","ContactDetails", _
    "http://www.deltabis.com/Contact")

objXmlTW.WriteStartElement("image")
```

It is within this element that we want to write the data about our image. We first declare a byte array to store the bytes returned during each read.

```
Dim bytesToRead As Integer = 100
Dim base64Buffer(bytesToRead) As Byte
```

We then continue to read from the `BinaryReader` while there are still bytes to read. The loop will terminate when the number of bytes to read is less that the number bytes read (that is, the buffer was not filled entirely). Each iterate reads a number of bytes into the `base64Buffer` array, and then all of the bytes written to this buffer are then written to the `XmlTextWriter` instance, and encoded using the `WriterBase64()` method.

```
'do this while there are still characters
Do
   readByte = binRead.Read(base64Buffer, 0, bytesToRead)
   objXmlTW.WriteBase64(base64Buffer, 0, readByte)
Loop While (bytesToRead <= readByte)
```

Next, the XML image, then the `ContactDetails` root element, and finally the XML document itself are closed.

```
'close image element
objXmlTW.WriteEndElement()

'close root
objXmlTW.WriteEndElement()

'Write XML Declaration
objXmlTW.WriteEndDocument()
```

To ensure that the data is actually written back to the base file stream, we call the `Flush()` method and then finally the `Close()` method is called to close the `XmlTextWriter` stream (and hence the base stream `FileStream`).

```
objXmlTW.Flush()
objXmlTW.Close()
```

The data is then displayed in the browser using the `ReadDocument()` method.

```
textBox1.Text += ReadDocument("..\\contactsWithImage.xml");
```

As you can see from the figure above, within the image element the data is encoded as base64.

> Note that an alternative to base64 encoding is to use binhex encoding, which can be achieved using the `WriteBinHex()` method. Again, this method takes a byte array as the first parameter, the second parameter is an integer of the first byte to encode in the byte array, and the final parameter is an integer of the number of bytes to encode. BinHex encoding is a common encoding format for the Mac and is defined at http://www.ietf.org/rfc/rfc1741 and uses binary and hexadecimal characters to encode the stream.

Let's now look at how we can decode our base64-encoded image and display the original image once more.

Try It Out: Decoding an Image

In this example we are going to look at how to *decode* the binary image we encoded in the last example and write it to a file on the user's drive. Although we are doing this locally, this XML file could have been sent anywhere in the world and the image that was embedded can still be extracted and saved!

1. Add a new button to the form and call it `Example 8`.

2. Double-click the button and add the following code to the event handler:

```
Private Sub button8_Click(ByVal sender As System.Object, ByVal e As _
    System.EventArgs) Handles button8.Click

    Dim xt As XmlTextReader = New XmlTextReader("..\\contactsWithImage.xml")

    'Read the image into a FileStream
    Dim fs As FileStream = New FileStream("..\\wroximage.gif", _
    System.IO.FileMode.Create)

    Dim bw As BinaryWriter = New BinaryWriter(fs)

    'Read binary data into array
    Dim readByte As Integer = 0
    Dim bytesToRead As Integer = 100

    'Create a buffer to hold the binary data
    Dim base64Buffer(bytesToRead) As Byte

    While (xt.Read())
      If (xt.Name = "image" And xt.NodeType = XmlNodeType.Element) Then
    Do
        readByte = xt.ReadBase64(base64Buffer, 0, bytesToRead)
        bw.Write(base64Buffer, 0, readByte)
    Loop While (readByte >= bytesToRead)
      End If
    End While

    bw.Flush()
    bw.Close()

    xt.Close()
End Sub
```

3. Save the file and run the application by pressing *F5*. When the application has started, click the **Example8** button and a new file called `wroximage.gif` will be created in the project directory. You can view this by browsing to the project directory using Windows Explorer. You can open the image in Internet Explorer or an image editor (such as Paint) and you will see the re-created image.

How It Works

To read in the XML document we created an `XmlTextReader` instance, with the path to the file we created earlier in the constructor.

```
XmlTextReader xt = new XmlTextReader("..\\contactsWithImage.xml")
```

Next, we know we are going to extract an image and write it to the file system, so we create a `FileStream` object pointing to the file `wroximage.gif` and create a `BinaryWriter` instance from this.

```
'Read the image into a FileStream
System.IO.FileStream fs = _
New System.IO.FileStream("..\\wroximage.gif",System.IO.FileMode.Create)
BinaryWriter bw = New BinaryWriter(fs)
```

Like in the previous example, we need a buffer to store the encoded data as it is read from the XML document, so we create a new byte array to do this.

```
Dim bytesToRead As Integer = 100

'Create a buffer to hold the binary data
Dim base64Buffer(bytesToRead) As Byte
```

We then read each node in the `XmlTextReader` until we find the image element where the encoded data can be found.

```
While (xt.Read())
   If (xt.Name = "image" And xt.NodeType = XmlNodeType.Element) Then
```

Within this section we use the `ReadBase64()` method of the `XmlTextReader`. We passed the buffer to read the data into, with 0 indicating we have to start at the first element of the byte array and the final parameter is the number of bytes to read. When the byte array is populated, the `Write()` method of the `BinaryWriter` instance will write the contents of the byte array to the stream. This continues while there is still encoded data within the XML document.

```
Do
   readByte = xt.ReadBase64(base64Buffer, 0, bytesToRead)
   bw.Write(base64Buffer, 0, readByte)
Loop While (readByte >= bytesToRead)
   End If
End While
```

When this process has completed, the BinaryWriter `Flush()` method is called to write the data to the underlying file stream and the stream is then closed (and hence so is the `FileStream`). Finally, the `XmlTextReader` stream is also closed.

```
bw.Flush()
bw.Close()

xt.Close()
```

We could use this technique to navigate to find the same image that was encoded in the previous Try It Out. This is a powerful means of keeping binary data with the XML document. However, it should be emphasized that working with binary data in XML files is quite inefficient and work is going on to determine the best way of doing this. One popular method is to use the MIME extensions commonly used with email to pass images with XML data. This is in fact one method used with the Simple Object Access Protocol; we discuss this in Chapter 11.

Summary

This chapter was much more practical than any of the chapters so far, as you start to gain a solid understanding of how to use XML and VB.NET with the `XmlTextReader` and `XmlTextWriter` classes. In this chapter we:

- ❑ Looked at the `XmlWriter` abstract class and discussed the important properties and methods of that class.

- ❑ Covered the only current concrete implementation of the `XmlWriter` class, the `XmlTextWriter` class.

- ❑ Continued our case study by using the writer to create the entire XML document including writing elements, attributes, CDATA sections, and character entities.

- ❑ Demonstrated a practical example of encoding and decoding an image that can be embedded directly within an XML document.

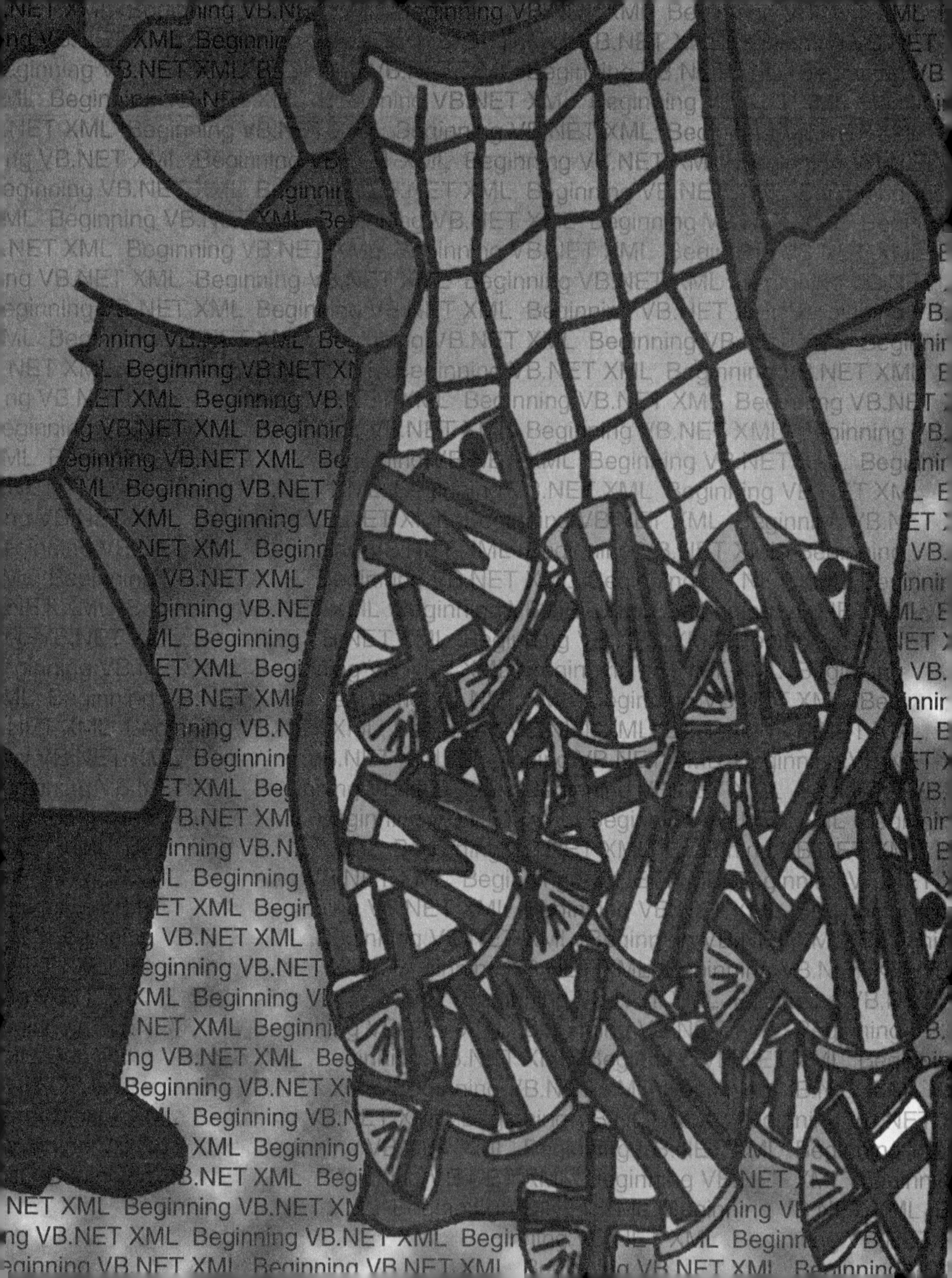
Beginning VB.NET XML

Implementation of the DOM in .NET

By now you will have a good understanding of XML and the technologies involved. You have also learned how to apply some of the most fundamental XML base classes to these technologies to see how you can create some very powerful applications very easily.

This chapter is going to look at how the Document Object Model (DOM) is implemented in the .NET Framework. We looked at the theory of the DOM in Chapter 3; it may be worth reading the start of Chapter 3 again to refresh your memory, as we are going to cover that material in more detail here. In short, we looked at the terminology used in XML and the Document Object Model, as well as the core interfaces provided by the DOM. We discussed namespaces and how qualified XPath queries can be created to select nodes from a document that uses namespaces. We will go into further detail about XPath in the following chapter.

In this chapter, you will learn:

- ❑ What the DOM is and how it differs from streaming models
- ❑ Using the XmlNode class
- ❑ Using the XmlDocument class
- ❑ Using the DOM with the ongoing case study

Before we start to go into any detail on the DOM, it is worth refreshing our minds by looking briefly at what the DOM is and how it is different from the streaming model discussed in the previous two chapters.

The Document Object Model

As should be familiar, the Document Object Model (DOM) the Document Object Model (DOM) class is an in-memory representation of an XML document. The DOM allows you to programmatically read, manipulate, and modify an XML document as defined by the W3C standard W3C DOM Level 1 and DOM W3C Level 2 specifications available at http://www.w3.org/TR/DOM-Level-2/core.html.

As we discussed previously, the DOM Core defines a set of objects and standard interfaces shown in the diagram below.

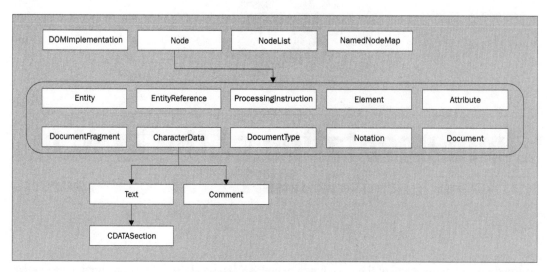

At the top of the interface hierarchy is the Node interface, representing any node in the XML document tree, from which every other node is derived – this is the interface we will look at in most detail in this chapter. Additionally, we will look at the NodeList and NamedNodeMap interfaces.

DOM versus Streaming Models

In Chapter 4 we discussed XmlReader and how it implements a streaming model, in much the same way that SAX does. We also described how streaming models differ from the Document Object Model and the advantages and disadvantages from a streaming point of view.

In real terms, DOM and streaming models can be used in quite different scenarios. Consider the case where you have data from your web site archived on a daily basis – from week to week the level of traffic may vary, so whereas one week you could have an XML file with a small number of entries, the next week it may contain a great deal more. If you wanted to display some data from this report in a web browser, you would be more likely to use a streaming model than the DOM because the DOM could take a noticeable length of time to load into memory and parse the XML document. The streaming model, however, would very quickly read through the data and return the information you are interested in. This scenario could also apply to indexes containing a list of information about documents on your site or archives of information where you are looking for a specific set of data. The DOM, however, is better suited to smaller documents or where you want to randomly access data within your document. So you may have a list of products ordered by a given customer and each of these has an Order ID defining the order item. The definition of this order may be later in the XML document and so you will want to get the ID and then access the definition of the order to write out a friendly name – this is much easier to achieve using DOM than a streaming model. This last point is important, because although the document may be large, if you intend to randomly access nodes in the document then you will be better using the DOM, because streaming will often require multiple reads to get random data.

Below are some scenarios where you will commonly use a streaming model:

- ❑ Reading an XML document containing information serialized from a database (that is, a table or set of tables in a database that have been converted to an XML equivalent).

- ❑ You want to build an invoice web page from a XML document containing invoice information or calculate a running total.

- ❑ Reading XML data that is asynchronous, such as data that comes from a remote web site via a web service. You may want to start processing the data immediately rather than wait for all of it to be transferred.

- ❑ Creating a large document where the data that is being written is retrieved asynchronously – this could be data that is retrieved from an HTTP POST such as a large invoice or a product catalog.

The DOM, on the other hand, will be most often used in the following cases:

- ❑ Creating a new XML document such as a person's name and address information from data in a Windows form or submitted via a web form

- ❑ Updating invoice information about a particular customer.

- ❑ Outputting a custom HTML document based on different parts of the XML document.

- ❑ Creating a new XML document based on parts of XML from the original document.

- ❑ Retrieving XML data from a remote web site or via an HTTP POST where the size of the data to be transferred is relatively small and so it can be transferred and immediately loaded.

Remember that the DOM creates a tree of the nodes in the document, and that this is built up and stored in memory before any processing on the document is done. This means two things – the first is an impact in the parsing and loading of the XML document, and the second is that memory is used while you work with the document. The latter point is generally not a significant issue unless the size of the document gets extremely large, but the first point is important. If you remember back to our streaming model discussion, you'll remember that it avoids this by never loading the entire document into memory. Instead it works sequentially through the XML document and either uses event handlers to do some work when finding a given node, or pulls the current node back to the application (as implemented by the `XmlReader` class).

From this point of view, streaming models offer some advantages over the DOM, such as potentially huge improvements in performance for very large documents, and filtering of the document to produce an alternative output.

The DOM, however, has its own advantages over streaming models, such as allowing editing of the document in memory, better support for other XML standard technologies such as XPath and Namespaces, and allowing random access to the document from any point. It also has the following properties:

- ❑ It is an official standard from the W3C

- ❑ It has a simple programming model, consisting of calling methods and properties

- ❑ You can randomly access the data in the document (for instance, use XPath to get to particular document fragments)

- ❑ Better integration with XPath, allowing it to be used to generate more complex queries (even joining nodes from different parts of the document at the same time) than the simple sequential queries provided by streaming

It is supported by many browsers, including Internet Explorer and Netscape Navigator.

One of the key points of the DOM is that it is read/write capable, and so allows direct updates to the tree in memory without redirecting to some other output. This makes it extremely efficient for adding, updating, or removing information from the structure.

.NET DOM Inheritance Model

Up to this point most of the work we have been doing using the DOM has been theoretical. We have used many of the types of nodes defined in the DOM when working with the readers and writers previously, so we at least have a basic knowledge of what these are. We met the `XmlNode` earlier when we looked at the `XmlNodeReader` in Chapter 4, but we never looked into much detail on the reader aspects. However, what you may have noticed was that the `XmlNode` node type could be used to store element nodes, attribute nodes, and any other kind of DOM nodes as defined in the earlier diagram. In fact the .NET Framework defines a class hierarchy that reflects the DOM architecture, with some additional classes to improve the usability of the classes.

The following diagram shows the .NET DOM inheritance model:

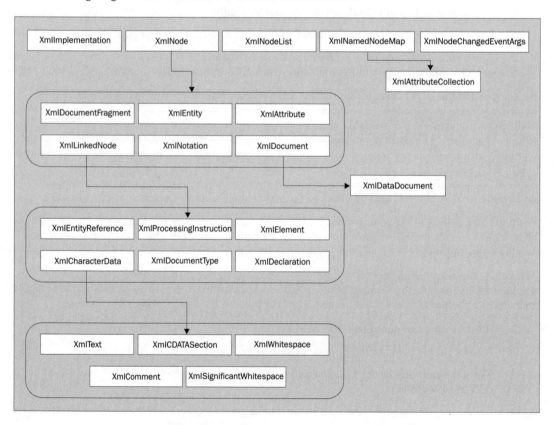

If you look back at the first figure in this chapter depicting the W3C DOM hierarchy, you will find an almost exact match between the interfaces defined in that and the interfaces defined in the .NET DOM hierarchy shown above. This is significant as it demonstrates that the .NET Framework does in fact conform to the standard DOM interfaces defined by the W3C. This means that developers don't have to learn new interfaces when they apply their existing knowledge of the DOM to .NET and even means that developers who typically work in other languages and environments don't have to learn new interface details if they want to work with the DOM. In fact in most cases you can take away the Xml prefix at the start of the name and it is the same name as the W3C interface. Once again the XmlNode is at the root of the hierarchy, with many other types inheriting from it.

We are going to look at what is provided in the .NET Framework to support the DOM interfaces; we will start by considering the XmlImplementation class, which forms the basis of the .NET DOM implementation.

The XmlImplementation Class

The XmlImplementation class allows you to create new XmlDocument objects representing empty XML documents using the CreateDocument() method. It can be used as follows:

```
Dim objXImp As XmlImplementation = new XmlImplementation()
Dim objXDoc As XmlDocument = objXImp.CreateDocument()
```

The XmlDocument class is discussed in detail later in the chapter. When XmlDocument instances are created using the same XmlImplementation instance, they share the same XmlNameTable – this is the table that contains the attribute and element names. These names are stored as CLR objects and so two XmlDocument instances with the same XmlNameTable can be compared using types rather than string comparison of element and attribute names.

The XmlNode Class

XmlNode is the abstract base class of every other node in the DOM and defines a whole host of members that are either inherited or overridden in the lower classes, providing access to elements, attributes, and other node types.

We are going to look at the XmlNode in detail very shortly, so we will defer discussion until the section called *The XmlNode Class* later.

The XmlNodeList Class

This class represents an ordered collection of nodes from an XML document and allows you to iterate through the nodes or access a given node. It is a live list, therefore any changes that you make to child nodes are reflected in the nodes returned by the methods and properties of XmlNodeList. This is useful when you have selected nodes from an XML document and want to do something with each node – so you could select all of the product element nodes from an XML file containing catalog data and return these as an XmlNodeList which you may iterate through and output the name of the product.

Typically the node list will be the result of an XPath query used with the XmlDocument class, this is discussed in the section on XmlDocument later in the chapter. XmlNodeList defines two public properties:

❑ Count – Returns an integer of the number of nodes in the XmlNodeList.

❑ ItemOf – Retrieves the node at a given index.

It also defines two public methods:

❑ GetEnumerator() – This provides a foreach style of iteration over the node list.

❑ Item() – This will return the node at the index (zero-based) given in the argument.

As an example, the following code snippet would output the name of each node in the node list. We will use the GetElementsByTagName() method of the XmlDocument class, which takes the name of the element you want to search for as a string, and then selects all descendant nodes that have that name, returning a NodeList containing references to the matching nodes.

```
. . .
Dim myNodeList As XmlNodeList = objXDoc.GetElementsByTagName("name")
Dim node As XmlNode

'Iterate through XmlNodeList
For Each node In myNodeList
   Console.WriteLine(node.Name & " in " & node.NamespaceURI & "\n")
'Next node
. . .
```

Alternatively, we can use a For loop to iterate through the node list and output the InnerText property of the current node.

```
. . .
Dim myNames As XmlNodeList = objXDoc.GetElementsByTagName("lastname")
Dim i As Integer = 0
For i = 0 To myNames.Count - 1
   Console.WriteLine(myNames(i).Name & " in " & myNames(i).InnerText & "\n")
Next
. . .
```

A collection of nodes can be stored as an XmlNodeList, which is an ordered collection of nodes that you can either access directly via an index, or iterate through. An XmlNodeList can contain a group of any kind of nodes and is often arrived at via an XPath query or while working up or down a DOM tree. So, for example, an XmlNodeList may contain:

❑ A collection of sibling element nodes at a given depth of the XmlDocument tree

❑ The attributes present on a given element node

The XmlLinkedNode class (shown in the previous diagram) is used to access nodes that can have siblings, such as elements and character data. The XmlCharacterData class derives a number of classes dealing with nodes such as text nodes, CDATA sections, and whitespace nodes.

The XmlNamedNodeMap Class

The W3C DOM `NamedNodeMap` interface and corresponding `XmlNamedNodeMap` .NET implementation provide access to a collection of nodes via their name or an index. This class defines a single `Count` property returning the number of nodes in the `XmlNamedNodeMap` collection. Beyond the `GetEnumerator()` method which basically does the same as the one for the `XmlNodeList`, there are four other methods defined by this class:

- ❑ `GetNamedItem()` – this method has two overloads and will return a given item when passed either the name of the `XmlNode` or the name of the `XmlNode` as well as the namespace it is in.

- ❑ `Item()` – this method will return the `XmlNode` at the index passed as an argument in `XmlNamedNodeMap` to the method.

- ❑ `RemoveNamedItem()` – this method has two overloads and removes the item from the `XmlNamedNodeMap` that is passed by name in the argument or the item passed by name as well as the namespace it is in.

- ❑ `SetNamedItem()` – this method takes an `XmlNode` as a parameter and adds it to the map, replacing an existing one if the names of the nodes are the same.

The following section of code will use the `GetNamedItem()` method discussed above to set the value of the `age` attribute of the document element to 28. It will then use the `RemoveNamedItem()` method to remove the `d-o-b` attribute from the document element node.

```
Dim attribMap As XmlNamedNodeMap = doc.DocumentElement.Attributes
Dim attribAge As XmlAttribute = CType(attribMap.GetNamedItem("age"), XmlAttribute)
attribAge.Value = "28"

attribs.RemovedNamedItem("d-o-b")
```

Note that when you are working with an XML document and you have updated the named node map, the underlying XML document will also be updated. So adding a new node using the `SetNamedItem()` method will also add a new node to the underlying `XmlDocument`.

You may prefer to use this over the `XmlNodeList` class when you want to work with names rather than indexes. For example, you may prefer to use `GetNamedItem("date")` rather than `Item(4)` – this is useful if items might be added to the node in question that would affect the indexes (that is, adding a new node before it would cause all indexes to increase by one).

The XmlAttributeCollection Class

The `XmlNamedNodeMap` class also derives an `XmlAttributeCollection` class, which represents a collection of attributes that can be accessed, modified, or removed. This is an extension by .NET to the W3C DOM Recommendation. This class, in fact, extends methods available in the `XmlNamedNodeMap` class quite extensively.

The XmlNodeChangedEventArgs Class

The last of our top-level .NET classes is the `XmlNodeChangedEventArgs` class; this allows you to assign event handlers to nodes within the `XmlDocument` so that you can perform some action when they are modified.

This class will handle the following events:

- ❑ NodeChanging – this event is raised when the Value property of a node is about to be changed.

- ❑ NodeChanged – this event is raised when the Value property of a node has been changed.

- ❑ NodeInserting – occurs when a node belonging to an XmlDocument instance is about to be inserted into another node.

- ❑ NodeInserted – occurs when a node belonging to an XmlDocument instance has been inserted into another node.

- ❑ NodeRemoving – this event is raised when a node is being removed from an XmlDocument.

- ❑ NodeRemoved – this occurs when the node has been removed from the XmlDocument.

The NodeChanging, NodeInserting, and NodeRemoving events allow you to insert some validation or checking rules before the value is finalized – so you can raise an exception if the intended value is invalid according to your business rules and the original state of the node will be restored.

This class is extremely useful for providing business rules for nodes in the XML document so that you can catch any errors before they are inserted. So, if you have an attribute node called age, you may want to know when someone intends to insert some value into this attribute so that you can check it is a valid integer and return an error if it is not, then cancel the insertion. Or, you may have a web form containing the list of orders made by a user that are stored in an XML file. If someone removes one of these orders from the XML file, you can catch this in the NodeRemoved event and update the user interface appropriately.

Additionally, this class defines four public properties:

- ❑ Action – this property will return Insert, Remove, or Change from the XmlNodeChangedAction enumeration depending on the type of node change event that is taking place.

- ❑ NewParent – this will return the value of the XmlNode parent node after the event completes. If the node has been removed it will return null.

- ❑ Node – this property will return the XmlNode that is being inserted, removed, or changed.

- ❑ OldParent – this will return the value of the XmlNode parent node before the event started or null if the node didn't have a parent.

Let's now look in detail at the XmlNode class, which is the abstract base class for all other nodes in the XML Document Object Model.

The XmlNode Class

Now that we have looked at the other classes at the top of the hierarchy, it is time to look at the XmlNode class, which is the base for all node types in the DOM. In fact, we have already looked in quite a bit of detail at the various types of nodes available in the previous two chapters, but it's now time to look at how these nodes are implemented and the functionality available with them.

What is XmlNode?

As all other nodes are derived from the XmlNode class, we will look at the properties and methods of that class and point out the differences of the other derived classes. We will point out in some places the template of how to use these members, but concrete examples will be given when we later come to look at the XmlDocument class.

The XmlNode itself is the abstract base class of every other node in the DOM and defines a whole host of members that are either inherited or overridden in the lower classes. So an element is a node, as is an attribute, a CDATA section and every entity reference within a text node. The great thing with .NET is that you can even extend these classes yourself, although it is recommended (to gain the additional and overridden members that may be added by each specific derived class) to derive the actual node type you want to extend, for example, XmlElement, rather than the XmlNode class itself.

What does XmlNode do?

The XmlNode class represents a single node in the XML document and provides the base methods and properties for navigating the DOM tree. It can use XPath to select a node, or set of nodes based on a given expression. Not only that, but in many XML classes in the .NET Framework, an XmlNode is often the return type, frequently within an XmlNodeList.

There is an XmlNodeType enumeration that contains all of the following node types and can be very useful when you want to do node testing. It is also better to use this enumeration rather than converting everything to strings for testing – firstly to improve efficiency and secondly to avoid errors in the names you write.

As the XmlNode class is the base class for the other node classes we mentioned above, it is worth looking at the members of this class, as they are common across these classes.

The methods and properties defined in the XmlNode class are therefore also available to the derived classes such as XmlElement and XmlAttribute. This means that an XmlNode instance can also represent an instance of an XmlElement, XmlAttribute, or other node types.

You could use the XmlNode class when you are iterating through the various nodes of an XML document where you don't know, up front, what type of node you may be working with. You can therefore use the XmlNode class to work with any kind of node and then use the XmlNodeType enumeration (for processing instruction, element, attribute, and so on) to get the specific type of the node and do some further processing specific to this type.

XmlNode Properties

We will now look at some of the more useful members.

The NodeType Property

The NodeType property returns the type of the current node, which is one of the XmlNodeType enumeration types shown in the bulleted list above. This is an important property as you may wish to provide some conditional functionality to be invoked when a particular node type, or node type in combination with some other property, has certain values.

The `XmlNodeType` enumeration has a member for each type of node, as we discussed in the XPath model in Chapter 3. Remember that many node types can have other node types as children, such as `Attribute`, which can have `Text` and `EntityReference` as children.

The following snippet shows how the `NodeType` property can be used when calling properties specific to a node.

```
While (xRead.Read())
    'Is this node an element?
    If (xRead.NodeType = XmlNodeType.Element)
        'Will return null for attributes
        Console.WriteLine(xRead.Attributes.Count)
    End If

    'Is this node an attribute?
    If (xRead.NodeType = XmlNodeType.Attribute)
        'Will only return owner element for attributes
        Console.WriteLine(xRead.OwnerElement.Name)
    End If

    'Etc
End While
```

In this case we iterate through each of the `XmlNode` nodes of the reader using the `Read()` method. We then check the type of the node, which we can get from the `NodeType` property of the node against the `XmlNodeType` enumeration. If the node is an `Element` node type, then we access the `Attributes` collection and the `Count` property will return the number of attributes attached to this element.

Similarly, if this is an attribute node, then we simply write out the name of the element to which this attribute is attached by using the `OwnerElement` property and then the `Name` property.

The Value Property

This property will get or set the text value of the current node, but varies depending on the `NodeType` of the current node. So while an `Attribute` may have a textual value, an `EndElement` node will have a `null` value. The following list states what is returned by the various node types:

❏   `Attribute` will have the value of the attribute returned

❏   `CDATA` returns the value of the CDATA section

❏   `Comment` returns the content on the comment

❏   `ProcessingInstruction` returns the content of the PI, excluding the target value

❏   `SignificantWhitespace` returns the whitespace between elements (in mixed content)

❏   `Text` will return the value of the text node

❏   `Whitespace` will return the whitespace within elements

❏   `XmlDeclaration` will have the content of the XML declaration

The other node types will all return `null` for the `Value` property.

The following snippet shows how the `Value` property can be used when calling properties specific to a node.

```
While (xRead.Read())
  'Is this node an element?
  If (xRead.NodeType = XmlNodeType.Element)
    'Will return null
    Console.WriteLine(xRead.Value)

    'Will return child text node content
    Console.WriteLine(xRead.InnerText)
  End If

  'Is this node an attribute?
  If (xRead.NodeType = XmlNodeType.Attribute)
    'Will return attribute value
    Console.WriteLine(xRead.Value)
  End If

  'Etc
End While
```

In this case we iterate through each of the `XmlNode` nodes of the reader using the `Read()` method. We again check the type of the node, which we can get from the `NodeType` property of the node against the `XmlNodeType` enumeration. If the node is an `Element` node type, we write out the `Value` of the element that will return null as stated above; the `InnerText` property, however, will write out a string of the text within the element.

Similarly, if this is an attribute node, then we can write out the `Value` property of the attribute, which will display the text value of the attribute.

The HasChildNodes Property

If you think back to Chapter 3 where we discussed parent nodes, child nodes, and sibling nodes, you'll remember that any given node may have a set of child nodes – for example, an `addresses` element may have a series of `address` elements for work and business. In this case, each `address` element is the child node of the `addresses` element, and the `addresses` element is the parent node of each of these `address` elements. Finally, each `address` element is a sibling node of each other `address` element as they are all at the same level with the same parent node.

Turning to the `HasChildNodes` property, this property returns `True` if the current node has any child nodes, otherwise `False`.

This is commonly used when you are going to iterate through the child nodes of some element and want to ensure that the node actually has child nodes prior to invoking the iteration.

Consider the following simple XML document:

```
<chapter>
  <para>
    Some text
  </para>
</chapter>
```

An example code fragment is:

```
If (objNode.hasChildNodes) Then
  'Do some work
End If
```

When `objNode` is the `<chapter>` element node, this will return `True`. When it is at the `<para>` element node it will also return `True` because there are child text nodes. However, when on the `text` node, it will return `False`.

The ChildNodes Property

This read-only property will return an `XmlNodeList` of the child nodes of the current node; otherwise it will return an empty `XmlNodeList`. This is commonly used with an index to return a node at a given position within the `XmlNodeList`, especially when iterating through the items of an `XmlNodeList`.

Consider the following simple XML document:

```
<chapter>
  <para>
    some text
  </para>
  <para>
    some more text
  </para>
</chapter>
```

The sample code fragment below shows how you may use this property in combination with the `HasChildNodes` property above:

```
If (objNode.hasChildNodes) Then
  Dim i As Integer
  For i=0 To objNode.ChildNodes.Count-1
    Console.Write(objNode.ChildNodes(i).Name)
  Next i
End If
```

When the context node is the `<chapter>` element node, this will write out to the console:

para
para

Notice that as the `ChildNodes` property returns the `XmlNodeList`, we can use the `Count` property of this class to give us the number of nodes in the list (two in this case), and then access each by index, and write the element name out using the `XmlNode Name` property.

The FirstChild and LastChild Properties

The `FirstChild` and `LastChild` properties of the `XmlNode` class are used to return the first child node of a given node and the last child node of a given node respectively; they both return `null` if there is no such node.

Remember that attribute nodes are not child nodes of element nodes. Calling `FirstChild` on an element node will return any child element nodes on that element.

Consider the following simple XML document:

```
<chapter title="Reading &amp; Writing">
  <para>
    some text
  </para>
  <para>
    some more text
  </para>
</chapter>
```

So, when on the `<chapter>` element node, the following lines will return the first `<para>` element node and the second `<para>` element node respectively.

```
Dim myFirstChild As XmlNode = objNode.FirstChild    'first para
Dim myLastChild As XmlNode = objNode.LastChild     'second para
```

If you are on the first `para` element, then the `FirstChild` property will return the `Text` node representing the text `some text`.

However, calling these methods on attributes will return the contents of the attribute, which can be made up of multiple node types, such as text and entity references.

The PreviousSibling and NextSibling Properties

The `PreviousSibling` property will return the `XmlNode` corresponding to the node prior to the current node at the same level in the hierarchy and `null` if there is no such node. Similarly, the `NextSibling` will return the `XmlNode` that is next in the document hierarchy at the same level as the current node.

So consider the following simple XML document:

```
<chapter title="Reading &amp; Writing">
  <paraA>
    some text
  </paraA>
  <paraB>
    some more text
  </paraB>
</chapter>
```

When the `<paraB>` element node is the current node, the following first line will return a `paraA` element node and the second line will return `null`.

```
Dim myPreviousSibling As XmlNode = objNode.PreviousSibling    'first paraA
Dim myNextSibling As XmlNode = objNode.NextSibling            'second null
```

The ParentNode Property

The `ParentNode` property will return an `XmlNode` that is the parent of the current node; in cases where the current node doesn't have a parent, it will return `Nothing`. The following table describes the nodes returned for this property.

NodeType	Return value of ParentNode
CDATA	This will return the element or entity reference containing the CDATA section. So, in the following code when the current node is the CDATA section, the `ParentNode` property will return para. `<para><![CDATA[some text]]></para>`
Comment	This will return the element or entity reference, document, or document type containing the comment node.
DocumentType	This will return the document node.
Element	When this is the current node, the `ParentNode` will return the parent element. If in the document root node then the document node will be returned.
EntityReference	The `ParentNode` of this is the element, attribute, or entity reference it is contained within.
ProcessingInstruction	The `ParentNode` of this node will return the document, element, document type, or entity reference containing the processing instruction.
Text	The `ParentNode` of this `XmlNode` will return the element, attribute, or entity reference containing the node.

The nodes `Attribute`, `Document`, `DocumentFragment`, `Entity`, and `Notation` will all return `Nothing` for this property, as they don't have parents.

The InnerText, InnerXml, and OuterXml Properties

Each of these properties is a Microsoft extension to the W3C Document Object Model, provided to make accessing the values of nodes easier than would be possible with standard DOM techniques.

The `InnerText` property is read/write capable and will return the concatenation of the text of the current node and all of the text nodes of the descendant child nodes. When you set this property, the child nodes will be replaced by the parsed contents of the string.

Consider working with the following simple XML document:

```
<chapter title="Reading &amp; Writing">
  <paraA>
    some text
  </paraA>
  <paraB>
    some more text
  </paraB>
</chapter>
```

If the current node is the paraA element node, then the InnerText property will return the string **some text**. Remaining on the same node, and setting the InnerText property to **some other text** would give the following XML:

```
<chapter title="Reading &amp; Writing">
  <paraA>
    some other text
  </paraA>
  <paraB>
    some more text
  </paraB>
</chapter>
```

Similarly, if the current node in our first example is the chapter element, then the InnerText property will return the string **some text some more text**.

Setting the InnerText property when on the chapter node to the string **some new text** would yield the following result.

```
<chapter title="Reading &amp; Writing">some new text</chapter>
```

The InnerXml property does a similar thing to the InnerText property, except that it also returns the nodes that are children of the current node, including the text. You can set the InnerXml property to a string value and this will set the child node of the current node to this value; if the current node cannot have child nodes (such as a text node) then an exception will be thrown. So, the following will output the string "**Display the InnerText of the chapter element: some new text**":

```
Dim doc as XmlDocument = new XmlDocument()
doc.LoadXml("<chapter title="Reading &amp; Writing">some new text</chapter>")

Dim element as XmlNode = doc.DocumentElement

Console.WriteLine("Display the InnerText of the chapter element: ")
Console.WriteLine(element.InnerText)
```

Finally, the OuterXml property will return everything that the InnerXml property returns, but it will also return the XML of the current node as well. Similarly, this property can be set to some string value.

So, contrasting `InnerXml` and `OuterXml` – consider when the current node is the `paraA` element of the following XML structure:

```
<chapter title="Reading &amp; Writing">
  <paraA>
    some text
  </paraA>
</chapter>
```

The `InnerXml` property will return the following fragment:

```
some text
```

The `OuterXml` property, however, will return the following:

```
<paraA>
    some text
</paraA>
```

Notice that the XML of the current element is returned, but not the parent XML element (that is, the `chapter` element is not returned).

Other Properties

There are several other abstract properties that are part of the `XmlNode` class and these are defined in the table below for convenience.

Property	Description
Attributes	This property will return an `XmlAttributeCollection` (discussed above) containing the attribute nodes when the current node is an element node. If this is called on another node type then it will return `null`.
BaseURI	This returns the Base URI of the current node, which is particularly important when an XML document is included in another. A common scenario would be the inclusion of external entities from one URI within XML documents in another URI.
IsReadOnly	This property will return `True` if the node is read-only, otherwise it will return `False`. This is a Microsoft extension to the DOM.

Note that a read-only node means that the node itself cannot be modified, but it can still be removed from the tree and inserted at some other location. |

Property	Description
Item	This is the indexer for the `XmlNode` and has two overloads returning an element node. The first is by name and the second takes the name and a namespace URI as arguments. This is a Microsoft extension to the DOM.
	So, for example, when on a given node, to get the `Value` property of the child element node called "`para`" which is in the "`urn:ns`" namespace, you may use the following code:
	`currEl("para","urn:ns").Value`
LocalName	The `LocalName` property will return the local name of the current node, which is the `Name` without any prefix. Hence, the `LocalName` property would return `title` for the XML element node `per:title`.
Name	The `Name` property returns the fully qualified name of the current node, therefore including any prefix.
NamespaceURI	The `NamespaceURI` property allows you to get the URI of the node. Where there is a prefix, this will be the namespace associated with the prefix, and where not, it will be the namespace that is in scope for the given node.
OwnerDocument	This property will return the `XmlDocument` to which the current node belongs and is used for creating nodes that are to be added to the document. This is a Microsoft extension to the DOM.
Prefix	This returns or sets the prefix of a given node and return `null` if a prefix doesn't exist, or an exception if you try to set a prefix on a node type that does not permit prefixes (such as a `text` node).
	Updating the value of this property changes the value of the `Name` property.

XmlNode Methods

Let's now look at the more useful methods that are part of the `XmlNode` class in the same way we looked at the properties above.

The SelectSingleNode() and SelectNodes() Methods

The `SelectSingleNode()` and `SelectNodes()` methods are in fact extensions to the Document Object Model core specification, but they have become so useful that they are almost considered standard methods of any DOM implementation (and in fact the Oracle XML parser implements two methods of the same name doing a similar thing).

The `SelectSingleNode()` method returns a single `XmlNode` based on an XPath query and has two overloads in the .NET implementation. The first simply takes the XPath query that you want to execute as an argument and the second takes a string representing an XPath query and an `XmlNamespaceManager` as arguments.

The `XmlNamespaceManager` represents a mapping of prefixes to namespaces and is used to qualify any prefixes used in your XPath string against valid namespaces. Within the namespace manager, you will add a prefix and associate this with one of the namespaces in the document – this is done for each namespace that you are going to select nodes from in your XPath expression. For each namespace in an XML document that qualifies a node that you want to select you must add an entry to the `XmlNamespaceManager` instance (there is an example at the end of this section). This takes the form:

```
nsManager.AddNamespace("myprefix", "http://www.wrox.com/ns#")
```

In this case `myprefix` is mapped to the namespace `http://www.wrox.com/ns#` and so XPath expressions can be qualified as `//myprefix:myNodes` to select all `myNodes` in the `myprefix` namespace. An example is shown further below.

An important note to remember from Chapter 3 is that in XPath you must qualify your query if the document instance you are selecting against has qualified nodes. In other words, if you have no default namespace in your document, you can use an XPath expression such as `//myNodes`. However, if you have a default namespace in your document you MUST use the `XmlNamespaceManager` to create a prefix that can qualify your query, so you may have `//myprefix:myNodes`.

The `XmlNamespaceManager` class is discussed in the next chapter.

We'll continue to work with the following XML document to illustrate how to use the `SelectSingleNode()` method.

```
<chapter title="Reading &amp; Writing">
  <para>
    some text
  </para>
  <para>
    some other text
  </para>
</chapter>
```

The following code will return the text node of the second `para` element node – that is, `some other text`:

```
Dim objNode As XmlNode = objXmlDoc.SelectSingleNode("/chapter/para[2]/text()")
```

The `SelectNodes()` method also has two overloads, one taking an XPath string and the other taking a string XPath expression as well as a `XmlNamespaceManager`. The difference is that this method will always return an `XmlNodeList` of the node or nodes that are selected by the expression. An empty `XmlNodeList` will be returned if no nodes are selected.

Continuing to work with the above XML instance, the following code will return two `XmlNodes` of the two `para` elements in the document.

```
Dim objNodes As XmlNodeList = objXmlDoc.SelectNodes("/chapter/para")
```

Finally, we mentioned that we have to use the `XmlNamespaceManager` if we want to qualify an instance. To demonstrate this, consider the following revised XML instance.

```
<chapter xmlns="urn:someNS" title="Reading &amp; Writing">
  <para>
    some text
  </para>
  <para>
    some other text
  </para>
</chapter>
```

In this case, even though the XML instance only uses a default namespace, we will have to qualify the XPath expression in order to select any of the nodes from the document (if you have a default namespace in your document you *must* use the XmlNamespaceManager to create a prefix that can qualify your query). This changes the way we implement the SelectSingleNode() method we discussed earlier to the following.

Look at the following snippet that shows how to use a qualified XPath expression to select nodes from the document above:

```
...
Dim ns As XmlNamespaceManager = New XmlNamespaceManager(objXmlDoc.NameTable)
ns.AddNamespace("p", "urn:someNS")

Dim p As XmlNode = objXmlDoc.SelectSingleNode("/p:chapter/p:para[2]/text()", ns)
...
```

In this case a new instance of an XmlNamespaceManager is required – this class takes a name table instance as a parameter that is created from the XmlDocument instance. This is because there is a default namespace and so we must qualify nodes in our XPath expression.

To do this we must first add a prefix to the namespace manager that is associated with the namespace that any of our nodes are qualified in. This is done by using the AddNamespace() method and in our case we associate the prefix p with the namespace urn:someNS – this is the default namespace of our XML document.

Following this we can actually perform the selection, using the SelectSingleNode() method (although you can use the SelectNodes() method also), with the namespace manager instance as the second parameter. Now, look at the XPath expression, /p:chapter/p:para[2]/text(). Each element that we select is preceded by the "p" prefix to qualify the node in the namespace. If we don't prefix any of these elements with a prefix then the node will NOT be selected.

The AppendChild() and PrependChild() Methods

The AppendChild() method takes an XmlNode as a parameter and adds it after the end of the last child node of the current node. When you are taking an XmlNode from the document and inserting it into a new position using the AppendChild() method, it is first removed from the document, then inserted into the new position in the document, and then the XmlNode inserted is returned.

To demonstrate, consider the XML fragment below:

```
<chapter xmlns="urn:someNS" title="Reading &amp; Writing">
  <paraA>
    some text
  </paraA>
  <paraB>
    some other text
  </paraB>
</chapter>
```

The call to `AppendChild()` is as follows, where `objNode` points to the text node **some text** in the `paraA` element node.

```
Dim objNode As XmlNode = objXmlDoc.AppendChild(objNode)
```

The resulting XML document is now as follows:

```
<chapter xmlns="urn:someNS" title="Reading &amp; Writing">
  <paraA></paraA>
  <paraB>
    some other text
  </paraB>
  some text
</chapter>
```

The `PrependChild()` method is a Microsoft extension to the DOM and is almost identical to the `AppendChild()` method, but rather than adding the node after the *last* child node of the current element, it adds the node before the *first* child node of the current element.

The InsertBefore() and InsertAfter() Methods

The `InsertBefore()` and `InsertAfter()` methods are very similar in that they both take two arguments, the first being the new `XmlNode` to insert and the second argument being the reference `XmlNode`.

The `InsertBefore()` method will insert the new `XmlNode` before the reference `XmlNode`, adding it to the start of the children of the current node if the reference `XmlNode` is null and removing the new `XmlNode` from the document if it is already in the tree. The `XmlNode` that is inserted is returned from this method.

Similarly, the `InsertAfter()` method will insert the new `XmlNode` after the reference `XmlNode`, inserting it at the start of the list of children of the current node if the reference node is null and removing the new `XmlNode` from the document if it already exists. The `XmlNode` that is inserted is returned from this method.

To demonstrate this, consider the XML fragment below:

```
<chapter title="Reading &amp; Writing">
  <para>
    <sentence>text in a sentence</sentence>
```

```
      some text
    </para>
    <para>
      some other text
    </para>
  </chapter>
```

When the current node is the `chapter` document root node, the new `XmlNode` is the `sentence` node (for example, it was selected using the `SelectSingleNode()` method) and the reference node is the second `para` `XmlNode`, then the method could be called as follows:

```
Dim objNode As XmlNode = objXmlDoc.InsertAfter(objSentenceNode, objParaNode)
```

The resulting XML document is now as follows:

```
<chapter title="Reading &amp; Writing">
  <para>
    some text
  </para>
  <para>
    some other text
  </para>
  <sentence>text in a sentence</sentence>
</chapter>
```

Alternatively, if the call had used the other method as follows:

```
Dim objNode As XmlNode = objXmlDoc.InsertBefore(objSentenceNode, objParaNode)
```

In this case the resulting XML document is now as follows:

```
<chapter title="Reading &amp; Writing">
  <para>
    some text
  </para>
  <sentence>text in a sentence</sentence>
  <para>
    some other text
  </para>
</chapter>
```

Notice that in both cases the newly inserted node is actually moved because it exists in the document. If the new node didn't exist in the document then it would be simply inserted at the appropriate position.

The ReplaceChild() Method

The `ReplaceChild()` method does a similar thing to the two methods above, but rather than inserting the new node before or after a reference node, the reference node is instead replaced.

The method takes a first parameter of the new XmlNode to insert and a second parameter of the XmlNode to be replaced. If the new XmlNode exists in the document it is first removed from the document before it is again inserted over the node to be replaced – the new node is returned from this method call.

Looking back at the examples immediately above, when the current node is the chapter document root node, the new XmlNode is the sentence node (for example, it was selected using the SelectSingleNode() method) and the node to be replaced is the second para XmlNode, then the method could be called as follows:

```
Dim objNode As XmlNode = objXmlDoc.ReplaceChild(objSentenceNode, objParaNode)
```

The resulting XML document is now:

```
<chapter title="Reading &amp; Writing">
  <para>
    some text
  </para>
  <sentence>text in a sentence</sentence>
</chapter>
```

Notice that the sentence node has been removed and put in the place of the second para element node.

Other Methods

There are several other abstract properties that are part of the XmlNode class and these are defined in the table below for convenience.

Method	Description
Clone()	This method will copy the current node and all of its sub-nodes and return the result as an XmlNode. Hence this method effectively duplicates the node. This is a Microsoft extension to the DOM.
CloneNode()	This method is very much like the one above, except that is also accepts a Boolean parameter. When True it indicates that the current node and all sub-nodes should be cloned – the exact same as the Clone() method above. When the parameter is set to False, this means that only the current node should be cloned.
CreateNavigator()	This method will create an XPathNavigator object for performing read-only navigation and transforms of the document or document fragment. We look in depth at the XPathNavigator class in the next chapter. This is a Microsoft extension to the DOM.
GetEnumerator()	This provides a foreach manner of iterating over the node list. This is a Microsoft extension to the DOM.

Method	Description
`GetNamespaceOfPrefix()`	This method takes a prefix as an argument and returns the namespace declaration that is in scope for that prefix for the current node (that is, finds the closest `xmlns` declaration). This is a Microsoft extension to the DOM.
`GetPrefixOfNamespace()`	This method complements the above method in that it takes a namespace as an argument and returns the prefix that has been defined for it that is in scope for the current node (that is, finds the closest `xmlns` declaration). This is a Microsoft extension to the DOM.
`Normalize()`	This method combines all adjacent text nodes into a single unified text node so that no two text nodes are adjacent. This is called a normal form and means that text nodes are separated by nodes, such as element nodes, comments, processing instructions, CDATA sections, and entity references.

The `Normalize()` method is useful for operations that require a particular document tree structure and ensures that the DOM view of a document is identical when saved and reloaded.

For example:

```
'Create a new document
Dim xmlDoc As XmlDocument = New XmlDocument()
Dim root As XmlNode = xmlDoc.CreateElement("root")


'Add new text nodes
root.AppendChild(xmlDoc.CreateTextNode("Steven"))
root.AppendChild(xmlDoc.CreateTextNode("Livingstone"))


Console.Write(root.ChildNodes.Count); '2 child nodes
root.Normalize()
Console.Write(root.ChildNodes.Count) '1 child nodes
```

Notice that is the first output two nodes are written because you have added two text nodes. However, after you have called the `Normalize()` method the two adjacent text nodes are combined into a single text node and so the next output shows only one text node.

Table continued on following page

Method	Description
RemoveAll()	This method will remove all the children and attributes of the current node. If the current node is an attribute and it is removed, but there is a default value assigned for this attribute (assigned for example using an XML Schema which we look at later), then a new attribute will immediately appear with the default value.
	This method is an extension to the DOM.
RemoveChild()	This method takes an XmlNode as an argument, which is the child node to be removed from the current node. The node that is removed is returned from this method.
Supports()	The Supports() method is useful for testing whether a given DOM implementation supports some feature.
	The first argument is a case-insensitive string representing the feature to test for and the second argument is also a string representing the DOM implementation version to test.
	Hence, the call Supports("xml","1.0") will return True, while the call Supports("xinclude","2.0") will return False.
	If you don't specify a version (that is, null) then all versions will be checked.
WriteContentTo()	This method takes an XmlWriter instance as an argument and saves all the children (from the InnerXml property) of the current node to this writer instance.
	This is also a DOM extension.
WriteTo()	This method takes an XmlWriter instance as an argument and saves the current node and all the children (from the OuterXml property) of the current node to this writer instance.
	This is also a DOM extension.

We have now looked at the XmlNode class in quite a bit of detail. The other XmlNode types all derive from this class, some being almost identical in implementation and others overriding some of these methods and adding their own methods and properties. We won't cover these all here as it's about time we started looking at some solid examples; however, the relevant members will be discussed when they come up.

One question you may have is about the differences between the XmlNode and the XmlWriter when it comes to creating and editing documents. The main difference is that the XmlNode members will be generally used to edit, update, and remove from an existing document whereas the XmlWriter will be used to create an entirely new document. When we look at the XmlDocument class next you will see some concrete implementations of the XmlNode members and the difference to the XmlWriter class discussed in the previous chapter will become apparent.

To look at implementing some of these features, we have to look at the `XmlDocument` class, which we will discuss next.

The XmlDocument Class

The `XmlDocument` class is the .NET representation of an XML document and implements the DOM Level 1 and DOM Level 2 core recommendations. It uses the `XmlNode` class very heavily, not only inheriting and overriding the `XmlNode` members, but also when working with the various types of `XmlNode` when adding, removing or updating the `XmlDocument`.

Using the `XmlDocument` class you can load a new instance of an `XmlDocument`, create a new `XmlDocument`, and even persist the document.

As an example of working with the `XmlDocument` class, let's consider the situation where you have a catalog of products stored in an XML file which can either be used by your web site or integrated with a partner web site requesting the XML file over the Internet. Rather than modify the document by hand, it is probable that you will want to programmatically modify its contents. You can do this using the `XmlDocument` class, by calling the `Load()` method with the path to the XML file. Once the file is loaded into the `XmlDocument` instance, you can use methods available in the Document Object Model (such as `CreateNode()` and `CreateAttribute()`) to add new products to the catalog. Similarly, you can use the `SelectNodes()` and `SelectSingleNode()` methods to find and modify existing products within the catalog. Finally, the `Save()` method of the `XmlDocument` class can then be used to save the updated XML document to disk.

Before we look at an example, let's have an overview of the important methods of this class. There are some properties and methods we won't discuss here, but they are very similar to properties and methods we have discussed when looking at `XmlNode` and `XmlReader` (such as `Name()`, `NameTable()`, `CloneNode()`, and so on) so for specific information on these look in the MSDN documentation.

The `XmlDocument` class has the `XmlDataDocument` sub-class which allows you to work with relational database structures as though they are XML documents.

Creating Nodes

The `XMLDocument` class has a whole bunch of `CreateXXX()` methods that allow you to create various `XmlNode` types such as elements, attributes, processing instructions, and others that can be inserted into the `XmlDocument`.

Each method is listed here with a brief description. Remember that these methods simply create the relevant `XmlNode`; the don't actually append it to the document, another method such as the `XmlNode` `AppendChild()` method must be used to actually add the node to the `XmlDocument`.

Method	Description
CreateAttribute()	Creates a new XmlAttribute node and has three overloads. The first simply takes the name of the attribute to create, the second takes the attribute name and namespace to qualify it in and the final overloads takes a prefix for the attribute, the attribute name, and the namespace the prefix should be associated with. This new XmlAttribute node can then be attached to some element using the SetAttributeNode() method of the XmlElement class.
CreateCDataSection()	Creates a new XmlCDataSection containing the data passed in the string argument to the method. The newly created XmlCDataSection node is returned.
CreateComment()	Creates a new XmlComment node containing the data specified as an argument to the method. The newly created XmlComment node is returned.
CreateDocumentFragment()	Creates a new XmlDocumentFragment node, which allows you to create a light XML document where you can add many types of nodes without working with the full XmlDocument. However, note that you can only insert the child nodes of the XmlDocumentFragment object and not the DocumentFragment node itself.
CreateDocumentType()	This method takes four parameters; the name of the document type to create, the public identifier for the document type, the system identifier for the type, and finally the internal DTD.
CreateElement()	Creates a new XmlElement node and has three overloads. The first simply takes the name of the element to create, the second takes the element name and namespace to qualify it in, and the final overload takes a prefix for the element, the element name, and the namespace the prefix should be associated with. This new XmlElement node can then be attached to an element using, for example, the AppendChild() method of the XmlNode class.
CreateEntityReference()	Creates an entity reference with the name specified in the argument to the method. When inserted into the document, the node created will be the relevant entity with that name for the document.

Method	Description
CreateNode()	This method has three overloads that allow you to create a new XmlNode instance. The first overload uses the first parameter as a string to identify the type of XmlNode to create (such as "element", "attribute", "text", and so on), the second parameter defines the name of the XmlNode to create, and the final parameter is the namespace that the new node should be associated with. The second overloaded method of CreateNode() is very similar to the previous overload, except that as the first parameter is passes an XmlNodeType object of the type of node to create. The final overload is the same as the previous method, except that it adds as the second parameter the prefix to the newly created node.
CreateProcessingInstruction()	Creates a new XmlProcessingInstruction node with the name specified in the first argument and the data specified in the second argument.
CreateSignificantWhitespace()	Creates a new XmlSignificantWhitespace node with the argument containing the whitespace characters to create. These characters can only be &#20; (space)
 (line feed)  (carriage return) and 	 (horizontal tab).
CreateTextNode()	Creates a new XmlText node with the text passed in the argument to the method.
CreateWhitespace()	Creates a new XmlWhitespace node with the argument containing the whitespace characters to create. These characters can only be &#20;
  and 	.
CreateXmlDeclaration()	Creates a new XmlDeclaration node with the first argument being the version ("1.0"), the second argument being the encoding for the document, and the final argument must be "yes" or "no" to indicate whether the document is standalone or not.

Load and Save

The XmlDocument class provides us with the core ability to load and save XML documents from specified locations or in memory streams. Let's first look at how the Load() method can be used to access XML documents.

Load() and LoadXml()

The Load() method has four overloads that all take a single parameter specifying where to get the document stream from, and by default, always preserves the whitespace in the document without doing any schema validation of the document (the XmlValidatingReader is used to do this).

```
Overloads Overridable Public Sub Load(Stream)
```

This first method overload takes a Stream object containing the XML document that is to be loaded.

```
Overloads Overridable Public Sub Load(string)
```

The second overload takes the URL of the file to load and can be either a local file or remote file.

```
Overloads Overridable Public Sub Load(TextReader)
```

The third overload takes an existing TextReader instance as its argument and loads the contained XML document.

```
Overloads Overridable Public Sub Load(XmlReader);
```

The final overload takes an XmlReader instance or any instance derived from XmlReader and builds a DOM instance from its contents. If the XmlReader is positioned at some node within the tree then the XML loaded is from this node onwards.

The LoadXml() method is a simple companion to the Load() method in that it loads any valid XML string as a XmlDocument instance. As an example, the following will load the XML in the parameter as a new XML document instance.

```
xdoc.LoadXml("<root><para>some para text</para></root>")
```

Try It Out: Loading a URL as an XmlDocument Instance

The first example we are going to look at is how to load an XML file into memory and write the result to the screen.

Note that all the sample code for this chapter is available for download from http://www.wrox.com. We will be storing sample code for this chapter within the following folder: C:\BegVBXML\Chapter06. You may, of course, use a different folder depending on what you prefer.

1. Create a new Windows Application called **Samples** and add a TextBox and a Button to the form – change the button's Text property to LoadURL. Also, change the Multiline property of the TextBox to True.

2. Add the following import statements to the start of the code file:

```
Imports System.Data
Imports System.Xml
```

3. Double-click on the button and enter the following code into the button event handler:

```
Private Sub button1_Click(ByVal sender As System.Object, _
                    ByVal e As System.EventArgs) Handles button1.Click
   Dim xdoc As XmlDocument = New XmlDocument()
   xdoc.Load("..\\sample.xml")

   TextBox1.Text = xdoc.OuterXml
End Sub
```

4. Now add a new XML file to the project, call it `sample.xml`, and enter the following XML into the document:

```
<?xml version="1.0" encoding="utf-8" ?>
<Catalog xmlns:test="uri:test">
  <Company email="celtic@deltabis.net" name="Celtic Productions">
    <ProductFamily familyID="pftops" LastUpdate="2001-08-26T18:39:09"
       buyersURI="http://www.deltabis.com/buyers/tops">
      <test:Product ProductID="CFC4">
        <color>black</color>
        <size>L</size>
        <price>32.99</price>
      </test:Product>
    </ProductFamily>
  </Company>
</Catalog>
```

5. Run this program and you will get the following output:

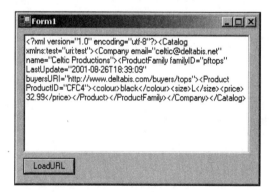

How It Works

This example illustrates the simplest possible scenario for loading an XML document into an `XmlDocument` instance. The `Load()` method was used, taking the path to the XML file as a parameter.

When loaded, we checked that we had actually read and parsed the file by writing out the content of the file using the `OuterXml` property of the `XmlDocument` class, as the current node will be the document root node.

If there is any problem in loading the XML document you will get an `XmlException` exception detailing the load or parse error and the `XmlDocument` instance stays null.

Try It Out: Loading an XmlReader Instance as an XmlDocument Instance

Next, we want to look at a common scenario where you have loaded an XML document using the `XmlReader` class, done some work and now want to pass a fragment of the document to the `XmlDocument` class to be able to use the DOM to work with it. This example demonstrates how this could be done.

1. In the **Samples** project, add a new button to the form and change the `Text` property to `Load XmlReader`.

2. Next, double-click on this button and add the following code to the event handler:

```
Private Sub button2_Click(ByVal sender As System.Object, _
                          ByVal e As System.EventArgs) Handles button2.Click
    ' Load a new XmlTextReader instance
    Dim xRead As XmlTextReader = New XmlTextReader("..\\sample.xml")

    ' Iterate through reader to get elements
    While (xRead.Read())

        If (xRead.NodeType = XmlNodeType.Element) Then

            ' Is the Product element in the uri:test namespace?
            If (xRead.LocalName = "Product" And xRead.NamespaceURI = "uri:test") Then
                Exit While
            End If
        End If
    End While

    ' Load this Product node into dom document
    Dim xdoc As XmlDocument = New XmlDocument()
    xdoc.Load(xRead)
    xRead.Close()

    textBox1.Text = textBox1.Text & "=== OuterXml ====="
    textBox1.Text = textBox1.Text & System.Environment.NewLine
    textBox1.Text = textBox1.Text & xdoc.FirstChild.OuterXml
    textBox1.Text = textBox1.Text & System.Environment.NewLine
    textBox1.Text = textBox1.Text & System.Environment.NewLine
```

```
textBox1.Text = textBox1.Text & "=== InnerXml ====="
textBox1.Text = textBox1.Text & System.Environment.NewLine
textBox1.Text = textBox1.Text & xdoc.FirstChild.InnerXml
textBox1.Text = textBox1.Text & System.Environment.NewLine
textBox1.Text = textBox1.Text & System.Environment.NewLine

textBox1.Text = textBox1.Text & "=== InnerText ====="
textBox1.Text = textBox1.Text & System.Environment.NewLine
textBox1.Text = textBox1.Text & xdoc.FirstChild.InnerText
textBox1.Text = textBox1.Text & System.Environment.NewLine
textBox1.Text = textBox1.Text & System.Environment.NewLine

textBox1.Text = textBox1.Text & "=== Value ====="
textBox1.Text = textBox1.Text & System.Environment.NewLine
textBox1.Text = textBox1.Text & xdoc.FirstChild.Value
End Sub
```

3. Finally, run the application and you will get the following output:

How It Works

We first load the sample XML document into an `XmlTextReader` instance as we looked at in previous chapters.

```
Dim xRead As XmlTextReader = New XmlTextReader("..\\sample.xml")
```

Following this, we used the `Read()` method of the `XmlTextReader` class to iterate through all of the nodes in the loaded XML document. Within this loop we first look for nodes that of the `XmlNodeType` `XmlElement` and when this is `True` we do some further processing. In this case, we check the `LocalName` and `NamespaceURI` properties of the `XmlElement` as check if the `LocalName` (that is, the element name) is `Product` and it is qualified in the namespace `uri:test`. When this is the case, we have found the element we are interested in and so we break out of the loop; otherwise we continue processing the nodes with the next `Read()` iteration.

```
While (xRead.Read())

  If (xRead.NodeType = XmlNodeType.Element) Then

    If (xRead.LocalName = "Product" And _
      xRead.NamespaceURI = "uri:test") Then
      Exit While
    End If
  End If
End While
```

At this point the `XmlTextReader` is positioned at the `Product` element node. We create an instance of the `XmlDocument` object class, and in the `Load()` method, we pass the `XmlTextReader`, which will load in only the `Product` node, and its child and attribute nodes as an XML document instance.

```
Dim xdoc As XmlDocument = New XmlDocument()
xdoc.Load(xRead)
xRead.Close()
```

When this has been done we can close the `XmlTextReader` and start to write the output to the screen.

```
textBox1.Text = textBox1.Text & "=== OuterXml ====="
textBox1.Text = textBox1.Text & System.Environment.NewLine
textBox1.Text = textBox1.Text & xdoc.FirstChild.OuterXml
textBox1.Text = textBox1.Text & System.Environment.NewLine
textBox1.Text = textBox1.Text & System.Environment.NewLine
```

This first block wrote out the `OuterXml` of the document root of this new `XmlDocument` instance – this is the XML including the current node and all its children and attributes. Notice that we use the `FirstChild` property of the `XmlDocument` instance to access the document element. This is because the newly created `XmlDocument` instance that we created when we passed in the `XmlTextReader` node is actually of `XmlNodeType` Document, and so we need to navigate to the child to access the actual document element. Much in the same way as in any XML document!

```
textBox1.Text = textBox1.Text & "=== InnerXml ====="
textBox1.Text = textBox1.Text & System.Environment.NewLine
textBox1.Text = textBox1.Text & xdoc.FirstChild.InnerXml
textBox1.Text = textBox1.Text & System.Environment.NewLine
textBox1.Text = textBox1.Text & System.Environment.NewLine
```

The second block wrote out the `InnerXml` of the document root of this new `XmlDocument` instance – this is the XML children and attributes of the current node and not the node itself.

```
textBox1.Text = textBox1.Text & "=== InnerText ====="
textBox1.Text = textBox1.Text & System.Environment.InnerText
textBox1.Text = textBox1.Text & xdoc.FirstChild.InnerXml
textBox1.Text = textBox1.Text & System.Environment.NewLine
textBox1.Text = textBox1.Text & System.Environment.NewLine
```

The third block wrote out the `InnerText` of the document root of this new `XmlDocument` instance – this is the concatenation of the text nodes of the child node of the current node (not the attribute nodes).

```
textBox1.Text = textBox1.Text & "=== Value ====="
textBox1.Text = textBox1.Text & System.Environment.NewLine
textBox1.Text = textBox1.Text & xdoc.FirstChild.Value
```

The final block wrote the `Value` property of the current node. Remember that this simply writes out the value of the current node, and as this is an element node it will have no value – this applies to nodes that can have explicit values, such as text nodes and entity nodes.

Save()

The `Save()` method also has four overloads that all take a single parameter specifying where the document stream should be written. The `PreserveWhitespace` property must be set to `True` to preserve the whitespace in the document and ensure that the XML document is written out in valid XML.

```
Overloads Overridable Public Sub Save(Stream)
```

This first method overload takes a `Stream` object specifying where the document is to be written. This is useful if, for example, you have some XML and want to cache it in a `MemoryStream` for use later in the application.

```
Overloads Overridable Public Sub Save(String)
```

The second overload takes the URL specifying where the XML document is to be saved. You may use this when a user had made updates to the XML document and you want to persist it to disk again.

```
Overloads Overridable Public Sub Save(TextWriter)
```

The third overload takes an existing `TextWriter` instance as its argument, and saves the output to this `TextWriter` instance. The `TextWriter` instance determines the encoding that the document will be written out in. You may save to a `TextWriter` instance if you wanted to use the `StringWriter` class (derived from `TextWriter`) to write the contents of an XML document to the screen (for example, in a text box).

```
Overloads Overridable Public Sub Save(XmlWriter)
```

The final overload takes an `XmlWriter` instance or any instance derived from `XmlWriter` and saves a DOM instance to the stream. This would be useful if you wanted to write the XML out using the encoding format specified on the `XmlWriter` – for example in a case where you may be appending to some other XML content.

Try It Out: Saving an XmlDocument Instance to a URL

A common scenario will be saving your XML document to some URL, typically locally. You could do this when creating a new purchase order for example or when you modify the existing details of a contacts XML file. Let's now look at how the `XmlDocument` does this.

1. In the **Samples** project, add a new button to the form and call this `Save URL`.

2. Next, double-click on this button and add the following code to the event handler.

```
Private Sub button3_Click(ByVal sender As System.Object, _
                        ByVal e As System.EventArgs) Handles button3.Click
    Const fPath As String = "..\\rootDoc.xml"

    ' load a string into a DOM document instance
    Dim xdoc As XmlDocument = New XmlDocument()
    xdoc.LoadXml("<root><para>some para text</para></root>")
    xdoc.Save(fPath)

    'Now retrieve the document
    Dim xNewdoc As XmlDocument = New XmlDocument()
    xNewdoc.Load(fPath)

    textBox1.Text = xNewdoc.OuterXml
End Sub
```

3. Run this program and you will get a file called `rootDoc.xml` created in the folder of your Visual Studio project and the following output:

How It Works

We initially define a location where the file is to be persisted and create a new instance of the `XmlDocument` class. Next we use the `LoadXml()` method of this class to parse and load a string representation of an `XmlDocument`; this can be any valid XML string that you may otherwise have in a document.

```
xdoc.LoadXml("<root><para>some para text</para></root>")
```

It is then simple to persist the document by calling the `Save()` method of the `XmlDocument` instance and passing the file location as a parameter.

```
xdoc.Save(fPath)
```

Finally, to demonstrate that the document has in fact been persisted, we separately use another `XmlDocument` instance to load the persisted XML document and display it to the user.

```
Dim xNewdoc As XmlDocument = New XmlDocument()
xNewdoc.Load(fPath)

textBox1.Text = xNewdoc.OuterXml
```

Try It Out: Saving an XmlDocument Instance to an XmlWriter Instance

Often we will have an `XmlWriter` object that we want to write to instead of a specified URL. This may be the case when we want to set specific properties on the `XmlWriter` instance (such as encoding) and then have them applied to the XML document that is loaded. We may want to work with the `XmlWriter` specifically (for example, you may have created a custom `XmlWriter` to use `XInclude` when writing the document out and want to use that to stream your document).

This example looks at saving to the `XmlTextWriter` class.

1. In the current **Samples** project, add a new button to the form and change the `Text` property to `Save TextWriter`.

2. Next, enter the following code into the button event handler:

```
Private Sub button4_Click(ByVal sender As System.Object, _
                          ByVal e As System.EventArgs) Handles button4.Click
    Const fPath As String = "..\\rootDoc2.xml"

    ' create a new text writer to the path above in Unicode
    Dim txtWrite As XmlTextWriter = New XmlTextWriter(fPath, _
        System.Text.Encoding.Unicode)

    ' load an XML string into a DOM document instance
    Dim xdoc As XmlDocument = New XmlDocument()
    xdoc.LoadXml("<?xml version='1.0' encoding='utf-8' ?>" _
        & "<root><para>some para text</para></root>")

    ' save the XML document to the text writer & hence file system
    xdoc.Save(txtWrite)

    txtWrite.Close()

    'Now retrieve the document
    Dim xNewdoc As XmlDocument = New XmlDocument()
    xNewdoc.Load(fPath)

    textBox1.Text = xNewdoc.OuterXml
End Sub
```

3. Run this program and you will get a file called `rootDoc2.xml` created in the folder of your Visual Studio project and the following output:

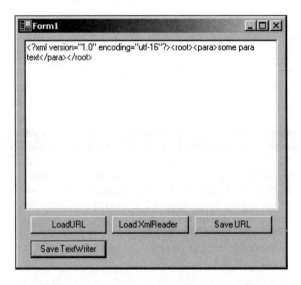

How It Works

This time after the file location has been defined, a new `XmlTextWriter` instance is created with the target of the defined file location and Unicode encoding – this means that all XML written using this writer will be encoded as Unicode, no matter what encoding it defines itself.

```
Dim txtWrite As XmlTextWriter = New XmlTextWriter(fPath,_
    System.Text.Encoding.Unicode)
```

Next, a similar XML document is loaded as before, and this time an XML declaration has been added stating that the encoding for the `XmlDocument` should be `UTF-8` encoding. When this is loaded, the `Save()` method is again called, this time passing the `XmlTextWriter` instance as an argument.

```
Dim xdoc As XmlDocument = New XmlDocument()
xdoc.LoadXml("<?xml version='1.0' encoding='utf-8' ?>" _
    & "<root><para>some para text</para></root>")
xdoc.Save(txtWrite)
```

This causes the `XmlDocument` XML to be written to the `XmlTextWriter` and hence persisted to file. Again the document is loaded and written to the text box to confirm that the method has worked.

An interesting note to make is that the encoding on the XML document is defined as `UTF-16` (also known as `Unicode`) rather than the `UTF-8` as stated by the XML input string. This is an important point to make, and you have to ensure that you don't make any assumptions about encoding when working with XML documents. In this case, the result will be that the content is encoded in UTF-16 encoding inherited from the `XmlWriter` instance rather than from the encoding defined on the XML declaration.

Iteration Through XmlDocument Instances

While working through the previous chapters, and especially this chapter, you may be thinking about the best way to work with document instances. For example, it is very common to iterate through an XML document looking for a specific node name, node type, or some other filter. You might do this to find the `product` elements in the XML instance with a `category` attribute containing a specific value. This would allow you to modify the `category` that all of these elements are related to and directly update the XML instance. Alternatively you may want to find all comment nodes within the XML document to build some kind of documentation that describes the XML document.

When working with the `XmlReader` derived classes the natural way to do this is using the `Read()` method, which will iterate through all nodes in the XML document and allow you to perform some action on them.

The closest equivalent in the DOM is a `XmlNodeList`, which is returned when you use XPath expressions and the `SelectNodes()` method of the `XmlDocument` class to filter the output nodes. You may consider the case where you could just save the resulting nodes to an `XmlTextReader` instance and use the `Read()` method to iterate though the nodes. However, apart from being a lot more work in creating the reader and saving to this reader, you would also have to ensure the reader was able to load the XML from the node list – in fact this would only work if a single node was returned otherwise you would have to wrap the nodes in the node list in some root element (only one top-level element can exist).

This sounds like an awful lot of work for something that should be simpler. Well, it is. The `XmlDocument` implementation and `XmlNode` class make the equivalent kind of recursive processes fairly simple. Why? Well, all nodes are ultimately derived from the `XmlNode` base class and so you can simply recursively pass an `XmlNode` object to the same method and evaluate its `XmlNode` type and perform some action.

This effectively allows us to walk the DOM tree, performing appropriate actions when we match specific nodes and node types.

Try It Out: Finding Elements with Recursion

This example will demonstrate an initial template (parts of the code are, specifically the recursive parts, reusable for your own application, where you would replace the parts specific for your application) for developing a recursive application that walks a DOM tree and writes out a purchase order of items ordered by a given company, as defined by an XML instance.

Currently there is support for outputting information on only one company, but I leave it as an exercise to extend the example. You may do this by creating a new class for company information and creating a new instance for each company and storing the data for each within public properties of that instance.

1. Add a new XML document to the **Samples** project called `sample2.xml` and enter the following XML.

```xml
<?xml version="1.0" encoding="utf-8" ?>
<Catalog xmlns:test="uri:test">
  <Company email="celtic@deltabis.net" name="Celtic Productions">
```

247

```
    <ProductFamily familyID="pftops" LastUpdate="2001-08-26T18:39:09"
      buyersURI="http://www.deltabis.com/buyers/tops">
      <test:Product ProductID="CFC4">
        <colour>black</colour>
        <size>L</size>
        <price>32.99</price>
      </test:Product>
      <test:Product ProductID="CFC5">
        <color>green</color>
        <size>M</size>
        <price>22.99</price>
      </test:Product>
    </ProductFamily>
  </Company>
</Catalog>
```

2. In the sample project we were working with earlier, add a new Class to the project by right-clicking on the project root of the **Samples** project and selecting **Add | Add New Item** and choose **Class**. Name the class `Recurse.vb`. Enter the following code into that class (note that this class is available with the download).

```vbnet
Imports System.Xml

Public Class Recurse
  ' Create a new global instance of the CatalogInfo structure
  Private _cInfo As CatalogInfo = New CatalogInfo()

  'Constructor - initialize structure to contain 10 items
  Public Sub New()
    _cInfo.NumItems = 0
    _cInfo.MyItems = Array.CreateInstance(GetType(Item), 10) 'initialize to 10
  End Sub

  ' Structure that holds all details about a single company
  Structure CatalogInfo
    Public CompanyName As String 'company's name
    Public EmailAddress As String 'company's email address
    Public NumItems As Integer 'number of items in the catalog
    Public MyItems() As Item 'array of ordered items

    'Override ToString() to return our own formatted string
    Public Overrides Function ToString() As String

      Dim strCompanyInfo As String = ""
      Dim strCompanyName As String = "Invoice for " _
           & Me.CompanyName & System.Environment.NewLine

      Dim strCompanyEmail As String = "Contact Address : " _
           & Me.EmailAddress & System.Environment.NewLine _
           & System.Environment.NewLine

      Dim strNumItems As String = "There are " & Me.NumItems _
```

```
                        & " items on order." & System.Environment.NewLine _
                        & "========================" & System.Environment.NewLine

        Dim ItemList As String = "The following items has been ordered." _
            & System.Environment.NewLine _
            & "--------------------------" _
            & System.Environment.NewLine

        Dim j As Integer = 0
        For j = 0 To MyItems.Length - 1

            If (MyItems(j).id Is Nothing) Then
                Exit For
            End If
            Dim id As String = "Item id " & MyItems(j).id
            Dim color As String = " was Color " & MyItems(j).color
            Dim size As String = ", Size " & MyItems(j).size
            Dim price As String = " and Price " & MyItems(j).price.ToString() _
                & "." & System.Environment.NewLine

            ItemList = ItemList & id & color & size & price
        Next

        strCompanyInfo = strCompanyName & strCompanyEmail & strNumItems _
            & ItemList

        Return strCompanyInfo
    End Function
End Structure

' Structure to contain details on an individual product item
Structure Item
    Public id As String      'item id
    Public color As String   'color of item
    Public size As String    'size
    Public price As Decimal   'price of item
End Structure

' Property that returns the formatted string of the company info
Public ReadOnly Property CatalogSummary() As String
    Get
        'Write out serialized structure info.
        Return _cInfo.ToString()
    End Get
End Property

'WalkTree() recursively iterates through nodes in the tree
Public Sub WalkTree(ByVal currNode As XmlNode)

    'Only iterate if there are any child nodes
    If (currNode.HasChildNodes) Then

        'Is child element node then walk tree
```

```
        Dim iNumChildNodes As Integer = currNode.ChildNodes.Count

        Dim i As Integer
        For i = 0 To iNumChildNodes - 1
          'Continue with the next node
          Dim nextNode As XmlNode = currNode.ChildNodes(i)

          Select Case (nextNode.NodeType)
            Case XmlNodeType.Document
            Case XmlNodeType.XmlDeclaration
            Case XmlNodeType.Element
              ElementNodeHandler(nextNode)
          End Select

          WalkTree(nextNode)
        Next
      End If
    End Sub

    ' Handles instances of a given node and stores its details
    Private Sub ElementNodeHandler(ByVal workNode As XmlNode)
      Select Case (workNode.LocalName)

        Case "Company"
          _cInfo.CompanyName = workNode.Attributes.GetNamedItem("name").Value
          _cInfo.EmailAddress = workNode.Attributes.GetNamedItem("email").Value

        Case "Product"
          _cInfo.NumItems = _cInfo.NumItems + 1
          _cInfo.MyItems(_cInfo.NumItems - 1).id = _
            workNode.Attributes.GetNamedItem("ProductID").Value

        Case "color"
          _cInfo.MyItems(_cInfo.NumItems - 1).color = workNode.InnerText
          _cInfo.MyItems(_cInfo.NumItems - 1).size = _
            workNode.NextSibling.InnerText
          _cInfo.MyItems(_cInfo.NumItems - 1).price = _
            Decimal.Parse(workNode.NextSibling.NextSibling.InnerText)

        Case "size"
        Case "price"
        Case Else
      End Select
    End Sub
End Class
```

3. Next return to the Windows form we were working with earlier and add a new button to the form and change the Text property to Recursion. Double-click on this button and add the following code to the handler.

```
Private Sub button5_Click(ByVal sender As System.Object, _
                ByVal e As System.EventArgs) Handles button5.Click
```

```
        Const fPath As String = "..\\sample2.xml"

        Dim xdoc As XmlDocument = New XmlDocument()
        xdoc.Load(fPath)

        'create a new instance and walk through the document hierarchy
        Dim xRec As Recurse = New Recurse()
        xRec.WalkTree(xdoc)

        textBox1.Text = xRec.CatalogSummary
    End Sub
```

Finally, run the application and click the **Recursion** button to get the following output:

How It Works

This example created a simple invoice of the product items that have been ordered by a company based on a simple XML document instance. Let's see how it worked.

When the button is clicked it invokes the recursion process by loading the `sample2.xml` file and passing it to an `XmlDocument` instance.

```
        Dim xdoc As XmlDocument = New XmlDocument()
        xdoc.Load(fPath)
```

Following this, an instance of the `Recurse` class is created and the `WalkTree()` method of this class is called, passing in the `XmlDocument` we instantiated earlier. This causes the recursion process to start from the root of the XML document.

```
        Dim xRec As Recurse = New Recurse()
        xRec.WalkTree(xdoc)
```

251

When complete, the `CatalogSummary` property of the `Recurse` class will return a formatted output summary of the catalog orders.

```
textBox1.Text = xRec.CatalogSummary
```

The Recurse Class

Let's look at the `Recurse` class, which contains the core functionality of this example. A global variable called `_cinfo` will be used to store information on a given company at runtime – this information will be stored in the `CatalogInfo` structure we look at shortly.

```
Private _cInfo As CatalogInfo = New CatalogInfo()
```

The constructor to this class simply initializes a `struct` that we used to store some information as we pass the XML document. It initializes a global counter of the number of items to zero and also creates a new array of `Item` types that contain details on given items as relates to a single company. This is then stored in the `MyItems` field of the `CatalogInfo` structure.

```
Public Sub New()
  cInfo.NumItems = 0
  cInfo.MyItems = Array.CreateInstance(GetType(Item), 10)
End Sub
```

You will notice that there is a `structure` called `CatalogInfo` that holds information on the catalog. The `structure` defines four public fields where we will be able to store data about our company. The first is the `CompanyName`, which is a `String`, as is the `EmailAddress` of the company. The third field is the `NumItems`, which is an integer number of items contained within the catalog. Finally, the `myItems` array is an array of `Item` entries, which is another `structure` that we will discuss next – this contains the items that are available.

```
Structure CatalogInfo
  Public CompanyName As String    'company's name
  Public EmailAddress As String 'company's email address
  Public NumItems As Integer 'number of items in the catalog
  Public MyItems() As Item    'array of ordered items

  Public Overrides Function ToString() As String
  'Formats output
  ...
  End Function
End Structure
```

There is also an override of the `ToString()` method – the purpose of this is to change the default output of the `ToString()` method of the `CatalogInfo` structure. Remember `ToString()` is defined in everything in .NET as it is inherited from the `System.Object` class. Rather than `ToString()` returning the name of the structure (that is, `CatalogInfo`), we override this to return a string which is a formatted representation of all of the data we have in the structure, including the company name, e-mail address and items associated with that company.

The `item` structure contains details on an individual item, such as the item ID, color, sized, and price of the item.

```
Structure Item
   Public id As String   'item id
   Public color As String   'color of item
   Public size As String   'size
   Public price As Decimal   'price of item
End Structure
```

The power in these structures comes as the developer can provide a simple property called `CatalogSummary` which calls the `ToString()` method of an instance of the `CatalogInfo` structure we looked at above and a formatted representation of the data within that instance is returned.

```
Public ReadOnly Property CatalogSummary() As String
  Get
    'Write out serialized structure info.
    Return _cInfo.ToString()
  End Get
End Property
```

How do we get that structure populated? Well, that is done by using a method called `WalkTree()`, which populates the structures with the data to be returned.

The `WalkTree()` method checks first if the current node actually has any child nodes, and when this is `True`, we continue in the code; otherwise we will come back out of the recursion and continue with a higher-level node.

```
If currNode.HasChildNodes Then
```

Next we determine the number of child nodes that are to be processed using the `ChildNodes` property of the current `XmlNode` and the `Count` property will return the number of child nodes.

```
Dim iNumChildNodes As Integer = currNode.ChildNodes.Count
```

We then iterate through each of these child nodes (we use a `for` loop, but you could equally have used a `foreach` iteration) and get the next node to process as one of these child nodes using the indexer of the `ChildNodes` property.

```
Dim nextNode As XmlNode = currNode.ChildNodes(i)
```

This means that we are now working through each of the `XmlNode` children and we want to determine what we want to do with this node. In some cases you may want to catch text nodes and do some processing to write out the `text` or `attribute` nodes and their values, the name of a company on a purchase order for instance. However, in this case we want to handle element nodes and so use a `switch` statement to determine when the `NodeType` of the next `XmlNode` is equal to an `Element`. When this is `True` we call a custom method that handles element nodes.

```
Case XmlNodeType.Element
   ElementNodeHandler(nextNode)
```

When this has been handled, we break out of the `switch` statement and again call the `WalkTree()` method to recurse down the tree, passing the current node as the argument. This is the key point. As every node is derived from the `XmlNode` class, we can pass all nodes back through this method recursively and handle it each time.

The `ElementNodeHandler()` method takes an `XmlNode` as an argument and checks its `LocalName` property to determine what action it should take. When we are on the `Company` element, the `GetNamedItem()` method of the `Attributes` property of an element node is passed the name of the attribute ("name" in this case) and returns its value.

```
Case "Company"
   _cInfo.CompanyName = workNode.Attributes.GetNamedItem("name").Value
```

A similar thing is done for the `Product` element nodes. When we match the `color` element node, we do something slightly different. We first get the value of the `color` element node by directly using the `InnerText` property. Its next sibling node is the `size` element, and so we use the `NextSibling` property of the element node and again the `InnerText`; the same thing is done for the next `price` sibling node.

Editing an XML Document

Earlier we mentioned that one of the advantages of the `XmlDocument` class and DOM model was that it could be used to perform updates on an XML document directly, unlike the streaming models we looked at earlier. Indeed, editing an XML document is one of the most common features and has excellent support in `XmlDocument` and related classes, such as the `CreateXXX()` methods mentioned above.

The following sections will look at how you can apply the XML classes in VB.NET to edit your XML documents.

Try It Out: Creating a New Node

The first thing we will look at is adding new product information to the existing document – this involves creating the various nodes and setting their values prior to inserting the node.

1. Add a new button to the form and give the button the text **Add Product**.

2. Double-click the button and enter the following code to the button event handler.

```
Private Sub button6_Click(ByVal sender As System.Object, _
                          ByVal e As System.EventArgs) Handles button6.Click
   'Looks at adding a new product element node and associates attributes & children

   'Create the XmlDocument.
   Dim xdoc As XmlDocument = New XmlDocument()
   xdoc.Load("..\\sample.xml")
```

```vb
'Create a document fragment.
Dim xdocFrag As XmlDocumentFragment = xdoc.CreateDocumentFragment()

'<test:Product/>
Dim newPrEl As XmlElement = xdoc.CreateElement("test", "Product", "uri:test")

'Add the ProductID attribute to the element
'<test:Product ProductID="MU78"/>
Dim newPrId As XmlAttribute = xdoc.CreateAttribute("ProductID")
newPrId.Value = "MU78"
newPrEl.Attributes.SetNamedItem(newPrId)

'Add color, size, and price children
Dim newColEl As XmlElement = xdoc.CreateElement("color")
newColEl.InnerText = "red" 'You can't use Value!
newPrEl.AppendChild(newColEl)

Dim newSzEl As XmlElement = xdoc.CreateElement("size")
newSzEl.InnerText = "M"
newPrEl.AppendChild(newSzEl)

Dim newPriceEl As XmlElement = xdoc.CreateElement("price")
newPriceEl.InnerText = "125.99"
newPrEl.AppendChild(newPriceEl)

'Add the children of the document fragment to the original document
xdocFrag.AppendChild(newPrEl)

Dim xProdFam As XmlElement = _
  CType(xdoc.SelectSingleNode("//ProductFamily"), XmlElement)
xProdFam.AppendChild(xdocFrag.FirstChild)

textBox1.Text = xProdFam.OuterXml
End Sub
```

3. Run this program and you will get the following output:

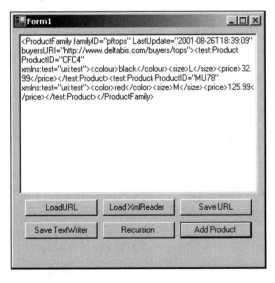

How It Works

Again the document is loaded into a new `XmlDocument` instance. As the `XmlDocument` itself may be large, it is much easier to create the XML we want to insert as a separate fragment, and then insert this whole fragment just once. There may be, depending of the size of the document, events that may be handled for the document, and other factors, some performance benefit in working with a fragment. It is also simpler for a developer to work on a simple fragment separate from the entire document, until the very last moment where you inject the fragment.

We therefore create a new `DocumentFragment` node, using the `XmlDocument` we created as the base document. A `DocumentFragment` is a `Document` object and is useful for cutting and rearranging document fragments. It can also have multiple child elements, unlike the `Document`, which can only have the root element as a child node.

We then start to create the fragment we want to insert, starting with the `Product` element node, which is qualified in the namespace `uri:test` and prefixed with the string test. This is done by called in the `CreateElement()` method of the `XmlDocument` instance as shown below:

```
Dim newPrEl As XmlElement = xdoc.CreateElement("test", "Product", "uri:test")
```

This gives us the XML fragment as follows:

```
<test:Product />
```

One this is done, we want to add the `ProductID` attribute to this element, and so the `CreateAttribute()` method is called with the name of the new attribute to create passed as the argument. The `Value` property is then used to set the value of this new attribute, and finally we have to attach the attribute to the `Product` element we just created.

```
Dim newPrId As XmlAttribute = xdoc.CreateAttribute("ProductID")
newPrId.Value = "MU78"
newPrEl.Attributes.SetNamedItem(newPrId)
```

The XML now looks as follows:

```
<test:Product ProductID="MU78" />
```

Following this, the `color` element is created and the value of this is set using the `InnerText` property. Like the attribute, elements must be attached to a parent, and so the `AppendChild()` method of the `Product` element node we created earlier is called, passing the new `color` element node as a parameter.

```
Dim newColEl As XmlElement = xdoc.CreateElement("color")
newColEl.InnerText = "red" 'You can't use Value!
newPrEl.AppendChild(newColEl)
```

Our XML fragment is now as follows:

```
<test:Product ProductID="MU78">
  <color>red</color>
</test:Product>
```

The `size` and `price` element nodes are then attached in a similar way to the `color` node, and then the entire document fragment is attached to the `DocumentFragment` node we created earlier.

```
xdocFrag.AppendChild(newPrEl)
```

Now we have to attach this fragment to the master document as a child node of the `ProductFamily` element node, so we use the `SelectSingleNode()` method and an XPath expression to return the `ProductFamily XmlNode`. Note that we use `//` in the XPath expression – this is not recommended when performance is of high importance, and you are better inserting the full path to the node (we won't as this is an example). When you use "`//`" in an XPath expression, it searches the entire document tree rather than the specific part of the document you are interested in – if your document is even a moderate size this will have a serious impact on performance.

```
Dim xProdFam As XmlElement = CType(xdoc.SelectSingleNode("//ProductFamily"), _
    XmlElement)
```

Notice that because we want to create an `XmlElement` node, we have to cast the return `XmlNode` from the `SelectSingleNode()` method. Finally, the `AppendChild()` method of this `XmlElement` node is used to add the contents of the `DocumentFragment` as a child; we have to add the `FirstChild` as we can't add the actual fragment itself.

```
xProdFam.AppendChild(xdocFrag.FirstChild)
```

The result is then written to the output.

```
textBox1.Text = xProdFam.OuterXml
```

Try It Out: Replacing Existing Nodes

The next scenario will look at the case where the user wants to change one of the items that have been ordered to some other item. In DOM terms, we want to replace the existing `Product` element node with a new element node containing the new data.

1. Add a new button to the form and give the button the text `Replace Product`.

2. Double-click the button and enter the following code to the button event handler.

```
Private Sub button7_Click(ByVal sender As System.Object, _
                        ByVal e As System.EventArgs) Handles button7.Click
    'Change the above to replace the order rather than add to it.

    'Looks at adding a new product element node and associates attributes & children

    'Create the XmlDocument.
    Dim xdoc As XmlDocument = New XmlDocument()
    xdoc.Load("..\\sample.xml")

    'Create a document fragment.
    Dim xdocFrag As XmlDocumentFragment = xdoc.CreateDocumentFragment()
```

```
                  '<test:Product/>
                  Dim newPrEl As XmlElement = xdoc.CreateElement("test", "Product", "uri:test")

                  'Add the ProductID attribute to the element
                  '<test:Product ProductID="MU78"/>
                  Dim newPrId As XmlAttribute = xdoc.CreateAttribute("ProductID")
                  newPrId.Value = "MU78"
                  newPrEl.Attributes.SetNamedItem(newPrId)

                  'Add color, size and price kids
                  Dim newColEl As XmlElement = xdoc.CreateElement("color")
                  newColEl.InnerText = "red" 'You can't use Value!
                  newPrEl.AppendChild(newColEl)

                  Dim newSzEl As XmlElement = xdoc.CreateElement("size")
                  newSzEl.InnerText = "M"
                  newPrEl.AppendChild(newSzEl)

                  Dim newPriceEl As XmlElement = xdoc.CreateElement("price")
                  newPriceEl.InnerText = "125.99"
                  newPrEl.AppendChild(newPriceEl)

                  'Add the children of the document fragment to the original document.
                  xdocFrag.AppendChild(newPrEl)

                  Dim xProdFam As XmlElement = _
                    CType(xdoc.SelectSingleNode("//ProductFamily"), XmlElement)
                  Dim xChildToGo As XmlElement = CType(xProdFam.ChildNodes(0), XmlElement)
                  xProdFam.ReplaceChild(xdocFrag.FirstChild, xChildToGo)
                  textBox1.Text = xProdFam.OuterXml
End Sub
```

3. Run this program and you will get the following output:

How It Works

This example is very similar to the last example where we added a given node. In this case we replace an existing node, so after we have selected the `ProductFamily` element node, we have to determine the child node that is to be replaced. In this case, we decide it is the first child node of this element using the `ChildNodes` property and indexer, and cast this `XmlNode` to an `XmlElement` node and return this node.

```
Dim xChildToGo As XmlElement = CType(xProdFam.ChildNodes(0), XmlElement)
```

Finally, the `ReplaceChild()` method is called on the `ProductFamily` element node; the document fragment contents are passed as the first parameter determining the new node, and the `XmlNode` child that is to be replaced is passed as the second parameter.

```
xProdFam.ReplaceChild(xdocFrag.FirstChild, xChildToGo)
```

Try It Out: Editing with InnerXml and InnerText

An alternative way to modify orders, or rather parts of orders, is to change the XML or text directly.

1. Add a new button to the form and give the button the text Change Order.

2. Double click the button and enter the following code to the button event handler.

```
Private Sub button8_Click(ByVal sender As System.Object, _
                          ByVal e As System.EventArgs) Handles button8.Click
    'Select and change the XML from <price>xxx</price> to
    '<price><currency type="dollars">xxx</currency></price>
    Dim xdoc As XmlDocument = New XmlDocument()
    xdoc.Load("..\\sample.xml")

    ' Get all of the price elements in the document
    Dim xList As XmlNodeList = xdoc.SelectNodes("//price")

    ' iterate through each node returned in the XmlNodeList
    Dim xNode As XmlNode
    For Each xNode In xList
      xNode.InnerXml = "<currency type=""dollar"">" & xNode.InnerText _
        & "</currency>"
    Next

    textBox1.Text = xdoc.OuterXml
End Sub
```

3. Run this program and click the **Change Order** button. You will get the following output:

How It Works

Again the XmlDocument instance is created from an XML file on disk. This time a list of all of the price element nodes are selected using the SelectNodes() method of the XmlDocument class, this will return an XmlNodeList of all of the price element nodes in this document.

```
Dim xList As XmlNodeList = xdoc.SelectNodes("//price")
```

When this list is returned, we use a For Each loop to iterate through each XmlNode in this XmlNodeList, and the InnerXml property of each XmlNode is changed to a new XML structure with the InnerText property being used to get the original text within the XmlNode.

```
Dim xNode As XmlNode
For Each xNode In xList
  xNode.InnerXml = "<currency type=""dollar"">" & xNode.InnerText _
    & "</currency>"
Next
```

The output from this section is therefore:

```
<currency type="dollar">22.99</currency>
```

Try It Out: Removing Nodes with XPath Queries

There are occasions when products are to be removed from the orders, and so this example looks at how this can be done with XPath and the SelectNodes() method.

1. Add a new button to the form and give the button the text Remove Product Info.

2. Double-click the button and add the following code to the button event handler:

```
Private Sub button9_Click(ByVal sender As System.Object, _
                          ByVal e As System.EventArgs) Handles button9.Click
    'Remove ProductFamily Nodes to just give a list of the companies who have made
    'orders
    Dim xdoc As XmlDocument = New XmlDocument()
    xdoc.Load("..\\sample.xml")
    Dim xList As XmlNodeList = xdoc.GetElementsByTagName("Company")

    Dim xNode As XmlNode
    For Each xNode In xList
      'Return those nodes with a URI
      Dim xProList As XmlNodeList = xNode.SelectNodes("ProductFamily")
      Dim xProNode As XmlNode
      For Each xProNode In xProList
        xNode.RemoveChild(xProNode)
      Next
    Next

    textBox1.Text = xdoc.OuterXml
End Sub
```

3. Run this program by clicking the **Remove Product Info** button and you will get the
following output:

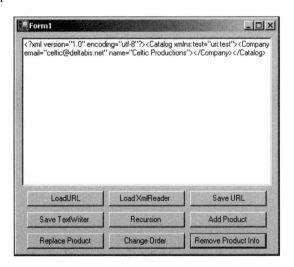

How It Works

This sample starts as always by loading the target XML document. However, the purpose is to return
only company information, so all product details should be removed. The first thing that is done is that
an `XmlNodeList` of all the `Company` element nodes is created using the `GetElementsByTagName()`
method, which takes the name of the element node you are searching for and returns an `XmlNodeList`
of the elements found. Thus, we have an `XmlNodeList` of `Company` elements.

261

```
Dim xList As XmlNodeList = xdoc.GetElementsByTagName("Company")
```

Next we want to iterate through this list and remove the `ProductFamily` elements and their children. So we start the iteration, and in each case get another `XmlNodeList` of all the `ProductFamily` elements within this company order.

```
For Each xNode In xList
    'Return those nodes with a URI
    Dim xProList As XmlNodeList = xNode.SelectNodes("ProductFamily")
```

With this list we again iterate through each `ProductFamily` node and call the `RemoveChild()` method of the original `Company` element node, passing the current `ProductFamily` element node as a parameter.

```
For Each xProNode In xProList
    xNode.RemoveChild(xProNode)
Next
```

This has the effect of removing each `ProductFamily` element node and all of its children and attributes, hence emptying the `Company` element of children. The result is as displayed in the figure above.

Try It Out: Importing Nodes from Other Documents

This final *Try It Out* will demonstrate how you can take orders from other XML documents and add them to the overall orders in the existing document. This involves importing the node rather than simply copying it, and this is what we will cover now.

1. Add a new button to the form and change the `Text` property to `Import Product Info`.

2. Double-click the button and enter the following code to the button event handler.

```
Private Sub button10_Click(ByVal sender As System.Object, _
                          ByVal e As System.EventArgs) Handles button10.Click
    'Importing Nodes from another XML document
    'Remove ProductFamily Nodes to just give a list
    'of the companies who have made orders

    'Load xml document
    Dim xdoc As XmlDocument = New XmlDocument()
    xdoc.Load("..\\sample.xml")

    Dim xdocImp As XmlDocument = New XmlDocument()
    xdocImp.Load("..\\sample2.xml")

    'Create an XmlNamespaceManager to resolve namespaces
    Dim nametab As NameTable = New NameTable()
    Dim nameMan As XmlNamespaceManager = New XmlNamespaceManager(nametab)
    nameMan.AddNamespace("p", "uri:test")

    'Get back product nodes in second doc that aren't in first
    Dim pNodes As XmlNodeList = xdocImp.SelectNodes("//p:Product", nameMan)
```

```
    'Iterate through XmlNodeList of Product elements
    Dim pNode As XmlNode
    For Each pNode In pNodes
        'Get back the value of the ProductID attribute on any Product elements.
        'The namespace manager is passed to resolve prefixes
        Dim pNodeImp As XmlNode = _
            xdoc.SelectSingleNode("//p:Product[@ProductID='" _
            & pNode.Attributes.GetNamedItem("ProductID").Value _
            & "']", nameMan)

        'If a node is not found in the main document then we want to import
        If pNodeImp Is Nothing Then 'node not found
            Dim importedNode As XmlNode = xdoc.ImportNode(pNode, True)

            ' add it as a child node to the main doc
            xdoc.SelectSingleNode("//ProductFamily").AppendChild(importedNode)
        End If
    Next

    textBox1.Text = xdoc.OuterXml
End Sub
```

3. Run the application and then click the Import Product Info button and you will get the following output:

How It Works

In this example, we took nodes from another XML document and merged it with another XML file. Initially both files were loaded.

```
Dim xdoc As XmlDocument = New XmlDocument()
xdoc.Load("..\\sample.xml")

Dim xdocImp As XmlDocument = New XmlDocument()
xdocImp.Load("..\\sample2.xml")
```

Next, an `XmlNamespaceManager` was created. This is needed to resolve and store namespaces. These namespaces allow you to associate nodes with a unique identifier such as a URL, which is then associated with some prefix to make referencing the namespace simpler (a document can however contain many namespaces, and hence different nodes throughout the document can be in different namespaces). This is required when you want to make qualified XPath queries. It requires a `NameTable` instance in its constructor, so we passed an empty instance. We then added the `uri:test` namespace to the cache and associated the prefix p with it. So all XPath queries in this namespace should be appended by the prefix `p:`.

```
Dim nametab As NameTable = New NameTable()
Dim nameMan As XmlNamespaceManager = New XmlNamespaceManager(nametab)
nameMan.AddNamespace("p", "uri:test")
```

With this set up, a qualified XPath query was made to return an `XmlNodeList` of the `Product` elements in the second XML document (that is, the one to be imported). Notice that the `XmlNamespaceManager` instance must be passed in this call to allow qualified queries to be made.

```
Dim pNodes As XmlNodeList = xdocImp.SelectNodes("//p:Product", nameMan)
```

We then iterate through each of the `Product` nodes returned from the document to be imported to try to determine which products are in the second XML document, but not in the first; this will determine the ones we want to import. We then use the `SelectSingleNode()` method of the first document (the importing document) to determine whether the `ProductID` attribute of each node in the second document exists in the first. Again, this must be qualified and so the `XmlNamespaceManager` must be passed.

```
For Each pNode In pNodes
    Dim pNodeImp As XmlNode = _
        xdoc.SelectSingleNode("//p:Product[@ProductID='" _
        & pNode.Attributes.GetNamedItem("ProductID").Value _
        & "']", nameMan)
```

If the `SelectSingleNode()` method did not return a node, then the `Product` from the second document does not exist in the first document and so we want to import it. To do this we must first call the `ImportNode()` method of the `XmlDocument` you are importing to and pass in the first parameter of the `XmlNode` you are wanting to import. The second parameter specifies whether you want to copy all child nodes; we do, so this is set to `True`.

```
If pNodeImp Is Nothing Then    'Node not found
    Dim importedNode As XmlNode = xdoc.ImportNode(pNode, True)
```

Finally, we find the `ProductFamily` element node in the first document and call its `AppendChild()` method with the imported node as a parameter, and now the node from the other document will be inserted into the first document.

```
    xdoc.SelectSingleNode("//ProductFamily").AppendChild(importedNode)
End If
```

Case Study

Let's finally continue with the case study and demonstrate how the techniques we have learned in this chapter can be applied. In this chapter, we will demonstrate a contact management application that allows you to:

❑ View the members of your contact list

❑ View details on an individual member

❑ Search for members by first, middle or last name

❑ Export your contacts to an XML file

❑ Import contacts from another XML file

Architecture

The application architecture contains three major components, the Application, the Import, and the Export as shown below.

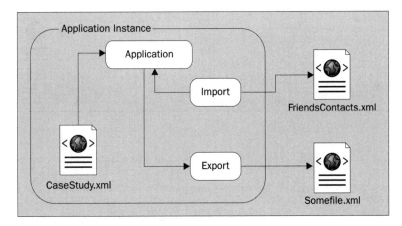

The Application contains the main logic that any user will work with, such as searching for users based on first name, middle name, or last name. It also allows users to select a specific user from a list provided and see more details about that user.

The second part is the ability to export contacts. If a user wants either move the contact list to another machine or share the contact list with another user, then the export functionality can be used to achieve this by creating an XML document on the file system.

The final part of the architecture is the Import facility, which will allow a user to import contacts that have been exported by another user. This facilitates the sharing of contacts among users.

This architecture can be mapped to an application context by defining the Application section above as a form (this could be a Windows Form or Web Form – in our case we use a Windows Form called Form 1). This will contain the core functionality as well as the import and export functions. The data for the contacts, both the local contacts and any contacts to be imported, are stored in XML files which act as the data tier for the purposes of this application (if the number of contacts increases dramatically they you may want to move the data in the data tier to a relational database).

Also, as the size of the XML files is relatively small we can load the files into XmlDocument instances – this allows us to perform filters and inserts/deletions directly on the document and persist it to disk.

Sequence Diagram

When working with the application, there is a sequence of events that occur, some automatically within the application and others as the result of a user action.

The following diagram shows the sequence of events when working with the application.

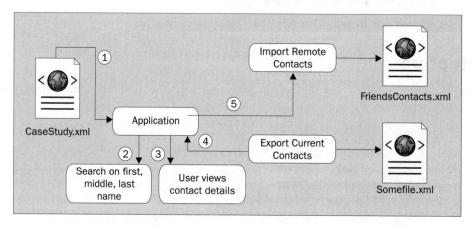

Let's look at what happens in each step.

1. The application loads the XML file CaseStudy.xml file containing contact details for the user

2. A user can choose to search for another user based on a first, middle, or last name

3. The details of an existing contact or contact(s) that have been retrieved can then be viewed

4. The user has the option of exporting the current contacts to an XML file on the file system (the location is determined by the user)

5. The user can also import contact details from another user's XML contact list on the file system

Let's now look at the application in a little more detail.

Application Details

Let's start the case study by looking at the XML file that holds all your contact information, `CaseStudy.xml`; this currently contains a single contact.

```
<?xml version="1.0" encoding="utf-8"?>
<ct:ContactDetails updateDate="20021201T14:00"
    xmlns:ct="http://www.deltabis.com/Contact">

  <!--This document contains contact information.-->
  <contact title="d2p1:Mr." xmlns:d2p1="http://www.deltabis.com/ns/titles/">
    <name>
      <first>Steven</first>
      <middle />
      <last>Livingstone-Perez</last>
    </name>
    <ct:notes>CEO of NTA Li&copy;mited, producer of the ProPortal&#xA9; system
      at http://www.deltabis.net. Security token is:
        <![CDATA[<securityAlgorithm>88hhdhddhs8*&W^H¥@HKJW)~~d<ssssowowo>>
        sswooowsw&(*&&^£&DJnxxj</securityAlgorithm>]]>
    </ct:notes>
  </contact>
</ct:ContactDetails>
```

The first thing that a user will do when this application is run is to view the members that are currently in the contact list. We look at loading these contacts now.

Loading User Contacts

The figure below shows the first screen that a user sees when this application is launched. Of immediate interest is that the Contacts list box that contains each of the contacts contained in the XML file; in this case my contact list has me.

In the event handler for the form load we have a method that is called to populate the listbox; this method is called `PopList()`.

```
Private Sub Form1_Load(ByVal sender As System.Object, _
                       ByVal e As System.EventArgs) Handles MyBase.Load
    'Initialise ListBox with all first and second names of contact list
    PopList(listBox1)
End Sub
```

The `PopList()` method takes as a parameter the `ListBox` control that you want to populate and doesn't return any value. The first thing it does is remove any previous items from the listbox. Following this, the `CaseStudy.xml` file is loaded into an `XmlDocument` instance and all of the name elements of each contact are returned as a `XmlNodeList` result from a `SelectNodes()` method.

```
Private Sub PopList(ByVal lBox As ListBox)
    listBox1.Items.Clear()

    'load the XML document get all name element nodes
    Dim xdoc As XmlDocument = New XmlDocument()
    xdoc.Load("..\\CaseStudy.xml")
    Dim xList As XmlNodeList = xdoc.SelectNodes("//name")
```

Finally, this `XmlNodeList` is iterated through and a new item is added to the `ListBox` in the form "lastname, firstname". The third child node of the current name element is the `last` element node and the first child node is the `first` element node.

```
    Dim xNode As XmlNode
    For Each xNode In xList
      lBox.Items.Add(xNode.ChildNodes(2).InnerText _
        & ", " & xNode.ChildNodes(0).InnerText)
    Next
End Sub
```

When one of the items in the contact list is clicked on, the application retrieves any notes about that user from the XML document and displays the information as shown below:

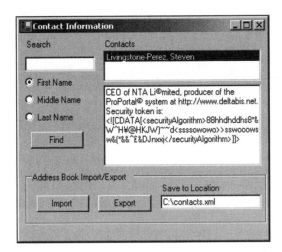

The `SelectedIndexChanged()` event handler of the `ListBox` first gets the text that is displayed for that item. It then manipulates the string to return the first name and the last name of the contact. Finally, the `DisplayNotes()` method is called, passing the first name and surname, and the result is written to the screen.

```
Private Sub listBox1_SelectedIndexChanged(ByVal sender As System.Object, _
    ByVal e As System.EventArgs) Handles listBox1.SelectedIndexChanged

  Dim itemtext As String = listBox1.GetItemText(listBox1.SelectedItem)
  Dim firstname As String = itemtext.Split(",")(1).Trim().ToString()
  Dim surname As String = itemtext.Split(",")(0).Trim().ToString()

  textBox2.Text = DisplayNotes(firstname, surname)
End Sub
```

The `DisplayNotes()` method simply loads the `CaseStudy.xml` document and calls the `SelectSingleNode()` method to find a single node where the contents of the `first` element match the first name passed, and the contents of the `last` element match the surname passed. When this is found, we know that the `Notes` element is the next sibling element of this name element, so the `NextSibling` property is used and its `InnerXml` property returns the marked up content of the notes for this contact.

```
Private Function DisplayNotes(ByVal firstname As String, _
                    ByVal surname As String) As String

  Dim xdoc As XmlDocument = New XmlDocument()
  xdoc.Load("..\\CaseStudy.xml")

  'Get the details of the notes element which is a sibling node next to the name
  'element node that has the persons first and last names matching
  Dim Notes As String = xdoc.SelectSingleNode("//name[first=""" _
    & firstname + """ and last=""" _
    & surname + """]").NextSibling.InnerXml

  Return Notes
End Function
```

This is great when we want to see a list of our users, but what happens when the list is large or we want to filter our contacts. Let's now see how the XML DOM can be used to perform this work.

Searching for Contacts

In the textbox below the **Search** label, you can enter in a string representing a person's **First Name**, **Middle Name**, or **Last Name** (specified by setting the radio buttons) and click the **Find** button to query the list for contacts that match your criterion.

When a contact or several contacts are found, a message box displays the number of contacts found and displays the information for each of those contacts.

When the **Find** button is clicked, the following event handler is invoked. The code determines which radio option has been selected, and then invokes the `FindContact()` method with the query also passed as a parameter.

```
Private Sub button3_Click(ByVal sender As System.Object, _
                          ByVal e As System.EventArgs) Handles button3.Click
    If (RadioButton1.Checked) Then
      FindContact("first", TextBox1.Text)
    ElseIf (RadioButton2.Checked) Then
      FindContact("middle", TextBox1.Text)
    Else
      FindContact("last", TextBox1.Text)
    End If
End Sub
```

Again the `XmlDocument` is instantiated and an `XmlNodeList` of name element nodes is created by combining whether we are querying the `first`, `middle`, or `last` element nodes and what the query string actually is.

```
Private Sub FindContact(ByVal type As String, ByVal query As String)
    Dim xdoc As XmlDocument = New XmlDocument()
    xdoc.Load("..\\CaseStudy.xml")

    'Get matching names
    Dim xList As XmlNodeList = xdoc.SelectNodes("//name[" + type _
      & "=""" + query + """]")
```

Next, a message box shows the user how many name elements were found using the `Count` property of the `XmlNodeList`. After this, each `XmlNode` in this node list is iterated through, and the `InnerText` property of each child node outputs the full name of the contact, the `Notes` element node, and the next sibling, is also appended to the output string.

```
    MessageBox.Show("There are " & xList.Count & " contacts matching your query.")

    ' iterate through each node and get contacts full names
    Dim xNode As XmlNode
    For Each xNode In xList
```

```
        Dim Message As String = ""
        Message = xNode.ChildNodes(0).InnerText _
           & " " + xNode.ChildNodes(1).InnerText _
           & " " + xNode.ChildNodes(2).InnerText

        Message = Message & "\n\nNotes\n====================" _
           & vbNewLine & xNode.NextSibling.InnerText

        MessageBox.Show(Message)
    Next
End Sub
```

Exporting Contacts

Often you may want to move your contact list to some other location. In our application we can output the XML contact information we have to a file location of our choice. The figure below shows an example of exporting the current contact list by clicking the Export button and setting the file location to C:\contacts.xml.

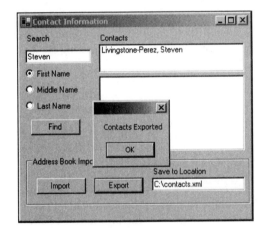

The output XML file is displayed in Internet Explorer as follows:

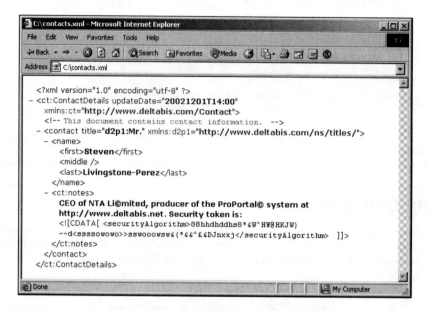

```
  C:\contacts.xml - Microsoft Internet Explorer                        _ □ x
 File    Edit    View    Favorites    Tools    Help

 Back  ▾  → ·  ⊗  ⊡  ⌂   Search   Favorites   Media   ⊙  ⊟▾ ⊜ ⊠ ⊟ ⊗
 Address  C:\contacts.xml                                               ▾

   <?xml version="1.0" encoding="utf-8" ?>
 - <ct:ContactDetails updateDate="20021201T14:00"
     xmlns:ct="http://www.deltabis.com/Contact">
     <!-- This document contains contact information. -->
 - <contact title="d2p1:Mr." xmlns:d2p1="http://www.deltabis.com/ns/titles/">
   - <name>
       <first>Steven</first>
       <middle />
       <last>Livingstone-Perez</last>
     </name>
   - <ct:notes>
       CEO of NTA Li©mited, producer of the ProPortal© system at
       http://www.deltabis.net. Security token is:
       <![CDATA[ <securityAlgorithm>88hhdhddhs8*&W^H¥@HKJW)
       ~~d<sssowowo>>sswooowsw&(*&&^£&DJnxxj</securityAlgorithm>  ]]>
     </ct:notes>
   </contact>
 </ct:ContactDetails>

  Done                                                  My Computer
```

When the **Export** button is clicked, the event handler below is called. It checks that a path has been entered to save the file and calls the `ExportContacts()` method, passing the file location as a parameter.

```
Private Sub Button2_Click(ByVal sender As System.Object, _
                          ByVal e As System.EventArgs) Handles Button2.Click
  If textBox3.Text.Trim().Length > 0 Then
    ExportContacts(textBox3.Text)
  End If

  MessageBox.Show("Contacts Exported")
End Sub
```

The `ExportContacts()` method itself loads the current contact list as an `XmlDocument` instance, and then calls the `Save()` method with the new file location as a parameter.

```
Private Sub ExportContacts(ByVal fPath As String)
  Const fOrigPath As String = "..\\CaseStudy.xml"
  Dim xdoc As XmlDocument = New XmlDocument()
  xdoc.Load(fOrigPath)

  xdoc.Save(fPath)
End Sub
```

Importing Other Contacts

If we have exported our contact list, it is equally likely that we are going to want to import our contact list or someone else's contact list. In this case, we want to import the contacts from the file `FriendsContacts.xml` who are not already in our contact list.

This file is shown below:

```xml
<?xml version="1.0" encoding="utf-8"?>
<ct:ContactDetails updateDate="20021201T14:00"
    xmlns:ct="http://www.deltabis.com/Contact">
  <!--This document contains contact information.-->
  <contact title="d2p1:Mr." xmlns:d2p1="http://www.deltabis.com/ns/titles/">
    <name>
      <first>Mark</first>
      <middle />
      <last>O&apos;Sullivan</last>
    </name>
    <ct:notes>ABCD Corp. French Translator for technical services.</ct:notes>
  </contact>
  <contact title="d2p1:Mrs." xmlns:d2p1="http://www.deltabis.com/ns/titles/">
    <name>
      <first>Maureen</first>
      <middle />
      <last>O&apos;Sullivan</last>
    </name>
    <ct:notes>CTO of ABCD Corp. in UK ventures.</ct:notes>
  </contact>
</ct:ContactDetails>
```

This file has two contacts that are not available in our XML file. Any contacts that already exist in our main XML document will not be imported. To import, the Import button is clicked and you are notified when the process is complete and your contact list is refreshed.

Now that these contacts have been imported, you can now query for names that previously could not be found in the database.

If you export the newly updated contacts file, you will get the following output in Internet Explorer:

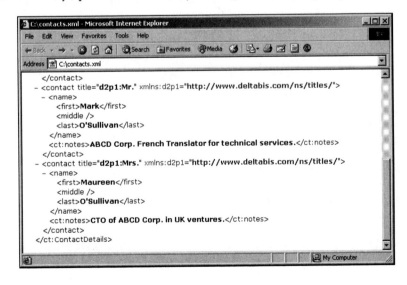

When the Import button is clicked, the following event handler is called. This first calls the `ImportContacts()` method to import the contacts from the other contact list, and then refreshes the listbox to display the latest list of users.

```
Private Sub Button1_Click(ByVal sender As System.Object, _
                          ByVal e As System.EventArgs) Handles Button1.Click
  If (textBox3.Text.Trim().Length > 0) Then
    'Import any contacts
    ImportContacts(textBox3.Text)
  End If

  ' Refresh the contact display list
  PopList(listBox1)
  MessageBox.Show("Contacts Imported")
End Sub
```

The `ImportContacts()` method starts by loading the XML document containing the contacts and the XML document of the contacts that are to be imported into two separate `XmlDocument` instances.

```
Private Sub ImportContacts(ByVal FriendFilePath As String)
  Dim FilePath As String = "..\\CaseStudy.xml"

  'Importing Nodes from another XML document
  'Remove ProductFamily Nodes to just give a list of the companies who have
  'made orders
  Dim xdoc As XmlDocument = New XmlDocument()
  xdoc.Load(FilePath)

  Dim xdocImp As XmlDocument = New XmlDocument()
  xdocImp.Load(FriendFilePath)
```

Next, a list of the contact element nodes is returned in an `XmlNodeList`. An `XmlNamespaceManager` instance is then populated so that we can qualify any queries in the `http://www.deltabis.com/Contact` namespace.

```
'Get back product nodes in second doc that aren't in first
Dim pNodes As XmlNodeList = xdocImp.SelectNodes("//contact")

'create an XmlNamespaceManager to resolve namespaces
Dim nametab As NameTable = New NameTable()
Dim nameMan As XmlNamespaceManager = New XmlNamespaceManager(nametab)
nameMan.AddNamespace("ns", "http://www.deltabis.com/Contact")
```

The following code will look very familiar, as is it is almost identical to what we used in the importing example we worked with earlier. This will determine which contacts are not in the contact list and import these from the second document to the first contact document. Notice that this time, it uses the `XmlNamespaceManager` instance (which binds a prefix to a namespace within the XML document) to qualify the `ContactDetails` element in the `SelectSingleNode()` query. This is required because the namespace `http://www.deltabis.com/Contact` is the default namespace.

```
Dim pNode As XmlNode
For Each pNode In pNodes
    'get back any contacts that have the first and last name suggested
    Dim pNodeImp As XmlNode = _
        xdoc.SelectSingleNode("//contact/name[first=""" _
        & pNode.FirstChild.ChildNodes.Item(0).InnerXml _
        & """ and last = """ _
        & pNode.FirstChild.ChildNodes.Item(2).InnerXml & """]")

    ' the node was not found in the main document
    If (pNodeImp Is Nothing) Then 'node not found
        'Import the node to the main document
        Dim importedNode As XmlNode = xdoc.ImportNode(pNode, True)

        'Append this node to the main document
        xdoc.SelectSingleNode("//ns:ContactDetails", _
            nameMan).AppendChild(importedNode)
    End If
Next
```

Finally, this new contact list is persisted and overwrites the original contact list.

```
    xdoc.Save(FilePath)
End Sub
```

You may look at extending this case study with some of the following exercises:

❑ We suggest you try to improve on the model with the addition of further contact details such as telephone and e-mail details.

❑ You may look at adding new/edit/delete features in a new form to edit some of the existing contact details as well as add new contacts.

❑ You could also add in validation by using the DOM events to catch modifications to the data and raise errors when the changes fail validation.

What Did We Learn?

This part of the case study has taught us how to employ DOM techniques within a sample application. The `XmlDocument` is a very useful representation of an XML file when you are required to query for data, such as the first, middle, and last names in our application. Of course the XPath queries themselves could have been far more difficult (such as case-sensitivity), depending on your requirements.

You will also have seen how the `XmlNamespaceManager` is required for qualified queries – it is important that this is a major point that you take away from this chapter as it is a common problem for beginners. The `XPathExpression` can be useful beyond simply compiling the expressions to make them more efficient, as you saw when we included sort criteria on our queries.

Finally, you will have seen how simple it is to transport XML between applications. The same principles allow you to integrate your application with other applications that were written by third parties, not knowing your XML structure. The XML data you have could, for example, be imported into Microsoft Outlook (with some customization and using Extensible Stylesheet technology which we meet in a couple of chapters) or some other similar application.

275

Summary

This chapter looked in depth at the XML Document Object Model and how it is implemented and used in the .NET Framework. We started the chapter by looking at the difference between the DOM model and the streaming model we discussed in previous chapters.

We examined the DOM inheritance model and went into detail specifically on the XmlNode type, as this is the base for all the other node types that are used in the DOM implementation. We examined many of the properties and methods of the XmlNode class and demonstrated how these can be used in practice.

We continued with a look at the XmlDocument class, which is a concrete implementation where we can work with the XmlNode and derived types. We demonstrated how to work with the numerous properties and methods of the XmlDocument and XmlNode classes, in particular creating nodes and importing nodes was discussed.

The chapter concluded with an in-depth example of applying the principles of this chapter to our ongoing case study. Here we looked at how to list contacts, search and filter contacts, as well as import contacts from other address books. We also mentioned how this model can be extended.

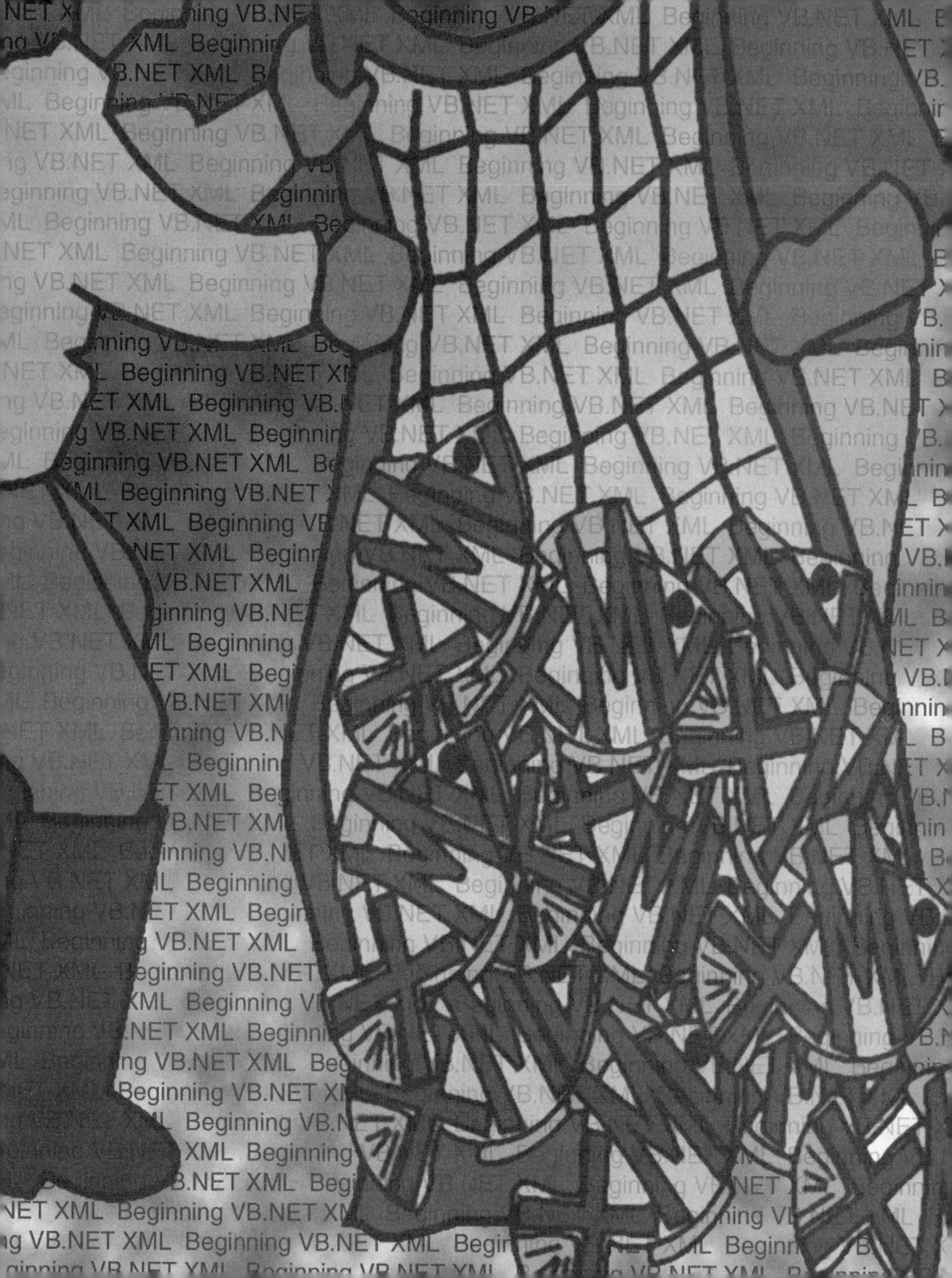
Beginning VB.NET XML

XPath and .NET

We have now covered a great deal of the functionality available in the XmlDocument and related classes. We have looked at how to use the XmlNode base class and how to load an XML document. We have also looked at how simple navigation can be done with the XmlDocument class.

In this chapter we are going to extend our understanding of working with the DOM in .NET and discuss how XPath can be used in .NET to achieve complex navigation and filtering on our XML documents. We are also going to look at the basics of how serialization (and de-serialization) of classes can be done directly in .NET using XML.

In this chapter, you will learn:

❑ What is the System.Xml.XPath namespace

❑ The XPathDocument class

❑ The XPathNavigator class

❑ When to use XPathNavigator

❑ How XPath can be used effectively with the XmlDocument class

❑ Custom XPathNavigator classes

❑ XML Serialization

❑ Using XPathNavigator with the ongoing case study

The support for XPath in .NET is primarily provided through the System.Xml.XPath namespace. It supports the W3C XML Path Language 1.0 available at http://www.w3.org/TR/xpath.

The System.Xml.XPath Namespace

The `System.Xml.XPath` namespace is the core namespace for working with XPath in .NET. Although `System.Xml.XmlDocument` supports some simple XPath queries using the `SelectSingleNode()` and `SelectNodes()` methods, this namespace provides classes for performing optimized read-only XPath queries against any data source, allowing compilation of expressions to improve performance. The more complex your queries become the more efficient a compiled query becomes.

In fact, the XPath namespace constitutes the following five classes:

❑   `XPathDocument` – Provides a data store for your XML documents that is optimized for XPath querying and XSLT processing.

❑   `XPathException` – The exception thrown if errors occur while executing an XPath expression.

❑   `XPathExpression` – Represents a compiled XPath expression, which can be used to improve the performance of your queries.

❑   `XPathNavigator` – Provides navigation facilities for the XML document. However, this is read-only, and unlike the `XmlDocument` class, does not support editing. This class can also feed into the XSLT classes discussed in the next chapter to perform optimized XML transformations.

❑   `XPathNodeIterator` – Provides iteration capabilities over an XPath node set.

Before we start on the details of this chapter, it is probably a good idea if you are new to the XPath language to read over the relevant sections in Chapter 3. If you are confident you now understand XPath, let's start by looking in some more detail at the classes discussed above.

XPath Classes in .NET

When working with classes such as the `XmlDocument` and `XmlNode` classes, you will remember that they had some ability to perform XPath queries using the `SelectSingleNode()` and `SelectNodes()` methods. These methods provide some fairly basic functionality in allowing any XPath query to be used to get a set of nodes back from a target XML document; however, that is all they offer.

Astute readers will also have noticed that the `XmlDocument` and `XmlNode` classes both provide a `CreateNavigator()` method. This method can be used to create an instance of an `XPathNavigator` class and can be used for querying any data source using XPath – all it requires is that the store implements the `IXPathNavigable` interface. You can even create your own custom object representing a data store (such as a database or file store) that can use the `XPathNavigator` class, so long as the class implements the `IXPathNavigable` interface.

As the `XmlDataDocument` class also inherits from the `XmlDocument` class, it also supports the `XPathNavigator` class (again via the `CreateNavigator()` method) so you can even perform XPath queries on relational data held in a dataset (we look at Datasets in Chapter 12).

Finally there is the XPathDocument class, which is like a stripped-down version of the XmlDocument class. The class is a read-only data model and therefore you cannot edit the XML stored within an XpathDocument. In this way the overhead associated with the DOM managing the modifications doesn't exist. The XPathDocument class doesn't maintain any node identity, nor does it check the document against the requirements of the XML DOM; the class only allows you to perform XPath queries. The XPathDocument class is also the recommended store for performing XSL transforms, which we'll look at later in the book.

Again, in common with the classes discussed above, the XPathDocument class uses the CreateNavigator() method to create an XPathNavigator instance, which can be used to perform queries over the document.

In fact, once we have created an XPathNavigator instance over a store (such as XmlDocument, XmlNode or XPathDocument) we can use methods that are a combination of many of the methods available in the XmlDocument and XmlReader classes. Examples are MoveToRoot(), MoveToParent(), Select(), and SelectChildren().

We now have three main techniques for accessing XML data:

❑ XmlDocument and XPathNavigator – provide in-memory view of data and editing facilities, and checks for XML conformance, as well as providing events for data modification

❑ XmlReader – provides read-only optimized sequential access to the data

❑ XPathDocument and XPathNavigator – provides in-memory read-only optimized random access to XML data

There are some similarities between the XmlReader and XPathDocument classes in terms of functionality and even at the method level. However, the XPathDocument still has to parse the XML document into memory and so will be slower for large documents than the XmlReader.

The XPathDocument Class

The XPathDocument class is like a stripped-down version of the XmlDocument class discussed in the last chapter. It doesn't offer the extent of functionality provided by the XmlDocument class, but provides six overloads for its constructor to create a new XPathDocument instance. It also provides a CreateNavigator() method to create an instance of the XPathNavigator class (this is the next class to be discussed).

The overloads for the XPathDocument constructor are as follows:

Constructor	Description
Sub New(Stream)	Allows you to pass a stream of bytes into the constructor, such as an XML data stream stored in memory.
Sub New(String)	Creates a new XPath document from the URL specified.
Sub New(TextReader)	Uses a TextReader object as an argument to specify the document to be loaded.

Table continued on following page

Constructor	Description
`Sub New(XmlReader)`	Takes an `XmlReader` instance, which is also a read-only view of the document. We can still use the `XmlReader` object as normal (moving around, and so on) and then come back to the `XPathDocument` object and it will automatically update itself for the current position in the `XmlReader`. This is in contrast to the `Stream`/`String`/`TextReader` versions which load the document in one go.
`Sub New(String, XmlSpace)`	This constructor also takes a URL as a parameter, but its second argument allows you to specify how to support whitespace in the document. If the `XmlSpace` parameter is set to `XmlSpace.Default` then only significant whitespace is preserved; otherwise `XmlSpace.Preserve` keeps all the whitespace in the document.
`Sub New(XmlReader, XmlSpace)`	Takes an `XmlReader` representing the XML document, and again an `XmlSpace` parameter as above to indicate how whitespace should be handled.

When using the `XmlReader` overloaded constructor, if the `XmlReader` instance is positioned on an `XmlNode`, the `XPathDocument` class will load the `XmlNode` and all of its children, hence allowing you to load only a fragment of an XML document. If, however, the `XmlReader` is positioned on an `XmlNode` type that is invalid as the root of a document, such as `XmlAttribute`, then the reader will read each following node until it finds a node that would be a valid document element node and loads from that point instead. In the case where the fragment is actually a set of sibling nodes (and remember that an XML document must have a single top-level root element!), this class will wrap them in a root node to create a valid XML document fragment.

Due to the host of constructors available, this class can, in fact, represent many different data sources as an XPath document; for example, you may have data in SQL Server that you want to perform queries against. The `XmlDataDocument` class allows you to access this data as an XML document, but the `XPathDocument` class allows an optimized view of that data for performing XPath queries against the data.

Try It Out: Creating an XPathDocument from a URL

This example is fairly short and simple, but just demonstrates how to load our case study XML document instance from a file location into an `XPathDocument` class. We don't yet do anything with it, but we will shortly.

> *Note that all the sample code for this chapter is available for download from http://www.wrox.com. We will be storing sample code for this chapter within the following folder: C:\BegVBXML\Chapter07. You may, of course, use a different folder depending on what you prefer.*

1. Create a new Windows Application project, call it Examples, and add a new Button control to the form. Change the button's Text property to URL XPathDocument.

2. Add the following XML document, containing details on personal contact information, to the project, and call the file `CaseStudy.xml` (alternatively this is available in the code download and should be put in the `Examples` root directory).

```xml
<?xml version="1.0" encoding="utf-8"?>
<ct:ContactDetails updateDate="20021201T14:00"
xmlns:ct="http://www.deltabis.com/Contact">
  <!--This document contains contact information.-->
  <contact title="d2p1:Mr." xmlns:d2p1="http://www.deltabis.com/ns/titles/">
    <name>
      <first>Steven</first>
      <middle />
      <last>Livingstone-Perez</last>
    </name>
    <ct:notes>CEO of NTA Li©mited, producer of the ProPortal© system at
http://www.deltabis.net. Security token is:
<![CDATA[<securityAlgorithm>88hhdhddhs8*&W^H¥@HKJW)~~d<ssssowowo>>sswooowsw&(*&&^£
&DJnxxj</securityAlgorithm>]]></ct:notes>
  </contact>
  <contact title="d2p1:Mr." xmlns:d2p1="http://www.deltabis.com/ns/titles/">
    <name>
      <first>Diego</first>
      <middle>Adriano</middle>
      <last>Perez</last>
    </name>
    <ct:notes>Latest addition to the Perez family.</ct:notes>
  </contact>
</ct:ContactDetails>
```

3. Double-click the button and add the following to the top of the code:

```vb
Imports System.Xml
Imports System.Xml.XPath
```

4. Now add the following code to the event handler for the button:

```vb
Private Sub Button1_Click(ByVal sender As System.Object, _
                          ByVal e As System.EventArgs) Handles Button1.Click
    'Load XPath document using XPathDocument class
    Dim xpDoc As XPathDocument = New XPathDocument("..\\CaseStudy.xml")
    MessageBox.Show("Created XPathDocument from URL")

    'Load XPath document using XPathDocument class with whitespace
    xpDoc = New XPathDocument("..\\CaseStudy.xml", XmlSpace.Preserve)
    MessageBox.Show("Created XPathDocument from URL with whitespace preserved.")

    Dim xRead As XmlTextReader = New XmlTextReader("..\\CaseStudy.xml")
    Dim xpdoc2 As XPathDocument = New XPathDocument(xRead)
    MessageBox.Show("Created XPathDocument from XmlReader")
End Sub
```

5. Run this application and you will get three messages after each of the instances of the XPathDocument classes have each been created. You will get the following when the XmlReader has been created.

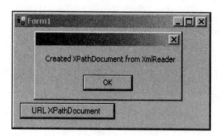

How It Works

In this example the XPathDocument class was used because the size of the XML file was quite small and we didn't have to modify the document in any way – we need it open for read-only queries. If we had needed to modify the contents of the XML document we would have used an XmlDocument instance.

We then used the XmlReader class to load the document, which is more suitable when the file is quite a bit larger and when you don't have to perform any queries on it – in other words you are happy with retrieving the data in a forward-only manner and random access to the document is not required.

Let's now look at the XPathNavigator class, which represents any store as a read-only XML document, thereby allowing XPath queries to be run against it.

The XPathNavigator Class

The XPathNavigator class provides us with a read-only view over a store represented as an XML document – the underlying store can be any format you want, such as a relational database or CSV file, but the XPathNavigator itself will act as though the store is in XML format. It is very fast and efficient and is optimized to work with the XslTransform class we discuss later, which is responsible for performing XSL transforms where the structure of an XML document is transformed to another structure. You cannot use this when you want to modify the underlying store, however, as it is read-only; in this case it would be better to use some sort of representation of the data that allows it to be modified such as the XmlDocument class for XML.

The XPathNavigator class can be invoked by many classes in .NET via the CreateNavigator() method. This method is available in any class that implements the IXPathNavigable interface, such as XmlDocument, XmlNode (and derived classes such as XmlElement), XmlDataDocument, and of course the XPathDocument classes.

As was touched on above, any class that implements the IXPathNavigable interface can use the XPathNavigator class to perform XPath queries over the data structure that it represents. This structure can be XML data as is the case with the XmlDocument class, or semi-structured data such as a file system.

As the XPathNavigator class is a fundamental class in working with XPath, it's worth looking at the members of this class, which we'll do now.

It was mentioned earlier that the `XPathNavigator` class contains many methods that are available in the `XmlDocument` and `XmlReader` classes, such as `Select()` and `MoveTo()`. There are also methods available for working with namespaces, notably `MoveToNamespace()`, `MoveToFirstNamespace()`, and `MoveToNextNamespace()` – we discuss these shortly. While we work through these members, it is worth looking back and comparing the discussions that were made in earlier sections on the `XmlDocument` and `XmlReader` members – mainly because many of them are functionally the same.

We will therefore concentrate on the differences here and you can refer to the discussion on the `XmlDocument` class for further information.

XPathNavigator Properties

We have met the properties of this class in other classes that we discussed earlier (such as the `XmlDocument` and `XmlNode` classes), so we won't reiterate them again here.

XPathNavigator Methods

The methods of the `XPathNavigator` class are similar to those of the `XmlReader` class; we will not mention in any detail those that are the same.

Those methods that are the same are:

- ❑ `Equals`
- ❑ `GetHashCode`
- ❑ `GetType`

We are going to cover most of the methods available in the `XPathNavigator` class; however, we are going to break at points during the discussion to demonstrate how they are used in *Try It Out* sections. This should allow you to advance your understanding as you move to the more in-depth methods in later pages.

The MoveTo() Method

This method takes another `XPathNavigator` instance as an argument and moves the current `XPathNavigator` to that position in the XML document, returning `True`. This will only work, of course, if the other `XPathDocument` specified as a parameter defines a node that also exists in the current XML document; if it doesn't this method would return `False`.

The MoveToFirstChild() Method

This method will move to the first child node of the current node, and will only work for the root and element nodes since these are the only XPath node types that can have children. It will return `True` when there is a child node, and `False` when there are no child nodes.

The MoveToRoot() Method

This is a useful method as it takes you straight to the root of the document, ignoring whitespace, comments, and processing instructions and will position the `XPathNavigator` at the root of the current XML document.

The MoveToId() Method

The `MoveToId()` method is useful when you have defined an `ID` type in a DTD or Schema that is to uniquely identify certain elements. You can pass in, as a parameter, the string representing the ID you are looking for, and the `XPathNavigator` will be positioned on that node, and will return `True`. If it can't find such a node, the position of the `XPathNavigator` will be unchanged and `False` will be returned.

The MoveToAttribute(), MoveToFirstAttribute(), and MoveToNextAttribute() Methods

The `MoveToAttribute()` method takes the local name and namespace URI as parameters and will move to the attribute matching those values on the current element node. It will return `True` when this move is successful, and `False` when the `XPathNavigator` is not positioned on an element node or there are no attributes matching the specified values.

The `MoveToFirstAttribute()` method, however, is simpler in that it will just move to the first attribute defined in document order on the element node. It will then return `True` when this move is successful, and `False` when there are no attributes defined on the current element or when the `XPathNavigator` is not positioned on an `XmlElement` node type.

Finally, the `MoveToNextAttribute()` can be used to move to the next attribute when positioned on an `attribute` node type. It will return `True` when this is successful, or `False` when there are no attributes, no more attributes, or the `XPathNavigator` is not positioned on an `attribute` node.

Try It Out: Working with Attributes

To illustrate how we can use these methods, let's return to the sample we were working with above in our last *Try It Out*.

1. Add a new button to the form and give it the `Text` property **Attributes**. In addition, add a new `TextBox` with the `Multiline` property set to `True`.

2. Double-click on the button and add the following code to the event handler:

```
Private Sub Button2_Click(ByVal sender As System.Object, _
                          ByVal e As System.EventArgs) Handles Button2.Click
    'Stores header information
    Dim headerText As String = ""

    'Working with IDs in the XPathNavigator
    Dim xpDoc As XPathDocument = New XPathDocument("..\\CaseStudy.xml")
    Dim xpNav As XPathNavigator = xpDoc.CreateNavigator()

    textBox1.Text = ""

    'Get to root of document
    xpNav.MoveToRoot()
    xpNav.MoveToFirstChild()
    headerText = "Currently positioned at "

    textBox1.Text = textBox1.Text & headerText & xpNav.Name _
        & System.Environment.NewLine
```

```
      'MoveTo the updateDate attribute
      Dim fUpDate As Boolean = xpNav.MoveToAttribute("updateDate", String.Empty)
      headerText = "Found updateDate attribute? "

      textBox1.Text = textBox1.Text & headerText & fUpDate _
        & System.Environment.NewLine

      'MoveTo the first attribute
      xpNav.MoveToFirstAttribute()
      headerText = "Found first attribute called "

      textBox1.Text = textBox1.Text & headerText & xpNav.Name _
        & System.Environment.NewLine

      'MoveTo the next attribute
      fUpDate = xpNav.MoveToNextAttribute()
      headerText = "Another attribute found? "

      textBox1.Text = textBox1.Text & headerText & fUpDate _
        & System.Environment.NewLine
End Sub
```

3. Run this application by pressing the *F5* key and you will get the following output after clicking the **Attributes** button:

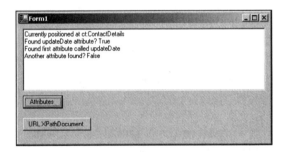

How It Works

The intention of this sample is to read the values of the root element and any attributes and write them to the output. We used an `XPathDocument` class to read in an XML document as we only intend to do XPath queries on the content and it can be read-only (a document loaded into an `XPathDocument` instance cannot be changed) as we don't want to modify the content. An `XPathNavigator` instance is also created to allow us to query the document using XPath statements.

Let's look at the code in the sample, which is concerned with the document element node of the sample XML file.

```
<?xml version="1.0" encoding="utf-8"?>
<ct:ContactDetails updateDate="20021201T14:00"
    xmlns:ct="http://www.deltabis.com/Contact">
...
```

The first important piece of code to note here is that when the button is clicked, the XML sample file is loaded as an `XPathDocument` instance and a new `XPathNavigator` instance is then created.

```
Dim xpDoc As XPathDocument = New XPathDocument("..\\CaseStudy.xml")
Dim xpNav As XPathNavigator = xpDoc.CreateNavigator()
```

Following this, we first call the `MoveToRoot()` method, which will move to the document root and then call the `MoveToFirstChild()` method discussed above; however, this will move to the first child of the document root, which in this case happens to be the document root element, ignoring the prolog element.

```
xpNav.MoveToRoot()
xpNav.MoveToFirstChild()
```

Next, the `MoveToAttribute()` method is called, passing `updateDate` as the attribute name we are looking for. We specify that there is no namespace using `String.Empty` (or you can use `nothing`) and store the Boolean return value in a variable.

```
Dim fUpDate As Boolean = xpNav.MoveToAttribute("updateDate", String.Empty)
```

This then places us on the `updateDate` attribute, so we write out that the search for this attribute on the document element was `True`, as stored in the variable.

The next method we call is the `MoveToFirstAttribute()` method which will move to the first attribute defined on the current element node, which in this case is still the `updateDate` attribute node. We write out the value of this attribute node to confirm this.

```
xpNav.MoveToFirstAttribute()
```

Finally, while still on the `updateDate` attribute node, we call the `MoveToNextAttribute()` method which should return `False` as there are no more attributes defined on the document element in our instance.

```
fUpDate = xpNav.MoveToNextAttribute()
```

We write this out to ensure that it is indeed the case.

Let's continue looking at the `MoveXXX()` navigation methods available to use in the `XPathNavigator` class.

The MoveToFirst(), MoveToNext(), MoveToPrevious(), and MoveToParent() Methods

The `MoveToFirst()` method moves the `XPathNavigator` to the first sibling of the current node. The first sibling is a node at the same level as the current node, but is first in document order (in other words the first sibling comes before the current node and any other node at that level). This will return `True` if there is a first sibling and it moves to this node, otherwise it will return `False` when there is no first sibling or the `XPathNavigator` instance is positioned on an attribute node.

The `MoveToNext()` method does a similar thing, but moves to the next sibling node of the current `XmlNode` in document order. If this is successful it returns `True` and moves to the next sibling, and returns `False` if there is no next sibling, or we are on an attribute node, and stays positioned at the current node.

The `MoveToPrevious()` method is the opposite of the last method and will move to the previous sibling node defined in document order. If there is no previous sibling node or we are on an attribute node this will return `False` and stay at the current position, otherwise it returns `True` and moves to the previous sibling node.

Finally, the `MoveToParent()` method moves to the parent node of the current `XmlNode`. This will only return `True` and move to the parent when the current node has a parent node; otherwise it will return `False`. Attributes, text, and namespaces go to an element node, and all the rest go to an element or the root. The root node itself doesn't have a parent node.

Try It Out: Moving Around the Document

Let's look at how we can use these methods to work with our sample document.

1. Add a new button to the form and call it `Moving`.

2. Double-click on the button and add the following code to the event handler:

```
Private Sub Button3_Click(ByVal sender As System.Object, _
                          ByVal e As System.EventArgs) Handles Button3.Click
    'Stores header information
    Dim headerText As String = ""
    headerText = "Currently positioned at "

    'Working with IDs in the XPathNavigator
    Dim xpDoc As XPathDocument = New XPathDocument("..\\CaseStudy.xml")
    Dim xpNav As XPathNavigator = xpDoc.CreateNavigator()

    textBox1.Text = ""

    'Get to root of document
    xpNav.MoveToRoot()
    textBox1.Text = textBox1.Text & headerText & xpNav.NodeType.ToString() _
        & System.Environment.NewLine

    'Move to ContactDetails
    xpNav.MoveToFirstChild()
    textBox1.Text = textBox1.Text & headerText & xpNav.Name &
System.Environment.NewLine

    'Move to Comment
    xpNav.MoveToFirstChild()
    textBox1.Text = textBox1.Text & headerText & xpNav.NodeType.ToString() _
        & System.Environment.NewLine

    'Move to contact
    xpNav.MoveToNext()
    textBox1.Text = textBox1.Text & headerText & xpNav.Name _
        & System.Environment.NewLine

    'Move to name
```

```
xpNav.MoveToFirstChild()
textBox1.Text = textBox1.Text & headerText & xpNav.Name _
  & System.Environment.NewLine

'Move to first
xpNav.MoveToFirstChild()
textBox1.Text = textBox1.Text & headerText & xpNav.Name _
  & System.Environment.NewLine

'Positioned at the first child element node
textBox1.Text = textBox1.Text & headerText & xpNav.Name _
  & System.Environment.NewLine

'Move to middle element node
xpNav.MoveToNext()
textBox1.Text = textBox1.Text & headerText & xpNav.Name _
  & System.Environment.NewLine

'Move to last element node
xpNav.MoveToNext()
textBox1.Text = textBox1.Text & headerText & xpNav.Name _
  & System.Environment.NewLine

'Move to middle element node
xpNav.MoveToPrevious()
textBox1.Text = textBox1.Text & headerText & xpNav.Name _
  & System.Environment.NewLine

'Move to first element node
xpNav.MoveToFirst()
textBox1.Text = textBox1.Text & headerText & xpNav.Name _
  & System.Environment.NewLine

'Move to parent name element node
xpNav.MoveToParent()
textBox1.Text = textBox1.Text & headerText & xpNav.Name _
  & System.Environment.NewLine
End Sub
```

3. Run this application, click the Moving button and you will get the following output.

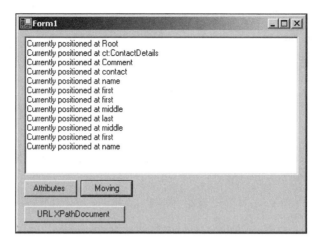

How It Works

In this example, we look at the following XML fragment from the sample XML file.

```
<?xml version="1.0" encoding="utf-8"?>
<ct:ContactDetails updateDate="20021201T14:00"
    xmlns:ct="http://www.deltabis.com/Contact">
  <!--This document contains contact information.-->
  <contact title="d2p1:Mr." xmlns:d2p1="http://www.deltabis.com/ns/titles/">
    <name>
      <first>Steven</first>
      <middle />
      <last>Livingstone-Perez</last>
    </name>
...
```

When the button is clicked, new `XPathDocument` and `XPathNavigator` instances are created again. We then navigate to the root of the document, which is the node before the document element node.

```
'Get to root of document
xpNav.MoveToRoot()
```

Calling the `MoveToFirstChild()` at this point will move the navigator to the `ContactDetails` document element node. The text "Currently positioned at ct:ContactDetails" is shown to indicate this.

```
'Move to ContactDetails
xpNav.MoveToFirstChild()
```

Then we move to the next node, which is a comment node. We want to get to the `<contact>` element so we skip the comment node by calling the `MoveToNext()` method which moves to the next sibling, which is the contact element node, and then display this in the textbox.

```
'Move to Comment
xpNav.MoveToFirstChild()
textBox1.Text = textBox1.Text & headerText & xpNav.NodeType.ToString() _
  & System.Environment.NewLine

'Move to contact
xpNav.MoveToNext()
textBox1.Text = textBox1.Text & headerText & xpNav.Name _
  & System.Environment.NewLine
```

Following this, we move to the first child node of the `contact` node, which is the `name` node, and then finally to the `first` element child node.

```
'Move to name
xpNav.MoveToFirstChild()
textBox1.Text = textBox1.Text & headerText & xpNav.Name _
  & System.Environment.NewLine

'Move to first
xpNav.MoveToFirstChild()
textBox1.Text &= headerText & xpNav.Name & System.Environment.NewLine
```

We are now positioned on the element called `first` which has the value `Steven`.

We again call the `MoveToNext()` method which moves to the next sibling of this element, with this being the empty `middle` element node. The `MoveToNext()` method is called again and this moves to the element node called `last`. At this point we use the `MoveToPrevious()` method to move the navigator back to the middle element.

```
xpNav.MoveToPrevious()
```

We again call the `MoveToFirst()` method to return us to the first element node. Finally, the `MoveToParent()` method can be called to move the navigator back to the parent name element node.

```
xpNav.MoveToParent()
```

We are going to continue looking at the navigation methods provided by the `XPathNavigator`. Specifically we will look at navigating a document that uses namespaces.

The MoveToNamespace(), MoveToFirstNamespace(), and MoveToNextNamespace() Methods

These three methods allow you to navigate the namespace axis to retrieve namespace nodes on the current element node (it returns `False` if it is called on any other node type). The `MoveToNamespace()` method takes the name of the namespace node to navigate to – the name is the prefix of the namespace node. If the move to the node with this name is successful then `True` is returned from this method, or else `False` is returned.

The `MoveToFirstNamespace()` method moves to the first namespace node of the current element and has two overloads. The first overload takes no parameters and simply moves to the first namespace node of the current element. The second overload takes an `XmlNamespaceScope` instance as a parameter, which is an enumeration having the following values:

- ❑ XmlNamespaceScope.All – all namespaces including the implicit XML namespace will be available. This is the same as the no parameter overload.

- ❑ XmlNamespaceScope.ExcludeXml – all namespaces excluding the implicit XML namespace will be available.

- ❑ XmlNamespaceScope.Local – only the namespaces defined on that node will be available.

Note that you cannot state exactly which node these calls will move to when called as the order is not defined.

The MoveToNextNamespace() has the same overloads as the MoveToFirstNamespace() method, but moves to the next namespace node on the element node.

Try It Out: Moving Through Namespaces

Let's look at how we can use these methods to work with our sample document.

1. Add a new button to the form and call it **Namespaces**.

2. Double-click on the button and add the following code to the event handler:

```
Private Sub Button4_Click(ByVal sender As System.Object, _
                          ByVal e As System.EventArgs) Handles Button4.Click
    'Stores header information
    Dim headerText As String = ""

    'Working with IDs in the XPathNavigator
    Dim xpDoc As XPathDocument = New XPathDocument("..\\CaseStudy.xml")
    Dim xpNav As XPathNavigator = xpDoc.CreateNavigator()

    textBox1.Text = ""

    'Get to root of document
    xpNav.MoveToRoot()
    'Move to ContactDetails
    xpNav.MoveToFirstChild()

    headerText = "Namespace is "
    Dim FoundNs As Boolean

    'Move to namespace with ct prefix
    FoundNs = xpNav.MoveToNamespace("ct")
    textBox1.Text &= "Found = " & FoundNs & ". " & headerText _
        & xpNav.Name & " and " _
        & xpNav.Value _
        & System.Environment.NewLine

    xpNav.MoveToParent()
    'Move to first namespace on element
```

```
      FoundNs = xpNav.MoveToFirstNamespace(XPathNamespaceScope.ExcludeXml)
      textBox1.Text &= "Found = " & FoundNs & ". " & headerText _
        & xpNav.Name & " and " _
        & xpNav.Value _
        & System.Environment.NewLine

      'Move to namespace node
      FoundNs = xpNav.MoveToNextNamespace(XPathNamespaceScope.ExcludeXml)
      textBox1.Text &= "Found = " & FoundNs & ". " & headerText _
        & xpNav.Name & " and " _
        & xpNav.Value _
        & System.Environment.NewLine
   End Sub
```

3. Run this application, click the **Namespaces** button and you will get the following output:

How It Works

In this example, we look at the following XML fragment from the sample XML file:

```
<?xml version="1.0" encoding="utf-8"?>
<ct:ContactDetails updateDate="20021201T14:00"
    xmlns:ct="http://www.deltabis.com/Contact">
```

When the button is clicked, new XPathDocument and XPathNavigator instances are created once more. We then navigate to the root of the document, which is the node before the document element node. Calling the MoveToFirstChild() at this point will move the navigator to the ContactDetails document element node.

```
      'Get to root of document
      xpNav.MoveToRoot()
      'Move to ContactDetails
      xpNav.MoveToFirstChild()
```

We next use the MoveToNamespace() method and pass in the prefix of the namespace we are looking for, which will move the navigator to the xmlns definition on this element.

```
FoundNs = xpNav.MoveToNamespace("ct")
```

We then call the `MoveToFirstNamespace()` method; notice that we have to explicitly call the `MoveToParent()` method before this because the navigator is currently positioned on an `XmlNamespace` node, and calling the `MoveToFirstNamespace()` method when not on an element node always returns `False`. So, now that we are positioned on the element node, we call this method and specify the `XPathNamespaceScope` in the parameter, which determines what namespaces are to be considered (for example, in our case we tell it to ignore the XML namespace that is present on every element node by default).

```
xpNav.MoveToParent()
'Move to FirstNamespace on element
FoundNs = xpNav.MoveToFirstNamespace(XPathNamespaceScope.ExcludeXml)
```

Finally, the `MoveToNextNamespace()` method is called, which returns `False` because there are no more namespace definitions on this element node.

```
FoundNs = xpNav.MoveToNextNamespace(XPathNamespaceScope.ExcludeXml)
```

Now we move on to look at the methods available in the `XPathNavigator` class for selecting parts of the document we are interested in.

Selecting Parts of Documents

The methods exposed by the `XPathNavigator` class for selecting parts of an XML document are what give us the power of random access to the document using XPath queries, similar to what was available in the `SelectSingleNode()` and `SelectNodes()` methods that we looked at when we discussed the `XmlDocument` class.

The `XPathNavigator` class, however, goes beyond simple select queries and actually provides optimized additional methods for selecting specific node types during your query. For example, you can select just all the children based on your XPath query using the `SelectChildren()` method or select all ancestors using the `SelectAncestors()` method. It is possible for you to implement this kind of functionality using XPath queries yourself, but the .NET methods have been optimized for doing this (as well as making your code writing easier!).

Remember from our discussion on the Document Object Model that, given a node in a document, its child nodes are all nodes that lie one level below this node in the tree. Its parent node is the node immediately above the node in the tree. Its descendant nodes are all nodes including the children, the children's children (grandchild nodes), and so on. Finally, its ancestor nodes are all nodes above it in the tree, including the parent node, the parent of the parent node (grandparent), and so on.

With that in mind, we start with the `Select()` method – the most general of the selection methods.

The Select() Method

The `Select()` method of the `XPathNavigator` class allows you to select an XML node using an XPath query, enabling you to return parts of the XML document based on specified criteria. This provides a powerful ability to access non-sequentially the nodes of the document you are interested in.

There are in fact two overloads to this method: the first being a simple XPath query as a `String`, and the latter being to pass an `XPathExpression` instance as a parameter. The `XPathExpression` class is discussed below, but represents a compiled XPath expression.

The context of the query is the starting point of the selection, which is the current node that the navigator is placed on. The result of the query is an `XPathNodeIterator` instance containing pointers to the nodes that were selected (and so allow you to make direct updates on these nodes if desired). You can then use the methods and properties of the `XPathNodeIterator` to access these nodes and their values.

When you have a XPath expression that involves namespaces, you have to use the `XPathExpression` overload of this method. We won't discuss this just now, as we will look at this class later in the chapter.

The SelectAncestors() Method

This method will select all the nodes that are ancestor nodes of the current node and that match the specified criteria. There are two overloads for this method, both returning an `XPathNodeIterator` pointing to the selected nodes.

The first takes an `XPathNodeType` as the first parameter and a Boolean value to indicate whether to also include the context node in the query. The `XPathNodeType` can be one of the following values:

- ❑ `All` – All node types will be returned
- ❑ `Attribute` – An attribute node will be returned
- ❑ `Comment` – A comment node will be returned
- ❑ `Element` – An element node will be returned
- ❑ `Namespace` – A namespace node will be returned
- ❑ `ProcessingInstruction` – A processing instruction (remember that the XML declaration is NOT a processing instruction)
- ❑ `Root` – The document root node will be returned
- ❑ `SignificantWhitespace` – A node with whitespace characters and `xml:space` set to preserve
- ❑ `Text` – The child text node of an element
- ❑ `Whitespace` – A node with only whitespace characters and no significant whitespace

The second overload takes the local name of an element as the first parameter, a namespace URI as the second parameter, and a Boolean to indicate whether to include the context node.

The SelectDescendants() Method

The `SelectDescendants()` method is very similar to the `SelectAncestors()` method, and in fact has the same two overloads, again both returning `XPathNodeIterator` instances.

The SelectChildren() Method

The `SelectChildren()` method will select all child nodes of the current node that match the specified criteria. It has two overloads.

The first overload will take an `XPathNodeType` as a parameter and filter the results based on this. The second overload will take a local name and namespace URI of an element, and filter the nodes based on these parameters. Again, this returns an `XPathNodeIterator` instance.

Try It Out: Selecting Nodes

Let's look at how we can use these methods to work with our sample document.

1. Add a new button to the form and call it `Select Nodes`.

2. Double-click on the button and add the following code to the event handler:

```
Private Sub Button5_Click(ByVal sender As System.Object, _
                          ByVal e As System.EventArgs) Handles Button5.Click
    Dim xpDoc As XPathDocument = New XPathDocument("..\\CaseStudy.xml")
    Dim xpNav As XPathNavigator = xpDoc.CreateNavigator()

    Dim xpIter As XPathNodeIterator = xpNav.SelectDescendants( _
      "ContactDetails", "http://www.deltabis.com/Contact", True)

    'Get to the ContactDetails node itself
    xpIter.MoveNext()
    textBox1.Text = ""
    textBox1.Text &= "Found context element " _
      & xpIter.Current.Name _
      & System.Environment.NewLine

    'Get all the last name nodes
    Dim xpIterNoFirst As XPathNodeIterator = _
      xpNav.SelectDescendants("last", String.Empty, False)

    While (xpIterNoFirst.MoveNext())
      textBox1.Text = textBox1.Text + "Found last name " _
        & xpIterNoFirst.Current.Value _
        & System.Environment.NewLine

      'Get the contact node for each of these people
      Dim xpIterCont As XPathNodeIterator = _
        xpIterNoFirst.Current.SelectAncestors("contact", String.Empty, False)

      xpIterCont.MoveNext()
      textBox1.Text &= "This last name has the title " _
        & xpIterCont.Current.GetAttribute("title", String.Empty) _
        & System.Environment.NewLine
    End While
End Sub
```

3. Run this application, click the **Select Nodes** button and you will get the following output:

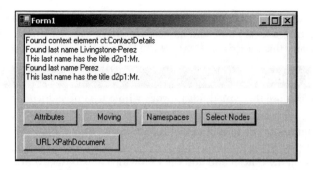

How It Works

In the same way as the previous example we load the document into an XPathDocument and create a navigator instance from it. When this is done, we will be positioned at the root of the document, and so we use the SelectDescendants() method to find the ContactDetails element. We specify that this is qualified in a namespace in the second parameter.

```
Dim xpIter As XPathNodeIterator = xpNav.SelectDescendants("ContactDetails", _
    "http://www.deltabis.com/Contact", True)
```

When this is executed, we are returned an XPathNodeIterator instance with a single element, which is the only ContactDetails element. We get to this node by calling the MoveNext() method; until we call this we are not yet positioned on this node in the iterator. We can then use the Current property of the XPathNodeIterator class to access properties on the XmlNode and write out some information.

```
'Get to the ContactDetails node itself
xpIter.MoveNext()
textBox1.Text = ""
textBox1.Text &= "Found context element " _
  & xpIter.Current.Name _
  & System.Environment.NewLine
```

Next, while positioned on the ContactDetails document element, the SelectDescendants() method is called and the element named last is specified in the first parameter with no namespace qualification in the second argument. This will select all elements in the document that have the name last.

```
Dim xpIterNoFirst As XPathNodeIterator = xpNav.SelectDescendants("last", _
    String.Empty, False)
```

With a list of selected nodes, we loop though the XPathNodeIterator and do some work with each node that is found, initially writing out the contents of the last element.

```
While (xpIterNoFirst.MoveNext())
  textBox1.Text = textBox1.Text + "Found last name " _
    & xpIterNoFirst.Current.Value _
    & System.Environment.NewLine

    'Get the contact node for each of these people
```

```
        Dim xpIterCont As XPathNodeIterator = _
          xpIterNoFirst.Current.SelectAncestors("contact", String.Empty, False)

      xpIterCont.MoveNext()
      textBox1.Text &= "This last name has the title " _
        & xpIterCont.Current.GetAttribute("title", String.Empty) _
        & System.Environment.NewLine
    End While
```

Still in this loop, we use the `SelectAncestors()` method to work our way back up the tree from the current node to find the first contact element node.

```
      Dim xpIterCont As XPathNodeIterator = _
        xpIterNoFirst.Current.SelectAncestors("contact", String.Empty, False)
```

There will be a single contact node for each `last` element, so we just call the `MoveNext()` method directly to consume the node and write out the value of the title attribute node on the relevant contact element. We do this for each contact element node that is found for successive last names.

We will now move on to look at how to compile and extend XPath queries using some of the more advanced methods of the `XPathNavigator` class.

The Compile() Method

The `Compile()` method of the `XPathNavigator` class is used to compile a string representation of an XPath query into an `XPathExpression` instance, and hence gain a performance improvement.

We will look at the `XPathExpression` class below.

The Evaluate() Method

The `Evaluate()` method of the `XPathNavigator` class fills in an area that was missing in previous parsers, the ability to evaluate a XPath expression and return a typed value, such as the sum of particular node values in a document. The result of this call is a typed value that is one of the following:

❑   Boolean

❑   Number

❑   String

❑   Node set

There are in fact three overloads of this method.

The first overload takes a simple `String` representing the XPath expression to evaluate and returns an object of one of the above types. The second overload takes an `XPathExpression` object and also returns a typed result. The final overload takes an `XPathExpression` instance as well as an `XPathNodeIterator` instance that defines the context for the XPath expression (rather than the current node).

We will look at an example of this after we have discussed the `Matches()` method.

The Matches() Method

The Matches() method of the XPathNavigator class returns a Boolean value indicating whether the current node matched the XSLT pattern. This method has two overloads. The first overload takes a simple String expression and the second overload takes an XPathExpression instance.

Note that the Matches() method uses XLST patterns to define the criterion. We will meet XSLT templates in the next chapter, which also use XSLT Patterns, but for now you just need to know that they offer a subset of what is offered by XPath. In short, an XSLT pattern must evaluate to a specific and well defined node-set – or none at all. You can also only use the child or attribute axes (as well as "//") although any XPath expression can be used in the predicate. If we have a single value then the match is made on that, if we have a node set then a match can be made on any of returned nodes.

Try It Out: Evaluating and Matching

This *Try It Out* will look at how to use the Evaluate() and Matches() methods with our sample document.

1. Add a new button to the form and change its Text property to Evaluate.

2. Double-click on the button and add the following code to the event handler:

```
Private Sub Button6_Click(ByVal sender As System.Object, _
                          ByVal e As System.EventArgs) Handles Button6.Click
    Dim xpDoc As XPathDocument = New XPathDocument("..\\CaseStudy.xml")
    Dim xpNav As XPathNavigator = xpDoc.CreateNavigator()

    'Set the maximum numbers of contacts in the address book
    Dim MaxContacts As Integer = 25
    Dim curNumCont As Integer = Convert.ToInt32(xpNav.Evaluate("count(//contact)"))
    Dim numContLeft As Integer = MaxContacts - curNumCont

    'Inform the user the space left in the address book
    textBox1.Text = ""
    textBox1.Text &= "You can have " _
      & numContLeft.ToString() _
      & " more contacts in your list." _
      & System.Environment.NewLine

    'Test the nodes
    Dim middleNames As XPathNodeIterator = xpNav.SelectDescendants _
            ("name", String.Empty, False)
    While (middleNames.MoveNext())
      If (middleNames.Current.Matches("name[child::last]")) Then
        middleNames.Current.MoveToFirstChild()
        middleNames.Current.MoveToNext()
        middleNames.Current.MoveToNext()

        textBox1.Text = textBox1.Text + "Contact :" _
          & middleNames.Current.Value _
          & " is added." _
          & System.Environment.NewLine
      End If
    End While
End Sub
```

3. Run this application, click the **Evaluate** button and you will get the following output:

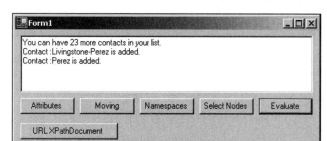

How It Works

Again we load the document into an `XPathDocument` and create a navigator instance from it. We then specify a variable that holds the maximum number of contacts allowed in the address book, currently 25.

```
Dim MaxContacts As Integer = 25
```

Next, we can use the `Evaluate()` method along with the XPath count function to tell us the number of contact element nodes in the document. This is one way of doing it – there are other ways, such as the `Count` property of an `XmlNodeList`. When we have this, we have to convert it to an integer in order to be able to do the subtraction, and so we use the `Convert` class to do this. This gives us the number of contacts that are now allowed.

```
Dim curNumCont As Integer = Convert.ToInt32(xpNav.Evaluate("count(//contact)"))
Dim numContLeft As Integer = MaxContacts - curNumCont
```

We then get all the name element nodes in the document and iterate though each, testing for those that have the `last` element defined (all of them in this case) using the `Matches()` method with the XSLT pattern `name[child::last]`.

```
Dim middleNames As XPathNodeIterator = xpNav.SelectDescendants("name", _
   String.Empty, False)
While (middleNames.MoveNext())
   If (middleNames.Current.Matches("name[child::last]")) Then
```

When there is a match, we move to the first child of the name element, the `first` element; then the `MoveToNext()` takes us to the middle element and another `MoveToNext()` takes us to the last element. We then write the text content of this element to the output as a list.

```
middleNames.Current.MoveToFirstChild()
middleNames.Current.MoveToNext()
middleNames.Current.MoveToNext()
```

Other Methods

There are several other abstract methods that are part of the `XPathNavigator` class and these are defined in the table below for convenience.

Method	Description
Clone()	This method will create a new XPathNavigator instance located at the same position as the original XPathNavigator instance.
ComparePosition()	This method can be used to compare the position of the current XPathNavigator against the XPathNavigator passed in the argument, and will return either Before, After, Same or Unknown. Unknown is likely when the two nodes being compared are in different document trees.
GetAttribute()	This returns the attribute with the local name and URI specified as parameters. This only works on element nodes and does not look at the children.
GetNamespace()	This returns the namespace of the local name specified as a parameter. This also only works on element nodes and does not look at the children.
IsDescendant()	This returns True if the XPathNavigator specified as an argument is a descendant of the current navigator – this means that it is positioned at a descendant node of the navigator.
IsSamePosition()	This is True when the current XPathNavigator and the XPathNavigator specified in the argument are at the same position in the document.
ToString()	Returns the textual value of the current node. The content returned depends on the NodeType of the node.

The performance of the evaluation of XPathNavigator XPath queries can be significantly improved by using the XPathExpression class, which allows you to compile an expression that is to be reused more than once. Let's look at this class now.

The XPathExpression Class

The XPathExpression class has been mentioned a few times in this chapter and encapsulates a compiled XPath expression, which is more powerful than a string-based XPath query. This is a very useful class when you are intending to use an expression multiple times, because it will be compiled and therefore you will get better performance than if it were not compiled.

It also allows you to add powerful sorting capabilities to your expressions and add namespace context to resolve prefixes that may be used in the expression.

When the Compile() method is called on an XPathNavigator instance, the XPath expression itself is compiled to produce an XPathExpression instance.

Properties

There are two read-only properties defined by this class.

❑ The `Expression` property – This property simply returns a string-based representation of the compiled XPath expression.

❑ The `ReturnType` property – This property will contain the `XPathResultType` of the compiled expression.

The `XPathResultType` can be one of the following:

❑ `Any` – Any of the XPath types defined below

❑ `Boolean` – a Boolean `True` or `False`

❑ `Error` – this compiled expression does not evaluate to a correct XPath type

❑ `Navigator` – a tree fragment

❑ `NodeSet` – a collection of nodes

❑ `Number` – a number

❑ `String` – a string

Methods

There are three important methods to know about – the others are inherited from the `System.Object` base class.

The AddSort() Method

This method has two overloads and allows you to sort the nodes that are selected by the XPath expression.

The first overload takes a first parameter, which is the sort key either specified as a string or as a compiled `XPathExpression`. The second parameter is an `IComparer` interface derived class; this is used to compare two objects.

The second overload also takes a first parameter. The second parameter is an `XmlSortOrder` value, which is either `Ascending` or `Descending`. The third parameter is an `XmlCaseOrder` value determining how capitals and lower cases should be sorted; the three options are `LowerFirst`, `None`, or `UpperFirst`. The fourth parameter is a `String` value indicating the language culture to sort on; `"en-GB"` for example. The final parameter is the `XmlDataType` that should be used for the sort and is either `Number` or `Text`.

The Clone() Method

The `Clone()` method will create a new instance of a current `XPathExpression`, which will be the same as the existing expression.

The SetContext() Method

The `SetContext()` method allows you to specify an `XmlNamespaceManager` for resolving namespaces that are to be used in the XPath query, and so the relevant `XmlNamespaceManager` is its only argument.

Try It Out: Creating and Using an XPathExpression

Let's now enhance the sample by allowing the performance to be optimized through compiling of a query into an XPath expression as well as adding some sorting capability to demonstrate the properties and methods we have looked at in covering the XPathExpression class.

1. Add a new button to the form and change its Text property to Context.

2. Double-click on the button and add the following code to the event handler:

```
Private Sub Button7_Click(ByVal sender As System.Object, _
                          ByVal e As System.EventArgs) Handles Button7.Click
    Dim xpDoc As XPathDocument = New XPathDocument("..\\CaseStudy.xml")
    Dim xpNav As XPathNavigator = xpDoc.CreateNavigator()

    'Bind the namespace
    Dim xmlNM As XmlNamespaceManager = New XmlNamespaceManager(xpNav.NameTable)
    xmlNM.AddNamespace("ct", "http://www.deltabis.com/Contact")

    'Create the XPathExpression, set the XPathExpression to the XmlNamespaceManager
    ' and add the sort to the XPathExpression
    Dim xpEx As XPathExpression = xpNav.Compile("/ct:ContactDetails/contact/name")
    xpEx.SetContext(xmlNM)
    xpEx.AddSort("first", XmlSortOrder.Ascending, XmlCaseOrder.None, "", _
      XmlDataType.Text)

    'Run the query
    Dim xIter As XPathNodeIterator = xpNav.Select(xpEx)

    textBox1.Text = ""
    textBox1.Text &= "Ordered by first name." _
      & System.Environment.NewLine

    While (xIter.MoveNext())
      Dim xIterLast As XPathNodeIterator = xIter.Current.Select("last")
      xIterLast.MoveNext()
      Dim xIterFirst As XPathNodeIterator = xIter.Current.Select("first")
      xIterFirst.MoveNext()

      textBox1.Text = textBox1.Text + xIterFirst.Current.Value _
        & " " _
        & xIterLast.Current.Value _
        & System.Environment.NewLine
    End While
End Sub
```

3. Run this application and click the Context button. You will get the following output:

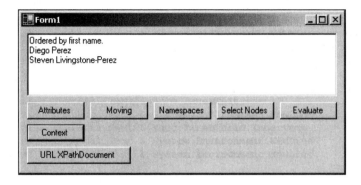

How It Works

After loading the XML document into an `XPathDocument` instance and creating a new navigator from this, we create a new `XmlNamespaceManager` instance because we want to create an XPath expression that has to use namespaces; to do this an `XmlNamespaceManager` must be specified. In this case, we add a single entry to the cache, which binds the prefix `ct` to the namespace `http://www.deltabis.com/Contact`.

```
Dim xmlNM As XmlNamespaceManager = New XmlNamespaceManager(xpNav.NameTable)
xmlNM.AddNamespace("ct", "http://www.deltabis.com/Contact")
```

Next, we create a new `XPathExpression` instance by compiling the XPath query `/ct:ContactDetails/contact/name`, which will return all of the name element nodes in the document, using the `Compile()` method. It will only do this if the name element nodes are the children of the contact node.

```
Dim xpEx As XPathExpression = xpNav.Compile("/ct:ContactDetails/contact/name")
```

The `SetContext()` method of the `XPathExpression` class is then used to associate the `XmlNamespaceManager`, and hence all namespace bindings defined by this, with this `XPathExpression` instance.

```
xpEx.SetContext(xmlNM)
```

Now when we return each of the name nodes, we want to order them by the first name of the person in alphabetical order and with the case of the name having no effect. We therefore add the following sorting expression to this `XPathExpression` instance.

```
xpEx.AddSort("first", XmlSortOrder.Ascending, XmlCaseOrder.None, "", _
    XmlDataType.Text)
```

Once this has been defined, we can actually execute the query, and this is done using the `Select()` method on the `XPathNavigator` object as follows:

```
Dim xIter As XPathNodeIterator = xpNav.Select(xpEx)
```

After this, we can just iterate through the `XPathNodeIterator`. We get the value of the last and first elements of each node, and format the result to the output.

```
While (xIter.MoveNext())
  Dim xIterLast As XPathNodeIterator = xIter.Current.Select("last")
  xIterLast.MoveNext()
  Dim xIterFirst As XPathNodeIterator = xIter.Current.Select("first")
  xIterFirst.MoveNext()

  textBox1.Text = textBox1.Text + xIterFirst.Current.Value _
    & " " _
    & xIterLast.Current.Value _
    & System.Environment.NewLine
End While
```

Custom Navigators

We have already discussed the `XmlReader` and `XmlWriter` abstract classes that can be used to read in an XML document as a stream or write XML data. The potential of these is actually very powerful because, as they are abstract, you can implement them in your own code and override the methods and properties. This means, for example, that you can change the `Read()` method to your own custom implementation which may actually read the data from a relational database rather than an XML file. Similarly you may choose to make the `WriteNode()` method of the `XmlWriter` class write data to a relational database rather than an XML file. You can do a similar thing for the `XPathNavigator` class. Why would you want to do this? You may want to allow navigation over data stores other than those in XML format, such as the file structure on a computer, the directory structure, the registry, or another hierarchical structure.

However, a good question is when to create a custom class derived from the `XmlReader` class and when to create a custom class derived from the `XPathNavigator` class. Sometimes it is obvious when you shouldn't use the `XPathNavigator` class. For example, if the programmable interface of the underlying structure supports only streaming or a firehose cursor (a forward, read-only cursor) then you should derive your custom class from the `XmlReader` class – otherwise you are going to have to deal with caching issues, and so on, to provide a hierarchical structure.

Also, if you're creating a model of a very large data structure (such as the entire directory system on your computer or the registry) and you don't want to perform any querying to create it (other than reading in the data piecemeal and perhaps doing some processing) then you are better using a streaming model as it offers better performance. In this case you may want to get all of the names of the files in your file system with a specific attribute.

If, however, your underlying source supports moving in any direction, or it is not too large, or if you want to be able to query the data (or transform it using XSLT), then you can use the `XPathNavigator` class, which will use a hierarchical tree to model the underlying structure. This will allow efficient random querying of the document as you saw when working with the DOM. In cases like this you may want to get all files from the file system created later than a particular date and then return a list of their parent folders.

To create a custom navigator you have to derive it from the `XPathNavigator` class, and override the properties of the `XPathNavigator` class shown below:

BaseURI	IsEmptyElement	NameTable	Value
HasAttributes	LocalName	NodeType	XmlLang
HasChildren	Name	Prefix	

So, if you were working with objects in the file system you may use the `FileSystemInfo` class to get details on a specific file, representing the directory structure as a store accessible using the `XFileNav` class. This class is derived from the `XPathNavigator` class. If you were reading directories from the file system on your local computer you know that there would be no `Prefix` because the folder is not qualified in any namespace. So, in this case you would want to return an empty string when an application accesses this property:

```
Public Overrides ReadOnly Property Prefix() As String
   Get
      Return String.Empty
   End Get
End Property
```

You also have to provide custom implementations for the following methods that access attribute information:

GetAttribute()	MoveToFirstAttribute()
MoveToAttribute()	MoveToNextAttribute()

You can override the `GetAttribute()` method of the `XPathNavigator` class as shown below. This will mean that a consumer of this class can simply use `GetAttribute("type")` to get the type extension of a given file, rather than using object-specific properties.

```
Public Function GetAttribute(name As String) As String
   Select Case name
      Case "type"
         Return objFileInfo.Extension
      Case "size"
         Return objFileInfo.Length
      Case "CreateTime"
         Return objFileInfo.CreationTime
   End Select
   Return ""
End Function
```

The following methods also have to be overridden:

Clone()	MoveToNext()
IsSamePosition()	MoveToParent()
MoveTo()	MoveToPrevious()
MoveToFirst()	MoveToRoot()
MoveToFirstChild()	NamespaceURI()
MoveToId()	

Similarly, you may override the `MoveToFirstChild()` method to open the directory you are working in and go to the first file or directory within that directory (the `OpenDir()` method is again part of our directory object and simply opens the directory and automatically goes to the first child file or directory).

```
Public Overrides Function MoveToFirstChild() As Boolean
   Return myFileObject.OpenDir()
End Function
```

Finally, the following namespace accessors must be overridden:

GetNamespace()	MoveToFirstNamespace()
MoveToNamespace()	MoveToNextNamespace()

You can override the `GetNamespace()` method to return an empty string because no namespaces are used in this case.

```
Public Overrides Function GetNamespace(name As String) As String
   Return String.Empty
End Function
```

It is left as an exercise to the reader to look into the example in the MSDN documentation at http://msdn.microsoft.com/msdnmag/issues/01/09/code/XML0109.exe of creating an `XPathNavigator` for the file system and implement one for a directory structure and other navigators. You will have to override the members discussed above in order to accomplish this.

XML Serialization

You may have had times while developing your applications when you wished there was a more flexible way of moving application data to another program, computer, or environment (either local or remote), and be able to re-create your previous state. Similarly there are times when you have application data stored in one or more classes and committing this data would result in an incomplete database update or an unfinished XML instance, because a user has left the application before filling in all the details.

Object persistence is only one possible use of serialization. Serialization is the process of transforming the state data of an object into a flat data stream. Another use is when objects must be sent from one location to another over the network. In order to do this the object needs to be converted from its in-memory representation to another format, which is suitable for sending over the network (or for saving on the disk). Deserialization is a complementary process of recreating objects from flat data stream created with serialization. Later in the book we look at web services and remoting, which deal with these object serialization for transport issues.

XML serialization allows you to:

- ❏   Serialize the data to disk and later de-serialize it in another application or environment.

- ❏   Serialize the current state of the application data and later, when you come to work with the application again, you can de-serialize the data instance and repopulate the various classes with the working data.

For many years, developers have created various techniques for serializing data, extremely important in the current days of distributed applications. However, they have found it difficult as many non-standard practices have emerged. Technologies such as NDR (DCOM), XDR (Sun RPC), and CDR (CORBA) allow data to be serialized and passed around, but as these data formats were based on the ordering of the raw data, then reordering or even interpretation of these formats was difficult. They were efficient of course, but interoperating between different formats was very difficult. XML provides us with the ability to mark up the data values so that they can be interpreted independent of the source application formatting. Technologies such as SOAP, XML-RPC, and remoting now use XML as the basis of providing serialized object communication in a distributed environment.

The .NET Framework has serialization support built right into the basics; in fact the .NET Framework itself uses serialization in areas such as remoting. Remoting is a technique where the current state of an object can be serialized as XML to be sent over some form of transport (such as HTTP or TCP).

The `System.Runtime.Serialization` and `System.Xml.Serialization` namespaces provide the base classes for working with serialization in the .NET Framework. The `System.Xml.Serialization` namespace provides methods to serialize the public properties and public fields of a class as XML elements and/or attributes. There are some limitations that are important to know before working within this namespace – the first is that it can **only** serialize public properties and fields – it cannot serialize private data. So if you want to serialize your object instance as XML you must either (a) store all of the important fields as public properties and fields or (b) have some kind of routine that puts your private fields into public properties or fields prior to serialization. This is not a big deal with most applications and so isn't regarded as a serious limitation.

The second limitation is that you cannot serialize object graphs with this namespace (you can serialize the data and shape, but not the type information of those other objects), which means you can only serialize the immediate object you are working in and not the objects that the object itself accesses. Again this is not generally a serious limitation as the data you are interested in will often be in the main object you are working with. XML serialization provides no type information or assembly information and only the data within the classes is serialized.

If you need to serialize private data members or object graphs, then you need to look into the `System.Runtime.Serialization.Formatters.Binary` namespace, which provides this facility. However, this will not store data in an XML format, but in a proprietary binary format.

The opposite of serialization is deserialization – the action of taking the serialized data (whether that is in XML format or not) and recreating the object with the data it had in it prior to serialization. Again the same restrictions apply to the System.Xml.Serialization and System.Runtime.Serialization namespaces (that is, you cannot deserialize a class with private data using the XML serialization namespace).

How does Serialization work?

Serialization can work slightly differently depending on the circumstances. If you want to save all private data within an application, then use one of the formatter classes of the System.Runtime.Serialization.Formatters namespace. For example, you may use the BinaryFormatter class in the System.Runtime.Serialization.Formatters.Binary namespace for a binary output format. However, if you only need to serialize public data, then you can use the XmlSerializer class to persist the data as XML, a preferred technique, especially when the data is required to be passed between varying applications and environments. Although you can only persist public data, you should not be put off this technique if you also need to persist some private data; however, you would be required to write serializer and de-serializer specific methods for coping with such circumstances. We will look at this shortly.

We will use XML serialization again later in Chapters 10 and 11 on XML Schemas.

The XmlSerializer Class

The XmlSerializer class is the core class that enables XML serialization and de serialization in the .NET Framework. It has three core methods that can be called but no properties; it also has a constructor with 7 overloads; which can be used to create an instance of this class. There is an eighth constructor overload that is protected and is only used by the .NET Framework.

There are three core methods:

- ❑ Serialize()
- ❑ Deserialize()
- ❑ CanDeserialize()

The Serialize() method takes a class instance and creates an XML instance representing the current state of the class in a specified output. The output can be a Stream, TextWriter, or XmlWriter instance depending on the object passed as an argument to the call.

Similarly, there is a Deserialize() method which deserializes an XML instance and creates a class instance representation of the data. The input instance that contains the XML instance can be a Stream, TextReader, or an XmlReader.

Finally, the CanDeserialize() method returns a Boolean True or False determining whether the XML instance can in fact be deserialized, and takes an XmlReader instance containing the document as an argument.

Try It Out: Basic Serialization

Serialization can get very complex, so it is important that you understand the basic principles and effects by using this technique within your application. This example demonstrates a simple method of serializing some contact information; it would obviously have to be improved in real life, but you should understand some of the basic concepts from this sample.

1. Create a new **Console Application** project called `serialization`. Now add a new class to this project (right-click on the application and select **Add | Add Class...**).

2. Name the new class file `Contacts.vb` and add the following code:

```
Imports System.Xml.Serialization

Public Class Contacts
    Private CtName As String = ""
    Public myElement As System.Xml.XmlElement

    Public Property ContactName() As String
      Get
        Return CtName
      End Get
      Set(ByVal Value As String)
        CtName = Value
      End Set
    End Property
End Class
```

3. Now, rename the original `Module1.vb` file to `serialization.vb`. Add the following code to the start of the file:

```
Imports System.Xml
Imports System.Xml.Serialization
Imports System.Text
```

4. Finally, add the following code to the `Module` method in this file:

```
Sub Main()
    'Serialize
    Dim MyContactCollection As Contacts = New Contacts()
    MyContactCollection.ContactName = "Roberto Perez"

    Dim xtw As XmlTextWriter = New XmlTextWriter _
        ("..\\CSinstance.xml", Encoding.UTF8)
    Dim xs As XmlSerializer = New XmlSerializer(GetType(Contacts))

    xs.Serialize(xtw, MyContactCollection)
    xtw.Close()
End Sub
```

5. Compile the application and then run it by pressing *F5*. The application will run but give you no output.

How It Works

When you ran this application, you got no visible output, mainly because the application was written as a console application to illustrate the fact that much of the work done by the XmlSerialization class goes unnoticed. However, if you open Windows Explorer and navigate to the folder where you created the above console application, you will see a file called CSinstance.xml.

Double-click on this file to open it in Internet Explorer and you will see the following:

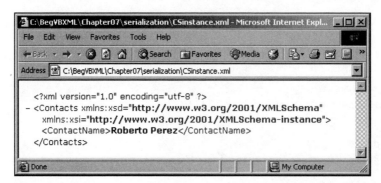

Basically, an XML file has been created storing some values that you created in the class instance prior to serialization. There is some additional information on the root element – don't worry too much about this as we will look at what this means when we look at serialization in the chapters on XML Schemas. However, this basically relates the current instance to any existing XML Schema information required for strong typing in XML.

What else happened? Well, we created a new instance of the Contacts class as normal and set the contact name as per normal as well.

```
Dim MyContactCollection As Contacts = New Contacts()
MyContactCollection.ContactName = "Roberto Perez"
```

Note that the ContactName property that was set is defined as public in the Contacts class; even though it is a private variable that stores the value, it is still accessible via a public property. Had we tried to serialize without adding this public property (that is, a set and no get) we would not have had the variable content output to the XML file.

```
Public Property ContactName() As String
  Get
    Return CtName
  End Get
  Set(ByVal Value As String)
    CtName = Value
  End Set
End Property
```

Back in the `serialization.vb` file, a new `XmlTextWriter` instance was also initialized to a given path with a file name `CSinstance.xml` and UTF-8 encoding. A new instance of an `XmlSerializer` class was created using the type of the `Contacts` class as an argument to its constructor.

```
Dim xtw As XmlTextWriter = New XmlTextWriter _
        ("..\\CSinstance.xml", Encoding.UTF8)
Dim xs As XmlSerializer = New XmlSerializer(GetType(Contacts))
```

Finally, the `Serialize()` method was called, which states the target of the serialization in the first parameter and the class instance to be serialized in the second parameter, in our case the `Contacts` instance. Finally the text writer instance is closed to persist the file.

```
xs.Serialize(xtw, MyContactCollection)
xtw.Close()
```

Notice that the output XML instance uses the class name (`Contacts` in this case) as the **root** element and the public properties of the class are serialized as child element nodes, with the value of the property set to the child text node of these element nodes. The public variable `myElement` is not serialized because it contains nothing.

Try It Out: Basic Deserialization

So now we have serialized a class instance to an XML instance, how do we go in reverse and at a later time get our class instance back from the XML serialized instance? Let's look at how this can be done for our sample above.

1. Return to the `serialization.vb` file we were just working with and go to the `Main()` method just below the `Close()` method. Enter the code highlighted below:

```
Imports System.Xml
Imports System.Xml.Serialization
Imports System.Text

Module Module1

  Sub Main()
    'Serialize
    Dim MyContactCollection As Contacts = New Contacts()
    MyContactCollection.ContactName = "Roberto Perez"

    Dim xtw As XmlTextWriter = New XmlTextWriter("..\\CSinstance.xml", _
                                          Encoding.UTF8)
    Dim xs As XmlSerializer = New XmlSerializer(GetType(Contacts))

    xs.Serialize(xtw, MyContactCollection)
    xtw.Close()

    'Deserialize
    Dim MyOldContactCollection As Contacts = New Contacts()
    Dim xOlds As XmlSerializer = New XmlSerializer(GetType(Contacts))
```

313

```
      Dim xt As XmlTextReader = New XmlTextReader("..\\CSinstance.xml")
      MyOldContactCollection = CType(xOlds.Deserialize(xt), Contacts)
      xt.Close()

      Console.WriteLine(MyOldContactCollection.ContactName)
      Console.ReadLine()
   End Sub

End Module
```

2. Run the application and you will get the following output:

How It Works

This time we did the reverse of our previous work and created a new class instance from the XML document we had previously created. An instance of a `Contacts` class was again created, as well as an instance of an `XmlSerializer` class with the type of the `Contacts` class as an argument.

```
Dim MyOldContactCollection As Contacts = New Contacts()
Dim xOlds As XmlSerializer = New XmlSerializer(GetType(Contacts))
```

Following this, we can then get the data from our XML instance to populate this class instance. The `XmlTextReader` class reads the `CSinstance.xml` file into a text reader instance – this is the source of our XML data and the same as the name of the file we created earlier (although of course it could be any URL).

```
Dim xt As XmlTextReader = New XmlTextReader("..\\CSinstance.xml")
```

The `Deserialize()` method of the `XmlSerializer` class can then be called with the `XmlTextReader` instance as a parameter and to enable the `Contacts` instance to be populated, the result of this deserialization must be cast to a `Contacts` class. The `XmlTextReader` can then be closed, as the `Contacts` instance will be populated.

```
MyOldContactCollection = CType(xOlds.Deserialize(xt), Contacts)
xt.Close()
```

To demonstrate that this is indeed the case, we simply write out the value of the `ContactName` property to the console (the `ReadLine()` method is simply to allow you to view the result without the console window closing).

Serialization Attributes

There may be cases where you want the output of the XML instance to be structured in a different way from the default XML instance created by serializing the class instance. For example, you may want to ensure your class conforms to a company format for purchase orders that uses XML namespaces. Namespaces are not written out during serialization (because the class contains no XML namespace information). The `SystemAttribute` class has a .NET Framework base class that is extended to the `System.XmlSerialization` namespace allowing declarative information to be applied to members of a class to further control how it is to be interpreted by the CLR.

We will now discuss three of the various classes that are available to customize the output of serialization: `XmlRootAttribute` (also written as `XmlRoot`), `XmlElementAttribute` (also written as `XmlElement`), and `XmlAttributeAttribute` (also written as `XmlAttribute`).

Each attribute declaration is entered just before the member that you want to alter the structure for. For example, you may want to change the root element name, or alter the document default namespace, so you would define this at the class level. Alternatively, you may want to alter the name of the element in the XML document for a field; this may be because the field name is invalid XML or that the XML is invalid VB code.

The definition is of the form:

```
<attributeClass(ClassProperty1, ClassProperty2 ...)>
member
```

The XmlRootAttribute Class

The `XmlRootAttribute` class, also written as `XmlRoot`, is applied to public class declarations and will represent the root element of all the definitions that are serialized within this class. This attribute declaration can also be applied to structures, enumerations, and interfaces.

The key properties available to this class are:

❑ `DataType` – this can be used to specify a specific XML Schema data type.

❑ `ElementName` – this allows you to set an alternative root element name for the class.

❑ `IsNullable` – states whether this value can be serialized to be `nothing`, as can be defined by XML Schema instances (`xsi:nil`).

❑ `Namespace` – gets or sets the namespace for the root element.

We will go into more detail on the `DataType` and `IsNullable` properties in Chapter 11.

So, consider the following class fragment:

```
Public Class Contacts
  'code...
End Class
```

When serialized as normal, this will give the following output:

```
<Contacts />
```

However, you can alter the output of this by using attributes in the following manner:

```
<XmlRootAttribute(Namespace:="uri:mt", ElementName:="ct")>
Public Class Contacts
   'code
End Class
```

This would then be serialized as follows:

```
<ct xmlns="uri:mt" />
```

The XmlElementAttribute Class

The `XmlElementAttribute` class, also written as `XmlElement`, is applied to public fields or properties and allows you to state that a given item should be serialized as an element with custom properties defined. The class can be applied several times to a field that returns an array of objects; it can be used to specify, using the `Type` property, different types that can be inserted into the array. There is also the ability to map to XML Schema types, discussed in Chapter 11.

The key properties available to this class are:

- ❑ `DataType` – this can be used to specify a specific XML Schema data type. Discussed in more detail in Chapter 11.

- ❑ `ElementName` – this allows you to set the element name for a field or property.

- ❑ `Form` – this determines whether the serialized item should be qualified or not; this is part of XML Schema definitions.

- ❑ `IsNullable` – states whether this value can be serialized to be null, as can be defined by XML Schema instances (`xsi:nil`). We look at this property in further detail in Chapter 11.

- ❑ `Namespace` – gets or sets the namespace given to the element that is created when the class is serialized.

- ❑ `Type` – Sets the object type used to represent the element.

So, consider the following public field definitions:

```
Public FirstName As String = "Diego"
```

When serialized as normal, this will give the following output:

```
<FirstName>Diego</FirstName>
```

However, you can alter the output of this by using attributes in the following manner:

```
<XmlElement(ElementName:="ChristianName")>
Public FirstName As String = "Diego"
```

This would then be serialized as follows:

```
<ChristianName>Diego</ChristianName>
```

The XmlAttributeAttribute Class

The `XmlAttributeAttribute` class, also written as `XmlAttribute`, is applied to public fields or properties and allows you to state that a given item should be serialized as an attribute on the root element, rather than the default element. There is also the ability to map to XML Schema types, as discussed in Chapter 11.

The key properties available to this class are:

- ❑ `AttributeName` – this allows you to set the attribute name.
- ❑ `DataType` – this can be used to specify a specific XML Schema data type for the attribute generated by the `XmlSerializer`. Discussed in Chapter 11.
- ❑ `Form` – this determines whether the serialized item should be qualified or not; this is part of XML Schema definitions. We discuss this in Chapter 11.
- ❑ `Namespace` – with this you can find out or set the namespace of the attribute element.

So, consider the following public field definitions:

```
Public UniqueId As String = "CT8272"
```

When serialized as normal, this will give the following output:

```
<Contacts UniqueId="CT8272" />
```

However, you can alter the output of this by using attributes in the following manner (so that it is an XML recognized ID type):

```
<XmlAttribute(AttributeName := "ID")>
  Public UniqueId As String = "CT8272"
```

This would then be serialized as follows:

```
<Contacts ID="CT8272" />
```

Try It Out: Changing the Serialized Structure

To illustrate the concept of attributes during serialization, let's take the previous simple XML document and add attributes to it to alter the output structure when it is serialized (this is **serialization2** in the code download).

1. Return to the `Contacts.vb` file we were working with earlier.

2. Alter the code to reflect the changes highlighted below:

```
Imports System.Xml.Serialization
```

```
<XmlRootAttribute(Namespace:="http://www.deltabis.com/ContactInstance", _
  ElementName:="SingleContact")> _
Public Class Contacts
  Private CtName As String = ""
  Public myElement As System.Xml.XmlElement

  <XmlAttributeAttribute("FullName")> _
  Public Property ContactName() As String
    Get
      Return CtName
    End Get
    Set(ByVal Value As String)
      CtName = Value
    End Set
  End Property
End Class
```

3. Run the application and then look at the `CSinstance.xml` created and you will see a new format as shown below:

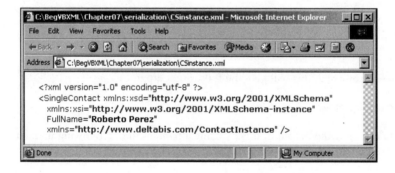

How It Works

This time we used the `XmlRoot` class to define the output format for the `Contacts` class definition, which *as* the class definition will be the root element for anything defined within this class. Within this attribute, we have stated that we want the root element to be qualified in the `http://www.deltabis.com/ContactInstance` namespace, and rather than have the default root element name as the class name (`Contacts` in this case), we state that we want the root `ElementName` to be `SingleContact`.

```
<XmlRootAttribute(Namespace:="http://www.deltabis.com/ContactInstance",
ElementName:="SingleContact")> _
Public Class Contacts
```

This will cause the output of the root element to be:

```
<SingleContact xmlns=" http://www.deltabis.com/ContactInstance" />
```

Also, we state that we want to define in the `ContactName` property an attribute of the previously defined element (the root element in this case) and we want the attribute name to be `FullName`; this is done using the `XmlAttributeAttribute` class.

```
<XmlAttributeAttribute("FullName")> _
Public Property ContactName() As String
```

This adds to the root element definition to create the following output:

```
<SingleContact FullName="Roberto Perez" xmlns=" http://www.deltabis.com/ContactInstance" />
```

Serialization with Multiple Classes

In almost every application there are going to be references to multiple classes. Additionally, there are going to be references to multiple classes even within the classes you are working with, and you may not have developed some of these! You will have no control over this, so how does serialization work in this arena? How can you ensure that the data you have populated in other class instances is also serialized along with the classes that you created? Well, in fact the .NET Framework (and specifically the `XmlSerialization` class) does most of the work for you and will serialize all of the data from the public properties and fields.

The `XmlSerialization` class will directly serialize any class instance you create, as long as they can be serialized themselves. By default, all classes derived from `Object` are serializable (as `Object` itself is defined to be serializable).

Try It Out: Serialization with an Uncontrolled Class Instance

To demonstrate how the .NET Framework can work to extend serialization to classes that are not under your control, we will look at an example where an `XMLElement` instance is being created within the `Contacts` class we worked with above. This XML document will simply store some of the data within the class as an XML instance – what we do with this XML document instance is not defined (you may write it to a data store). This example is the **serialization3** project in the download for this chapter.

1. Modify the `Contacts.vb` file to reflect the changes highlighted in the code below:

```
Imports System.Xml.Serialization

<XmlRootAttribute(Namespace:="http://www.deltabis.com/ContactInstance",_
  ElementName:="SingleContact")> _
Public Class Contacts
  Private CtName As String = ""
  Public NameElement As System.Xml.XmlElement

  <XmlAttributeAttribute("FullName")> _
  Public Property ContactName() As String
```

```
    Get
      Return CtName
    End Get
    Set(ByVal Value As String)
      CtName = Value
    End Set
  End Property

  Public Sub CreateXmlDoc()
    NameElement = New System.Xml.XmlDocument().CreateElement("FirstName")
    NameElement.InnerText = CtName
  End Sub
End Class
```

2. Now modify the Main method of the serialization.vb file as indicated below:

```
Sub Main()
  'Serialize
  Dim MyContactCollection As Contacts = New Contacts()
  MyContactCollection.ContactName = "Roberto Perez"
  MyContactCollection.CreateXmlDoc()

  Dim xtw As XmlTextWriter = New XmlTextWriter _
        ("..\\CSinstance.xml", Encoding.UTF8)
  Dim xs As XmlSerializer = New XmlSerializer(GetType(Contacts))
  ...
End Sub
```

3. Run the application and then check the CSinstance.xml file and you will see the following output:

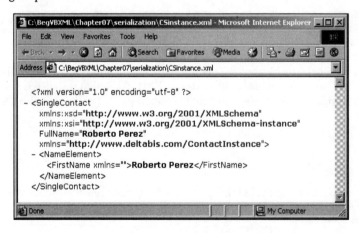

How It Works

You can see from the XML instance above that the serialized XML document now contains information on the XML element instance we created and populated. We did this by first defining the NameElement XmlElement variable to be public – very important if its contents are to be serialized.

```
Public NameElement As System.Xml.XmlElement
```

A `public` method was also added to this class, which can then be called by a client to initialize the `NameElement` variable to contain some data. In this case, it simply creates a child element called FirstName and sets it to a text value.

```
Public Sub CreateXmlDoc()
   NameElement = New System.Xml.XmlDocument().CreateElement("FirstName")
   NameElement.InnerText = CtName
End Sub
```

Next, we added a single line of code to the `serialization.vb` file, which calls the above method to give it some values.

```
MyContactCollection.CreateXmlDoc()
```

So when this is run, the serializer will work through the main class instance, which will define the root element. It then works though the class, serializing the fields and properties, as well as serializing any classes defined within this class and so on.

We're going to end our discussion on XML serialization for the moment. We will look at it further in Chapter 11 when we have discussed the XML Schema Definition Language, but we will not be going into great detail as the subject is so large. For further information look at the MSDN documentation and read *Professional XML for .NET Developers*, from Wrox Press (ISBN 1-86100-531-8).

Improving the Case Study

We are going to improve part of the case study here and leave the remaining parts for you to implement as an exercise. Specifically, we are going to improve the searching and querying facility by using the `XPathDocument` class and many of the other classes we have discussed in this chapter.

So, let's look at the `FindContact()` method that we previously created and improve this. This new case study can be found in the **Case Study** project within the download folder for this chapter. This method will allow someone looking for a contact to choose to search by first, middle or last name, specify a name to search for and have the results of the search displayed to them.

```
Private Sub FindContact(ByVal type As String, ByVal query As String)
   'Read-only querying to be done at this point
   Dim xpDoc As XPathDocument = New XPathDocument("..\\CaseStudy.xml")
   Dim xpNav As XPathNavigator = xpDoc.CreateNavigator()

   Dim xmlNM As XmlNamespaceManager = New XmlNamespaceManager(xpNav.NameTable)
   xmlNM.AddNamespace("ct", "http://www.deltabis.com/Contact")

   Dim xpExpr As XPathExpression = xpNav.Compile("/ct:ContactDetails/contact/" _
      & "name[starts-with(" & type & ","""" & query & """)]")

   xpExpr.SetContext(xmlNM)
   xpExpr.AddSort("first", XmlSortOrder.Ascending, XmlCaseOrder.None, "",_
               XmlDataType.Text)
```

```
        Dim xpNodeIt As XPathNodeIterator = xpNav.Select(xpExpr)
        MessageBox.Show("There are " & xpNodeIt.Count & " contacts matching your
                        query.")

    While (xpNodeIt.MoveNext())
      Dim Message As String = ""
      xpNodeIt.Current.MoveToFirstChild()

      Message = xpNodeIt.Current.Value

      xpNodeIt.Current.MoveToNext()
      Message = Message & " " & xpNodeIt.Current.Value

      xpNodeIt.Current.MoveToNext()
      Message &= " " & xpNodeIt.Current.Value

      xpNodeIt.Current.MoveToParent()
      xpNodeIt.Current.MoveToNext()

      Message = Message &" " & vbNewLine & "Notes" & vbNewLine _
        & "=====================" & vbNewLine _
        & xpNodeIt.Current.Value

      MessageBox.Show(Message)
    End While
  End Sub
```

In the previous example, we used an `XmlDocument` instance to load the XML document that was to be selected against. However, this provides us with more functionality than we need (and hence a larger hit on performance) because we don't require editing functionality. We therefore use an `XPathDocument` class to load the XML document and create a new `XPathNavigator` instance.

```
    Dim xpDoc As XPathDocument = New XPathDocument("..\\CaseStudy.xml")
    Dim xpNav As XPathNavigator = xpDoc.CreateNavigator()
```

We create an `XmlNamespaceManager` instance that caches the mappings between prefixes and namespaces that will be used to qualify our XPath queries.

```
    Dim xmlNM As XmlNamespaceManager = New XmlNamespaceManager(xpNav.NameTable)
    xmlNM.AddNamespace("ct", "http://www.deltabis.com/Contact")
```

Then we create a compiled `XPathExpression` instance; note that we also use the XPath `starts-with` function to allow you to specify the start of the string in the query.

```
    Dim xpExpr As XPathExpression = xpNav.Compile("/ct:ContactDetails/contact/" _
      & "name[starts-with(" + type + ",""" + query + """)]")
```

We next use the `SetContext()` method to associate the `XmlNamespaceManager` instance with the `XPathExpression` instance to allow namespace queries to be resolved. We also use the `AddSort()` method to state that we want to order by the value of the `first` attribute in alphabetical order.

```
xpExpr.SetContext(xmlNM)
xpExpr.AddSort("first", XmlSortOrder.Ascending, XmlCaseOrder.None, "", _
XmlDataType.Text)
```

Following this, we can execute the `Select()` method and this will return a list of items that matched our query. We then inform the user how many matches were found by the query.

```
Dim xpNodeIt As XPathNodeIterator = xpNav.Select(xpExpr)
MessageBox.Show("There are " & +xpNodeIt.Count _
   & " contacts matching your query.")
```

The method then iterates through each returned item and, as we are at the `name` element node, we call the `MoveToFirstChild()` method to get to the `first` element node.

```
While (xpNodeIt.MoveNext())
  Dim Message As String = ""
  xpNodeIt.Current.MoveToFirstChild()

  Message = xpNodeIt.Current.Value
```

Next we call the `MoveToNext()` method which takes us to the next sibling node of the `first` element node which is the `middle` node. This is repeated again to access the final `last` element node.

```
   xpNodeIt.Current.MoveToNext()
   Message = Message & " " & xpNodeIt.Current.Value

   xpNodeIt.Current.MoveToNext()
   Message = Message & " " & xpNodeIt.Current.Value
```

After we have access each of the child nodes, we call the `MoveToParent()` method which takes the navigator to the name element node again; the `MoveToNext()` method will take us to the `notes` sibling node.

```
   xpNodeIt.Current.MoveToParent()
   xpNodeIt.Current.MoveToNext()

   Message = Message & " " & vbNewLine & vbNewLine _
     & "Notes" & vbNewLine _
     & "====================" & vbNewLine _
     & xpNodeIt.Current.Value

   MessageBox.Show(Message)
End While
```

So, if someone is looking for anyone whose first name starts with the letter "D", they would type "D" into the search box, ensure the **First Name** is selected and click the **Find** button. The result from the query is shown below:

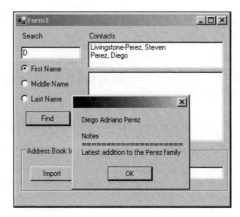

Summary

We now have a good knowledge of the classes, methods, and properties available within the System.Xml.XPath namespace and what they can be used for. We also know a bit about serialization in XML and how that can be used for saving working snapshots of your classes.

You are now in a position to create powerful, optimized applications that allow you to retrieve information from an XML document based on complex XPath queries. The XPathNavigator class is extremely powerful and the most efficient way to access data from an XML document when working with XPath. You can also start to look at some of the more powerful capabilities of working with serialization in XML – this will allow you to persist instances of your classes and retrieve them when required.

We covered the following areas in this chapter:

- ❑ What the System.Xml.XPath namespace is
- ❑ The XPathDocument class
- ❑ The XPathNavigator class
- ❑ When to use XPathNavigator
- ❑ Custom XPathNavigator classes
- ❑ XML Serialization
- ❑ Using XPathNavigator with the ongoing case study

We suggest you experiment with these classes to improve what we have done thus far with the case study. One exercise is to look at writing a custom XPathNavigator class to represent a Visual Studio solution. This may contain details on the type of project (Windows Form, Console, and so on) and type of file (Class file, XML file, and so on) that can be queried by the user.

Another exercise would be to look at improving the case study to support customized ordering of the selected information (for example, order by first, middle, or last name). You could even extend the case study to allow users to enter new user information and use the serialization classes to suspend and resume the entry of data at any point.

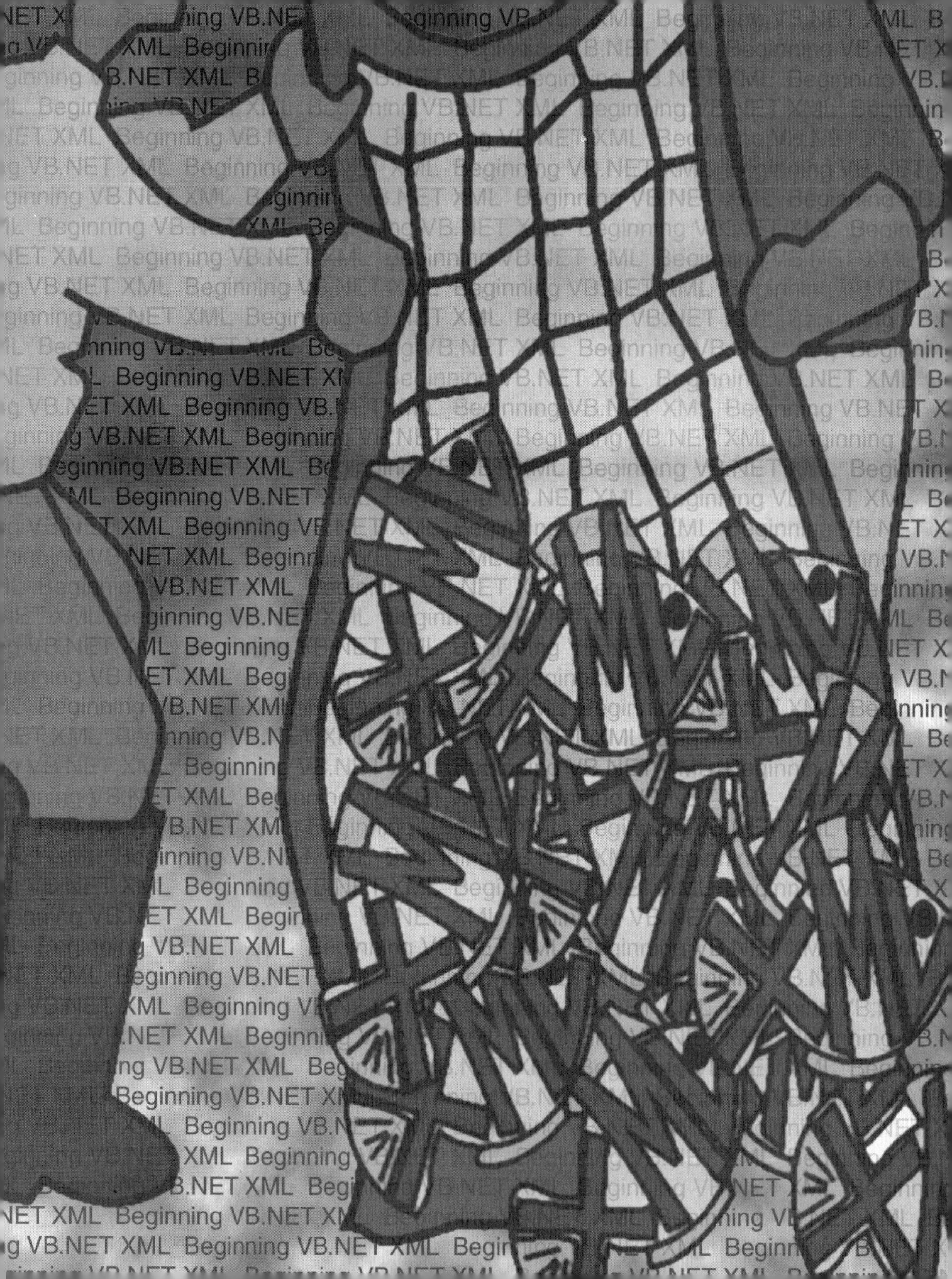
Beginning VB.NET XML

XSLT

In this chapter we are going to look at the **XSL Transformation Language** (**XSLT**) and the support available for it in the .NET Framework. XSLT is used to take an XML document and output it in another format, such as an HTML page or another XML document (although we aren't limited to these formats). This transformation is based on the contents of the XML document, through matching elements and attributes within the document.

In this chapter, you will learn:

- ❑ The XSLT elements
- ❑ Matching templates in XSLT
- ❑ How XSLT allows iteration and conditional logic
- ❑ Functions in XSLT
- ❑ How whitespace works in XSLT
- ❑ The XslTransform class
- ❑ How .NET transforms stylesheets
- ❑ How VB scripting is supported
- ❑ How XSLT interacts with the environment

Before we go on to look at XSLT is in detail we will:

- ❑ Discuss why and when XSLT is required
- ❑ Demonstrate some scenarios where XSLT would be most useful when working with XML

When is it Used?

There are two key areas where XSL can be useful, and you will likely use both at some point when working with XML structures:

❑ Formatting

❑ Transformations

Formatting

So how does it help with formatting? Well, more and more information is being stored as XML either permanently (in a file structure) or temporarily (to mark up the results of a database query) and writing these directly to the output that is intended for a human reader is not very useful. XML is not a great structure for an end user, who is not interested in the XML, to attempt to read and extract any meaning from it. As an example, look at the figure below, which is an example of the contact details XML structure we have been working with throughout the book.

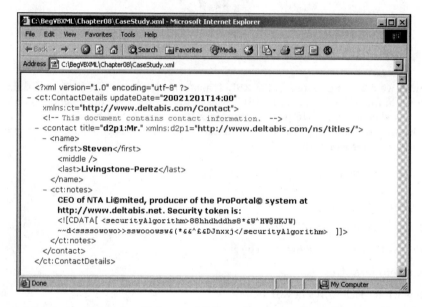

To most users this isn't going to be all that useful. Sure, the data is there, but it really isn't friendly to someone who is non-technical and expecting to get any information from this. This is where XSL formatting comes in. It would be a lot better if this page were marked up as HTML so that users can read the data as they would any other web page. XSL can be used on this XML document to re-structure it into something more user-friendly, such as the display shown on the next page.

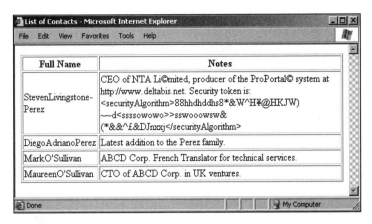

This is a lot more readable, and the transformation would work no matter how much information is contained in the source document. What's more, with XSL formatting you can use Cascading Stylesheet (CSS) formatting and other HTML element formatting (such as H1 for headers). In fact, you may tailor the output for unusual clients, such as a PDA or mobile phone – XSL supports this as well using similar techniques.

However, as we said a few paragraphs ago, there is another major use for XSL – transformations – so let's look at this now.

Transformations

In the past, issues such as the ordering or structure of data, whether that be in communications or data stored in a document, has caused problems because when some other application comes to read the data, it is not in the format it expects. Of course we are never going to get everybody to adapt their applications to work with a single data format, so let's do it the other way round – adapt the data to fit the application.

Consider purchase orders in old Electronic Data Interchange (EDI) applications where the data is in a specific format. Different applications use the data in different ways, conforming to different document structures, so when a new application wanted to use the purchase order details, a lot of work was required to have the application extract the data and ensure each piece of data was where it was expected to be. This is a huge issue when you take your business online and expect to provide business-to-business services. Can you expect everyone to conform to your standard? Even in the case of EDI where there were global standards, they were still expensive to implement for custom applications (and let's face it, we almost always create a custom application or customize an existing product) because of the specific ordering of the data and the resources required to create enterprise-level applications on top of this. It got worse when you went outside your network where everyone wanted their own view of the data they thought was important to them.

It would be much easier for organizations to use any purchase order structure (or any other structure for that matter) they want and simply transform the input data format to one that is appropriate for their application. What's more, their application may only want a fraction of the data that is available (for example, the company name for a company registration database) and so they may want to get only the data they are interested in and format it in some way that the receiving application will be happy with. The following diagram illustrates how XSLT would play an important role in transformations.

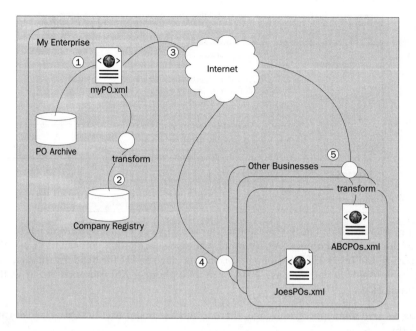

The sequence may be as follows:

1. Within your enterprise some application creates a Purchase Order in `myPO.xml` and submits the details to a database containing an archive of purchase orders. For example (and remember this is a very much simplified version of the far more complex real world!):

```
<po myid="876363">
  <company name="ABC Ltd" id="73338" />
  <orders>
    <order quantity="3" sku="8272C" />
    <order quantity="8" sku="622B" />
  </orders>
</po>
```

2. The purchase order contains the name and ID of the company that it is being submitted to and these details are recorded in a Company Registry database. The application that records these details needs only the name of the company and its ID, so an XSLT transforms the `myPO.xml` structure to a simpler structure containing only these details. Such a structure may resemble the following:

```
<CompanyInfo>
    <Name id="73338">ABC Ltd</Name>
</CompanyInfo>
```

3. Each purchase order represented as XML is sent through the Internet to each business that is to deal with the order.

4. The application that handles purchase orders for the ABC Ltd company expects them to be in the following format and so another transform must be made before the application uses the data.

```
<order from="876363">
    <orderItems>
        <item num="3">8272C</item>
        <item num="8">622B</item>
    </orderItems>
</order>
```

Therefore an XSLT file will transform the incoming data into this new format.

5. Finally, Joe Corp expects the data to be in some alternative format (we won't write another – I'm sure you get the picture of the random formats of data structures) and so the data from "My Enterprise" must also be transformed prior to being used by its purchase order application.

You now see how XSLT can be used at many hubs (connection areas) of the enterprise – internally and externally. This is one of the main reasons why XSLT was created – to enable data that is stored in an XML format to be transformed to one or more formats that don't even necessarily exist when the structure is defined.

In fact the output of using XSLT doesn't even have to be XML – you can take in an XML document and transform it to a Comma-Separated Variable (CSV) format if that is what the receiving application expects. XSLT in this respect can be a hub for integrating disparate applications, internal and external, together using a series of transforms. We will see how that can be done in this chapter.

One final note on this is that you don't need to view the formatting and transforming of XSLT separately. They can be combined and used where appropriate – for example you may want to transform the incoming purchase order to your internal format and then use an XSL Stylesheet to display the data to the user. This is also a common scenario.

Now that we have some understanding of exactly why XSLT exists, let's look at it in more detail.

The XSL Language

The **Extensible Stylesheet Language** (XSL) is a styling and transformation language within the XML family of technologies. XSL has two constituent technologies known as **XSL-Formatting Objects** (XSL-FO) and **XSL Transformations** (XSLT).

We haven't looked (nor will we look) at XSL-FO, mainly because it is not supported in .NET, nor is it supported by either of the main commercial browsers (Internet Explorer and Netscape Navigator). Its main purpose is to extend the ideas behind Cascading Stylesheets and allow rich formatting such as color, layout, and font control, which is currently carried out by CSS (or directly in the HTML document). It is only one half of XSL, however – in this chapter we intend to concentrate on **XSL Transformations** (XSLT), which is supported by .NET and Internet Explorer (you will learn later how you can also support any other browser when working on the server). In addition, XSLT involves **both** the formatting and transformation aspects we discussed earlier.

To find out more about XSL-FO, go to http://www.w3.org/TR/xsl. The specification of XSLT itself is found at http://www.w3.org/TR/xslt.

When you come to work with XSL you may come across a version of XSL that you are unfamiliar with. This version is based on a pre-standard XSL that was submitted to the W3C and was implemented by Microsoft to give developers the power of using XSL early. This draft version was never standardized, but has remained in use due to the development base it built up prior to a standards-based XSL processor being available. We aren't going to look at the support for the pre-standard XSL implementation. If you want to find out more about this, look at *XML Application Development with MSXML 4.0*, from Wrox Press (ISBN 1-86100-589-X) for more details.

There is also a standards-based implementation of XSL that was written according to the W3C XSL Transformations (XSLT) Version 1.0 recommendation, which can be found at http://www.w3.org/TR/xslt. This is the XSLT specification that is supported by the XSL classes in the .NET Framework (we discuss browser support later in the chapter).

XSLT Principles

As mentioned earlier, XSLT allows the transformation of some input XML document to an alternative output structure that may or may not be XML – it is possible for example to transform an XML document to CSV format.

But how does it know what elements and attributes within the source XML document to take and transform to the output? For example, if we have a `<company>` element within the source XML document and this is supposed to be output as a header tag within a H1 element in the output HTML document – how exactly does XSLT do this?

It does this by using rules, or **patterns**, that query the structure and data of the source XML document and when a given pattern is found within the XML document, we say that there has been a **match**. So what is a pattern in XSLT? The following sentences are English language versions of typical XSLT queries:

❑ Match the root element of the document

❑ Match the `company` element nodes (there may be more than one)

❑ Match `company` element node with a child text node with the value "ABC Ltd"

❑ Match any `order` element that has a `quantity` attribute with a value more than 3

Each pattern represents a single **template**, defining a rule containing instructions that determine what is to happen when that particular pattern within the source XML document is found, or is matched. An example may be, "When a company element is found, take its contents and write it out as an HTML H1 element with the name of the company as its contents" – we will see how this works shortly. An XSLT document will typically contain many of these templates.

How are these templates then used? Well, the XSLT processor will load the XML document into a tree structure, like the in-memory tree structure used when we looked at the Document Object Model tree. Once this is done the XSLT can operate on the source XML document by using the **templates** to match **patterns** within the document. The following diagram illustrates the process:

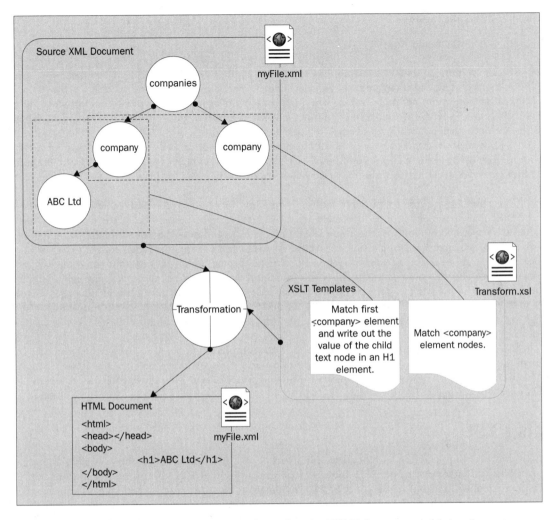

The transformation examines the templates defined in the XSLT document, applying the patterns defined for these templates to all nodes in the source XML document that match the template.

Most of us are familiar with programming languages such as C, C#, VB, VB.NET, JavaScript, and so on, where we write code detailing exactly what the computer is to do, and in what order. This is known as imperative or **procedural** programming. When we looked at the XmlReader examples, we had a well defined set of actions that a class instance would perform:

❑   Create a new instance of the reader

❑   Get a reference to the XML document

❑   Read through the document

❑   Read each node and if a node has the name X, then do this

❑   Write the results

❑   Close the reader

You will have noticed that XSLT is not like this and it is often this change in how you tackle applications that provides most of the learning curve for web-based applications. XSLT is based on a **declarative** programming model where you don't specify how something is to be done or even denote a specific order. In XSLT we provide conditions that when satisfied cause something to happen. When they are not satisfied, nothing happens – that piece of code will act as if it is not there. The XmlReader and XmlDocument classes are great for doing certain specific things based on the nodes in an XML file, but in order to provide the same functionality (where we transform the entire source document that XSLT provides us with), we would have to write a lot of code.

XSLT is based on the concept of **functional** programming, which forms the basis of languages such as Lisp and Scheme. The set of templates that make up the stylesheet define a fragment of the input XML file that should be operated on (for instance, that matches the pattern) and describe how it should be output. This structure means that there are no side-effects, except when you use some external code such as C# or JScript code. As an example, you can define global variables and initialize them, but you cannot change their values. This may sound strange, but the idea behind this is that you can process any given template in any order without having to perform the full transform process again. In a procedural language, however, a change to a global variable may affect the order that the methods can be called in (for example GetName(id) may not be able to be called until SetId() is called to initialize the global variable id).

In XSLT order is unimportant. You simply add in the templates you want to be matched and the ordering is taken care of by the processor. It will implicitly process templates that match nodes higher in the hierarchy before it processes templates for nodes further down. Therefore, you can be a lot more flexible when using XSLT.

Using XSL

XSL has been supported in various forms for a number of years on the Microsoft platform, directly with the MSXML parser that comes with Internet Explorer or in other applications by working with the separately downloadable version of MSXML. The main reason for having a separate download was so that the XML support in the parser could be improved upon and used with your applications without having to release new versions of Internet Explorer for every update. It also means that MSXML can be used to transform a document in one of two ways:

❑   Directly by browsing to the XML document itself with Internet Explorer.

❑   Programmatically by specifying the XML file to be transformed and the XSL stylesheet to be used to perform the transform.

Directly browsing XML documents and having them transformed by XSLT is fairly popular when you are able to guarantee that the end browser supports XSL – for example, Internet Explorer browsers 5.5 and above. This is the technique we looked at above and simply requires a processing instruction in the XML document with a URL reference to the stylesheet that should perform the processing. The following diagram shows how this process works:

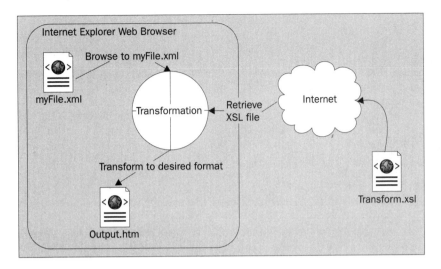

Programmatic transforms are the main way in which XSLT is currently used, for one good reason – you can use transforms on the server to output HTML (or any other desired output) for clients who do not support transforming XSL stylesheets (that is, the client doesn't have an XSL processor).

You also have the ability to write script on the clients to perform the same kind of transforms, but this is less popular as it again depends on Internet Explorer or a client-side XSL processor being available. You may choose to use client-side scripts when you want to pass some information into the stylesheet (we see how you do this later) or when you are dynamically building the XML document on the client.

The architecture of these programmatic solutions is shown in the following diagram.

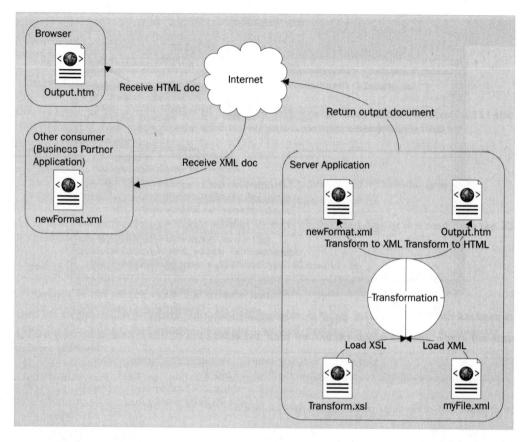

In this case, a client makes a request – the client being anything, from a web browser to another application, making a request to a URL. On the server, the application will load both the XML and XSL documents it's using and then the transformation engine will be called. Depending on the type of request (for example, as flagged in the querystring, or a different URL being called), the transform will output a different document type. This may be pure HTML that is supported by every browser – in this case the application will never know that you used XML and XSL as it sees only the resultant HTML. This is great as it still allows you to separate the data in your XML file from the presentation details stored in the XSL file. In the second case, we may have an application from a business partner and they expect the XML to be in an alternative format, so the transform is again performed on the server and the partner's application sees only the XML result – in the appropriate format. What's more, this concept can be applied to *any* end device – as long as the transform is designed to output the correct format for that device, be that a mobile phone, a personal digital assistant, or another application.

This is the primary reason for performing XSL transforms on the server – it opens you up to a much wider range of end devices if you are required to support them at some point in the future – this is particularly true in the business-to-business arena where new business partners may be quite common.

One question that has not yet been answered is how Cascading Stylesheets (CSS) plays a role in all of this. Is it now redundant? Or is there something that it can still give us?

XSL and CSS

Cascading Stylesheets have been around for a long time and have provided basic formatting for the content within browsers. In no way has this been superceded by XSL, and in fact CSS continues to be worked upon to provide support for devices other than browsers – version 3 is currently in working draft.

> **Details of CSS can be found at** http://www.w3.org/Style/CSS/.

XSLT itself is purely for transforming and formatting – not styling. This is a key point because Cascading Stylesheets are purely for styling – details such as positioning, font types, colors, and the like are the domain of CSS. It is for this reason that using CSS *with* XSLT is actually recommended. Here are some scenarios that indicate where this is appropriate:

❑   XML and XSLT can be used on the server to create HTML output that is styled using CSS. This allows full backward compatibility with existing browsers.

❑   We can use XML with CSS and write directly to the client. Most browsers support viewing of XML documents, and CSS can be used directly in these documents to display the XML document in a readable format. This technique is discussed in detail in *XML Application Development with MSXML 4.0*, from Wrox Press (ISBN 1-86100-589-X), in Chapter 7.

❑   We can use XML and XSLT on the client using CSS to style the formatted content. This is similar to the first point above, but the actual XML and XSLT (along with the CSS) are sent directly to the client.

You may have noticed earlier that we mentioned that the XSL 1.0 Recommendation is broken into two key parts. We have been discussing XSLT, used for formatting and transforming documents, but there is another part used for styling the output, called Formatting Objects (XSL-FO), and more details can be found at http://www.w3.org/TR/xsl. XSL-FO is not very well supported at the moment, but it contains some functionality that is very much similar to CSS and will likely compete with CSS at some point in the future (when better support arrives for it). However, whereas CSS was developed more for adding styling to existing document formats such as HTML, XSL-FO has been developed to work with documents formatted as XML. Here are some of the differences between CSS and XSL-FO:

❑   XSL-FO uses XML syntax for its definitions, whereas CSS is not XML.

❑   XSL-FO is a new styling standard giving opportunity for conformance among the major browsers in the same way XML (and related technologies such as XSLT) have been well accepted. CSS, however, has been out for a long time and support varies among browsers (although it is still quite well supported).

❑   CSS is simpler than XSL-FO (the functionality available in XSL-FO is extensive), but the variance of support in browsers had made this issue more complex than it need be.

❑   Finally, and most importantly, XSL-FO has no support in the main commercial browsers and so CSS remains the styling language of choice for the near future.

You should now have a pretty good understanding of why we use XSL and where it fits into the grand scope of XML technologies and software development. For information on the support that is available on the client and on the server for using XSL, see Appendix B.

The XSL Namespace

If you remember back to our discussions on namespaces throughout the book you will remember that they are a way of collecting together terms that have the same meaning into a single vocabulary. So namespaces can be used to distinguish the element address, meaning an address in computer memory, from the geographical address of a person. This is important to prevent names with the same spelling (but different meaning) from clashing.

Namespaces are also commonly used to group together elements that have some significance to the XML parser. This is possible because the XML parser knows that certain namespace definitions are significant and are to be handled by some XML processor. In the case of XSLT, this is the XSLT processor. What this means is that any elements within an XML document that are qualified in the XSLT namespace will be processed by the XSLT parser which will perform some function based on the type and/or content of the element.

The namespace that is associated with XSLT is http://www.w3.org/1999/XSL/Transform, and so any elements that are qualified under this element will be processed by the XSLT processor. There is a predefined set of elements that can be used within this namespace and so you can't just use any element or an exception will be thrown – we discuss the supported elements later in this chapter.

Quite commonly the prefix xsl is bound to the XSLT namespace and so you will typically see template definitions as follows:

```
<xsl:template match="/">
  ...
</xsl:template>
```

Note that the template element is now qualified in the http://www.w3.org/1999/XSL/Transform namespace and so it will be understood and processed by the XSLT processor. You can of course make the prefix anything you want, but all elements within this namespace will be processed by the XSLT processor.

At this point you should have a fairly good understanding of some of the key concepts of XSLT, so it's time to start looking at how to use XSLT. The easiest way to understand how to create XSL is to take a look at a simple example.

Anatomy of a Simple XSL Example

This simple example will take a simple XML document containing some content, process the content of this XML file using an XSL stylesheet, and output an HTML file containing this processed content.

> **In order to view this example, you should have Internet Explorer 5.5 or above installed.**

Consider the XML file, simple.xml, shown next.

```
<?xml version="1.0" encoding="utf-8"?>
<content>
  <text>
    <p>hello world</p>
  </text>
</content>
```

When this is viewed in Internet Explorer, you will see the following:

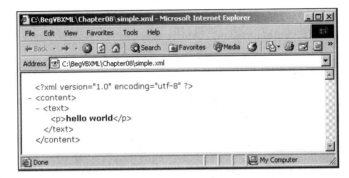

The output is *almost* the exact text from the XML document in simple.xml. There is some formatting done, for example inserting the dashes before the elements that can be expanded and collapsed. This is not a feature of XML – this is a feature of Internet Explorer (IE). IE has a built-in XSLT stylesheet, which takes any valid XML file and applies some very basic formatting so that it is a bit more readable when viewed in the browser. Of course, when you actually create an application you are going to want to format the XML in some format other than this basic format provided by Internet Explorer. How do we do this? We use an XML Processing Instruction.

Adding a Processing Instruction

A Processing Instruction (PI) will tell the XML parser that it is to use an stylesheet other than the built-in stylesheet to format the document.

> **The XSL processing instruction is not part of the XSLT or XPath standards and instead has its own W3C Recommendation, which you can find at http://www.w3.org/TR/xml-stylesheet.**

The basic processing instruction for XSLT is defined as follows:

```
<?xml-stylesheet href="" type=""?>
```

There are two mandatory attributes on the `xml-stylesheet` PI – the `href` attribute and the `type` attribute. The `href` attribute has a value specifying the URL of the stylesheet that will be used to format or transform the XML document – it is also called the principal stylesheet. In addition, the `type` attribute must be present to indicate the language in which the stylesheet is written – this is because although we will concentrate on XSL stylesheets in this chapter, the type can also be a Cascading Stylesheet (used for simply formatting the presentation of the data such as simple fonts and colors). With XSLT, the value of the `type` attribute should be `"text/xsl"` and this is what you will see with all examples in this chapter. There are additional optional attributes defined on this element as discussed below:

- ❑ `title` – this can be used to give a title to a stylesheet. It is useful where you have multiple stylesheets in a document and you want the user to be able to choose which one to use. As an example, you may have a stylesheet for formatting for a web browser and another for transforming the data for a Braille browser for the blind.

- ❑ `media` – this can be used to specify the output medium. Because XML can be transformed to almost any output, you can have outputs for "print" and "projection" and other output as defined in the HTML 4.0 specification.

- ❑ `charset` – this attribute cannot be used with XSLT stylesheet as the encoding is actually defined by the XML document itself.

- ❑ `alternate` – if the value of this is "no" then this is the preferred stylesheet in a group of stylesheets, or else it is "yes" to indicate it is an alternative stylesheet.

So, returning to the example, the processing instruction that will be used to transform our XML document is shown below:

```
<?xml-stylesheet type="text/xsl" href="simple.xsl"?>
```

The `type` attribute is set to `"text/xsl"` to indicate that it is an XSLT stylesheet that we want to use to process the document. The location of the stylesheet, which we will create below, is set in the `href` attribute to `simple.xsl`. This file is in the same directory as the XML document. The extension `".xsl"` is not required, but generally the extension is either `".xsl"` or `".xslt"`.

The processing instruction is added as shown below:

```
<?xml version="1.0" encoding="utf-8"?>
<?xml-stylesheet type="text/xsl" href="simple.xsl"?>
<content>
  <text>
    <p>hello world</p>
  </text>
</content>
```

With the XML document in place, it's time to create the XSLT stylesheet that is going to format the document.

Creating the Stylesheet

Every XSLT stylesheet must contain a root element, just like every XML document. This will be either the `stylesheet` element or the `transform` element – the names of both are completely interchangeable. The reason for having them both is simply to allow you to indicate what the main intention of the stylesheet is: to format an XML document (`stylesheet`) or transform the XML document (`transform`) into some other format. Remember, there is no difference between formatting a XML document using a stylesheet or transforming a document using a stylesheet. The terms are used simply to indicate the intention of the document to a human user – they are interpreted the same by an XSLT processor.

The stylesheet element will contain at least one namespace declaration, which is the W3C standard namespace `xmlns:xsl="http://www.w3.org/1999/XSL/Transform"`. The prefix is typically "xsl", although it can be anything you want as long as it is used consistently throughout the document.

The `version` attribute is also required and will correspond to the version of XSLT being used. The .NET XSL parser supports version 1.0 of the specification (although it does provide some support for features that will come in version 2.0).

An example of what we know so far is:

```
<xsl:stylesheet version="1.0"
  xmlns:xsl="http://www.w3.org/1999/XSL/Transform" />
```

Within this `stylesheet` (or `transform`) element, you can place `template` elements that match particular elements in the XML document, which will be processed by the XSLT processor – we look at the `stylesheet` element in more detail shortly.

Other than the `template` element that we will discuss in detail below, the `value-of` element will output some text value defined in the source XML document. The `value-of` element is the most common way of outputting information from the source XML document to the resultant document. It simply outputs the value of the selected node as a text value and is defined as follows:

```
<xsl:value-of select="expression" disable-output-escaping="yes | no" />
```

The `select` attribute uses an XPath expression, which selects a node based on the context node and any returned node-set is converted to a string. If a node-set is selected containing more than one item, then the output of this will be the text value of the first node in document order.

The `disable-output-escaping` attribute is used to control output escaping of special characters and defaults to no. For example, if the value of the selected node is < and the `disable-output-escaping` attribute was set to no, then it will be escaped and the output value will be <. However, if this attribute is set to yes, then it will not be escaped and instead will be parsed resulting in the < character being output.

Let's create a simple example that demonstrates how to create a stylesheet and apply it to an XML document; this will allow us to discuss in more detail the various parts of stylesheets.

Try It Out: Creating a Simple Stylesheet

This process will involve creating a stylesheet, creating an XML document, and then applying the transform and viewing the result.

Note that all the sample code for this chapter is available for download from http://www.wrox.com. We will be storing sample code for this chapter within the following folder: C:\BegVBXML\Chapter08. You may, of course, use a different folder depending on what you prefer.

1. Create a new file using your preferred text editor and enter the following XSL code:

```xml
<?xml version="1.0" encoding="utf-8"?>
<xsl:stylesheet version="1.0"
  xmlns:xsl="http://www.w3.org/1999/XSL/Transform">

  <xsl:template match="p">
    <html>
      <head></head>
      <body>
        The message is
        <xsl:value-of select="." />.
      </body>
    </html>
  </xsl:template>

</xsl:stylesheet>
```

2. Save this file as simple.xsl.

3. Create another new file and enter the following XML:

```xml
<?xml version="1.0" encoding="utf-8"?>
<?xml-stylesheet type="text/xsl" href="simple.xsl"?>
<content>
  <text>
    <p>hello world</p>
  </text>
</content>
```

4. Save this as simple.xml in the same folder as the simple.xsl file you created above.

5. Open simple.xml in Internet Explorer and you will see the following result:

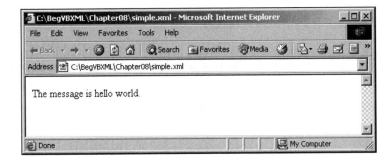

How It Works

Notice that the XSL document `simple.xsl` is also an XML document and has the root `stylesheet` element, which is prefixed in this case by `xsl`, this is bound to the namespace `http://www.w3.org/1999/XSL/Transform`, the XSL namespace as defined in the W3C specification.

Within this root element we have a `template` element containing a `match` attribute, which will match some element, in this case, any p element in the source XML document. We then define some HTML within this template – any elements written that are not qualified in the XSL namespace (in other words all elements not prefixed with `xsl` in this case) are not processed and are copied directly to the output document.

The `<value-of>` element will then copy the text node `The message is hello world` to the `<body>` element of the output.

The HTML result document, which is what the transform actually displayed in Internet Explorer, is as follows:

```
<html>
  <head></head>
  <body>
    The message is hello world.
  </body>
</html>
```

When the p element was matched, it caused the template with the stylesheet to be processed. This stylesheet defines some HTML elements that are not processed by the XSLT processor (as they are not associated with the XSLT namespace!) and so they were copied "as is" directly to the output. Within the `<body>` element, the `<xsl:value-of>` element asked for the text value of the context node, which in turn got the content within the `<p>` element in the source XML document, which is `hello world`. This value was written directly to the output along with the rest of the document, in the place where the `xsl:value-of` was placed – that is, after the text `The message is` – and so gave `The message is hello world`.

This concludes our initial example, so let's look at creating stylesheets in a little more detail.

Creating XSLT Stylesheets

We have now seen an example of creating a stylesheet, so let's look in more detail at the elements and functions involved, which are defined by the W3C standard. Each stylesheet also follows a fairly similar structure:

- ❑ A root `stylesheet` element qualified in the XSL namespace, indicating this is an XSL document
- ❑ A series of `template` elements that match patterns in the target XML document
- ❑ Some discrete functional templates performing some desired output
- ❑ Other XSL elements contained within these templates performing other functionality

Let's look in detail at what these elements are.

Using the XSLT Elements

There are quite a lot of elements that are part of the XSL language, but there are some core elements that you will use more commonly than others. We are going to look at all of these, but concentrate on the more common elements. Let's start by looking at template patterns and matching, which is an important part of stylesheet design.

Patterns, Matching, and Templates

So far we have managed to discuss the concepts of templates and pattern matching without going into any detail as to how they are actually accomplished at the code level. How does a pattern get defined and then used with some XML source?

The first thing that you will be glad to know is that you have met the syntax of patterns before – when we discussed XPath. In the same way that we used XPath in the DOM earlier in the book to select nodes based on set expressions, XSLT used exactly the same concepts. As the XSLT document is processed against the source XML file, each pattern that is defined using XPath will be used to return nodes that are found by this expression. So, for example, in the figure we looked at above, all `<company>` elements could be matched with the expression `"//company"` – very much the same as the XPath expressions we looked at in the DOM chapters.

Using XPath expressions will be fairly familiar to you because you have used them in previous chapters, but when it comes to XSLT, things are very slightly different – or should we say more restricted.

The patterns that are used in XSLT do use XPath syntax, but it is restricted in that the result **must** be a node-set; in other words, returning Boolean values or string results is not allowed. This makes sense as you are trying to find patterns of nodes within the source XML document and a pattern that returns an absolute value will be specific to a given node. The XPath expressions allowed in XSLT are termed **XSL Patterns**. As an example, while `"//company[1]"` would return a node-set containing a single node pointing to the first company element (or an empty node-set if there are none), the pattern `"//company[1]/text()"` returns the string value of that node and so is invalid. Similarly, `"//company[1]/text()='ABC Ltd'"` returns a Boolean `true` if the text node of the first company element is equal to "ABC Ltd" and so this is **not** a valid XSL pattern.

When a given pattern returns a non-empty node-set, in other words nodes are returned from the XSL pattern expression, this is called a **match**. So we say that a pattern **matches** nodes within the source XML document when that pattern returns a non-empty node-set for a given expression. Some examples of valid XSL pattern expressions are as follows:

- ❏ `"//company"` – matches all company elements in the document and returns them in a node-set
- ❏ `"//company/address"` – matches any address element nodes that are the children of company nodes and returns these address elements in a node-set

As we go through the chapter you will see more complex examples and XSL patterns that extend beyond the simple queries we have shown above (such as selecting element nodes based on the value of their attribute nodes). But we will continue with our discussion for the moment on using patterns.

A single pattern is almost never enough, and in fact most transforms are going to need a use a series of patterns that do different things. For example, while you may write the name of the company to a H1 element, you may also want to write the orders submitted by that company and its delivery address in two separate tables. We have to have some way of listing the patterns that are to be evaluated and also what is to happen when a match is made. These details are stored in individual **templates**, which are used in an XSLT document to define a pattern that is to be matched and what is to be done when that template is matched.

Every XSLT document will have at least one template, although most will have many more. The basic syntax of a template is as follows:

```
<template match="pattern">
  <!-- do something -->
</template>
```

The `template` keyword is defined in the XSLT specification and defines a template as we discussed above. The actual pattern is the value of the `match` attribute on the template element. The contents of the template element determine what is to be done when this pattern has been matched (that is, a non-empty node-set is returned for this pattern).

As a simple example, the following pattern will write out `Found the first company.` when the expression `"//company[1]"` is matched (it may, for example, be part of the creation of an HTML output document).

```
<template match="//company[1]">
  Found the first company.
</template>
```

The actual value of the match expression can get quite complex, as can the contents of the template. We will see more complex cases as we work through this chapter – for now we are gaining an understanding of some of the fundamental concepts of XSLT.

Another fundamental concept is that of **context**, which determines the node currently being processed – let's look at context now.

Context and Template Matching

When we looked at the *Context in XPath* section in Chapter 3 we defined the context node as the "starting node" for XPath expressions. So, consider the following XML fragment.

```
<?xml version="1.0"?>
<person age="25">
  <name>
     <firstname>Graham</firstname>
     <middlename>Mark</middlename>
     <lastname>Livingstone</lastname>
  </name>
</person>
```

So, if some XPath expression was "/person" then the context node, or starting point, would be the document root (the parent node of the document element, which you cannot see) and this expression would select the <person> element, which is the document element. In a subsequent XPath expression, for example "name/firstname", the person document element would be the context node and so the XPath expression would be relative to that node – in other words it could be written "/person/name/firstname". A further XPath query would have this firstname element as the context node and so writing "text()" would be the same as "/person/name/firstname/text()".

The idea of the context node makes working with XPath a lot easier as you don't have to write huge XPath expressions for every selection. For example, in the above document if you wanted the firstname and middlename elements above you could use the expressions "/person/name/firstname/" and "/person/name/middlename/". However, it would be better if we could first set the *starting point* for the second expression to the name element and then just access the firstname and middlename child elements with simple relative expressions; in other words "/person/name" sets the name element as the context node and then "firstname" gets the firstname element and "middlename" the middlename element. This second technique becomes extremely important when documents get more complex as in the real world.

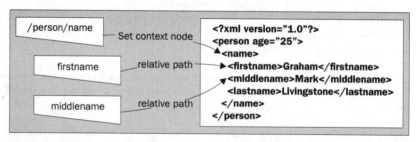

In XSLT, the context node is very important – even more so than when working with the DOM. This is because every template in an XSLT document is evaluated according to the context node, which changes as the XSLT document is processed. The first template that is processed will be evaluated with respect to the document root, which is the context node before any other templates have been processed. Within this template you will instruct the XSLT processor to continue and evaluate the other templates that have been specified in the document – this process is repeated until all templates have been processed. Each template that you indicate to be processed is processed based on the context provided by the previous template – and that context changes as you work through all the templates. As an example, let's consider again the following XML document:

```
<?xml version="1.0"?>
<person age="25">
  <name>
    <firstname>Graham</firstname>
    <middlename>Mark</middlename>
    <lastname>Livingstone</lastname>
  </name>
</person>
```

The templates that have been defined to process this document are as follows (this is only an example and there is a bit more to templates, which we will look at later – for example, you don't use comments to indicate what templates to process – there is a keyword for this as we will see shortly):

```
<template match="/">
  <!--process next template -->
</template>

<template match="person">
  <!--process next template -->
</template>

<template match="name">
  <!--process next template -->
</template>

<template match="firstname">
  <!--Write out first name-->
</template>

<template match="middlename">
  <!--Write out middle name-->
</template>

<template match="lastname">
  <!--Write out last name-->
</template>
```

The first template will match the document root node – the parent of the document element node. We then tell the XSLT processor to evaluate the next template using the document root as the context – the "/" XPath match pattern causes a match on the document element and sets this to the context node. The next template that will match will be the one with person as the match attribute. This is because the person is evaluated relative to the document root context node and this has a <person> child element node and so this template is equivalent to "/person", which will return a node-set containing a single node.

This template then indicates that the next template should be processed with the <person> element now being the context node. So the next template that matches is the <name> element as this element is a child of the <person> element. Again this template instructs the other templates to be processed setting the context node to the <name> element.

Now, the processor looks at the stylesheet to see what templates have patterns that match at this level. Well, in fact the last three match, because `firstname`, `middlename`, and `lastname` are ALL child nodes of the context node – the `name` element has these three elements as children. Therefore, what the XSLT processor does is evaluate each template in document order, and when it has evaluated each template, it will move to the next one. So the `firstname` template is evaluated first, then the `middlename`, and finally the `lastname` template.

In fact, what's better is that you can make the templates as simple or as complex as you like and moving into a given template can cause as many other templates to be invoked as is necessary. For example, the template above matching the `firstname` may invoke other templates that return information from any other part of the document. This is where the power of template processing comes in. We look at some powerful examples of template matching later in the chapter.

Templates are extremely important when working with XSLT, but they have to be encapsulated within a root element that defines that this is an XSLT stylesheet we are working with. Let's look at this root element before continuing our discussion on template matching.

The Root Stylesheet Element

This is perhaps the most significant element as it is the root element for the stylesheet and contains all other XSLT elements. A template for this is as follows:

```
<xsl:stylesheet id="id" version="number"
  xmlns:xsl="http://www.w3.org/1999/XSL/Transform">

</xsl:stylesheet>
```

You can also use `<xsl:transform>` rather than `<xsl:stylesheet>` for this element – there is absolutely no difference other than the name of the element. The semantic difference is mainly to better indicate the purpose of the stylesheet.

This element will contain at least one namespace declaration, which is the W3C standard namespace `xmlns:xsl="http://www.w3.org/1999/XSL/Transform"` – although the prefix is commonly `xsl`, it can be anything you want as long as it is used consistently throughout the document.

The `id` attribute can be used to uniquely identify this node within the XML document and allows for embedding and reference to multiple XSL documents. This is useful because an XML document can actually have the XSL document (or multiple XSL documents) embedded within the XML document rather than as a separate document. It is important to be able to distinguish between them in the case of multiple stylesheets.

The `version` attribute will correspond to the version of XSLT being used and the .NET XSL parser supports version 1.0 of the specification (although it does provide some support for features that will come in version 2.0).

From what we know so far, we would have an XSL stylesheet with the following template.

```
<xsl:stylesheet id="mainStyle" version="1.0"
  xmlns:xsl="http://www.w3.org/1999/XSL/Transform">
  <!--other elements-->
</xsl:stylesheet>
```

This alone doesn't do very much for us (it does absolutely nothing in fact); the real power of XSL transforms comes with template matching, which is what we'll cover now.

Template Matching

As we discussed above, XSLT works fundamentally by matching patterns, and these patterns typically match some document structure – as simple as an element name or as complex as an element at a specific context position with some specific attribute node. In fact, templates will generally match a pattern that uses XSL Patterns syntax discussed earlier, to match a given document fragment structure.

Template matching is done using the `<xsl:template>` element – notice that we now use the `xsl` prefix to qualify the element in the XSLT namespace. The `template` element has a `match` attribute that defines the pattern that is to be matched. As a simple example, consider the following XML fragment, which is similar to what we have seen in the case study we have been working with throughout the book.

```
<?xml version="1.0" encoding="utf-8"?>
<ContactDetails">
  <!--other content -->
</ContactDetails>
```

The XPath expression "/" will match the root `ContactDetails` element, and in XSLT this fact can be used to create a template that will have its contents invoked when the root element is found. So the following template can be created to match the root element.

```
<xsl:template match="/">
...
</xsl:template>
```

Within this template, the root element will be the context element (that is, the starting element for any code within this element) and you can do something based on this element or invoke other templates that will match other parts of the XML document. The XSL processor will work from the bottom of the stylesheet to the top checking for templates that match the structure of the XML document. The first match that is found will be invoked, and if no match is found then there are some default templates that are invoked. Default or built-in templates can often be confusing because they can, for example, output the text within the XML elements even though you don't actually have any template explicitly doing this in the stylesheet.

Until otherwise instructed, the executable file used for the examples below can be found in the `transform\bin` *folder.*

Try It Out: Template Matching

It's time to get practical and have a look at exactly what happens in practice. In this example we are going to look at the simplest possible case, which will validate the discussions above. We will take a simple XML document, match the root element, and write out some text indicating that the root element has been found.

The sample application is called **transform.exe** and will be used for most examples in this chapter – it is a simple executable that uses the .NET `System.Xml` and `System.Xml.Xsl` classes to read in both an XML document and the XSL that is entered in the application, performs a transform, and writes the result to the screen. You will see how to do this yourself in the next chapter, but the purpose of this chapter is to familiarize you with XSLT, so we won't be going into the application code. The code is available in the download.

1. The XML file that will be used for this example is called `example1.xml` and should be in the project root directory. It contains the following XML:

```xml
<?xml version="1.0" encoding="utf-8"?>
<ContactDetails>
  Contact Details entered here.
</ContactDetails>
```

2. Enter the following XSLT into the top textbox and ensure the **Example 1** radio button is selected.

```xml
<xsl:stylesheet version="1.0" xmlns:xsl="http://www.w3.org/1999/XSL/Transform">
  <xsl:template match="/ContactDetails">
    <xsl:value-of select="." />
  </xsl:template>
</xsl:stylesheet>
```

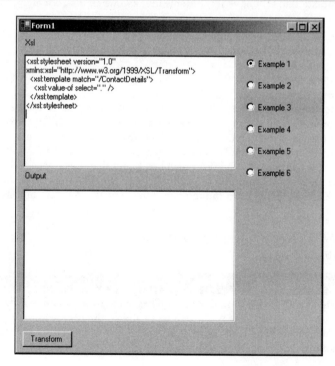

3. Click the Transform button and you will get this output in the bottom textbox:

Contact Details entered here.

How It Works

The first thing that we did was add the root `stylesheet` element that is required for all XSLT documents (or `transform`, of course!). On this the `version` attribute must be specified as `"1.0"` as this is the version of XSLT supported in the current .NET Framework. Also, the `xsl` prefix was associated with the XSLT namespace.

```
<xsl:stylesheet version="1.0" xmlns:xsl="http://www.w3.org/1999/XSL/Transform">
```

Next, we added a template with a match attribute of `"/ContactDetails"`, which will select any `ContactDetails` element that is a child node of the root node.

```
<xsl:template match="/ContactDetails">
  <xsl:value-of select="." />
</xsl:template>
```

Within the `template` we have a `<value-of>` element, which has a select attribute with the value `"."`. As discussed earlier this is an XPath statement relative to the context node. The context node in this template will be the `ContactDetails` element and so the XPath expression `"."` (meaning "this node") in the `<value-of>` element will concatenate all child text nodes of this element (that is, `Contact Details entered here.`) and return it as a string.

When the template pattern is matched, we write out a simple message to the screen as follows:

Contact Details entered here.

The example we used looked at creating a template for the root element – that is, the element within the document that encapsulates all of the other elements. But what happens when we want to match one of these other elements? We looked at this earlier when we discussed templates, but it's worth trying an example to see what happens – you will find a couple of interesting results.

There are actually a couple of ways to do this, either by leaving the XSL processor to work though the template and find any templates whose pattern matches a given element, or to explicitly tell the parser to match a specific element. We look at the latter later on, but let's look at the simplest method of creating templates to match elements other than the root element.

Try It Out: Searching For a Child Element

How do we seek out a particular child element from an XML document that we need to perform some processing on? This Try It Out will demonstrate how to do this by extending the example we worked on earlier.

1. Open the `example1.xml` file that was used in the last *Try It Out* in a text editor and change its contents to read as follows:

```
<?xml version="1.0" encoding="utf-8"?>
<ContactDetails>
  <contact>contact details</contact>
</ContactDetails>
```

2. Enter the following XSLT into the top textbox and ensure the **Example 1** checkbox is selected.

```
<xsl:stylesheet version="1.0" xmlns:xsl="http://www.w3.org/1999/XSL/Transform">
  <xsl:template match="/ContactDetails/contact">
    <xsl:value-of select="." />
  </xsl:template>
</xsl:stylesheet>
```

3. Click the Transform button and you will get this output in the bottom textbox:

contact details

4. Again modify the example1.xml file to include another contact element as shown below:

```
<?xml version="1.0" encoding="utf-8"?>
<ContactDetails>
  <contact>contact details 1</contact>
  <contact>contact details 2</contact>
</ContactDetails>
```

Save the file.

5. Use the same XSLT in the top textbox as before and ensure the **Example 1** radio button is selected.

```
<xsl:stylesheet version="1.0" xmlns:xsl="http://www.w3.org/1999/XSL/Transform">
  <xsl:template match="/ContactDetails/contact">
    <xsl:value-of select="." />
  </xsl:template>
</xsl:stylesheet>
```

6. Click the Transform button and you will get this output in the bottom textbox:

contact details 1contact details 2

How It Works

The goal is to find the contact element within the XML document and do something when it is found. So within the match attribute on the template element, we have changed "/ContactDetails" to "/ContactDetails/contact". This means "return the contact elements that are children of the ContactDetails element that is a child of the root node", which in this case is any contact elements that are children of the document element. In this case there is a single contact element and so a node-set with a single contact element is processed and this contact element will be the context node. Again the <value-of> element will write out the string representation of the text node of this element, which will be "contact details".

What happens if we have two `contact` elements – which one is selected? Well, as we demonstrated in Step 6, in fact all nodes are selected that match the pattern and a node-set is returned containing all the matching nodes. In this case, the expression (this is also called a **location path**) "/ContactDetails/contact" returned a node-set containing the two child contact elements. What the XSLT processor will then do is iterate through each node one by one, changing the context node to each new node in the node-set and then processing the template. This is how we get the text of the two `contact` elements output.

This is an important note to make – if the pattern specified in the template matches more than one node, it will return a node-set containing all of those nodes and iterate through the node set, applying the template to each node in turn. There is no need for you to explicitly tell it to do so, as you would have to do in procedural code such as C# or VB.

Built-in Template Rules

This leads to another interesting point; above we mentioned that there is an alternative way of creating your templates as well as using the full location path (for example, /ContactDetails/contact). Consider modifying the last XSLT document we worked with to read as follows:

```
<xsl:stylesheet version="1.0" xmlns:xsl="http://www.w3.org/1999/XSL/Transform">
    <xsl:template match="contact">
        <xsl:value-of select="." />
    </xsl:template>
</xsl:stylesheet>
```

If you run this stylesheet against the previous XML document, you will again get the following output:

contact details 1contact details 2

So, how did this template match the `contact` element? We know that before any template is processed the context node is the document root (that is, the parent of the root element) – but the only child element of this is the `ContactDetails` element. So how does the processor select the `contact` element? To understand this we need to look at built-in templates.

When an XSLT document is processed and there is no matching template for a node that is found, one of the built-in template rules is invoked.

There are four built-in template rules according to the XSLT standard that perform any functionality (you don't see any of the built-in templates) that are invoked based on the type of node that is being processed.

1. When there is no `template` element for the root node (`/`), then a built-in template will be processed that matches this node. This template is very simple and just tells the processor to process the children of the root node.

2. When any element node is found in the document (for example, "ContactDetails") and there is no template for that element, then the built-in template for elements will be processed. This will simply tell the processor to process any children of that element node.

3. When an attribute node is found and there is no matching template, the XSLT processor built-in template will simply copy the string value of the attribute to the output.

4. Finally, when any text node is found in the XML document, that text value will be copied directly to the output. For other nodes, such as comment, processing instruction, and namespace, there is no action taken.

Looking back at our example, we should now be able to appreciate what has happened. Firstly, the XSLT document is processed and the root node will be found in the XML document. There is no template in the XSLT document to process this node, so the built-in rule (Step 1 above) will be invoked that tells the processor to process the child nodes of this element. The only child element is the `ContactDetails` element; but there is no template for this, so Step 2 above will cause the built-in template rule for elements to be processed. This tells the processor to process any child nodes of the `ContactDetails` element. The child nodes of this are the two contact elements (which are in fact sibling nodes); there **is** of course a `template` for these with the match attribute containing `"contact"`.

As there are two `contact` element nodes, a node-set containing these two elements is created and the template processed for each. The template itself is nothing exciting and simply tells the processor to copy the text node of each contact element to the output.

Hang on – these built-in template rules are great because you don't have to explicitly write in every template that you are going to want to be processed, but what if you really *don't want* the nodes to be processed? A good example is text nodes; you don't *always* want to write the text within the elements to the output. For example, you may want to write out some text indicating that a contact element has been found, but not write out the entire text content of that element (remember it is the concatenation of all child text nodes that is copied to the output).

To do this you can create an empty template within the stylesheet that will match the text node. Remember, the XSLT processor will look through the entire XSLT document from bottom to top of the first template that matches that node and it is only when it has not found any that the built-in template will be invoked. This template would look like the following:

```
<xsl:template match="text()" />
```

As you progress through some of the more complex examples, you will see how useful overriding some of the built-in templates can be.

However, as useful as the built-in templates are for processing the XML document, they don't give you much control over what the XSLT document does. The XSLT processor will simply process all of the templates in the order that they are found – this gives you little control of the placing of the output in the resultant document (unless you are lucky enough that everything is just written out in that order). A further complication is that once you match a node that is the parent of some other node, the XSLT processor will not process any children of that node.

Let's look at how you can control how the processing of templates is done.

Controlling Template Processing

It is important that you understand when you should control template processing and when you can leave it to the built-in templates. The best way to illustrate the lack of control you have with the built-in template rules is with an example.

Try It Out: Matching Multiple Elements Within an XML Document

How do we ensure that we are searching through all elements in the document, even if a match is found? This Try It Out will demonstrate how to do this by extending the example we worked on earlier.

1. Staying with the last *Try It Out* example, enter the following XSLT into the top textbox and ensure the **Example 1** radio button is selected.

```
<xsl:stylesheet version="1.0" xmlns:xsl="http://www.w3.org/1999/XSL/Transform">
  <xsl:template match="/">
    Matched Document Root
  </xsl:template>

  <xsl:template match="contact">
    <xsl:value-of select="." />
  </xsl:template>
</xsl:stylesheet>
```

2. Click the Transform button and you will get the following output in the bottom textbox:

Matched Document Root

How It Works

From the XSLT used in the last *Try It Out*, we modified the XSLT document to now match the root of the XML document as well as the `contact` element.

```
  <xsl:template match="/">
    Matched Document Root
  </xsl:template>
```

From your current understanding of templates you may think that the root element is matched, writes out **Matched Document Root** and then continues processing, and the built-in template for the `ContactDetails` element will tell the processor to process the child nodes. This would cause the second template to be matched and processed. However, when we ran this transform we got the following output.

Matched Document Root

This no doubt leads you to the question – why did it not match the `contact` element? There is a pretty good reason. When the processor matches a node and processes its template, unless it is explicitly told to do so within that template, it will **not** process any child element nodes – the built-in template for elements is only used when a template doesn't match a parent element node. In the case above, the template for the root node was fired, but it didn't indicate anything about processing child nodes, so the processing terminated there. So, to reiterate this important point; if the XSLT processor matches a template with a given node, unless explicitly told to do so, it will not process any child elements of that node.

When the node that is matched is the root node, none of the elements in the document are processed because this is the parent node of all element nodes in the document. Even when this is the document element node, as this node is also the parent of all other element nodes, no other templates for element nodes will be processed (in fact only processing instructions and comment nodes before this will be processed as these come before the document element). To ensure that the child nodes *are* processed, you can use the `<apply-templates>` element – let's look at this now.

Processing Templates with xsl:apply-templates

We have the problem that templates are not processed for nodes if a template that matched one of the ancestor nodes (parent, parent's parent, and so on) did not explicitly tell the processor to do so. To resolve this we can use another of the XSL keywords – `apply-templates`.

At its most basic, you can simply use `apply-templates` as follows:

```
<xsl:apply-templates />
```

There is a lot more to this element and we will discuss that shortly. This version, however, will do everything we need at the moment; it will simply tell the XSLT processor to continue processing templates for that node. It should be placed with the template at the position where you want the output from the other templates that are processed to appear. So, in the following case, the output from the other templates that are processed will be within the opening `<b>` and closing `</b>` tags.

```
<xsl:template match="/">
  <b><xsl:apply-templates /></b>
</xsl:template>
```

In this case, the output from the other templates will appear after the `</b>` tag (and most likely in the wrong place!).

```
<xsl:template match="/">
  <b></b><xsl:apply-templates />
</xsl:template>
```

So, it's important to place your `apply-templates` in the correct place. Going back to our discussion of the `example1.xml` file discussed above, let's look at an example of applying templates.

Try It Out: Matching Elements With Applied Templates

The following Try It Out will enable the processor to work through the XML document, processing any template that is matched This *Try It Out* will demonstrate how to do this by extending the example we worked on earlier.

1. Staying with the last *Try It Out* example, enter the following XSLT into the top textbox and ensure the Example 1 radio button is selected.

```
<xsl:stylesheet version="1.0" xmlns:xsl="http://www.w3.org/1999/XSL/Transform">
    <xsl:template match="/">
        Matched Document Root
```

```
      <xsl:apply-templates />
    </xsl:template>

    <xsl:template match="contact">
       <xsl:value-of select="." />
    </xsl:template>
  </xsl:stylesheet>
```

2. Click the Transform button and you will get this output in the bottom textbox:

Matched Document Root
contact details 1contact details 2

How It Works

In this stylesheet we again match the root node and first write out the text Matched Document Root. After this we use the `<xsl:apply-templates>` element, which will tell the XSLT processor to process any templates for child nodes of the context node (which is of course the root node) and copy the output to this position (that is, overwrite the `apply-templates` keyword).

What happens next is that the `ContactDetails` node will be found and as there is no template for this, the built-in template will tell the XSLT processor to continue processing the child nodes of the `ContactDetails` element. Finally, a node-set containing the two `contact` elements is created and the processor will iterate through each and process the contents of that template. All that is processed is a `<value-of>` element, which will copy the contents of each `contact` element to the output.

Thus far we have seen that the XSLT processor will work through the nodes of the XML document and find any templates that match it and process them, processing child nodes where instructed.

One other scenario that is quite common is where you want to reorder the information from the XML document or process templates that rely on the order that nodes are processed by the XSLT processor. So, although the contact element may be processed, you may want to add information from a node elsewhere in the document. Let's look at how the `<apply-templates>` element can be used in these situations.

Extending apply-templates

When you want to explicitly control the ordering of content from an XML document or invoke templates in a different order than the XSLT processor will do, you should use `apply-templates`. In fact you can also use this to prevent a single template from doing everything – much like in procedural coding where you create a set of methods in a class rather than a single method that does everything.

The `<apply-templates>` element helps us in these scenarios because it optionally has a `select` attribute, which takes an XPath expression that will return a node-set containing the node(s) that match the XPath expression (which is relative to the context node in the current template) and will then search for a template in the XSLT document to process the node-set. This is defined as follows:

```
  <xsl:apply-templates select="expression" />
```

Each node in the node-set will be iterated through and the selected template processed for each. Some examples are as follows:

❏ `<xsl:apply-templates select="contact" />`
   Select the child `contact` elements of the context node and process templates for this node-set.

❏ `<xsl:apply-templates select="contact/name" />`
   Select the `name` elements that are children of the `contact` elements children of the context node and process templates for this node-set.

❏ `<xsl:apply-templates select="contact/name/@age" />`
   Select the `age` attribute of the `name` elements that are children of the `contact` elements that are children of the context node and process templates for this node-set.

There are a wide variety of expressions that can be created all using XPath, so we'll use a *Try It Out* to demonstrate how the `<apply-templates>` element can be further used.

Try It Out: Customizing HTML output using apply-templates

This example is going to demonstrate how `apply-templates` can be used to create a customized HTML output from our XML document. To provide a basis for a good example, we can extend the XML file we were working with earlier. We will continue to use the `transform.exe` file.

1. The following XML is the sample XML file `example2.xml` in the project.

```xml
<?xml version="1.0" encoding="utf-8"?>
<ContactDetails>
  <contact age="27">
    <name>
      <first>Steven</first>
      <middle />
      <last>Livingstone-Perez</last>
    </name>
  </contact>
  <contact age="25">
    <name>
      <first>Loreto</first>
      <middle>Amelia</middle>
      <last>Livingstone-Perez</last>
    </name>
  </contact>
</ContactDetails>
```

2. Enter the following XSLT into the top textbox and ensure the **Example 2** radio button is selected.

```xml
<xsl:stylesheet version="1.0" xmlns:xsl="http://www.w3.org/1999/XSL/Transform">
  <xsl:template match="/">
  <html>
    <head>My contact details</head>
    <body>
      <xsl:apply-templates select="ContactDetails/contact/name" />
    </body>
  </html>
```

```
    </xsl:template>

  <xsl:template match="name">
    <br/> Age : <xsl:value-of select="ancestor::contact/@age" />
    <br/>
    Name : <xsl:value-of select="last" />, <xsl:value-of select="first" />
  </xsl:template>
</xsl:stylesheet>
```

3. Click the Transform button and the output is as follows – notice that it is in HTML.

```
<html><head>My contact details</head><body><br /> Age : 27<br />
Name : Livingstone-Perez, Steven<br /> Age : 25<br />
Name : Livingstone-Perez, Loreto</body></html>
```

How It Works

In this case we have a template that matches the root node and writes out an HTML template.

```
<xsl:template match="/">
<html>
  <head>My contact details</head>
  <body>
```

Next the `apply-templates` element is placed after the `<body>` element and before the closing `</body>` element, and so this is where any output from the `apply-templates` processing will be copied to.

```
    <xsl:apply-templates select="ContactDetails/contact/name" />
  </body>
</html>
</xsl:template>
```

The `select` attribute of the `apply-templates` element is `"ContactDetails/contact/name"`, which will select all of the `name` elements within the document that are children of the `contact` element, which in turn are children of `ContactDetails` elements. The `ContactDetails` element itself must be a child of the context node, which is the root node in this case. This returns a node-set containing the two `name` elements within our document and applies any templates within the document for these nodes.

The template with the `match="name"` attribute is then processed and so each name element becomes the context node. The first `value-of` selects an `ancestor` node (parent, parent's parent, and so on) called `contact` and then selects the attribute node called `age` and copies the value of that node to the output.

The second `value-of` element selects the child element of the context node (that is, the `name` element) called `last` from the document and copies the text value of this node to the output and the final `value-of` selects the child called `first` and does the same thing.

You will have noticed that the output you get is not formatted in any way. This is deliberate and an important point to understand – it is very different from HTML in this manner – whitespace is significant and no formatting of the document is done without your instructions. With HTML on the other hand, all whitespace is converted to a single whitespace character and nicely formatted. We look at whitespace issues later in the chapter.

Using `apply-templates` as described above can be very powerful and allows you to control the processing of templates – it is very unlikely you will ever create a stylesheet where you can rely solely on the processor – you will almost always have to control the processing. We look at some of the advanced capabilities of the `apply-templates` element later in the chapter, but for now let's continue with templates.

Templates and Namespaces

Although we now have a good understanding of working with templates our knowledge is slightly unrealistic, because we don't yet know what to do when the source XML document uses namespaces. Namespaces are being increasingly used in XML documents, so it is essential that we understand how we can match elements in other namespaces.

When we are working with namespaces there are two things that we must do with our XML document. The first is to declare the namespace(s) within our XSLT document and associate it/them with a prefix(es). The second is to update the `match` attribute on any `template` to qualify any nodes in the location path that are in a namespace in the source XML document.

This is best illustrated with an example.

Try It Out: Qualified Template Matching

In this example we are going to look at how we can continue to use our templates to process a modified XML document that uses namespaces. It is likely that most XML documents you come to work with will use namespaces so this is an important topic.

1. The XML file that will be used for this example is called `example3.xml` and should be in the project root directory. It contains the following XML.

```
<?xml version="1.0" encoding="utf-8"?>
<ct:ContactDetails xmlns:ct="http://www.deltabis.com/Contact">
  <contact>
    <name>
      <first>Josefa</first>
      <middle>Ignacia</middle>
      <last>Bustamenta</last>
    </name>
  </contact>
  <contact>
    <name>
      <first>Diego</first>
      <middle>Adriano</middle>
      <last>Perez</last>
    </name>
```

```
      </contact>
    </ct:ContactDetails>
```

2. Enter the following XSLT into the top textbox. Ensure that the **Example 3** radio button is selected:

```
<xsl:stylesheet version="1.0" xmlns:xsl="http://www.w3.org/1999/XSL/Transform"
  xmlns:ct="http://www.deltabis.com/Contact">

 <xsl:template match="ct:ContactDetails">
  <xsl:apply-templates select="contact" />
  </xsl:template>

  <xsl:template match="contact">
    Name : <xsl:value-of select="name/first" />
  </xsl:template>
</xsl:stylesheet>
```

3. Click the **Transform** button and you will get this output in the bottom textbox:

```
Name : Josefa
Name : Diego
```

How It Works

The first thing you have to ensure is that any namespaces in the XML document that qualify elements you will be matching on are also defined in the XSLT document. This ensures that you can qualify any of your XPath expression in the XSLT document, be that for `match` attributes or `select` attributes. This is exactly what we have done in the above XSLT document:

```
<xsl:stylesheet version="1.0" xmlns:xsl="http://www.w3.org/1999/XSL/Transform"
  xmlns:ct="http://www.deltabis.com/Contact
```

Next, we modify the `<xsl:template>` element to now match on the qualified name of the `ContactDetails` element; without the `ct` prefix (or rather a prefix that expands to the `http://www.deltais.com/Contact` namespace) this would not match anything.

```
<xsl:template match="ct:ContactDetails">
  Found ContactDetails
</xsl:template>
```

When the template pattern is matched, we write out the output to the screen:

```
Name : Josefa
Name : Diego
```

Namespaces Everywhere

XSLT gives us plenty of options when it comes to working with namespaces. However, one side-effect is that any namespaces that are in the XSLT document, other than the XSLT namespace itself, are *also* copied to the output – this means that a consumer of your output XML document may end up with an array of namespaces. However, there are times when you may have a namespace defined within the stylesheet for internal purposes only (such as to collect some custom-defined elements) and you don't want this copied to the output XML document – mainly because these elements will be of use only to your stylesheet. You will not have seen that thus far because we have written text nodes to the output and not elements – this will affect writing elements in HTML or any other XML format. To illustrate, consider the last *Try It Out* (Qualified Template Matching) and modify the template matching the contact element node as follows:

```
<xsl:stylesheet version="1.0" xmlns:xsl="http://www.w3.org/1999/XSL/Transform"
  xmlns:ct="http://www.deltabis.com/Contact">

  <xsl:template match="ct:ContactDetails">
    <xsl:apply-templates select="contact" />
  </xsl:template>

  <xsl:template match="contact">
    <name><xsl:value-of select="name/first" /></name>
  </xsl:template>
</xsl:stylesheet>
```

This time when the application is run, you will get the following output:

```
<name xmlns:ct="http://www.deltabis.com/Contact">Josefa</name><name
xmlns:ct="http://www.deltabis.com/Contact">Diego</name>
```

The problem here is that the namespaces from the XSLT document have also been copied to the output along with the elements – even though you never declared these namespaces on those elements (or likely never intended them to be copied out). The situation gets more complex when there are multiple namespaces, so how can we control those namespaces in our output?

The answer actually lies in one of the first XSLT elements we looked at, the stylesheet element. The outline for the <stylesheet> element can now be extended as follows:

```
<xsl:stylesheet id="id" version="number"
extension-element-prefixes="NCNames"
exclude-result-prefixes="NCNames"
xmlns:xsl="http://www.w3.org/1999/XSL/Transform">

</xsl:stylesheet>
```

The extension-element-prefixes attribute contains a whitespace-delimited list of prefixes. Each prefix is mapped to some namespace as part of a namespace declaration as shown below:

```
<xsl:stylesheet version="1.0" xmlns:xsl="http://www.w3.org/1999/XSL/Transform"
  xmlns:oracle="http://www.oracle.com/XSL/Transform/java"/>
```

In this case, the prefix `oracle` was mapped to the namespace `http://www.oracle.com/XSL/Transform/java`. The reason this can be powerful is that when specific parsers read an XSL stylesheet, elements that are qualified in specific namespaces have significant meaning. So, elements qualified in the `http://www.w3.org/1999/XSL/Transform` namespace are significant to all XSL processors because this defines the standard XSL elements and the processor knows how to process those elements. However, to extend functionality, parsers can also implement their own custom pieces of functionality. To state that a given element is part of some custom implementation it has to be qualified in a namespace that is significant to the parser reading the document. In the case of the Oracle XSL processor, any elements that are qualified in (and hence have a prefix mapped to) the namespace `http://www.oracle.com/XSL/Transform/java` will be handled specially by the Oracle processor and implement some specific functionality. This way XSLT engines are able to use this attribute to declare their own special features. These are called **extension elements**.

Finally, the `exclude-result-prefixes` attribute takes a whitespace-delimited list of prefixes associated with namespaces that are defined in the source XSLT document but are not to be output to the resultant XML document. This is important because the namespace declarations are always copied across and applied even to any elements you may create yourself within the XSLT document. This prevents the namespace from being applied to all of these elements. Note, however, that any elements in the source XML document qualified in this namespace will still retain the prefix and namespace association.

Try It Out: Excluding Namespaces

We are starting with a simple example to demonstrate the concept of how namespace prefixes can be removed from the output and when they cannot be removed. This is important when you are transforming an XML document and don't want all of the namespaces applied to every element that is copied across. This is especially useful when working with external applications that don't expect those namespace definitions to be there and so may get confused, such as when they cannot find an element that was mistakenly qualified using the wrong namespace. It also helps reduce the size of the file, which can be important in distributed scenarios because unnecessary namespace declarations don't appear on every element.

1. The XML file that will be used for this example is called `example4.xml` and should be in the project root directory. It contains the following XML:

```
<?xml version="1.0" encoding="utf-8"?>
<ct:ContactDetails xmlns:ct="http://www.deltabis.com/Contact">
  <contact>
    <name>
      <first>Daniel</first>
      <middle />
      <last>Livingstone</last>
    </name>
  </contact>
</ct:ContactDetails>
```

2. Ensure the **Example 4** radio button is selected and enter the following XSLT into the top textbox:

```
<xsl:stylesheet version="1.0" xmlns:xsl="http://www.w3.org/1999/XSL/Transform"
xmlns:ct="http://www.deltabis.com/Contact" exclude-result-prefixes="ct">
```

```
    <xsl:template match="/">
      <Envelope>
        <xsl:copy-of select="*" />
      </Envelope>
    </xsl:template>
  </xsl:stylesheet>
```

3. Click the Transform button and you will get the following output:

```
<Envelope><ct:ContactDetails
xmlns:ct="http://www.deltabis.com/Contact"><contact><name><first>Daniel</first><middle />
<last>Livingstone</last></name></contact></ct:ContactDetails></Envelope>
```

How It Works

The top textbox takes the full XSLT document that is to perform the transform and the bottom textbox is the output from the transform using the example4.xml document in the code downloads. The root element of the example4.xml document is defined as follows:

```
<ct:ContactDetails xmlns:ct="http://www.deltabis.com/Contact">
...
</ct:ContactDetails>
```

The idea of the transform is to wrap this and the entire document in an Envelope element for passing the document through some other system. We use the exclude-result-prefixes="ct" attribute definition to say that we don't want to copy the ct prefix and namespace definition to other outputted elements (the Envelope element in this case). Don't worry about the xsl:template element quite yet, as we will cover it later; in this case it will simply invoke its contents when the root of the XML document is found – that is, when it finds the ct:ContactDetails element.

This therefore outputs the XML code as follows:

```
<Envelope>
  <ct:ContactDetails xmlns:ct="http://www.deltabis.com/Contact">
    ...
  </ct:ContactDetails>
</Envelope>
```

Had we not used the exclude-result-prefixes attribute on the stylesheet root element in the stylesheet, we would have got the following output because the namespace declaration would have been copied and declared on the Envelope element and declared at a global level.

```
<Envelope xmlns:ct="http://www.deltabis.com/Contact">
  <ct:ContactDetails>
    ...
  </ct:ContactDetails>
</Envelope>
```

This would happen for every element that was created in the stylesheet that didn't come from the original XML document. So, if we added a <test> sibling element to this template as follows:

```
<xsl:stylesheet version="1.0" xmlns:xsl="http://www.w3.org/1999/XSL/Transform"
xmlns:ct="http://www.deltabis.com/Contact" exclude-result-prefixes="ct">
  <xsl:template match="/">
    <Envelope>
      <xsl:copy-of select="*" />
    </Envelope>

    <test>...</test>
  </xsl:template>
</xsl:stylesheet>
```

We would get the following output:

```
<Envelope xmlns:ct="http://www.deltabis.com/Contact">
  <ct:ContactDetails>
    ...
  </ct:ContactDetails>
</Envelope>
<test xmlns:ct="http://www.deltabis.com/Contact">...</test>
```

In this case, the `ct` namespace has been copied to the `test` element, even though it doesn't ever use it – using `exclude-result-prefixes` we can prevent all this unnecessary copying of namespace declarations.

This may or may not be an issue, but when there are many namespace definitions this can be a useful way to make the output document more readable or smaller when size is of concern.

Advanced Templates

Now that we understand the basic concepts of working with XSLT and templates, we can move on to some slightly more advanced concepts. We are going to look at `priority`, which determines which of your templates are processed when there are multiple templates matching a given node, and then we will look at some advanced scenarios of `apply-templates`.

Templates and Priority

Looking back at the template definition earlier, we can extend it to also have a `priority` attribute, which allows matching templates to be ordered by some predefined priority:

```
<xsl:template name="QName" match="pattern" priority="number">
</xsl:template>
```

The more specific templates are given a higher priority by default than those that are less specific. What do we mean by this? Well, when we define XPath patterns to match elements, we can have multiple patterns that match at certain times during evaluation.

For example, you may have a template that matches a `name` element that has an empty `middle` child element as well as another template that matches a non-empty `first` element child of a `name` element. Take the following XML fragment as an illustration:

```
<name>
  <first>Steven</first>
  <middle />
  <last>Livingstone-Perez</last>
</name>

<name>
  <first>Diego</first>
  <middle>Adriano</middle>
  <last>Perez</last>
</name>
```

You may do this because you want to do some special processing for names that have no middle name, and treat all others as first name elements. The obvious problem here is that unless you pay attention to how you order your templates in the document, you may not get the desired result: remember the stylesheet works from bottom to top looking for the most specific template.

First of all, by default the template that has the most specific match, no matter where it is in the document, will always be invoked. What is a "specific match"? In the XML document above you may have a template that matches any <name> element; for example, <template match="name" />. A more specific match would be a template that matches any <name> element that has a <first> element child node; for example, <template match="name[first]" />. Yet a more specific match would be a template that matches any <name> element that has a <first> element child node whose child text node is equal to "Diego"; for example, <template match="name[first='Diego']" />. The templates are all examples of matching any <name> element occurrence, but each gets slightly more specific on exactly what the node details must be for that template to be invoked.

So, in the following templates, the bottom template will match any name element with a first child element that has a text node value equal to Diego; the second template will always match any name element that has a child first element; if there is no child first element, then the top-most template will be invoked.

```
<xsl:template match="name">
  matched name
</xsl:template>
<xsl:template match="name[first]">
  matched name with first child element
</xsl:template>
<xsl:template match="name[first='Diego']">
  matched name with first child element whose value is Diego
</xsl:template>
```

This may not seem like a great surprise because you will typically have made the second template more specific for some reason. However, consider the situation where you want to create a template that matches a name element that has a child element called last. This is defined as follows:

```
<xsl:template match="name[last]">
  matched name with last element
</xsl:template>
```

```
<xsl:template match="name[first]">
  matched name with first child element
</xsl:template>
```

In this case there are two templates that by default have equal priority; that is, they both match a name element that has a specified child element node. When a given name element has both a child element called last and a child element called first, which of these templates is invoked? The answer, you may have guessed, is the second or bottom-most template, because the processor will work from the bottom up. In this case that may be fine and you could argue that you just ensure that your templates are ordered correctly when working with them, but that is easier said than done, especially in a more complex stylesheet that may involve many templates that match at various parts of the document.

There are in fact a set of default priorities that determine when a given match is to override a match elsewhere in the XSLT document. The priorities are actually a signed integer value between 0 and 9 with the higher number indicating a higher priority and lower number indicating a lower priority. Patterns with 0 are the default common patterns.

The priority of a template is determined as follows:

❑   Patterns such as node(), text(), and * are not very commonly selected and so have a low default priority of -0.5.

❑   Patterns of a name or attribute are very common and have a default priority of -0.25.

❑   Qualified Patterns match only on given namespace axes and so are more specific than the others and have a default priority of 0.0.

❑   Other specific patterns are given default priorities of 0.5; such as name[first].

❑   You can also assign your default priorities to templates as real numbers; the W3C recommendation defines no limit on the value of priorities; although the .NET documentation indicates a limit of 9, we found the priority can actually be any integer value as per the W3C Recommendation. If the priority of a given template is important in the implementation then it is better to assign your own default priority rather than rely on the default ones so as to ensure the correct template is used and also to optimize the performance of the stylesheet.

Let's try out how to use the priority attribute.

Try It Out: Assigning Priority

We will continue with the "transform" sample application we were working with in the last *Try It Out*. This will demonstrate how priorities can be used to ensure that templates are processed in the order you actually expect them to be, even when there are conflicting template expressions.

1.   We will use the example4.xml file we used in the previous example, it should be in the project root directory. It contains the following XML.

```
<?xml version="1.0" encoding="utf-8"?>
<ct:ContactDetails xmlns:ct="http://www.deltabis.com/Contact">
  <contact>
    <name>
```

```
        <first>Daniel</first>
        <middle/>
        <last>Livingstone</last>
      </name>
    </contact>
  </ct:ContactDetails>
```

2. Enter the following XSLT into the top textbox. Ensure that the **Example 4** radio button is selected.

```
<xsl:stylesheet version="1.0" xmlns:xsl="http://www.w3.org/1999/XSL/Transform"
  xmlns:ct="http://www.deltabis.com/Contact" >

  <xsl:template match="name[last]" priority="1">
    matched name
  </xsl:template>

  <xsl:template match="name[first]">
    matched name with first child element
  </xsl:template>

  <xsl:template match="text()" />
</xsl:stylesheet>
```

3. Click the Transform button and you will get the following output in the bottom textbox (don't worry about the whitespace; this will be explained later in the chapter).

matched name

How It Works

If no priority were taken into consideration for this example, then the bottom template would always be invoked for the name elements that have both first and last child elements. However, we always want the top template to be processed whether there are first elements or not. Of course, we could just make sure that this template was closer to the bottom of the stylesheet than the second template, but when there are more than a couple of templates, this ordering can make things even more confusing. Worse yet, if anything is moved the output of the stylesheet may change. It is much better to just say that no matter where this template appears, it should always be processed before certain other templates. Priorities give us this ability.

In the above case, we wanted to ensure that the default template invocation was changed to have the top template always invoked over the second template when they are both matched. To do this, we assigned the top template a higher priority than the second template. The second template will have a default priority of 0.5, so setting the priority of the top template to any real number higher than this will cause it to be invoked instead. To make things simple, we chose to set the priority to 1.

```
<xsl:template match="name[last]" priority="1">
```

You will notice that another template has been added that doesn't seem to do anything.

```
<xsl:template match="text()" />
```

It actually does the necessary job of preventing all the text nodes in the document from being written to the output. This happens because there are no templates to match the text nodes within the XML document so a default template will copy all of the text nodes to the output and you will get a concatenated list of all the text nodes in the document. To prevent these from being output, simply match any text nodes using the XPath `text()` function and leave the template empty.

As an aside you will have noticed that the content within the templates is output with whitespace surrounding it. This is because in XML whitespace is significant and any whitespace in your XSLT documents is usually output with the content. We will discuss whitespace and how to control it later in the chapter.

Template Modes

There are going to be times when we create an XSLT document, but want it to act slightly differently depending on the situation it is used in. For example, you may have a single stylesheet where the output should be different depending on some starting condition; such as if you determine the output needs to be different (for example, HTML, XML, or WAP) then you may perform much of the same functionality within the stylesheet, but the output may be slightly different. As an example, consider the following description of what a given stylesheet for the contact details should do for different outputs.

- ❏ Match the `ContactDetails` element
- ❏ Get the value of the `outputFormat` attribute
- ❏ If the value of this attribute is `html` then output the content as HTML (that is, process the templates for HTML output)
- ❏ If the value of this attribute is `xml` then tell the stylesheet to output the content as XML using the templates specified for XML output
- ❏ Copy the result to the output

Note that in the second and third steps, we use an **attribute** (although we show alternatives later in the chapter) that determines whether the stylesheet should output HTML or XML. Rather than creating two stylesheets to perform very similar transformations, but creating different outputs, XSLT lets us specify that a given template applies in one circumstance (for example, HTML output) and another should be used in another circumstance (for example, XML output). This attribute is called `mode`.

The `mode` attribute is a qualified name with an optional prefix and allows a template to be run multiple times for a given pattern, meaning that we can have multiple templates for a given pattern, but only the one in the selected `mode` is invoked. By default there is no `mode`.

Of course if there is no mode by default then how do we put the stylesheet processor into a certain mode or change mode? The way to do this is using the `<apply-templates>` element again, which also has a `mode` attribute, which takes the name of the `mode` that you want to apply the templates in. This then selects the nodes matching this expression and returns a node-set, which it then processes with the templates in the XSLT document in the mode specified.

Let's demonstrate this with a *Try It Out.*

369

Try It Out: Templates and Modes

In this example, we are going to use modes to output the result of an XSL transformation in two formats – the first is HTML and the second is XML. Typically you will only output one of these formats, but both are shown here for completeness. Later in the chapter we look at how you can influence the mode that will be used from outside the XSLT document.

1. We will again use the `example4.xml` file for this example. It contains the following XML:

```xml
<?xml version="1.0" encoding="utf-8"?>
<ct:ContactDetails xmlns:ct="http://www.deltabis.com/Contact">
  <contact>
    <name>
      <first>Daniel</first>
      <middle />
      <last>Livingstone</last>
    </name>
  </contact>
</ct:ContactDetails>
```

2. Ensure that the Example 4 radio button is selected and enter the following XSLT into the top textbox:

```xml
<xsl:stylesheet version="1.0" xmlns:xsl="http://www.w3.org/1999/XSL/Transform"
    exclude-result-prefixes="ct" xmlns:ct="http://www.deltabis.com/Contact">

  <xsl:template match="ct:ContactDetails">
    <xsl:apply-templates select="contact" mode="xml" />
  </xsl:template>

  <xsl:template match="contact">
    <html>
      html output
    </html>
  </xsl:template>

  <xsl:template match="contact" mode="xml">
    <Envelope>
      xml output
    </Envelope>
  </xsl:template>

  <xsl:template match="text()" />
</xsl:stylesheet>
```

3. Click the Transform button and you will get the following output:

```xml
<Envelope>
   xml output
</Envelope>
```

How It Works

This example illustrated how you can use modes to generate different output. The default mode allows the `ContactDetails` element to be selected, but within it we changed the mode to `xml`. By default the template that matches the `contact` element will be processed as it has no mode – this is what we have seen in all of our previous examples. However, within the first template we change the mode from the default to `xml`.

```
<xsl:template match="ct:ContactDetails">
  <xsl:apply-templates select="contact" mode="xml" />
</xsl:template>
```

This will then work through the nodes in the XML document and look for templates in the stylesheet in the `xml` mode. Notice that both the `<apply-templates>` and `<template>` elements must have matching modes for this to work. This generates the following output because there is a `contact` element node in the source XML document.

```
<Envelope>
    xml output
</Envelope>
```

Notice that the HTML templates are never processed because they are in a different mode. Modes are even more useful when we come to look at importing other stylesheets because we can have control over the templates that are processed, despite the "default" templates in the imported document.

Template Parameter and Sorting

The application of templates can be even more powerful than what we have discussed earlier – beyond selecting nodes and processing them in a particular mode, we can also pass information to the templates via parameters and even sort the nodes that have been selected in the node-set.

Parameters are useful when we want to make a template more generic or don't want to store static information within it. They are similar to parameters in a method for a procedural language, such as VB or C#. For example, they could be used to pass a link to someone's web site that you selected from some other part of an XML document to a template showing details about the person.

Sorting in XSLT is very useful and can be used to sort numbers as well as strings.

The template for the `apply-templates` element is shown below:

```
<xsl:apply-templates select="expression" mode="mode">
  <xsl:with-param />
  <xsl:sort />
</xsl:apply-templates>
```

As was mentioned earlier, the `select` attribute takes an XPath expression that will select a node or set of nodes within the stylesheet. The `mode` attribute is used to specify the mode that a template should be in when matching a pattern allowing different outputs for similar templates based on the operating mode.

Within the `<apply-templates>` element you can specify two other elements: the first is the `<with-param>` element and the second is the `<sort>` element. The `<with-param>` element is used to pass parameters to the matching template. However, the parameter will only be available to the template if a `param` element with the same name is declared within the matching template (discussed later). Otherwise the parameter will be ignored. As an example, you may have the following `<apply-templates>` element:

```
...
<xsl:apply-templates select="expression">
  <xsl:with-param name="myParam" select="paramValue"/>
</xsl:apply-templates>
...
```

The `name` attribute specifies the name of that parameter, `myParam` in this case, and the `select` attribute is an expression that can return a node-set as well as a simple string value – we will come to a section later, *Parameters and Variables*, where we discuss this.

The `template` would get the parameter as follows, where the `param` element must have a `name` attribute value that is the same as the name of the `with-param` attribute that was used when the `apply-templates` was called:

```
<xsl:template match="expression">
  <xsl:param name="myParam" />
</xsl:template>
```

To get the value of the `myParam` parameter, we use the dollar sign with the `value-of` element as follows:

```
<xsl:value-of select="$myParam" />
```

The `sort` element can occur many times and states the nodes that should be ordered in the node-set that is then selected, and it is this ordered node-set that is then used by the matching template. If there is no sort order provided then the document order is used.

```
...
<xsl:apply-templates select="expression">
  <xsl:sort select="node" />
</xsl:apply-templates>
...
```

Let's try out an example with parameters and sorting.

Try It Out: Template Parameters and Sorting

Continuing with the transform example, we are now going to look at how we can pass a simple parameter to a template and also how the node-set resulting from an `apply-templates` can be sorted.

1. The XML file that will be used for this example is called `example5.xml` and should be in the project root directory. It contains the following XML:

```
<?xml version="1.0" encoding="utf-8"?>
<ct:ContactDetails updateDate="20021201T14:00"
   xmlns:ct="http://www.deltabis.com/Contact">
  <contact>
    <name>
      <first>Rebekkah</first>
      <middle>Helen</middle>
      <last>Anderson</last>
    </name>
  </contact>
</ct:ContactDetails>
```

2. Ensure the Example 5 radio button is selected and enter the following XSLT into the top textbox of the `transform` application:

```
<xsl:stylesheet version="1.0" xmlns:xsl="http://www.w3.org/1999/XSL/Transform"
   exclude-result-prefixes="ct" xmlns:ct="http://www.deltabis.com/Contact">

<xsl:template match="ct:ContactDetails">
  <xsl:apply-templates select="contact">
    <xsl:with-param name="lastUpdated" select="@updateDate"/>
    <xsl:sort select="name/last" />
  </xsl:apply-templates>
</xsl:template>

<xsl:template match="contact">
  <xsl:param name="lastUpdated" />

  Contact updated at <xsl:value-of select="$lastUpdated" />
  has the name <xsl:value-of select="name/last" />,
  <xsl:value-of select="name/first" />.
</xsl:template>
</xsl:stylesheet>
```

3. Click the Transform button and you will get the following output:

```
Contact updated at 20021201T14:00
has the name Anderson,
Rebekkah.
```

How It Works

Let's first look at how the `<apply-templates>` element was used when the root element was matched.

```
<xsl:apply-templates select="contact">
  <xsl:with-param name="lastUpdated" select="@updateDate"/>
  <xsl:sort select="name/last" />
</xsl:apply-templates>
```

The `select` attribute selects any `contact` child elements of the context node and hence will invoke the only other template in the stylesheet that will match this expression. Within this `apply-templates` we do two things; the first is to create a new parameter called `lastUpdated`, which is given the value of the `updateDate` attribute on the root element and passed to the template using the `with-param` element. The second thing is to use the `sort` element to order the selected nodes alphabetically according to the text of the element node called `last` that is a child of the `name` element node (which is in turn a child element of the matched contact element nodes). For our XML source document, this produces a node-set with two items.

The template that matches this pattern has `contact` as the value of the `match` attribute on the template element.

```
<xsl:template match="contact">
  <xsl:param name="lastUpdated" />

  Contact updated at <xsl:value-of select="$lastUpdated" />
  has the name <xsl:value-of select="name/last" />,
  <xsl:value-of select="name/first" />.
</xsl:template>
```

Within this template, one of the first things that we do is to define a parameter called `lastUpdated`. This is needed so that the parameter that was passed from the `<apply-templates>` element can be passed into this template and read from at some point.

Within the template, the first of the parameters outputs the value of the `lastUpdated` variable, and so that we can tell the parser that this is a variable (rather than an element for example), we have to prefix it with a dollar sign. The second `value-of` element uses an XPath expression that selects that child `last` element of the name element, which itself is a child of the contact element node. Finally, `value-of` does the same, but for the element node called `first`.

Calling your Own Templates

There are going to be times when you have some reusable functionality that may be used throughout the stylesheet and appears within many templates – this is like a reusable method in XSL that can be called to perform some common functionality. A common example is the creation of tables in HTML or repeatable fragments of XML. For this reason, the `<call-template>` element allows you to force a given template to be invoked at any time. It is similar to the `<apply-templates>` element in that it invokes some predefined template within the stylesheet, but is different in that it does this by using a name to specify the template rather than some pattern based on the XPath expression.

The `call-template` element is defined as follows:

```
<xsl:call-template name="QName" />
```

The name attribute of this element is the name of the `xsl:template` that we want to invoke. The template we are calling does not need to have a `match` attribute, but it can if desired; it just happens that when using the `call-template` element, the `match` attribute is ignored (although it can still be used by the `apply-templates` element).

The template itself is not much different from what we have been working with previously, except that rather than a `match` attribute, it uses a `name` attribute. Note also that the context does not change when using the `call-template` element as you are simply calling a template.

Try It Out: Calling a Template

To illustrate the usefulness of the `call-template` element, let's look at how we can use this to insert line breaks between contacts in the stylesheet.

1. The XML file that will be used for this example is called `example5.xml` and should be in the project root directory. It contains the following XML:

```xml
<?xml version="1.0" encoding="utf-8"?>
<ct:ContactDetails updateDate="20021201T14:00"
   xmlns:ct="http://www.deltabis.com/Contact">
  <contact>
    <name>
      <first>Rebekkah</first>
      <middle>Helen</middle>
      <last>Anderson</last>
    </name>
  </contact>
</ct:ContactDetails>
```

2. Ensure the **Example 5** radio button is selected and enter the following XSLT into the top textbox of the `transform` application:

```xml
<xsl:stylesheet version="1.0" xmlns:xsl="http://www.w3.org/1999/XSL/Transform"
    exclude-result-prefixes="ct" xmlns:ct="http://www.deltabis.com/Contact">

   <xsl:template match="ct:ContactDetails">
      <xsl:apply-templates select="contact" />
   </xsl:template>

   <xsl:template match="contact">
     <xsl:value-of select="name/last"/>, <xsl:value-of select="name/first"/>
     <xsl:call-template name="linebreak" />
   </xsl:template>

   <xsl:template name="linebreak">
=====================
   </xsl:template>

</xsl:stylesheet>
```

3. Next click the **Transform** button and you will get the following output.

Anderson, Rebekkah

=====================

How It Works

This time we add the `<call-template>` element immediately after the last and first name element values are written out.

```
<xsl:call-template name="linebreak" />
```

This will call the template with the name attribute `linebreak` and write its contents to the output.

```
<xsl:template name="linebreak">
=====================
</xsl:template>
```

This will happen for each contact element in the source XML document. In a more complex scenario you may want to put some more complex markup within the `linebreak` template.

XSL Iteration

Iteration in XSL is done using the `<for-each>` element, which iterates through the context node-set determined by the `select` attribute. This element is defined as follows:

```
<xsl:for-each select="expression">
</xsl:for-each>
```

The node-set is selected by the expression given in the `select` attribute and each source element you work through in the node-set becomes the new context node for any expressions evaluated within the `<for-each>` element.

Try It Out: XSL for-each

This example will work through each contact in the sample XML document and write out the first and last name of the contact along with any notes associated with that contact.

1. The XML file that will be used for this example is called `example6.xml` and should be in the project root directory. It contains the following XML:

```
<?xml version="1.0" encoding="utf-8"?>
<ct:ContactDetails updateDate="20021201T14:00"
  xmlns:ct="http://www.deltabis.com/Contact">
  <contact>
    <name>
      <first>Steven</first>
      <middle />
      <last>Livingstone-Perez</last>
    </name>
  </contact>
  <contact>
    <name>
      <first>Diego</first>
      <middle />
```

```
        <last>Perez</last>
      </name>
    </contact>
  </ct:ContactDetails>
```

2. Ensure the **Example 6** radio button is selected and enter the following XSLT into the top textbox of the `transform` application:

```
<xsl:stylesheet version="1.0" xmlns:xsl="http://www.w3.org/1999/XSL/Transform"
  exclude-result-prefixes="ct" xmlns:ct="http://www.deltabis.com/Contact">

  <xsl:template match="ct:ContactDetails">
    <xsl:for-each select="contact/name">
      <xsl:value-of select="last"/>, <xsl:value-of select="first"/>.
    </xsl:for-each>
  </xsl:template>

</xsl:stylesheet>
```

3. Next click the **Transform** button and you will get the following output:

```
Livingstone-Perez, Steven.
    Perez, Diego.
```

How It Works

We have a single template in this example that will match the root element. Within this element we have a `<for-each>` element with the XPath expression selecting the `contact/name` nodes, which will return a node-set with two elements.

```
<xsl:for-each select="contact/name">
```

Within this `<for-each>` element we have two `<value-of>` elements. Notice that both `select` elements that are child nodes of the name element, indicating that the context node within the `for-each` changes to the current node within the node-set.

Conditional Logic

Like almost all programming languages, XSL provides the ability to perform conditional logic within the stylesheet in the form of `if` elements and `choose` elements.

The if Conditional

The `if` element allows conditional constructs within templates in the stylesheet, similar to the `if` keyword in procedural languages, and is used for simple "if *condition* then *do something*" constructs. It is defined as follows:

```
<xsl:if test="expression">
</xsl:if>
```

The `test` attribute is an XPath expression that is required and must return `True` or `False`: if the return value is `True` then the content of the `if` element is invoked, otherwise it is not. The element can only occur within a `template` element and the rules that determine whether `True` or `False` is returned are as follows:

- ❏ If the expression returns a node-set containing at least one node (that is, non-empty node set), then it is regarded as `True`; otherwise it is `False`

- ❏ If the expression returns a non-empty string then it is regarded as `True`; otherwise `False`

- ❏ If the expression returns a number it is regarded as `True`, otherwise it is `False`

So the following example will process the contents of the `if` element when there is an `age` attribute on the context node:

```
<xsl:template match="contact">
  <xsl:if test="@age">do something</xsl:if>
</xsl:template>
```

This works because it is a Boolean test – if the `age` attribute exists, it is `True`; if it does not exist, then it is `False`.

The following example will process the `if` element if the age is 25.

```
<xsl:template match="contact">
  <xsl:if test="@age='25'">do something</xsl:if>
</xsl:template>
```

The following example will process the `if` element if the `age` is greater than 25.

```
<xsl:template match="contact">
   <xsl:if test="@age &gt; 25">do something</xsl:if>
</xsl:template>
```

> **This example works because you can evaluate numeric values in XSLT using `&gt;` for > (greater than) and `&lt;` for < (less than) – this is because < and > are reserved XML characters (specifically < will cause a problem because the parser will think you are opening a new element!) and so they must be escaped by their character entity equivalent.**

Another common use of the `if` element is to perform tests based on the position of the node you are currently processing (the context node) in the node-set that is currently being processed (the context node-set). This is common, for example, where you have a template that matches more than one node and you want to determine the last node so that you can format the output accordingly – for example, you may add commas (`,`) after each value that is output, but after the last value you want to add a period (`.`) rather than a comma to terminate the sentence. This can be done using the `if` element and two built-in XPath functions; `position()` and `last()`.

The `position()` function returns the integer value of the context node in the context node-set (that is, the collection of all nodes that are being processed). Therefore, for the first node, the position function will return 1, for the second 2, and so on.

The `last()` function returns the position of the last node in the node-set; this is also the number of nodes in the node-set, also call the **context size**. So, if there are 5 nodes in the node-set, the `last()` function returns 5.

These can be used in combination with the `if` element to modify the output based on the current node. For example, the following outputs a comma after each node, except the last where it outputs a period.

```
<xsl:stylesheet version="1.0" xmlns:xsl="http://www.w3.org/1999/XSL/Transform"
    exclude-result-prefixes="ct" xmlns:ct="http://www.deltabis.com/Contact">
<xsl:template match="ct:ContactDetails">
  <xsl:for-each select="contact/name">
    <xsl:value-of select="first" />
    <xsl:if test="position()!=last()">, </xsl:if>
    <xsl:if test="position()=last()">.</xsl:if>
  </xsl:for-each>
</xsl:template>

</xsl:stylesheet>
```

The template within this stylesheet used a `<for-each>` element to select all of the name elements and then iterates through these, using the `test` attribute of the `if` element to compare the value of the `position()` function to the value of the `last()` function; if they are not the same, `False` is returned and a comma is output. If they *are* the same then `True` is returned and a period is output.

The output from this (transforming the XML from the last example) will be:

Steven, Diego.

Making Choices with xsl:choose

The other conditional element is the `choose` element, which is combined with the `when` and `otherwise` elements to provide conditional processing in XSLT. It is used as follows:

```
<xsl:choose>
  <xsl:when test="Boolean expression">
  </xsl:when>
  <xsl:otherwise>
  </xsl:otherwise>
</xsl:choose>
```

All elements must be wrapped in a `choose` element and this element must contain one or more `when` elements and optionally an `otherwise` element. You will likely see the similarities to the `Select` statement in VB, where the `when` element is equivalent to the `Case` keyword and the `otherwise` is equivalent to the `Else` keyword.

You can have multiple when elements with different conditions; each when element must have a test attribute containing an expression that evaluates to true or false. When it evaluates to true the content of that when element is invoked and afterwards the choose element is exited. When none of the when elements evaluate to true, the content of the otherwise element is invoked. As a simple example, consider revising the last example where we used the if element to use the choose element to determine the character to output after each value (a comma or period). The changes are highlighted below:

```
<xsl:stylesheet version="1.0" xmlns:xsl="http://www.w3.org/1999/XSL/Transform"
   exclude-result-prefixes="ct" xmlns:ct="http://www.deltabis.com/Contact">

   <xsl:template match="ct:ContactDetails">
     <xsl:for-each select="contact/name">
       <xsl:value-of select="first" />
       <xsl:choose>
         <xsl:when test="position()!=last()">, </xsl:when>
         <xsl:otherwise>.</xsl:otherwise>
       </xsl:choose>
     </xsl:for-each>
   </xsl:template>
</xsl:stylesheet>
```

The template within this stylesheet uses a for-each element to select all of the name elements and then iterates through these, using a choose element and within this the test attribute of the when element to compare the value of the position() function to value of the last() function. If they are not the same, False is returned and a comma is output; if they are, the contents of the otherwise element is processed and a period is output.

The output from this (again transforming the XML from the last example) will be:

Steven, Diego.

Try It Out: Conditional Logic

This example will use conditional logic to determine whether a given user has a first name and output a message to the screen. Again we are using the transform.exe application.

1. The XML file that will be used for this example is called example6.xml and should be in the project root directory. It contains the following XML:

```
<?xml version="1.0" encoding="utf-8"?>
<ct:ContactDetails updateDate="20021201T14:00"
   xmlns:ct="http://www.deltabis.com/Contact">
  <contact>
    <name>
      <first>Steven</first>
      <middle/>
      <last>Livingstone-Perez</last>
    </name>
  </contact>
  <contact>
    <name>
```

```
        <first>Diego</first>
        <middle>Adriano</middle>
        <last>Perez</last>
      </name>
    </contact>
</ct:ContactDetails>
```

2. Ensure the Example 6 radio button is selected and enter the following XSLT into the top textbox of the `transform` application:

```
<xsl:stylesheet version="1.0" xmlns:xsl="http://www.w3.org/1999/XSL/Transform"
   exclude-result-prefixes="ct" xmlns:ct="http://www.deltabis.com/Contact">

<xsl:template match="name">
     =====================
   <xsl:value-of select="first" />
     <xsl:text> </xsl:text>
   <xsl:value-of select="last" />?
   <xsl:choose>
     <xsl:when test="middle!=''">Yes</xsl:when>
     <xsl:otherwise>No</xsl:otherwise>
   </xsl:choose>
</xsl:template>

<xsl:template match="text()" />
</xsl:stylesheet>
```

3. Next click the Transform button and you will get the following output:

```
=====================
Steven Livingstone-Perez?
No
=====================
Diego Perez?
Yes
```

How It Works

Each `name` element is matched by the `template` element and within this the first and last names are written out – notice the use of the `text` element, which ensures that there is a space between the first and last name due to the whitespace handling of XSLT, which we will discuss later.

We then use the `choose` element to do our conditional processing. In the first case we have a `when` element, which has a `test` attribute that determines whether the `middle` child element is empty or not and if this is the case then `Yes` is written to the output. If this is not the case then the `otherwise` element is invoked and writes out `No` to the output.

Parameters and Variables

Quite often, as in procedural code, you want to influence the processing of the stylesheet or part of a template via some external mechanism. XSLT provides two ways to do this using either parameters or variables. Parameters are used to pass values either into a stylesheet or a template, very much in the same way as parameters are used for methods in procedural code.

Variables, however, can be global to the stylesheet or local to a given template (or even local to other elements such as `for-each`) and can be set to some value that can then influence the processing. One major and very distinct difference between XSLT variables and variables you will meet when working with procedural code is that **they can only be set once**. In other words, once a variable has been set either globally or locally, it cannot be set again within the same scope. We will see what implications this has shortly.

Parameters

Parameters can be passed to stylesheets or templates and allow influence over the processing of the stylesheet or an individual template. A parameter is defined using the `param` element and allows a default value to be set; it is defined as follows:

```
<xsl:param name="QName" select="expression">
</xsl:param>
```

The `name` attribute sets the name by which the parameter will be referenced and the `select` expression sets the parameter, the value of which can be a simple text value or a tree fragment. The `param` element can appear only as a child of a `stylesheet`, `transform`, or `template` element and inherits the value of any parameter passed to one of these if the passed parameter has the same name. If not, it uses the default value and if there is no specified default value then it contains an empty string.

So, if you are passing a value from outside the stylesheet (this is done programmatically and we'll see how to do this later), you should use a parameter (or parameters depending on how many individual values you want to pass in) and the parameter should have a name (the same as the external parameter name) and be defined as an immediate child of the `stylesheet` element.

```
<xsl:stylesheet ...>
  <xsl:param name="myExternalName" />
</xsl:stylesheet>
```

What if a value is not passed in and you try to reference this in the stylesheet? It will be initialized to an empty string and may cause a problem for any templates using this value. You can also set a default value that is only used when the variable is not initialized:

```
<xsl:stylesheet ...>
  <xsl:param name="myExternalName" select="'myDefaultValue'" />
</xsl:stylesheet>
```

The `select` attribute is an XPath expression that will initialize the parameter to some value. Notice that when you initialize a string value, you *must* wrap it in single quotes or the value will be treated as an XPath expression and will set the parameter value to an empty node-set.

The other scenario where you will use parameters is to pass a value to a template using an `<apply-templates>` or `<call-template>` element. We earlier looked at passing parameters in the *Template Parameter and Sorting* section, so refer back to that for an example. However, let's see how to do this using the `<call-template>` element.

To pass the parameter using `call-template` you would use the combination of a `call-template` and `template` elements as follows:

```
<xsl:template match="contact">
  <xsl:call-template name="myTemplate">
    <xsl:with-param name="myParam" select="@userID" />
  </xsl:call-template>
</xsl:template>
```

The `template` definition would be defined as follows:

```
<xsl:template name="myTemplate">
  <xsl:param name="myParam" />
  ...
</xsl:template>
```

The `with-param` element will pass the `userID` attribute to the `myTemplate` template. This template should immediately define a `param` element with the same name as the parameter that has been passed, that is, `myParam`.

Variables

Global and local variables can be created in XSLT to contain text values or tree fragments that can be used within the stylesheet or template – they do not take values from external sources, for example being passed into the stylesheet or template. The variable element is defined as follows:

```
<xsl:variable name="QName" select="expression">
</xsl:variable>
```

The `name` attribute sets the name by which the variable will be referenced, and the `select` attribute defines an expression that will set the value of the variable. Alternatively, you can omit the `select` expression and set the value of the variable to the content within the variable element.

If you want to assign a string value to a variable, then you must remember to enclose the value in single quotes, as follows:

```
<xsl:variable name="day" select="'Monday'" />
```

You can then use this variable within a template to perform some processing as follows:

```
<xsl:template name="myTemplate">
  <xsl:choose>
    <xsl:when test="$day='Monday'">No news today</xsl:when>
```

```
      <xsl:when test="$day='Wednesday'">No news today</xsl:when>
      <xsl:otherwise>View news section</xsl:otherwise>
   </xsl:choose>
</xsl:template>
```

If you are assigning a number, however, you don't have to do this:

```
<xsl:variable name="dayNumber" select="1" />
```

You can also use an XPath expression to determine the value of a variable:

```
<xsl:variable name="day" select="@day" />
```

Finally, the value of a variable can be an XML fragment as follows:

```
<xsl:variable name="days">
   <xsl:for-each select="@day">
      <dayname><xsl:value-of select="." /></dayname>
   </xsl:for-each>
</xsl:variable>
```

This will create a variable called `days` with the value of the `day` attribute enclosed in `dayname` elements. For example:

```
<dayname>Monday</dayname>
<dayname>Tuesday</dayname>
<dayname>and so on...</dayname>
```

You can then use this variable within a template to perform some processing as follows:

```
<xsl:template name="myTemplate">
   <xsl:for-each select="msxsl:node-set($days)/dayname">
      <xsl:choose>
         <xsl:when test="$days='Monday'">We have news today</xsl:when>
         <xsl:otherwise>No news today</xsl:otherwise>
      </xsl:choose>
   </xsl:for-each>
</xsl:template>
```

Notice that the `<for-each>` element can be used to iterate through the variable as though it is an actual node-set. To do this, however, you have to use an extension function (a function not defined by XSLT, but defined by the XSLT processor to do some particular function) called `node-set` that takes a string representation of a XML document fragment and converts it to an actual node-set. We look at this later when we discuss functions in XSLT.

The main difference between the param and variable elements is that a param element can be set outside the context in which it is declared – which is why you can pass external values to parameters. Variables on the other hand are set at some point in the stylesheet and cannot be overridden or changed within that scope. So if a variable is locally declared within a for-each iteration, it can be changed during each iteration as it goes out of scope each time, but it *cannot* be changed within the <for-each> element as it is still in scope – much like a variable in a for loop in procedural code. Hence, a variable does not have the concept of a default value.

Variables are typically most useful when there is a piece of processing that you do multiple times and could improve performance by doing it once and storing it for later reference; for example counting or accessing tree fragments. It is also useful when you come to work with fragments that come from other documents – there is a function called the document() function that takes a URI followed by an XPath expression (for example, document.xml/root/ContactDetails) and returns a document fragment; we look at this when we discuss XPath functions.

Using variables is not required when creating stylesheets, but they can create much cleaner, reusable code, which will benefit you in the longer term.

Managing Whitespace with xsl:text

The xsl:text element can be a very important element when controlling output and whitespace. Writing your code within a stylesheet on multiple lines, with whitespace characters to format the stylesheet, generally means that the whitespace is copied to the output and your results can be unexpected (as we have seen in our examples). Alternatively, you can wrap your formatting over multiple lines or with whitespace involved, and use the text element to ensure that whitespace you don't intend to be copied to the output is not.

The text element is used to output text nodes directly to the output and is defined as follows:

```
<xsl:text disable-output-escaping="yes | no" />
```

The disable-output-escaping attribute is used to control output escaping of special characters and defaults to no. For example, if the value of the selected node is < and if the disable-output-escaping attribute is set to no, then it will be escaped and the output value will be <. However, if this attribute is set to yes, then it will not be escaped and instead will be parsed resulting in the < character being output. This element can have no other XSL elements as child nodes.

For example, consider the following template:

```
<xsl:template match="name[middle!='']">
  first name <xsl:value-of select="first" />
  second value <xsl:value-of select="middle" />
  third value <xsl:value-of select="last" />


      ===============
</xsl:template>
```

We want to match name elements where the middle name is not empty. When we have done that, we use lines to nicely format the output with an underline. The result is as follows:

```
first name Diego
second value Adriano
third value Perez


         ===============
```

This isn't really the format we wanted. We are most likely looking to have all the information on one line with a line drawn underneath. To do this, however, we have to do something like the following:

```
<xsl:stylesheet version="1.0" xmlns:xsl="http://www.w3.org/1999/XSL/Transform"
    xmlns:ct="http://www.deltabis.com/Contact">

  <xsl:template match="name[middle!='']">
    <xsl:text>first name </xsl:text> <xsl:value-of select="first" />
    <xsl:text> second name </xsl:text> <xsl:value-of select="middle" />
    <xsl:text> third name </xsl:text><xsl:value-of select="last" />
    <xsl:text>&#xD;&#xA;</xsl:text>
    <xsl:text>=============================================</xsl:text>
  </xsl:template>
  <xsl:template match="text()"/>
</xsl:stylesheet>
```

This produces the following output (note the change in whitespace overall).

```
first name Diego second name Adriano third name Perez
=============================================
```

In this case we use five instances of the text element to achieve the correct result. The first three simply output the strings first name, second name, and third name, each followed by the relevant value – note that you cannot include value-of within the text element! An interesting point to note here is that all whitespace nodes outside the text element are removed, so whereas before we had whitespace before the strings, we no longer have these. What this also means is that we had to explicitly put a space in the text elements.

The fourth text element contains the Unicode characters for a carriage return and linefeed, so that we can have a return after the first line. The final line simply outputs a line under what we have output using the text element to omit surrounding whitespace.

Other XSLT Elements

We have discussed the core elements used when working with XSLT. There are many more XSLT elements that you will use during the creation of your stylesheets; for more information on these see either *XSLT Programmer's Reference 2nd Ed.*, by Michael Kay (ISBN 1-86100-506-7) or http://www.w3c.org/TR/xslt#element-syntax-summary.

XSLT Functions

In previous chapters, we defined some XPath functions that can be used with either the DOM or in XSLT. However, there are some functions that are exclusive to XSLT and they are worth mentioning here.

- ❑ current() – this function returns a node-set that has the current node as its only member. This is not always the context node when you are working with predicates in your XPath expressions.

- ❑ document(object, node-set) – this function allows you to access external XML resources. If you provide a single string then it is treated as a URI and the XML document at that URI is retrieved as a node-set. If the single argument is a node-set then it treats each node as a string URI, retrieves the XML document at each URI, and returns the unions of these documents. If there are two arguments, then the first is treated as before, but the second argument is a node-set indicating the base URL, used for the relative URL in the first argument. If the parameter list is empty, then the result is the XML source of the XSLT itself.

- ❑ element-available(string) – this function returns true if the particular instruction or extension element passed as a parameter is available for use.

- ❑ format-number(number, string, string) – this function converts a number for human reading. The first argument is the number to convert, the second is the format pattern, and the last is optional, describing the decimal format. See the decimal-format element above for more details on available options.

- ❑ function-available(string) – this function tests the parser and returns a Boolean true if the function specified in the argument is available in the function library.

- ❑ generate-id(node-set) – this returns a string of ASCII characters that uniquely identifies the node in the node-set in document order. If there is no argument then the context node is used.

- ❑ key(name, value) – this function will retrieve the key defined by the XSL key element with the specified name and filter the results based on the specified value.

- ❑ msxsl:node-set(string) – this extension function allows you to convert tree fragments into node-sets. This is important when you have an XML fragment but want to be able to use an xsl:for-each on it, for example for iterate through the nodes on it. You **must** first convert it to a node-set from an XML string fragment using this function. The node-set extension function itself is defined in the namespace urn:schemas-microsoft-com:xslt, which is a special namespace recognized by the Microsoft XSL parsers.

- ❑ system-property(string) – this allows you to access environment properties with the string argument being a valid system property. The current values are version, vendor, vendor-url, and msxsl:version.

- ❑ unparsed-entity-uri(string) – this function provides access to declarations of unparsed entities in the DTD of the source document. It returns the URI of the unparsed entity; for example, the URI to a JPG image.

Let's look at an example of using the popular document() function. You may have a remote XML document, b.xml, defined as follows, which defines the days of the week where a particular news section is available:

```
<days>
  <day>Monday</day>
  <day>Tuesday</day>
  <day>Friday</day>
</days>
```

You may have the following XML document processing the main XML document a.xml:

```
<xsl:stylesheet version="1.0" xmlns:xsl="http://www.w3.org/1999/XSL/Transform"
   xmlns:msxsl="urn:schemas-microsoft-com:xslt">
   <xsl:template match="day">
     <xsl:variable name="days" select="document('b.xml'/days)" />
     <xsl:variable name="today" select="." />

     <xsl:for-each select="msxsl:node-set($days)">
       <xsl:if test="$today=day">There is news today</xsl:if>
     </xsl:for-each>
   </xsl:template>
</xsl:stylesheet>
```

This will create a variable called days and the document() function will be used to get the b.xml file; from this you can then select a particular node-set using a normal XPath expression such as 'b.xml'/days, which selects the document element days.

Notice that the for-each element can be used to iterate through the variable as though it is an actual node-set; to do this, however, you have to use the extension function called msxsl:node-set(), which takes a string representation of an XML document fragment and converts it to an actual node-set. The prefix of this function, msxsl, must be declared in the root of the stylesheet as xmlns:msxsl="urn:schemas-microsoft-com:xslt" because when the processor finds this function call, this namespace binding will tell it that the processor itself can process this function as an extension function.

XSLT and Whitespace

We have often mentioned the whitespace issues of working with XSLT in the discussions in this chapter and there are good reasons for this. When we talk of whitespace, we mean those invisible characters that are part of any XML document we create and often have an effect on its output. You may wonder why this seems to be such a big deal and think surely it would have been discovered before now. Well, as most of us have been working in HTML, the whitespace issues are masked.

The rules of HTML ensure that whitespace is kept to a minimum, so two consecutive whitespace characters in HTML are collapsed to a single whitespace, and new lines are always ignored (which is why we need the <br> tag) and so we never need to worry about them. In XML we cannot ignore whitespace issues because the invisible characters are present in most documents and can radically affect our output. The XML attribute xml:space allows us to control whitespace to some extent within the source XML document; this will always override any whitespace handling in the XSLT document.

It is important to understand that when we talk of whitespace we often mean those characters that occur between element nodes – in other words, whitespace text nodes. This does not necessarily include the text nodes within these elements. So, consider the following string <a> <b>hello </b> </a> – the whitespace between <a> and <b> is a whitespace text node and may or may not be significant – the XSL parser will strip this to a single space. However, the whitespace after the text hello is part of the text and is not a whitespace text node.

One way of controlling the whitespace in our output is to use the XSL text element, which sends literal text to the output and so the whitespace within this element is retained. To explicitly insert whitespace nodes, we can also use the Unicode character references such as <xsl:text> </text> which would represent a single space and would be preserved.

We should now have a fairly good understanding of the XSL language and how to create stylesheets. Now let's look at how you can use XSLT and stylesheets in .NET in the next chapter.

Summary

In this chapter we look at the Extensible Stylesheet Language (XSL) and how it can be implemented using the .NET classes. In particular we covered the following:

- ❏ The XSLT elements
- ❏ Matching templates in XSLT
- ❏ How XSLT allows iteration and conditional logic
- ❏ Functions in XSLT
- ❏ How whitespace works in XSLT

This chapter has taught you the beginnings of the XSLT language, but there is a lot to XSLT and in fact one of the best ways to understand XSLT fully and know the power that it offers is to actually use it! Let's now move on and see how we can exploit the abilities of XSLT with the .NET classes.

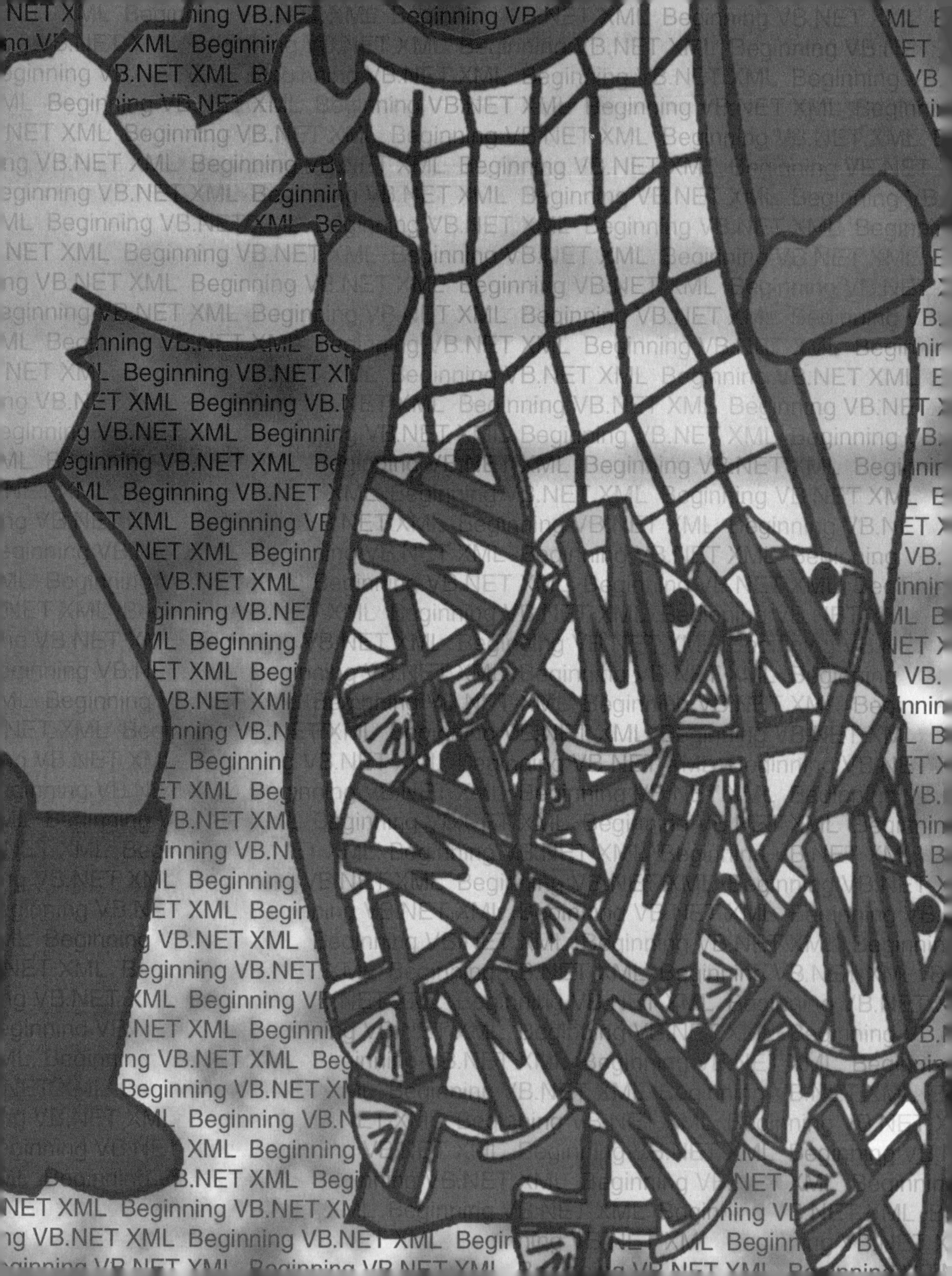
Beginning VB.NET XML

XSLT in .NET

Up to this point you will have a good understanding of how to create stylesheets to format and transform XML documents. However, when developing applications using XML and XSLT, as discussed in the previous chapter, you need a way to programmatically transform an XML document with a stylesheet. Whether this is as HTML to write to a browser, or XML to write to some other application, the mechanism remains the same.

The .NET Framework provides us with classes that allow us to do all of the above. In fact, with the .NET classes, the following is possible:

❑ Transform an XML document on the server to HTML that can be written to any browser, such as Internet Explorer or Netscape Navigator.

❑ Transform an XML document on the server to some other XML format for display on some other device that uses an XML format. An example is the Wireless Application Protocol (WAP) that is used on mobile phones.

❑ Transform an XML document to an alternative XML format in an internal network when integrating applications that require alternative XML formats.

❑ Transform an XML document to an alternative XML format for use in a business-to-business scenario where the partner uses an alternative XML format.

There are many other scenarios where you may find XML and XSLT solve your problems; in addition to these examples, you can also pass in external information to the template allowing them to be used in scenarios where user or application personalization may be important.

Let's look at .NET support for XSLT.

The .NET XSLT classes

XSLT support in .NET is provided via the System.Xml.Xsl namespace and supports the W3C 1.0 recommendation defined at http://www.w3.org/TR/xslt.

The main classes provided by this namespace that you will use when working with XSLT are shown below. We discuss all of these except XsltContext, which is generally useful in advanced scenarios where you are defining your own custom functions and is material for an advanced book.

❑ XslTransform – this class allows you to transform an XML document using an external XSLT stylesheet. This is the core class allowing you to actually take an XML document and transform it with a stylesheet; for example, you may have an XML document on the server and when a user makes a request for it (typically via an .aspx dynamic web page), it is dynamically transformed on the server into HTML and sent to the browser.

❑ XsltArgumentList – this class allows you to pass external parameters or objects into the stylesheet. You will use this with the above XslTransform class when you want to pass parameters into the XSLT document; as an example, you may want to write the logon name of the person within the XSLT transform and so you pass the users logon name as a parameter to the stylesheet. Additionally you can create a custom class that exposes functions that can be used within the stylesheet to extend the functionality available with XSLT (for example, a simple FirstToUpper() function that converts the first characters of a string to upper case).

❑ XsltException – this class represents an exception that is thrown while the stylesheet is being processed. This will be available for any exceptions that occur during the lifetime of the XSLT document. The next class defines exceptions specifically for compile-time problems when the stylesheet is being loaded.

❑ XsltCompileException – this class contains the exception that is thrown by the load() method when there is a problem with the XSLT document itself. It derives from the above class and so gives information specific to a compile-time problem. This is a useful class for getting error details specific to the XSLT when the load() method of the XslTransform class is called.

❑ XsltContext – The XsltContext class derives from the XmlNamespaceManager class and, as such, is responsible for managing any namespaces used within the XSLT document that map back to any functions or parameters called when using an XPath expression. This is particularly powerful for adding your own custom functions within the XSLT document. The msxsl namespace used with the node-set() function is an example of a Microsoft extended function.

The XslTransform Class

The XslTransform class is used to load a stylesheet and transform a specified XML document to a specified output. The two main methods of this class are:

❑ Load() – this method loads a specified XSLT document including any stylesheets that have been referenced using import or include elements.

❑ Transform() – this method transforms a specified XML document using the loaded stylesheet and writes the results to the specified output.

Loading Stylesheets

The Load() method of the XslTransform class has 8 overloads as defined below.

❑ Load(IXPathNavigable) – this method loads a stylesheet typically contained in an XmlNode or XPathDocument instance. The instance must implement the IXPathNavigable interface to be used in this method.

❑ Load(String) – this method loads the stylesheet at the URL specified as an argument to the method.

❑ Load(XmlReader) – this method takes an XmlReader instance of a stylesheet as its argument.

❑ Load(XPathNavigator) – this method loads the stylesheet contained in the XPathNavigator class; you typically create an instance of an XPathNavigator class by using the CreateNavigator() method of the XmlNode or XPathDocument classes.

❑ Load(IXPathNavigable, XmlResolver) – this method is the same as the first method discussed above, but additionally it takes an instance. The first method uses a default XmlResolver instance, so you only need this method when you need custom resolution of referenced stylesheets. For further information on the XmlResolver class visit http://msdn.microsoft.com/library/en-us/cpref/html/ frlrfSystemXmlXmlResolverClassTopic.asp

❑ Load(String, XmlResolver) – like the previous method this takes custom resolver if the default is insufficient. The string parameter is the URL of the stylesheet.

❑ Load(XmlReader, XmlResolver) – this method also allows a custom resolver to be specified.

❑ Load(XPathNavigator, XmlResolver) – this method also allows a custom resolver to be specified.

Let's look at an example of the XslTransform class in our next two *Try It Out* sections – the first loads the XSLT document from a file location and the second loads the document from an XmlTextReader instance.

Try It Out: Loading a Stylesheet from a File

In this example we are going to look at loading a stylesheet from a file – this is common where you have an archive of your collection of stylesheets on the file system. This demonstrates the XslTransform class we discussed above and shows the Load() method being used to load an XSL document.

> *Note that all the sample code for this chapter is available for download from http://www.wrox.com. We will be storing sample code for this chapter within the following folder: C:\BegVBXML\Chapter09. You may, of course, use a different folder depending on what you prefer.*

1. In Visual Studio .NET, create a new VB Windows Application project called XslLoad and add a single button to the form changing the Text property to Load.

2. Create a new XSL File called style.xsl and add the following to the file:

```
<xsl:stylesheet version="1.0" xmlns:xsl="http://www.w3.org/1999/XSL/Transform">
  <xsl:template match="/">
    <names>
      <xsl:apply-templates />
```

```
    </names>
  </xsl:template>

  <xsl:template match="name">
    <name><xsl:value-of select="last" />, <xsl:value-of select="first" /></name>
  </xsl:template>
</xsl:stylesheet>
```

3. Double-click the button and at the top of the file, import the following namespaces:

```
Imports System.Xml.Xsl
```

4. In the button event handler and enter the following code:

```
Private Sub Button1_Click(ByVal sender As System.Object, _
  ByVal e As System.EventArgs) Handles Button1.Click
  Dim filename As String = "..\\style.xsl"

  Try
    'Load the stylesheet.
    Dim Xsl As XslTransform = New XslTransform()
    Xsl.Load(filename)

    MessageBox.Show(filename & " has been loaded.")
  Catch compEx As XsltCompileException
    MessageBox.Show("Compile Error : " & compEx.InnerException.Message)
  Catch ex As Exception
    MessageBox.Show("General Error : " & ex.Message)
  End Try
End Sub
```

5. Run the application and click the button and you will get a message saying the file was successfully loaded.

6. Modify the `style.xsl` file and change the namespace declaration to `http://www.w3.org/2000/XSL/Transform`. Again click the button and you will get the following message:

Compile Error : The wrong namespace was used for XSL. Use 'http://www.w3.org/1999/XSL/Transform'.

OK

How It Works

The stylesheet itself is fairly simple, so we will go straight to the code. First, we had to import the `System.Xml.Xsl` namespace that contains the `XslTransform` class we are going to use.

A `Try...Catch` statement was then used to try to load the XSL file from the location specified in the filename variable. To load this file, a new instance of the `Transform` class was created and then the `load()` method was called passing in the path to the `style.xsl` file.

```
Dim Xsl As XslTransform = New XslTransform()
Xsl.Load(filename)
```

If this was successfully loaded, a message is shown to the user in a message box. However, if there is an exception there are two handlers. The first is for `XsltCompileException` exceptions, which we used in Step 5. This will catch any problems that occur with the stylesheet as it is being compiled – in our case it realized that the namespace we had declared was not the one recognized as the `Xsl` namespace and so an exception was thrown. Notice that we have to use the `InnerException` property to get at the actual error – the message property will give you the general error that occurred (for example, there was a problem with file `style.xsl`).

```
MessageBox.Show(filename & " has been loaded.")
```

Any other exceptions are caught by the general exception handler in the last catch block and will display the appropriate message. This will display errors when the stylesheet itself is invalid – for example, not a valid XML document.

Now let's look at how a similar thing can be done when the stylesheet is loaded from an `XmlTextReader`.

Try It Out: Loading a Stylesheet from a Text Reader

It is common for you to have to load a new instance of the `XslTranform` class from a reader of some kind; this reader may have been populated from a file or from dynamically created XSLT using the Document Object Model. It may even be a cached stylesheet that was held in memory and you now want to use it for a transform. In this example we will initialize the reader from a stylesheet entered by the user and load this stylesheet.

1. Back in the XslLoad project add a new button to the form, and change the `Text` property to ReaderLoad. Also add a new multi-line `TextBox` control to the form, wide enough to view the contents of the `style.xsl` file.

2. Double-click the ReaderLoad button and at the top of the file, import the following namespaces:

```
Imports System.Xml
```

3. Now enter the following code into the event handler for this button (`Button2`):

```
Private Sub Button2_Click(ByVal sender As System.Object, _
    ByVal e As System.EventArgs) Handles Button2.Click
  Dim xStyleRead As XmlTextReader = _
    New XmlTextReader(textBox1.Text, XmlNodeType.Document, Nothing)

  Try
    'Load the stylesheet.
    Dim Xsl As XslTransform = New XslTransform()
    Xsl.Load(xStyleRead)
```

```
      MessageBox.Show("The Stylesheet has been loaded.")
   Catch compEx As XsltCompileException
      MessageBox.Show("Compile Error : " & compEx.InnerException.Message)
   Catch ex As Exception
      MessageBox.Show("General Error : " & ex.Message)
   End Try
End Sub
```

4. Run the application, copy the code from the `style.xsl` file into the textbox, and click the **ReaderLoad** button. You will get a message saying the file was successfully loaded.

5. Modify the `style.xsl` file removing the `version` attribute and its value. Now click the **ReaderLoad** button again and you will get the following message:

Compile Error : Missing mandatory attribute 'version'.

OK

How It Works

We had to import the `System.Xml` namespace this time because we are going to use the `XmlTextReader` class, which can be found in this namespace.

Next a new `XmlTextReader` instance was created to load in the text of the textbox as a new XML document instance.

```
Dim xStyleRead As XmlTextReader = _
   New XmlTextReader(TextBox1.Text, XmlNodeType.Document, Nothing)
```

The first parameter to the `XmlTextReader` is a string of the fragment that you want to load in; the second parameter is the node type it represents, in this case it is a full XSL document, and finally the last value is null as there is no parser context to pass.

Within the `Try` block, a new instance of an `XslTransform` object is created and then the `Load()` method takes reader as an argument and loads the XSLT document.

```
Dim Xsl As XslTransform = New XslTransform()
Xsl.Load(xStyleRead)
```

The rest of the document is the same as the previous example.

Once we have actually loaded the document we are going to want to perform the transform – this is what we cover next.

Transforming Stylesheets

We so far have shown how to load a stylesheet and so we want to know how to actually perform the transform on the XML document. Transforms are executed using the XslTransform class and in particular the Transform() method which actually invokes the transform itself. Chapter 7 discussed the IXPathNavigable interface and the XPathDocument class and you may want to refamiliarize yourself with those classes as they are commonly used within this method.

The Transform() method of the XslTransform class has 9 overloads as defined below.

❑   Transform(IXPathNavigable, XsltArgumentList) – this method will transform the XML document specified in the first argument which is an object implementing the IXPathNavigable interface which is typically the XmlNode or XPathDocument instances. The second argument can be used to pass in an XsltArgumentList instance as discussed later in this section. This allows external parameters and objects to be passed to the Xsl document. The result of the transformation is returned as an XmlReader instance.

❑   Transform(String, String) – this method takes the input URL of the XML file to transform and the second argument specifies the output URL where the result should be written to.

❑   Transform(IXPathNavigable, XsltArgumentList, Stream) – this is the same as the first method, except the result is written to the specified Stream.

❑   Transform(IXPathNavigable, XsltArgumentList, TextWriter) – this is the same as the first method, except the result is written to the specified TextWriter.

❑   Transform(IXPathNavigable, XsltArgumentList, XmlWriter) – this is the same as the first method, except the result is written to the specified XmlWriter.

❑   Transform(XPathNavigator, XsltArgumentList) – this method will transform the XML document specified in the XPathNavigator instance. The result of the transformation is returned as an XmlReader instance.

❑   Transform(XPathNavigator, XsltArgumentList, Stream) – this method is the same as the previous method, but writes the result of the transform to the specified Stream.

❑   Transform(XPathNavigator, XsltArgumentList, TextWriter) – this method is the same as the previous method, but writes the result of the transform to the specified Textwriter.

❑   Transform(XPathNavigator, XsltArgumentList, XmlWriter) – this method is the same as the previous method, but writes the result of the transform to the specified XmlWriter.

The following examples will take you through practical examples of the XslTransform and XsltCompileException classes. You can either view the examples from the code download in the Chapter09 folder or create the examples yourself.

Try It Out: Performing a Simple Transform

Before we look at more complex cases, it's worth looking at how we can perform transforms using some simple cases. In this first case we are going to show how to transform a document on the file system.

1.   Back in the XslLoad project add a new button to the form, setting its Text property to FileTransform.

2. Add a new XML file called `example.xml` to the root of the project and add the following XML to it (you may recognize it as `example6.xml` from the last chapter):

```xml
<?xml version="1.0" encoding="utf-8"?>
<ct:ContactDetails updateDate="20021201T14:00"
xmlns:ct="http://www.deltabis.com/Contact">
  <contact>
    <name>
      <first>Steven</first>
      <middle />
      <last>Livingstone-Perez</last>
    </name>
  </contact>
  <contact>
    <name>
      <first>Diego</first>
      <middle>Adriano</middle>
      <last>Perez</last>
    </name>
  </contact>
</ct:ContactDetails>
```

3. Double-click the **FileTransform** button and enter the following code into the event handler for this button.

```vb
Private Sub button3_Click(ByVal sender As System.Object, _
  ByVal e As System.EventArgs) Handles button3.Click
  Dim xStyleRead As XmlTextReader = _
  New XmlTextReader(textBox1.Text, XmlNodeType.Document, Nothing)

  Try
    'Load the stylesheet.
    Dim Xsl As XslTransform = New XslTransform()
    Xsl.Load(xStyleRead)
    Xsl.Transform("..\\example.xml", "..\\output.xml")

    Dim xr As XmlTextReader = New XmlTextReader("..\\output.xml")
    xr.MoveToContent()
    textBox1.Text = xr.ReadOuterXml()
    xr.Close()
  Catch compEx As XsltCompileException
    MessageBox.Show("Compile Error : " & compEx.InnerException.Message)
  Catch ex As Exception
    MessageBox.Show("General Error : " & ex.Message)
  End Try
End Sub
```

4. Run the application and enter the following XSLT document into the textbox:

```xml
<xsl:stylesheet version="1.0" xmlns:xsl="http://www.w3.org/1999/XSL/Transform">
  <xsl:template match="/">
```

```
    <names>
      <xsl:apply-templates />
    </names>
  </xsl:template>

  <xsl:template match="name">
    <name><xsl:value-of select="last" />, <xsl:value-of select="first" /></name>
  </xsl:template>
</xsl:stylesheet>
```

5. Click the FileTransform button and the following output will be displayed in the textbox:

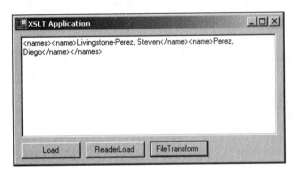

How It Works

Again the stylesheet entered into the textbox is read into an `XmlTextReader` instance and loaded into an `XslTransform` instance.

Once the XSLT is loaded, the `Transform()` method is called; the path to the file we want to transform called `example.xml` is the first parameter and the file we want to write to is the second parameter, `output.xml`.

```
Xsl.Transform("..\\example.xml", "..\\output.xml")
```

After this we have some code that validates that the document was actually written:

```
Dim xr As XmlTextReader = New XmlTextReader("..\\output.xml")
xr.MoveToContent()
textBox1.Text = xr.ReadOuterXml()
xr.Close()
```

An `XmlTextReader` instance then loads the `output.xml` file, which is where we wrote the result of the transform. When this is done we will be at the document root, so we call the `MoveToContent()` method which will move the reader to the document element. Now that we are at this node, the `ReadOuterXml()` method can be called to return the entire XML of this document and this is written to the textbox. The reader is then closed.

The resultant XML is as follows (you can see this by opening `output.xml` in the project root):

<names><name>Livingstone-Perez, Steven</name><name>Perez, Diego</name></names>

Maximum Performance with XPathDocument

So far we have demonstrated loading XML documents from the file system and the `XmlTextReader`, but .NET provides another class that is optimized for loading XML documents that are intended to be used in XSL transformations; this is the `XPathDocument` class. This section will look at how you can maximize the performance of your transforms by using the `XPathDocument` class.

The `XPathDocument` class that we discussed in Chapter 7 stated that it was read-only and hence provided maximum performance for working with XSLT transforms. One of the overloads the `Transform()` method takes is any class that implements the `IXPathNavigable` interface as a first parameter (in fact it can also take an `XPathNavigator` instance, which can be created from any `IXPathNavigable` class).

The `XPathDocument` class, `XmlDocument` class, and `XmlNode` class all implement the `IXPathNavigable` interface and so any of these can be the first argument to the `Transform()` method.

The simplest method to use in this case is where you want to transform an `XPathDocument` and have no parameters to pass to the stylesheet (we'll see how to pass parameters later).

```
Transform(IXPathNavigable, XsltArgumentList) As XmlReader
```

This returns the result of the transform to an XML reader. So, you may have the following snippet:

```
xpDoc As System.Xml.XPath.XPathDocument _
    = New System.Xml.XPath.XPathDocument(("..\\example.xml"))

'Load the stylesheet.
Dim xsl As XslTransform = new XslTransform()
xsl.Load("..\\style.xsl")
Dim xr As XmlReader = xsl.Transform(xpDoc, Nothing)

xr.MoveToContent()
result = xr.ReadOuterXml()
xr.Close()
```

In this case the `example.xml` file is loaded as an `XPathDocument` instance. The stylesheet is also loaded into a new `Transform` instance and then the `Transform()` method is called. The `Transform()` method itself first takes the `XPathDocument` instance in the first parameter and null in the second because there are no parameters being passed to the stylesheet. This time the transform is written to an `XmlReader` instance and so we can directly read the XML within this reader (much quicker than having to read from the file system!).

There are times when you want to perform a transform and not necessarily have it written out immediately. For example, you may want to perform schema validation (see the next chapter) before it is written to another application, or you may want to transform it again (common in a multi-application scenario). Let's look at how we can use the `MemoryStream` class with the `XslTransform` class to transform an instance and keep it in memory.

Try It Out: Optimized Transforms to Memory

This Try It Out will look at using the `MemoryStream` class with the `XslTransform` class to cache transforms in memory.

1. Back in the XslLoad project add a new button to the form, called MemoryTransform.

2. Double-click the MemoryTransform button and enter the following code at the top of the code:

```
Imports System.Xml.XPath
Imports System.IO
```

3. Now enter the following code into the event handler for this button (`Button4`):

```
Private Sub Button4_Click(ByVal sender As System.Object, _
    ByVal e As System.EventArgs) Handles Button4.Click
    'Create a new MemoryStream instance to store transform
    Dim ms As MemoryStream = New MemoryStream()

    'Load XML document as XPathDocument instance
    Dim xpDoc As XPathDocument = New XPathDocument(("..\\example.xml"))

    Try
        'Load the stylesheet.
        Dim Xsl As XslTransform = New XslTransform()
        Xsl.Load("..\\style.xsl")
        Xsl.Transform(xpDoc, Nothing, ms)

        'Do something with memory stream
        'Another transform perhaps

        Dim sr As StreamReader = New StreamReader(ms)
        sr.BaseStream.Seek(0, SeekOrigin.Begin)
        textBox1.Text = sr.ReadToEnd()
        ms.Close()
        sr.Close()
    Catch compEx As XsltCompileException
        MessageBox.Show("Compile Error : " & compEx.InnerException.Message)
    Catch ex As Exception
        MessageBox.Show("General Error : " & ex.Message)
    End Try
End Sub
```

4. Run the application and enter the follow XSLT document into the stylesheet:

```
<xsl:stylesheet version="1.0" xmlns:xsl="http://www.w3.org/1999/XSL/Transform">
  <xsl:template match="/">
    <names>
      <xsl:apply-templates />
    </names>
  </xsl:template>
```

```
    <xsl:template match="name">
      <name><xsl:value-of select="last" />, <xsl:value-of select="first" /></name>
    </xsl:template>
  </xsl:stylesheet>
```

5. Click the MemoryTransform button and the following output will be displayed in the textbox:

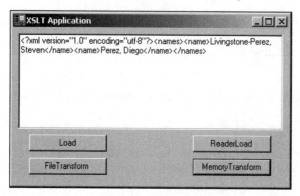

How It Works

The first thing that was done was to create a new `MemoryStream` instance to store the result of our transform:

```
Dim ms As MemoryStream = New MemoryStream()
```

Following this, the XML file was loaded into a new `XPathDocument` instance:

```
Dim xpDoc As XPathDocument = New XPathDocument(("..\\example.xml"))
```

Once the stylesheet is loaded, again the `Transform()` method was called, this time the first parameter being the `XPathDocument` instance again, the second being null (we aren't passing any parameters) and the third parameter is the `Stream` that we want to write to, in this case the `MemoryStream` instance.

```
Xsl.Transform(xpDoc, Nothing, ms)
```

After the transform has been processed, you will have the result of the transform in memory. At this point you may want to pass it to another class to do something with it, or perhaps store it in memory for later use or even pass it to some remote application using web services, which we meet at the end of the book.

```
Dim sr As StreamReader = New StreamReader(ms)
sr.BaseStream.Seek(0, SeekOrigin.Begin)
TextBox1.Text = sr.ReadToEnd()
ms.Close()
sr.Close()
```

A `StreamReader` instance is then created which will read the data from the `MemoryStream` instance; before we can read anything, however, the `Seek()` method of the `BaseStream` property of the `StreamReader` instance (which is, of course, actually our `MemoryStream` instance!) has to be set back to the beginning (as the transform leaves the position of the `MemoryStream` reader at the end of the stream).

Finally, the `ReadToEnd()` method of the `StreamReader` reads the contents of the `MemoryStream` instance and the result is written to the textbox.

```
<?xml version="1.0" encoding="utf-8"?><names><name>Livingstone-Perez,
Steven</name><name>Perez, Diego</name></names>
```

Finally the `MemoryStream` and `StreamReader` instances are both closed.

Transforming XML Documents – Real World Examples

We now have enough information to be able to actually perform the kind of transform you would expect in a real world application. In the next two examples, we are going to work through the transform of an XML document to HTML – this is typical of many web applications that have to write content to a browser for user interaction.

Following this, we will show how to transform the same XML document to an alternative XML format. The most common scenario for this is where the original XML document is being transformed for some other application to consume.

Try It Out: Transforming an XML Document to HTML

This example will show you how to create an HTML document output from the detailed XML document we have been using for our case study. You can also run this application by clicking on the `transformXml2Html.exe` executable in the `Chapter09` code download folder.

1. In Visual Studio .NET, create a new VB Windows Application project called TransformXml2Html.

2. Create a new XML file called `CaseStudy.xml` in the `transformXml2Html` project folder. This has been slightly modified from previous versions to contain phone, fax, and e-mail information:

```
<?xml version="1.0" encoding="utf-8"?>
<ct:ContactDetails updateDate="20021201T14:00"
xmlns:ct="http://www.deltabis.com/Contact">
  <!--This document contains contact information.-->
  <contact title="d2p1:Mr." xmlns:d2p1="http://www.deltabis.com/ns/titles/">
    <name>
      <first>Steven</first>
      <middle />
      <last>Livingstone-Perez</last>
    </name>
    <contactInfo>
      <item type="phone">72993</item>
      <item type="phone">2933</item>
      <item type="fax">98484</item>
      <item type="email">steven@someaddress.com</item>
      <item type="email">ntw_uk@hotmail.com</item>
    </contactInfo>
    <ct:notes>CEO of NTA Li©mited, producer of the ProPortal© system at
    http://www.deltabis.net. Security token is:
```

```
      <![CDATA[<securityAlgorithm>88hhdhddhs8*&W^H¥@HKJW)
      ~~d<ssssowowo>>sswooowsw&(*&&^£&DJnxxj
      </securityAlgorithm>]]></ct:notes>
   </contact>
   <contact title="d2p1:Mr." xmlns:d2p1="http://www.deltabis.com/ns/titles/">
     <name>
       <first>Diego</first>
       <middle>Adriano</middle>
       <last>Perez</last>
     </name>
     <contactInfo>
       <item type="phone">82662</item>
       <item type="fax">00283</item>
       <item type="email">diego@someaddress.com</item>
     </contactInfo>
     <ct:notes>Latest addition to the Perez family.</ct:notes>
   </contact>
</ct:ContactDetails>
```

3. Now add two multi-line `TextBox` controls, a button (**Transform to HTML**), and two labels (**XSL Stylesheet** and **HTML Output**) to the form, so the interface looks similar to that used in the `transform.exe` example we worked with in the previous chapter.

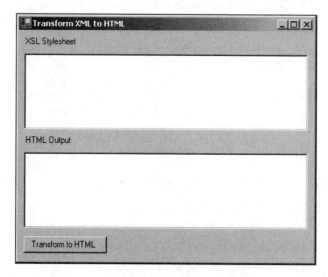

4. Import the following namespaces into the code, by adding these at the top of `form1.vb`

```
Imports System.Xml
Imports System.Xml.Xsl
Imports System.Xml.XPath
Imports System.IO
```

5. Double-click the button and enter the following code into the event handler for this button.

```vb
Private Sub Button1_Click(ByVal sender As System.Object, _
    ByVal e As System.EventArgs) Handles Button1.Click
  TextBox2.Text = ""

  'Load a new XmlTextReader instance
  Dim xStyleXmlRead As XmlTextReader = New XmlTextReader("..//CaseStudy.xml")

  'Create a new XPathDocument instance with the reader
  Dim xStyleDoc As XPathDocument = _
    New XPathDocument(xStyleXmlRead, XmlSpace.Preserve)
  xStyleXmlRead.Close()

  'Initialize a navigator from this
  Dim xStyleNav As XPathNavigator = xStyleDoc.CreateNavigator()

  'Create a new text reader instance for the stylesheet from the text entered
  Dim xStyleRead As XmlTextReader = _
    New XmlTextReader(textBox1.Text, XmlNodeType.Document, Nothing)

  'Load the doc into a transform class
  Dim xTran As XslTransform = New XslTransform()
  xTran.Load(xStyleRead)
  xStyleRead.Close()

  Dim sw As StringWriter = New StringWriter()
  xTran.Transform(xStyleNav, Nothing, sw)

  TextBox2.Text = sw.ToString()

  sw.Close()
End Sub
```

6. Now build and run the application entering the following XSLT into the top textbox.

```xml
<xsl:stylesheet version="1.0" xmlns:xsl="http://www.w3.org/1999/XSL/Transform"
    xmlns:ct="http://www.deltabis.com/Contact">

  <xsl:output method="html" doctype-public="-//W3//DTD HTML 4.0 Transitional//EN"
/>

  <xsl:template match="ct:ContactDetails">
    <html>
      <head>
        <title>List of Contacts</title>
      </head>
      <body>
        <table border="1">
          <tr>
            <th>Name</th>
            <th>Phone</th>
            <th>Fax</th>
            <th>Email</th>
```

```
            </tr>
            <xsl:apply-templates />
          </table>
        </body>
      </html>
    </xsl:template>

    <xsl:template match="contact">
      <tr>
        <td><xsl:apply-templates select="name" /></td>
        <td>
          <xsl:apply-templates select="contactInfo/item[@type='phone']">
            <xsl:sort select="@type" data-type="number" order="descending" />
          </xsl:apply-templates>
        </td>
        <td>
          <xsl:apply-templates select="contactInfo/item[@type='fax']">
            <xsl:sort select="@type" data-type="number" order="descending" />
          </xsl:apply-templates>
        </td>
        <td>
          <xsl:apply-templates select="contactInfo/item[@type='email']">
            <xsl:sort select="@type" data-type="text" order="ascending" />
          </xsl:apply-templates>
        </td>
      </tr>
    </xsl:template>

    <xsl:template match="name">
      <xsl:value-of select="first" />
      <xsl:text> </xsl:text>
      <xsl:value-of select="middle" />
      <xsl:text> </xsl:text>
      <xsl:value-of select="last" />
    </xsl:template>

    <xsl:template match="item">
      <xsl:choose>
        <xsl:when test="@type='email'">
          <a href="mailto:{.}"><xsl:value-of select="." /></a>
          <xsl:if test="position()!=last()">, </xsl:if>
        </xsl:when>
        <xsl:otherwise>
            <xsl:value-of select="." />
            <xsl:if test="position()!=last()">, </xsl:if>
        </xsl:otherwise>
      </xsl:choose>
    </xsl:template>
</xsl:stylesheet>
```

7. Click the button and you will get the following output in the bottom textbox.

```
<!DOCTYPE html PUBLIC "-//W3//DTD HTML 4.0 Transitional//EN" >
<html xmlns:ct="http://www.deltabis.com/Contact">
 <head>
  <META http-equiv="Content-Type" content="text/html; charset=utf-16">
  <title>List of Contacts</title>
 </head>
 <body>
  <table border="1">
   <tr>
    <th>Name</th>
    <th>Phone</th>
    <th>Fax</th>
    <th>Email</th>
   </tr>
   <tr>
    <td>Steven  Livingstone-Perez</td>
    <td>72993, 2933</td><td>98484</td>
    <td><a href="mailto:steven@someaddress.com">steven@someaddress.com</a>,
       <a href="mailto:ntw_uk@hotmail.com">ntw_uk@hotmail.com</a></td>
   </tr>
   <tr>
    <td>Diego Adriano Perez</td>
    <td>82662</td>
    <td>00283</td>
    <td><a href="mailto:diego@someaddress.com">diego@someaddress.com</a></td>
   </tr>
  </table>
 </body>
</html>
```

8. To demonstrate this in a browser, copy this code into an HTML file, say `test.htm`; view it in a browser and you will get the following output:

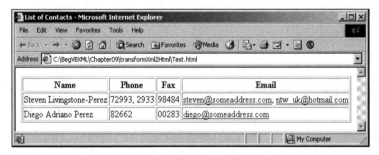

How It Works – The XSLT

The XSLT used many of the elements we have discussed earlier in the book and so should be familiar to you. Specifically, the `output` element was used with the method attribute set to `html` to indicate the output is to be in HTML format. Additionally, the `doctype-public` attribute specifies the DTD used for HTML 4.0, often spotted at the top of most HTML pages you create.

407

```
<xsl:output method="html" doctype-public="-//W3//DTD HTML 4.0 Transitional//EN" />
```

Notice that the XML declaration is not written when you are outputting HTML markup because the `<xsl:output>` element knows that HTML documents do not have an XML declaration and so it does not copy it to the output.

Another point of note is within the template that matches the contact elements. There are a series of `<apply-templates>` elements used to access the `<item>` elements defined in the `<contactInfo>` element; each contains a `type` attribute which has the value `phone`, `fax`, or `email` to define the type of information within the element.

```
<xsl:apply-templates select="contactInfo/item[@type='phone']">
  <xsl:sort select="@type" data-type="number" order="descending" />
</xsl:apply-templates>
```

The XPath predicate used on the `apply-templates` `select` attribute indicates that we want the parser to select all `<item>` elements whose `type` attribute contains the value `phone`. This will return a node-set containing all of these elements and we furthermore define a `sort` element to order this information. Notice that because these are numeric telephone numbers, we specify that the `data-type` is `number` (rather than the default `text`) and we also order from highest to lowest by setting the `order` attribute to `descending`.

The template that is matched by this is the `item` template as follows:

```
<xsl:template match="item">
  <xsl:choose>
    <xsl:when test="@type='email'">
      <a href="mailto:{.}"><xsl:value-of select="." /></a>
      <xsl:if test="position()!=last()">, </xsl:if>
    </xsl:when>
    <xsl:otherwise>
      <xsl:value-of select="." />
      <xsl:if test="position()!=last()">, </xsl:if>
    </xsl:otherwise>
  </xsl:choose>
</xsl:template>
```

Notice that within this template we use a `choose` element to determine when the `test` attribute of the `item` element contains the value `email`, as we want to wrap this in an anchor, a tag, otherwise we just write out the value. When the value is `email`, an anchor tag is created with the value set to the value of the contact node – that is, the text value within the `item` element, which will be the e-mail address. The curly braces `{}` are used here as a shortcut to the `<value-of>` element.

```
<a href="mailto:{.}"><xsl:value-of select="." /></a>
```

After this we want to break up multiple elements of the same type by a comma.

```
<xsl:if test="position()!=last()">, </xsl:if>
```

This works because the `<apply-templates>` that calls this template creates an ordered node-set of matching elements (as discussed above). We then use the `test` attribute of the `if` element to check if the `position()` of the current node in the node-set is equal to the position of the `last()` node. If it is not then we have multiple nodes, and so a comma is written out. A similar thing is done for the other types.

The rest of the XSLT document should be fairly familiar, so let's move on and look at the VB.NET code used to produce this output.

How It Works – The VB.NET code

This first thing that is done is to load in the case study XML document to an `XmlTextReader` instance.

```
Dim xStyleXmlRead As XmlTextReader = New XmlTextReader("..//CaseStudy.xml")
```

An `XPathDocument` instance is created from the `XmlTextReader` instance, using the `XmlSpace.Preserve` parameter to ensure that no whitespace is removed from the XML document when it is parsed (because by default whitespace text nodes will be removed). The `XmlTextReader` instance is then closed.

```
Dim xStyleDoc As XPathDocument = _
   New XPathDocument(xStyleXmlRead, XmlSpace.Preserve)
xStyleXmlRead.Close()
```

The `Transform()` method requires an `XPathNavigator` instance of the XML document, so we use the `CreateNavigator()` method of the `XPathDocument` instance to do this.

```
Dim xStyleNav As XPathNavigator = xStyleDoc.CreateNavigator()
```

Next, an `XmlTextReader` instance is created from the XSLT text entered into the first textbox, specifying the second parameter to indicate that it is a full XML document.

```
Dim xStyleRead As XmlTextReader = _
   New XmlTextReader(textBox1.Text, XmlNodeType.Document, Nothing)
```

Next, a `XslTransform` instance is created and the `XmlTextReader` instance representing the stylesheet is loaded using the `Load()` method.

```
Dim xTran As XslTransform = New XslTransform()
xTran.Load(xStyleRead)
```

We next create an instance of the `StringWriter` class and `Transform()` the XML document writing the output directly to this `StringWriter` instance – very useful when you are planning to directly write out the entire output.

```
Dim sw As StringWriter = New StringWriter()
xTran.Transform(xStyleNav, Nothing, sw)
```

We then use the `ToString()` method of the `StringWriter` class that will write the entire transformed XML document to the second textbox and finally close the `StringWriter` stream.

409

```
textBox2.Text = sw.ToString()
sw.Close()
```

Try It Out: Transforming an XML Document to XML

This example is similar to the example above, except that it will show how to output the XML document to some other XML document format. This is common where you are integrating with either some existing application or some business partner and have to transform the XML into their format. We will continue to work with the example we created in the last *Try It Out*.

1. In the top box, enter the following XSLT:

```
<xsl:stylesheet version="1.0" xmlns:xsl="http://www.w3.org/1999/XSL/Transform"
  xmlns:ct="http://www.deltabis.com/Contact">

  <xsl:output method="xml" omit-xml-declaration="yes" indent="yes"/>

  <xsl:template match="ct:ContactDetails">
    <ListOfContacts>
      <xsl:apply-templates select="contact" />
    </ListOfContacts>
  </xsl:template>

  <xsl:template match="contact">
    <person xmlns:d2p1="http://www.deltabis.com/ns/titles/">
      <xsl:attribute name="name">
        <xsl:value-of select="name/first" />
        <xsl:text> </xsl:text>
        <xsl:value-of select="name/last" />
      </xsl:attribute>
      <xsl:copy-of select="contactInfo/item"/>
    </person>
  </xsl:template>
</xsl:stylesheet>
```

2. Click the button to make the transform and you will get the following output:

```
<ListOfContacts xmlns:ct="http://www.deltabis.com/Contact">
  <person name="Steven Livingstone-Perez" xmlns:d2p1="http://www.deltabis.com/ns/titles/">
    <item type="phone">72993</item>
    <item type="phone">2933</item>
    <item type="fax">98484</item>
    <item type="email">steven@someaddress.com</item>
    <item type="email">ntw_uk@hotmail.com</item>
  </person>
  <person name="Diego Perez" xmlns:d2p1="http://www.deltabis.com/ns/titles/">
    <item type="phone">82662</item>
    <item type="fax">00283</item>
    <item type="email">diego@someaddress.com</item>
  </person>
</ListOfContacts>
```

How It Works

In this example, we wanted to take the input XML format, filter it, and copy some of the details into another XML structure as defined below.

```
<ListOfContacts xmlns:ct="http://www.deltabis.com/Contact">
  <person name="..."
    xmlns:d2p1="http://www.deltabis.com/ns/titles/">
    <item type="phone">...</item>
  </person>
  ...
</ListOfContacts>
```

Within the stylesheet, we use the `<output>` element to indicate that we are outputting XML using the `method` attribute, and the `omit-xml-declaration` attribute is set to `yes`, so the XML declaration is removed from the output. Finally, the `indent` attribute is set to `yes` so that the output formatting is visually more pleasant (the text output above is exactly as it appears on the screen).

```
<xsl:output method="xml" omit-xml-declaration="yes" indent="yes"/>
```

We then match the `ContactDetails` root element, and within this create the root element of the new XML document we are creating, the root element being called `ListOfContacts`. Within this new element, we use the `<apply-templates>` element to select any `contact` template in the document.

```
<xsl:template match="ct:ContactDetails">
  <ListOfContacts>
    <xsl:apply-templates select="contact" />
  </ListOfContacts>
</xsl:template>
```

We match this in the template with the value `contact` for the `match` attribute and immediately create a `person` element. The http://www.deltabis.com/ns/titles/ namespace is defined on this element; if it is not, then this namespace will be shown on every child element that is copied across – since this is the parent element of these, the namespace will apply to all of them.

```
<person xmlns:d2p1="http://www.deltabis.com/ns/titles/">
```

Next we use the XSL attribute element to create a new attribute called `name` which is a combination of the first and last names.

Finally, we use the `<copy-of>` element, and select all the `<item>` elements for the given contact and copy the elements across exactly as they are, including attributes and text nodes.

```
<xsl:copy-of select="contactInfo/item"/>
```

Scripting in Stylesheets

Performing transforms as we discussed above using pure XSLT is generally satisfactory; however, there are times when XSLT doesn't offer you quite what you need and you need to extend its capabilities. Such situations are:

❏ You may want to write some routine that is not available in native XSLT – for example, you may want to write a `FirstToUpper()` function, for example, that converts the first character of the string passed as a parameter to its capital equivalent. Furthermore, you may want to add the capability for complex mathematical calculations in your XSLT.

❏ You may want to improve the efficiency or make simpler something that is already available in XSLT. String manipulation is a good example and you may write a `ToLower()` method that converts an entire string to lower case. Typically in XSLT you would have to use the `translate()` function, which can get quite ridiculous when performing many string manipulations (you have to declare every letter in the alphabet in upper and lower case!).

❏ You may store your data in an external database or remotely and want to access it within your XSLT transform. Personalization data is a prime example.

Scripting and extension functions in XSLT allow you to achieve all of this functionality. The specification allows the use of extension elements and, in particular, the .NET XSLT processor allows the embedding of procedural script blocks, which can be written in VB.NET, C#, VB, Jscript, JavaScript, or VBScript.

To define a script block you need to do the following three things:

❏ On the root stylesheet element, bind the msxsl prefix to the namespace urn:schemas-microsoft-com:xslt and create another prefix bound to your own custom namespace which will define the namespace that your own functions reside within. So, for example, if your extension elements are in the namespace `urn:myNamespace`, you could define it as follows:

```
<xsl:stylesheet version="1.0" xmlns:xsl=http://www.w3.org/1999/XSL/Transform
  xmlns:msxsl="urn:schemas-microsoft-com:xslt" xmlns:myns="urn:myNamespace">
```

❏ Create a script block using the `msxsl:script` element and within this create your VB.NET functions. It is advisable that you wrap everything within the `msxsl:script` element in a CDATA section to ensure that any special XML characters (for example & characters) are not interpreted as XML (and cause a parse error).

❏ Reference your functions using the `prefix:function()` syntax. You can pass parameters to the functions you have defined in the normal way, but the value you pass in can be an XPath expression that evaluates to the value to be passed in. Note that you can use XPath functions such as `number()` to convert the type passed in to the type expected by the method signature defined in the script block (see example below).

The scripting example in the following *Try It Out* section provides a working example of how this is put into practice, so refer to that for implementation details.

You should really only use procedural scripting when you really need it – that is, functionality only attainable via scripting techniques or .NET classes. Often many things that you want to do can be equally done using pure XSLT and XPath; using the embedded scripting obviously has some performance implications for the processing of the stylesheet as the processor has to separately handle the functions associated with an alternative namespace and map them to their code block in the XSLT. There are *some* cases with string manipulation where using procedural code may provide better usability and efficiency; a good example is converting characters to upper or lower case.

Support for .NET Classes

You can access the .NET classes from within the script blocks in the stylesheets in similar ways to how you do it in normal classes. The slight difference is that you don't have a `using` statement, so you have one of two options.

The first is that the following classes are implicitly available in the script blocks.

- ❏ System
- ❏ System.Collection
- ❏ System.Text
- ❏ System.Text.RegularExpressions
- ❏ System.Xml
- ❏ System.Xsl
- ❏ System.XPath
- ❏ System.VisualBasic

To use other classes, you must qualify the full namespaces to the class, but this is a perfectly feasible technique. You would reference the `StringBuilder` class for example as follows:

```
Dim sb As System.Text.StringBuilder = New System.Text.StringBuilder(origStr)
```

The script that uses these classes must again be placed within an `msxsl:script` block discussed earlier, where the `msxsl` prefix is mapped to the special namespace urn:schemas-microsoft-com:xslt. So, the following example will convert the first letter of any string to upper case. It uses the string manipulation facilities of VB.NET within the stylesheet.

```
...
<msxsl:script implements-prefix="rules" language="VB">
  <![CDATA[
  Public Function ToUpper(ByVal origStr As String) As String
    Dim ch As Char = origStr.ToCharArray(0, 1)(0)
    Dim firstUp As String = ch.ToString().ToUpper()

    origStr = origStr.Remove(0, 1)
    origStr = origStr.Insert(0, firstUp)

    Return origStr
  End Function
  ]]>
</msxsl:script>
...
```

Within the stylesheet, you may have the following element, where the context node has the value `steven`:

```
<xsl:value-of select="rules:ToUpper(.)" />
```

The output would then be `Steven`.

In this example, we improve on the above function by using the `StringBuilder` class, which is part of the `System.Text` namespace and is far more efficient at concatenation for working with strings.

```
<xsl:stylesheet version="1.0" xmlns:xsl="http://www.w3.org/1999/XSL/Transform"
  xmlns:msxsl="urn:schemas-microsoft-com:xslt">

  <msxsl:script implements-prefix="rules" language="VB">
    <![CDATA[
      Dim sb As System.Text.StringBuilder = New System.Text.StringBuilder(origStr)

      Dim ch As Char = origStr.ToCharArray(0, 1)(0)
      Dim firstUp As String = ch.ToString().ToUpper()

      sb.Remove(0, 1)
      sb.Insert(0, firstUp)
      Return sb.ToString()
    ]]>
  </msxsl:script>

</xsl:stylesheet>
```

Let's look at an example of using scripting in a full example.

Try It Out: Scripting in XSLT

This example will demonstrate how you can use procedural languages within the XSLT stylesheet. We are going to implement a business rule using VB.NET within the stylesheet. This business rule is part of a contact management application and any phone or fax number that is less than 10,000 will be regarded as a local number and the text (**Local Number**) will be written to the user interface.

The stylesheet will extend the one we worked with earlier when we created the HTML output. We will also continue to use the TransformXml2Html project we created earlier.

1. In the top textbox enter the following XSLT – the highlighted parts are where the stylesheet is different from the one we worked with earlier.

```
<xsl:stylesheet version="1.0" xmlns:xsl="http://www.w3.org/1999/XSL/Transform"
  xmlns:ct="http://www.deltabis.com/Contact"
  xmlns:msxsl="urn:schemas-microsoft-com:xslt"
  xmlns:rules="http://www.deltabis.com/busrules"
  exclude-result-prefixes="rules msxsl ct">

  <xsl:output method="html"
    doctype-public="-//W3//DTD HTML 4.0 Transitional//EN" />

  <msxsl:script implements-prefix="rules" language="VB">
    <![CDATA[
    Public Function LocalNumber(ByVal Number As Integer) As String
      If (Number < 10000) Then
```

```
      Return "(Local Number)"
    Else
      Return ""
    End If
  End Function
  ]]>
</msxsl:script>

<xsl:template match="ct:ContactDetails">
  <!--Insert code from XML to HTML conversion here-->
</xsl:template>

<xsl:template match="contact">
  <!--Insert code from XML to HTML conversion here-->
</xsl:template>

<xsl:template match="name">
  <!--Insert code from XML to HTML conversion here-->
</xsl:template>

<xsl:template match="item">
  <xsl:choose>
    <xsl:when test="@type='email'">
      <a href="mailto:{.}"><xsl:value-of select="." /></a>
      <xsl:if test="position()!=last()">, </xsl:if>
    </xsl:when>
    <xsl:otherwise>
      <xsl:value-of select="." />
      <xsl:value-of select="rules:LocalNumber(number(.))" />
      <xsl:if test="position()!=last()">, </xsl:if>
    </xsl:otherwise>
  </xsl:choose>
</xsl:template>
</xsl:stylesheet>
```

2. Click the button to transform the XML document and you will get the following HTML output.

```
<!DOCTYPE html PUBLIC "-//W3//DTD HTML 4.0 Transitional//EN" >
<html>
  <head>
    <META http-equiv="Content-Type" content="text/html; charset=utf-16">
    <title>List of Contacts</title>
  </head>
  <body>
    <table border="1" ID="Table1">
      <tr>
        <th>Name</th>
        <th>Phone</th>
        <th>Fax</th>
        <th>Email</th>
      </tr>
      <tr>
```

```
            <td>Steven Livingstone-Perez</td>
            <td>72993, 2933(Local Number)</td>
            <td>98484</td>
            <td>
              <a href="mailto:steven@someaddress.com">
                steven@someaddress.com</a>,
              <a href="mailto:ntw_uk@hotmail.com">
                ntw_uk@hotmail.com</a></td>
        </tr>
        <tr>
            <td>Diego Adriano Perez</td>
            <td>82662</td>
            <td>00283(Local Number)</td>
            <td>
            <a href="mailto:diego@someaddress.com">
              diego@someaddress.com</a></td>
        </tr>
      </table>
    </body>
</html>
```

3. Like earlier, you can copy and paste this into some HTML document to view the output; this will give something like the following:

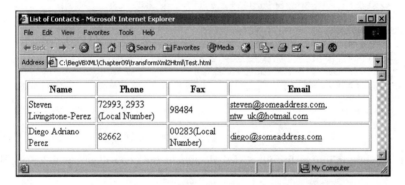

How It Works

On the root stylesheet element, we have to add some new namespace definitions that associate prefixes with the Microsoft extension URI urn:schemas-microsoft-com:xslt and our own defined namespace http://www.deltabis.com/busrules. Additionally, we don't want all of these namespaces to appear in the HTML document, so we use the exclude-result-prefixes attribute to remove the namespaces associated with the rules, msxsl and ct prefixes.

```
<xsl:stylesheet version="1.0" xmlns:xsl="http://www.w3.org/1999/XSL/Transform"
  xmlns:ct="http://www.deltabis.com/Contact"
  xmlns:msxsl="urn:schemas-microsoft-com:xslt"
  xmlns:rules="http://www.deltabis.com/busrules"
  exclude-result-prefixes="rules msxsl ct">
```

Further on in the stylesheet we can actually define a script section. This uses the `msxsl:script` extension element with the `implements-prefix` attribute being set to `rules` (the prefix associated with our namespace above) and the language is set to VB.

```
<msxsl:script implements-prefix="rules" language="VB">
  <![CDATA[
  Public Function LocalNumber(ByVal Number As Integer) As String
    If (Number < 10000) Then
      Return "(Local Number)"
    Else
      Return ""
    End If
  End Function
  ]]>
</msxsl:script>
```

Again, we should wrap our code in a CDATA section to ensure that any special XML characters are escaped. This `LocalNumber()` function is fairly simple (in fact you can do this in pure XSLT, but it is done this way for illustrative purposes) and just returns some text if the number is less than 10,000, otherwise it returns an empty string.

Later in the stylesheet we can invoke this function by using the prefix we defined separated by a colon and then the `LocalNumber()` function name. The parameter passed to this function is a normal XPath expression that, in this case, gets the value of the local item tag. As we know this is a number, we use the XPath `number()` function to convert this (which is also required by the VB.NET function).

```
<xsl:value-of select="rules:LocalNumber(number(.))" />
```

Arguments in XSLT

The power of XSLT comes in its ability to be able to define modularized stylesheets that can inherit and reuse other stylesheets. Often, however, there are variations on how these stylesheets are going to act based on their implementation environment; usually not known until run time and when working in the environment. Good examples of things we may not know until the stylesheet is processing are device dependency, language, encoding, and output format.

Additionally there are many things that cannot be done directly in XSLT and would probably require you to insert procedural script blocks. The main problem with this, however, is that although script blocks are great for simple reusable functionality, when you want to do something a little more complex (maybe interact with a database), you want to follow standard enterprise practices such as allowing code reuse and removing the code detail from the stylesheet. In this case you want to build .NET components that can be used from any application, including XSLT stylesheets.

XsltArgumentList Class

Passing arguments in XSLT is done using the `XsltArgument` class. This class allows you to pass parameters to a stylesheet or associate an existing class with it. You can use parameters for passing personalization information, such as the user's name, preferred color scheme, or information about the device the client is using. This allows you to influence the stylesheet depending on whether a user is using a browser or a personal digital assistant. External objects are very useful for accessing sources such as databases that your XSLT will not have access to, or for performing complex logic that is not available within the stylesheet (such as mathematical algorithms).

The `XsltArgumentList` class of the `System.Xml.Xsl` namespace allows you to pass external arguments to the stylesheet. This is advantageous over embedded procedural script blocks because it makes the stylesheets smaller, less cluttered with script blocks, and allows much more reuse and isolation of the code. You can also pass other XML node fragments to the stylesheet using this method, which allows for the combination of XML data from multiple sources.

The `XsltArgumentList` class provides the necessary methods to enable working with arguments to an XSLT stylesheet. This class has no properties and the following main methods.

- `AddExtensionObject()` – This method adds a reference to an external object using the first parameter as the namespace to associate this object in the stylesheet and the second parameter as an instance of the object.

- `AddParam()` – This method allows you to add a parameter to the stylesheet with an associated value. The first argument is the name of the parameter, the second is the namespace to associate this parameter with (typically an empty string), and the final parameter is the parameter value to pass in.

- `Clear()` – This removes all objects and parameters associated with the `XsltArgumentList` instance.

- `GetExtensionObject()` – This returns the object (value) associated with the namespace passed in the argument.

- `GetParam()` – This returns the object (value) associated name of the parameter passed in the first argument and with the namespace passed in the second argument.

- `RemoveExtensionObject()` – This removes a specific extension object associated with the namespace passed as an argument.

- `RemoveParam()` – This removes a specific parameter with the name parameter and associated with the namespace passed as an argument.

Let's first look at how we can pass parameters to XSL stylesheets using the `XsltArgument` class.

Passing Parameters

The `XsltArgument` class we have been discussing allows you to pass parameters to the stylesheet, which is an important feature in making the stylesheet more reusable and flexible. Let's try out working with parameters.

Try It Out: Pass in a Parameter

We will continue to work with and extend the TransformXml2Html sample we created earlier to illustrate how parameters can be used to influence your stylesheets. This example will allow you to show the name of a user (from a personalization directory, for example) along with some custom coloring that has been determined outside the stylesheet.

1. Add a new button control to the form, naming it **Add parameters**. Double-click the button and add the following code to the event handler.

```
Private Sub Button2_Click(ByVal sender As System.Object, _
    ByVal e As System.EventArgs) Handles Button2.Click
```

```
    textBox2.Text = ""

    'Load a new XmlTextReader instance
    Dim xStyleXmlRead As XmlTextReader = New XmlTextReader("..//CaseStudy.xml")

    'Create a new XPathDocument instance with the reader
    Dim xStyleDoc As XPathDocument = _
      New XPathDocument(xStyleXmlRead, XmlSpace.Preserve)
    xStyleXmlRead.Close()

    'Initialize a navigator from this
    Dim xStyleNav As XPathNavigator = xStyleDoc.CreateNavigator()

    'Create a new text reader instance for the stylesheet from the text entered
    Dim xStyleRead As XmlTextReader = _
      New XmlTextReader(textBox1.Text, XmlNodeType.Document, Nothing)

    'Load the doc into a transform class
    Dim xTran As XslTransform = New XslTransform()
    xTran.Load(xStyleRead)
    xStyleRead.Close()

    Dim LoggedOnUser As String = "Steven Livingstone"
    Dim bgColor As String = "yellow"

    Dim xArgList As XsltArgumentList = New XsltArgumentList()
    xArgList.AddParam("username", "", LoggedOnUser)
    xArgList.AddParam("color", "", bgColor)

    Dim sw As StringWriter = New StringWriter()
    xTran.Transform(xStyleNav, xArgList, sw)

    textBox2.Text = sw.ToString()

    sw.Close()
End Sub
```

2. Add the XSLT that can be found in `param.xslt` in the code downloads to the top textbox. Note that this XSLT is the same as that used in the *Try It Out: Scripting in XSLT* section, except for the lines highlighted below:

```
<xsl:output method="html"
  doctype-public="-//W3//DTD HTML 4.0 Transitional//EN" />
```

```
<xsl:param name="username" select="'unknown'" />
<xsl:param name="color" select="'white'" />
```
```
.
.
.
<xsl:template match="ct:ContactDetails">
  <html>
    <head>
```

```
            <title>List of Contacts</title>
          </head>
          Welcome back <b><xsl:value-of select="$username" /></b>.
          <body bgcolor="{$color}">
            .
            .
            .

</xsl:template>
```

3. Now run the application and click the **Add parameters** button; you will get the following after the output code has been pasted into an HTML file and viewed in a browser.

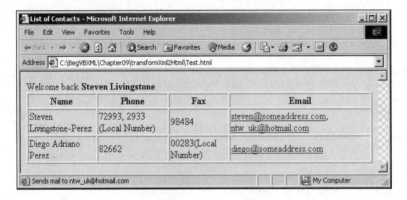

4. Modify the values of the `LoggedOnUser` and `bgColor` variables in the VB.NET code and see how this affects the code output.

How It Works

When adding parameters to the stylesheet, there are a number of things you have to do.

❑ You first create an instance of the `XsltArgumentList` class and use the `AddParam()` method to add a parameter with the name of the parameter as the first argument and the value of the parameter as the second argument. In this case the parameter is called `paramName` and the value is specified in `paramValue`.

```
Dim xArgList As XsltArgumentList = new XsltArgumentList()
xArgList.AddParam("paramName","",paramValue)
```

❑ You then add the namespace you have associated with the parameter you are passing in to the root of the stylesheet element. In this case we did not qualify the parameter in any namespace, so we did not have to do this step.

❑ In the stylesheet you add a XSL `param` element to the top of the stylesheet with the same name as the parameter you are intending to pass in. You can then define a `param` element within the stylesheet as follows:

```
<xsl:stylesheet version="1.0" xmlns:xsl="http://www.w3.org/1999/XSL/Transform"
  xmlns:ct="http://www.deltabis.com/Contact">

  <xsl:param name="paramName" select="'defaultValue'" />
  .
  .
  .
```

Notice that the parameter must have the same name as the passed parameter. You can also use the `select` attribute to set a default value; if this is a text value, you must enclose this in single quotes or you will be unable to access the value (numbers do not require the quotes).

❑ Finally you reference the value of the parameter using the dollar sign and the name of the parameter. You can get the value of the parameter using normal XSL techniques as follows:

```
<xsl:stylesheet version="1.0" xmlns:xsl="http://www.w3.org/1999/XSL/Transform"
  xmlns:ct="http://www.deltabis.com/Contact">
  .
  .
  .
  <xsl:param name="paramName" select="'defaultValue'" />

  <xsl:template match="/">
    <xsl:value-of select="$paramName" />
  </xsl:template>
</xsl:stylesheet>
```

So in view of this, looking at the VB.NET code, the first thing we did is define two variables with initial parameters for the username and background color; of course in a real world application this would be dynamically determined by some authentication mechanism.

```
Dim LoggedOnUser As String = "Steven Livingstone"
Dim bgColor As String = "yellow"
```

Next we created an instance of the `XsltArgumentList` class and used the `AddParam()` method to add the two values as parameters to the stylesheets. The first parameter was called `username`; it was not qualified in any namespace taking the value of the `LoggedOnUser` variable. The second parameter was called `color` and took the value of the `bgColor` variable.

```
Dim xArgList As XsltArgumentList = New XsltArgumentList()
xArgList.AddParam("username", "", LoggedOnUser)
xArgList.AddParam("color", "", bgColor)
```

Finally, when the `Transform()` method was called, this `XsltArgumentList` instance was passed in as the second argument to the method call.

```
xTran.Transform(xStyleNav, xArgList, sw)
```

The transform was then processed.

The XSLT Stylesheet

At the top of the stylesheet we had to define two parameters that had the same names as the parameters we were passing in so that the values could be passed through. Hence, we have a parameter called `username` and another called `color`. They are both given default values using the `select` attribute, as we discussed in the last chapter when looking at parameters. This means if no parameter is passed in then the parameters will get these default values, and if parameters *are* passed in then they will override these default values. Remember that string values must be enclosed within single quotes (' '), otherwise you will not be able to use them as the value will be an empty string.

```
<xsl:param name="username" select="'unknown'" />
<xsl:param name="color" select="'white'" />
```

Later in the stylesheet we used the values passed into the parameter to provide some customization. The `username` parameter was used to give a welcome message to the user. The `color` parameter was used to specify a value for the background color of the web page as defined by the `bgcolor` attribute.

```
Welcome back <b><xsl:value-of select="$username" /></b>.
<body bgcolor="{$color}">
```

Working with External Objects

To pass an object to the stylesheet there are a number of things that must be done. These are:

❑ Create an instance of the `XsltArgumentList` class and use the `AddExtensionObject()` method to add a parameter with the namespace to associate with the object as the first argument and the object instance as the second argument

❑ Add the namespace you have associated with the extension you are passing in to the root of the stylesheet element associated with some prefix

❑ Reference the value of the parameter using the prefix associated with the above defined namespace, followed by the method and passing in any required parameters

Let's try out working with parameters to enforce these ideas.

Try It Out: Working with External Objects

This example will extend the example we worked with in the previous *Try It Out* to add the ability to create some output based on computation from another custom class. In this case it will determine the city that the telephone or fax number belongs to based on the first digit (of course in real life it would be far more complex!).

1. Add a new button to the TransformXml2Html sample project form, change its `Text` property to **External Objects**, double-click on it, and then add the following code to the event handler. The code is similar to the code for the last *Try It Out* with the additions highlighted.

```
Private Sub Button3_Click(ByVal sender As System.Object, _
    ByVal e As System.EventArgs) Handles Button3.Click
    TextBox2.Text = ""
```

```
'Load a new XmlTextReader instance
Dim xStyleXmlRead As XmlTextReader = New XmlTextReader("..//CaseStudy.xml")

'Create a new XPathDocument instance with the reader
Dim xStyleDoc As XPathDocument = New XPathDocument(xStyleXmlRead, _
   XmlSpace.Preserve)
xStyleXmlRead.Close()

'Initialize a navigator from this
Dim xStyleNav As XPathNavigator = xStyleDoc.CreateNavigator()

'Create a new text reader instance for the stylesheet from the text entered
Dim xStyleRead As XmlTextReader = New XmlTextReader(textBox1.Text, _
   XmlNodeType.Document, Nothing)

'load the doc into a transform class
Dim xTran As XslTransform = New XslTransform()
xTran.Load(xStyleRead)
xStyleRead.Close()

Dim LoggedOnUser As String = "Steven Livingstone"
Dim bgColor As String = "yellow"

Dim xArgList As XsltArgumentList = New XsltArgumentList()
xArgList.AddParam("username", "", LoggedOnUser)
xArgList.AddParam("color", "", bgColor)

Dim Locator As Locator = New Locator()
xArgList.AddExtensionObject("http://www.deltabis.net/locator", Locator)

Dim sw As StringWriter = New StringWriter()
xTran.Transform(xStyleNav, xArgList, sw)

textBox2.Text = sw.ToString()

sw.Close()
End
```

2. Additionally, add a new class to the project called `Locator`. This class should contain a single method as shown below.

```
Public Class Locator
   'Finds the city a number is based in.
   'Real world application would likely use a database
   Public Function FindCity(ByVal Number As Integer) As String
      Dim city As String = ""
      Dim FirstNumber As String = Number.ToString().Substring(0, 1)

      Select Case (FirstNumber)
         Case "0"
            city = "Glasgow"
         Case "1"
```

```
      city = "Oslo"
   Case "2"
      city = "London"
   Case "3"
      city = "Milan"
   Case "4"
      city = "Santiago"
   Case "5"
      city = "Winnipeg"
   Case "6"
      city = "Seoul"
   Case "7"
      city = "Osaka"
   Case "8"
      city = "Sydney"
   Case "9"
      city = "New York"
   Case Else
      city = "Unknown"
   End Select

   Return city
   End Function
End Class
```

3. Run the application and add the contents of the stylesheet `object.xslt`, which can be found in the code download, to the top textbox. This is the same as the `param.xslt` file before, with the additions highlighted in the fragments below:

```
<xsl:stylesheet version="1.0" xmlns:xsl="http://www.w3.org/1999/XSL/Transform"
   xmlns:ct="http://www.deltabis.com/Contact"
   xmlns:msxsl="urn:schemas-microsoft-com:xslt"
   xmlns:rules="http://www.deltabis.com/busrules"
   xmlns:locator="http://www.deltabis.net/locator"
   exclude-result-prefixes="rules msxsl ct">

   ...

      <xsl:otherwise>
        <xsl:value-of select="." />
        <xsl:value-of select="rules:LocalNumber(number(.))" />
        <b>[City : <xsl:value-of select="locator:FindCity(number(.))" />]</b>
        <xsl:if test="position()!=last()">, </xsl:if>
      </xsl:otherwise>
   ...
```

4. Click the **External objects** button to invoke the transformation and then copy the resultant code to an HTML file and view it in a browser. You will get the following output:

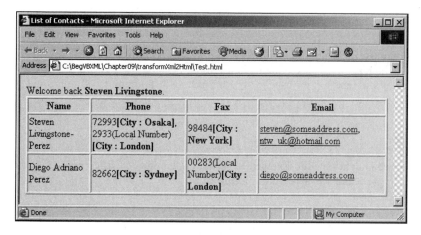

How It Works

The first piece of VB.NET code is the `Locator` class, which is simply a class with a single method that takes in a number, gets its first digit and returns the name of a city based on a case statement. There is no reason why this class could not connect to a database or even a web service.

Following the steps outlined above, we first create an instance of the `XsltArgumentList` class and use the `AddExtensionObject()` method. The first parameter to add to the `AddExtensionObject()` method is the namespace that the extension object is to be associated with inside the stylesheet. This namespace must also be declared and associated with a prefix within the stylesheet.

In this case the namespace is `http://www.deltabis.net/locator` and the object is `Locator`.

```
Dim xArgList As XsltArgumentList = New XsltArgumentList()
    ...
Dim Locator As Locator = New Locator()
xArgList.AddExtensionObject("http://www.deltabis.net/locator", Locator)
```

Next, at the top of the stylesheet on the root element we add the namespace, associated with the `locator` prefix that is associated with the extension object (note we also add this prefix to the `exclude-result-prefixes` attribute to ensure it is not written to the output).

```
<xsl:stylesheet version="1.0" xmlns:xsl="http://www.w3.org/1999/XSL/Transform"
  xmlns:ct="http://www.deltabis.com/Contact"
  xmlns:msxsl="urn:schemas-microsoft-com:xslt"
  xmlns:rules="http://www.deltabis.com/busrules"
  xmlns:locator="http://www.deltabis.net/locator"
  exclude-result-prefixes="rules msxsl ct">
```

To invoke any of the methods, you simply use the prefix with a colon and then the method name, with relevant parameters. This works in a similar way to the `msxsl:script` element. So finally in the stylesheet, we can call this method by specifying the locator prefix, followed by a colon and the `FindCity()` method that we want to call.

```
<b>[City : <xsl:value-of select="locator:FindCity(number(.))" />]</b>
```

Notice that in the parameter to the method we use an XPath expression to return the value of the context node (which is the item element). In addition, because the FindCity() method expects an Integer type as a parameter, we use the XPath number() function to do this conversion.

Summary

In this chapter we look at how the Extensible Stylesheet Language (XSL) can be implemented using the .NET classes. In particular we covered the following:

❑ The XslTransform class

❑ How to perform some simple XSLT transforms, both to files and into memory

❑ How .NET transforms stylesheets

❑ How VB scripting is supported

❑ XSLT interacting with the environment via parameters and external objects

The next chapter will start to deal with the functionality available in XML Schemas.

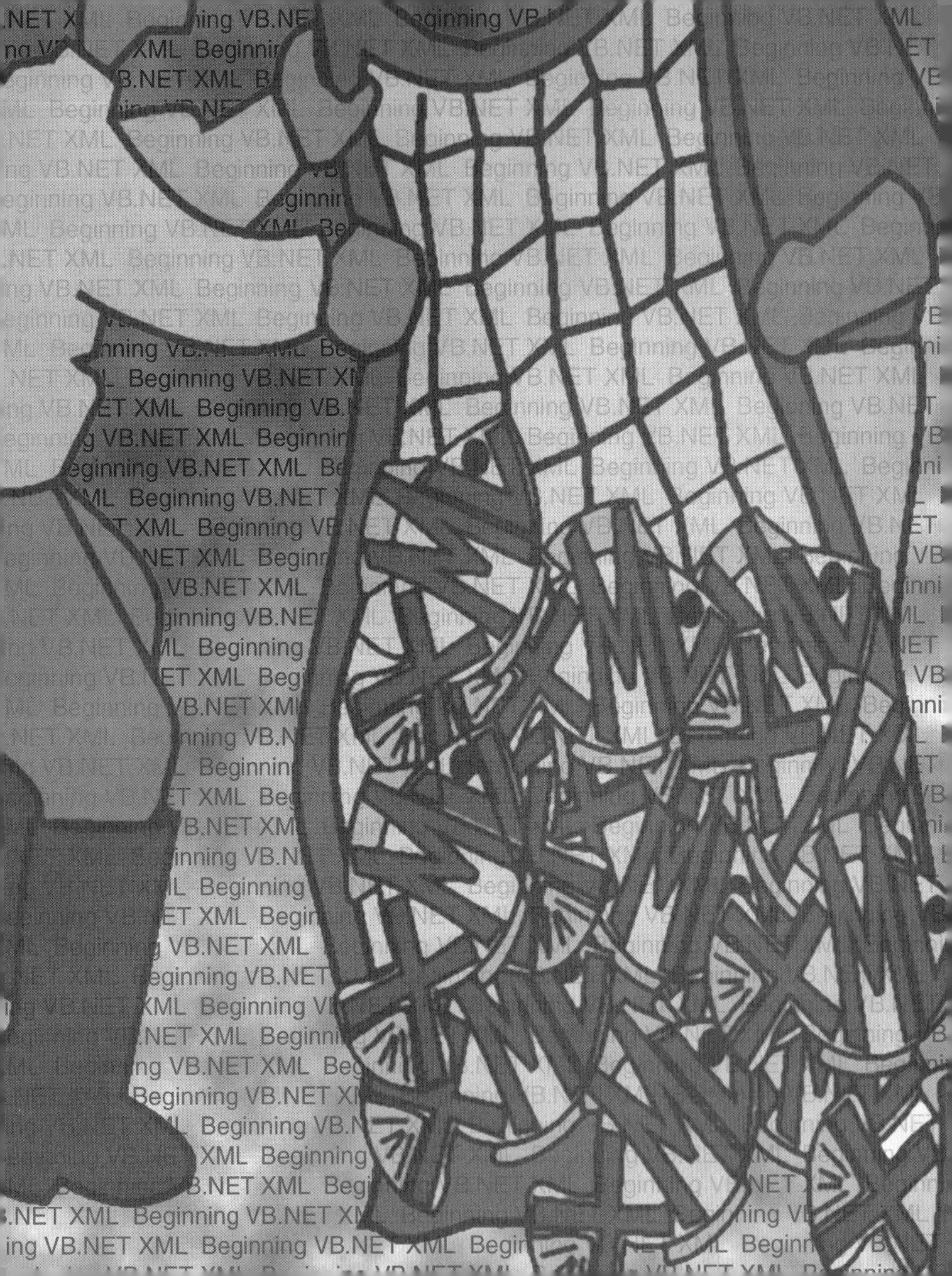
Beginning VB.NET XML

XML Schema – Background, Language, and General Use

In the previous chapter we looked at the Extensible Stylesheet Language which is just one of the technologies that can be used with XML. We discussed how it could be used to read in an XML document and output multiple formats of the document, such as HTML and any XML format (for example, an XML file describing our contacts).

In this chapter we are going to start to look at the XML Schema Language, which is a more recent, but extremely important addition to the XML family and will essentially replace Document Type Definitions (discussed in Chapter 2). It allows us to define the permitted structure and content of an XML document, and to validate that the XML document is of a given structure before it is transformed using XSLT (see Chapter 8). Schemas can be used in a wide variety of places, ranging from the simple validation of a document to the validating of XML documents for business applications, and web services.

In this chapter, we will cover:

- ❏ The role of XML Schema Definitions (XSD)
- ❏ Validating an XML document using an XSD
- ❏ The XML Schema language
- ❏ Data Type support in XSD
- ❏ Complex Types and Content Models
- ❏ Introduction to how XSD data types map to .NET data types
- ❏ Techniques for validating Schemas
- ❏ Working with Schemas inline
- ❏ Modularization of Schemas
- ❏ Improving the case study using XML Schemas

The Role of XML Schemas (XSD)

An XML Schema or XSD (XML Schema Definition) is a means by which we set the grammar that an XML Document must adhere to, to be considered well-formed and valid.

Just to recap, a well-formed XML document is one that complies with certain syntactical rules outlined in the XML specification. If we are using XSDs, the document will also have to adhere to the structure determined by that. An XSD is an XML advance on DTD (Data Type Definition) technology. Although DTDs are very popular, they have disadvantages, which include learning yet another language and technical weaknesses (for example, is not strongly-typed – see Chapter 2 for more information on DTDs). By using XSDs we are using the same XML language as our XML documents and gaining from having more control of our data.

Well-Formed and Valid XML Schemas

One of the main reasons for the success of XML is its adaptability to almost any situation. XML can be used on any platform, integrated with any application, stored in many data stores and it can even be used to send details about an object from one computer to another computer, which can then re-create the object (this process is known as serialization). Even the structure of the XML itself is extremely flexible, allowing the creator of an XML document to decide the hierarchy an XML document is going to use, which items are going to be elements, which are going to be attributes and even what namespaces to qualify these in.

However, over-zealous use may turn these potential benefits into a disadvantage if we are unable to control or manage this flexibility. This is where the first role of the XSD (XML Schema) comes into play; it is a way to define the structure of an XML document so that we can rely on getting a parser error if an XML document does not comply with the rules that we define in our XSD, or are implicit in the well-formedness rules of XML.

To make our XSDs effective, though, we need to consider the following important aspects:

- ❑ Consistency of Data Structures
- ❑ Selecting a Vocabulary
- ❑ Validation/Maintaining Control of Data

Consistency in Data Structures

One of the key potential problems in working with XML is variation in document format. With XML everybody has the capability of creating their own data structure based on how they see the data and how it should be represented. If you take even a simple purchase order example we can see how many variations are possible to represent the data:

```
<po id="PO7363" department="IT">
  <itemsOrdered>...</itemsOrdered>
</po>
```

```
<order internalNumber="7363">
  <item dept="IT">...</item>
  <item dept="HR">...</item>
  <item dept="IT Development">...</item>
</order>
```

```
<poid idref="PO7363">
</poid>
<orderdetail id="PO7363">
  <item dept="IT">...</item>
  <item dept="HR">...</item>
  <item dept="IT Development">...</item>
</orderdetail>
```

The variation in these XML structures, containing essentially the same information, would make it almost impossible for any application to support all of them. More than just the structure being different, even the names given to the elements and attributes differ.

In this type of situation, we have two options. If, for example, we had a large group of companies, we may have a business rule that requires that we offer the different definitions of a purchase order. This is possible as we could develop XSD for each and include them in the respective XML documents. However, if we decided that we did need to merge, consolidate, or compare the different purchase orders, then we may use the XML transformation methodology of XSLT.

XSLT will allow you to convert any of the above XML formats to the other. But is this *really* what you want to do within every application? The overhead of transforming every operation is one thing, but the detection of what format is being used, deciding on the appropriate stylesheet and then the transform process will definitely impact on performance. This is not to mention having to write stylesheets for every new format. Internally, this could cause considerable work.

It would be easier if we could define a single structure and and have every application using that structure for storing the data in XML. Then transforms wouldn't be required. In a world of mergers, acquisitions, and corporate re-engineering, change has become a constant and while transformations may be the key, keep in mind that there are efficiency benefits to be gained if we can judicially control the number and variety of structural transformations.

Choosing a Vocabulary

Because XML is so flexible there may be many times where the flexibility that XML offers results in data or element naming ambiguity. For example we may want to separately display in an XML document data from two companies in a company group: company 'A' has an element called PurchaseOrderID and it is an integer, while company 'B' also has an element called PurchaseOrderID but it is a string data type. Each company has its own XSD. To overcome this ambiguity problem, in our XML document we can include the names of the different namespaces, of respective XSDs, to fully qualify each PurchaseOrderID element.

Data Control (XML Document Validity)

The final consideration is, how to control what is valid data and can be held in a given XML document? This type of problem is more clearly illustrated if we consider that somebody may equally write "two" rather than "2" for the numOrders attribute. Or if your company has six departments, then it would certainly help if your purchase order application had a value indicating which department (for example, "IT") this order was made from rather than just a blank. In fact, what's to prevent blanks from appearing anywhere in the document?

This brings us to the second role of XSD, that of defining valid data. From our discussions with the users we may formulate common business rules or facts to be, that a purchase order ID must identify the department and that the quantity is an integer, cannot be null, and must be greater than zero. In this example one design approach may be to develop an XSD for each department, so that it encapsulates the common and respective rules, and then reference each XSD in an XML document. Another design choice may be to standardize all business rules or facts across departments and hold them in one XSD.

So now that we have an overview of the XSD concept, let's get more acquainted.

So, What is a Schema?

We saw earlier that a schema is a "means by which we set the grammar that an XML document must adhere to, to be considered well-formed and valid." So before we develop our own schema we first need to consider the background issues that go into defining the grammar of what becomes a schema.

Background to Defining a Schema

When working with XSD there is an almost identical requirement to provide the kind of schema language that we use in relational database systems. A VB.NET class may map to a database table or to an XSD element; the table's fields or columns, which map to the class's properties, may map to the child elements or attributes of the element. Furthermore, we need to decide on what we will accept as valid data types and relationships between our XML documents in a very comparable way to the relational database model. XML is much more flexible than a database; there are additional concepts such as what elements are allowable within other elements and what attributes may be attached to a given element, but the basic concepts are similar.

To demonstrate, consider the following XML fragment:

```
  . . .
    <contact contactid="7662">
      <name>
        <first>Steven</first>
        <middle />
        <last>Livingstone-Perez</last>
      </name>
    </contact>
  . . .
```

Here the <contact> element could be regarded as a record within a database table called Contacts. The contactid attribute could be the value of the contactid column within that table that allows an integer value. This equates to ContactId, in our fictitious relational database, where ContactId in the Contacts table may be the primary key to the NameID in the Names table. This would map to the <name> child element of the <contact> element in the XML document.

The `Names` table itself would have four columns called `NameID`, `First`, `Middle`, and `Last`. The `First` and `Last` columns could both be defined to contain strings (`varchar` in database terminology) and the middle column would also be defined as a `string`, but could be defined to allow `null` values.

Validation

In XML, the data and the schema are generally completely separate documents, although a schema may be inline (that is, it is actually included in the XML document itself – we discuss this shortly). In fact the XML document can be a group of documents and the schema can be a group of schemas. There are generally three steps involved in any process where an XML document is validated against the constraints in the schema:

1. The XML document is loaded

2. The schema document is loaded

3. The XML document is *validated* against the schema

The XML document and schema document have to be brought together to perform the validation. They can sit on completely different servers and even be on different sides of the world.

When the validation occurs, the XML parser will check that the document structure is valid and well-formed. This might involve checking that the child elements of an element are one of those allowed and defined in the schema or that any attributes that are used on an element are permitted and whether the actual content within these nodes is valid as defined by the schema. An example of this might be a schema which states that the day attribute of a weekday element must be an integer value rather than a string (that is, 1 rather than "Monday" or "one").

At this stage we still haven't looked at an actual schema, because to appreciate them we first need to consider the schema background and also take a look at the schema language itself. Let's do this now.

The XML Schema Definition Language

The XML Schema Definition Language (XSDL) is a normal 'XML document' that is written in XML using a 'definition' style XML language. This is made up of elements, attributes, namespaces, and all the other nodes you would find in a typical XML document. In this section, we are going to break down the various parts of an XSD document that we develop with XSDL.

What Elements can Appear?

At the very least, an XSD document contains the following:

❑ The `schema` root element and XML Schema namespace definition

❑ An `element` definition

Schema Root Element

The Schema Root Element is the root of any XSD and contains the constraints of the Schema as well as the XML Schema namespace definition, any other namespace definitions, version information, language information, and some other attributes. Any XSD file must define one and only one schema root element.

This can be defined as follows:

```
<xsd:schema xmlns:xsd="http://www.w3.org/2001/XMLSchema">

    . . .

</xsd:schema>
```

The namespace definition is essential to creating XSDL constraints and allows us to associate the elements, attributes and types that have been defined in the schema document through using the prefix assigned to the namespace; here we have used xsd, but it can be any prefix you desire.

Elements

Elements in XSDL are declared using the element tag and the simplest way to define an element is as follows:

```
<xsd:element name="first" type="xsd:string" />
```

There are a series of attributes that can also be applied to this element to form constraints on the element. The type attribute, as used here, is very flexible and can refer to one of the many XML Schema built-in data types or the name of a simple or complex type – these are all discussed later in the chapter. The following definition would limit the value of the age element to an integer:

```
<xsd:element name="age" type="xsd:integer" />
```

As a simple example, the following schema will define an element called first which can take any string value.

```
<xsd:schema xmlns:xsd="http://www.w3.org/2001/XMLSchema">
  <xsd:element name="first" type="xsd:string" />
</xsd:schema>
```

Hence a valid XML instance would be as follows:

```
<?xml version="1.0"?>
<first>Steven</first>
```

Notice that the schema element is the root element of the XSD document and the xsd prefix is qualified in the W3C namespace for Schemas. The first element is defined as a child of the schema root element and must be of string type; note that when an element (or attribute) is declared as a child of the schema root element (an immediate child; not a grandchild) it is known to be declared at the **global level**.

Limiting Occurrences

You can also define the minimum and maximum number of times that an element may appear within its parent element using the minOccurs and maxOccurs attributes. The minOccurs attribute must contain a value equal to or greater than zero, where zero means that the element is optional. The maxOccurs attribute must also be an integer value greater than or equal to zero, and additionally it can have the value unbounded, which means that there is no limit on the maximum number of appearances. The default value for both the minOccurs and maxOccurs is 1 so if you do not specify these attributes, then the element is expected to occur once as a child of the parent node.

As a result, setting minOccurs to zero and setting a limit on the maxOccurs attribute would mean that the element may or may not occur, but if it does occur then its appearances are limited by the value specified in the maxOccurs attribute.

This schema says that the first element must appear once and only once.

```
<xsd:element name="first" type="xsd:string" />
```

So a valid instance would be:

```
<first>Steven</first>
```

This example says that the first element *must* appear once and may appear a maximum of three times.

```
<xsd:element name="first" type="xsd:string" maxOccurs="3" />
```

So, this is also a valid instance:

```
<first>Steven</first>
<first>Loreto</first>
<first>Daniel</first>
```

This final example says that the first element *must* appear at least twice and may appear any number of times greater than this.

```
<xsd:element name="first" type="xsd:string" minOccurs="2" maxOccurs="unbounded" />
```

So this instance would be invalid as there are too few element instances:

```
<first>Steven</first>
```

The following table outlines the effects of combinations of the minOccurs and maxOccurs attributes.

minOccurs	maxOccurs	Number of Child Element(s)
1 (Default)	1 (Default)	One and only one.
0	1	Zero or one.
0	Unbounded	Zero or more.
1	Unbounded	One or more.

Now that we have a basic understanding of the background of schemas and XSDL, let's create a very simple schema to apply what we understand so far.

Try It Out: A Simple Schema that Deals with Undeclared Elements

Note that all the sample code for this chapter is available for download from http://www.wrox.com. We will be storing sample code for this chapter within the following folder: C:\BegVBXML\Chapter10. You may, of course, use a different folder depending on what you prefer.

1. If you want to use the code from the code download, you can find the files for the following example in the Example folder. If you are going to write your own files, type the following code into a text editor and save it as instance.xml in the folder you have chosen to store this example's files in;

```xml
<?xml version="1.0"?>
<name>
  <first>Steven</first>
  <middle />
  <last>Livingstone-Perez</last>
</name>
```

2. Next we need to write our XML Schema document, so type in the following text and save it as schema.xsd.

```xml
<xsd:schema xmlns:xsd="http://www.w3.org/2001/XMLSchema">
  <xsd:element name="name">
    <xsd:complexType>
      <xsd:sequence>
        <xsd:element name="first" type="xsd:string" />
        <xsd:element name="middle" type="xsd:string" />
        <xsd:element name="last" type="xsd:string" />
      </xsd:sequence>
    </xsd:complexType>
  </xsd:element>
</xsd:schema>
```

3. In this schema document we have defined an element called name using the element tag. We can state that there is a set of child elements by declaring these within this element in a complexType element; we then use a sequence element, which says that the elements must appear in the document in the order they are defined. complexType and sequence elements are discussed further a little later in the chapter.

4. This can be tested by running the following command from a command prompt:

example.exe instance.xml schema.xsd

You must, of course, ensure that the command prompt is pointing at the directory where your code is being held. So for our example, this would involve typing `cd c:\BegVBXML\Chapter10` at the command prompt, if your code was held in the directory we suggested at the start of this example.

> **Note: The three steps that we discussed earlier will all happen at this stage, that is Step 1. The XML document is loaded; Step 2. The schema document is loaded; Step 3. The XML document is *validated* against the schema, and if everything is valid and well-formed we get the following result.**

Let's now see what happens when we add in an element that we haven't included in our schema.

Open the `instance.xml` document and add the element illustrated in the code below and save the file as `instance1b.xml`.

```
<?xml version="1.0"?>
<name>
  <first>Steven</first>
  <middle />
  <last>Livingstone-Perez</last>
  <age>27</age>
</name>
```

Run the application again by typing **example.exe instance1b.xml schema.xsd** at the command line. You should get the following output:

This message is telling you that the XML Schema document does not define an `age` element as a child of the `name` element.

To now fix this and ensure that the validation executes correctly by making the following modification to `schema.xsd` and save this as `schema1b.xsd`.

```
<xsd:schema xmlns:xsd="http://www.w3.org/2001/XMLSchema">
  <xsd:element name="name">
    <xsd:complexType>
      <xsd:sequence>
        <xsd:element name="first" type="xsd:string" />
        <xsd:element name="middle" type="xsd:string" />
        <xsd:element name="last" type="xsd:string" />
        <xsd:element name="age" type="xsd:integer" />
      </xsd:sequence>
    </xsd:complexType>
  </xsd:element>
</xsd:schema>
```

We have now added a new definition for an `age` element, which must be an integer. One other thing to remember though is that in defining this element in our schema, we have decided on a data type that we will permit for this element. Therefore, if we were to modify `instance1b.xml` again and change the value within the `<age>` element to **"Age 27"** and save this as `instance1c.xml`:

```
<?xml version="1.0"?>
<name>
  <first>Steven</first>
  <middle />
  <last>Livingstone-Perez</last>
  <age>Age 27</age>
</name>
```

Then run the application again by typing **example.exe instance1c.xml schema1b.xsd** at the command line, you should get the following output:

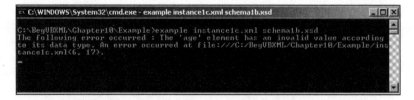

In this case, the **"Age"** text of **"Age 27"** was invalid according to the definition for the `age` element, which has an integer data type assigned to it and so an exception was thrown.

So from this brief discussion we can see how easy it is to develop and use an XSD to define and control valid and well-formed data in an XML document. Now we will further explore what we can do with XSD, as we look at referencing elements and substitution.

Referencing Elements and Substitution

When working with XML documents, you may find yourself using the same element multiple times. Rather than define this element multiple times within the schema, you can declare it at a global level (as a child of the `schema` root element) and reference it from anywhere within the schema. This saves you from redefining the element multiple times, as well as ensuring a consistent definition of a given element.

This referencing is done using the `ref` attribute on an `element` tag. The following would reference the element `first` defined in the schema and would also make `first` reusable in other definitions within the schema.

```
<xsd:schema xmlns:xsd="http://www.w3.org/2001/XMLSchema">
  <xsd:element name="first" type="xsd:string" />
  <xsd:element name="name">
    <xsd:complexType>
      <xsd:sequence>
        <xsd:element ref="first" />
      </xsd:sequence>
    </xsd:complexType>
  </xsd:element>
</xsd:schema>
```

In addition to referencing elements, there are times when you want to change the name of the element for a particular audience, but still retain the same meaning as the original definition. As an example, your XML file may be updated to enable it to be used by Spanish users, and so rather than use `first`, you may prefer to use `primero` (the Spanish for first). To accomplish this, you can use the `substitutionGroup` attribute, which basically allows you to specify another element definition in the schema that should replace the element it's defined on.

So the previous schema could be modified to read:

```
<xsd:schema xmlns:xsd="http://www.w3.org/2001/XMLSchema">
  <xsd:element name="primero" type="xsd:string" substitutionGroup="first"/>
  <xsd:element name="first" type="xsd:string" />
  <xsd:element name="name">
    <xsd:complexType>
      <xsd:sequence>
        <xsd:element ref="first" />
      </xsd:sequence>
    </xsd:complexType>
  </xsd:element>
</xsd:schema>
```

This allows the following two XML instances to be valid according to the above schema and mean the same thing:

```
<?xml version="1.0"?>

<name>

  <first>Steven</first>

</name>
```

```
<?xml version="1.0"?>

<name>

  <primero>Steven</primero>

</name>
```

Setting Default and Fixed Values

Even when we have managed to define an element as a specific type and have defined even a simple structure for our content, there are going to be times when we want to set a default value for that element or even set a fixed value so that it cannot be changed.

439

As an example, consider a form where a user enters contact details. The first time a user does this you may want to assume a default value for the sex of the user (let's say, Male). Once the contact has entered their details, if they want to modify them, you may want to prevent certain values from being modified. So, once someone entered Male when they submitted the details, you would want to make sure that they're not able to change the sex to Female when they update their details.

To accomplish the first of these there is the `default` attribute, which can be used to specify the default value of an XML element if no value is given for it in the XML document. To prevent a value from being changed, there is the `fixed` attribute, which is used to indicate the value of an element that cannot be changed or overridden. The following example is where we have a `City` element that defaults to the value `Glasgow` and a `Country` element that is fixed at the value `Scotland`, which can never be changed.

```
<xsd:element name="City" type="xsd:string" default="Glasgow"/>
<xsd:element name="Country" type="xsd:string" fixed="Scotland"/>
```

Finally, there is the `nillable` attribute, which states that no value has been assigned for a given element (different from an empty string!). This should be set to `True` or `False`. So for the following example, we're allowing a "middle" name element to have no value assigned.

```
<xsd:element name="middle" type="xsd:string" nillable="true" />
```

To use the `nil` attribute within an XML document instance, you must make a namespace declaration of `http://www.w3.org/2001/XMLSchema-instance` on the XML document root element and qualify the `nil` attribute within this namespace; it is normally associated with the `xsi` prefix. This is then used to set the `nillable` attribute to `True` as `xsi:nil="true"`.

```
<?xml version="1.0"?>
<name xmlns:xsi="http://www.w3.org/2001/XMLSchema-instance">
  <first xsi:nil="true" />
</name>
```

Controlling Structure with Compositors

To this point we have only learned how to create documents that contain sequences of elements; from our current knowledge, an element may or may not appear, but if it does, it must appear in a certain position. Also, we don't have any control over a situation where elements are mutually exclusive; that is where element A or element B can occur, but not both.

We may decide that we want elements to appear in any order as long as they all appear. Consider our previous example XML document;

```
<?xml version="1.0"?>
<name>
  <first>Steven</first>
  <middle />
  <last>Livingstone-Perez</last>
  <age>Age 27</age>
</name>
```

There is a way to specify that we don't mind if the `<last>`, `<middle>`, or `<first>` elements appear first, using a **compositor** – a methodology that enables us to subtly to define our structure of elements. You have already met one compositor in the `sequence` element that defines how the fragment may be composed – that is defining a list of elements that must appear in the order specified in the schema (or not appear if they are optional).

The `all` compositor allows the elements you define to appear in any order. Child elements of the `all` element are required by default and may only appear a maximum of one time – you can set the `minOccurs` attribute to 0 to indicate that the element is optional (the `minOccurs` and `maxOccurs` can also be set on the `all` element itself to apply to all the elements it defines).

So, we could create a schema like the one, which includes the `all` compositor (this schema is **schema1d.xml** in the code download):

```
<xsd:schema xmlns:xsd="http://www.w3.org/2001/XMLSchema">
  <xsd:element name="name">
    <xsd:complexType>
      <xsd:all minOccurs="0">
        <xsd:element name="first" type="xsd:string" />
        <xsd:element name="middle" type="xsd:string" />
        <xsd:element name="last" type="xsd:string" />
      </xsd:all>
    </xsd:complexType>
  </xsd:element>
</xsd:schema>
```

The elements defined within the `xsd:all` element can be defined in any order and can also appear in an XML document in any order.

There is one other compositor that we have not yet looked at, which is the `choice` element. The `choice` element allows you to specify one of a multiple of declarations, and is useful for mutually exclusive cases. So, for example, the following schema declares the content model of our `<name>` element using a `<choice>` declaration:

```
<xsd:schema xmlns:xsd="http://www.w3.org/2001/XMLSchema">
  <xsd:element name="name">
    <xsd:complexType>
      <xsd:choice>
        <xsd:element name="first" type="xsd:string" />
        <xsd:element name="middle" type="xsd:string" />
        <xsd:element name="last" type="xsd:string" />
      </xsd:choice>
    </xsd:complexType>
  </xsd:element>
</xsd:schema>
```

Using this schema, within the instance document we have been using, we could include only the `<first>` element, only the `<middle>` element, or only the `<last>` element. We would not be able to include more than one of the elements within the instance.

Defining Attributes

We can define attributes in XSDL in much the same way as we define elements, but the level of restriction is greater. They can only be simple types, and therefore, they can only contain text and have no children. There are also fewer attributes that can be applied to `attribute` element definitions, as shown below.

❑   `default` – the initial default value that can be overridden.

❑   `fixed` – the set value of an attribute that cannot be changed or overridden.

❑   `form` – determines the local value of the `attributeFormDefault`.

❑   `id` – the unique ID of the attribute in the Schema document.

❑   `name` – the name of the attribute.

❑   `ref` – a reference to a previous attribute definition.

❑   `type` – the XSD type of this attribute, or a simple type.

❑   `use` – how the attribute is used.

The `default`, `fixed`, `name`, `ref` and `type` attributes are the same as those defined for the `element` tag; note however that as mentioned at the start of this section, the `type` is limited to simple types. We will look at the `form` attribute later in the chapter, so let's look at the `use` attribute, which we haven't yet discussed. A simple definition for an attribute is:

```
<xsd:attribute name="age" type="xsd:integer" />
```

The `use` attribute takes one of the values `optional`, `prohibited`, or `required`. `optional` indicates that the attribute isn't mandatory, `prohibited` is used when you are reusing a predefined set of attribute definitions and don't want one of the attributes from that group to be reused (that is, you want to filter out that attribute from the group) and `required` means that the attribute is mandatory.

Creating Attributes

We have focused our discussion on elements but an alternative is to use attributes to represent this data, so rather than build up a structure based on a hierarchy of elements as we have done in our 'name' example above, we could insert attributes into an element. Thus 'first', 'middle' and 'last' would be attributes of the 'name' element rather than child elements of the 'name' element.

In our developer's community there are differing opinions about whether to favor elements or attributes: simply put it's about design choice and evaluating what is appropriate given the circumstances. In a nutshell, elements are preferred by some developers when they need the flexibility to split an element by inserting child elements; this can't be done with an attribute.

Elements may also be preferred because they are more readable and the relational structure is obvious. On the other hand some developers prefer attributes because they tend to be less wordy than elements, are intuitive for developers that have HTML experience, and may also be transmitted more quickly as they can consume less bandwidth.

So by no means is the choice of elements or attributes clear-cut; we suggest that it is a case-by-case decision, however when a developer is uncertain about permanency and correctness of the structure of data, then the flexibility of elements may be a deciding factor in making the design choice.

Adding attributes to an XML Schema document can be done in much the same way as we defined elements. The following is the simplest definition for an attribute:

```
<xsd:attribute name="age" type="xsd:integer" />
```

This defines an attribute called `age` whose value must be an `integer` type. When this is added to a schema, it must be the child of the `schema` element, the child of a `complexType` or the child of an `attributeGroup` element. As we discuss later in the chapter a `complexType` is a type used when " you want to define an element that contains child elements and/or attributes", and an `attributeGroup` element is an element that is used when we "need to group attributes for inheritance and reuse using the `xsd:attributeGroup` element."

To attach the attribute to an element it should be either defined or referenced immediately after the compositor within the `complexType` definition. As an example, to add the above attribute to an element called `first`, we would have to define the schema as follows:

```
<xsd:schema xmlns:xsd="http://www.w3.org/2001/XMLSchema">
  <xsd:element name="name">
    <xsd:complexType>
      <xsd:sequence>
        <xsd:element name="first" type="xsd:string" />
      </xsd:sequence>
      <xsd:attribute name="age" type="xsd:integer" />
    </xsd:complexType>
  </xsd:element>
</xsd:schema>
```

This would validate this XML instance (`instance1g.xml`):

```
<?xml version="1.0"?>
<name age="27">
  <first>Steven</first>
</name>
```

Note that, unlike elements, attributes are optional by default and so the `use="optional"` attribute on attributes is, well, *optional*. So the following instance would also be valid according to the above schema:

```
<?xml version="1.0"?>
<name>
  <first>Steven</first>
</name>
```

If you want to say that the attribute must appear in the instance then set the value of the `use` attribute to `required` (`schema1g.xsd`);

443

```
<xsd:schema xmlns:xsd="http://www.w3.org/2001/XMLSchema">
  <xsd:element name="name">
    <xsd:complexType>
      <xsd:sequence>
        <xsd:element name="first" type="xsd:string" />
      </xsd:sequence>
      <xsd:attribute name="age" type="xsd:integer" use="required"/>
    </xsd:complexType>
  </xsd:element>
</xsd:schema>
```

You can even define an attribute at a global level and use the ref attribute to reference it as shown in the next schema:

```
<xsd:schema xmlns:xsd="http://www.w3.org/2001/XMLSchema">
  <xsd:attribute name="age" type="xsd:integer" use="required"/>
  <xsd:element name="name">
    <xsd:complexType>
      <xsd:sequence>
        <xsd:element name="first" type="xsd:string" />
      </xsd:sequence>
      <xsd:attribute ref="age" />
    </xsd:complexType>
  </xsd:element>
</xsd:schema>
```

Finally, like elements, attributes can specify default and fixed values. Like before, consider the case where a user who has registered has defined their title (for example, Mr, Miss, or Mrs) and their age (say 27). When the user looks again at their data, you may assume a default value for their title (that is, the one they chose before – I'm using "Sir"!). You could also fix the age attribute if the application already knows their date of birth and could calculate their current age from this. To prevent the user from modifying this manually, you could set the value as fixed. The following XML schema would accomplish this:

```
<xsd:schema xmlns:xsd="http://www.w3.org/2001/XMLSchema">
  <xsd:attribute name="age" type="xsd:integer" fixed="27"/>
  <xsd:element name="name">
    <xsd:complexType>
      <xsd:sequence>
        <xsd:element name="first" type="xsd:string" />
      </xsd:sequence>
      <xsd:attribute ref="age" />
      <xsd:attribute name="title" type="xsd:string" default="Sir" />
    </xsd:complexType>
  </xsd:element>
</xsd:schema>
```

Now you can create the following XML instance (instance1h.xml) that would be validated by the above schema.

```
<?xml version="1.0"?>
<name title="Sir">
  <first>Steven</first>
</name>
```

However, the following schema would be *invalid* – not because of my loss of title, but because the age attribute value has been modified and this has a `fixed` value in the schema (if you changed this value from "28" to "27" it would be valid).

```
<?xml version="1.0"?>
<name age="28" title="Mr">
  <first>Steven</first>
</name>
```

Now we have enough knowledge to create a basic schema to validate our XML documents. We don't intend to cover every single element in this chapter – for others you may need to look at the MSDN documentation, http://www.w3c.org/XML/Schema, or *Professional XML Schemas* (ISBN 1-86100-547-4) from Wrox Press.

Next we look more closely at the details of XSDL by looking at data types.

XML Schema Data Types

XML Schemas offer a rich set of built-in data types that you can use to define the allowable types in your elements. They are made up of **primitive** and **derived** data types. Primitive data types are the most basic data types from which all other data types are created, like `string`, `double`, `decimal`, `Boolean` and `time`. Derived data types are types that can be layered on top of the primitive data types to provide a bit more control over their possible values, examples being `integer`, `nonNegativeInteger`, `long`, `positiveInteger` and `byte`,

In addition XML provides **data type facets** which allow you to further restrict the value of these data types by allowing you to layer additional constraints such as limiting the length of a string, specifying the maximum allowable value of an integer or specifying a set of enumerable values from which one can be chosen.

Beyond this, you can even build your own **custom types** when required that can define not only specific data type definitions (such as a "PhoneNumber" data type), but you can define even more advanced data types that can define an entire structure (such as the elements, attributes and their data types – "address" is an example).

There are two kinds of these data types defined by XSD; **simple types** and **complex types**. Simple types are the building blocks of any XML Schema document and are used when you are defining an element that contains only character data and no child elements or attributes. Complex types are used when you want to create a more complex content model for an element containing child elements, or if you want the element to have attributes.

As we progress through the section on data types we should keep in mind how this all fits in with the data type methodology that we have in VB.NET; can you spot the similarities between XML's primitive, derived, custom, simple and complex types with VB.NET's primitive, derived, structure, and class types?

Common Data Types

Rather than go through every primitive and derived data type, let's pick out some of the most common and see how they can be used in your XML Schema documents. A full reference can be found in the MSDN documentation or at the W3C site at http://www.w3.org/TR/xmlschema-2/.

Primitive Data Types

Primitive data types are the basic building blocks of every data type you work with in XML Schema. The XML Schema language builds upon these types as well as providing data types to create your own custom types.

Some of the most common primitive data types are:

❑   boolean – can be 1 (True) or 0 (False).

❑   dateTime – an ISO 8601 abbreviated date with optional time part – from the Gregorian calendar in the form CCYY-MM-DDThh:mm:ss. An example is "2002-09-25T07:23:12-02:00" which means that the time given (after T) is two hours behind Universal Co-Ordinated Time (UTC). You can also write this as 2002-09-25T05:23:12Z" where Z indicates that the time is with respect to UTC and so the two hours difference is taken away from the local time (just after the T).

❑   decimal – Represents arbitrary precision decimal numbers.

❑   string – character data (for example, "Glasgow Celtic").
In DTD it was CDATA, for example, <!ATTLIST author age CDATA #IMPLIED>

To illustrate how they can be used, first consider the following XML file (instanceB.xml):

```
<?xml version="1.0"?>
<ContactDetails lastUpdated="2002-09-25T19:13:12Z">
  <name local="true">
    <first>Steven</first>
    <middle />
    <last>Livingstone-Perez</last>
  </name>
  <rate>10.34</rate>
<ContactDetails>
```

We *could* just validate the new lastUpdated and local attributes as well as the new rate element using a string data type, but that is weak validation – as long as it was a valid string it would pass validation, even if "sometime" was the value of the lastUpdated attribute! Fortunately we can use some of the primitive data types that we have with XML Schema to provide stronger validation against these nodes. The lastUpdated attribute is a date and time combination and so we can use the dateTime data type. The local attribute (indicating if the contact is geographically local) can only take a True or False, so we can use the Boolean type for that. Finally, the contents of the rate element are monetary value and we can use the decimal primitive type to validate this.

The following XML Schema (schemaB.xsd) will validate the above XML document;

```
<xsd:schema xmlns:xsd="http://www.w3.org/2001/XMLSchema">
  <xsd:element name="ContactDetails">
    <xsd:complexType>
      <xsd:sequence>
```

```
            <xsd:element ref="name" />
            <xsd:element name="rate" type="xsd:decimal" />
          </xsd:sequence>
          <xsd:attribute name="lastUpdated" type="xsd:dateTime" />
        </xsd:complexType>
      </xsd:element>

      <xsd:element name="name">
        <xsd:complexType>
          <xsd:sequence>
            <xsd:element name="first" type="xsd:string" />
            <xsd:element name="middle" type="xsd:string" />
            <xsd:element name="last" type="xsd:string" />
          </xsd:sequence>
          <xsd:attribute name="local" type="xsd:boolean" />
        </xsd:complexType>
      </xsd:element>
    </xsd:schema>
```

The first element defines the ContactDetails root element, and this defines a sequence element containing a reference to the name element definition and a new rate element. This rate element is specified as a decimal data type, so it can be used to validate numbers containing decimals.

```
<xsd:element name="rate" type="xsd:decimal" />
```

Additionally a new lastUpdated attribute is defined immediately after the sequence element and the data type is set to be dateTime which will allows us to specify a date and time using a standard format.

```
<xsd:attribute name="lastUpdated" type="xsd:dateTime" />
```

Later the name element is defined and within this the first, middle and last elements are defined as string types. Also the local attribute is defined as an XSD Boolean type attached to the name element.

```
<xsd:attribute name="local" type="xsd:boolean" />
```

Derived Data Types

Often we can improve the level of validation by using the derived types – these types further restrict the values allowed by the primitive data types. Some of the most common derived data types are:

- ❑ int – Represents an integer with a minimum value of -2,147,483,648 and maximum of 2,147,483,647. Derived from long derived type.

- ❑ nonNegativeInteger – Represents an integer that is greater than or equal to zero (for example, 98). Derived from integer derived type.

- ❑ nonPositiveInteger – Represents an integer that is less than or equal to zero. A nonPositiveInteger consists of a negative sign (-) and sequence of decimal digits (for example, -98). Derived from integer derived type.

- ❑ positiveInteger – Represents an integer that is greater than zero (for example, 1). Derived from nonNegativeInteger derived type.

❑   short – Represents an integer with a minimum value of -32,768 and maximum of 32,767. Derived from int datatype.

As an example you may improve the range of values allowed for the age attribute (currently any positive or negavtive integer number) to positiveInteger – that is, a number that has to be greater than 0 (you cannot be less than zero years of age and are unlikely to be writing XML at 0 years!).

```
<xsd:attribute name="age" type="xsd:positiveInteger" />
```

Simple Types

Although we get a lot of power from the built-in data types, there are many occasions where just a data type to constrain the possible values of your data just isn't enough. It may be useful to say that someone's age can only be any possible positive integer, but I doubt many of have met 27,000 year old people – however, with the positiveInteger type, someone could define that as their age. This idea of deriving data types from other data types is a very powerful capability and allows you to create reusable data types that can be used in many different schema documents (we should how to import schemas later).

However, before we start to look in depth at how to create these simple type data types, its worth looking at **data type facets**, which are constraining elements provided by XML Schema that allow you to solve the above problems.

Data Type Facets

The ability to use the above data types to improve validation is certainly an improvement on the basic string validation we had at the start of the chapter. However, sometimes we need to provide some absolute constraints on top of the data types to get strict validation.

You may want to put a limit on the number of characters in the middle attribute – for example, you may only want the initial rather than the full middle name. In this case you would want to put a restriction on the length of the string to be a maximum of 1 character.

As another example, you may want to have better control over the title that can be defined for a given contact – for example, limit the value to one of a set of enumerated values. You may even want to combine some of these restrictions to provide a more concrete constraint – such as a value that is a currency and is within a range.

This kind of functionality can be accomplished in XML Schema using **data type facets**, which allow you to apply such restrictions. These data type facets are used to further constrain the values of the data type on a simpleType.

Before we look at a couple of examples, the following are the full list of facets that can be used to constrain the permissible values.

❑   enumeration – a specified set of values separated by whitespace (for example, 1 2 3 4 5). This constrains a data type to the specified values.

❑   fractionDigits – value with specific maximum number of decimal digits in the fractional part. (for example, fractionDigits="1" would mean 36.4 and 45.9 are valid).

❑   length – Number of units of length. Units of length depend on the data type, so the length of a string is measured in characters, whereas the length for base64Binary is measured in Octets (8 bits). This value must be a nonNegativeInteger.

❑   maxExclusive – Upper bound value, so all values are less than this value (for example, a maxExclusive value of 10 would mean all values should be under 10). This value must be the same data type as the inherited data type.

❑   maxInclusive – Maximum value (for example, a maxInclusive value of 10 would mean all values should be under, or equal to, 10). This value must be the same data type as the inherited data type.

❑   maxLength – Maximum number of units of length (for example, a maxLength of 5 would mean there could be a maximum of 5 units of length). The units of length depend on the data type.

❑   minExclusive – Lower bound value, so all values must be greater than this value (for example, a minExclusive value of 10 would mean all values should be greater than 10). This value must be the same data type as the inherited data type.

❑   minInclusive – Minimum value (for example, a minInclusive value of 10 would mean all values should be greater than, or equal to, 10). This value must be the same data type as the inherited data type.

❑   minLength – Minimum number of units of length (for example, a minLength of 5 would mean there could be a minimum of 5 units of length). Units of length depend on the data type and this value must be a nonNegativeInteger.

❑   pattern – Specific pattern that the data type's values must match and the pattern value must be a regular expression. This constrains the data type to literals that match the specified pattern.

❑   totalDigits – Value with specific maximum number of decimal digits.

❑   whiteSpace – Value must be one of preserve (the whitespace in the value is not changed), replace (all tabs, line-feeds and carriage returns are replaced by a space), or collapse (does what replace does and then remove contiguous and trailing and leading spaces). The facet constrains values derived from the string data type.

When applying facets to a data type, you use the restriction element; the restriction element has an attribute called base, which contains the value of the data type you want to apply further restrictions to. The data type you restrict can be either one of the built-in data types or an existing simple type definition, which we look at in the next section. Within the restriction element you place the data type facets and their applicable values to further constrain the type.

The restriction element is defined as follows:

```
<restriction
  id="ID"
  base="QName" />
```

The id attribute is a unique identifier for the restriction element within the schema document and the base attribute is set to a built-in XSD data type or an existing simple type definition and is the type that is being restricted (and can use namespaces to qualify the type). The restriction element also uses **data type facets** to further restrict the value, such as length, minInclusive, and maxInclusive.

As an example, the following restriction limits the minimum length of a string to four characters:

```
<xsd:restriction base="xsd:string">
  <xsd:minLength value="4"/>
</xsd:restriction>
```

An additional facet can also be added to limit the maximum length of the above string to ten characters.

```
<xsd:restriction base="xsd:string">
  <xsd:minLength value="4"/>
  <xsd:maxLength value="10"/>
</xsd:restriction>
```

The following example sets the allowable values of an integer (int data type) to between 1 and 100 (which could be applied to the age attribute as discussed earlier – we see how in the next section):

```
<xsd:restriction base="xsd:int">
  <xsd:minInclusive value="1"/>
  <xsd:maxInclusive value="100"/>
</xsd:restriction>
```

As a final example, we can create a set of enumerable values based on the string data type from which one has to be chosen as follows. This is done using multiple entries of the enumeration facet for each possible value:

```
<xsd:restriction base="xsd:string">
   <xsd:enumeration value="FirstValue" />
   <xsd:enumeration value="SecondValue" />
   <xsd:enumeration value="ThirdValue" />
</xsd:restriction>
```

So how do we actually use these restrictions? They are used when working with simple types, which is what we move on to discuss now.

Creating Simple Types

Simple types are custom data types that create further constraints on the possible values of a node. Common simple type definitions are "TelephoneNumber" (specifying a specific format for telephone numbers rather than just a list of numbers), "Age" (as looked at above, limiting the possible age values), "Title" (allowing a choice from a limited set of "Mr", "Mrs", and so on) and "Price" (allowing monetary values to be specified). Let's look at how we can create these custom data types using the simpleType element.

There are two ways a simple type can be used – the first is directly on an element element if it has no attributes or child elements – the second is as a simpleType element.

So we could define an element called age that takes any valid positive integer as follows:

```
<element name="age" type="xsd:positiveInteger" />
```

Similarly, you may define an element for a person's first name as follows:

```
<element name="first" type="xsd:string" />
```

With XSD you can restrict the valid integer values, or length or a person's name. For this, you can use a `simpleType` element, which is defined as follows:

```
<simpleType
   id= "ID"
   name="NCName"
   final="(#all | (list | union | restriction))" />
```

The `id` should uniquely identify the `simpleType` element within the document and the `name` cannot use the colon character. A `simpleType` cannot contain elements and cannot have attributes – it is basically a value, or set of values according to the rules defined within the `simpleType`, which is derived from the existing XSD types or other `simpleType` definitions.

We can demonstrate how to create `simpleType` definitions using the data type facets we created in the last section. In the first case we may create a "PersonsName" simple type that can be used to limit the minimum length of a person's first name to four characters as follows:

```
<xsd:simpleType name="PersonsName">
  <xsd:restriction base="xsd:string">
    <xsd:minLength value="4"/>
  </xsd:restriction>
</xsd:simpleType>
```

This can then be applied to an element definition using the `type` attribute as with any built-in data type. We use it below to specify that the value of the `first` element must be at least four characters in length:

```
<xsd:element name="first" type="PersonsName" />
```

So a valid instance of this element would be:

```
<first>Steven</first>
```

The following instance using only an initial would be invalid:

```
<first>S</first>
```

We can further restrict the `PersonsName` simple type to be a maximum length as follows:

```
<xsd:simpleType name="PersonsName">
  <xsd:restriction base="xsd:string">
    <xsd:minLength value="4"/>
    <xsd:maxLength value="10"/>
  </xsd:restriction>
</xsd:simpleType>
```

Again we can use it to specify that the value of the `first` element must be at least four characters in length, but a maximum of ten characters:

```
<xsd:element name="first" type="PersonsName" />
```

So a valid instance of this element would be:

```
<first>Steven</first>
```

The following instance containing the full name would be invalid:

```
<first>Steven Livingstone</first>
```

We can also improve the earlier definition of the `age` attribute by defining a custom `age` simple type as follows:

```
<xsd:simpleType name="PersonsAge">
  <xsd:restriction base="xsd:int">
    <xsd:minInclusive value="1"/>
    <xsd:maxInclusive value="100"/>
  </xsd:restriction>
<xsd:simpleType>
```

We can then apply it to the `age` attribute as follows:

```
<xsd:attribute name="age" type="PersonsAge" />
```

So a valid instance of this attribute (using its definition on the `name` element as earlier) would be:

```
<name age="27">...</name>
```

The following instance, containing a very much older me, would be invalid:

```
<name age="127">...</name>
```

Let's now try a full example to see `simpleType` definitions in use.

Try It Out: Restriction with simpleType Elements and Enumerations

Constraining the possible entries within a large XML document is essential in gaining correct data that will be used by your application. Whether it's for a user interface or an internal function, knowing that the data entered is valid according to your business rules is essential. Incorrect data may make no sense to the consumer or even break the application itself. Restricting such data values using simple type definitions can prevent many of these kinds of problems from occurring in the first place.

Here we are going to restrict the values of the `first` element in our schema to ensure that the length of a person's first name is within a desired range. We will also limit the valid options that can be entered against the `title` element in our schema using enumerations.

1. Create a new XML Schema file called `schema2.xsd` and enter the following details.

```
<xsd:schema xmlns:xsd="http://www.w3.org/2001/XMLSchema">
  <xsd:element name="name">
    <xsd:complexType>
      <xsd:sequence>
        <xsd:element name="first" type="PersonsFirstname"
          minOccurs="0" maxOccurs="1" default="John" />
        <xsd:element name="middle" type="xsd:string"
          minOccurs="0" maxOccurs="unbounded" nillable="true" />
        <xsd:element name="last" type="xsd:string"
          minOccurs="1" maxOccurs="1" default="Doe"/>
      </xsd:sequence>
      <xsd:attribute name="title" type="PersonsTitle" default="Mr."/>
    </xsd:complexType>
  </xsd:element>
  <xsd:simpleType name="PersonsFirstname">
    <xsd:restriction base="xsd:string">
      <xsd:minLength value="4"/>
      <xsd:maxLength value="10"/>
    </xsd:restriction>
  </xsd:simpleType>
  <xsd:simpleType name="PersonsTitle">
    <xsd:restriction base="xsd:string">
      <xsd:enumeration value="Mr." />
      <xsd:enumeration value="Mrs." />
      <xsd:enumeration value="Miss." />
    </xsd:restriction>
  </xsd:simpleType>
</xsd:schema>
```

2. Create a new XML document called `instance2.xml` and enter the following code:

```
<?xml version="1.0"?>
<name>
  <first>Steven</first>
  <middle />
  <last>Livingstone-Perez</last>
</name>
```

3. At the command line, navigate to the folder containing the `example.exe` file and enter the following at the command prompt:

```
example.exe instance2.xml schema2.xsd
```

Hit *Enter* and the file will be successfully validated.

4. Alter the `instance2.xml` file to read as follows:

```
<?xml version="1.0"?>
<name>
  <first>S</first>
  <middle />
  <last>Livingstone-Perez</last>
</name>
```

5. Re-run the command:

```
example.exe instance2.xml schema2.xsd
```

and you will get the following output:

6. To test our schema restrictions on the `title` element, load `instance2.xml` and make the highlighted changes below. Save the file as `instance3.xml`:

```
<?xml version="1.0"?>
<name title="Mr.">
  <first>Steven</first>
  <middle />
  <last>Livingstone-Perez</last>
</name>
```

7. At the command line, navigate to the folder containing the `example.exe` file and enter the following at the command prompt:

```
example.exe instance3.xml schema2.xsd
```

Hit *Enter* and the file will be successfully validated.

8. Alter the `instance3.xml` file to read as follows:

```
<?xml version="1.0"?>
<name title="Mrr.">
  <first>Steven</first>
  <middle />
  <last>Livingstone-Perez</last>
</name>
```

9. Re-run the command line and you will get the following output.

How It Works

In this case we created a `simpleType` element with the name `PersonsFirstname`. The `restriction` element has been used with a base type of the built-in XSD `string` data type, which means that the value of this node can only be a `string` type. However, we further restrict the length of the string; `minLength` says that the string must be at least four characters in length and `maxLength` means that the string cannot be more than 10 characters in length.

```
<xsd:simpleType name="PersonsFirstname">
 <xsd:restriction base="xsd:string">
   <xsd:minLength value="4"/>
   <xsd:maxLength value="10"/>
 </xsd:restriction>
</xsd:simpleType>
```

We can therefore use this definition on an element or attribute node as the value of the `type` attribute to restrict its content to strings of between four and ten characters; in our case we do this for the element called `first`.

```
<xsd:element name="first" type="PersonsFirstname" minOccurs="0" maxOccurs="1"
 default="John" />
```

In the first test case, the value of the `first` element was "`Steven`", which is six characters in length and so is validated.

```
<first>Steven</first>
```

In the second case we changed the content of this element to the initial "`S`" which is of course a single character and will fail validation.

```
<first>S</first>
```

This produced the following error message; "The 'first' element has an invalid value according to its data type". This tells us which element is in error.

Following this, we altered our XML instance to test our `PersonsTitle` restrictions. The `restriction` element also uses a base type of the built-in XSD `string` data type, but this time, we further restrict the possible values of the string using the `enumeration` facet. We set this to be `Mr`, `Mrs`, and `Miss`.

```
<xsd:simpleType name="PersonsTitle">
 <xsd:restriction base="xsd:string">
```

```
        <xsd:enumeration value="Mr." />
        <xsd:enumeration value="Mrs." />
        <xsd:enumeration value="Miss." />
      </xsd:restriction>
    </xsd:simpleType>
```

We have also added an attribute node definition after the `sequence` element and set the
`PersonsTitle` as the value of the `type` attribute to restrict its content to one of these strings. It is set
to default to the string `"Mr."`.

```
  <xsd:attribute name="title" type="PersonsTitle" default="Mr."/>
```

In the first test case, the value of the first element was `"Mr."` which is a valid entry in the enumeration list.

```
  <name title="Mr.">
```

In the second case we illustrated what may happen when text is incorrectly entered.

```
  <name title="Mrr.">
```

The validation error message that is written to the console indicates indeed that the `title` attribute has
failed validation.

> **XSDL data types function easily alongside the native, derived, and custom types that
> we can develop with VB.NET. In VB.NET we have a process called serialization that is
> accessed via the `System.Xml.Serialization` namespace. This will serialize or
> convert a custom object and its native data types into XML equivalents and store it in
> an XML file on the file directory: the reverse process is to deserialize. The XSD and
> the XML files that we develop are the basis from which we can exchange data by using
> XML (and XLST) to bridge the disparate application or incompatible platform divide.**

Complex Types

Although simple type definitions allow us to ensure the value of a given element or attribute is within a
certain range, or of a given type or combinations of these, it doesn't allow us to say anything about the
structure of a type. For example, we know that the parts that make up an address are fairly standard
(house number, floor, building, street name, city, and so on), so it would make sense to be able to define
an "address" type that allow an application to define a home address, or business address using a
standard format. This would make it a lot easier for our applications to read as it has an idea of the
format it is in. You can imagine similar constructs being used for credit card sections on a web page, for
example – they all are based on fairly common parts. It would be good to define this structure once and
have it reused in other places. In XML Schemas, this kind of complex structure and typing can be
achieved by using `complexType` elements, which use all of the `simpleType` and built-in data type
definitions we have discussed throughout this chapter.

In contrast to `simpleType` elements, `complexType` elements may contain elements and attributes, and are what you will use to create the structure of an XSD Schema. If you want to define an element that contains child elements and/or attributes then you must use a `complexType` element. You can define templates for certain structures (such as an "Address" type) using `complexType` definitions that contain details on the elements and attributes allowed for that type – this definition may use other `complexType` and `simpleType` definitions to create a content model (much like a template of the structure for that type).

Complex types can be declared at a global level (that is, as a direct child element of the root `schema` element) and must have a `name` attribute defining how they should be referred to. A `mixed` attribute also states whether character data is allowed as a child of this element and defaults to `false` (that is, you are only allowed elements).

Complex types that are declared as a child of an `element` tag and have no `name` attribute are called **anonymous** types; these types are not reusable in the schema and are generally specific to the element. These are useful when you have a unique grouping of elements and attributes that are not likely to be used outside a particular element.

You typically use complex types to define a more complex set of reusable elements and/or attributes, such as for fully defining someone's full name, full address, or job description. A given `complexType` element may even use other `complexType` elements and will likely use `simpleType` and built-in type definitions.

You could declare a `complexType` for an element as follows.

```
<xsd:element name="first" type="FirstNameType" />
```

This declares a `complexType` called `FirstNameType` which will constrain the value of the `first` element – this may be as simple as limiting the number of characters in the string or more complex such as an expression.

The best way to understand the use of `complexType` elements is to work on an example.

Try It Out: Using Complex Type Elements

The purpose of this Try It Out is to show you how to take existing schema definitions and improve the reusability by moving definitions into a named `complexType` element definition. We will use this definition to contain the data constraints required when creating someone's name.

1. Create a new XML Schema file called `schema4.xsd` and enter the following:

```
<xsd:schema xmlns:xsd="http://www.w3.org/2001/XMLSchema">
  <xsd:element name="Contacts">
   <xsd:complexType>
    <xsd:sequence>
      <xsd:element ref="name" />
      <xsd:element name="friendsName" type="FullName"
        maxOccurs="10" />
      <xsd:element name="Notes">
       <xsd:complexType>
```

```
          <xsd:sequence maxOccurs="unbounded">
            <xsd:element name="entry" type="xsd:string" />
          </xsd:sequence>
        </xsd:complexType>
      </xsd:element>
    </xsd:sequence>
  </xsd:complexType>
</xsd:element>

<xsd:element name="name" type="FullName" />
<xsd:complexType name="FullName">
 <xsd:sequence>
  <xsd:element name="first" type="PersonsFirstname"
    minOccurs="0" maxOccurs="1" default="John" />
  <xsd:element name="middle" type="xsd:string"
    minOccurs="0" maxOccurs="unbounded" nillable="true" />
  <xsd:element name="last" type="xsd:string"
    minOccurs="1" maxOccurs="1" default="Doe" />
 </xsd:sequence>
 <xsd:attribute name="title" type="PersonsTitle" default="Mr." />
</xsd:complexType>
```

```
<xsd:simpleType name="PersonsFirstname">
 <xsd:restriction base="xsd:string">
  <xsd:minLength value="4" />
  <xsd:maxLength value="10" />
 </xsd:restriction>
</xsd:simpleType>
<xsd:simpleType name="PersonsTitle">
 <xsd:restriction base="xsd:string">
  <xsd:enumeration value="Mr." />
  <xsd:enumeration value="Mrs." />
  <xsd:enumeration value="Miss." />
 </xsd:restriction>
</xsd:simpleType>
</xsd:schema>
```

2. Open `instance3.xml` and save the file as `instance4.xml` (no changes required).

3. At the command line, navigate to the folder containing the `example.exe` file and enter the following at the command prompt:

```
example.exe instance4.xml schema4.xsd
```

Hit *Enter* and the file will be successfully validated.

How It Works

The root element is defined as `Contacts` and defines a `sequence` of child elements. The first is a reference to a predefined `name` element, which is defined at a global level in the document.

```
<xsd:element ref="name" />
```

The definition of this name element structures it to conform to that of the FullName complex type definition as specified in the type attribute below. This complexType element is defined globally and the definitions that are used to define the <name> element are placed within this type – this means that you have a reusable collection of elements stored within this complex type.

```
<xsd:complexType name="FullName">
  <xsd:sequence>
   <xsd:element name="first" type="PersonsFirstname"
    minOccurs="0" maxOccurs="1" default="John" />
   <xsd:element name="middle" type="xsd:string"
    minOccurs="0" maxOccurs="unbounded" nillable="true" />
   <xsd:element name="last" type="xsd:string"
    minOccurs="1" maxOccurs="1" default="Doe" />
  </xsd:sequence>
  <xsd:attribute name="title" type="PersonsTitle" default="Mr." />
  </xsd:complexType>
```

Notice that the complexType definition contains elements and attributes which themselves make use of existing simple type definitions allowing powerful reuse of your custom data types.

The reusability of such types is demonstrated with the definition of the friendsName element, which is also of type FullName – the only difference (from the name element above) being that there can be up to 10 instances of this element.

```
<xsd:element name="friendsName" type="FullName" maxOccurs="10" />
```

The final element definition demonstrates the use of an anonymous complex type. The Notes element simply contains a list of entries for each time a note is added. This is a very basic structure and so it's not worth creating a whole new complexType definition for such a simple element. Instead we determine that the entry element can contain any string contents and may be repeated as many times as required.

```
<xsd:element name="Notes">
  <xsd:complexType>
   <xsd:sequence maxOccurs="unbounded">
    <xsd:element name="entry" type="xsd:string" />
   </xsd:sequence>
  </xsd:complexType>
</xsd:element>
```

Grouping and Attributes

Within many of the more complex definitions we create to define any XML document, there are going to be sets of elements, attributes or combinations of both that are always used together. For example, you may group together the first, middle and last names into a single group, or group together the city and country elements of a full address. There is an overlap between grouping and complex types, but you can generally improve the ability to reuse and share element and attribute definitions that are often found together by grouping them and then using these groups within the complex type definitions.

Grouping can be used to group element and attribute definitions and to extend complexType definitions and promote reuse and inheritance of element definitions. A group element can optionally use a name attribute definition to allow it to be referenced via the ref attribute on another group.

The `minOccurs` and `maxOccurs` attributes are used to define how many times the group can be repeated in the containing element, and both of these attributes default to `1`. The value of `minOccurs` must be equal to or greater than zero (zero implying that the group is optional) and `maxOccurs` takes a value equal to or greater than zero, with the value `unbounded` indicating unlimited occurrences. These are only used when the `group` is referred to within the containing XML Schema `element` definition.

To group elements, we use the `group` element combined with a `sequence`, `choice`, or `all` compositor child element (these were covered earlier in this chapter). The following is an example of using the `choice` element to choose a city, where the `choice` child element determines that we will have to select one from our `CityChoice` group.

```
<xsd:group name="CityChoice">
  <xsd:choice>
    <xsd:element name="Glasgow" type="xsd:string" />
    <xsd:element name="Santiago" type="xsd:string" />
    <xsd:element name="New York" type="xsd:string" />
  </xsd:choice>
</xsd:group>
```

This could then be referenced within the schema as follows:

```
<xsd:element name="City">
  <xsd:group ref="CityChoice" minOccurs="1" maxOccurs="1" />
</xsd:element>
```

Using the `sequence` element we now have the following group, which requires that you define a `region` before you define the `CityChoice`.

```
<xsd:group name="Address">
  <xsd:sequence>
    <xsd:element name="region" type="xsd:string" />
    <xsd:group ref="CityChoice" />
  </xsd:sequence>
</xsd:group>
```

Finally, the `all` element implies that all elements may appear once and only once (or not at all), in any order, and must be unique throughout the content. Its content can only be elements and it is limited to the top level of a content model.

The following is an example of a valid use of the `all` element, which allows the items of a `Name` group to be in any order.

```
<xsd:group name="Name">
  <xsd:all>
    <xsd:element name="first" type="xsd:string" />
    <xsd:element name="middle" type="xsd:string" />
    <xsd:element name="last" type="xsd:string" />
  </xsd:all>
</xsd:group>
```

Of course, if we find ourselves wanting to group elements, we also need to group attributes for inheritance and reuse using the `xsd:attributeGroup` element. So if we had a group of attributes that were used often it would be easy to reuse them – it also makes the schema much easier to read.

We could create a simple group of attributes as follows:

```
<xsd:attributeGroup name="contactAttribs">
  <xsd:attribute name="city" type="xsd:string" />
  <xsd:attribute name="country" type="xsd:string" />
  <xsd:attribute name="age" type="xsd:integer" />
</xsd:attributeGroup>
```

The `attributeGroup` definition can then be used within the definition of a `complexType` element as follows:

```
<xsd:element name="contact">
  <xsd:complexType>
    <xsd:attributeGroup ref="contactAttribs" />
  </xsd:complexType>
<xsd:element>
```

So we can then have a fragment that would validate against this definition as follows:

```
...
<contact city="Glasgow" country="Scotland" age="27" />
...
```

Other attribute groups can be nested within an attribute group and they should appear at the end of a complex type definition, just before the closing `complexType` tag.

simpleContent

What you will have come to learn as you go through the sections within this chapter is that one of the main goals of XML Schema is to allow you to build and reuse data type definitions, from the simple built-in data types provided by XML Schema to the simple type definitions which allow you to provide much stricter validation on the possible values of an element or attribute. Reuse can be very powerful, but you may already be questioning how good this actually is. Sure, you can define a subset of titles for a user to choose from or an enumeration of countries from which a user can choose one or more, but in *my* case it isn't always that simple because we don't use *this* title and we definitely need *those* countries to be added to the list of enumerable values. Does that mean you have to define another new type, copy all of the content from the existing type, amend it for your use and hence lose any relation to the validation originally provided by the definition in the first place? You'll be glad to know that the answer is no; XML Schema allows you to extend and restrict details on existing data types, whether they be the built-in data types or the simple type custom data types. This is done using the `simpleContent` element.

The `simpleContent` element is used to restrict or extend an existing built-in data type or simple type within the complex type definition. It can also be used to restrict the values of an `element` definition. It *must* contain a `restriction` or `extension` child element and can *only* be a child of a `complexType` element definition.

The advantage of the simpleContent element is that you can achieve great code reuse by deriving from existing simpleType definitions to extend and restrict the types you have created. This can be as simple as deriving the string data type or as complex as extending an existing simpleType definition and adding attribute definitions to it.

So the following definition could be used to restrict the value of the houseNumber element to an integer with an attribute called houseType that has one of a set of enumeration values.

```
<xsd:element name="houseNumber">
  <xsd:complexType>
    <xsd:simpleContent>
      <xsd:extension base="xsd:int">
        <xsd:attribute name="houseType">
          <xsd:simpleType>
            <xsd:restriction base="xsd:string">
              <xsd:enumeration value="flat"/>
              <xsd:enumeration value="tenement"/>
              <xsd:enumeration value="bungalow"/>
              <xsd:enumeration value="detached"/>
            </xsd:restriction>
          </xsd:simpleType>
        </xsd:attribute>
      </xsd:extension>
    </xsd:simpleContent>
  </xsd:complexType>
</xsd:element>
```

The complexType must be the parent of any simpleContent definition. We then use the extension element because we want to extend the content of this element. We could equally have used restriction if we wanted to restrict the content of this element based on a type.

We define the base attribute on this extension (or restriction) element and this says that we are extending the element with the type of the content within this element being an integer, but the element itself is being extended beyond simply containing an integer to also contain an attribute defining the type of house.

The attribute called houseType is defined and given a base type of string and so values of this attribute are restricted to string data types, followed by a further restriction to a set of enumeration values as we saw earlier using the enumeration facet.

Remember that when working with XML Schema there can be many ways to achieve the same thing. In the above example we could equally have created a houseType data type with the enumerations defined as local to that definition. It is up to the designer of the XML Schema document to decide the preferred techniques for creating the document constraints.

Content Models

Content Models in XSD define allowable content in the elements that may appear in the structure of your schema. We have already looked at mechanisms of creating content models when we discussed the sequence, choice, group, and all elements. Content models are used to restrict the elements, attributes, and types used within your XML document and determine the level to which a user can, or cannot, add their own elements and attributes within an XML instance.

The following are all content models in XSDL:

Any

This is the default content model when an element is declared in XML in that it can contain text, elements and whitespace. You will find this very useful if you want to be able to allow the contents of the elements to be added to without the person having to physically change the schema file.

In the case below, we want the name element to contain *any* other names that we may not have thought of when the schema was created – maidenName being an example.

```
<xsd:schema xmlns:xsd="http://www.w3.org/2001/XMLSchema">
  <xsd:element name="name">
   <xsd:complexType>
    <xsd:sequence>
      <xsd:element name="first" type="xsd:string" />
      <xsd:element name="middle" type="OtherNames" />
      <xsd:element name="last" type="xsd:string" />
    </xsd:sequence>
   </xsd:complexType>
  </xsd:element>
  <xsd:complexType name="OtherNames">
   <xsd:sequence>
    <xsd:any namespace="##any" processContents="lax"
      minOccurs="0" maxOccurs="unbounded"/>
   </xsd:sequence>
  </xsd:complexType>
</xsd:schema>
```

The xsd:any element in the sequence can be used to state the allowable additions for this type (and hence within the middle element to which it is applied). The first is the namespace attribute, which can be any of the following:

- ##any – this means that elements from any namespace can be present.
- ##other – elements from any namespace other than the target namespace of the parent of this element can be present (remember an import may change the target namespace of an element)
- ##local – elements that are not qualified in a namespace can be used.
- ##targetNamespace – any element from the target namespace of the parent of this element can be present (remember an import may change the target namespace of an element).
- (List) – this can be a space-delimited list of valid namespaces of any elements to be added such as your own custom namespaces, ##targetNamespace, and ##local.

The processContents attribute states what is to be done to validate any elements that are created here. It can be one of three values:

- strict – this means that the XML processor **must** obtain the schemas associated with those namespaces and validate any elements and attributes.

❑ `lax` – this is similar to `strict`, except that no errors occur if the processor is unable to find the schema documents (but an error will occur if the schemas are found and an element fails validation).

❑ `skip` – there will be no attempt to get the schema documents to validate the XML document.

A valid instance for the above schema would therefore be:

```
<?xml version="1.0"?>
<name>
  <first>Steven</first>
  <middle>
    <nameInSpain>Esteban</nameInSpain>
  </middle>
  <last>Livingstone-Perez</last>
</name>
```

Empty

Empty elements prevent any text or elements from appearing as children to the element that is declared as being empty and is useful if you wanted to ensure that no child elements or text, or even whitespace can be within this element. Consider an application which contains a section listing products that can be ordered by users and another section which contains the items ordered by that user. You want to prevent the user from adding any orders to the document until they have registered. You can therefore restrict the element from containing any content until the user has registered and then you can update the schema (dynamically as seen in the next chapter) to specify a particular type for that element (such as `OrderType`).

However, it is slightly complex to define an `empty` type in XSD as you don't explicitly declare that the element should be `empty`, rather you restrict it using the `xsd:anyType` type, discussed above – doing this means the element may only carry attributes. The following is an example of a complex type that is empty and allows only the `age` attribute.

```
<xsd:schema xmlns:xsd="http://www.w3.org/2001/XMLSchema">
  <xsd:element name="contact">
    <xsd:complexType>
      <xsd:complexContent>
        <xsd:restriction base="xsd:anyType">
          <xsd:attribute name="age" type="xsd:integer" />
        </xsd:restriction>
      </xsd:complexContent>
    </xsd:complexType>
  </xsd:element>
</xsd:schema>
```

Note two points. The `complexContent` element is required to indicate that the content for the `complexType` is to be extended or restricted – in our case it is to be restricted so the `restriction` element is used. The `restriction` element takes the `base` type you wish to restrict, and because we want to restrict everything, we use the `xsd:anyType` type. This allows an instance like the following:

```
<contact age="78"><!--Nothing allowed in here--></contact>
```

Element

This is what we have been previously discussing when we looked at creating complex types. Note that complex types can be both named and anonymous. They are named when they are given a "name" attribute, and so they can be reused throughout the Schema. They are anonymous when they are defined without a name within an `<element>` tag and defined only for that element. We discussed named and anonymous types earlier in this chapter.

Mixed

The final content model is `mixed` which can contain a mixture of text, content and attributes. We declare a content type of `mixed` by setting the `mixed` attribute on a `complexType` element to `true`.

So, for example, the following is a mixed `complexType` for describing a person's first name.

```
<xsd:schema xmlns:xsd="http://www.w3.org/2001/XMLSchema">
<xsd:element name="contact">
  <xsd:complexType mixed="true">
  <xsd:sequence>
    <xsd:element name="first" type="xsd:string" />
  </xsd:sequence>
  </xsd:complexType>
</xsd:element>
</xsd:schema>
```

An instance with this element could be:

```
<?xml version="1.0"?>
<contact>His first name is<first>Steven</first>.</contact>
```

Notice that the `contact` element contains text as well as the `first` element.

XSD Data Types Compared with .NET Data Types

To be able to (almost) seamlessly work between the XML world and the .NET world we need mappings between the data types that are defined for each. So if we have an element that has been defined as a `Boolean` in XML Schema, how does .NET represent this `Boolean` value? Slightly more complex, how does .NET represent an `ENTITY` or `negativeInteger` XSD data type? Conversely, how do XML Schemas represent .NET data types? How does the `Int32` type map to XML Schemas or even an `int16` or `Single`?

XML Schema data types are defined in the `XmlSchemaDataType` class, and the following table defines the mapping of XML Schema data types to .NET data types.

XML Schema Data Type	.NET Data Type	XML Schema Data Type	.NET Data Type
anyURI	System.Uri	long	System.Int64
base64Binary	System.Byte[]	month	System.DateTime
Boolean	System.Boolean	Name	System.String
Byte	System.SByte	NCName	System.String
Date	System.DateTime	negativeInteger	System.Decimal
dateTime	System.DateTime	NMTOKEN	System.String
decimal	System.Decimal	NMTOKENS	System.String[]
Double	System.Double	nonNegativeInteger	System.Decimal
duration	System.TimeSpan	nonPositiveInteger	System.Decimal
ENTITIES	System.String[]	normalizedString	System.String
ENTITY	System.String	NOTATION	System.String
Float	System.Single	positiveInteger	System.Decimal
gDay	System.DateTime	QName	System.Xml.XmlQualifiedName
gMonthDay	System.DateTime	short	System.Int16
gYear	System.DateTime	string	System.String
gYearMonth	System.DateTime	time	System.DateTime
hexBinary	System.Byte[]	timePeriod	System.DateTime
ID	System.String	token	System.String
IDREF	System.String	unsignedByte	System.Byte
IDREFS	System.String[]	unsignedInt	System.UInt32
int	System.Int32	unsignedLong	System.UInt64
integer	System.Decimal	unsignedShort	System.UInt16
language	System.String		

In the next and following chapters we will see that this mapping is important when it comes to working with XML documents in .NET and serializing .NET data to XML documents as well.

We now have a fuller appreciation of XSDL, and how it is used to develop an XSD that reflects a set of data and business rules, but now we have to rise above that level of detail and discuss the different techniques of applying a schema.

Schema Validation Techniques

Up until this point in the chapter, we have concentrated on creating schemas that can validate our XML documents and have yet to look at how we actually perform the validation process itself. When an XML document is sent to us from a business partner or someone enters details into an XML document or an application within the enterprise receives XML data from another application, we have to bring the document and schema together to perform the validation.

There are three techniques available to us:

❏ Specify the XML Schema file to be used to validate the document within the XML document itself.

❏ Have the XML Schema file within the XML document (and not as a separate file).

❏ Use programmatic techniques to associate an XML Schema with an XML document and invoke the validation process.

In this section we will demonstrate how all these techniques are possible, but the next chapter goes into detail on how to perform programmatic validation with XML Schema.

Validation and Namespaces

The first technique of validation is to provide information within the XML document itself that can indicate to the parser the details of the XML Schema that is to validate this document. The most basic form of this is as follows:

```
<contact xmlns:xsi="http://www.w3.org/2001/XMLSchema-instance"
    xsi:noNamespaceSchemaLocation="someURI">
...
</contact>
```

> You can see an example of this if you go back to the Examples directory and run "examples.exe schema7.xml schema7.xsd" which will cause the XML instance to be validated against the schema document.

The namespace `xmlns:xsi="http://www.w3.org/2001/XMLSchema-instance"` is required and is a reference to the XML Schema namespace for instances. You must provide this if you intend to validate your XML instances directly with no programmatic techniques. The `xsi:noNamespaceSchemaLocation` attribute contains the URI of an XSD document that is to validate the XML instance and is only used when the XML document does not require validation against any qualified nodes (that is, nodes bound to a given namespace). Programmatic assignment of an XSD Schema actually overrides any internally defined association.

There is a slightly more complex, but also more common, technique for specifying validation information within the XML document. This is because this technique also caters for namespaces within the XML document; with the use of namespaces becoming essential to most documents, you will tend to make use of this technique more frequently. The following template shows how this technique works:

```
<contact xmlns:xsi="http://www.w3.org/2001/XMLSchema-instance"
    xmlns:a="namespace1" xmlns:b="namespace2" xmlns:z="namespaceN"
    xsi:schemaLocation="namespace1 uri1 namespace2 uri2 namespaceN uriN">
    ...
</contact>
```

We use the `schemaLocation` attribute as a hint to the processor on how to associate nodes defined within the document, bound to given namespaces, against XML Schema documents that will validate those nodes. So the `schemaLocation` attribute first takes the namespace and then the URI of the document to perform the validation; this is repeated for each namespace and XML Schema document. So in the above example, all nodes within the current document that are in the `namespace1` namespace will be validated against the XML Schema document at the location `uri1`.

A schema document itself is also viewed as a collection of types and definitions that all belong to a single namespace, which is called the **target namespace**. This target namespace associates the definitions of an XML Schema document with a single target namespace URI, independent of all other namespace declarations within that XML Schema document. The most basic form of this is shown below:

```
<xsd:schema xmlns:xsd="http://www.w3.org/2001/XMLSchema"
    xmlns="namespace1" xmlns:a="namespace1" xmlns:z="namespaceN"
    targetNamespace="namespace1">
    ...
</xsd:schema>
```

Try It Out: Namespace Validation

We are now going to demonstrate how you can validate an XML document by directly placing the schema location information within the XML file. This is a useful technique when an XML file is to be passed around, perhaps from application to application or even between business partners. It is easy for the XML file and its accompanying XML Schema document to get separated and then you could be unable to validate the XML file; however, if the details are specified within the XML file itself, then you only need to pass around a single document which points to a specific URL for validation.

We will also need to use a different executable for this example. This is because we now only need one parameter, as the schema information is stored within the file.

1. Change to the `Example2` project directory in the code downloads and create a new XML Schema file called `schema8.xsd`. Enter the following code into this:

```
<xsd:schema targetNamespace="http://www.deltabis.com/Contact"
  xmlns:xsd=http://www.w3.org/2001/XMLSchema
  xmlns="http://www.deltabis.com/Contact">

  <xsd:element name="ContactDetails" type="ContactDetails" />
  <xsd:complexType name="ContactDetails">
    <xsd:sequence minOccurs="1" maxOccurs="1">
      <xsd:element name="name" type="Name" minOccurs="1" maxOccurs="1" />
    </xsd:sequence>
  </xsd:complexType>
```

```
      <xsd:complexType name="Name">
       <xsd:sequence>
        <xsd:element name="first" type="PersonsFirstname"
          minOccurs="0" maxOccurs="1" default="John" />
        <xsd:element name="middle" type="xsd:string"
          minOccurs="0" maxOccurs="unbounded" nillable="true" />
        <xsd:element name="last" type="xsd:string"
          minOccurs="1" maxOccurs="1" default="Doe" />
       </xsd:sequence>
       <xsd:attribute name="title" type="PersonsTitle" default="Mr." />
      </xsd:complexType>
      <xsd:simpleType name="PersonsFirstname">
       <xsd:restriction base="xsd:string">
        <xsd:minLength value="4" />
        <xsd:maxLength value="10" />
       </xsd:restriction>
      </xsd:simpleType>
      <xsd:simpleType name="PersonsTitle">
       <xsd:restriction base="xsd:string">
        <xsd:enumeration value="Mr." />
        <xsd:enumeration value="Mrs." />
        <xsd:enumeration value="Miss." />
       </xsd:restriction>
      </xsd:simpleType>
     </xsd:schema>
```

2. In the same directory, create a new XML file called `instance8.xml` and add the following to the document.

```
<ct:ContactDetails xmlns:ct="http://www.deltabis.com/Contact"
   xmlns:xsi="http://www.w3.org/2001/XMLSchema-instance"
   xsi:schemaLocation="http://www.deltabis.com/Contact schema8.xsd">
  <name title="Mr.">
    <first>Steven</first>
    <middle />
    <last>Livingstone-Perez</last>
  </name>
</ct:ContactDetails>
```

3. At the command prompt type:

```
example2.exe instance8.xml
```

Press *Enter* and the file will be successfully validated.

How It Works

The XML Schema file itself was a shortened version of the one you worked with earlier. However, there were a few new lines at the top of the file:

```
<xsd:schema targetNamespace="http://www.deltabis.com/Contact"
   xmlns:xsd="http://www.w3.org/2001/XMLSchema"
   xmlns="http://www.deltabis.com/Contact">
   ...
</xsd:schema>
```

Now there are two namespace definitions within the document, the XML Schema namespace and our own custom namespace. What this means is that any **globally** defined elements or attributes are qualified in the default namespace that *we* have defined – that is, the ContactDetails element is qualified in the namespace http://www.deltabis.com/Contact.

Within the XML document instance we define it so it uses namespaces.

```
<?xml version="1.0"?>
<ct:ContactDetails xmlns:ct="http://www.deltabis.com/Contact"
   xmlns:xsi="www.w3.org/2001/XMLSchema-instance"
   xsi:schemaLocation="http://www.deltabis.com/Contact contact.xsd">
...
</ct:ContactDetails>
```

So, a namespace is defined on the root element that associates the ct prefix with the namespace http://www.deltabis.com/Contact. We can then use the schemaLocation attribute to associate all elements defined within this namespace in the instance document with the XML Schema document found at contact.xsd. The XSD also has a target namespace of this URI and so validation can be invoked.

Programmatic Validation

The .NET Framework offers classes that allow you to perform dynamic validation of an XML document using a specified XML Schema document. Details of programmatic validation of XML Schemas are discussed in the next chapter.

Inline Schemas

Inline schemas are schemas that are included in the actual XML document that they validate. This offers the obvious advantage of having one file containing both sets of information; the disadvantage is that reuse is lost and the file size increases. You may like the idea of using this technique if you have XML documents that are passed around to applications or business partners who do not have access to the locations where your schemas are stored. Additionally you may prefer not to use separate documents in these cases in case the documents get separated from each other and you lose any validation.

The inline schema has the following general format:

```
<wrapperElement>
   <xsd:schema>
   ...
   </xsd:schema>
```

```
    <root>
    ...
    </root>
  </wrapperElement>
```

The wrapper element can be called anything you like and is only used to wrap the combination of the schema and the instance. Therefore, at the first child element of this wrapper element you will have the XSD Schema element, as shown. The second child will be the root of the actual XML document that is to be validated by the inline schema.

Try It Out: Using an Inline Schema

In this example we are going to show how we could apply inline schema validation to any of the examples we have been working with in this chapter. We will work with a slightly simplified version of the last few schemas we have been working with (simply to save space!).

1. Navigate to the folder containing the **Example2** project and you will see `Example2.exe`.

2. Create a new XML file called `instance9.xml`, add the following code to it, and save the file.

```
<data>
  <xsd:schema xmlns:xsd="http://www.w3.org/2001/XMLSchema">
    <xsd:element name="name">
  <xsd:complexType>
  <xsd:sequence>
    <xsd:element name="first" type="xsd:string"
      minOccurs="0" maxOccurs="1" default="John" />
    <xsd:element name="middle" type="xsd:string" minOccurs="0"
      maxOccurs="unbounded" nillable="true" />
    <xsd:element name="last" type="xsd:string" minOccurs="1"
      maxOccurs="1" default="Doe" />
  </xsd:sequence>
  <xsd:attribute name="title" type="PersonsTitle" default="Mr." />
  </xsd:complexType>
    </xsd:element>
    <xsd:simpleType name="PersonsTitle">
  <xsd:restriction base="xsd:string">
    <xsd:enumeration value="Mr." />
    <xsd:enumeration value="Mrs." />
    <xsd:enumeration value="Miss." />
  </xsd:restriction>
    </xsd:simpleType>
  </xsd:schema>
  <name title="Mr.">
    <first>Steven</first>
    <middle />
    <last>Livingstone-Perez</last>
  </name>
</data>
```

3. Open a command prompt in the folder containing the `example2.exe` file and enter the following command:

```
example2.exe instance9.xml
```

Hit *Enter* and the file will be successfully validated.

4. Now modify the instance9.xml file and change the value of the title attribute on the name element to Mrr. near the end of the file and re-run the validation. This time you will be shown the following validation message:

How It Works

The data wrapper element is used to wrap the XML and XSD combination. The first child element of this node is the XML Schema document that we have been working with.

```
<?xml version="1.0" ?>
<data>
    <xsd:schema xmlns:xsd="http://www.w3.org/2001/XMLSchema">
    ...
    </xsd:schema>
    <name>
    ...
    </name>
</data>
```

Schema Modularization

It may be that you want to maintain a central source of XML schemas within your enterprise from which other developers can create new schemas using these components. You may even use the schemas of applications and business partners locally and over the Internet to build your schemas. In XML Schemas, the import and include elements allow you to reuse existing schemas rather than re-entering them every time.

Including Schemas

The include element is the simplest way of doing this and simply adds the elements defined in the schema to the including schema. It is essential to note that for this to work the targetNamespace property of the included schema must have the same namespace as the targetNamespace attribute of the including schema or have no targetNamespace defined at all. The last point means that your XML instance document doesn't need to know anything about these modularized schemas and so we can work as we have been doing thus far.

When you define a `targetNamespace` for a given XSD file, all references to elements defined within that document must by either the target namespace or in another namespace to which they belong.

Try It Out: Including XML Schema Documents

This example will demonstrate how you can include data from other XML Schema documents to improve the modularity of your design. We will again use a slightly different executable to be able to dynamically associate a namespace with the schemas in these examples.

1. Navigate to the folder containing the **Example3** project and you will find `Example3.exe`.

2. Create a new XML Schema file called `schema10.xsd` and enter the following code into it:

```
<xsd:schema targetNamespace="http://www.deltabis.com/Contact"
    xmlns:xsd="http://www.w3.org/2001/XMLSchema"
    xmlns="http://www.deltabis.com/Contact">
  <xsd:include schemaLocation="schema10inc.xsd" />
  <xsd:element name="ContactDetails" type="ContactDetails" />
  <xsd:complexType name="ContactDetails">
    <xsd:sequence minOccurs="1" maxOccurs="1">
      <xsd:element name="name" type="Name" minOccurs="1" maxOccurs="1" />
    </xsd:sequence>
  </xsd:complexType>
  <xsd:complexType name="Name">
    <xsd:sequence>
      <xsd:element name="first" type="PersonsFirstname" minOccurs="0"
          maxOccurs="1" default="John" />
      <xsd:element name="middle" type="xsd:string" minOccurs="0"
          maxOccurs="unbounded" nillable="true" />
      <xsd:element name="last" type="xsd:string" minOccurs="1" maxOccurs="1"
          default="Doe" />
    </xsd:sequence>
    <xsd:attribute name="title" type="PersonsTitle" default="Mr." />
  </xsd:complexType>
</xsd:schema>
```

3. Create another XML Schema file called `schema10inc.xsd` and enter the following code:

```
<xsd:schema xmlns:xsd="http://www.w3.org/2001/XMLSchema">
  <xsd:simpleType name="PersonsFirstname">
    <xsd:restriction base="xsd:string">
      <xsd:minLength value="4" />
      <xsd:maxLength value="10" />
    </xsd:restriction>
  </xsd:simpleType>
  <xsd:simpleType name="PersonsTitle">
    <xsd:restriction base="xsd:string">
      <xsd:enumeration value="Mr." />
      <xsd:enumeration value="Mrs." />
      <xsd:enumeration value="Miss." />
    </xsd:restriction>
  </xsd:simpleType>
</xsd:schema>
```

4. Create a new XML file called `instance10.xml` and enter the following XML code:

```
<ct:ContactDetails xmlns:ct="http://www.deltabis.com/Contact">
  <name title="Mr.">
    <first>Steven</first>
    <middle />
    <last>Livingstone-Perez</last>
  </name>
</ct:ContactDetails>
```

5. At the command line, navigate to the folder containing the `example3.exe` file and enter the following at the command prompt:

example3.exe instance10.xml schema10.xsd

Hit *Enter* and the file will be successfully validated.

6. Now modify the `instance10.xml` file and change the value of the `title` attribute on the name element to `Mrr.` and re-run the validation. This time you will be shown a validation error message similar to that in the last *Try It Out*.

How It Works

In this example we create a new default namespace definition in the namespace `http://www.deltabis.com/Contact`. Now in order to create a valid target namespace, we must set the `targetNamespace` attribute to one of the namespaces defined in the document; of course in our case, beyond the XML Schema namespace, we only have one declaration so this becomes our target namespace.

```
<xsd:schema xmlns:xsd="http://www.w3.org/2001/XMLSchema"
    xmlns="http://www.deltabis.com/Contact"
    targetNamespace="http://www.deltabis.com/Contact">
```

We also want to include the simple type definitions that we have now removed from the current XML Schema file and put into `schema10inc.xsd`, and so we use the `include` element with the `schemaLocation` pointing to this file. Note that the `include` element **must** be declared at the top of the file, before any templates are defined.

```
<xsd:include schemaLocation="schema10inc.xsd" />
```

Now, when we don't specify the target namespace as the default namespace, a prefix pointing to the target namespace is required to qualify the types that are referenced. In this case we need to prefix type references with the prefix `ct` as shown below.

```
<xsd:element name="name" type="Name" minOccurs="1" maxOccurs="1" />
<xsd:element name="previousName" type="ct:PreviousName" minOccurs="1"
    maxOccurs="1" />
<xsd:element name="ContactFamilyInfo" type="MaleFamilyInfo" minOccurs="0"
    maxOccurs="1"/>
```

The same qualified type references are required for other definitions within the XML Schema; this includes the value of base attributes of `extension` or `restriction` elements.

The `schema10inc.xsd` file is a very basic XSD, with no namespace qualification and importantly, no target namespace; therefore it falls into the target namespace defined in the `schema10.xsd` file.

The last thing that is done is the updating of the XML instance file to reflect that the root element is now qualified in a namespace. This requires the namespace that was the target namespace of the XSD file to be defined, and the root element qualified in this namespace. Remember that it is only the elements that have been defined **globally** (that is, a child of the `schema` element) in the XSD that have to be qualified in this way – in our case this applies only to the `ContactDetails` element.

```
<ct:ContactDetails xmlns:ct="http://www.deltabis.com/Contact">
...
</ct:ContactDetails>
```

Importing Schemas

Including schemas as discussed above is a simple way of using XML Schema files that either define no `targetNamespace` in the document or have been defined with the same `targetNamespace` (typically to deliberately break the files into smaller components).

However, it is not always the case that the target namespace values are the same; and when you get to the Internet and business partner relationships, it is very seldom that your target namespace and the one of your business partner (or application) are the same. This means that you cannot use the `include` element to bring these components together – instead you have to look at the XML Schema `import` element.

Reuse of schemas with different target namespaces can also be accomplished via the `import` element, which is used when you want to reference types without necessarily bringing them into your schema. In this case you identify the namespace to be imported *as well as* the location of the schema.

Once you have specified the location of the schema document to import as well as the target namespace to use, you must also declare that target namespace within the importing document. So, you find the target namespace of the document you want to import, declare that namespace within the main XML schema document and associate this namespace with a prefix.

Once that is done, if you wish to use any definition (`element`, `attribute`, `simpleType`, `complexType`) from the imported schema, you must qualify that type by using the prefix in front of it (for example, `myprefix:importedType`).

The most effective way to understand this process is to look at an example.

Try It Out: Importing Other XML Schema Documents

This example will demonstrate how you can include data from other XML Schema documents to improve the modularity of your design.

1. Copy the file `schema10.xsd` that you created in the last *Try It Out* and make the modifications as highlighted in the file below. Save the file as `schema11.xsd`.

```
<xsd:schema xmlns:xsd="http://www.w3.org/2001/XMLSchema"
    xmlns:ct="http://www.deltabis.com/Contact"
    xmlns:st="urn:simpleTypeDefns"
    targetNamespace="http://www.deltabis.com/Contact">

  <xsd:import namespace="urn:simpleTypeDefns" schemaLocation="schema11inc.xsd" />

  <xsd:element name="ContactDetails" type="ContactDetails" />
  <xsd:complexType name="ContactDetails">
    <xsd:sequence minOccurs="1" maxOccurs="1">
      <xsd:element name="name" type="Name" minOccurs="1" maxOccurs="1" />
    </xsd:sequence>
  </xsd:complexType>
  <xsd:complexType name="Name">
    <xsd:sequence>
      <xsd:element name="first" type="st:PersonsFirstname"
          minOccurs="0" maxOccurs="1" default="John" />
      <xsd:element name="middle" type="xsd:string" minOccurs="0"
          maxOccurs="unbounded" nillable="true" />
      <xsd:element name="last" type="xsd:string" minOccurs="1"
          maxOccurs="1" default="Doe" />
    </xsd:sequence>
    <xsd:attribute name="title" type="st:PersonsTitle" default="Mr." />
  </xsd:complexType>
</xsd:schema>
```

2. Copy the file schema11inc.xsd that you created in the last *Try It Out*, make the modifications as highlighted in the file below, and save the file as schema9inc.xsd.

```
<xsd:schema xmlns:xsd="http://www.w3.org/2001/XMLSchema"
    xmlns="urn:simlpeTypeDefns"
    targetNamespace="urn:simpleTypeDefns">
  <xsd:simpleType name="PersonsFirstname">
  <xsd:restriction base="xsd:string">
    <xsd:minLength value="4"/>
    <xsd:maxLength value="10"/>
  </xsd:restriction>
  </xsd:simpleType>

  <xsd:simpleType name="PersonsTitle">
  <xsd:restriction base="xsd:string">
    <xsd:enumeration value="Mr." />
    <xsd:enumeration value="Mrs." />
    <xsd:enumeration value="Miss." />
  </xsd:restriction>
  </xsd:simpleType>
</xsd:schema>
```

3. Copy instance10.xml and rename the copied file instance11.xml.

4. At the command line, navigate to the folder containing the example3.exe file and enter the following at the command prompt:

```
example3.exe instance11.xml schema11.xsd
```

Hit *Enter* and the file will be successfully validated.

5. Now modify the `instance11.xml` file and change the value of the `title` attribute on the name element to "Mrr." and re-run the validation. You should again see a validation error message similar to that in the last *Try It Out*.

How It Works

In this example we first added a new namespace declaration to the schema root element of the main XSD file.

```
xmlns:st="urn:simpleTypeDefns"
```

Following this we imported the XML Schema file `schema11inc.xsd` and, because this is in a different namespace to the `targetNamespace` of the current document, we also specified the `targetNamespace` of the imported document in the `namespace` attribute. Notice that this is the same as the namespace associated with the `st` prefix above. This is required because we can now qualify elements and types in the imported XSD in this namespace.

As an example of this, the `title` attribute is set to the `PersonsTitle` simple type, which is defined in the imported XML Schema file. Because of this, the reference to the type must be qualified and so the `st` prefix must be used.

```
<xsd:attribute name="title" type="st:PersonsTitle" default="Mr."/>
```

Similarly, this is repeated for any definition referencing the `PersonsFirstName` simple type, which is also defined in the imported file.

No modifications are required to the XML instance. If there are global elements referenced from your imported schema, however, you will have to qualify these in the XML instance in the appropriate namespace.

Common Uses of Schemas

Schemas will become an essential part of working with XML, but you may be wondering where you could currently find schemas being used. As they are relatively new there are still ideas and applications surfacing that use XML Schemas in different ways from what has been seen before. However, here are some of the most common and effective scenarios for using a schema at the time of writing.

Validating Documents

One of the most basic problems with XML documents at the moment, whether they were created manually using an editing tool, using the DOM, or by an XSLT transform process, is ensuring that the resultant XML document is actually in a well-defined format. Remember that by well-formed we are describing the condition by which a given document is valid according to the XML 1.0 specification. This is an important process whether you are writing the XML file, storing the XML within a column in a database, or displaying it in an XML reader (such as Microsoft Word).

When they are not in a well-defined format, it is very difficult to intelligently read the data from them – it is even trickier if the elements and attributes are named differently from what we are expecting. How are we supposed to write an application that reads data from an XML file if both its structure and element names vary?

This is a basic problem that schemas have been created to solve. You can create a schema that defines the structure and content of an XML document and at a point, whether during the creation of the document, or during the reading of the document, you validate the document against its schema. The diagram below illustrates this process:

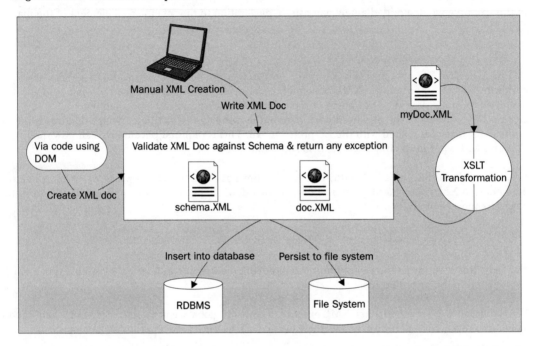

In this scenario, whenever an XML document is created, the resultant document will be validated against a schema. This allows us to ensure that before any data is written to a database or saved to the file system that it is valid according to the rules set out in the schema. If there is a problem during the validation process, an exception will be raised to the client and it must handle what to do next. Typically it will display a message indicating where in the XML document the problem lies (for example, you cannot have an <address> element as a child of a <name> element).

Application Integration

Increasingly, XML is seen as a vehicle to get data from one application to another application in your enterprise. Legacy applications on a mainframe can be exposed to the Internet via an intermediate application, using XML as the data transport format. Furthermore, applications running on UNIX can communicate with web applications running on Windows, again using XML as the data transport format. Even distributed Windows-based applications within the enterprise could expose a simple XML interface to allow direct communication using XML.

The main source of error, however, is when the data being communicated is either not well-formed or not valid data (according to the consuming application). So, although the following XML fragment may be valid for the `UpdateOrder()` method Java object on a UNIX box:

```
<order oid="8762"></order>
```

if the following is the XML that is sent to it from the Windows client:

```
<order ordid="PC8762">...</order>
```

we will have two problems. The first is that the Java application won't be able to find an attribute called `oid` because in the Windows VB application it is called `ordid`. The second is that, whereas the VB application uses a `PC` before each of the order identification numbers, the Java application does not. This will cause the entire application to fail.

Ideally, the Windows application could use a schema to ensure that the data it was sending to the legacy Java application was in fact correctly formatted and the data within it was valid for that application. If the validation were to fail, then it still has the details locally and so can update the XML fragment to read correctly, revalidate and then send the XML to the UNIX-based application.

Business Partner Integration

In some situations you may come to an agreement with a business partner to work using the same closed XML document structure (in other words you decide on the structure and data yourselves). In this case you can use a schema to ensure that any XML data that is sent between them is valid. The validation is done locally and if the document is valid it is then sent to the partner; otherwise it has to be updated to correct the problems.

However, there is another option. It is becoming increasingly popular to use repositories of schema documents, held on the Internet, that are common throughout the industry. In this case all your current and future business partners can format their data according to a single model, and this model can be validated by a single schema from any application. The following example demonstrates this for a purchase order schema.

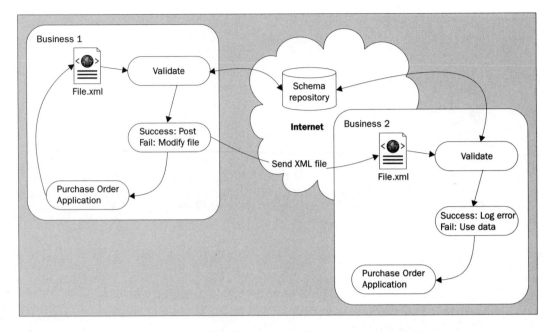

In this case, Business 1 creates a new XML purchase order, File.xml, which is to be posted to a partner site (Business 2). After it is created, it is first validated; this process reads the schema file from the central repository and checks to see whether the XML document is valid according to the constraints in this schema. If the file is valid then the XML file is posted to the partner site; otherwise it is returned to the purchase order application with the details of the problem.

When Business 2 receives the XML file, the first thing it does is validate it against the relevant schema in the central repository. This means the file has been validated twice, which is fairly common in the real world, where business partners could have limited knowledge of each other. An enterprise sending XML details to one of its own remote offices may validate only once, for example, when the application is received by Business 2. If validation is successful then the data is integrated into the application and processed. If there is a failure the error is logged and Business 1 may be automatically contacted or otherwise.

Case Study – Create an XSD Schema

In this section we are going to demonstrate an XML Schema for the case study we have been working on thus far. We will build a full XML Schema that will be able to validate the CaseStudy.xml file and notify us of an invalid structure or any invalid content values. This idea will allow us to progress to the next chapter where we look at the code used to perform the validation.

Throughout this chapter, hints have been given to you as to how this is going to look and so you will notice some of the code being reused. Other parts of interest will be explained to you.

> **The code for this section can be found in the** `XmlDocVal` **project folder in the code download.**
>
> **To validate the** `CaseStudy.xml` **document against the XML Schema document, you go to the** `XmlDocVal` **project and run the following at the command line.**
>
> `xmldocval CaseStudy.xml contact.xsd`

The XML document instance called `CaseStudy.xml` is as follows:

```xml
<?xml version="1.0"?>
<ct:ContactDetails xmlns:ct="http://www.deltabis.com/Contact"
    updateDate="1999-12-01"
    xmlns:xsi="http://www.w3.org/2001/XMLSchema-instance"
    xsi:schemaLocation="http://www.deltabis.com/Contact contact.xsd">
  <name title="Mr.">
    <first>Steven</first>
    <middle>S.</middle>
    <last>Livingstone</last>
  </name>

  <contactInfo>
    <item type="phone">72993</item>
    <item type="phone">2933</item>
    <item type="fax">98484</item>
    <item type="email">steven@someaddress.com</item>
    <item type="email">ntw_uk@hotmail.com</item>
  </contactInfo>

  <homeAddress xsi:type="ct:UKAddress">
    <name>Steven Livingstone</name>
    <street>6 Brackla Avenue</street>
    <city>Glasgow</city>
    <postcode>CB11JR</postcode>
  </homeAddress>

  <workAddress xsi:type="ct:USAddress">
    <name>IBM Corporation</name>
    <street>7829 San Calle</street>
    <city>San Jose</city>
    <state>CA</state>
    <zip>90210</zip>
  </workAddress>

  <ct:notes>hello</ct:notes>
</ct:ContactDetails>
```

This is quite an extension to the XML instance we have been working with previously. We can now hold name information, contact information, home and work details and any associated notes about the contact. Notice that again a prefix has been associated with the `http://www.deltabis.com/Contact` namespace. This prefix, however, is only required on the `ContactDetails` and `notes` elements as these are the only ones that have been globally declared in our XSD files (as you will see).

The main XML Schema file, called `contact.xsd`, is as follows and this is the file that the XML instance is validated against.

```
<schema targetNamespace="http://www.deltabis.com/Contact"
    xmlns="http://www.w3.org/2001/XMLSchema"
    xmlns:ct="http://www.deltabis.com/Contact">

  <annotation>
    <documentation xml:lang="en">
      Schema for Contact Information.
      Includes: address.xsd
    </documentation>
  </annotation>

  <!-- include address constructs -->
  <include schemaLocation="address.xsd"/>

  <element name="ContactDetails" type="ct:ContactDetails"/>

  <complexType name="ContactDetails">
    <annotation>
      <documentation>
        All ContactDetails which takes name, homeAddress,
        an optional work Address and any number of additional
        notes about the person. The update date is also stored
        as an attribute.
      </documentation>
    </annotation>
    <sequence minOccurs="1" maxOccurs="1">
      <element name="name" type="ct:name" minOccurs="1"
          maxOccurs="1" />
      <element name="contactInfo" type="ct:contactInfo"
          minOccurs="1" maxOccurs="1" />
      <element name="homeAddress" type="ct:Address" minOccurs="1"
          maxOccurs="1" />
      <element name="workAddress" type="ct:Address" minOccurs="0"
          maxOccurs="1" />
      <element ref="ct:notes" minOccurs="0" maxOccurs="unbounded"/>
    </sequence>
    <attribute name="updateDate" type="date"/>
  </complexType>

  <complexType name="name">
    <annotation>
      <documentation>
```

```
        Person's name as firstname middlename lastname.
        Middle name takes the value "I." where I is the
        initial.
        Additionally, there is an attribute enumeration.
      </documentation>
    </annotation>
    <sequence>
      <element name="first" type="string"/>
      <element name="middle">
        <simpleType>
          <restriction base="string">
            <pattern value="[A-Z]\."/>
          </restriction>
        </simpleType>
      </element>
      <element name="last" type="string"/>
    </sequence>
    <attribute name="title" type="ct:title"/>
</complexType>

<complexType name="contactInfo">
  <annotation>
    <documentation>
      Contact Information for the individual.
      Should only have email, phone and fax.
    </documentation>
  </annotation>
  <sequence minOccurs="1" maxOccurs="1">
    <element name="item" minOccurs="1" maxOccurs="unbounded">
      <complexType>
        <simpleContent>
          <extension base="string">
            <attribute name="type"
                   type="ct:contactMethods" />
          </extension>
        </simpleContent>
      </complexType>
    </element>
  </sequence>
</complexType>

<element name="notes" type="string"/>

<!-- Title Derivations -->
<simpleType name="title">
  <restriction base="string">
    <enumeration value="Mr." />
    <enumeration value="Mrs." />
    <enumeration value="Ms." />
    <enumeration value="Miss." />
    <enumeration value="Dr." />
    <enumeration value="Rev." />
    <enumeration value="Sir." />
```

```
      </restriction>
    </simpleType>

    <!-- Contacts -->
    <simpleType name="contactMethods">
      <restriction base="string">
        <enumeration value="phone" />
        <enumeration value="fax" />
        <enumeration value="email" />
      </restriction>
    </simpleType>
  </schema>
```

The first thing that may strike you is that we no longer use the xsd prefix. As was stated earlier, this is just a prefix you choose to use; it is common to make the XML Schema namespace the default namespace and so you don't have to qualify every element. We have done that here.

Again we have the usual namespace declarations at the top of the file and the definition of the targetNamespace attribute. As is appropriate for real world scenarios, we have also inserted documentation explaining each of the elements that are used throughout the document.

The contents of the address.xsd file are included in this file; this file has the same target namespace as the current one (see below), so we can use include rather than import.

```
<include schemaLocation="address.xsd"/>
```

Notice that when we define the homeAddress and workAddress elements, we set their type to be the Address complex type, which is defined in the included file and in the namespace associated with the ct prefix.

```
<element name="homeAddress" type="ct:Address" minOccurs="1" maxOccurs="1" />
<element name="workAddress" type="ct:Address" minOccurs="0" maxOccurs="1" />
```

Next, notice that the validation of the middle element has been improved. It is now restricted to a string type, but further to this, the pattern element is used to define a regular expression that any string will be tested against. The regular expression is [A-Z]\.. which means that the value of the middle element can be any upper case letter followed by a period; in other words an initial!

```
<element name="middle">
  <simpleType>
    <restriction base="string">
      <pattern value="[A-Z]\."/>
    </restriction>
  </simpleType>
</element>
```

The definition of the `contactInfo` complex type is interesting because it defines an element that can have an attribute. If the attribute was defined right after the sequence element, then it would apply to the element that this `complexType` is assigned to. But it is *supposed* to apply to the `item` child element. To achieve this, we define the element and use no `type` attribute. Next we create a `complexType` element as a child of this. Next the `simpleContent` element can be used because we are going to extend using an attribute and no complex types. So below this we use the `extension` element (we want to add the attribute definition to that of the element) and set the base type of this to string. This means that the content of the `item` element will have to be a string. We then define the attribute we want to add, called `type`, and the *type* of this is the `contactMethods` simple type.

```
<sequence minOccurs="1" maxOccurs="1">
  <element name="item" minOccurs="1" maxOccurs="unbounded">
    <complexType>
      <simpleContent>
        <extension base="string">
          <attribute name="type" type="ct:contactMethods" />
        </extension>
      </simpleContent>
    </complexType>
  </element>
</sequence>
```

The rest of this XSD are fairly simple `simpleType` definitions defining limitations on the `title` and `contact` details.

The included XSD document `address.xsd` is as follows:

```
<schema targetNamespace="http://www.deltabis.com/Contact"
        xmlns="http://www.w3.org/2001/XMLSchema"
        xmlns:ct="http://www.deltabis.com/Contact">

  <annotation>
    <documentation xml:lang="en">
      Addresses Schema, used in Contact.xsd.
    </documentation>
  </annotation>

  <complexType name="Address">
    <annotation>
      <documentation xml:lang="en">
        Addresses contains the name, street and city.
      </documentation>
    </annotation>
    <sequence>
      <element name="name"   type="string"/>
      <element name="street" type="string"/>
      <element name="city"   type="string"/>
    </sequence>
  </complexType>

  <complexType name="USAddress">
```

```
      <annotation>
        <documentation xml:lang="en">
          Specific US Addresses based on the Address type.
          Adds the state enumeration and zip.
        </documentation>
      </annotation>
      <complexContent>
        <extension base="ct:Address">
          <sequence>
            <element name="state" type="ct:USState"/>
            <element name="zip"   type="positiveInteger"/>
          </sequence>
        </extension>
      </complexContent>
    </complexType>

    <complexType name="UKAddress">
      <annotation>
        <documentation xml:lang="en">
          Specific UK Addresses based on the Address type.
          Adds postcode enumeration.
        </documentation>
      </annotation>
      <complexContent>
        <extension base="ct:Address">
          <sequence>
            <element name="postcode" type="ct:UKPostcode"/>
          </sequence>
        </extension>
      </complexContent>
    </complexType>

    <simpleType name="USState">
      <restriction base="string">
        <enumeration value="AK"/>
        <enumeration value="AL"/>
        <enumeration value="AR"/>
        <enumeration value="CA"/>
        <!-- list of others ... -->
      </restriction>
    </simpleType>

    <simpleType name="Postcode">
      <restriction base="string" />
    </simpleType>

    <!-- simple type definition for UKPostcode -->
    <simpleType name="UKPostcode">
      <restriction base="ct:Postcode">
        <pattern value="[A-Z]{2}\d\d[A-Z]{2}" />
      </restriction>
    </simpleType>
  </schema>
```

The first thing to note is that the target namespace is the same as the previous XML Schema file.

First an `Address` type is defined, which has fairly basic element definitions within it.

```
<complexType name="Address">
  <annotation>
    <documentation xml:lang="en">
      Addresses contains the name, street and city.
    </documentation>
  </annotation>
  <sequence>
    <element name="name"   type="string"/>
    <element name="street" type="string"/>
    <element name="city"   type="string"/>
  </sequence>
</complexType>
```

The main reason this is of interest is because it acts as the base type for two other derived types, which are the complex types `USAddress` and `UKAddress`. The `USAddress` extends the `Address` type, adding a set of values based on a `USState` enumeration type and a `PostCode` simple type definition.

The `UKAddress` type also adds a postcode definition, but because it is different from a US zip code, an alternative simple type definition is used. This type again uses a regular expression to test any entry with to ensure it is in the format "XX00XX", where X is any letter and 0 is any number.

```
<simpleType name="UKPostcode">
  <restriction base="ct:Postcode">
    <pattern value="[A-Z]{2}\d\d[A-Z]{2}" />
  </restriction>
</simpleType>
```

You can test that the XML document is actually valid by going to the `XmlValDoc` project directory and at the command prompt type:

`XmlDocVal CaseStudy.xml`

Hit *Enter* and the following will be displayed:

If you modify the `postcode` element in `CaseStudy.xml` file to the following and revalidate.

```
<postcode>CB11JRD</postcode>
```

You will get the following output indicating that it is an invalid UK postcode.

We will demonstrate how this can be integrated with the GUI application in the next chapter, which focuses on the .NET side of XML Schemas.

Summary

This chapter taught you a great deal about the XML Schema language and its usage. We discussed the following:

❑   The role of XML Schema Definitions (XSD)

❑   Validating an XML document using an XSD

❑   The XML Schema language

❑   Data Type support in XSD

❑   Complex Types and Content Models

❑   Introduction to how XSD data types map to .NET data types

❑   Techniques for validating schemas

❑   Working with schemas inline

❑   Modularization of schemas

❑   Improving the case study using XML Schemas

In the next chapter we move on to look at how schemas can be used programmatically using .NET.

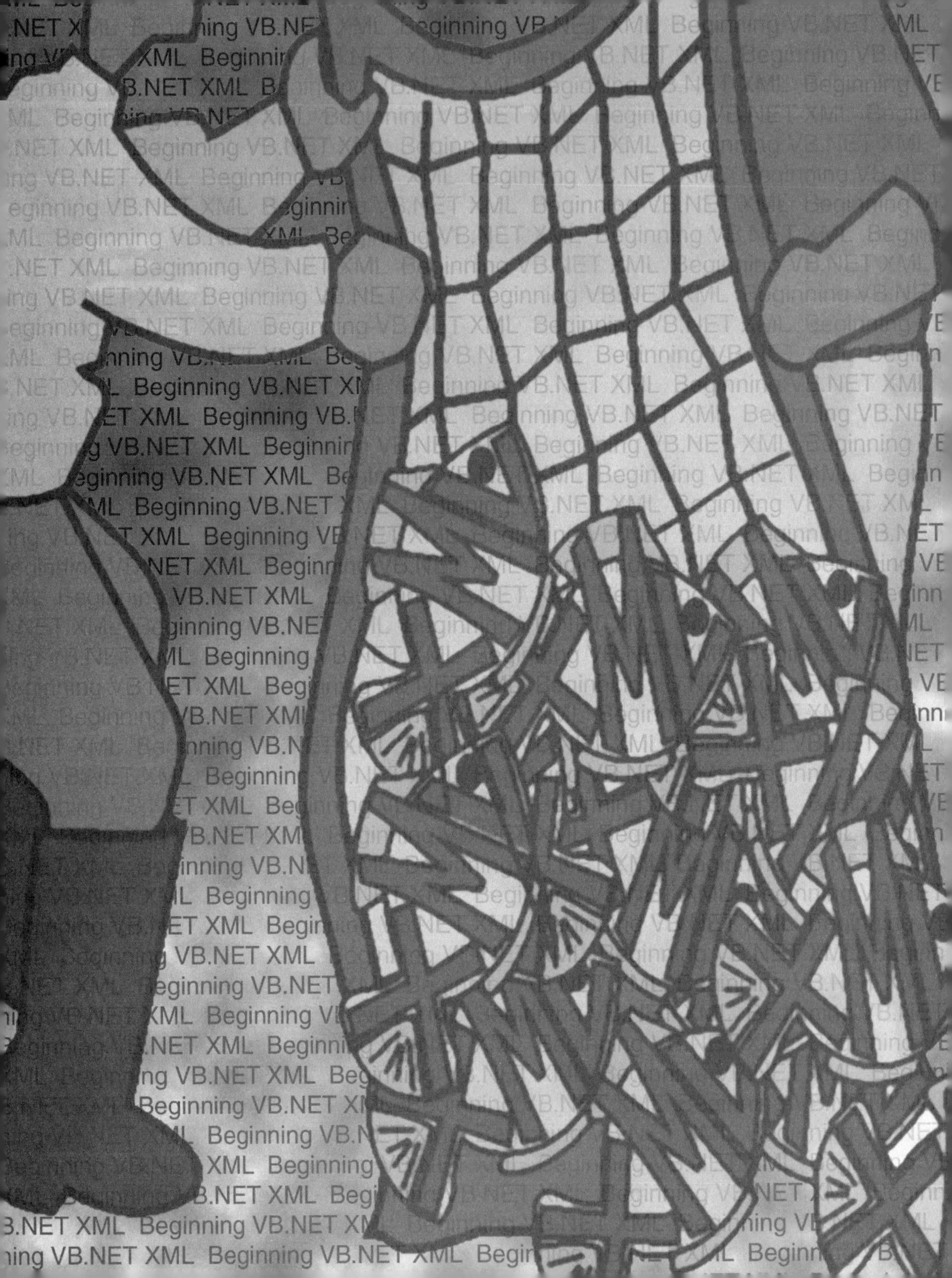
Beginning VB.NET XML

XML Schemas and .NET

In the last chapter we discussed the theoretical and practical aspects of the XML Schema language as defined by the W3C. We looked not only at the elements and attributes of the language, but also at how XML Schema documents are used with XML document instances. We deliberately avoided adding too much information on .NET and instead concentrated on the aspects of the XML Schema Definition (XSD).

In this chapter we are going to extend our knowledge of XML Schema to the world of .NET. We will look at the programmatic techniques of creating schema documents as well as how to validate XML instances against these documents using .NET classes.

In this chapter, you will learn:

- ❏ How to edit schemas in Visual Studio .NET
- ❏ Programmatic Validation of XML
- ❏ XSD and Serialization with the `xsd.exe` utility
- ❏ How to enhance our case study with what we have learned in the last two chapters

Using the Schema Editor in Visual Studio .NET

The Visual Studio .NET IDE offers the easiest way to graphically create XML Schema documents. This is ideal for users who would rather not get into the depths of XML Schema. Using Visual Studio .NET allows the user to create a schema fairly quickly and you can even import an existing XML Schema document and have VS.NET create a graphical view for you.

Generate a Schema from an XML Document

If you want to quickly create an XML Schema document that will validate an instance then you can use Visual Studio to create the schema for you based on the XML instance. To demonstrate how this can be done, we can use the following XML instance, which we've called `FirstTest.xml`:

```xml
<?xml version="1.0" encoding="utf-8" ?>
<ct:ContactDetails xmlns:ct="http://www.deltabis.com/Contact">
  <first>Steven</first>
  <last>Livingstone</last>
</ct:ContactDetails>
```

If you open this in the Visual Studio .NET IDE, you can even get a simple graphical view that some users may prefer when entering data to an instance.Click the **Data** button at the bottom left of the IDE and you will get a view like the following:

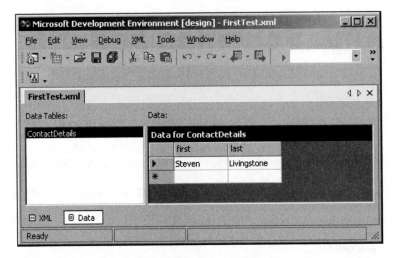

Go back to the XML window and select the **XML I Create Schema** option and a new file called document called `FirstTest.xsd` will be created in the project.

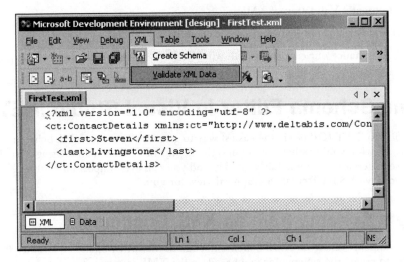

Click the **XML** box at the bottom left of the IDE to view the actual XML document.

The code created will be similar to the following:

```xml
<?xml version="1.0" ?>
<xs:schema id="NewDataSet" targetNamespace=http://www.deltabis.com/Contact
    xmlns:mstns="http://www.deltabis.com/Contact"
    xmlns="http://www.deltabis.com/Contact"
    xmlns:xs="http://www.w3.org/2001/XMLSchema"
    xmlns:msdata="urn:schemas-microsoft-com:xml-msdata"
    attributeFormDefault="qualified" elementFormDefault="qualified">
  <xs:element name="ContactDetails" msdata:Prefix="ct">
    <xs:complexType>
      <xs:sequence>
        <xs:element name="first" form="unqualified"
            type="xs:string" minOccurs="0" />
        <xs:element name="last" form="unqualified"
            type="xs:string" minOccurs="0" />
      </xs:sequence>
    </xs:complexType>
  </xs:element>
  <xs:element name="NewDataSet" msdata:IsDataSet="true"
    msdata:Locale="en-GB" msdata:Prefix="ct"
    msdata:EnforceConstraints="False">
    <xs:complexType>
      <xs:choice maxOccurs="unbounded">
        <xs:element ref="ContactDetails" />
      </xs:choice>
    </xs:complexType>
  </xs:element>
</xs:schema>
```

If we now look at a manually created version of the schema document that we will create later in the chapter, we can see some significant differences as well as similarities:

```xml
<xsd:schema xmlns:xsd="http://www.w3.org/2001/XMLSchema"
    xmlns:ct="http://www.deltabis.com/Contact"
    targetNamespace="http://www.deltabis.com/Contact">

  <xsd:element name="ct:ContactDetails" type="ct:PersonsFirstname" />

  <xsd:complexType name="Name">
    <xsd:sequence>
      <xsd:element name="first" type="ct:PersonsFirstname"
        minOccurs="0" maxOccurs="1" default="John" />
      <xsd:element name="middle" type="xsd:string"  minOccurs="0"
        maxOccurs="unbounded" nillable="true" />
      <xsd:element name="last" type="xsd:string" minOccurs="1"
        maxOccurs="1" default="Doe"/>
    </xsd:sequence>
  </xsd:complexType>
```

```
    <xsd:simpleType name="PersonsFirstname">
      <xsd:restriction base="xsd:string">
        <xsd:minLength value="4"/>
        <xsd:maxLength value="10"/>
      </xsd:restriction>
    </xsd:simpleType>
  </xsd:schema>
```

The XML Schema prefix itself is different, but remember that prefixes are always resolved to a namespace, so the prefix can be anything you want. There are also some extra namespaces that have been added by the generator (these are generally useful when the XML Schema is being mapped to a DataSet representation of a database table and will provide data type mapping, for example), adding some metadata that is used by the IDE when reading the instance back in and generating the diagrammatic view.

Notice that the ContactDetails element in the VS-generated schema is defined within the complexType, rather than separately as we did manually – this means there is no reuse of the type because it is anonymous and hence cannot be referred to from any other element or complex type definition. This is not a big issue for the IDE, although it does result in larger XML Schema documents. Notice also that the automatically generated schema has the root element NewDataSet, which actually contains the XML document instance and is recognized by the editor when reading this schema.

One important point about this is that the dynamically generated schema doesn't in fact represent our business rules fully. The instance document didn't have a middle element defined, because it is optional, so the schema doesn't know about this and therefore doesn't define it in the schema. This is one of the limitations of reverse engineering schema documents from XML instances. It is best to avoid using this technique except in the simplest of circumstances where you want to have a simple XML Schema document validating a relatively simple XML document instance. However, if you want to avoid the details of XML Schemas then you may find that this gives you a head start in the development of your schema.

You can even view this instance graphically by clicking the Schema button at the bottom left of the IDE. Doing this will generate a graphical view of the XML Schema as follows:

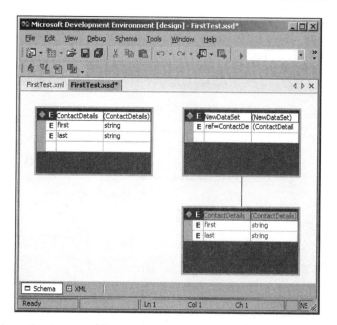

The next step up from this is to actually use the graphical capabilities of the IDE to create a schema document, this is what we are going to look at now.

Try It Out: Creating a Schema from Scratch

Let's now dynamically create a Schema to validate the XML instance we have been looking at (shown below), using .NET:

> *Note that all the sample code for this chapter is available for download from http://www.wrox.com. We will be storing sample code for this chapter within the following folder: C:\BegVBXML\Chapter11. You may, of course, use a different folder depending on what you prefer. The XML you will need for this example is the following:*

```
<?xml version="1.0" encoding="utf-8" ?>
<ct:ContactDetails xmlns:ct="http://www.deltabis.com/Contact">
  <first>Steven</first>
  <last>Livingstone</last>
</ct:ContactDetails>
```

1. Start a new Windows project and call it SOMSamples.

2. We need to create a new XML Schema document, so right-click on the project, select **Add**, then **Add New Item**, and choose **XML Schema** from the **Templates** window. Call this new schema GraphSchema.xsd. Click the **Schema** button at the bottom left; if you are not taken to the graphical view ensure that you can see the toolbox window – the toolbox windows should display on the **XML Schema** tab only. Finally ensure that you have the **Properties** windows open as you will be using this frequently to set the values of many of the attributes of the XML Schema.

25

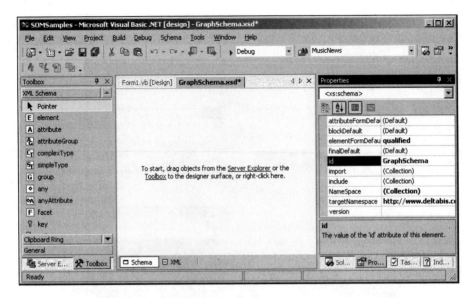

3. In Properties change the targetNamespace to http://www.deltabis.com/Contact.

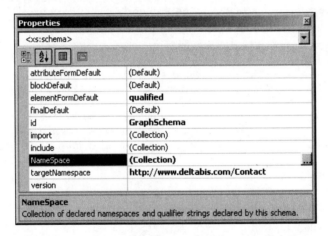

4. Click on Namespace in Properties, click on the button labeled with the ellipsis (...), and then click the Add button. In the Properties section, click on the value field of NameSpace and enter the namespace http://www.deltabis.com/Contact. Change the value of the Qualifier field to ct, which is the prefix associated with this namespace. Finally, select Close.

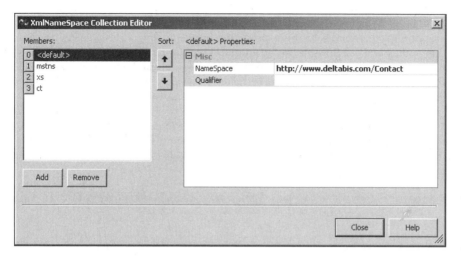

We are now going to create the main content of the schema document. It is best to start by defining the types you are going to use and then create the elements and structures that are going to use these types. This is similar to the method that is used to dynamically create a schema using the schema Object Model. The Schema Object Model, or SOM, was provided by Microsoft to achieve the same functionality as the DOM for XML documents. Using the SOM, you can read schema documents from a file location or have them dynamically created in memory, then compile and validate an XML instance (which may also be dynamically generated).

5. So, first we need to create a `simpleType` that defines our constraints on a person's first name. Click on the `simpleType` icon in the toolbox and drag it onto the schema diagram. Give it the name PersonsFirstname and keep its Base field equal to string to restrict it to string types only. In the schema design window, click on the box under the ST icon and from the drop-down choose Facet. Change the drop-down to minLength and set the value field to 4. Repeat this for maxLength, setting the value field to 10.

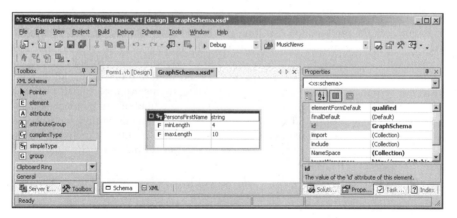

6. Next we need to create a `complexType` that defines our `Name` type that will group the elements together and set various properties on them. Drag a `complexType` element from the toolbox and call it `Name`. In the graphical representation in the schema design form, click on the row below to add a new element and call it first. In the value field, select the PersonsFirstName simple type from the drop-down list. In the Properties window, set the property default to John, minOccurs to 0 and maxOccurs to 1.

7. In the next row, create a middle element of type `String` and set minOccurs to 0, maxOccurs to unbounded, and nillable to true. Finally create another row of an element called last. Set the minOccurs to 1, maxOccurs to 1 and default to Doe. The diagram should now look something like the figure below:

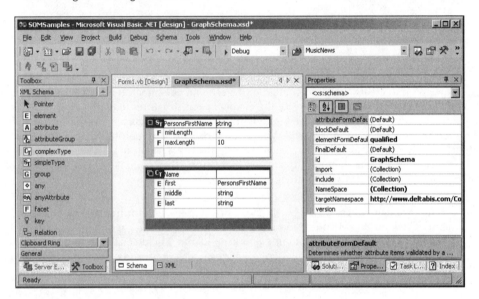

8. Finally we need to create the root element that brings these definitions together, so drag a new element from the toolbox and this time give it the name ContactDetails. Note that this isn't strictly necessary when working directly with the schema designer in this case. The schema designer creates the targetNamespace as the default namespace by default and you are unable to remove the default namespace – or even set it to null – hence all elements in this case will be qualified. However, as we are working to our instance, which does qualify the elements in this way, we will use the prefix. The value field of this element also should be qualified to be Name(ct) (although, again, as this is the default namespace when using the designer it would be qualified in any case). Doing this will automatically enter the elements defined by the `Name` `complexType` element into the definition for this element. The full schema diagram is shown on the following page.

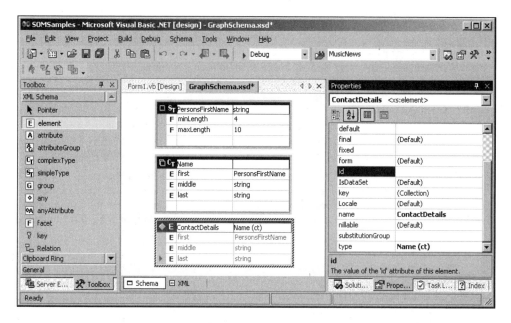

9. We can now test our instance against this schema by adding the `FirstTest.xml` file to the project. Now go to the XML view (rather than the Data view because this doesn't have a facility for validation). Set the targetSchema property in the Properties window for this document to be the same as the targetNamespace of the schema we just created (http://www.deltabis.com/Contact). This makes an association in Visual Studio .NET between these documents.

10. Now click the XML item in the menu bar and choose Validate XML Data. You will get no error messages returned and the following will appear at the bottom of the window:

```
No validation errors were found.
```

The schema we just created is shown below.

```xml
<?xml version="1.0" encoding="utf-8" ?>
<xs:schema id="GraphSchema" targetNamespace="http://www.deltabis.com/Contact"
    elementFormDefault="qualified" xmlns="http://www.deltabis.com/Contact"
    xmlns:mstns="http://www.deltabis.com/Contact"
    xmlns:xs="http://www.w3.org/2001/XMLSchema"
    xmlns:ct="http://www.deltabis.com/Contact ">
  <xs:simpleType name="PersonsFirstname">
    <xs:restriction base="xs:string">
      <xs:minLength value="4" />
      <xs:maxLength value="10" />
    </xs:restriction>
  </xs:simpleType>
  <xs:complexType name="Name">
    <xs:sequence>
```

```
            <xs:element name="first" type="ct:PersonsFirstname"
                minOccurs="0" maxOccurs="1" default="John" />
            <xs:element name="middle" type="xs:string" minOccurs="0"
                maxOccurs="unbounded" nillable="true" />
            <xs:element name="last" type="xs:string" minOccurs="1"
                maxOccurs="1" default="Doe" />
        </xs:sequence>
    </xs:complexType>
    <xs:element name="ContactDetails" type="ct:Name" />
</xs:schema>
```

If you compare this schema to the one we manually created earlier, shown below, you will see that there is a very close similarity. In fact the main differences you will note are that the order is slightly different and that the XML Schema annotations for working with datasets have been added to the dynamically-generated schema. The prefix used is also different from the one we worked with, but this isn't an issue as they both map to the same namespace.

```
<xsd:schema xmlns:xsd="http://www.w3.org/2001/XMLSchema"
    xmlns:ct="http://www.deltabis.com/Contact"
    targetNamespace="http://www.deltabis.com/Contact">

    <xsd:element name="ct:ContactDetails" type="ct:PersonsFirstname" />

    <xsd:complexType name="Name">
        <xsd:sequence>
            <xsd:element name="first" type="ct:PersonsFirstname"
                minOccurs="0" maxOccurs="1" default="John" />
            <xsd:element name="middle" type="xsd:string"  minOccurs="0"
                maxOccurs="unbounded" nillable="true" />
            <xsd:element name="last" type="xsd:string" minOccurs="1"
                maxOccurs="1" default="Doe"/>
        </xsd:sequence>
    </xsd:complexType>

    <xsd:simpleType name="PersonsFirstname">
        <xsd:restriction base="xsd:string">
            <xsd:minLength value="4"/>
            <xsd:maxLength value="10"/>
        </xsd:restriction>
    </xsd:simpleType>
</xsd:schema>
```

Using the IDE is a great way to create an initial template schema. For simple and straightforward XML instances, they are very easy and quick to create. In fact, for the majority of your VB.NET applications, you can use the IDE to create your schemas. However, for more complex applications, it is likely that you will find it more of an advantage to know and understand the XML Schema Language in order to shape your XML Schemas to do exactly what you want.

Programmatic Validation of XML

Programmatic validation of XML instances in the .NET Framework is done using the `XmlValidatingReader` class that we discussed briefly in Chapter 4. This class is derived from the `XmlReader` abstract class and is basically the `XmlTextReader` class with validation layered on top. The `XmlTextReader` itself performs no validation and simply provides the ability to load in the XML document. This added validation is intended to provide you with the ability to check the XML document against a DTD or XML Schema before you read the contents of the document.

Overview of XmlValidatingReader

We have already looked at the `XmlReader` class in depth, but it's worth looking again at the `XmlValidatingReader`. This class has three constructors, a `ValidationType` property, `Schemas` property, and a `SchemaType` property.

XmlValidatingReader Constructors

XmlValidatingReader(XmlReader)

This takes an existing `XmlReader` instance containing the XML instance that you intend to validate. It is used when you have already used an `XmlReader` derived class to load the XML file; you use the `XmlValidatingReader` to provide validation of the XML document stored in the `XmlReader` instance. The following example code snippet shows how this may be used.

```
//Load file into XmlTextReader instance
Dim objXTRead as XmlTextReader = new XmlTextReader (strXMLfile)

//load XmlTextReader instance into validating reader
dim objXValRead as XmlValidatingReader = new XmlValidatingReader (objXTRead)
```

XmlValidatingReader(String, XmlNodeType, XmlParserContext)
XmlValidatingReader(Stream, XmlNodeType, XmlParserContext)

These constructors take either a `String` or a `Stream` representation of the XML fragment that you want to validate followed by the node type of this fragment (`Element`, `Attribute`, or `Document`) and finally the parser context for the processing to occur. The parser context is defined by `XmlParserContext`, which defines a set of XML properties to be used during the validation, such as the base URI to be used for resolving any file references within the XML document, encoding, namespace information, the `xml:lang` scope, the `xml:space` scope, and even DTD information.

A simple example using a string representation is shown below:

```
Dim objXValRead As XmlValidatingReader = _
New XmlValidatingReader("<name age='27'><first>Steven</first></name>",
                        XmlNodeType.Element, Nothing)
```

This example will load the XML fragment `"<name age='27'><first>Steven</first></name>"` as an `element` node.

XmlValidatingReader Properties

The `ValidationType` property is used to specify the type of schema that will be validated against, which is one of `auto` (determined by the reader itself), `DTD`, `XDR`, `None`, or `Schema`. These values are defined in the `ValidationType` enumerator, which is part of the `System.Xml` namespace. This property must be set if the schema that you are validating against is external to the document – as we are discussing XSD, this will be `ValidationType.Schema`.

Note however, that if you set the `ValidationType` property to a schema type other than `Auto`, and the schema that is used to validate the document is not of that type, an exception will be thrown. For example, if you say that the schema is `ValidationType.Schema` and a `DTD` is found within the document or assigned programmatically, then an exception will be thrown. Additionally if no Schema is found within the document or assigned programmatically, then an exception will also be thrown when you set the validation type to anything other than `Auto` or `None` (there is no schema information in this case). In fact, you can use `ValidationType.Auto` to ensure that even if there is no schema assigned, there will not be an error – this will also choose whatever schema is available to validate the document, whether it's an XSD or other type of schema.

The `Schemas` property is a member of the `XmlValidatingReader` class and allows you to create a cache of schemas associated with namespaces that can then be used to validate your XML document. These schemas are stored in the `XmlSchemaCollection` class, which is also discussed shortly.

The `SchemaType` property is read-only and can be used to provide information on the type of validation that is being performed on the current node. So, when validating using a Schema, you can query it to find the type of validation (for example, `datatype`, `simpleType`, or `complexType` - for more information on types, see the Schema Datatypes reference in the Appendix). When validating using DTDs the `SchemaType` property returns null. This property can be useful if you are mapping your XML data to a relational database or some other application and want to know the type of a part of the data. For example, you may want to check whether the `"day"` attribute has been defined as an integer or string (for example, `"1"` as opposed to `"Monday"`) so that when stored in a database (or passed to some method), it's native type can be used. It provides us with a much stronger programming model.

Let's now take a look at how to actually tackle this validation of XML.

Validation Using XmlValidatingReader

`XmlValidatingReader` provides the simplest method of validating because you simply have to read in the XML document and use the `XmlValidatingReader` to check if the document is valid. The first step of validation is to provide some information within the XML document itself that can give the parser the details of the XML Schema document that is to validate this document. The namespace `xmlns:xsi="http://www.w3.org/2001/XMLSchema-instance"` is required and is a reference to the XML Schema namespace for instances. You must provide this if you intend to validate your XML instances directly with no programmatic techniques.

```
<?xml version="1.0"?>
<name xmlns:xsi="http://www.w3.org/2001/XMLSchema-instance"
  xsi:noNamespaceSchemaLocation="schema1.xsd">
```

```
   <first>Steven</first>
   <middle />
   <last>Livingstone-Perez</last>
</name>
```

The noNamespaceSchemaLocation attribute specifies the location of the schema to use for validation. It has been defined on the root with its value set to the URL location of the XML Schema file; in this case it is schema1.xsd. The noNamespaceSchemaLocation attribute is only used when the XML document does not require validation against any qualified nodes (that is, nodes bound to a given namespace). As the nodes within this document are not bound to any namespace, we are able to use the noNamespaceSchemaLocation attribute. An alternative method is discussed in the next example.

The XML Schema that validates this instance is shown below:

```
<xsd:schema xmlns:xsd="http://www.w3.org/2001/XMLSchema">
  <xsd:element name="name">
    <xsd:complexType>
      <xsd:sequence>
        <xsd:element name="first" type="PersonsFirstname"
           minOccurs="0" maxOccurs="1" default="John" />
        <xsd:element name="middle" type="xsd:string"
           minOccurs="0" maxOccurs="unbounded" nillable="true" />
        <xsd:element name="last" type="xsd:string"
           minOccurs="1" maxOccurs="1" default="Doe"/>
      </xsd:sequence>
    </xsd:complexType>
  </xsd:element>

  <xsd:simpleType name="PersonsFirstname">
    <xsd:restriction base="xsd:string">
      <xsd:minLength value="4"/>
      <xsd:maxLength value="10"/>
    </xsd:restriction>
  </xsd:simpleType>
</xsd:schema>
```

This document is also in its most basic form. It has no namespace definitions (other than the XML Schema namespace definition) and so we don't need to use the targetNamespace.

To programmatically validate this is fairly simple; first we would need to create an XmlTextReader instance and load in the specified XML file. Once this is done you have to use an XmlValidatingReader instance and pass in the XmlTextReader instance as a parameter to its constructor to create a new validating instance.

```
Dim objXTRead As XmlTextReader = New XmlTextReader(filename)
Dim objXValRead As XmlValidatingReader = New XmlValidatingReader(objXTRead)
```

Next you can use a `While` loop with the `Read()` method to read the XML document from the reader; if you don't insert any code in this loop then this will simply read through each node in the XML document, validate it against the schema and throw an exception if a validation error occurs causing the validation process to immediately terminate. Alternatively you can put code within this loop (such as the code we discussed when we looked in detail at the `XmlTextReader` in Chapter 4 – checking for node types, getting values, and so on) and validation is done with an exception being thrown when there is a problem.

```
While (objXValRead.Read())
End While
```

When complete you should close both readers.

```
objXTRead.Close()
objXValRead.Close()
```

Notice that we didn't explicitly specify the validation type; the parser will work out the type of validation to be used by examining the XML document to be processed and getting any schema information present within that document. Alternatively you can explicitly specify this by adding the following line just before you call the `Read()` method. It is usually best to explicitly specify, even if it's just to make the code more readable.

```
objXValRead.ValidationType = ValidationType.Schema
```

Try It Out: Validating with Schema Information inside XML Instance

This example is going to look at how to create a simple tool that will validate any XML instance that has its schema information (or lack of) stored within the XML instance itself.

1. Create a new VB console project called **Validation**, rename the `module.vb` file to `validation.vb` and add the following namespace reference:

```
Imports System.Xml
```

2. Next add the following private method to the class (we will leave discussion of error handling until the next example).

```
Private Sub ValidateDocument(ByVal strXMLDocName As String)
    Dim strXMLfile As String = strXMLDocName

    'read the xml file we want to validate
    Dim objXTRead As XmlTextReader = New XmlTextReader(strXMLfile)

    'layer validation on top
    Dim objXValRead As XmlValidatingReader = _
        New XmlValidatingReader(objXTRead)

    'set it to XML Schema validation
    objXValRead.ValidationType = ValidationType.Schema
```

```
            'invoke validation process
            While (objXValRead.Read())
            End While

            'close readers
            objXTRead.Close()
            objXValRead.Close()

            Console.WriteLine("Validation Completed for " & strXMLDocName)
            Console.ReadLine()
        End Sub
```

3. Next add the code highlighted below to the `Main()` method.

```
Sub Main(ByVal CmdArgs() As String)
    'Put user code to initialize the page here
    Dim strLocalFile As String = "../" + CmdArgs(0).ToString

    ValidateDocument(strLocalFile)
End Sub
```

4. Now add the files `instance10.xml`, `schema10.xsd` and `schema10inc.xsd` to the project; they can be found in the code download for this chapter or last chapter, or written from the code given below;

instance10.xml

```xml
<ct:ContactDetails xmlns:ct="http://www.deltabis.com/Contact"
    xmlns:xsi="http://www.w3.org/2001/XMLSchema-instance"
    xsi:schemaLocation="http://www.deltabis.com/Contact schema10.xsd">

    <name title="Mr.">
      <first>Steven</first>
      <middle />
      <last>Livingstone-Perez</last>
    </name>
</ct:ContactDetails>
```

schema10.xsd

```xml
<xsd:schema targetNamespace="http://www.deltabis.com/Contact"
xmlns:xsd="http://www.w3.org/2001/XMLSchema"
xmlns="http://www.deltabis.com/Contact">
    <xsd:include schemaLocation="schema10inc.xsd" />
    <xsd:element name="ContactDetails" type="ContactDetails" />
    <xsd:complexType name="ContactDetails">
      <xsd:sequence minOccurs="1" maxOccurs="1">
        <xsd:element name="name" type="Name" minOccurs="1" maxOccurs="1" />
      </xsd:sequence>
    </xsd:complexType>
    <xsd:complexType name="Name">
```

```
      <xsd:sequence>
        <xsd:element name="first" type="PersonsFirstname" minOccurs="0"
                     maxOccurs="1" default="John" />
        <xsd:element name="middle" type="xsd:string" minOccurs="0"
                     maxOccurs="unbounded" nillable="true" />
        <xsd:element name="last" type="xsd:string" minOccurs="1" maxOccurs="1"
                     default="Doe" />
      </xsd:sequence>
      <xsd:attribute name="title" type="PersonsTitle" default="Mr." />
    </xsd:complexType>
  </xsd:schema>
```

schema10inc.xsd

```
<xsd:schema xmlns:xsd="http://www.w3.org/2001/XMLSchema">
    <xsd:simpleType name="PersonsFirstname">
        <xsd:restriction base="xsd:string">
            <xsd:minLength value="4" />
            <xsd:maxLength value="10" />
        </xsd:restriction>
    </xsd:simpleType>
    <xsd:simpleType name="PersonsTitle">
        <xsd:restriction base="xsd:string">
            <xsd:enumeration value="Mr." />
            <xsd:enumeration value="Mrs." />
            <xsd:enumeration value="Miss." />
        </xsd:restriction>
    </xsd:simpleType>
</xsd:schema>
```

5. Open the file `instance10.xml` and modify the root element to read as the highlighted code below. (This only applies to the `instance10.xml` from the previous chapter download)

```
<ct:ContactDetails xmlns:ct="http://www.deltabis.com/Contact"
  xmlns:xsi="http://www.w3.org/2001/XMLSchema-instance"
  xsi:schemaLocation="http://www.deltabis.com/Contact schema10.xsd">
...
</ct:ContactDetails>
```

6. Build the application. From the command prompt, navigate to the `bin` directory of the project. The path would be C:\BegVBXML\Chapter11\Validation\bin for our example, but will obviously depend on where you have stored your project. Run the application via a command prompt using the line:

```
validation.exe instance10.xml
```

The schema will now successfully validate, as shown below:

```
Select Command Prompt - validation.exe instance10.xml                    _ □ x
Microsoft Windows 2000 [Version 5.00.2195]
(C) Copyright 1985-2000 Microsoft Corp.

C:\>cd C:\begvbxml\chapter11\validation\bin

C:\BegVBXML\Chapter11\Validation\bin>validation.exe instance10.xml
Validation Completed for ../instance10.xml
```

How It Works

The `System.Xml` namespace must be used in this case because that is the location of the `XmlReader` derived classes and, for our needs, the `XmlValidatingReader` class.

The `ValidateDocument()` method takes the location of the document to validate as a parameter from the `Main()` function and loads this document into an `XmlTextReader` instance.

```
Dim objXTRead As XmlTextReader = New XmlTextReader(strXMLfile)
```

This reader instance is then loaded into an `XmlValidatingReader` instance on which we can then place some validation; the validation itself isn't done at this point, remember. We explicitly set the `ValidationType` property to `Schema` because we know we are validating against a XML Schema document.

```
Dim objXValRead As XmlValidatingReader = New XmlValidatingReader(objXTRead)
objXValRead.ValidationType = ValidationType.Schema
```

At this point we are ready to start the validation process and so we call the `Read()` method while looping through each node in the document. As it does this each node is validated and at this point any node that fails validation will cause an exception to be raised and written to the output.

```
While (objXValRead.Read())

End While
```

Finally, if all so far has been successful, then both the text reader and validating reader are closed and a message is written to the output (note that the `ReadLine()` at the end of the code simply prevents the console window from closing immediately after the application has executed).

```
objXTRead.Close()
objXValRead.Close()

Console.WriteLine("Validation Completed for " & strXMLDocName)
Console.ReadLine()
```

The XML instance itself contains all of the schema details. The namespace of the document, as well as the schema to associate with this namespace, is defined within the document and the reader doesn't have to know about this explicitly; it will perform the appropriate validation when it finds these references.

Validation with Schema Details in Code

Programmatic schema validation is the more complex, but most powerful way of validating XML instances against XML Schema documents. It allows you to improve the overall performance of your schema validations by allowing you to create a cache of XML Schema documents that can be held in memory and hence don't need to be reloaded for every validation. This is a huge advantage over loading files from disk or even across the Internet.

Programmatic validation also allows you to override any references to schema documents within the XML instance. This means that although you may have a reference to a schema within the XML document for validation, perhaps for some very basic validation against top-level elements to ensure a basic structure to your XML document, you can override this reference programmatically (without having to remove all of the references within the XML documents).

Validating an Instance

When validating an XML instance against a schema there are a series of steps that you have to complete in your class.

First you have to get the XML Schema file loaded into an instance of a reader. When this is done, create a new instance of an `XmlSchemaCollection` class.

```
Dim objXTReadSchema As XmlTextReader = New XmlTextReader(strXMLSchemaFile)
Dim objXSchColl As XmlSchemaCollection = New XmlSchemaCollection()
```

Following this, you can add each loaded schema to the `XmlSchemaCollection` class, which will act as a cache for mapping namespaces to schemas. This is done using the `Add()` method; in the case below `String.Empty` is used to indicate that there is no default namespace – that is, a null namespace.

```
objXSchColl.Add(String.Empty,objXTReadSchema)
```

> In the case where there is a null namespace (or `String.Empty` as here), the XML Schema will not have a target namespace.

Alternatively you can put a real namespace in here and so the schema in the second parameter will validate nodes in the given namespace. You can add as many namespace to schema mappings as desired in order to validate your instance.

Next we can read in the XML instance we intend to validate and then load the newly created reader into an `XmlValidatingReader`, which allows us to apply validation details for the instance.

```
Dim objXTRead As XmlTextReader = New XmlTextReader(strXMLfile)
Dim objXValRead As XmlValidatingReader = New XmlValidatingReader(objXTRead)
```

The `Schemas` property then uses the `Add()` method to associate the schemas defined in our schema collection with the reader.

```
objXValRead.Schemas.Add(objXSchColl)
```

Up to this point, no validation has actually occurred; you have been setting up the environment for validation.

To start the validation process, you iterate through the XML instance using the `Read()` method to read each node in the document. As each node is read it is validated against the respective schema by selecting the schema from the cache that matches the namespace of each node that is validated and checking the constraints of that node.

If there are any problems the processing is exited and an `XmlSchemaException` exception is thrown.

```
Try
  While (objXValRead.Read())
  End While
Catch e As Exception
  Console.WriteLine(e.Message)
End Try
```

Once we have completed the validation process the schema, text, and validating readers should be closed.

```
objXTReadSchema.Close()
objXTRead.Close()
objXValRead.Close()
```

Let's look in detail at the `XmlSchemaCollection` class as it is important to working with schemas.

XmlSchemaCollection

The `XmlSchemaCollection` class is essential for dynamically validating XML instances against schema documents (XSD, XDR documents), whether they are XSD files or dynamically created XSD documents as discussed later in the chapter. The collection is a cache of schemas that are stored in memory and can be quickly accessed to validate an XML document.

There are two constructor overloads to this class. The first constructor takes no parameters and creates a new schema cache instance.

```
Public Sub New()
```

The second and more commonly used constructor takes a name table instance as a parameter and creates a new schema cache.

```
Public Sub New(XmlNameTable)
```

The key methods for this class are the `Add()` and `Contains()` methods.

Add()

Individual schema documents are cached in a schema collection using the `Add()` method, which has four overloads:

```
Public Function Add(String, String) As XmlSchema
Public Function Add(XmlSchema) As XmlSchema
Public Sub Add(XmlSchemaCollection)
Public Function Add(String, XmlReader) As XmlSchema
```

The first, and most common overload, is where you add a namespace as the first parameter and the schema document to associate with this namespace in the second parameter.

The second overload takes an XmlSchema object that represents an XML Schema document, where its targetNamespace is used to identify the schema and how it should be used to validate an instance. It returns the XmlSchema object representing the document that has been added to the collection.

The third overload is where you add an existing XmlSchemaCollection instance, which already has schema associations.

The final overload allows you to pass a namespace as the first parameter and the second parameter is an XmlReader instance containing the schema document to validate against.

Contains()

The Contains() method allows you to determine whether a given XML Schema document is in the schema collection. You may find this method useful if your schema list is dynamically created or read from a cache (for example in a web-based application), where the schemas available are not under the sole control of your application.

There are two overloads:

```
Public Function Contains(String) As Boolean
Public Function Contains(XmlSchema) As Boolean
```

You can pass either a namespace or an XmlSchema instance as a parameter and it determines whether a schema associated with this namespace is in the schema collection.

Properties

There are three properties available for this class.

The Count property will return the number of namespaces defined in this XmlSchemaCollection instance.

```
Public ReadOnly Property Count As Integer
```

The NameTable property returns the default XmlNameTable instance used in this XmlSchemaCollection instance.

```
Public ReadOnly Property NameTable As XmlNameTable
```

The Item property will return the XML Schema instance that is associated with the specified namespace.

```
Public Default ReadOnly Property Item(ByVal namespace As String) As XmlSchema
```

Try It Out: Dynamic Validation of an XML Instance

This next *Try It Out* is going to look at how to dynamically validate an XML instance. We are going to modify the XML instance we have been working with to also contain details on books that the contact has ordered.

1. Create a new VB console project called **DynamicValidation**, rename the `module.vb` file to `validation.vb` and add the following namespace reference:

```
Imports System.Xml
Imports System.Xml.Schema
```

2. Add the following private method to the class:

```
Private Sub ValidateDocument(ByVal strXMLDocName As String, _
                             ByVal strXMLSchemaFile As String)
  Dim strXMLfile As String = strXMLDocName

  'Load the Schema file into a reader instance
  Dim objXTReadSchema As XmlTextReader = New XmlTextReader(strXMLSchemaFile)

  'Load the Schema file into a reader instance
  Dim objXTReadSchemaEcom As XmlTextReader = New XmlTextReader("..\\ecom.xsd")

  'Create a new collection to cache the schemas
  Dim objXSchColl As XmlSchemaCollection = New XmlSchemaCollection()

  'Add a new schema to the collection
  objXSchColl.Add("http://www.deltabis.com/Contact", objXTReadSchema)
  objXSchColl.Add("http://www.wrox.com/ecom", objXTReadSchemaEcom)

  'Read the XML file we want to validate
  Dim objXTRead As XmlTextReader = New XmlTextReader(strXMLfile)

  'Layer validation on top of this
  Dim objXValRead As XmlValidatingReader = New XmlValidatingReader(objXTRead)

  'Add Schema cache to object
  objXValRead.Schemas.Add(objXSchColl)

  'Invoke validation process
  Try
    While (objXValRead.Read())
    End While
  Catch e As Exception
    Console.WriteLine("The following error occurred : " & e.Message)
  Finally

    'Close readers
    objXTReadSchema.Close()
    objXTReadSchemaEcom.Close()
```

```
      objXTRead.Close()
      objXValRead.Close()
   End Try

   Console.WriteLine("Validation Completed for " & strXMLDocName)
   Console.ReadLine()
End Sub
```

3. Next add the code highlighted below to the `Main()` method.

```
   Sub Main(ByVal CmdArgs() As String)
      'Put user code to initialize the page here
      Dim strLocalFile As String = "../" + CmdArgs(0).ToString
      'Dim strLocalSchemaFile As String = "../" + CmdArgs(1).ToString

      ValidateDocument(strLocalFile, strLocalSchemaFile)
   End Sub
```

4. Now add the files `instance10.xml`, `schema10.xsd`, and `schema10inc.xsd` to the project; they are the same files you used in the last Try It Out and can also be found in the code download for this chapter. Copy each of these files and rename them to `instance11.xml`, `schema11.xsd`, and `schema11inc.xsd` respectively – we need to make a couple of modifications to these files.

5. Open the file `instance11.xml` and modify the code to the following:

```
<ct:ContactDetails xmlns:ct=http://www.deltabis.com/Contact
    xmlns:ecom="http://www.wrox.com/ecom">
  <name title="Mr.">
    <first>Steven</first>
    <middle />
    <last>Livingstone-Perez</last>
  </name>
  <ecom:books>
    <book>Professional XML 2nd Edition</book>
    <book>Beg VB.NET XML</book>
  </ecom:books>
</ct:ContactDetails>
```

6. Modify the `schema11.xsd` file in the areas highlighted below:

```
...
<xsd:include schemaLocation="schema11inc.xsd" />
...
<xsd:complexType name="ContactDetails">
  <xsd:sequence minOccurs="1" maxOccurs="1">
    <xsd:element name="name" type="Name" minOccurs="1" maxOccurs="1" />
    <xsd:any namespace="##any" processContents="strict"/>
  </xsd:sequence>
</xsd:complexType>
...
```

7. Create a new XML Schema file called `ecom.xsd` and add the following code:

```
<xsd:schema targetNamespace="http://www.wrox.com/ecom"
    xmlns:xsd="http://www.w3.org/2001/XMLSchema"
    xmlns="http://www.wrox.com/ecom">
  <xsd:element name="books" type="bookOrdered" />
  <xsd:complexType name="bookOrdered">
    <xsd:sequence minOccurs="1" maxOccurs="1">
      <xsd:element name="book" type="xsd:string"
              minOccurs="1" maxOccurs="unbounded" />
    </xsd:sequence>
  </xsd:complexType>
</xsd:schema>
```

8. Build the program, and then open a command prompt. Navigate to the bin directory underneath your project, and run the application with the command:

dynamicvalidation.exe instance11.xml schema11.xsd

The schema will successfully validate.

9. Again open the `instance11.xml` file and change the `title` attribute on the `name` child element from "Mr." to "Sr." and again do Step 8. You will get the following message:

10. Rename "Sr." back to "Mr." as we will work with this in a later example.

How It Works

The definition of the `ContactDetails` complex type within the `schema11.xsd` file was modified slightly:

```
<xsd:complexType name="ContactDetails">
  <xsd:sequence minOccurs="1" maxOccurs="1">
    <xsd:element name="name" type="Name" minOccurs="1" maxOccurs="1" />
    <xsd:any namespace="##any" processContents="strict" />
  </xsd:sequence>
</xsd:complexType>
```

The any element in this case says that after the name element, there can by any element from any namespace – indicated by setting the namespace attribute to the wildcard "##any", but any element must be validated by a schema or an error will occur – indicated by the "strict" value of the processContents attribute.

This will allow you to validate the modifications to the `schema11.xml` file that added new elements within this namespace:

```
<ct:ContactDetails xmlns:ct=http://www.deltabis.com/Contact
    xmlns:ecom="http://www.wrox.com/ecom">
...
  <ecom:books>
    <book>Professional XML 2nd Edition</book>
    <book>Beg VB.NET XML</book>
  </ecom:books>
</ct:ContactDetails>
```

The `books` elements are qualified in the `http://www.wrox.com/ecom` namespace and so will be validated by the `ecom.xsd` schema – we see how the two are associated in the code we look at next.

Looking at the code, the `System.Xml` namespace must be used in this case because that is the location of the `XmlReader` derived classes and in our case the `XmlValidatingReader` class. Also the `System.Xml.Schema` namespace must be declared as this is where the `XmlSchemaCollection` class can be found.

The `ValidateDocument()` method takes the location of the document to validate as well as the location of the schema to use for validation as parameters from the `Main()` function and loads the schema documents (including the new `ecom.xsd` schema) into `XmlTextReader` instances. It then creates a new instance of a schema collection cache and specifies that the namespaces `http://www.deltabis.com/Contact` and `http://www.wrox.com/ecom` should be associated with the schema documents we have just loaded.

```
objXSchColl.Add("http://www.deltabis.com/Contact",objXTReadSchema)
objXSchColl.Add("http://www.wrox.com/ecom",objXTReadSchemaEcom)
```

Notice that the namespace of the first of these is the same as the `targetNamespace` of the schema document `schema11.xsd` that we loaded.

```
<xsd:schema xmlns:xsd="http://www.w3.org/2001/XMLSchema"
    xmlns:ct="http://www.deltabis.com/Contact"
    targetNamespace="http://www.deltabis.com/Contact">
...
```

The second is the `targetNamespace` of the `ecom.xsd` file:

```
<xsd:schema targetNamespace="http://www.wrox.com/ecom"
    xmlns:xsd="http://www.w3.org/2001/XMLSchema"
    xmlns="http://www.wrox.com/ecom">
...
```

Next, the reader instance is loaded into an `XmlTextReader` instance and then into an `XmlValidatingReader` instance that we can then place some validation on. The `Add()` method of the `Schemas` property (of the validating reader) is then used to associate the cache of schemas with this XML document instance.

```
objXValRead.Schemas.Add(objXSchColl)
```

We now start the validation process and so we call the `Read()` method while looping through each node in the document. This time we have wrapped the reading process in `Try...Catch...Finally` statements to catch any `XmlSchemaException` errors that may occur and this allows us to present the error on the screen in our desired format, rather than the default message box provided by the .NET Framework.

```
Try
  While (objXValRead.Read())
  End While
Catch e As Exception
  Console.WriteLine("The following error occurred : " & e.Message)
Finally
  'close readers
  objXTReadSchema.Close()
  objXTReadSchemaEcom.Close()
  objXTRead.Close()
  objXValRead.Close()
End Try
```

When any node fails validation against the XML Schema document, an `XmlSchemaException` will be raised and the `Catch` statement will handle the error and write out the problem. When this is done the `Finally` statement is automatically run to close the documents and the document processing has completed.

Handling Exceptions and Using the ValidationEventHandler

We ended the last section by discussing the handling of errors in the validation process, using `Try...Catch` statements. This is useful when you want the process to stop as soon as any node has failed validation and you want to exit the application.

Often, however, you will want to validate the entire document and handle each validation error as it occurs, and either write it directly or buffer it to write all errors when the process has completed. This gives the advantage of you being able to programmatically decide what errors are serious enough for you to stop validation and what errors could be listed and corrected by the client and resubmitted.

We can add a `ValidationEventHandler` event to the validating reader that can accomplish this for us and allow us to decide what we want to do with errors. This will ensure that no matter how many validation errors we get during the validation process, they will all be handled by the event handler and we can later report these errors as a whole. We will however continue to use other exception handling (such as `Try...Catch` blocks) which will handle errors other than schema validation errors.

To add a handler for a validation error, you use the following code:

```
AddHandler objXValRead.ValidationEventHandler, _
    AddressOf ValidationEventHandler
```

This says that the event handler for any validation errors is the method `ValidationEventHandler()` and this must also be defined in the class. This method is defined as follows:

```
      Private Sub XMLDocumentValidationCallBack(ByVal sender As Object, _
                                    ByVal args As ValidationEventArgs)
        Console.WriteLine(args.Exception.Message)
      End Sub
```

The `ValidationEventHandler` delegate is defined and must have two parameters; the first is the `sender` object and the second is the arguments of the validation. This latter parameter is a class that can be used to extract the schema exception details such as `Exception`, `Message`, and `Severity`. This is discussed next.

Using the Event Handler

Within the validation event handler class we have access to several properties that we can use to determine how serious the error is and any error information associated with the validation problem.

The most useful properties are `LineNumber`, returning the number of the line in the instance where the validation problem occurred; `LinePosition`, which is the position on that line where the validation failed, and `Message`, which is the message raised by the exception. These can be used to find exactly where in the XML instance the problem lies.

The `Severity` property returns one of the `XmlSeverityType` enumeration values which is either `Error`, indicating that a node failed validation against the XML Schema or `Warning`, indicating that no schema is available to validate a particular node during a larger validation process.

The `Message` property simply returns a text representation of the validation error that occurred. Detailed error information is available through the `Exception` property, which returns an `XmlSchemaException` class. This has a number of useful properties that provide rich validation information.

Try It Out: XSD Validation of an XML Document

We are now going to look at how we can validate an XML document and use the event handler to catch any exceptions during validation. This is an important part of intelligent exception handling and providing error details customized to your environment. For example, although we present these details to a screen, they could equally be logged in a log file or the event viewer for later analysis.

1. Go back to the `validation.vb` class we worked with in the `DynamicValidation` project (`DynamicValidation2` in the code download) and add the highlighted line below to the `ValidateDocument()` method.

```
    Private Sub ValidateDocument(ByVal strXMLDocName As String, _
                             ByVal strXMLSchemaFile As String)
        Dim strXMLfile As String = strXMLDocName

        'Load the Schema file into a reader instance
        Dim objXTReadSchema As XmlTextReader = New XmlTextReader(strXMLSchemaFile)

        'Load the Schema file into a reader instance
        Dim objXTReadSchemaEcom As XmlTextReader = _
            New XmlTextReader("..\\ecom.xsd")
```

```
                'Create a new collection to cache the schemas
                Dim objXSchColl As XmlSchemaCollection = New XmlSchemaCollection()

                'Add a new schema to the collection
                objXSchColl.Add("http://www.deltabis.com/Contact", objXTReadSchema)
                objXSchColl.Add("http://www.wrox.com/ecom", objXTReadSchemaEcom)

                'Read the xml file we want to validate
                Dim objXTRead As XmlTextReader = New XmlTextReader(strXMLfile)

                'Layer validation on top of this
                Dim objXValRead As XmlValidatingReader = _
                  New XmlValidatingReader(objXTRead)

                'Add Schema cache to object
                objXValRead.Schemas.Add(objXSchColl)

                'Assign event handler for validation
                AddHandler objXValRead.ValidationEventHandler, _
                  AddressOf XMLDocumentValidationCallBack

                'Invoke validation process
                Try
                   While (objXValRead.Read())
                   End While
                Catch e As Exception
                   Console.WriteLine("The following error occurred : " & e.Message)
                Finally
                     'Close readers
                   objXTReadSchema.Close()
                   objXTReadSchemaEcom.Close()
                   objXTRead.Close()
                   objXValRead.Close()
                End Try

                Console.WriteLine("Validation Completed for " & strXMLDocName)
                Console.ReadLine()
            End Sub
```

2. Next add the event handler after this method, at the end of the class:

```
        Private Sub XMLDocumentValidationCallBack(ByVal sender As Object, _
                                                  ByVal args As ValidationEventArgs)
            If (args.Severity = XmlSeverityType.Error) Then
                Console.WriteLine("\n***** XML Schema Validation Error*****")
                Console.WriteLine(args.Exception.Message)
            End If
        End Sub
```

3. Run the application in a command prompt window (you will again need to navigate to this, so you can use the following to position your command prompt at the correct location):

cd ..\..\dynamicvalidation2\bin

4. Type the following command:

```
dynamicvalidation2.exe instance11.xml schema11.xsd
```

the schema will successfully validate.

5. Again open the `instance11.xml` file and change the element `last` to `surname` (remember to change the closing element as well) and repeat the steps from Step 3. You will get the following message:

6. Rename the element `surname` back to `last` to keep the file in its original state for later use.

How It Works

There isn't too much of a difference here from the validation code we used earlier to dynamically validate the XML instance. However, this time extra validation code has been added. In the first case we added an event handler for any validation problems.

```
AddHandler objXValRead.ValidationEventHandler, _
    AddressOf XMLDocumentValidationCallBack
```

This assigns the method `XMLDocumentValidationCallBack` to handle these problems. This method is defined at the end of the class and simply checks the severity of the problem. If it is an error then it writes out a message indicating that an error has occurred. Note that processing continues no matter how many validation errors occur, so we can get a log of every error in the document. This is generally better than repeatedly fixing and running the instance.

XSD and Serialization with xsd.exe

The `xsd.exe` utility, or XML Schema Definition Tool, can be used to serialize classes as XML instances as well as take XML Schema documents and create classes from them.

Try It Out: Creating a XML Schema from a Class

Here we demonstrate how `xsd.exe` can be used to create an XML Schema document that describes a class that could then be used to validate serialized instances – as we saw in Chapter 7.

1. To demonstrate this example, create a new VB Class Library project called **SimpleClass**.

> The **xsd.exe** utility can typically be found in the **\Program Files\Microsoft Visual Studio .NET\FrameworkSDK\Bin** folder. For the purposes of this sample, copy this executable to the **SimpleClass** project and put the file in the **bin** directory.

2. Rename the file called `module.vb` to `SimpleClass.vb` and add the following code (available in the download):

```
Public Class Simple
  Public SpeakString As String = Nothing

  Public Sub Speak(ByVal name As String)

    SpeakString = "Hello " & name & "."
  End Sub
End Class
```

3. We then compile this as `SimpleClass.dll` and run the `xsd.exe` utility on it, with the following on the command line from the root project directory (C:\BegVBXML\Chapter11\SimpleClass):

xsd bin\SimpleClass.dll

This will generate a file called `schema0.xsd` in the same directory. If you examine the contents of this file you will get the following:

```
<?xml version="1.0" encoding="utf-8"?>
<xs:schema elementFormDefault="qualified"
   xmlns:xs="http://www.w3.org/2001/XMLSchema">
  <xs:element name="Simple" nillable="true" type="Simple" />
  <xs:complexType name="Simple">
    <xs:sequence>
      <xs:element minOccurs="0" maxOccurs="1" name="SpeakString"
          type="xs:string" />
    </xs:sequence>
  </xs:complexType>
</xs:schema>
```

You can see from this that a new element definition has been created for the class called `Simple` and its type is set to a `complexType` element called `Simple` also. This `complexType` defines a `sequence` element and within this is the `SpeakString` public field that will actually be serialized (remember only public fields will be serialized).

Creating a Class from an XML Schema

If we can create an XML Schema document from a class then it is only right that we can create a class from an XML Schema document. Consider the following XML Schema document that will validate an XML document containing some basic user information. Create a new XML Schema file called `profile.xsd` in the `SimpleClass` project and add the following code to it.

```
<?xml version="1.0" encoding="utf-8"?>
<xs:schema elementFormDefault="qualified"
   xmlns:xs="http://www.w3.org/2001/XMLSchema">
  <xs:element name="Info" nillable="true" type="NameAndCity" />
  <xs:complexType name="NameAndCity">
    <xs:sequence>
      <xs:element name="name" type="xs:string" minOccurs="1" maxOccurs="1" />
      <xs:element minOccurs="0" maxOccurs="1" name="HomeTown"
          type="city" />
    </xs:sequence>
  </xs:complexType>

  <xs:simpleType name="city">
    <xs:restriction base="xs:string">
      <xs:enumeration value="Glasgow" />
      <xs:enumeration value="Edinburgh" />
      <xs:enumeration value="Aberdeen" />
    </xs:restriction>
  </xs:simpleType>
</xs:schema>
```

We then compile this into `SimpleClass.dll` and run the `xsd.exe` utility on it, with the following on the command line:

```
xsd /c /language:vb profile.xsd
```

This will generate a file called `profile.vb` in the same directory. If you examine the contents of this file you will get the following:

```
'---------------------------------------------------------------------
' <autogenerated>
'     This code was generated by a tool.
'     Runtime Version: 1.0.3705.288
'
'     Changes to this file may cause incorrect behavior and will be lost if
'     the code is regenerated.
' </autogenerated>
'---------------------------------------------------------------------

Option Strict Off
Option Explicit On

Imports System.Xml.Serialization

'
'This source code was auto-generated by xsd, Version=1.0.3705.288.
'

'<remarks/>
<System.Xml.Serialization.XmlRootAttribute("Info", [Namespace]:="", _
IsNullable:=true)> _
```

```
Public Class NameAndCity

    '<remarks/>
    Public name As String

    '<remarks/>
    Public HomeTown As city

    '<remarks/>
    <System.Xml.Serialization.XmlIgnoreAttribute()>  _
    Public HomeTownSpecified As Boolean
End Class

'<remarks/>
Public Enum city

    '<remarks/>
    Glasgow

    '<remarks/>
    Edinburgh

    '<remarks/>
    Aberdeen
End Enum
```

If you look in detail at the file you can see that the `NameAndCity complexType` definition has actually been translated to a class called `NameAndCity`. However, an attribute has been applied to this because the root element is actually called `Info` – different from the class name. The two elements of the sequence are defined as public fields; the first is of type `string` and the second is of type `city`, which is an enumeration defined further down in the class. Notice that the `HomeTownSpecified` Boolean value is used because this element has been defined as optional in the XSD and so this may not be used (that is, `HomeTownSpecified=false`).

This is a primer to what you can do with the `xsd.exe` utility and intended to illustrate that it can be used with any class, not just when working with data sets. We discussed and demonstrated serialization in Chapter 7, but mentioned that XML Schema has a big part to play in serialization. We will see examples of that in the next chapter when we look at ADO.NET, which uses XML Schema to serialize database tables as XML.

Let's apply some of the knowledge we have gained within this chapter now to improve our case study application.

Case Study – Improving with Validation

We are going to extend the case study we have been working with to add a process that validates that any external contacts that we are going to import conform to a standard structure, as defined by an XML Schema.

> **This example can be found in the `CaseStudy` folder, launched by clicking the `CaseStudy.vbproj` file.**

The XML Schema document that imported contacts must be validated against is defined below and can be found in `Contacts.xsd` in the download.

```xml
<xsd:schema xmlns:xsd="http://www.w3.org/2001/XMLSchema"
  xmlns:ct="http://www.deltabis.com/Contact"
  xmlns:title="http://www.deltabis.com/ns/titles/"
  targetNamespace="http://www.deltabis.com/Contact">
  <xsd:annotation xml:lang="en">
    <xsd:documentation>
      Contact Information
    </xsd:documentation>
  </xsd:annotation>

  <xsd:include schemaLocation="ContactsInc.xsd" />

  <xsd:element name="ContactDetails" type="ct:ContactDetails" />

  <xsd:element name="notes" type="xsd:string" />

  <xsd:complexType name="ContactDetails">
    <xsd:sequence minOccurs="1" maxOccurs="unbounded">
      <xsd:element name="contact">
        <xsd:complexType>
          <xsd:sequence>
            <xsd:element name="name" type="ct:Name"
              minOccurs="1" maxOccurs="1" />
            <xsd:element ref="ct:notes" />
          </xsd:sequence>
          <xsd:attribute name="title"
            type="ct:PersonsTitle" default="title:Mr."/>
        </xsd:complexType>
      </xsd:element>
    </xsd:sequence>
    <xsd:attribute name="updateDate" type="xsd:dateTime" />
  </xsd:complexType>

  <xsd:complexType name="Name">
    <xsd:sequence>
      <xsd:element name="first" type="ct:PersonsFirstname"
        minOccurs="0" maxOccurs="1" default="John" />
      <xsd:element name="middle" type="xsd:string" minOccurs="0"
        maxOccurs="unbounded" nillable="true" />
      <xsd:element name="last" type="xsd:string" minOccurs="1"
        maxOccurs="1" default="Doe"/>
    </xsd:sequence>
  </xsd:complexType>

</xsd:schema>
```

The schema root element is defined with two namespaces, one being the main namespace, that is `http://www.deltabis.com/Contact`, which is also the target namespace for the document. The other namespace is used for qualifying title names and is `http://www.deltabis.com/ns/titles/`.

```
<xsd:schema xmlns:xsd="http://www.w3.org/2001/XMLSchema"
  xmlns:ct="http://www.deltabis.com/Contact"
  xmlns:title="http://www.deltabis.com/ns/titles/"
  targetNamespace="http://www.deltabis.com/Contact">
...
</xsd:schema>
```

The definitions from the `ContactsInc.xsd` schema are also included; this has the same target namespace as the current document, so we can use `include` rather than `import`.

```
<xsd:include schemaLocation="ContactsInc.xsd" />
```

There are only two global element definitions, which are the `<ContactDetails>` and `<notes>` elements; because they are global, the default is that they both have to be qualified in any instances they are used in. The first element is defined as being of the type `ContactDetails` and the second is simply the built-in XSD `string` type.

```
<xsd:element name="ContactDetails" type="ct:ContactDetails" />
<xsd:element name="notes" type="xsd:string" />
```

The `ContactDetails` complex type is defined to contain a `<contact>` element that must occur at least once and can occur as many times as required.

```
<xsd:complexType name="ContactDetails">
  <xsd:sequence minOccurs="1" maxOccurs="unbounded">
    <xsd:element name="contact">
      ...
    </xsd:element>
  </xsd:sequence>
  <xsd:attribute name="updateDate" type="xsd:dateTime" />
</xsd:complexType>
```

Within the definition of the `<contact>` element we additionally create a new anonymous `<complexType>` element definition, which in turn contains two elements and an attribute definition.

```
<xsd:complexType>
  <xsd:sequence>
    <xsd:element name="name" type="ct:Name"
        minOccurs="1" maxOccurs="1" />
    <xsd:element ref="ct:notes" />
  </xsd:sequence>
  <xsd:attribute name="title"
      type="ct:PersonsTitle" default="title:Mr."/>
</xsd:complexType>
```

The first element is called `<name>` and it's defined (later in the schema) as the user-defined `Name` type; it must occur one time only. The second element definition actually references the `<notes>` element that was defined globally. Because this was defined globally it will have to be qualified in the instance; you will see this later in the instance. After the definition of the `<sequence>` element an attribute is defined for the `<contact>` element called `title`; the value of this must be one of the enumeration values defined in the `PersonsTitle` simple type (it must be qualified in the target namespace) definition in the included schema that we look at next. It defaults to the value "Mr.".

Finally the `Name` complex type we mentioned earlier is defined and this is a sequence of the elements `<first>`, `<middle>`, and `<last>`; we have met and discussed these in previous sections so we won't go over these again.

```
<xsd:complexType name="Name">
  <xsd:sequence>
    <xsd:element name="first" type="ct:PersonsFirstname"
        minOccurs="0" maxOccurs="1" default="John" />
    <xsd:element name="middle" type="xsd:string"  minOccurs="0"
        maxOccurs="unbounded" nillable="true" />
    <xsd:element name="last" type="xsd:string" minOccurs="1"
        maxOccurs="1" default="Doe"/>
  </xsd:sequence>
</xsd:complexType>
```

The included schema we mentioned earlier was called `ContactsInc.xsd` and defines the simple types that are used in the main schema. It is shown below.

```
<xsd:schema xmlns:xsd="http://www.w3.org/2001/XMLSchema"
  targetNamespace="http://www.deltabis.com/Contact"
  xmlns:ct="http://www.deltabis.com/Contact"
  xmlns:title="http://www.deltabis.com/ns/titles/">
  <xsd:simpleType name="PersonsFirstname">
    <xsd:restriction base="xsd:string">
      <xsd:minLength value="4"/>
      <xsd:maxLength value="10"/>
    </xsd:restriction>
  </xsd:simpleType>

  <xsd:simpleType name="PersonsTitle">
    <xsd:restriction base="xsd:string">
      <xsd:enumeration value="title:Mr." />
      <xsd:enumeration value="title:Mrs." />
      <xsd:enumeration value="title:Miss." />
    </xsd:restriction>
  </xsd:simpleType>
</xsd:schema>
```

The root schema element is defined in the same way as the previous schema. The first simple type that is defined is the `PersonsFirstName` that we discussed in previous sections. The second simple type is the `PersonsTitle` type that is restricted based on the XSD string data type and is an enumeration of qualified values. Qualified values give us the added advantage of allowing for globally defined titles.

The XML document that we want to import into the application is the `FriendsContacts.xml` file we discussed at the end of Chapter 7. It is shown again below.

```
<?xml version="1.0" encoding="utf-8"?>
<ct:ContactDetails updateDate="2002-12-01T14:00:00"
  xmlns:ct="http://www.deltabis.com/Contact">
  <!--This document contains contact information.-->
```

```
    <contact title="title:Mr." xmlns:title="http://www.deltabis.com/ns/titles/">
      <name>
        <first>Mark</first>
        <middle />
        <last>O&apos;Sullivan</last>
      </name>
      <ct:notes>ABCD Corp. French Translator for technical services.</ct:notes>
    </contact>
    <contact title="title:Mrs."
    xmlns:title="http://www.deltabis.com/ns/titles/">
      <name>
        <first>Maureen</first>
        <middle />
        <last>O&apos;Sullivan</last>
      </name>
      <ct:notes>CTO of ABCD Corp. in UK ventures.</ct:notes>
    </contact>
  </ct:ContactDetails>
```

Now that we have the instance as well as the various schema validation documents, we need to connect this functionality with the application we have been building. We need to add in some code for the form. First we need to specify that we are going to use the `System.Xml.Schema` namespace in addition to the `System.Xml` namespace.

```
Imports System.Xml
Imports System.Xml.Schema
```

A `ValidateDocument()` method is also added to the code. This takes the location of the XML document to validate as an argument and specifies the location of the schema to validate against.

```
'Validates a file against the XML instance
Private Sub ValidateDocument(ByVal strXMLDocName As String)

  Dim strXMLSchemaFile As String = "..\\Contacts.xsd"
  Dim strXMLfile As String = strXMLDocName
```

An `XmlTextReader` instance gets the schema file and creates a new schema collection, adding the schema to this cache.

```
  'Read in schema file
  Dim objXTReadSchema As XmlTextReader = New XmlTextReader(strXMLSchemaFile)

  'Create new collection
  Dim objXSchColl As XmlSchemaCollection = New XmlSchemaCollection()

  'Add schema to the collection cache
  Try
    objXSchColl.Add("http://www.deltabis.com/Contact", objXTReadSchema)
  Catch Ex As Exception
    MessageBox.Show(Ex.Message)
  End Try
```

Next the document instance is loaded into an `XmlValidatingReader` instance and the schema cache is added to the schemas for this reader. An event handler is also assigned to handle any validation problems when the instance is read.

```
'Read in XML instance
Dim objXTRead As XmlTextReader = New XmlTextReader(strXMLfile)
Dim objXValRead As XmlValidatingReader = _
    New XmlValidatingReader(objXTRead)

'Add Schema cache to object
objXValRead.Schemas.Add(objXSchColl)

'Assign event handler for validation
AddHandler objXValRead.ValidationEventHandler, _
    AddressOf XMLDocumentValidationEvent
```

Finally the reader is read and if any validation problems are found the user will be notified of the problems at this point.

When completed all readers are closed.

```
'Validate the file
Try
  While (objXValRead.Read())
  End While
Catch e As Exception
  MessageBox.Show("The following error occurred : " & e.Message)
Finally
  objXTReadSchema.Close()
  objXTRead.Close()
  objXValRead.Close()
End Try
```

The event handler for validation problems uses a global variable to store whether there were any validation problems; this variable is simply used as a flag indicating to the `ImportContacts()` method that the validation of the file to import had failed and to terminate the importing process.

```
Dim ValidationFailed As Boolean = False

Private Sub XMLDocumentValidationEvent(ByVal sender As Object, _
                                ByVal args As ValidationEventArgs)

If (args.Severity = XmlSeverityType.Error) Then
  _ValidationFailed = True
  MessageBox.Show("The contacts could not be imported : " _
    & args.Exception.Message)
End If
```

Finally the `ImportContacts()` method must be modified to call the `ValidateDocument()` method as well as stop importing the contacts if the validation fails.

```
Private Sub ImportContacts()
    Dim FilePath As String = "..\\CaseStudy.xml"
    Dim FriendFilePath As String = "..\\FriendsContacts.xml"

    'Validates against XML Schema
    ValidateDocument(FriendFilePath)

    If Not _ValidationFailed Then
        ...
    End If
End Sub
```

As a final point, to demonstrate that this validation process works we change the `title` attribute of the first contact in `FriendsContacts.xml` from `Mr.` to `Snr.` and re-run the validation process. The following message will be reported to indicate that the validation has failed.

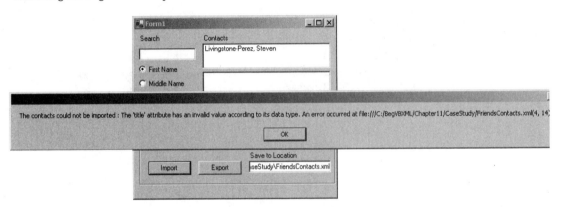

Summary

In this chapter we looked at how XML Schema is utilized in .NET and supporting tools. In particular we covered the following topics:

- ❑ Editing Schemas in Visual Studio .NET
- ❑ Programmatic Validation of XML
- ❑ XSD and Serialization with the `xsd.exe` utility
- ❑ Enhancements to our case study with what we have learned in the last two chapters

XML Schema is not the simplest of languages to learn, but the benefits offered can vastly improve your XML applications and lower the cost when working with systems integration and third party businesses. In the next chapter we go on to look at some of the most important aspects of how XML is used in ADO.NET.

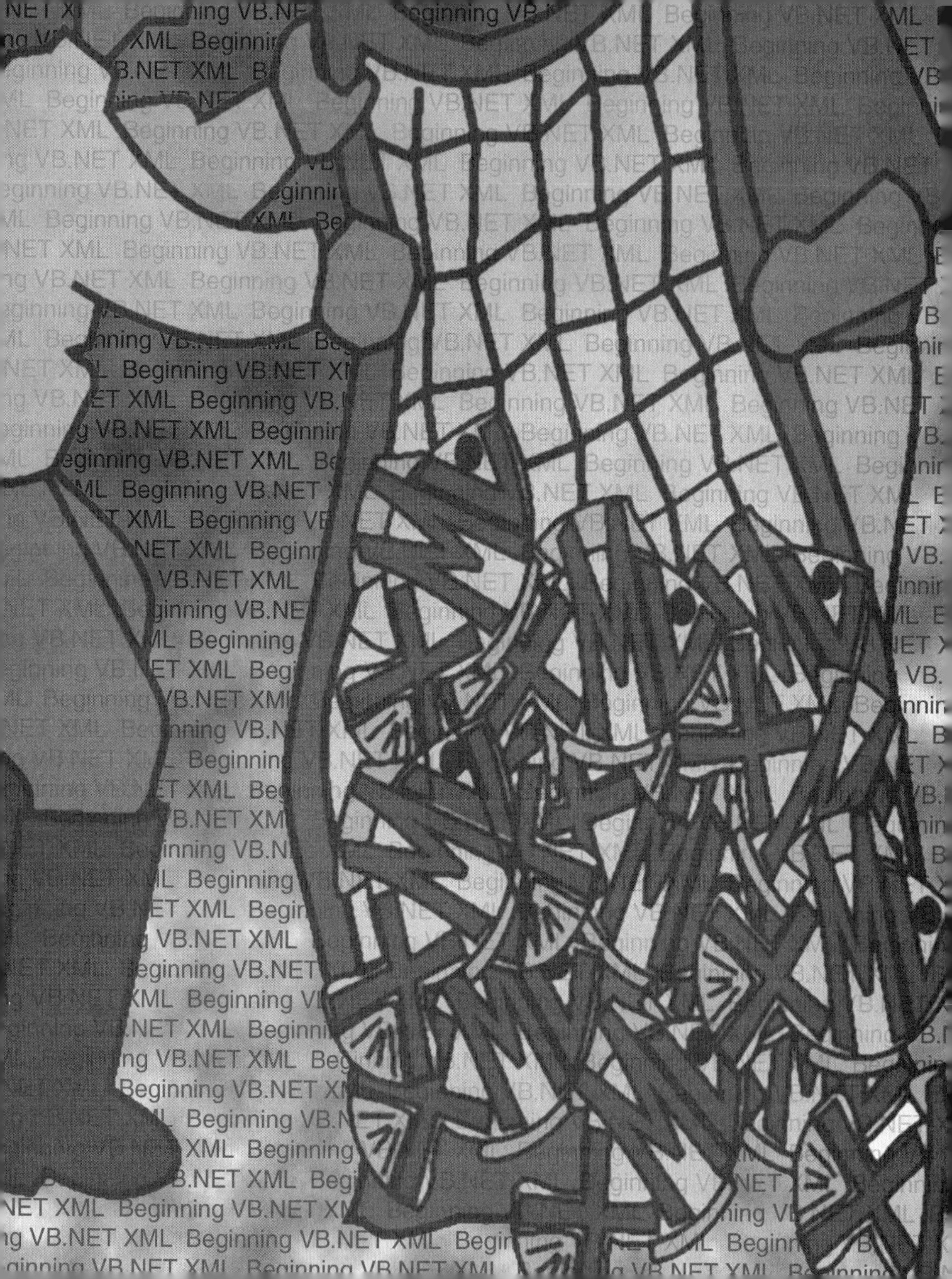
Beginning VB.NET XML

XML in ADO.NET

Throughout this book so far we've seen how we can represent data in an XML format, using elements, attributes, namespaces, and so on. It will probably come as no surprise to learn that ADO.NET, the collection of classes in the .NET Framework designed for working with data, contains a lot of functionality for working with XML data, and for writing data as XML.

For the benefit of those of you who are less familiar with it, ADO.NET is the new data access model for .NET applications, replacing and improving upon traditional ADO technology (used predominantly in ASP 3 and Visual Basic 6 applications) in many ways. The most significant improvement comes from its tight integration with XML, which will be our main focus throughout the chapter. We're going to briefly introduce the ADO.NET model and look at some examples to show how we can use it, then we'll move on to look at how XML fits in to the picture. We won't be looking at all of the ADO.NET features in this book, so for a more thorough discussion, you may want to refer to either *Beginning VB.NET Databases*, from Wrox Press, (ISBN 1-86100-555-5), or, for more of a fast-paced overview, you could refer to *Fast Track ADO.NET*, from Wrox Press (ISBN 1-86100-760-4).

In this chapter, we're going to look at:

- ❑ A quick refresher of what the .NET data providers are, and how they are used
- ❑ The different .NET data provider classes (`Connection`, `Command`, `DataReader`, `DataAdapter`, and `DataSet`) that are used to work with data sources
- ❑ How to read and write XML using the `DataSet`
- ❑ What the `XmlDataDocument` class provides for us

If you are already familiar with the basic workings of ADO.NET, you will probably find the first part of this chapter to be familiar ground that may serve as a useful refresher. And while we can use wizards in Visual Studio .NET to automatically generate a lot of code for us, we'll look at adding code by hand so that we can retain control over what techniques are used, and gain a better understanding of how to structure our code.

ADO.NET Overview

ADO.NET is a library of classes, interfaces, enumerations, and other tools that provide a structured and efficient toolkit for data access. ADO.NET provides functionality to developers writing managed code similar to the functionality provided to native COM developers by ADO.

ADO.NET is designed to enable the following:

❑ Seamless integration with the .NET Framework and provide a simple and intuitive way to access and work with relational data.

❑ Improved interoperability of web applications by using XML to share disconnected data across disparate systems.

❑ Extensibility – ADO.NET is fully extensible making it easier to integrate 3rd party and legacy data formats and databases.

❑ Tight integration with XML. XML support is built into ADO.NET at a fundamental level, bridging the gap between relational and hierarchical XML data, and offering great flexibility for developers of data-driven applications.

Now we have some idea of what ADO.NET is about, let's move on to look in some detail at the various classes that comprise ADO.NET.

.NET Data Providers

We'll start off by looking at the .NET data providers, whose primary function within the .NET Framework is to act as an interface between applications and data sources. They are used for retrieving data from a data source and reconciling changes to the data back to the data source. There are two namespaces supplied with .NET that contain classes for connecting to two different types of data sources:

.NET data provider namespaces	Description
System.Data. SqlClient	SQL Server .NET Data Provider for Microsoft SQL Server version 7.0 or later. It is optimized for accessing SQL Server and communicates with it directly by using the internal Tabular Data Stream (TDS) application-level protocol of SQL Server.
System.Data.OleDb	OLE DB .NET Data Provider for data sources exposed using OLE DB. Recommended for middle-tier applications using Microsoft SQL Server 6.5 or earlier. Also recommended for single-tier applications using Microsoft Access databases, or any other OLEDB provider that supports the proper OLEDB interfaces. Connecting to data sources using the OleDb classes is a bit slower than using the SqlClient classes because we have to pass through more connectivity layers to reach our data sources.

There are also additional providers available for download and subsequent installation:

.NET data provider namespaces	Description
`System.Data.Odbc`	An Open Database Connectivity (ODBC) .NET Data Provider is available as a separate download at http://msdn.microsoft.com for connecting to ODBC data sources (which tend to be older data sources that don't have an OLE DB provider). It provides native access to ODBC drivers in the same way that the OLE DB .NET Data Provider provides access to native OLE DB providers
`System.Data.SqlXml`	SQLXML (XML for SQL Server) is a downloadable and fully supported feature pack that extends the XML capabilities of SQL Server 2000. This namespace contains the managed providers that allow .NET code to take advantage of these enhanced XML features. The latest version is available for download at http://msdn.microsoft.com/sqlxml/
`System.Data. OracleClient`	This provider has been written to provide a similar service to that provided by the classes in the `SqlClient` namespace, as it connects directly to the Oracle database. It can be downloaded from: http://www.microsoft.com/downloads/release.asp?ReleaseID=37805.

The classes contained within each of these namespaces are all very similar in usage, but they have different prefixes corresponding to the connection method being used, for example, the `SqlClient` implementation of the `Connection` class is `SqlConnection`, whereas the `OleDb` equivalent is `OleDbConnection`, and so on.

> **We'll be using the `SqlClient` namespace for the examples in this chapter, so in each case when we are discussing functionality provided by various classes, we could equally be referring to any of the other data providers.**

A .NET data provider is comprised of four core objects: `Connection`, `Command`, `DataReader`, and `DataAdapter`.

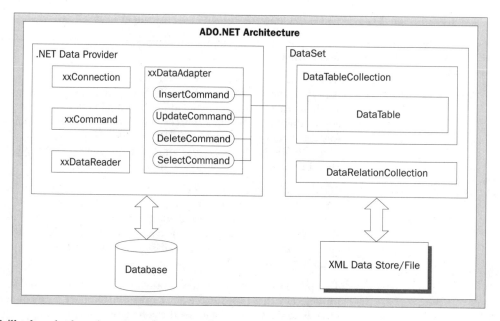

We'll take a look at these four objects in a bit more detail, and look at a couple of simple examples to show them in action.

The Connection Class

The Connection class establishes a connection to a specific data source and handles the security settings required to access the data source.

The Connection class defines several methods, including:

❑ Open() – Opens a database connection with the property settings specified by the ConnectionString.

❑ Close() – Closes the connection to the database. This is the preferred method of closing any open connection.

❑ CreateCommand() – Creates and returns a SqlCommand object associated with the SqlConnection.

Among its properties are the following:

❑ ConnectionString – Gets or sets the connection string used to open a SQL Server database.

❑ ConnectionTimeout – Gets the time to wait while trying to establish a connection before terminating the attempt and generating an error.

Let's look at the most commonly used connection strings for connecting to a database via the SqlConnection and OleDbConnection classes.

Standard Security

When a client connects to SQL Server with a username and password pair, SQL Server compares the supplied credentials against those stored in its system tables (note that connections that rely on username and password pairs are called non-trusted connections). If the supplied pair is not matched, authentication fails and the user receives an error message.

```
"Provider=sqloledb;Data Source=machineName;Initial Catalog=databaseName;
   User Id=userName;Password=password"
```

This is a sample connection string to an OLE DB data source, using the `OleDb` classes, to a database (specified in the intital `Catalog` attribute) that resides on a particular database server (specified in the `Data Source` attribute). We then specify the appropriate user name and password combination in the last two attributes.

A similar process occurs when connecting to a SQL Server database using the `SqlClient` classes, for example:

```
"Data Source=machineName;Initial Catalog= databaseName;
   User Id=userName;Password=password"
```

Putting this in context, we could connect to the SQL Server Pubs sample database residing on the local machine, using the default (and extremely hackable) administrator `sa` account and a blank password:

```
Dim cnString As String
cnString = "Data Source=localhost;user id=sa;password=;Initial Catalog=pubs"
Dim myConnection As SqlConnection
myConnection = New SqlConnection(cnString)
```

> When working on your own applications, it is strongly recommended that you assign a strong password to your administrator account and avoid ever having an account with a blank password to protect your data.

Trusted Connection

Windows Authentication Mode allows SQL Server 2000 to rely on the built-in Windows security policy to authenticate users. Connections made to the server using this mode are known as trusted connections. As an example, the following line of code represents a basic connection string using an `OleDbConnection` class that uses a trusted connection:

```
"Provider=sqloledb;Data Source=machineName;Initial Catalog= databaseName;
   Integrated Security=SSPI"
```

And if we use the `SqlConnection` class instead, our code would appear as follows:

```
"Data Source=machineName;Initial Catalog= databaseName; Integrated Security=SSPI"
```

Note that instead of using `Integrated Security=SSPI`, we could also use `Integrated Security=True`, as this is functionally equivalent.

The Command Class

The `Command` class executes a SQL command against a data source. We can use the `Command` class to access to database commands to return data, modify data, run stored procedures, and send or retrieve parameter information.

Several methods provided by this class are shown below:

❑ `ExecuteReader()` – This method executes commands that return rows

❑ `ExecuteNonQuery()` – This method executes commands such as Transact-SQL INSERT, DELETE, UPDATE, and SET statements

❑ `ExecuteScalar()` – This method retrieves a single value, such as the identity of an inserted row, from a database

❑ `ExecuteXmlReader()` – This method sends the `CommandText` to the connection and builds an `XmlReader` object

There are also several commonly used properties of this class:

❑ `CommandText` – Gets or sets the SQL statement or stored procedure to execute at the data source

❑ `CommandType` – Gets or sets a value indicating how the `CommandText` property is to be interpreted. Command type can be any one of three values:

    ❑ `StoredProcedure` – The name of a stored procedure

    ❑ `TableDirect` – When the `CommandType` property is set to `TableDirect`, the `CommandText` property should be set to the name of the table or tables to be accessed

    ❑ `Text` – A SQL string that could be a simple query, or could amend, insert, or even delete data from our database, for example: `"SELECT * FROM tbl_authors"`

❑ `ConnectionString` – Gets or sets the string used to open a SQL Server database

The following is a brief example of creating a new `SqlCommand` object:

```
Dim selectQuery As String = "SELECT * FROM stores"
Dim cmd As SqlCommand = New SqlCommand(selectQuery)
```

We'll look at an example of using this class in just a moment.

The DataReader Class

The `DataReader` class reads a forward-only, read-only stream of rows from a data source. Using the `DataReader` is very fast, and compared to using a `DataSet` (as we'll see shortly), it can increase application performance and reduce system overhead because only one row at a time is ever in memory, making it an especially good choice if we are retrieving large amounts of data.

The `DataReader` class defines many public methods, the most commonly used being:

- ❏ `Read()` – Advances the `SqlDataReader` to the next record.
- ❏ `Close()` – Closes the `SqlDataReader` object.

Let's look at a simple example of how we implement the `DataReader`. Once we've created a connection object, and specified a SQL query for our `command` object (which we can use to retrieve specified rows from our data source), we can then create a `DataReader` by calling `ExecuteReader()` method of the `Command` object to retrieve the required rows from a data source, as shown in the following example.

```
Dim rdr As SqlDataReader
rdr = cmd.ExecuteReader()
```

The `Read()` method of the `DataReader` object is then used to obtain a row from the results of the query. Here we iterate through a `DataReader` object, returning two columns from each row. Note that each column of the returned row can be accessed by passing the name or ordinal reference of the column, for example `rdr(0)`, to the `DataReader`, but for optimal performance we use accessor methods (accessor method column values should be accessed in their native data types, for example `DateTime`, `Guid`, `Int32`, `String`, and so on):

```
While rdr.Read()
   Console.WriteLine(rdr.GetInt32(0) + " " + rdr.GetString(1))
End While
rdr.Close()
```

The DataAdapter Class

The `DataAdapter` class populates a `DataSet` and resolves updates to the data back to the data source.

The `DataAdapter` has many properties and methods, too numerous to cover here, so we'll concentrate on the few we'll be using in this chapter. Let's look at the methods first.

- ❏ `Fill()` – Fills the `DataSet` with data from the database.
- ❏ `Update()` – Updates the data in the database based on changes to the data held in the `DataSet`

And four properties that we'll encounter in this chapter:

- ❏ `InsertCommand` – used to insert new records into the data source
- ❏ `DeleteCommand` – used to delete records from the data source
- ❏ `SelectCommand` – used to select records from the data source
- ❏ `UpdateCommand` – used to update records in the data source

These properties all use either a SQL statement or a stored procedure to affect the required records. We'll see some examples of the `DataAdapter` in action after we've looked at the `DataSet` class.

The CommandBuilder Class

Another class worth mentioning here is the `CommandBuilder`. The `CommandBuilder` auto-generates the `UpdateCommand`, `InsertCommand`, and `DeleteCommand` SQL statements used by the `DataAdapter` to write any changes to data held in a `DataSet` back to the underlying data source on a call to the `DataAdapter`'s `Update` method.

There are several public methods defined by this class, but there are three of particular interest:

❑ `GetDeleteCommand()` – Gets the automatically generated `SqlCommand` object required to perform deletions on the database when an application calls `Update` on the `SqlDataAdapter`.

❑ `GetInsertCommand()` – Gets the automatically generated `SqlCommand` object required to perform inserts on the database when an application calls `Update` on the `SqlDataAdapter`.

❑ `GetUpdateCommand()` – Gets the automatically generated `SqlCommand` object required to perform updates on the database when an application calls `Update` on the `SqlDataAdapter`.

And there's one public property of several we're interested in:

❑ `DataAdapter` – Gets or sets a `SqlDataAdapter` object for which T-SQL statements are automatically generated.

Although the `SqlCommandBuilder` can only be used for single table updates, we'll see in a later example just how convenient it can be in that particular scenario.

The DataSet Class

The `DataSet` is the object at the heart of ADO.NET's disconnected data processing model. It is effectively a disconnected cache of relational data. The diagram below shows the `DataSet` object model:

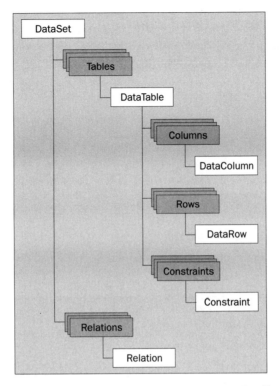

From the diagram we can see that the DataSet is made up of several collections (shown in grey): Tables, Columns, Constraints, and Relations, which describe the relational structure of the data. It also contains a collection of Rows, which represent the actual data.

Each DataTable object represents one table of in-memory relational data. The Columns collection for a particular DataTable contains a collection of all the table's columns (DataColumn objects), its Rows collection contains a collection of its rows (DataRow objects), and the Constraints collection, you guessed it, contains a collection of all the table's constraints. There are two types of constraint objects: ForeignKeyConstraints that define rules for how related child records should be updated when a record in a master table is updated or deleted, and UniqueConstraints which guarantees that column values are unique. The Relations collection contains a collection of DataRelation objects that establish a relationship between a parent and child tables based on a common key, such as a product ID number. We'll look at Relations in more detail later.

Data Access Strategy

Choosing correctly between the DataSet and DataReader classes to access your data can provide substantial performance gains. When we populate a DataSet, we're actually using a DataReader behind the scenes to obtain the data, which means that using a DataSet just for reading data is wasteful as there is another layer you need to go through. The DataSet represents the whole of your data in memory, whereas the DataReader can process data row by row, which in some ways is analogous to the DOM versus SAX relationship for processing XML. To help you make a more informed choice between the DataSet and the DataReader, we've outlined the two basic scenarios you'll encounter on the next page:

Data Retrieval and Presentation Scenario

Use the `DataReader` wherever the functionality of the `DataSet` isn't required, for example when no modification of the data is required, like when simply displaying data on a Web Form:

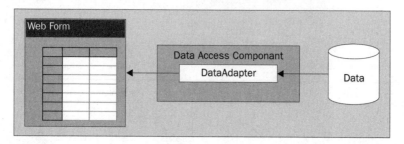

Disconnected Processing Scenario

Use the `DataSet` if you want to do any of the following:

❑   Remote data between tiers or from an XML Web Service

❑   Interact with data dynamically, such as binding to a Windows Forms control or combining and relating data from multiple sources

❑   Cache data locally in your application

❑   Provide a hierarchical XML view of relational data and use XSL Transformations or XPath Queries on your data

❑   Perform extensive processing on your data without requiring an open connection to the data source, which frees the connection to be used by other clients

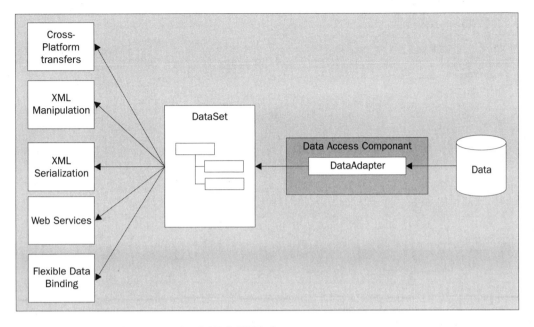

Let's move on to our first example of ADO.NET classes in action.

In this first example we'll create and fill a `DataSet` using the results obtained from a simple query performed on the sample Pubs database shipped with SQL Server 2000. We'll be using this database in all of our examples.

If you don't have SQL Server, you can use the SQL Server 2000 Desktop Engine (MSDE). If you have a copy of Visual Studio .NET, MSDE can be installed as part of this package, or after installation from the .NET samples. For more information about MSDE, you can refer to http://www.microsoft.com/sql/techinfo/development/2000/MSDE2000.asp for availability and installation instructions.

Try It Out: Binding a DataSet to a DataGrid

This example will perform a simple query on our database and display our results in a `DataGrid` on a Windows form.

> *Note that all the sample code for this chapter is available for download from http://www.wrox.com. We will be storing sample code for this chapter within the following folder:* `C:\BegVBXML\Chapter12`. *You may, of course, use a different folder depending on what you prefer.*

1. Create a new VB.NET Windows Application and call it **DisplayingData**.

2. Next, drag a `DataGrid` control and a `Button` control from the toolbox onto the form. Set the `Text` property of the button to **Run Example**. Then set the `AlternatingBackColor` property of the `DataGrid` in the **Properties** pane to an appropriate color, as shown below:

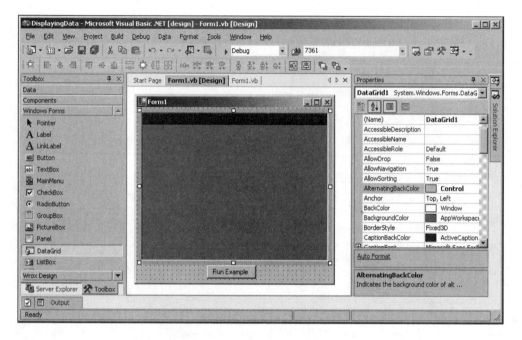

3. Double-click on the Run Example button to go to the code view. Add the following namespace directives at the top of the code:

```
Imports System.Data
Imports System.Data.SqlClient
```

4. Then add the code shown below to the Button1_Click() event handler.

```
Private Sub Button1_Click(ByVal sender As System.Object, e As System.EventArgs) _
                    Handles Button1.Click
```

```
Try
    Dim cnString As String = "data source=localhost;" & _
                        "initial catalog=pubs;Integrated Security=SSPI"

    'Specify SQL server-specific connection string
    Dim myConnection As New SqlConnection(cnString)

    'Create command text for DataAdapter
    Dim myCommandText As String = "SELECT au_lname, au_fname, " & _
                        "address FROM authors"

    'Open connection
    myConnection.Open()

    'Create DataAdapter object
    Dim myAdapter As New SqlDataAdapter(myCommandText, myConnection)
```

```
    'Create DataSet
    Dim myDataSet As New DataSet()

    'Fill DataSet
    myAdapter.Fill(myDataSet, "authors")

    'Close connection
    myConnection.Close()

    'Set the DataSource property of the DataGrid
    DataGrid1.DataSource = myDataSet.Tables("authors")

  Catch ex As SqlException

    MsgBox(ex.ToString())

  End Try
End Sub
```

5. Run the project and click the button – the `DataGrid` should be displayed on the form as shown below:

How It Works

We first import the relevant namespaces at the top of our code file so that we can use classes in our code without including the full namespace qualifier each time:

```
Imports System.Data
Imports System.Data.SqlClient
```

The next step is to create and open a connection to our database. Because connecting to a database could sometimes generate errors, we've included all of our code within a `Try...Catch` block. In our example, we've used Integrated Security to connect to our data store, though you could use SQL Server authentication if you preferred. We then use our connection string to open a new connection object:

```
Try
  Dim cnString As String = "data source=localhost;" & _
                           "initial catalog=pubs;Integrated Security=SSPI"

  'Specify SQL server-specific connection string
  Dim myConnection As New SqlConnection(cnString)
```

> Note that this example assumes you have a database configured to reside on the local machine as a root instance, not a named instance. If you have installed MSDE from the .NET Samples, you may need to use `(local)\NetSDK` instead of `Localhost` for your data source. For more information on connecting to different databases, you may want to refer to *Beginning VB.NET Databases,* fromWrox Press ISBN: 1-86100-555-5.

Next we build our SQL query and pass it to the `SqlDataAdapter` constructor along with the `Connection` object:

```
'Create command text for DataAdapter
Dim myCommandText As String = "SELECT au_lname, au_fname, " & _
                              "address FROM authors"

'Open connection
myConnection.Open()

'Create DataAdapter object
Dim myAdapter As New SqlDataAdapter(myCommandText, myConnection)
```

We can now create a new `DataSet` instance and populate it with data using the `Fill()` method of the `DataAdapter`:

```
'Create DataSet
Dim myDataSet As New DataSet()

'Fill DataSet
myAdapter.Fill(myDataSet, "authors")
```

We can now close our connection and display the results of our query in our data grid:

```
'Close connection
myConnection.Close()

'Set the DataSource property of the DataGrid
DataGrid1.DataSource = myDataSet.Tables("authors")
```

Our final act is to finish with a `Catch` section, which will handle any errors incurred while attempting to run the example:

```
Catch ex As SqlException

  MsgBox(ex.ToString())

End Try
```

If an exception is thrown, for example if you specify a non-existent SQL Server, if your SQL Server service isn't running, or if your user credentials fail authentication, a message box will pop up with details of the error giving you some idea of where your code has gone wrong.

Working with Data in a DataTable

Now that we've seen how to fill a `DataSet` with data from a database and display it, we can then manipulate that data in a `DataTable`. By manipulation, we mean adding new data, amending existing data, or deleting data, and when we're working with offline data, this process could get a little tricky. Imagine if you made some changes to your data while working offline, and one of your colleagues made a different change to the same record and updated the data source. When you go back online to update your data, you will need to deal with the two conflicting updates in the most appropriate manner.

There are numerous classes available to us when we are working with our data that contain methods and properties that can be used to track the state of each row that we may alter, add, delete, and so on, and we are able to track any changes that are made to the data between the time at which the `DataSet` was populated, and the time when we are ready to update our data source. We're not going to look at these in detail in this book, since we want to concentrate on the XML functionality available to us when using ADO.NET. Let's simply look at a quick example of making a change to an offline `DataSet`, then updating the database.

Because the `DataSet` is disconnected from the underlying data source, the changes we make offline won't be propagated back to the database unless we explicitly do so. This can be done by calling the `Update` method of the `DataAdapter`.

When the `Update` method is called, the `DataAdapter` analyzes the changes that have been made and when a change to a `DataRow` is encountered, it uses the `InsertCommand`, `UpdateCommand`, or `DeleteCommand` to process the change. The appropriate command is selected on the basis of the Row's `RowState`. Let's see a very simple example:

Try It Out: Updating a Data Source

In this example we'll fill a table in a dataset with all the rows from the `authors` table, then we'll find a particular author and change their address. The changes will then be propagated back to the database.

> **1.** Create a new VB.NET console application project called **DBUpdates** and add the following two namespace references at the very top of the `Module1.vb` file:

```
Imports System.Data
Imports System.Data.SqlClient
```

2. Next add the following code to the `Main()` method:

```
Dim cnString As String
cnString = "data source=localhost;initial catalog=pubs;Integrated Security=SSPI;"

'Create new SqlConnection object
Dim myConnection As New SqlConnection(cnString)

'Open connection
myConnection.Open()

'Create command text for DataAdapter
Dim myCommandText As String = "SELECT * FROM authors"

'Create DataAdapter object
Dim myAdapter As New SqlDataAdapter(myCommandText, myConnection)

'Create CommandBuilder to build SQL commands
Dim myBuilder As New SqlCommandBuilder(myAdapter)

'Create DataSet
Dim myDataSet As New DataSet()

'Fill DataSet
myAdapter.Fill(myDataSet, "authors")

Dim authTable As DataTable
authTable = myDataSet.Tables("authors")

'Find record and modify
Dim foundRows As DataRow()
foundRows = authTable.Select("au_fname = 'Innes' AND au_lname='del Castillo'")
PrintRows(foundRows, "author details before change")
foundRows(0)("address") = "22 Sandy Shores, Burntisland"
PrintRows(foundRows, "author details after change")

myAdapter.Update(myDataSet, "authors")

'Close connection
myConnection.Close()
Console.ReadLine()
```

3. Add the `PrintRows()` method below `Main()`

```
Sub PrintRows(ByVal foundRows As DataRow(), ByVal label As String)
  Dim r As DataRow
  Dim c As DataColumn
```

```
      If (foundRows.Length <= 0) Then
        Console.WriteLine("no records found")
        Return
      End If

      For Each r In foundRows
        Console.Write(label + ":")
        For Each c In r.Table.Columns
          Console.WriteLine(c.ColumnName + " = " & r(c) & "    ")
        Next
        Console.WriteLine()
      Next
  End Sub
```

4. Run the code by pressing *Ctrl-F5*. The console output should look like this:

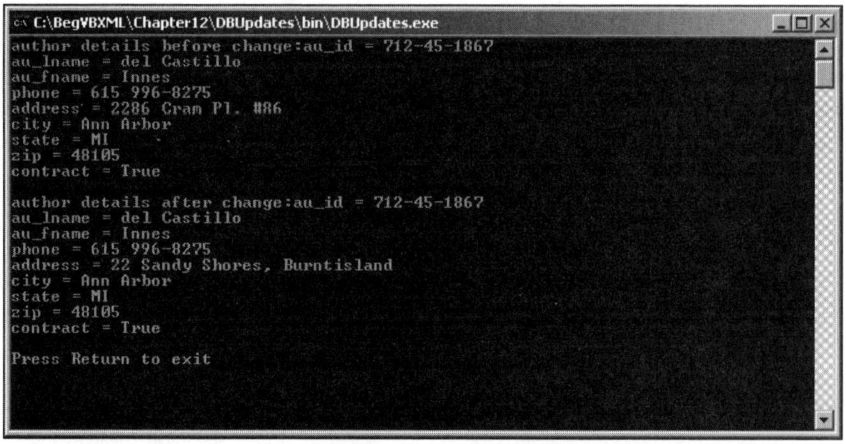

How It Works

We set up our connection string and open the connection as we have done before:

```
Dim cnString As String
cnString = "data source=localhost;initial catalog=pubs;Integrated Security=SSPI;"

'Create new SqlConnection object
Dim myConnection As New SqlConnection(cnString)

'Open connection
myConnection.Open()
```

Next we create the command text for the `DataAdapter`, which initializes the `SqlDataAdapter`'s `SelectCommand` property.

```
'Create command text for DataAdapter
Dim myCommandText As String = "SELECT * FROM authors"
```

```
'Create DataAdapter object
Dim myAdapter As New SqlDataAdapter(myCommandText, myConnection)
```

We then construct a `CommandBuilder` object passing the `SqlDataAdapter` as an argument to its constructor to automatically build the UPDATE command for the `DataAdapter`.

```
'Create CommandBuilder to build SQL commands
Dim myBuilder As New SqlCommandBuilder(myAdapter)
```

We create and fill our `DataSet` with the results of our database SELECT:

```
'Create DataSet
Dim myDataSet As New DataSet()

'Fill DataSet
myAdapter.Fill(myDataSet, "authors")
```

Find the author in the `DataTable` and modify his address:

```
'Find record and modify
Dim foundRows As DataRow()
foundRows = authTable.Select("au_fname = 'Innes' AND au_lname='del Castillo'")
PrintRows(foundRows, "author details before change")
foundRows(0)("address") = "22 Sandy Shores, Burntisland"
PrintRows(foundRows, "author details after change")
```

Then call `Update` to propagate the changes back to the database:

```
myAdapter.Update(myDataSet, "authors")
```

Finally, we close the connection:

```
myConnection.Close()
```

We then use the `PrintRows()` method to iterate through our columns and rows to display the appropriate details.

> *We'll use this method again later in this chapter, so to speed up this process, you might want to copy the method to a custom toolbar. Simply right-click on the toolbox pane, and select **Add Tab**. Type a name for your tab, for example, **My Snippets**. All you have to do then is expand the new tab, select the whole of the method you want to reuse and drag it to the toolbar. Whenever you need to reuse the method, you can drag it back into your code.*

Relationships

So far we've looked at getting data from a single table only. But there will be many occasions when you'll be working with multiple tables that are related in some way. Filling a `DataSet` with data from two related tables requires two queries to access the tables separately. The relationship between the two tables is then explicitly defined by the `DataRelation` class. The relationship is created between matching columns in the "parent" and "child" tables via the `DataColumn` class. The "parent" table is that containing the Primary Key, the "child" table containing the Foreign Key. In the example below, the `AuthorID` column relates the two tables in a one-to-many relationship. What this means in English is that any one author may have published one or several books. The Primary Key (PK) is the `AuthorID` column in the Authors table, with the Foreign Key (FK) being the `AuthorID` column in the Titles table.

Authors Table		Titles Table	
Name	AuthorID (PK)	AuthorID (FK)	Title
Deborah Barrett	1001	1003	Beginning C# XML
Siegfried McDougal	1002	1003	Dummies Guide to Notepad
Harry Planter	1003	1003	Professional CharMap .NET

Let's look at an example that helps us to understand how we can populate a `DataSet` with data from multiple tables. Later on in the chapter we can look at how we can represent this sort of data as XML.

Try It Out: Populating a DataSet from Multiple Tables

In this example we'll add the `authors` and `titleauthor` tables to a `DataSet` and create a relationship between them so we can find all the `title_ids` associated with each author.

1. Create a new VB.NET console application project called **Relationships** and add the following two namespace references at the very top of the `Module1.vb` file:

```
Imports System.Data
Imports System.Data.SqlClient
```

2. Next add the following code to the `Main()` method.

```
Dim myDataSet As DataSet
myDataSet = fillDS()
Dim myDR As DataRelation
myDR = myDataSet.Relations("AuthTitles")

'Print out the nested authors and their author ids
Dim authRow As DataRow
Dim titleRow As DataRow

For Each authRow In myDataSet.Tables("authors").Rows
  Console.WriteLine("Author ID:" & authRow("au_id") & " Name: " & _
      authRow("au_fname") & " " & authRow("au_lname"))
  For Each titleRow In authRow.GetChildRows(myDR)
```

```
      Console.WriteLine(vbTab & "Title ID: " & titleRow("title_id"))
   Next
Next

Console.ReadLine()
```

3. Add the following method under the `Main()` method:

```
Function fillDS() As DataSet
   Dim cnString As String
   cnString = "data source=localhost;initial catalog=pubs;" & _
            "Integrated Security=SSPI;"

   'Create a new SqlConnection object
   Dim myConnection As New SqlConnection(cnString)

   'Open connection
   myConnection.Open()

   'Create command text for author DataAdapter
   Dim myAuthorCommandText As String = ("SELECT au_id, au_lname, " & _
                                  "au_fname, address FROM authors")

   'Create command text for title DataAdapter
   Dim myTitleCommandText As String = ("SELECT au_id, title_id FROM " & _
                                  "titleauthor")

   'Create DataAdapter objects for each table
   Dim myAuthorAdapter As New SqlDataAdapter(myAuthorCommandText, myConnection)
   Dim myTitleAdapter As New SqlDataAdapter(myTitleCommandText, myConnection)

   'Create DataSet
   Dim myDS As New DataSet()

   'Fill the dataset
   myAuthorAdapter.Fill(myDS, "authors")
   myTitleAdapter.Fill(myDS, "titleauthor")

   'Get the DataColumn objects from two DataTable objects in the DataSet.
   Dim parentCol As DataColumn
   Dim childCol As DataColumn

   parentCol = myDS.Tables("authors").Columns("au_id")
   childCol = myDS.Tables("titleauthor").Columns("au_id")

   'Create DataRelation between authors and titles.
   Dim authorTitleRel As New DataRelation("AuthTitles", parentCol, childCol)

   'Add the relation to the DataSet.
   myDS.Relations.Add(authorTitleRel)

   'Close connection
   myConnection.Close()
   Return myDS
End Function
```

4. Compile and run the project. The output in the console will be as below:

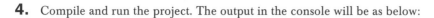

```
C:\BegVBXML\Chapter12\Relationships\bin\Relationships.exe                    _ □ X
Author ID:672-71-3249 Name: Akiko Yokomoto
        Title ID: TC7777
Author ID:712-45-1867 Name: Innes del Castillo
        Title ID: MC2222
Author ID:722-51-5454 Name: Michel DeFrance
        Title ID: MC3021
Author ID:724-08-9931 Name: Dirk Stringer
Author ID:724-80-9391 Name: Stearns MacFeather
        Title ID: BU1111
        Title ID: PS1372
Author ID:756-30-7391 Name: Livia Karsen
        Title ID: PS1372
Author ID:807-91-6654 Name: Sylvia Panteley
        Title ID: TC3218
Author ID:846-92-7186 Name: Sheryl Hunter
        Title ID: PC8888
Author ID:893-72-1158 Name: Heather McBadden
Author ID:899-46-2035 Name: Anne Ringer
        Title ID: MC3021
        Title ID: PS2091
Author ID:998-72-3567 Name: Albert Ringer
        Title ID: PS2091
        Title ID: PS2106

Press any key to continue_
```

How It Works

The screenshot below is an extract of the Pubs database diagram showing the relationship between the `authors` and `titleauthor` tables. The line joining the two tables tells us there is a primary key-foreign key relationship between the tables, with the primary key being the `au_id` column in the `authors` table.

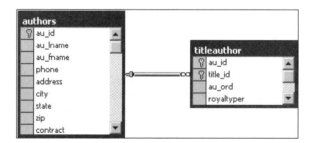

In the `fillDS()` method we fill our `DataSet` and create the relationships between the two tables (we'll use this function extensively throughout the rest of the chapter, so you may want to keep a copy of it handy as we described with the `PrintRows()` method earlier). The parent column in our `DataRelation` is the `au_id` column in the `authors` table, with the child being the `au_id` column in the `titleauthor` table. We've created `DataColumn` instances for both of these:

```
'get the DataColumn objects from two DataTable objects in the DataSet
Dim parentCol As DataColumn
Dim childCol As DataColumn

parentCol = myDS.Tables("authors").Columns("au_id")
childCol = myDS.Tables("titleauthor").Columns("au_id")
```

Next we create the `DataRelation`. The first parameter passed in the `DataRelation` constructor string is the name of the relation:

549

```
'create DataRelation between authors and titles.
Dim authorTitleRel As New DataRelation("AuthTitles", parentCol, childCol)
```

The next step is to add the `DataRelation` we just created to the `DataSet`:

```
'add the relation to the DataSet.
myDS.Relations.Add(authorTitleRel)
```

Now the relationship is set up, we can begin processing our results. We need to set up a `For Each` loop to display the `title_id` for each author.

```
For Each authRow In myDataSet.Tables("authors").Rows
  Console.WriteLine("Author ID:" & authRow("au_id") & " Name: " & _
      authRow("au_fname") & " " & authRow("au_lname"))
  For Each titleRow In authRow.GetChildRows(myDR)
    Console.WriteLine(vbTab & "Title ID: " & titleRow("title_id"))
  Next
Next
```

Notice here we're iterating the `Rows` collection in this example using a `For Each` loop. The nested `For Each` loop displays all `titleRows` associated with the current `authRow`. The related rows are returned by the `GetChildRows` method of `DataRow`.

The DataSet and XML

We've looked in some depth at the `DataSet` in the previous sections of the chapter, but from a relational data perspective. We'll concentrate now on the `DataSet`'s support for XML.

`DataSets` can also be filled from an XML stream or document. Conversely, the contents of a `DataSet` can be written as an XML stream or document. So, without further ado (pardon the pun), let's take a look at the various methods provided by the `DataSet` for reading and writing XML and XML Schemas.

Methods	Description
GetXml	Returns a string containing an XML representation of the data stored in the DataSet.
GetXmlSchema	Returns a string containing the XML schema for the DataSet.
WriteXml	Writes the XML representation of the data in the DataSet class to a stream, file, TextWriter, or XMLWriter class. The schema can be optionally included with the XML.
WriteXmlSchema	Writes a string containing the XML Schema information to a stream or file.
ReadXml	Populates a DataSet class with the specified XML data read from a stream or file.
ReadXmlSchema	Loads the specified XML schema information into the current DataSet class.

Generating XML from a DataSet – the WriteXml() Method

There are a number of situations where having an XML representation of our `DataSet` would be desired. For instance, we might want to transfer the contents of the `DataSet` to a remote client over HTTP for use by another application, or we may want to pass it to a Web Service. We can write to several sources depending on how the generated XML will be used. We can optionally include the `DataSet` schema by specifying the `XmlWriteMode` – we'll say more about `DataSet` schemas later. For now, let's take a look at the various overloads we have at our disposal when using the `WriteXML()` method.

```
Overloads Public Sub WriteXml(Overload1, XmlWriteMode)
```

The `XmlWriteMode` is optional. If we ignore this for a moment, `Overload1` can be any one of the following:

Overload	Result
Stream	Writes `DataSet` data using the specified `System.IO.Stream`
String	Writes `DataSet` data to a specified file
TextWriter	Writes `DataSet` data using the specified `TextWriter`
XmlWriter	Writes `DataSet` data to the specified `XmlWriter`

If we also pass in an `XmlWriteMode` to the constructor, we have some more options about our output XML:

Method	Description
IgnoreSchema	Writes the current contents of the `DataSet` as XML data, without an XML Schema. This is the default.
WriteSchema	Writes the current contents of the `DataSet` as XML data with the relational structure as inline XML Schema (XSD).
DiffGram	Writes the entire `DataSet` as a `DiffGram`, including original and current values.

Let's see this in action by looking at an example.

Try It Out: Saving a DataSet as an XML Document

In this example we'll show how the contents of a `DataSet` can be persisted to an XML file. We'll also introduce the nested property of the `DataRelation` class.

1. Create a new VB.NET console application project called `SaveDataSetAsXML` and add the following two namespace references at the very top of the `Module1.vb` file:

```
Imports System.Data
Imports System.Data.SqlClient
```

2. Next add the following code to the `Main()` method:

```
Dim myDataSet As DataSet = fillDS()
Dim myDR As DataRelation = myDataSet.Relations("AuthTitles")

myDR.Nested = False
myDataSet.WriteXml("..\nestedFalse.xml")

myDR.Nested = True
myDataSet.WriteXml("..\nestedTrue.xml")
```

3. Add the `fillDS()` function we used in our previous example below `Main()`.

4. Compile and run the project. Two XML files called `nestedFalse.xml` and `nestedTrue.xml` should be created in the current working directory.

How It Works

The code fills the `DataSet` exactly as we did in the Relationships example earlier, but instead of writing the contents of the `DataSet` as we did before using nested `For Each` loops, we make a single call to `WriteXML()`. We've chosen in this example to write our XML using the default `XmlWriteMode` (by not specifying the mode our code will use the default) which excludes the inline XSD schema.

```
myDataSet.WriteXml("..\nestedFalse.xml")
```

We set the `DataRelation`'s `Nested` property **before** we write the XML to file.

```
myDR.Nested = false
```

We can control how the child rows of a relation are rendered in XML using the `Nested` property. Setting `Nested` to `True` ensures the `titleauthor` nodes are rendered as children of the corresponding author nodes as shown in the `nestedTrue.xml` below (the XML has been truncated because it's quite long).

```
<?xml version="1.0" standalone="yes"?>
<NewDataSet>
  <authors>
    <au_id>172-32-1176</au_id>
    <au_lname>White</au_lname>
    <au_fname>Johnson</au_fname>
    <address>10932 Bigge Rd.</address>
    <titleauthor>
      <au_id>172-32-1176</au_id>
      <title_id>PS3333</title_id>
    </titleauthor>
  </authors>
  <authors>
    <au_id>213-46-8915</au_id>
    <au_lname>Green</au_lname>
```

```
      <au_fname>Marjorie</au_fname>
      <address>309 63rd St. #411</address>
      <titleauthor>
        <au_id>213-46-8915</au_id>
        <title_id>BU1032</title_id>
      </titleauthor>
      <titleauthor>
        <au_id>213-46-8915</au_id>
        <title_id>BU2075</title_id>
      </titleauthor>
    </authors>
    ...
  </NewDataSet>
```

The contents of `nestedFalse.xml` below shows us how the XML looks when `Nested` is set to `false`.

```xml
<?xml version="1.0" standalone="yes"?>
<NewDataSet>
  <authors>
    <au_id>427-17-2319</au_id>
    <au_lname>Dull</au_lname>
    <au_fname>Ann</au_fname>
    <address>3410 Blonde St.</address>
  </authors>
  <authors>
    <au_id>486-29-1786</au_id>
    <au_lname>Locksley</au_lname>
    <au_fname>Charlene</au_fname>
    <address>18 Broadway Av.</address>
  </authors>
  ...
  <titleauthor>
    <au_id>213-46-8915</au_id>
    <title_id>BU1032</title_id>
  </titleauthor>
  <titleauthor>
    <au_id>409-56-7008</au_id>
    <title_id>BU1032</title_id>
  </titleauthor>
  ...
</NewDataSet>
```

Generating XML Schemas from a DataSet – the WriteXmlSchema() Method

The `WriteXmlSchema()` method enables us to write a `DataSet` structure as an XML schema. It has four overloads, similar to those of the `WriteXml()` method:

```
Overloads Public Sub WriteXmlSchema(Source)
```

Where the *Source* argument can again be either a `Stream`, `String`, `TextWriter`, or `XmlWriter`.

Let's see it in action:

Try It Out: Generating an XML Schema from a DataSet

1. Create a new VB.NET console application project called **GenerateXSDFromDataset** and add the following two namespace references at the very top of the `Module1.vb` file:

```
Imports System.Data
Imports System.Data.SqlClient
```

2. Next add the following code to the `Main()` method:

```
Dim myDataSet As DataSet = fillDS()
myDataSet.WriteXmlSchema("..\authTitle.xsd")
```

3. Add the `fillDS()` function we used in our previous example below the `Main()` method.

4. Compile and run the project. The XSD schema generated (`authTitle.xsd`) is written to the working directory for our project. The contents of this file are shown below:

```xml
<?xml version="1.0" standalone="yes"?>
<xs:schema id="NewDataSet" xmlns="" xmlns:xs="http://www.w3.org/2001/XMLSchema"
xmlns:msdata="urn:schemas-microsoft-com:xml-msdata">
  <xs:element name="NewDataSet" msdata:IsDataSet="true" msdata:Locale="en-GB">
    <xs:complexType>
      <xs:choice maxOccurs="unbounded">
        <xs:element name="authors">
          <xs:complexType>
            <xs:sequence>
              <xs:element name="au_id" type="xs:string" minOccurs="0" />
              <xs:element name="au_lname" type="xs:string" minOccurs="0" />
              <xs:element name="au_fname" type="xs:string" minOccurs="0" />
              <xs:element name="address" type="xs:string" minOccurs="0" />
            </xs:sequence>
          </xs:complexType>
        </xs:element>
        <xs:element name="titleauthor">
          <xs:complexType>
            <xs:sequence>
              <xs:element name="au_id" type="xs:string" minOccurs="0" />
              <xs:element name="title_id" type="xs:string" minOccurs="0" />
            </xs:sequence>
          </xs:complexType>
        </xs:element>
      </xs:choice>
    </xs:complexType>
    <xs:unique name="Constraint1">
      <xs:selector xpath=".//authors" />
      <xs:field xpath="au_id" />
    </xs:unique>
    <xs:keyref name="AuthTitles" refer="Constraint1">
      <xs:selector xpath=".//titleauthor" />
```

```
              <xs:field xpath="au_id" />
         </xs:keyref>
    </xs:element>
</xs:schema>
```

How It Works

A table is generated in the `DataSet` for every `complexType` child element of a schema element. The table structure is determined by the definition of the complex type. So, for our `authors` table we have:

```
<xs:element name="authors">
  <xs:complexType>
    <xs:sequence>
      <xs:element name="au_id" type="xs:string" minOccurs="0" />
      <xs:element name="au_lname" type="xs:string" minOccurs="0" />
      <xs:element name="au_fname" type="xs:string" minOccurs="0" />
      <xs:element name="address" type="xs:string" minOccurs="0" />
    </xs:sequence>
  </xs:complexType>
</xs:element>
```

The mapping process will create an "authors" `DataTable` with columns au_id, au_lname, au_fname, and address in the `DataSet`. For the `titleauthor` table we have the following:

```
<xs:element name="titleauthor">
  <xs:complexType>
    <xs:sequence>
      <xs:element name="au_id" type="xs:string" minOccurs="0" />
      <xs:element name="title_id" type="xs:string" minOccurs="0" />
    </xs:sequence>
  </xs:complexType>
</xs:element>
```

The mapping process creates a "titleauthor" `DataTable` from this with columns au_id and title_id in the `DataSet`.

The `<unique>` element in an XSD schema specifies the uniqueness constraint on an element or attribute, which maps to a unique constraint in the `DataTable` in the generated `DataSet`. So in this case the uniqueness constraint is being applied to the au_id column of the `authors` DataTable:

```
<xs:unique name="Constraint1">
  <xs:selector xpath=".//authors" />
  <xs:field xpath="au_id" />
</xs:unique>
```

The `<keyref>` element allows you to establish links between elements within a document. This is similar to a foreign key relationship in a relational database. If a schema specifies the `<keyref>` element, during the schema mapping process the element is converted to a corresponding foreign key constraint on the columns in the tables of the `DataSet`. By default, the `<keyref>` element also generates a relation, with the `ParentTable`, `ChildTable`, `ParentColumn`, and `ChildColumn` properties specified on the relation.

```
<xs:keyref name="AuthTitles" refer="Constraint1">
  <xs:selector xpath=".//titleauthor" />
  <xs:field xpath="au_id" />
</xs:keyref>
```

DiffGrams

The `DiffGram` format is used to identify current and original values in XML documents, highlighting the differences between the two. It is used implicitly when sending and receiving `DataSets` to and from an XML Web Service, and can be used by applications running on other platforms to send and receive data to or from a .NET application. This provides a very simple and flexible method for transmitting and returning relational data using XML Web Services. Worthy of note is that while the `DiffGram` format is used primarily as a serialization format for the contents of a `DataSet`, you can also use `DiffGrams` to modify data in tables in a SQL Server 2000 database.

Let's take a look at an example.

Try It Out: Saving a DataSet as a DiffGram

As we won't be looking at web services until the next chapter, we'll simply write the contents of our `DataSet` as a `DiffGram` to a file so we can examine it. We'll modify one of the rows in the `DataSet` before we write out the `DiffGram` so as to further illustrate the concept:

1. Create a new VB.NET console application project called `SaveDataSetAsDiffgram` and add the following two namespace references at the very top of the `Module1.vb` file:

```
Imports System.Data
Imports System.Data.SqlClient
```

2. Next add the following code to the `Main()` method:

```
Dim myDataSet As DataSet = fillDS()

Dim foundRows As DataRow()
foundRows = myDataSet.Tables("authors").Select("au_lname = 'del Castillo'")

PrintRows(foundRows, "author details before change")
foundRows(0)("address") = "new address, somewhere far away"
PrintRows(foundRows, "author details after change")

myDataSet.WriteXml("..\DiffGram.xml", XmlWriteMode.DiffGram)

Console.Readline()
```

3. Add the `fillDS()` and `PrintRows()` methods we used in previous examples below the `Main()` method.

4. Compile and run the project. The console output will be as shown in the figure below and a file called `DiffGram.xml` will have been created in the current working directory:

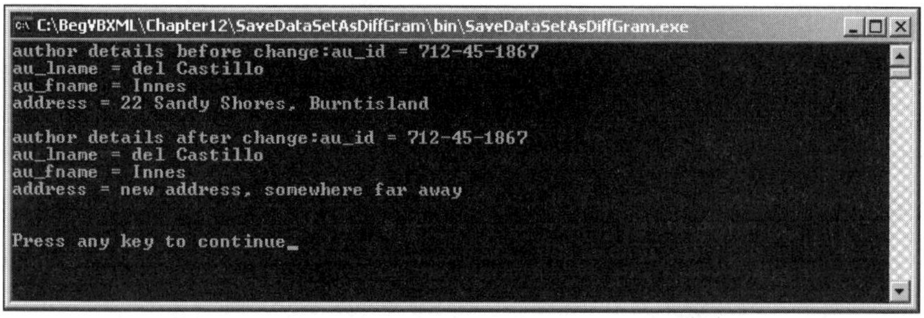

The contents of `DiffGram.xml` is shown below (note – the listing has been truncated because it's quite large):

```xml
<?xml version="1.0" standalone="yes"?>
<diffgr:diffgram xmlns:msdata="urn:schemas-microsoft-com:xml-msdata"
                 xmlns:diffgr="urn:schemas-microsoft-com:xml-diffgram-v1">
  <NewDataSet>
    <authors diffgr:id="authors1" msdata:rowOrder="0">
      <au_id>172-32-1176</au_id>
      <au_lname>White</au_lname>
      <au_fname>Johnson</au_fname>
      <address>10932 Bigge Rd.</address>
    </authors>
    ...
    <authors diffgr:id="authors14" msdata:rowOrder="13"
          diffgr:hasChanges="modified">
      <au_id>712-45-1867</au_id>
      <au_lname>del Castillo</au_lname>
      <au_fname>Innes</au_fname>
      <address>new address, somewhere far away</address>
    </authors>
    ...
    <titleauthor diffgr:id="titleauthor1" msdata:rowOrder="0">
      <au_id>213-46-8915</au_id>
      <title_id>BU1032</title_id>
    </titleauthor>
    ...
    <titleauthor diffgr:id="titleauthor13" msdata:rowOrder="12">
      <au_id>486-29-1786</au_id>
      <title_id>PC9999</title_id>
    </titleauthor>
    ...
  </NewDataSet>
  <diffgr:before>
    <authors diffgr:id="authors14" msdata:rowOrder="13">
      <au_id>712-45-1867</au_id>
      <au_lname>del Castillo</au_lname>
      <au_fname>Innes</au_fname>
      <address>2286 Cram Pl. #86</address>
    </authors>
  </diffgr:before>
</diffgr:diffgram>
```

How It Works

With the `DataSet` filled, we locate an author with the last name `del Castillo` using the `DataTable`'s `Select` method:

```
Dim foundRows As DataRow()
foundRows = myDataSet.Tables("authors").Select("au_lname = 'del Castillo'")
```

Next we change the author's address, writing the author's details to the console before and after the change using the `PrintRows` function we wrote for an earlier example:

```
PrintRows(foundRows, "author details before change")
foundRows(0)("address") = "new address, somewhere far away"
PrintRows(foundRows, "author details after change")
```

Finally we write the `DiffGram` to file:

```
myDataSet.WriteXml("..\DiffGram.xml", XmlWriteMode.DiffGram)
```

The `DiffGram` itself consists of 3 main blocks of data (2 of which are shown below):

```
<NewDataSet>
  <authors diffgr:id="authors14" msdata:rowOrder="13"
                      diffgr:hasChanges="modified">
    <au_id>712-45-1867</au_id>
    <au_lname>del Castillo</au_lname>
    <au_fname>Innes</au_fname>
    <address>new address, somewhere far away</address>
  </authors>
</NewDataSet>
```

This first block of data represents contains the `Current` row data. The `<NewDataSet>` element represents our `DataSet`. Notice the address element contains the new address. We know this row has been modified because the `diffgr:hasChanges` attribute is set to `"modified"`. The next block contains the `Original` version of the row data; the `<address>` element here contains the original address. Notice the use of the `diffgr:id` annotation to pair the elements in the `<diffgr:before>` and `<NewDataSet>` block:

```
<diffgr:before>
  <authors diffgr:id="authors14" msdata:rowOrder="13">
    <au_id>712-45-1867</au_id>
    <au_lname>del Castillo</au_lname>
    <au_fname>Innes</au_fname>
    <address>2286 Cram Pl. #86</address>
  </authors>
</diffgr:before>
```

The third block referenced earlier is not shown in our `DiffGram` output because it's an errors block and it's only written out if there are row errors. The errors would be contained within the `<diffgr:errors>` element and would be matched to elements in the `Current` block using the `diffgr:id` annotation.

Building a DataSet with XML

We can generate the relational structure of a `DataSet` and populate it with data from an XML document or stream using the `DataSet` class's `ReadXml()` method. The `ReadXml()` method has 8 overloads, all of which take the XML source and 4 of which take an optional `XmlReadMode` value as arguments.

```
Overloads Public Function ReadXml(Source, XmlReadMode) As XmlReadMode
```

The XML *Source* argument is one of `Stream`, `String`, `TextReader`, or `XmlReader`.

If we specify an `XmlReader` instance as the source (or any instance derived from `XmlReader`) a DOM instance is built from its contents. If you pass an `XmlReader` that is positioned on some node in the tree, `ReadXml` will read to the next element node and will treat that as the root element, reading until the end of the element node only. This does not apply if you specify that the `XmlReadMode` is `Fragment`.

Adding the `XmlReadMode` argument specifies how the XML data and a relational schema are read into the `DataSet`. The members of the `XmlReadMode` are shown in the table below (note that if we do not specify the `XmlReadMode`, it defaults to `Auto`):

XmlReadMode	Description
ReadSchema	Reads any inline schema and loads the data and schema.
IgnoreSchema	Ignores any inline schema and loads the data into the existing `DataSet` schema.
InferSchema	Ignores any inline schema and infers the schema from the structure of the XML data, then loads the data.
DiffGram	Reads a `DiffGram` and adds the data to the current schema. `DiffGram` merges new rows with existing rows where the unique identifier values match.
Fragment	Continues reading multiple XML fragments until the end of the stream is reached. Fragments that match the `DataSet` schema are appended to the appropriate tables. Fragments that do not match the `DataSet` schema are discarded.
Auto	This is the default. Examines the XML and chooses the most appropriate option in the following order: ❑ If the XML is a `DiffGram`, `DiffGram` is used. ❑ If the `DataSet` contains a schema or the XML contains an inline schema, `ReadSchema` is used. ❑ If the `DataSet` does not contain a schema and the XML does not contain an inline schema, `InferSchema` is used. For best performance you should set an explicit `XmlReadMode` if you know the format of the XML being read, since examining the XML takes some time.

It's worth at this point mentioning a bit about how the XSD schema maps to the internal relational structure of the `DataSet`. A `DataTable` is generated in the `DataSet` for each `<complexType>` child element of a schema element, but only when the `<complexType>` element is nested inside another `<complexType>` element. The table structure is determined by the definition of the complex type. We'll illustrate this with an example shortly, but first let's look at how the `DataSet` structure is inferred from an XML document.

The inference process first determines from the XML document which elements will be inferred as tables. From the remaining XML the inference process determines the columns for those tables. For nested tables the inference process generates nested `DataRelation` and `ForeignKeyConstraint` classes. The inference rules are summarized below:

❑   Elements that have attributes are inferred as tables.

❑   Elements that have child elements are inferred as tables.

❑   Elements that repeat are inferred as a single table.

❑   If the document or root element has no attributes, and no child elements that would be inferred as columns, it is inferred as a `DataSet`. Otherwise, the document element is inferred as a table.

❑   Attributes are inferred as columns.

❑   Elements that have no attributes or child elements, and do not repeat, are inferred as columns.

❑   For elements that are inferred as tables that are nested within other elements also inferred as tables, a nested `DataRelation` is created between the two tables. A new primary key column named `TableName_Id` is added to both tables and used by the `DataRelation`. A `ForeignKeyConstraint` is created between the two tables using the `TableName_Id` column.

❑   For elements that are inferred as tables and that contain text but have no child elements, a new column named `TableName_Text` is created for the text of each of the elements. If an element is inferred as a table and has text, but also has child elements, the text is ignored.

Let's see this at work in an example.

Try It Out: Populating a DataSet with XML

Let's first populate a `DataSet` with the `nestedFalse.xml` file we created earlier:

1. Create a new VB.NET console application project called **CreateDatasetFromXML** and add the following namespace reference at the very top of the `Module1.vb` file:

```
Imports System.Data
```

2. Next add the following code to the `Main()` method:

```
Dim myDataSet As New DataSet()
myDataSet.ReadXml("..\nestedTrue.xml")

Console.Write("Tables->" & vbNewLine)
Dim dt As DataTable
```

```
For Each dt In myDataSet.Tables
  Console.Write(dt.TableName & vbNewLine)
Next

Console.Write("Relations->" & vbNewLine)

Dim r As DataRelation

For Each r In myDataSet.Relations
  Console.Write(r.RelationName & vbNewLine & vbNewLine)
Next

'print out the nested authors and their author ids
Dim authRow As DataRow
Dim titleRow As DataRow

For Each authRow In myDataSet.Tables("authors").Rows
  Console.WriteLine("Author ID:" & authRow("au_id") & " Name: " & _
                    authRow("au_fname") & " " & authRow("au_lname"))
  For Each titleRow In authRow.GetChildRows("authors_titleauthor")
    Console.WriteLine(vbTab & "Title ID: " & titleRow("title_id"))
  Next
Next

Console.Readline()
```

3. Add the `nestedFalse.xml` and `nestedTrue.xml` files we created in the `SaveDataSetAsXML` example to the project by right-clicking on the project name in the solution explorer, and selecting **Add | Add Existing Item...** from the context menu. Navigate to the files on your system and add them to the solution.

4. Compile and run the project by pressing *Ctrl-F5*. The console output will be as shown in the figure below:

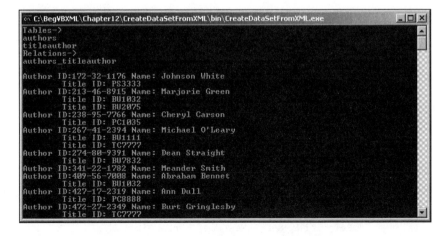

5. Now change the file name passed to `ReadXML` to be `nestedFalse.xml`:

```
Dim myDataSet As New DataSet()
myDataSet.ReadXml("..\nestedFalse.xml")
...
```

6. Compile and run the project again. The console output will be as shown in the figure below:

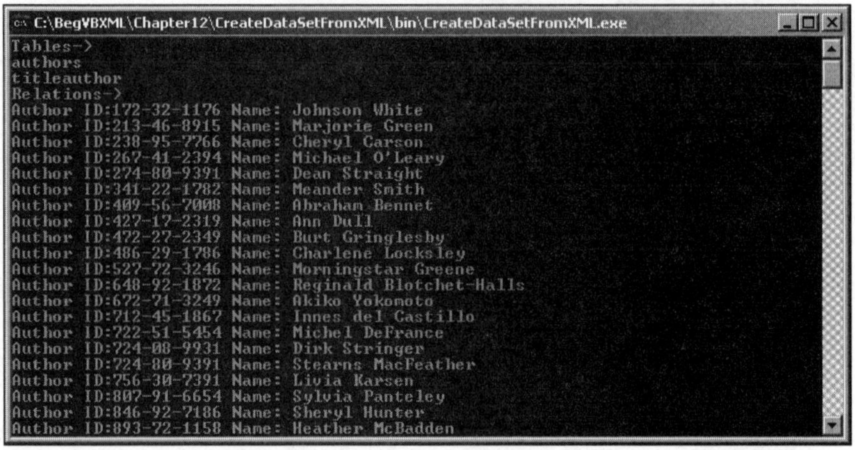

How It Works

First we define a new instance of the `DataSet` class:

```
Dim myDataSet As New DataSet()
```

Then we populate the `DataSet` with the `nestedTrue.xml` file using the `ReadXML` method.

```
myDataSet.ReadXml("..\nestedFalse.xml")
```

As the `nestedTrue.xml` file has no inline schema, and we defined no `XMLReadMode` on our call to `ReadXML`, and the XML is read using the default read mode of `InferSchema`. Thus, the internal schema of the `DataSet` is inferred from the structure of the XML document, following the inference rules we outlined earlier. The next section of code iterates through the `DataSet`'s `Tables` and `Relations` collections writing out the table and relation names respectively.

```
Console.Write("Tables->" & vbNewLine)
Dim dt As DataTable
For Each dt In myDataSet.Tables
  Console.Write(dt.TableName & vbNewLine)
Next

Console.Write("Relations->" & vbNewLine)
Dim r As DataRelation

For Each r In myDataSet.Relations
  Console.Write(r.RelationName & vbNewLine & vbNewLine)
Next
```

We can see from the output that two tables have been created in the `DataSet`, authors and titleauthors, and a relation called `authors_titleauthor`.

Finally we write out the authors and their associated `title_ids`:

```
Dim authRow As DataRow
Dim titleRow As DataRow
For Each authRow In myDataSet.Tables("authors").Rows
  Console.WriteLine("Author ID:" & authRow("au_id") & " Name: " & _
                    authRow("au_fname") & " " & authRow("au_lname"))
  For Each titleRow In authRow.GetChildRows("authors_titleauthor")
    Console.WriteLine(vbTab & "Title ID: " & titleRow("title_id"))
  Next
Next
```

We repeated the example using the `nestedFalse.xml` file to show the difference. You'll notice from the console output this time that no relationship has been inferred from the underlying data structure.

Building DataSets from XML Schema

The schema of a `DataSet` (its tables, columns, relations, and constraints) can be defined programmatically, using the `DataAdapter's Fill` or `FillSchema` methods, or can be loaded from an XML document or stream. To load `DataSet` schema information from an XML document or stream we can use the `DataSet's ReadXmlSchema` method. There are four different overloads of `ReadXmlSchema` available depending on the source of our XML:

```
Overloads Public Sub ReadXmlSchema(Source)
```

Where the *Source* can be either a `Stream`, `String`, `TextReader`, or `XmlReader`. Let's take a look at an example of this.

Try It Out: Generating a DataSet from an XML Schema

In this example we'll create a `DataSet` by reading `authTitle.xsd`, a schema we generated in an earlier example, then we'll populate the `DataSet` with our `nestedTrue.xml` file.

1. Create a new VB.NET console application project called **GenerateDataSetFromXSD** and add the following two namespace references at the very top of the `Module1.vb` file:

```
Imports System.Data
Imports System.IO
```

2. Next add the following code to the `Main()` method:

```
Dim myDataSet As New DataSet()
Dim xmlStream As New StreamReader("..\authTitle.xsd")
myDataSet.ReadXmlSchema(xmlStream)

'Write DataSet contents
myDataSet.WriteXml("..\beforeLoad.xml")
```

```
'Load DataSet
xmlStream = new StreamReader("..\nestedFalse.xml")
myDataSet.ReadXml(xmlStream,XmlReadMode.IgnoreSchema)

'Set nested to true
Dim myDR As DataRelation = myDataSet.Relations("AuthTitles")
myDR.Nested = true

'Write DataSet contents
myDataSet.WriteXml("..\afterLoad.xml")
```

3. Add the `nestedTrue.xml` and `authTitle.xsd` files created earlier to the project.

4. Run the project. Two XML files will be written to the current working directory called `beforeLoad.xml` and `afterLoad.xml`.

How It Works

The first thing we did in this example was to declare the required namespaces. You'll notice this time we've declared the `System.IO` namespace as we'll be using the overloaded versions of `ReadXMLSchema` and `ReadXML` that take an XML stream as the source.

Next we create our `DataSet` and load the XSD file into it:

```
Dim myDataSet As New DataSet()
Dim xmlStream As New StreamReader("..\authTitle.xsd")
myDataSet.ReadXmlSchema(xmlStream)
```

We write the `DataSet` contents to a file at this stage to show how it looks before we populate it with data.

```
'Write DataSet contents
myDataSet.WriteXml("..\beforeLoad.xml")
```

The `beforeLoad.xml` file is shown below:

```
<?xml version="1.0" standalone="yes" ?>
<NewDataSet />
```

We then read the XML stream into the `DataSet`:

```
'Load DataSet
xmlStream = new StreamReader("..\nestedTrue.xml")
myDataSet.ReadXml(xmlStream,XmlReadMode.IgnoreSchema)
```

Before we write the contents of the `DataSet` we set the `Nested` property of the `DataRelation` to be `true`:

```
'Set nested to true
Dim myDR As DataRelation = myDataSet.Relations("AuthTitles")
myDR.Nested = true
```

And finally we write the contents of the `DataSet` after loading:

```
'Write DataSet contents
myDataSet.WriteXml("..\afterLoad.xml")
```

The `afterLoad.xml` file is shown below (note the file has been truncated for brevity):

```
<?xml version="1.0" standalone="yes"?>
<NewDataSet>
  <authors>
    <au_id>172-32-1176</au_id>
    <au_lname>White</au_lname>
    <au_fname>Johnson</au_fname>
    <address>10932 Bigge Rd.</address>
    <titleauthor>
      <au_id>172-32-1176</au_id>
      <title_id>PS3333</title_id>
    </titleauthor>
  </authors>
  . . .
  <authors>
    <au_id>998-72-3567</au_id>
    <au_lname>Ringer</au_lname>
    <au_fname>Albert</au_fname>
    <address>67 Seventh Av.</address>
    <titleauthor>
      <au_id>998-72-3567</au_id>
      <title_id>PS2091</title_id>
    </titleauthor>
    <titleauthor>
      <au_id>998-72-3567</au_id>
      <title_id>PS2106</title_id>
    </titleauthor>
  </authors>
</NewDataSet>
```

Restricting the DataSet's view of an XML Instance

We can use an XML schema to narrow the `DataSet`'s view of an XML document, as the schema of the `DataSet` only needs to match the XML elements that you want to expose in your relational view. Let's modify our schema so that the `DataSet` can only see the author elements in our `nestedTrue.xml` document.

Try It Out: Limiting a DataSet's view of an XML document

1. Create a new VB.NET console application project called **RestrictingDataSetView** and add the following namespace reference at the very top of the `Module1.vb` file:

```
Imports System.Data
```

2. Next add the following code to the `Main()` method:

```
'Create DataSet from modified Schema
Dim newDataSet As New DataSet()
newDataSet.ReadXmlSchema("..\newAuthTitles.xsd")

'Load DataSet
newDataSet.ReadXml("..\nestedTrue.xml", XmlReadMode.IgnoreSchema)

'Write DataSet contents
newDataSet.WriteXml("..\afterLoad2.xml")
```

3. Next add the `authTitle.xsd` from the earlier examples to the project and remove those nodes highlighted below. Once you've removed the nodes, save the edited version of the schema as `newAuthTitle.xml`.

```
<?xml version="1.0" standalone="yes"?>
<xs:schema id="NewDataSet" xmlns="" xmlns:xs="http://www.w3.org/2001/XMLSchema"
xmlns:msdata="urn:schemas-microsoft-com:xml-msdata">
  <xs:element name="NewDataSet" msdata:IsDataSet="true" msdata:Locale="en-GB">
    <xs:complexType>
      <xs:choice maxOccurs="unbounded">
        <xs:element name="authors">
          <xs:complexType>
            <xs:sequence>
              <xs:element name="au_id" type="xs:string" minOccurs="0" />
              <xs:element name="au_lname" type="xs:string" minOccurs="0" />
              <xs:element name="au_fname" type="xs:string" minOccurs="0" />
              <xs:element name="address" type="xs:string" minOccurs="0" />
            </xs:sequence>
          </xs:complexType>
        </xs:element>
        <xs:element name="titleauthor">
          <xs:complexType>
            <xs:sequence>
              <xs:element name="au_id" type="xs:string" minOccurs="0" />
              <xs:element name="title_id" type="xs:string" minOccurs="0" />
            </xs:sequence>
          </xs:complexType>
        </xs:element>
      </xs:choice>
    </xs:complexType>
    <xs:unique name="Constraint1">
      <xs:selector xpath=".//authors" />
      <xs:field xpath="au_id" />
    </xs:unique>
    <xs:keyref name="AuthTitles" refer="Constraint1">
      <xs:selector xpath=".//titleauthor" />
      <xs:field xpath="au_id" />
    </xs:keyref>
  </xs:element>
</xs:schema>
```

4. Next, add the `nestedTrue.xml` file to the project.

5. When we run the project, the output is saved in `afterLoad2.xml`, an extract of which is shown below:

```xml
<?xml version="1.0" standalone="yes"?>
<NewDataSet>
  <authors>
    <au_id>172-32-1176</au_id>
    <au_lname>White</au_lname>
    <au_fname>Johnson</au_fname>
    <address>10932 Bigge Rd.</address>
  </authors>
  <authors>
    <au_id>213-46-8915</au_id>
    <au_lname>Green</au_lname>
    <au_fname>Marjorie</au_fname>
    <address>309 63rd St. #411</address>
  </authors>
  <authors>
    <au_id>238-95-7766</au_id>
    <au_lname>Carson</au_lname>
    <au_fname>Cheryl</au_fname>
    <address>589 Darwin Ln.</address>
  </authors>
  ...
</NewDataSet>
```

How It Works

Our schema now defines a subset of the full `nestedTrue.xml` document, and so the `DataSet` only has access to that subset of data, that is, the `<authors>` elements. The `<titleauthor>` elements contained in the `nestedTrue.xml` file are discarded by the `DataSet` on loading, so we've effectively lost half the data from our original document! Not that it is much of a problem for us, because we have the original source document on our hard disk. But imagine we had received the XML in the form of a serialized stream as part of some business process, and we were required to update a subsection of the data then pass the full document on to the next stage of the process. There is one way around this problem, and that's to synchronize our `DataSet` with an `XmlDataDocument` object. We'll talk more about the `XmlDataDocument` in the following section.

The XmlDataDocument Class

We've talked about the `XMLDocument` class and we've talked about the `DataSet`, so it's time to introduce the class that brings the functionality of them both together, the `XmlDataDocument`.

The `XmlDataDocument` breaks with tradition in that it allows us to view and manipulate a hierarchical and relational representation of our data simultaneously. Because the `XmlDataDocument` inherits from the `XmlDocument` class, we can navigate our relational data using the DOM, query it using XPath expressions, and apply XSLT transformations.

As the `XmlDataDocument` class inherits from `XmlDocument`, its properties and methods are essentially the same (for more information, you may want to refer back to the discussion in Chapter 6). Several methods have been overridden to work better with the `DataSet`. In addition to the overrides, there is a single property and two additional methods specific to the `XmlDataDocument` class that we'll encounter:

❑   The `DataSet` property – This property gets a `DataSet` that provides a relational representation of the data in the `XmlDataDocument`.

❑   `GetElementFromRow()` – This method takes a `DataRow` instance as its constructor and retrieves the `XmlElement` associated with that `DataRow`.

❑   `GetRowFromElement()` – This method takes an `XmlElement` instance as its constructor and retrieves the `DataRow` associated with that `XmlElement`.

As a simple illustration of the similarities between the `XmlDocument` and `XmlDataDocument` class let's revisit the *Loading a URL as an XmlDocument Instance* example in Chapter 6. The example will be identical except for the fact we'll be using the `XmlDataDocument` instead of the `XmlDocument`.

Try It Out: Loading a URL as an XmlDataDocument Instance

This example is similar to the *Loading a URL as an XmlDocument Instance* example in Chapter 6, which looked at how to load an XML file into memory and write the result to a Windows Form.

1.   Create a new Windows application, call it **LoadURLAsXMLDataDocument**, and add a textbox and button to the form – give the button the text **LoadURL**, and set the `Multiline` property to `True`.

2.   Double-click on the button and first add the following statement to the top of the file.

```
Imports System.Data
Imports System.Xml
```

3.   Next, enter the following code to the button event handler:

```
Private Sub Button1_Click(ByVal sender As System.Object, ByVal e As
System.EventArgs) Handles Button1.Click
    Dim xdoc As New XmlDataDocument()
    xdoc.Load("..\sample.xml")

    TextBox1.Text = xdoc.OuterXml
End Sub
```

4.   Now add a new XML file to the project, call it `sample.xml`, and enter the following XML into the document.

```
<?xml version="1.0" encoding="utf-8" ?>
<Catalog xmlns:test="uri:test">
  <Company email="celtic@deltabis.net" name="Celtic Productions">
    <ProductFamily familyID="pftops" LastUpdate="2001-08-26T18:39:09"
      buyersURI="http://www.deltabis.com/buyers/tops">
```

```
            <Product ProductID="CFC4">
              <color>black</color>
              <size>L</size>
              <price>32.99</price>
            </Product>
          </ProductFamily>
        </Company>
      </Catalog>
```

5. Run the program and you'll get the following output.

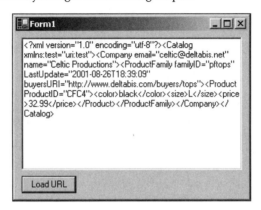

How It Works

The output obtained using the `XmlDataDocument` is the same as the output we obtained using the `XmlDocument`. This makes sense since, as we said earlier, the `XmlDataDocument` inherits all the `XmlDocument`'s methods and properties. The one main benefit the `XmlDataDocument` class provides over the `XmlDocument` class, however, is that it allows us to work with our data in a hierarchical and relational form simultaneously. Before we can do this, we must synchronize the `DataSet` and `XmlDataDocument`, and that is what we will look at in the next section.

Synchronizing with a DataSet

When synchronized, the `DataSet` and `XmlDataDocument` classes operate on the same collection of rows, so that if a change is made to the `XmlDataDocument`, the change will be reflected in the `DataSet` and vice versa. There are several ways to synchronize a `DataSet` and `XmlDataDocument` object, each of which are outlined below.

Providing a Hierarchical View of Existing Relational Data

You can populate a `DataSet` with a schema and data, then synchronize it with a new `XmlDataDocument`:

```
Dim myDataSet As New DataSet()
myDataSet.ReadXmlSchema("schema.xsd")
Dim xmlDoc As XmlDataDocument = New XmlDataDocument(myDataSet)
xmlDoc.Load("XMLDocument.xml")
```

Providing a Relational View of Existing Hierarchical (XML) Data

If you have XML data you want to work with as relational data, populate a `DataSet` with only a schema, synchronize it with an `XmlDataDocument`, and then load the XML into the `XmlDataDocument`. For obvious reasons, the table names and column names in the `DataSet` schema must match the names of the XML elements you want them synchronized with.

```
Dim myDataSet As New DataSet()
myDataSet.ReadXmlSchema("schema.xsd")
Dim xmlDoc As XmlDataDocument = New XmlDataDocument(myDataSet) 'synchronized!
xmlDoc.Load("XMLDocument.xml")
```

Providing a Relational View of Existing Hierarchical (XML) Data – Method 2

This is another method you can use if you have XML data you want to work with as relational data. Create a new `XmlDataDocument` and load it from an XML document, then access the relational view of the data using the `DataSet` property of the `XmlDataDocument`. The schema of the `DataSet` needs to be loaded before the data in the `XmlDataDocument` can be viewed using the `DataSet`. Again, the table names and column names in your `DataSet` schema must match the names of the XML elements that you want them synchronized with:

```
Dim xmlDoc As New XmlDataDocument()
Dim myDataSet As DataSet = xmlDoc.DataSet 'synchronized!
myDataSet.ReadXmlSchema("schema.xsd")
xmlDoc.Load("XMLDocument.xml")
```

Let's take a look at an example.

Try It Out: Synchronizing a DataSet with an XmlDataDocument

1. Create a new VB.NET console application project called **DataSetXMLDataDocumentSync1** and add the following namespace references at the very top of the `Module1.vb` file:

```
Imports System.Data
Imports System.Xml
```

2. Next add the following code to the `Main()` method:

```
'Create DataSet from Schema
Dim myDataSet As New DataSet()
myDataSet.ReadXmlSchema("..\authTitle.xsd")

'Load DataSet
myDataSet.ReadXml("..\nestedTrue.xml",XmlReadMode.IgnoreSchema)

'Synchronize the XmlDataDocument and Dataset
Dim xmlDoc As New XmlDataDocument(myDataSet)

Dim authorXML As XmlElement
Dim authRow As DataRow
```

```
'Write out values
For Each authRow In myDataSet.Tables("authors").Rows
  authorXML = xmlDoc.GetElementFromRow(authRow)
  Console.WriteLine("{0} {1}", _
                    authorXML.SelectSingleNode("./au_fname").InnerText, _
                    authorXML.SelectSingleNode("./au_lname").InnerText)
Next

Console.ReadLine()
```

3. Add the `nestedTrue.xml` and `authTitle.xsd` files from previous examples to the project.

4. Run the project. The output in the console should be as below:

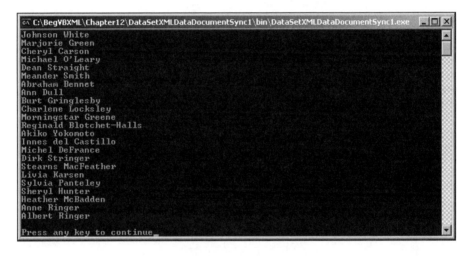

How it Works

As usual, the first thing we do is import the relevant namespaces.

```
Imports System.Data
Imports System.Xml
```

We create and populate the `DataSet` as we've done before:

```
'Create DataSet from Schema
Dim myDataSet As New DataSet()
myDataSet.ReadXmlSchema("..\authTitle.xsd")

'Load DataSet
myDataSet.ReadXml("..\nestedTrue.xml", XmlReadMode.IgnoreSchema)
```

Then we synchronize the `XmlDataDocument` and the `DataSet`:

```
'Synchronize the XmlDataDocument and Dataset
Dim xmlDoc As New XmlDataDocument(myDataSet)
```

The interesting part now is that because we've synchronized the two objects, we can obtain an `XmlElement` from any row using the `GetElementFromRow` method (we can also get any `DataRow` object given an `XmlElement` using the `GetRowFromElement` method). In the `For Each` loop we're iterating through the `Rows` collection of the "authors" `DataTable`, but we're getting the author names from the `XMLElement` using a simple XPath query.

```
Dim authorXML As XmlElement
Dim authRow As DataRow

'Write out values
For Each authRow In myDataSet.Tables("authors").Rows
  authorXML = xmlDoc.GetElementFromRow(authRow)
  Console.WriteLine("{0} {1}", _
                    authorXML.SelectSingleNode("./au_fname").InnerText, _
                    authorXML.SelectSingleNode("./au_lname").InnerText)
Next
```

Let's now take our example one step further and transform our XML representation of the `DataSet` into HTML using XSLT.

Try It Out: Transform the Contents of a DataSet

1. Create a new VB.NET console application project called **TransformDataSetContents** and add the following two namespace references at the very top of the `Module1.vb` file:

```
Imports System.Data
Imports System.Data.SqlClient
Imports System.Xml
Imports System.Xml.Xsl
Imports System.IO
```

2. Next add the following code to the `Main()` method:

```
Dim myDataSet As DataSet = fillDS()
Dim xmlDataDoc As XmlDataDocument = New XmlDataDocument(myDataSet)
Dim myXSLT As New XslTransform()
myXSLT.Load("..\XSLTFile.xslt")

Dim myFs As New FileStream("..\authors.htm", FileMode.Create, FileAccess.Write)
myXSLT.Transform(xmlDataDoc, Nothing, myFs)
myFs.Close()
```

3. Again, add the `fillDS()` method code we met earlier.

4. Add a new XSLT file called `XSLTFile.xslt` to the project and add the code below.

```xml
<?xml version="1.0" encoding="UTF-8" ?>
<xsl:stylesheet xmlns:xsl="http://www.w3.org/1999/XSL/Transform" version="1.0">

<xsl:template match="NewDataSet">
<head>
  <style type="text/css">
    table {font-family:Tahoma;font-size:8pt;}
    th {font-family:Tahoma;
        font-size:9pt;
        background-color:#3366CC;
        color:#FFFFFF}
    tr.alternate {background-color:#FFFF99;}
  </style>
</head>
<html>
  <body>
    <center>
      <table border="0" width="100%">
        <tr align="left">
          <th>Author</th>
          <th>Address</th>
          <th>Title ID</th>
        </tr>
        <xsl:apply-templates select="authors"/>
      </table>
    </center>
  </body>
</html>
</xsl:template>

<xsl:template match="authors">
  <tr>
    <xsl:if test="position() mod 2 = 0">
    <xsl:attribute name="class">alternate</xsl:attribute>
    </xsl:if>
    <td valign="top">
      <xsl:value-of select="au_fname"/>&#32;
      <xsl:value-of select="au_lname"/>
    </td>
    <td valign="top"><xsl:value-of select="address"/></td>
    <td><xsl:apply-templates select="titleauthor"/></td>
  </tr>
</xsl:template>

<xsl:template match="titleauthor">
  <xsl:value-of select="./title_id"/> <br/>
</xsl:template>

</xsl:stylesheet>
```

5. Run the project. A file called authors.htm will be created in the root of our project. When we look at this file in our browser, we see the following:

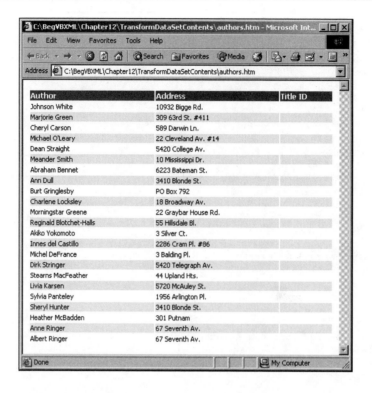

How it Works

First we fill the `DataSet`, then synchronize it with the `XmlDataDocument`:

```
Dim myDataSet As DataSet = fillDS()
Dim xmlDataDoc As XmlDataDocument = New XmlDataDocument(myDataSet)
```

Next we load the transform:

```
Dim myXSLT As New XslTransform()
myXSLT.Load("..\XSLTFile.xslt")
```

Then create a new `FileStream` instance, which creates the `.htm` file and initializes it for writing:

```
Dim myFs As New FileStream("..\authors.htm", FileMode.Create, FileAccess.Write)
```

The `XmlDataDocument` is then transformed and the resulting output streamed to our `.htm` file:

```
myXSLT.Transform(xmlDataDoc, Nothing, myFs)
```

Finally the `FileStream` is closed:

```
myFs.Close()
```

Summary

You'll hopefully now have a good appreciation for what ADO.NET is all about, and should be able to start integrating the functionality into your VB.NET applications.

In the first part of the chapter we focused on some basic techniques to demonstrate how the various ADO.NET classes can be used to perform common data access tasks. We learned how the .NET data providers act as an interface between applications and data sources, channeling data to and from the `DataSet`, and looked at the `DataSet` class in some depth covering areas such as:

- ❑   Accessing and modifying rows

- ❑   Data row versioning

- ❑   Data Binding (Web Forms, `DataGrids`)

- ❑   Table relationships

For the remainder of the chapter we endeavored to highlight how XML is integral to the new data access model, and to demonstrate the flexibility this provides. With this in mind we concentrated heavily on the interaction and integration of ADO.NET with XML in the latter half of the chapter. We looked firstly at how the `DataSet` can read and write XML in various formats, and then moved on to look at the role played by XSD schemas in defining its internal structure.

Finally we introduced the `XmlDataDocument` class, showing how it can be used to view and manipulate a relational and hierarchical representation of our data simultaneously, offering us the ability to navigate the relational data using the DOM, query it using XPath expressions, and apply XSLT transformations.

In the next chapter we'll look at two other key applications of the .NET Framework, Web Services and Remoting. The main focus will again be on how XML underpins the technologies.

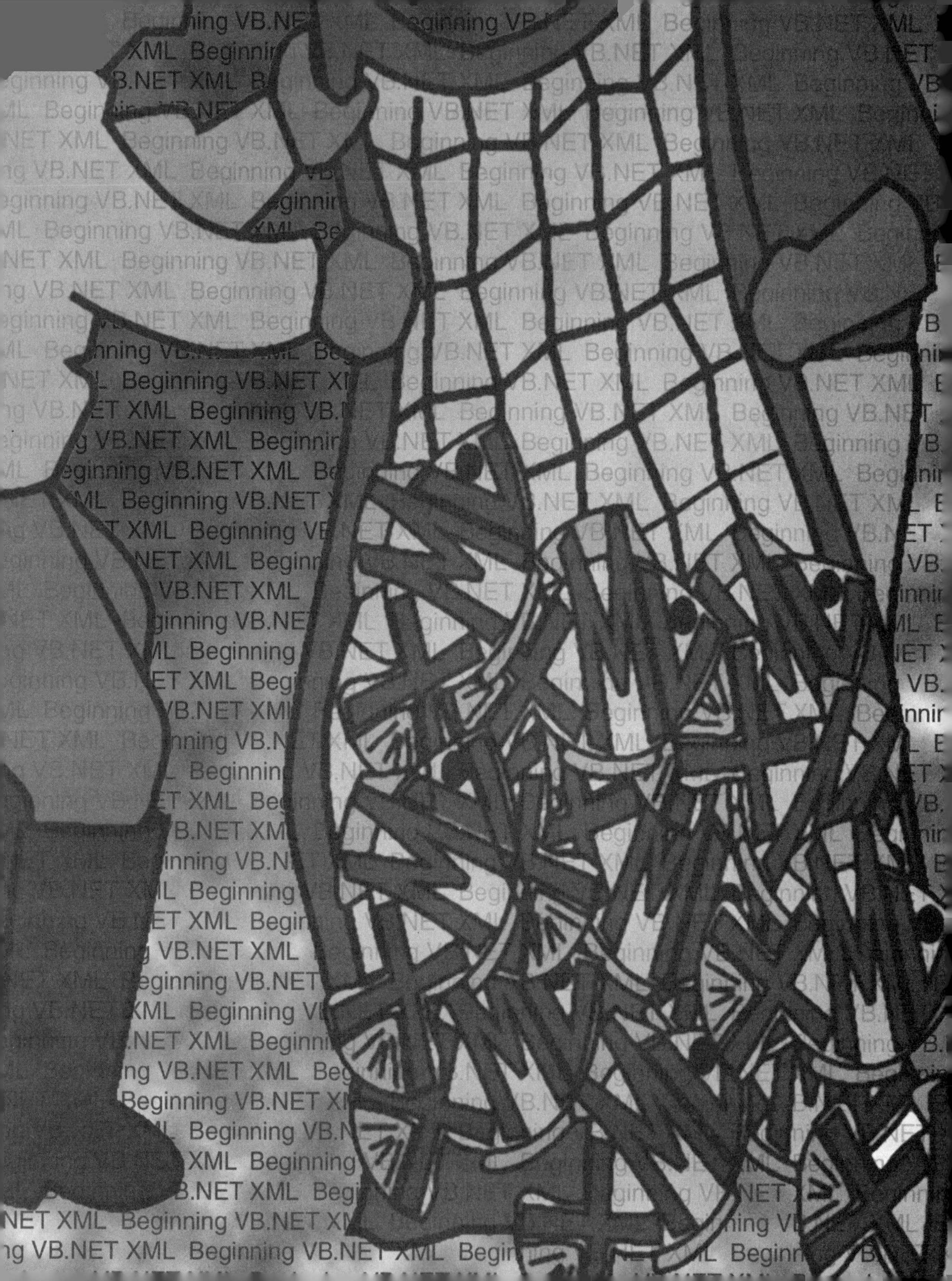
Beginning VB.NET XML

Web Services and Remoting

In the previous chapter, we discussed ADO.NET, one of the technologies provided by the .NET Framework. Since ADO.NET uses many of the underlying technologies, such as XML Schema, Serialization, and others, it could be regarded as an application of the .NET Framework.

In this chapter we will look at Web services, again more of an application of the underlying technologies offered by the .NET Framework.

In this chapter, you will learn about:

- ❏ Web services
- ❏ The Global XML Architecture
- ❏ What the Simple Object Access Protocol (SOAP) is and how it uses XML
- ❏ The XML based Web Service Description Language (WSDL)
- ❏ Microsoft's DISCO discovery XML document
- ❏ The Universal Description, Discovery and Integration Service
- ❏ Remoting and XML configuration files
- ❏ Using Web services with the case study

What are Web Services?

It is likely that you have heard of web services long before you picked up this book. It is fair to say that with XML, web services are the most talked-about technology that has been emerging over the last few years. It is important to realize, however, that it is exactly that – emerging. For the number of web service issues that have been solved over the last few years, there are many more that are being solved as this chapter is written.

A web service is a service that is accessible over a public or private network (such as the Internet or a corporate network), providing some functionality that may be consumed by another web service or some application. Web services are based on XML, which is used for describing the service as well as the communication with the service. Web services frequently use HTTP as the application protocol, but the progression is towards using web services over many protocols such as SMTP. This adoption of these fundamental standards allows services written in any language, on any platform, and in any geographical location to communicate with other web services.

Some great examples of this are the web service initiatives from Google and Amazon who have provided web service interfaces to allow you to query their directories and analyze results returned. More information on searching Google can be found at http://www.google.com/apis/ and more details about Amazon at http://www.amazon.com/webservices.

Furthermore, the .NET Framework itself is web service-centric. Although it has been possible to layer web services on top of existing components, or components that were developed before .NET, this was achievable by using add-on tools to adapt languages that were never designed with XML or web services in mind. An example of this is the SOAP Toolkit; this can be used to make COM components into web services. The .NET Framework, however, was developed with both XML and web services in mind and so web service capability has been integrated directly into the Framework and the Visual Studio .NET IDE. This has all been backed up by the Global XML Architecture, which is part of Microsoft's vision that we discuss below.

If you have previously worked with DCOM (or CORBA) then you will understand the difficulties associated in working with components that are on different computers. Application communication on Windows alone was difficult because each DCOM object had to be registered on every server it was to be accessed on – the same idea applied to working with CORBA. Accessing web services, on the other hand, can be as simple as requesting the URL for the service. Another problem with DCOM was that the protocols were proprietary and so communication between distributed objects were complex – in contrast web services are based on open standards.

DCOM could be even more problematic when working in a secure environment where ports were locked down and firewalls prevented most traffic from passing in or out of the enterprise. All this made for complicated and often expensive architecture decisions to be made when distributed components had to work on large networks (such as a corporate network or the Internet) and had to communicate with each other.

Web services, however, can operate over port 80, which is the HTTP port. This is allowed by nearly all firewalls, so it is possible for communication to occur into and out of the enterprise without creating any major security holes.

Another benefit that is being gradually realized, and presents much greater technical challenges, is the ability to provide and consume web services from distributed systems. Technical issues such as scalability, performance, failover, transactions, payment, trust, and many others are what Microsoft, IBM, and many of the largest companies are looking at just now, and what Microsoft and IBM term the **Global XML Architecture (GXA)**.

GXA – Global XML Architecture

If ever an important move in the web services world was to be made, the Global XML Architecture is it. The Global XML Architecture defines a platform consisting of a formal framework of protocols that can be used to create enterprise-level web services. It allows further protocols to be layered on top of this platform to define requirements such as security, reliability, and agreement between parties.

The idea behind the GXA is to improve the entire arena of web services, adding features such as security (which has a huge number of sub sections, such as trust, privacy, and so on), routing of web services, interoperability. An analogy is that the GXA will become the operating system of the web services world, providing a core of features and services that can be used by implementations without having to know the details – much in the way we make use of features such as Active Directory to provide authentication for the operating system.

There is, in fact, a set of core goals that the GXA hopes to accomplish:

❑ **Decentralization** and **Federation** will allow distributed components to work in a decentralized manner with no central authority, but will utilize the hierarchical nature of domain names to maintain identity and control over the services.

❑ **Modularity** of the GXA is of prime importance, allowing the user to use certain parts of the architecture, while not using others. This may allow you to not use the security protocols of GXA in one scenario, while still using the routing protocols.

❑ The **XML Information Set**, or **Infoset**, will be used to define GXA protocols, so that all definitions understand the same concepts when working with XML during communication. For more information on this see http://www.w3.org/TR/xml-infoset/.

❑ **Neutral transport** is also an important part of the GXA; SOAP is the message exchange format, but the underlying protocol may be HTTP or any other transport protocol, such as SMTP.

❑ **Application Domain neutrality** is the key of the core goals of the GXA. Web services at present allow applications to talk to each other from disparate systems in a distributed environment, but they do not state that any given application must fully implement, for example, its security model according to a given specification. The GXA defines a general-purpose model that is extensible in any given domain, so the protocol in any domain can be application-specific, as long as it provides the higher-level requirements as specified in the GXA.

We are still in the early stages of the GXA, with features such as security being provided by HTTP standards such as HTTPS, rather than web service-specific security protocols. Presently Microsoft is working on an XML-based virtual network protocol for web services that would sit on top of a protocol stack such as TCP/IP.

Where Are We Now?

So now we know the overall picture, where are we right now? Well, despite the amount of work that still needs to be done with web services architectures, .NET provides you with the fundamental building blocks to start creating web services. Not only that, but the standards that .NET uses are not going to be simply replaced when the GXA is finalized, but rather some of these standards are forming the basis of the GXA right now.

In particular, .NET offers the following components for creating web services:

❑ **SOAP** – This is the **Simple Object Access Protocol**, which along with XML RPC (another HTTP-based Web Service standard, and a precursor to SOAP) was the main driver for web services during its initial phases. This defines the structure of the XML messages that can be sent and received when invoking and consuming distributed components.

❑ **WSDL** – The **Web Services Discovery Language** came along not too long after the initial specifications of SOAP and is intended to describe any web service in an XML format. This document describes a web service in terms of messages using the XML Schema Language, and how they are bound to protocols, as well as some other details we will look at below.

❑ **DISCO** – **Discovery Protocol** is a Microsoft-based solution to tell consumers what a web service offers in terms of web services. For instance, knowing some URL, you can make a call to a DISCO document that will return an XML document detailing where to access various document types, such as documentation and WSDL documents.

❑ **UDDI** – The **Universal Description, Discovery, and Integration** service is like the bigger brother of DISCO documents and has a much wider scope. Whereas DISCO documents are provided to tell you what is available on a given server, UDDI is intended to provide a directory of global (or at least distributed) web services. Such a directory can be populated with web services, and searched by consumers for web services of particular types. The future idea is that dynamic discovery of web services based on specified criteria could be done, possibly by other web services.

We can see from the points above that there are two ways in which you can discover and use the same web services; the first and simplest to implement is via DISCO documents that describe the service(s) that you have to offer. A diagram of a typical session with a DISCO file is shown below:

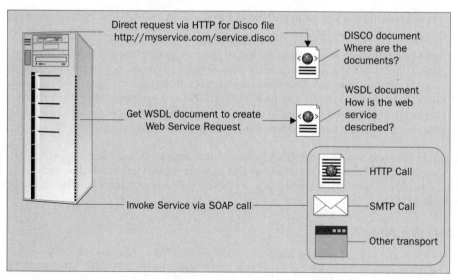

Additionally, there is the more complex UDDI version which is intended for situations where you don't know where your services reside, but you know the criteria you want – which can be as basic or complex as you like. The architecture is similar to that of the DISCO file, but involves a third party UDDI registry.

> Up to this point you may think that UDDI servers will be limited to authorized registries that you will have to interact with in order to use any web services. Although on the Internet it is very likely that a small number of set registries will appear, the next version of Microsoft's operating system, Windows .NET Server, will have a version running a UDDI server. This will be popular when you wish to host a set of managed web services within in an enterprise.

The following diagram illustrates this architecture:

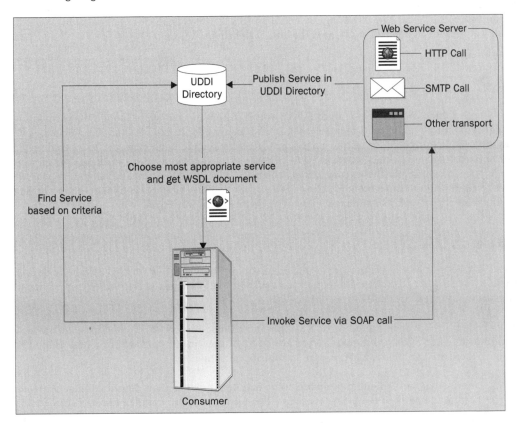

In this chapter we are going to focus on the higher-level involvement of XML in web services. We won't focus too much on the low-level detail as WSDL files are generated and consumed automatically and we won't normally need to change them manually. However, the intention is to show you how XML and .NET play their part in providing web services, both from an infrastructure and application point of view.

Web Services and .NET

Unlike the SOAP toolkit released from Microsoft to allow COM components to be exposed as web services, .NET provides the ability to web service-enable ASMX and ASHX files as web services within the core of the Framework. This allows any application on any environment from any geographic location to work with .NET web services – thus an in-house Unix e-commerce application could use a credit card web service written in VB. Equally, an e-commerce application written in .NET would be able to make use of some application exposed as a web service running on a Unix box.

Web services in .NET are exposed via ASP.NET `.asmx` files held on the web server or more directly via an `IHttpHandler` (the .NET equivalent of an ISAPI filter) `.ashx` implementation. We will create a full web service in the case study near the end of the chapter.

SOAP

The Simple Object Access Protocol, or SOAP as it is commonly known (although the acronym will no longer stand for anything in its next release), is what many people call web services, mainly as this is the communications protocol for web services and what most people have exposure to when developing web services. This is not only because SOAP was the prime activator of the work on web services that has happened over the last few years, but also because it is the furthest that developers of web services have to go in order to implement a web service – many toolkits hide the implementation details and make the interface look like a normal class, with method and properties.

What is SOAP?

SOAP is an application-level protocol using XML and primarily HTTP or HTTPS (although it is possible to use other communications protocols such as SMTP) to allow distributed applications to relay information by making remote procedure calls.

At its highest level it is described in an XML format, although many of the toolkits available for creating web services using SOAP never expose you to the XML used in its transport. In a typical SOAP request, there are two places XML is used to transmit information:

❑ The actual method and parameters to be invoked in the call are described in an XML format within the body of the SOAP message. The response is also detailed here.

❑ There are template SOAP elements that are present in almost every SOAP call and effectively wrap the method and parameters discussed above.

The **SOAP envelope** namespace is defined with each SOAP message, with a root `Envelope` element defining the SOAP message and encapsulating the body of the message, which itself is defined within the `Body` element. The `Body` element is in the same namespace as the `Envelope` element.

Let's take a look at the XML that is sent when a SOAP service is used.

Example SOAP Headers

For every SOAP message that is either requested or responded to, there is a series of headers and XML content that are present. The actual details can be very complex in some cases, so it is best to demonstrate these with a simple example.

Consider the following method that we have exposed as a web service:

```
MyMethod(ByVal MyParam As String) As String
```

It is important to remember that on many occasions you will not be exposed to the request and response details; you will work with the objects like any other object and not even see any XML being generated. However, to make full use of web services it is important to understand a little about what is going on underneath.

SOAP Request

The SOAP header and body that would be required for the method is as follows:

```
POST /MyLocation/MyPage.asmx HTTP/1.1
Host: ServerName
Content-Type: text/xml; charset=utf-8
Content-Length: length
SOAPAction: "http://tempuri.org/MyMethod"

<?xml version="1.0" encoding="utf-8"?>
<soap:Envelope xmlns:xsi="http://www.w3.org/2001/XMLSchema-instance"
  xmlns:xsd="http://www.w3.org/2001/XMLSchema"
  xmlns:soap="http://schemas.xmlsoap.org/soap/envelope/">
  <soap:Body>
    <MyMethod xmlns="http://tempuri.org/">
      <MyParam>myString</MyParam>
    </MyMethod>
  </soap:Body>
</soap:Envelope>
```

In this case the `length` and `myString` values will be replaced by the values calculated at run time depending on the values used. The `MyMethod()` method is mapped to the `MyMethod` element and it is qualified within the namespace `http://tempuri.org/MyMethod`. This namespace, however, would be changed in a production environment to contain a permanent namespace, probably based on your company's domain name that will allow consumers to uniquely refer to it.

Within this element the parameters for the method are defined, with the name of each parameter being the same as a child element of the `<MyMethod>` element. The WSDL document for the web service will state the parameters (and the return type) are of a specific data type. In this case, we have a single child element called `<MyParam>`; within this element the actual runtime value of the `<MyParam>` argument will be placed.

SOAP Response

When the SOAP method above is consumed by the web service, a method is executed and the response is received and wrapped again in a SOAP response instance.

```
HTTP/1.1 200 OK
Content-Type: text/xml; charset=utf-8
Content-Length: length

<?xml version="1.0" encoding="utf-8"?>
<soap:Envelope xmlns:xsi="http://www.w3.org/2001/XMLSchema-instance"
  xmlns:xsd="http://www.w3.org/2001/XMLSchema"
  xmlns:soap="http://schemas.xmlsoap.org/soap/envelope/">
  <soap:Body>
    <MyMethodResponse xmlns="http://tempuri.org/">
      <MyMethodResult>myString</MyMethodResult>
    </MyMethodResponse>
  </soap:Body>
</soap:Envelope>
```

As above, the `length` and `mystring` values are determined at execution time. The response is again wrapped in `Envelope` and `Body` elements. The result is wrapped in an element with the name of the method appended to "Response", so in our case we have an element called `MyMethodResponse` that is qualified in the web service namespace.

Within this element the actual result of the method is contained within an element with the method name appended to "Result", so in this case we have the string result within an element called `MyMethodResult`.

Try It Out: Create a Simple "Hello World" Web Service

In this Try It Out we are going to create a "hello world" example web service that we will consume later in the chapter.

> *Note that all the sample code for this chapter is available for download from http://www.wrox.com. We will be storing sample code for this chapter within the following folder:* `C:\BegVBXML\Chapter13`. *You may, of course, use a different folder depending on what you prefer.*

1. Launch Visual Studio .NET and create a new VB ASP.NET Web Service project. Set the name to HelloWorld, click the OK button and the new project will automatically be created in the HelloWorld virtual directory.

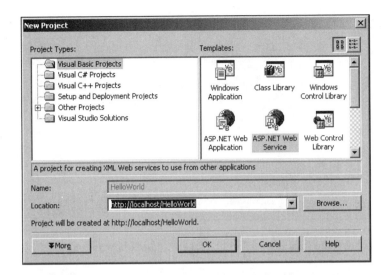

2. Right-click on the `Service1.asmx` file and click the **View Code** button. Make the changes highlighted in the code below. Notice that the actual method and the associated attribute (in the <> brackets) are uncommented from the generated file.

```
Imports System.Web.Services
```

```
<WebService(Namespace:="http://www.deltabis.net/services/hw/", _
  Description:="Hello World Company Test Service.", _
  Name:="HelloWorldService" )> _
Public Class Service1
    Inherits System.Web.Services.WebService

#Region " Web Services Designer Generated Code "
  ...
#End Region
```

```
  <WebMethod(BufferResponse:=True, _
    CacheDuration:=20, _
    Description:="Hello Method", _
    MessageName:="SayHello")> _
    Public Function HelloWorld(ByVal person As String) As String
    HelloWorld = "Hello " & person
  End Function
```

```
End Class
```

3. Right-click on the `Service1.asmx` file and click the **Set As Start Page** entry.

4. Press *F5* or hit the **Start** button; the web service will be compiled and the browser launched. You will be taken to the service help page, shown below. These pages are dynamically generated by the .NET Framework to aid you in the development and testing of your services:

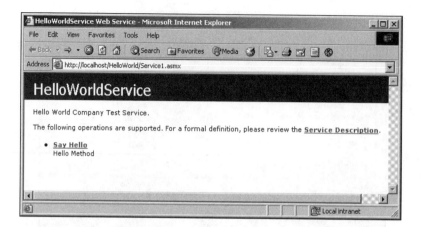

5. Click the SayHello link and you will be taken to the following page:

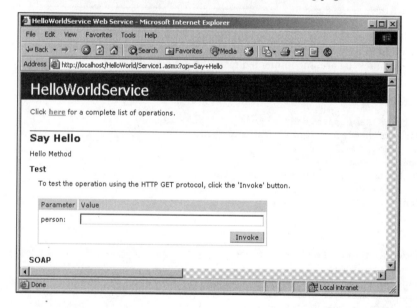

6. Type a name into the box (in my case I typed "Cochi") and click the Invoke button and you will get the following:

7. Return to the starting page at http://localhost/HelloWorld/service1.asmx and click the **Service Description** link.

8. You will be shown the WSDL file which dynamically generated by the .NET Framework and is used to describe the interface of the web service. Alternatively you can get the WSDL file for any .NET-enabled web service by adding **?WSDL** to the URL. We discuss the WSDL file in the next section.

How It Works

In Visual Studio .NET right-click on the `Service1.asmx` file and chose **Open With...** from the context menu and choose **Source Code (Text) Editor**. The file will open with a single directive, the `WebService` processing directive, as shown below:

```
<%@ WebService Language="vb" Codebehind="Service1.asmx.vb"
   Class="HelloWorld.Service1" %>
```

The `Language` attribute states that we are using VB.NET as the programming language for the web service and the `Codebehind` attribute specifies the code-behind page used for this web service. The `Class` attribute defines the class within the code-behind file that implements the web service.

The code-behind file is the file we made the modifications to earlier. It is defined within the namespace `HelloWorld` (this is automatically created from the name of the project), and significantly includes the `System.Web.Services` namespace.

```
Imports System.Web.Services
```

Web services typically inherit from the from the `WebService` class of the `System.Web.Services` namespace, which provides ASP.NET functionality such as application and session state, the `Request` and `Session` intrinsic objects. Our `Service1` class inherits from this class.

```
Public Class Service1
   Inherits System.Web.Services.WebService
```

Notice that prior to the class definition we add a `WebService` attribute. Attributes are commonly used in web services, as in serialization, to define some metadata about a given class or method. In this case, the `WebService` attribute is used to specify details about the class.

```
<WebService(Namespace:="http://www.deltabis.net/services/hw/", _
    Description:="Hello World Company Test Service.", _
    Name:="HelloWorldService")> _
```

The `Namespace` parameter of the `WebService` attribute defines the unique namespace that will define the web service; the `Description` is what is displayed when someone asks for a description of the service and the `Name` parameter defines the name that the service will be known as, for instance `HelloWorldService`.

There is a single public `HelloWorld()` method defined in this class, that takes a string representing the person to say hello to and returns a string `"Hello "` concatenated with the value of the `person` parameter. The `WebMethod` attribute is also defined on this method, which allows you to specify metadata about a method of a web service. If we don't include this attribute the method will not be available as a web service, nor will non-Public methods.

```
<WebMethod(BufferResponse:=True, _
    CacheDuration:=20, _
    Description:="Hello Method", _
    MessageName:="SayHello")> _
    Public Function HelloWorld(ByVal person As String) As String
    HelloWorld = "Hello " & person
End Function
```

The `BufferResponse` attribute tells the service to wait until the response is completely serialized as XML before returning the result to the client. The `CacheDuration` attribute will state how long the response for this method should be help in memory in the machine, potentially allowing you to improve the performance of your web service when there are a large number of requests. The `Description` attribute provides a short description of the web service method and the `MessageName` attribute defines the name by which this web method will be known to the client (for instance, a client will call the `SayHello()` method rather than the `HelloWorld()` method).

The web service was actually viewed at the appropriate URL, http://localhost/HelloWorld/Service1.asmx in this case. Notice that the name of the method on this page is called `SayHello`, which is the `Description` for the `HelloWorld()` method, almost like an alias. Clicking this link displays all the relevant details on the `HelloWorld()` method, with a button to invoke the service and some definitions on how it will be invoked for different bindings (SOAP, HTTP GET, and HTTP POST).

As was mentioned earlier, web services can be invoked in many ways depending on the binding, and in .NET you are given three fundamental ways of calling a service:

❑ As a SOAP call as discussed earlier

❑ Via a HTTP GET with the method and parameter details in the URL query string

❑ As an HTTP POST with the details posted to the web page

We'll come back to the SOAP version later, but, in our case, we clicked the Invoke button, which makes an HTTP GET call to the service. Have a look at the query that was made:

```
http://localhost/HelloWorld/Service1.asmx/SayHello?person=Cochi
```

The URL to the web service makes the URL up to the final slash character. After this slash character the method you want to call is specified, followed by a question mark and then a name-value pair of the parameter value you want to pass. In our case there is just the `person` parameter and the method name is `SayHello`. The result is a simplified version of the SOAP response we discussed earlier for a GET or POST:

```
<?xml version="1.0" encoding="utf-8" ?>
<string xmlns="http://www.deltabis.net/services/hw/">Hello Cochi</string>
```

As we said, when invoking or receiving services using the GET or POST methods, the data is much simpler than the equivalent SOAP calls. This simplicity, however, comes with limitations, such as the amount of data (in the case of the GET protocol), complexity with increasing amounts of data (in the case of POST), and limited structure – one of the major advantages of adopting an XML solution. In addition, a SOAP-based solution offers a more programmatic approach to working with web services in that it can be integrated and used within your applications like any other .NET component (rather than by a series of explicit HTTP requests). We will see an example of creating a SOAP client later in the chapter, but right now let's look at the SOAP request and response that are sent for this method.

The SOAP request XML is shown below, this response and request are for the same example as we used above for the HTTP GET running through the debugger:

```
<?xml version="1.0" encoding="utf-8"?>
<soap:Envelope xmlns:xsi="http://www.w3.org/2001/XMLSchema-instance"
  xmlns:xsd="http://www.w3.org/2001/XMLSchema"
  xmlns:soap="http://schemas.xmlsoap.org/soap/envelope/">
  <soap:Body>
    <SayHello xmlns="http://www.deltabis.net/services/hw/">
    <person>Cochi</person>
    </SayHello>
  </soap:Body>
</soap:Envelope>
```

Notice the `<SayHello>` element contains a single `person` parameter and it is also qualified in the unique namespace for this web service.

The SOAP response from this call is shown below:

```
<?xml version="1.0" encoding="utf-8"?>
<soap:Envelope xmlns:xsi="http://www.w3.org/2001/XMLSchema-instance"
  xmlns:xsd="http://www.w3.org/2001/XMLSchema"
  xmlns:soap="http://schemas.xmlsoap.org/soap/envelope/">
  <soap:Body>
    <SayHelloResponse xmlns="http://www.deltabis.net/services/hw/">
      <SayHelloResult>Hello Cochi</SayHelloResult>
    </SayHelloResponse>
  </soap:Body>
</soap:Envelope>
```

The response contains a single result in the `SayHelloResult` element, which is the return string "Hello Cochi".

We look at a more detailed example of working with a real web service in the *Case Study* section later in the chapter.

WSDL

WSDL (often pronounced "whiz-dull") or the Web Service Description Language, is an XML grammar used to describe the public interface for a web service, specifying its public methods and parameters. This WSDL file is a contract for message formats that can be exchanged between the service provider and the service client. So, a WSDL file can be published and read by a client wanting to use a web service, this client will then know what format the messages must take in order to communicate with that service and the format of the responses that will be returned.

When we created our web service a WSDL file was also created describing the web service to consumers of the service; we saw a WSDL file in Step 8 of the previous *Try it Out*. If you used IDL when working with COM or CORBA, then WSDL is the equivalent for web services, but in contrast, WSDL is platform, operating system, and language neutral.

Before we go on to look at an example file, we are going to look at what WSDL is, where it came from, and where it is used.

> **The WSDL specification can be found at** http://www.w3.org/TR/wsdl.html

The purpose of WSDL is to completely describe a web service to a consumer, such as the methods available and how these methods are called. WSDL considers the network- or web- service as an end point that operates on document-orientated messages or procedure-orientated data. Each operation and procedure is first abstractly defined, then bound to transport protocols (such as HTTP), and finally the message formats are defined.

The key to WSDL was the adoption of the XML Schema standard to describe the message formats which provides a language independent way of providing strong type details about the parameters and return values for a web service, .NET for example has mappings between XML Schema built-in data types and the data types used in .NET. We discussed this in the last chapter.

How is WSDL Used?

WSDL is powerful in that it allows a web service to abstract the definitions of its methods and arguments from the consumer and define a contract on how a consumer can interact with the web service. It maps the methods and parameters in the programming language of choice to typed element definitions in an XML instance using XSD definitions to define the types. It also defines the different transport protocols that the web service supports and how the methods are transported across these protocols.

This is extremely important in the adoption of web services, as it means the full power of web services can be adopted without learning all the technical details of schemas and transport protocols. Furthermore, because WSDL is comprised completely of XML, any WSDL-aware application can automatically read the description of a web service from this file and even call methods and pass the necessary parameters without the explicit need to manually write code to call those methods.

What's more, WSDL for a given web service is used to create a proxy class in a chosen language, which can then be used like any other class, with methods and properties to call. The .NET runtime does this either through `WSDL.exe` or VS.NET. We will see an example of this later.

Simple WSDL File

The simplest way to discuss what a WSDL file offers is to look at a simple example of one. The following WSDL file (it is not a physical file as it is dynamically generated by the .NET Framework) is what is created for the simple HelloWorld web service we created earlier at http://localhost/HelloWorld/service1.asmx?WSDL. It is best viewed in Internet Explorer, but in Mozilla you can view it by right-clicking and selecting View Source.

The root element of the document is the `definitions` element, which wraps the rest of the WSDL document and is qualified in the default namespace `http://schemas.xmlsoap.org/wsdl/`. On this element are a number of namespace definitions that are used throughout the document.

The prefix `s` maps to the XML Schema namespace for creating our type definitions using XSD later in the document.

```
<definitions xmlns:http="http://schemas.xmlsoap.org/wsdl/http/"
  xmlns:soap="http://schemas.xmlsoap.org/wsdl/soap/"
  xmlns:s="http://www.w3.org/2001/XMLSchema"
  xmlns:s0="http://www.deltabis.net/services/hw/"
  xmlns:soapenc="http://schemas.xmlsoap.org/soap/encoding/"
  xmlns:tm="http://microsoft.com/wsdl/mime/textMatching/"
  xmlns:mime="http://schemas.xmlsoap.org/wsdl/mime/"
  targetNamespace="http://www.deltabis.net/services/hw/"
  xmlns="http://schemas.xmlsoap.org/wsdl/">
```

The actual services are defined using 6 major elements (`<types>`, `<message>`, `<portType>`, `<binding>`, `<service>`, and `<port>`), which we will now look at. First there is the `types` element definition. This is perhaps the most important definition within the document as it defines the request and response using XML Schema Language (XSL). To start with there is the attribute name, if that is not available we then use the method type, along with the allowable parameter types for the request and then the response (the method name appended to `"Response"`) along with the typed name of the return type for the method.

```
<types>
  <s:schema elementFormDefault="qualified"
    targetNamespace="http://www.deltabis.net/services/hw/">
    <s:element name="SayHello">
      <s:complexType>
        <s:sequence>
```

```
                   <s:element minOccurs="0" maxOccurs="1" name="person" type="s:string" />
                 </s:sequence>
               </s:complexType>
             </s:element>
             <s:element name="SayHelloResponse">
               <s:complexType>
                 <s:sequence>
                   <s:element minOccurs="0" maxOccurs="1"
                     name="SayHelloResult" type="s:string" />
                 </s:sequence>
               </s:complexType>
             </s:element>
             <s:element name="string" nillable="true" type="s:string" />
          </s:schema>
       </types>
```

Notice that the `targetNamespace` attribute is defined as the unique namespace that has been defined for this web service; in this case it is `http://www.deltabis.net/services/hw/`, but this would change with your web services. The element named `<SayHello>` is defined to contain a single parameter called `person`, which is an XSD string data type. Similarly, the return value from the web service is also defined as an element called `<SayHelloResponse>` containing a single element called `<SayHelloResult>`, also of type string.

Following the type definitions, we can get down to defining the actual messages that go in and out of the service. There is a `<message>` element definition for each request and response for each protocol that is used to communicate with the service. In this case there are message definitions for SOAP, HTTP GET, and HTTP POST. The `message` name is the name of the method, followed by the transport mechanism and then either `In` or `Out` depending on the direction of the message. Within each `message` element there is a `<part>` element, which defines the parameters and their type mappings. Notice that each reference is qualified with the namespace bound to the prefix `s0`, which happens to be the unique namespace we assign to the web service, and also the target namespace of the XML Schema definition we created above. This allows us to link our XML Schema definitions directly with the messages that go in and out of the web service.

```
<message name="SayHelloSoapIn">
  <part name="parameters" element="s0:SayHello" />
</message>
<message name="SayHelloSoapOut">
  <part name="parameters" element="s0:SayHelloResponse" />
</message>
<message name="SayHelloHttpGetIn">
  <part name="person" type="s:string" />
</message>
<message name="SayHelloHttpGetOut">
  <part name="Body" element="s0:string" />
</message>
<message name="SayHelloHttpPostIn">
  <part name="person" type="s:string" />
</message>
<message name="SayHelloHttpPostOut">
  <part name="Body" element="s0:string" />
</message>
```

You can also see above that the SOAP transport takes far more structured parameters, whereas the HTTP GET and POST methods simply take strings. Notice that the output of each of these allow a custom string element, this is the same as any XSD `<string>` element, but it can also be `null`.

Following this, there are a series of `<portType>` elements, which is an abstract definition of the operations supported by each protocol, the name of the operation is the same as the method name, as well as the `input` and `output` messages which are referenced in the `message` attribute. The name of each `<portType>` is the name of the service followed by the protocol that the operation(s) is being defined for. If we haven't supplied an attribute value, it is the name of the class. This applies to `portTypes`, bindings, and service elements.

```
    <portType name="HelloWorldServiceSoap">
    <operation name="HelloWorld">
      <documentation>Hello Method</documentation>
      <input name="SayHello" message="s0:SayHelloSoapIn" />
      <output name="SayHello" message="s0:SayHelloSoapOut" />
    </operation>
  </portType>
  <portType name="HelloWorldServiceHttpGet">
    <operation name="HelloWorld">
      <documentation>Hello Method</documentation>
      <input name="SayHello" message="s0:SayHelloHttpGetIn" />
      <output name="SayHello" message="s0:SayHelloHttpGetOut" />
    </operation>
  </portType>
  <portType name="HelloWorldServiceHttpPost">
    <operation name="HelloWorld">
      <documentation>Hello Method</documentation>
      <input name="SayHello" message="s0:SayHelloHttpPostIn" />
      <output name="SayHello" message="s0:SayHelloHttpPostOut" />
    </operation>
  </portType>
```

Up until this point we have been defining abstract definitions describing the web service itself. Next, the `<binding>` element is using to bring together the definitions with concrete protocols. Each `<binding>` element is set to the type of abstract `portType` defined earlier that corresponds to that protocol. There is a one-to-one mapping between bindings and `portTypes` and also between operations. So the SOAP `<binding>` is of the type equal to the `portType` definition for SOAP, associating the abstract method definitions with this `<binding>`. The child `<binding>` element associates this binding with some transport protocol, in this case, the SOAP HTTP transport. The operation is defined and associated with the absolute method at that URI, as well as a definition of the `<input>` and `<output>` parameters, which in this case are not encoded due to being set as `literal`.

```
    <binding name="HelloWorldServiceSoap" type="s0:HelloWorldServiceSoap">
    <soap:binding transport="http://schemas.xmlsoap.org/soap/http"
      style="document" />
    <operation name="HelloWorld">
      <soap:operation soapAction="http://www.deltabis.net/services/hw/SayHello"
        style="document" />
      <input name="SayHello">
```

```
          <soap:body use="literal" />
      </input>
      <output name="SayHello">
        <soap:body use="literal" />
      </output>
    </operation>
  </binding>
  ...
```

Although not shown, <binding>s are also created for HTTP GET and HTTP POST <binding>s. Finally the actual service elements are set, these define the view that a consumer will primarily see – this is the address element bound to the correct namespace of the web service for each <binding>; in our case the SOAP, GET, and POST <binding>s all use the same web address.

```
    <service name="HelloWorldService">
      <documentation>Hello World Company Test Service.</documentation>
      <port name="HelloWorldServiceSoap" binding="s0:HelloWorldServiceSoap">
        <soap:address location="http://localhost/HelloWorld/Service1.asmx" />
      </port>
      <port name="HelloWorldServiceHttpGet" binding="s0:HelloWorldServiceHttpGet">
        <http:address location="http://localhost/HelloWorld/Service1.asmx" />
      </port>
      <port name="HelloWorldServiceHttpPost" binding="s0:HelloWorldServiceHttpPost">
        <http:address location="http://localhost/HelloWorld/Service1.asmx" />
      </port>
    </service>
  </definitions>
```

Each protocol (SOAP, HTTP POST, HTTP GET) has a port associated with it that defines the binding for that port and the address where that the actual service for that binding can be found.

That covers a relatively simple case of working with a WSDL file. If you have not used WSDL before, then it is likely that you are a bit in awe of the amount of information available in a single document. It can be quite complex, but remember that most of the time you will be hidden from much of these details. The key to WSDL is knowing what the various sections mean and being able to browse through it (when there is no documentation available) if and when necessary and have a reasonable understanding of the bindings, types, methods, return values, and protocols supported by a web service; the rest can be implemented by .NET.

Try It Out: Creating a "Hello World" Web Service Proxy

Once you have a WSDL file you can create a proxy class for any client wanting to access your service in any .NET language. Of course, other languages can access that service; they would just need to create the appropriate proxy for their language using the WSDL file provided.

1. Open a command window in the directory Program Files\Microsoft Visual Studio .NET\FrameworkSDK\Bin and locate the wsdl.exe file, typically found in the directory.

2. Copy the file to the C:\BegVBXML\Chapter13 directory and type the following at the command line:

wsdl /language:vb "http://localhost/HelloWorld/Service1.asmx?WSDL"

3. Once this has completed, open the `HelloWorldService.vb` file in a text editor. The filename is generated from the name of the service in the WSDL file.

4. You will get something like the following:

```vb
'-----------------------------------------------------------------------------
' <autogenerated>
'     This code was generated by a tool.
'     Runtime Version: 1.0.3705.288
'
'     Changes to this file may cause incorrect behavior and will be lost if
'     the code is regenerated.
' </autogenerated>
'-----------------------------------------------------------------------------


Option Strict Off
Option Explicit On


Imports System
Imports System.ComponentModel
Imports System.Diagnostics
Imports System.Web.Services
Imports System.Web.Services.Protocols
Imports System.Xml.Serialization


'
'This source code was auto-generated by wsdl, Version=1.0.3705.288.
'

'<remarks/>
<System.Diagnostics.DebuggerStepThroughAttribute(), _
  System.ComponentModel.DesignerCategoryAttribute("code"), _
  System.Web.Services.WebServiceBindingAttribute(Name:="HelloWorldServiceSoap", _
[Namespace]:="http://www.deltabis.net/services/hw/")> _
Public Class HelloWorldService
   Inherits System.Web.Services.Protocols.SoapHttpClientProtocol

   '<remarks/>
   Public Sub New()
     MyBase.New
     Me.Url = "http://localhost/HelloWorld/Service1.asmx"
   End Sub

   '<remarks/>
   <System.Web.Services.Protocols.SoapDocumentMethodAttribute(_
     "http://www.deltabis.net/services/hw/SayHello", _
     RequestElementName:="SayHello", _
     RequestNamespace:="http://www.deltabis.net/services/hw/", _
     ResponseElementName:="SayHelloResponse", _
     ResponseNamespace:="http://www.deltabis.net/services/hw/", _
     Use:=System.Web.Services.Description.SoapBindingUse.Literal, _
     ParameterStyle:=System.Web.Services.Protocols.SoapParameterStyle.Wrapped)>_
```

595

```
    Public Function HelloWorld(ByVal person As String) As
<System.Xml.Serialization.XmlElementAttribute("SayHelloResult")> String
    Dim results() As Object = Me.Invoke("HelloWorld", New Object() {person})
    Return CType(results(0),String)
    End Function

    '<remarks/>
    Public Function BeginHelloWorld(ByVal person As String, ByVal callback As
System.AsyncCallback, ByVal asyncState As Object) As System.IAsyncResult
    Return Me.BeginInvoke("HelloWorld", New Object() {person}, callback,
asyncState)
    End Function

    '<remarks/>
    Public Function EndHelloWorld(ByVal asyncResult As System.IAsyncResult) As
String
    Dim results() As Object = Me.EndInvoke(asyncResult)
    Return CType(results(0),String)
    End Function
End Class
```

How It Works

The wsdl.exe utility is available to create a SOAP proxy class (the /protocol: switch can be used to create HttpGet, HttpPost, or custom protocol classes) in a number of the .NET languages. The /language: switch can be used to create VB.NET and JScript.NET proxy classes also, although if the switch is left out then the language defaults to C#. These can then be included in any client that wants to consume the service, when we create a proxy the runtime builds the exact same public interface as the real class. The developer can just create the client using the proxy class as if it were the real class, and when the actual request is made, the proxy itself takes control of the request, makes an SOAP call to the web service, and returns the result to the client code. The interesting thing is that you never see any XML; you call the method and pass parameters as with any other class, and the result that is returned to you is a final type, such as a string or int.

> More details on the wsdl.exe utility can be found if you search for "Creating an XML Web Service Proxy" in the MSDN Library.

When you use the WSDL utility there are a number of options available to you to create the proxy class – all parameters except the URL of the service are optional. When we specified the full URL to the WSDL file on the web server, the utility created a proxy class by the name of the web service. In our case this was HelloWorldService.vb and was placed in the current directory. We will see how to use the proxy file later in the chapter, but let's look a little at its contents first.

Notice that the HelloWorldService class is derived from the SoapHttpClientProtocol class, which provides the functionality required by a SOAP client. Its constructor initialized the target URL of the service to the URL of our web service. Additionally there are some attributes used by the class when binding to the service.

Next, there are three method definitions, which may seem strange in that we only defined the one. The first one is, as we expect, the `HelloWorld()` method; it has some attributes defined on it that you could see in the WSDL document, such as the `RequestElementName` and `ResponseElementName` parameters. The other two methods that are available are `BeginHelloWorld()` and `EndHelloWorld()`, which are for asynchronous calls to the web service service. For more in formation on this see *Beginning .NET Web Services with VB.NET*, from Wrox Press (ISBN 1-86100-725-6).

Within the VS.NET arena, there is an alternative to the `wsdl.exe` utility, which is easier and more likely to be used when you have direct access to the web service. This involves simply adding a reference to the client code, which will retrieve the WSDL details over HTTP and create a local proxy for your code. Functionally this is the same as using `wsdl.exe` but it is all done in the background. This is obviously more difficult, however, when working in development environments that may not have HTTP access to the service, or when you are a company distributing a software product with built-in web service client functionality. In these cases the proxy will be more popular.

Discovery – DISCO

Up until this point, knowing where to look for web services and the various document types that are considered part of web services has been easy because we know exactly where to look. More commonly you won't know the exact URL of a web service or its WSDL document, and this gets even more complex when you consider a more automated process where your client can find a web service it wants to use.

Microsoft has therefore created a simple solution for single servers using DISCO documents. DISCO documents allows a client to discover the web service offered by a given web server, the documentation for the service and how you can interact with that service (via WSDL). You simply create a `.disco` file and place it in the virtual root where the web service `.asmx` file is found. This document simply contains links to other documents that describe the web service. With Visual Studio .NET, this DISCO file is automatically created for you.

There are in fact two versions of DISCO documents – the first, and most common is the static DISCO document (`.disco`), which is defined by the designer of the web service and points to the relevant documents. The second is a dynamic DISCO document (`.vsdisco`) which actually creates a static DISCO document on the fly when a request for it is made by recursing through the sub-directories looking for `.asmx` and `.disco` files.

Let's look at each of these in a little more detail.

Static DISCO Files

Static DISCO files are XML files and are created by adding a new file with the `.disco` extension to the virtual root of the web service you are working with. The name of the DISCO file is typically the name of the web service following by a `.disco` extension. The DISCO file itself uses a root `<discovery>` element, which must be qualified in the default namespace `http://schemas.xmlsoap.org/disco/` as shown below:

```
<?xml version="1.0" encoding="utf-8" ?>
<discovery xmlns="http://schemas.xmlsoap.org/disco/">
</discovery>
```

Within this root element you add the references to other discovery documents, services and schemas that may be of interest to clients. The `<discoveryRef>` element is used to reference other DISCO discovery documents on the server and the `ref` attribute points to the actual physical document, as follows:

```
<?xml version="1.0" encoding="utf-8" ?>
<discovery xmlns="http://schemas.xmlsoap.org/disco/">
  <discoveryRef ref="/Services/default.disco" />
</discovery>
```

You can also reference the WSDL document using the `<contractRef>` element (`contractRef` is for referencing WSDL docs), which must be qualified in the namespace `http://schemas.xmlsoap.org/disco/scl/`. The `ref` attribute references the actual WSDL document, and you can also use a `docRef` attribute to point to a file that discusses the web service documentation in this case they point to the `HelloWorld` service we worked with earlier. So we can extend the above document as follows:

```
<?xml version="1.0" encoding="utf-8" ?>
<discovery xmlns="http://schemas.xmlsoap.org/disco/"
  xmlns:scl="http://schemas.xmlsoap.org/disco/scl/">
  <discoveryRef ref="/Services/default.disco" />
  <scl:contractRef ref="Service1.asmx?WSDL" docRef="Service1.asmx" />
</discovery>
```

Static DISCO files can be created in Visual Studio .NET by right-clicking on the root of the project hosting the web service, selecting **Add** and then **Add New Item...** The **Static Discovery File** icon can then be selected and the file name added; typically the name of the file is the same name as the web service.

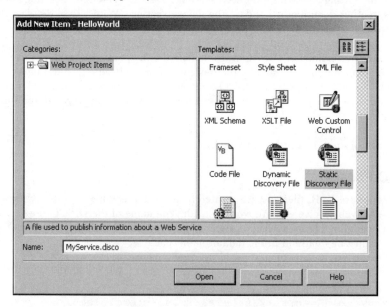

When this is created the root `<discovery>` element is all that is added to the file – you have to manually add the rest of the XML document using the elements discussed above.

Try It Out: Add a Static DISCO File to our Web Service

This will add a new static DISCO file that we will use this in an example shortly

1. Return to the HelloWorld web service we were working on earlier and add a new static discovery file called `HelloWorld.disco` to the project root.

2. Add the following to this file:

```
<?xml version="1.0" encoding="utf-8" ?>
<discovery xmlns="http://schemas.xmlsoap.org/disco/"
    xmlns:scl="http://schemas.xmlsoap.org/disco/scl/">
    <scl:contractRef ref="Service1.asmx?WSDL" docRef="Service1.asmx" />
</discovery>
```

Dynamic DISCO Files

Dynamic DISCO files, in contrast, are dynamically created whenever a request for a `.vsdisco` file is requested. Requests for files with this extension are handled by `Web.Services.Discovery.DiscoveryRequestHandler` which will create a DISCO document based on the `.asmx` and `.disco` resources found in the virtual root and its subdirectories. For every web service found, a new `<contractRef>` element is created with the `ref` attribute pointing to the WSDL document and the `docRef` attribute which points to the actual web service.

So, consider the following web directory structure:

```
\InetPub
        \wwwroot
                \HelloWorld (virtual root)
                        Service1.asmx
                        web.config
                        HelloWorld.vsdisco
```

The `.vsdisco` file is also an XML document, but is slightly different from the DISCO file, as follows:

```
<?xml version="1.0" encoding="utf-8" ?>
<dynamicDiscovery xmlns="urn:schemas-dynamicdiscovery:disco.2000-03-17">
  <exclude path="_vti_cnf" />
  <exclude path="_vti_pvt" />
  <exclude path="_vti_log" />
  <exclude path="_vti_script" />
  <exclude path="_vti_txt" />
  <exclude path="Web References" />
</dynamicDiscovery>
```

You can see that the root element is called `<dynamicDiscovery>` and the namespace is different with a date specific part detailing when the dynamic discovery document was created. A series of `<exclude>` elements with a `path` attribute detail folders, these don't have to be dynamically checked for appropriate documents.

If a request was made directly for the file `HelloWorld.vsdisco` we were working with earlier, then by default .NET doesn't recognize that the `.vsdisco` files are to be processed (probably as they are more resource-intensive than static files, but it would still make sense to enable them by default and allow you to turn them off!) and so you will just get the XML output. You must add the following to the `web.config` file to allow them to be accessed:

```
<configuration>
  <system.web>
    ...
    <httpHandlers>
      <add verb="*" path="*.vsdisco"
        type="System.Web.Services.Discovery.DiscoveryRequestHandler,
        System.Web.Services, Version=1.0.3300.0, Culture=neutral,
        PublicKeyToken=b03f5f7f11d50a3a" validate="false"/>
    </httpHandlers>
  </system.web>
</configuration>
```

Now, if a request was made directly for the file `Hello.vsdisco`, for example by a .NET application or even an application on another platform that understands the format of the DISCO document, and makes an HTTP request for the DISCO document via the web service (for example, `http://localhost/HelloWorld/HelloWorld.vsdisco`), then a document similar to the following `.disco` document will be dynamically created and returned.

```
<?xml version="1.0" encoding="utf-8"?>
<discovery xmlns:xsd=http://www.w3.org/2001/XMLSchema
  xmlns:xsi=http://www.w3.org/2001/XMLSchema-instance
  xmlns="http://schemas.xmlsoap.org/disco/">

  <contractRef ref=http://localhost/HelloWorld/Service1.asmx?wsdl
    docRef="http://localhost/HelloWorld/Service1.asmx"
    xmlns="http://schemas.xmlsoap.org/disco/scl/" />

  <discoveryRef ref="http://localhost/HelloWorld/HelloWorld.disco" />
</discovery>
```

Try It Out: Consuming a Web Service

This example demonstrates how to use a static DISCO file to create a web service client.

1. Create a new VB Windows Application project called HelloWorldServiceClient.

2. Now right click on the References folder and select the Add Web Reference item.

3. This will bring up the Add Web Reference dialog box; in the Address bar, enter http://localhost/HelloWorld/HelloWorld.disco as the URL and hit *Enter*. This will display the DISCO document we entered earlier in a dialog box as shown below:

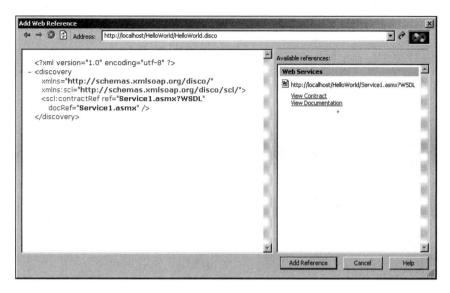

The **View Contract** link displays the WSDL document; you don't need to do this when adding a new web reference, but it is useful to check the description document anyway. The **View Documentation** link will take you to a page we saw earlier, which lists the available methods and their descriptions for the web service.

4. Click the **Add Reference** button (you must still be viewing the `HelloWorld.disco` file before you do this) and the `HelloWorld.disco`, `Service1.wsdl`, and a proxy class `reference.vb` is dynamically created for you on the client (you can't see the proxy class).

5. Add a button to the Windows form and double-click on the button to open the event handler for the button. Enter the following code into this section:

```
Private Sub Button1_Click(ByVal sender As System.Object, _
  ByVal e As System.EventArgs) Handles Button1.Click
  Dim ws As HelloWorldServiceClient.localhost.HelloWorldService = _
    New HelloWorldClient.localhost.HelloWorldService()

  MessageBox.Show(ws.HelloWorld("Everyone"))
End Sub
```

6. Press the *F5* key or **Start** button to run the application. Click the button and you will get the following response.

How It Works

In this example we worked through using a local web service, but it could quite easily have been any service on any server. We discovered the web services when we specified the location of our DISCO file. This was parsed and the links to the WSDL file and documentation were displayed in the window on the right.

When we clicked the **Add Reference** button, Visual Studio automatically downloaded the WSDL file, static DISCO file and also created a proxy class that could be used to call the web service. This can be found by using the **Show All Files** option in VS.NET, the find is called `reference.vb`. If you open this file, you will see the contents are almost exactly the same as that for the manual proxy we created earlier using the `wsdl.exe` utility.

Disco Redirects

Something you may have noticed is that it is often unlikely that a consumer is going to know the exact URL of the DISCO file that holds the details of the service they may be interested in.

There are two ways you can improve this. The first is to create a `default.htm` file in the virtual root that simply links through to the DISCO file. The file `default.htm` can be created and placed in the virtual root.

```
<html>
  <head>
    <link type="text/xml" rel="alternate" href="HelloWorld.disco" />
  </head>
</html>
```

Now, you can get the full details on the web service via the URL http://localhost/HelloWorld/. Additionally you could put a DISCO document on the root of the web site and refer to the other DISCO documents in the site; this way the consumer could just use the URL http://localhost and find all web services on the server.

Directories – UDDI

The Universal Description, Discovery and Integration (UDDI) Service, is a technical specification for the description, discovery, and integration of global web services. It is an essential part of web services as it allows a company to publish the web services it has to offer and allows some other company to discover that the service is available based on numerous search criterions. Much of the discovery of web services is currently done manually at the moment, although the idea behind UDDI is to provide a much more automated capability for applications to discover web services they need.

There are two main areas where UDDI is focused. The first is purely as a technical specification for building directories of web services, with the data stored as XML and the discovery mechanism being provided by the UDDI API specifications that allows you to search this data.

The second area is the UDDI Business Registry, which is a fully operational implementation of the UDDI technical specifications. Launched in May 2001 by Microsoft, Ariba, and IBM, the UDDI registry now enables anyone to search existing UDDI data. It also enables any company to register itself and its services. There are three versions of UDDI specification, version 1 was released in September 2000 and the latest, version 3, was released in July 2002.

UDDI takes the concepts behind DISCO and expands them to a global audience and is supported by various enterprise companies. However, it is really the concepts that are extended; the implementation is far more detailed and complex and although it has started to evolve, there is a lot of work to be done to ensure business level directories for web services.

UDDI is a web service itself and provides an API as well as an XML Schema based description of the messages and data structures required to interact with the directories. The idea is that globally there will be a limited number of directories that will allow publishers to add their own web services and consumers to search and use these services. Not only that, but the next generation of Windows Servers will have a UDDI component allowing your own Enterprise to host its own UDDI registry, perhaps for internal use and business partners.

UDDI Concepts

UDDI uses familiar business directory concepts, originating from the white/yellow/green sections of US phone books, to organize the directory into white pages, yellow pages, and green pages. The "white pages" contain name, address, contact information, and known identifiers for a business. "Yellow pages" include industrial categorizations based on standard taxonomies, and the "green pages" contain the technical specifications of the services exposed by the business.

The four core types of information are business entities, services, binding templates and models, which are related as shown below:

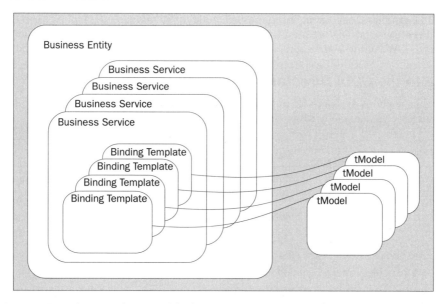

The **business entity** is the core element of the business and contains details on name, address, and contact information, as well as technical details on its services. Each of these **services** contains business and technical descriptions and categorizations of the service. Each service has a **binding template**, which has technical details on how to actually invoke the web service. Each of these links to a **tModel** that contains metadata about the service, such as its name, who published it, and URLs to the various technical documents that define the specification. This part is similar to a DISCO document. It may, for example, contain a URL that points to a WSDL document to define the contract for a web service wanting to interact with the service.

This so far defines the structure of the UDDI directory, but obviously information must be both retrieved and published. This is done through the UDDI API, which defines a series of methods that can be used to interrogate the directory, as well as publish your information to the directory. Alternatively, you can search and publish the directory using the online interfaces at the following locations:

❏ http://uddi.microsoft.com

❏ https://uddi.ibm.com/ubr/registry.html

❏ http://www.uddi.org/register.html

Additionally both IBM and Microsoft offer test directories that you can play around with while developing:

❏ https://www-3.ibm.com/services/uddi/testregistry/protect/registry.html

❏ http://test.uddi.microsoft.com/default.aspx

❏ http://uddi.rte.microsoft.com (beta of UDDI v2)

All interaction via this directory is done using XML and SOAP, but the high-level API protects users from having to work with XML. The functions available in this API are defined in the `Microsoft.Uddi` and `Microsoft.Uddi.Api` namespaces.

These UDDI namespaces are not part of the .NET Framework installation, so you have to download these at http://msdn.microsoft.com/library/en-us/Dnuddi/html/versuddisdk.asp. At the time of writing there is a download for UDDI v1 for Visual Studio .NET and a download of a beta version of UDDI v2 preview classes. When these are installed you will have a UDDI SDK and sample application.

Publishing to the UDDI Directory

There are four methods available for publishing data to the directory, three utility methods that are useful in this process and another four that can be used to remove details.

Method Name	Description
save_business()	Publishes new or updates existing complete businessEntity information
save_service()	Publishes new or updates existing service information for a specified business
save_binding()	Publishes new or updates existing binding information for a specified business
save_tModel()	Publishes new or updates existing complete tModel information
get_authToken()	Requests an authentication token from the UDDI node that can be used on future calls in place of the full authentication credentials
discard_authToken()	Discards an authentication token preventing its later use
get_registered_info()	Requests top-level details about entities that are currently managed by an authenticated user

Method Name	Description
delete_business()	Deletes an entire business registration from the node
delete_service()	Deletes a service from a business registration
delete_binding()	Deletes a binding from a service registration
delete_tModel()	Deletes a tModel registration from the binding

Try It Out: Publishing your Business Services to the directory

In this section we are going to publish a business to the UDDI registry.

1. Download and install the UDDI SDK from http://msdn.microsoft.com/library/en-us/Dnuddi/html/versuddisdk.asp – you want to download the **version 1 SDK** (1.76 beta) (not version 2) that is for .NET.

2. Now go to http://test.uddi.microsoft.com and register with the directory so you can then make updates. You will need to have a Microsoft Passport to do this; the e-mail address and password you register will be required for making the update.

3. Once you have done this you will be taken to the Administer page as shown below, which will have no businesses registered:

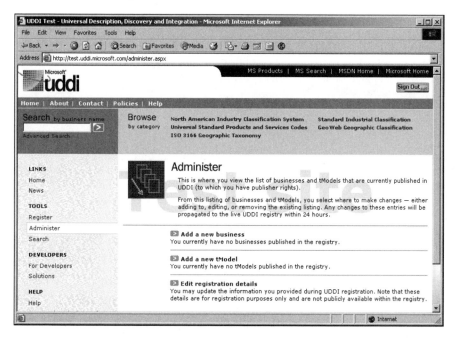

Next we want to actually add a business to this – within the test registry you are limited to a single business – so in the following steps we assume there are no businesses yet registered for your username.

4. In VS.NET create a new VB Windows Application project called **UDDItest** and add a reference to the `Microsoft.UDDI.SDK` namespace which is listed with the other .NET namespaces in the references list.

5. Add 1 `GroupBox` control, 6 `Label` controls, 5 `TextBox` controls, and 1 `Button` control to the form and arrange each of the items as shown below. Set the defaults as shown (or to something else if you prefer):

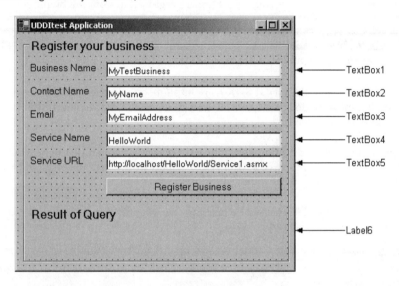

6. Press *F7* to switch to the code view of this form and add the following imports to the top of the file which will give us access to the UDDI classes:

```
Imports Microsoft.Uddi
Imports Microsoft.Uddi.Api
```

7. Return to the form, double-click the **Register Business** button, and add the following code. Remember to enter the `username` and `password` details within the code that you used to register to the UDDI site, otherwise you will not be able to run the sample.

```
Private Sub button1_Click(ByVal sender As System.Object, _
    ByVal e As System.EventArgs) Handles button1.Click
    'Get values from form into local variables
    Dim businessName As String = textBox1.Text
    Dim contactName As String = textBox2.Text
    Dim emailAddress As String = textBox3.Text
    Dim WebServiceName As String = textBox4.Text
    Dim WebServiceLocation As String = textBox5.Text

    'Change to appropriate server
    Microsoft.Uddi.Publish.Url = "https://test.uddi.microsoft.com/publish"
```

```
'Set username and password details
Microsoft.Uddi.Publish.User = "stv_wrox@hotmail.com"
Microsoft.Uddi.Publish.Password = "ntanet__"

'Add the information about the business we are creating
Dim sb As SaveBusiness = New SaveBusiness()
sb.BusinessEntities.Add()
sb.BusinessEntities(0).Name = businessName

'Create associated web service entry
sb.BusinessEntities(0).BusinessServices.Add()
sb.BusinessEntities(0).BusinessServices(0).Name = WebServiceName & "Service"

'Create BindingTemplate to say how web services can be accessed
sb.BusinessEntities(0).BusinessServices(0).BindingTemplates.Add()

'Add the specific web service
sb.BusinessEntities(0).BusinessServices(0).BindingTemplates(0). _
  Descriptions.Add(WebServiceName)

sb.BusinessEntities(0).BusinessServices(0).BindingTemplates(0). _
  AccessPoint.Text = WebServiceLocation

sb.BusinessEntities(0).BusinessServices(0).BindingTemplates(0). _
  AccessPoint.URLType = Microsoft.Uddi.Api.URLTypeEnum.Http

'Send to UDDI
Try
   MessageBox.Show("Xml being sent is " & sb.ToString())
   Dim bd As BusinessDetail = sb.Send()
Catch ue As UddiException
   label6.Text = ue.Message
   Return
Catch err As Exception
   label6.Text = err.Message
   Return
End Try

   label6.Text = "Your entry was saved in UDDI."
End Sub
```

8. Save this and either press the **Start** button or *F5* to run the application. When the form we designed earlier appears (unless you want to change any details), click the **Register Business** button. You will get a message box displaying the XML that is being submitted to the server:

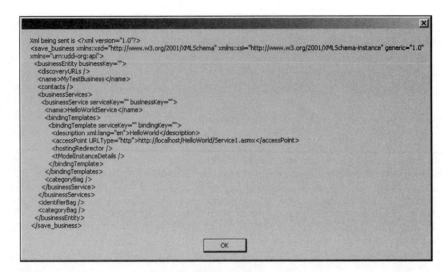

The business name is wrapped in the `<name>` element of the `<businessEntity>` parent node and the service and binding details are also entered in descendant nodes of this.

9. After clicking OK, about 10 seconds or so later you will get the following displayed:

Notice that it tells you that your data has been saved in the directory. To verify this, go back and log into the UDDI test directory at http://test.uddi.microsoft.com. When you view the Administer page (you can click the Administer link on the left of the screen if you desire) you'll see something like the following:

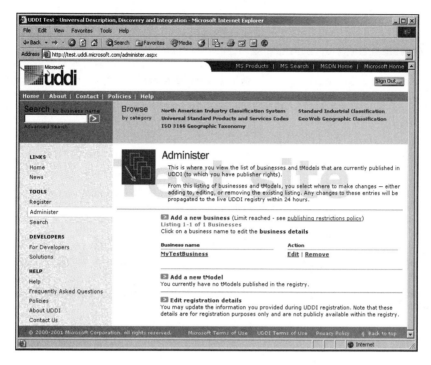

How It Works

To make any request to the UDDI registry you have to specify the URL of the server in the `Url` property of the `Publish` class. The appropriate `username` and `password` details must also be specified in order to be able to update the registry (they are not needed for read-only queries).

```
'Change to appropriate server
Microsoft.Uddi.Publish.Url = "https://test.uddi.microsoft.com/publish"

'Set username and password details
Microsoft.Uddi.Publish.User = "username"
Microsoft.Uddi.Publish.Password = "password"
```

We use the `SaveBusiness` class to publish new information about the business, the key property being the name of the business.

```
'Add the information about the business we are creating
Dim sb As SaveBusiness = New SaveBusiness()
sb.BusinessEntities.Add()
sb.BusinessEntities(0).Name = businessName
```

The `BusinessEntities` property can be used to insert information about multiple businesses, but we are only adding one and so use the index 0 in the brackets. Equally, the `BusinessServices` property can be used to add information about multiple services belonging to a business and so we add the information about the single HelloWorld service we have specified (which in this case points to the local service we created earlier, although no verification is done that this service exists).

```
'Create associated web service entry
sb.BusinessEntities(0).BusinessServices.Add()
sb.BusinessEntities(0).BusinessServices(0).Name = WebServiceName & "Service"
```

A `BindingTemplate` is then added which is used to associate access and description information about the service with the name we created – details such as the location of the service and how to access it (`Http` and `Https` are common, although `fax` and `phone` are possible as we can describe any abstract service).

```
'Create BindingTemplate to say how web services can be accessed
sb.BusinessEntities(0).BusinessServices(0).BindingTemplates.Add()

'Add the specific web service
sb.BusinessEntities(0).BusinessServices(0).BindingTemplates(0). _
   Descriptions.Add(WebServiceName)
sb.BusinessEntities(0).BusinessServices(0).BindingTemplates(0). _
   AccessPoint.Text = WebServiceLocation
sb.BusinessEntities(0).BusinessServices(0).BindingTemplates(0). _
   AccessPoint.URLType = Microsoft.Uddi.Api.URLTypeEnum.Http
```

When the information is complete, the `Send()` method invokes the request; underneath, however, everything is done as an XML message.

```
Dim bd As BusinessDetail = sb.Send()
```

You have now successfully registered a business and service with UDDI, so how do we get information back? Let's now look at querying the UDDI directory.

Querying the UDDI directory

There are four methods available for searching the directory and another five for actually retrieving the details.

Method Name	Description
find_business()	Finds the top-level information for one or more matching businesses
find_service()	Finds the top-level service information for a given business
find_binding()	Finds the top-level binding information for a given business
find_tModel()	Finds the top-level information for one or more matching tModels
get_businessDetail()	Gets the complete businessEntity information for one or more identified businesses
get_businessDetailExt()	Gets the extended businessEntity information for one or more identified businesses

Method Name	Description
`get_serviceDetail()`	Gets the complete information for one or more identified services
`get_bindingDetail()`	Gets the complete `bindingTemplate` information for one or more identified bindings
`get_tModelDetail()`	Gets the complete information for one or more identified `tModels`

Try It Out: Finding a Business and its Services

In this example we are going to look at how you can query one of the live UDDI registries to find a business and then return information about the services it offers.

1. Return to the UDDItest project we were working with in the last example, extend the size of the form, and add 1 GroupBox control, 2 TextBox controls, 1 Label control, and 1 Button control, with the values shown.

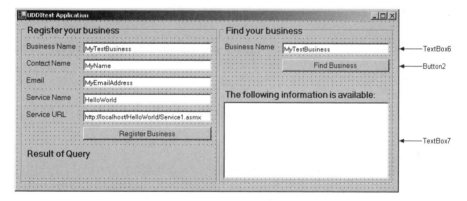

2. Now double-click the Find Business button and add the following code:

```
Private Sub button2_Click(ByVal sender As System.Object, _
    ByVal e As System.EventArgs) Handles button2.Click
    Dim businessName As String = textBox6.Text

    Try
        'UDDI Registry to connect to
        Inquire.Url = "http://test.uddi.microsoft.com/inquire"

        'Create instance to find business
        Dim business As FindBusiness = New FindBusiness()

        'Specify the name of the business to search for
        business.Name = businessName

        'Show XML
        MessageBox.Show("Get business details " & System.Environment.NewLine _
            & business.ToString())
```

```vb
'Make the request
Dim businessList As BusinessList = business.Send()

'Show XML
MessageBox.Show("Returned business details " _
  & System.Environment.NewLine _
  & businessList.ToString())

textBox7.Text = ""
textBox7.Text = textBox7.Text + "You searched the " _
  & businessList.Operator.ToString() & " registry." _
  & System.Environment.NewLine

'How many results?
textBox7.Text = textBox7.Text + "There were " & _
  businessList.BusinessInfos.Count.ToString() & _
  " matches for your search." + System.Environment.NewLine _
  & System.Environment.NewLine

'If there are any matching businesses
If (BusinessList.BusinessInfos.Count > 0) Then

  'Show the business provider's name
  textBox7.Text = textBox7.Text + businessList.BusinessInfos(0).Name _
    & " provides the following services :" _
    & System.Environment.NewLine _
    & System.Environment.NewLine

  'Output any services and their identifying keys
  Dim j As Integer = 0
  For j = 0 To businessList.BusinessInfos(0).ServiceInfos.Count - 1
    textBox7.Text = textBox7.Text + "***" _
      & businessList.BusinessInfos(0).ServiceInfos(j).Name

    Dim getsd As GetServiceDetail = New GetServiceDetail()

    getsd.ServiceKeys.Add( _
      businessList.BusinessInfos(0).ServiceInfos(j).ServiceKey)

    'Show XML Request
    MessageBox.Show("Get Service Detail :" _
      & System.Environment.NewLine _
      & getsd.ToString())

    Dim sd As ServiceDetail = getsd.Send()

    'Show XML Result
    MessageBox.Show("Service Detail : " _
      & System.Environment.NewLine _
      & sd.ToString())

    textBox7.Text = textBox7.Text + " can be accessed at " _
      & sd.BusinessServices(0).BindingTemplates(0).AccessPoint.Text _
```

```
                     & System.Environment.NewLine
        Next
      End If
    Catch ex As UddiException
      MessageBox.Show("UDDI exception: " & ex.Number & " - " & ex.Message)
    Catch ex As Exception
      MessageBox.Show("General exception: " & ex.Message)
    End Try
  End Sub
```

3. Now run the code and click the **Find Business** link. You will first get a display of the XML that is being set to the registry to request more information about the business.

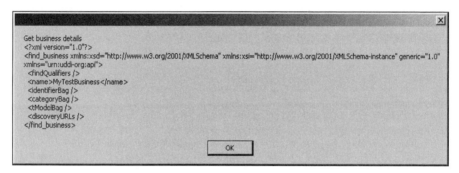

4. You will then receive information on the XML that is returned from the registry with the details of the business(es) found.

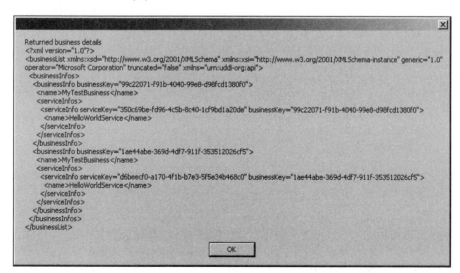

5. Next, the first service key of the first business is extracted from this XML and a request is made for the services offered by that business.

The `GetServiceDetail` class is serialized to the structure above, containing a single child element (in this case) with the service key to search for.

6. Finally the return XML from the registry containing the information about the specified service is displayed.

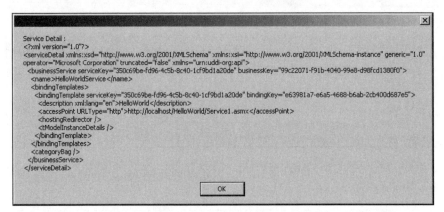

This XML will contain all of the details for the service key that was searched for and you can access the values within this structure via the properties on the `ServiceDetail` class. We only access the first `bindingTemplate` element.

7. When this has completed, you will get the result of your query displayed in the textbox at the bottom of the application:

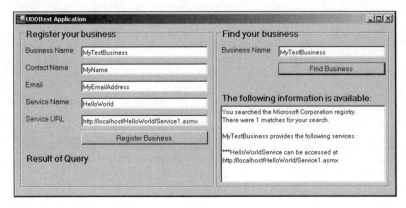

How It Works

The `FindBusiness` class again allows us to find any businesses with the specified name and this data is returned in XML format from the UDDI registry.

```
'Create instance to find business
Dim business As FindBusiness = New FindBusiness()

'Specify the name of the business to search for
business.Name = businessName
```

When this is returned, we can iterate through each of the returned businesses and find the name of any services that are associated with that business.

```
textBox7.Text = textBox7.Text + "You searched the " _
& businessList.Operator.ToString() & " registry." _
& System.Environment.NewLine
```

We create a new instance of a `GetServiceDetail` class that returns `ServiceDetail` objects when we request the details with the `Send()` method. We can add details of service keys to the `GetServiceDetail` class; we get these from the business information that was returned by calling the `Send()` method. In our code we only add the first service key that is returned.

```
Dim getsd As GetServiceDetail = New GetServiceDetail()
getsd.ServiceKeys.Add(businessList.BusinessInfos(0).ServiceInfos(j).ServiceKey)
```

Once the request has returned, we can get information about the binding between the business and the service; we get the access point which defines the location of the web service.

The `FindBusiness` class is mapped to the `find_business` element and the details of the properties of this class are serialized within this node, the business name being an example.

A `businessList` root element node contains all of the information of the businesses found and this element maps back to the `BusinessList` class. The details of the child nodes are abstracted by providing properties to access the values in the XML.

Now you can consume the web service in one of your applications. This is out of the scope for a single chapter so for more information on this see *Professional ASP.NET Web Services with VB.NET*, from Wrox Press (ISBN 1-86100-775-2). However, we leave it as an exercise for the reader to extend this application to discover other web services, perhaps using some advanced search criterion such as a service name search of the description field that is also returned with the web service from the UDDI registry.

The best way to understand the UDDI directory is to work with it using the namespaces and methods discussed above and use the test directories available. You can start by downloading the UDDI SDK, which is updated every few months, from http://msdn.microsoft.com/library/en-us/Dnuddi/html/versuddisdk.asp.

.NET Remoting

> An exhaustive discussion of .NET Remoting is outside the scope of this book. In this
> overview we intend to discuss how XML impacts on .NET Remoting, rather than
> looking at .NET Remoting as a whole.
>
> For further information on .NET Remoting, see *Professional ASP.NET Web Services
> with VB.NET,* from Wrox Press (ISBN 1-86100-775-2) and *Advanced .NET Remoting,
> from* Apress (ISBN 1-59059-062-7).

As powerful as web services are for remote communication between components, the overhead of
SOAP can sometimes be inefficient for intranet or local applications that don't necessarily need to
worry about conforming to standards as they are only intended to work with each other. In fact as the
size of the objects and data sets increases, the overhead of using SOAP as a serialization format for these
objects and data sets increases also. When you don't need to interoperate with other platforms and
languages that do not support the .NET Framework then you can look at a technology called .NET
Remoting. A good source for performance comparisons can be found at
http://www.dotnetremoting.cc/DotNetCentric/Articles/Remotingvs.ASP.NETWebServ.asp which looks
at the relative performance of working with ASP.NET web services against Remoting over HTTP; you
will find that the Remoting option is significantly more performant as the size of the objects and size of
the data increases. So, what is .NET Remoting?

.NET Remoting is a generic, extensible framework (library, set of classes) for inter-process
communication. So by using .NET Remoting classes we can establish communication between objects
that run in different processes, maybe also in different application domains, without regard to whether
these objects live on the same computer or on computers that are thousands of miles apart. .NET
Remoting allows us to write flexible, high-performance, distributed applications.

In the past this work was performed by distributed COM (or DCOM), which allowed you to call
methods on remote objects. However, DCOM itself was relatively inefficient and never worked well
over the Internet, mainly due to firewalls and other security issues.

The replacement for DCOM in the .NET Framework is .NET Remoting, which also improves the
capabilities offered by web services in situations where you don't have to worry about operating with
clients on other operating systems and environments. The term **Web Services Anywhere** has been
applied to Remoting as it can be used in any application to communicate over any transport protocol
(HTTP, TCP, and so on) with any kind of data encoding; however .NET Remoting is not web services.
This, of course, means that you can also use SOAP encoding over a HTTP channel as the
communication method for Remoting. There are significant performance issues with SOAP over HTTP
using Remoting, however, and ASP.NET web services offer much higher performance, but binary
encoded Remoting hosted in IIS provides even better performance than this.

What is Remoting – Architecture Overview

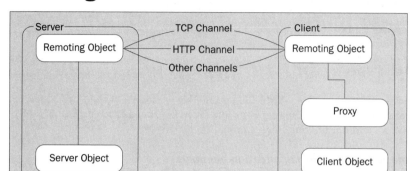

The **remote object** runs on the server and is never directly called on the client. Instead a **proxy** is created, which can then be used to call the methods of the server object. Communication between the client and server is done via a **channel**, which can be HTTP, TCP, or other protocols.

When a client calls a server method, a message is passed, containing details on the remote object method that was called and any parameters that are to be passed. A **formatter** is then used to encode the message before it is sent into the channel. The format of this encoded message can be SOAP to work with applications that are not written using any of the .NET languages, or encoding in a binary format (this is optimized as you don't have whitespace, angled brackets, and so on to encode along with the actual data) to improve speed and efficiency when working with other .NET components.

The .NET configuration of such a service can be done in compiled code. The problem is that this may change often and very likely increase in scope relatively often, requiring a recompilation each time. To improve on this, the entire configuration for remoting clients and server can be specified in an XML configuration file that is loaded at run time and allows changes to be made without compilation.

Remoting Configuration

As we mentioned, a configuration file is a very powerful mechanism that .NET brings to component development as it can be used to configure remoting applications without the details requiring to be compiled in the code. The following is an example of the client `config` file that is used in a `HelloWorld` client that we look at later in this chapter:

```
<?xml version="1.0" encoding="utf-8" ?>
<configuration>
  <system.runtime.remoting>
    <application name="HelloWorld">
      <client url="tcp://localhost:9000/HelloWorld">
        <wellknown type="HelloWorldRemotingClass.HelloWorld,
          HelloWorldRemotingClass"
          url="tcp://localhost:9000/HelloWorld/HelloWorldUri" />
```

617

```
        </client>
        <channels>
          <channel ref="tcp" />
        </channels>
      </application>
    </system.runtime.remoting>
  </configuration>
```

This configuration document is an XML file and the key elements of this XML document are as follows. A lot of the elements that we're looking at have a `displayName` attribute but it is only used by the configuration tool and not the remoting runtime.

<system.runtime.remoting> and <application elements>

The `<system.runtime.remoting>` element is a child of the root configuration element and contains the `<application>` elements for each application you want to define in the XML document. The `<application>` element itself uses a `name` attribute which, on the server, defines the name of the server application that is used by the client in the URL created to access the application.

<client>

The `<client>` element is used to configure client details for a given application. The `url` attribute on this element specifies both the protocol and root URL of the application to which the client will connect. The child `<wellknown>` element is used to specify the server-activated object that you want to call. The `type` attribute is important and specifies the type of the object, followed by a comma and then the assembly name of the type. If the type is in the Global Assembly Cache (GAC), then the strong name must be used, including version, culture, and public key information.

The `url` attribute is used to specify the object that is to be invoked. This is the URL to the class, as well as the URL of the object itself as specified in the server configuration file.

<service>

The `<service>` element is used when configuring the server application; it is in place of the `<client>` element and contains the `<wellknown>` element. The `mode` attribute of this element is either `SingleCall` or `Singleton`. When `SingleCall` is set, a new object instance will be created for each client that connects to the remote object; `Singleton` will mean that a single instance is created and used by all clients. The `type` attribute is the same as for the `<client>` element and the `objectUri` attribute specifies an endpoint for the object and is used by the client to specifically reference the object instance.

<channels> and <channel>

The `<channels>` element defines all the channels that the client or server will operate over. Each `<channel>` element contains details on each channel that will be available for transport. The `port` attribute specifies the port number that the defined protocol will work over.

The `ref` attribute can be used instead of the `type` attribute to specify a well-defined transport protocol as defined below. However, if you use a class and it's in the GAC (for instance, all .NET Framework base classes), then you must fully qualify the class, such as:

```
<channel type="System.Runtime.Remoting.Channels.Http.HttpChannel,
System.Runtime.Remoting, Version=1.0.3300.0, Culture=neutral,
PublicKeyToken=b77a5c561934e089" />
```

The following channel protocols are defined for the `ref`:

- ❑   Http
- ❑   HttpClient
- ❑   HttpServer
- ❑   Tcp
- ❑   TcpClient
- ❑   TcpServer

The following formatter `ref`s are also defined:

- ❑   Soap
- ❑   Binary

Creating Remoting Clients and Servers

There is quite a lot of information that can be specified in the configuration file, such as:

- ❑   Host application information
- ❑   The name of the objects
- ❑   The URI of the objects
- ❑   The Channels being registered
- ❑   The lease time details for server objects

The `config` file itself should have the same name as the executable followed by `.config`; so the application `Hello.exe` should have the configuration file name `Hello.exe.config` in the same folder as the executable. Let's create a simple remoting application that demonstrates the concepts we have been discussed above.

Try It Out: Creating a Remoting Server

In this first step, we are going to create a remoting server that can communicate over the TCP protocol, and that can be configured as necessary.

1.   Create a new VB Class Library project called HelloWorldRemotingClass.

2.   Change the name of the original `Class.vb` file to `HelloWorldClass.vb`, and replace the code inside with that below:

```
Public Class HelloWorld
  Inherits MarshalByRefObject
  'Says hello to someone.
  Public Function SayHello(ByVal Someone As String) As String
    Return "Hello " & Someone
  End Function
End Class
```

3. Build this class into the assembly `HelloWorldRemotingClass`.

4. Now create another project, a VB Console Application, called HelloWorldRemotingServer. Add a reference to the class we just created by right-clicking on the **References** folder and selecting the **Add Reference** item. Select the **Browse** button and browse to the HelloWorldRemotingClass directory (probably one directory up) and then open the bin folder and select the HelloWorldRemotingClass.dll and click the **Open** button. Finally click the **OK** button to add the reference.

5. Add the following code to the `.vb` file.

```
Imports System.Runtime.Remoting
Imports System.Runtime.Remoting.Channels
Imports HelloWorldRemotingClass

Module Module1

  Sub Main()
    Try
      RemotingConfiguration.Configure("..\HelloWorldRemotingServer.exe.config")
      System.Console.WriteLine("HelloWorldServer Listening")
      System.Console.WriteLine("Hit any key to exit.")
      System.Console.ReadLine()
    Catch Ex As Exception
      System.Console.WriteLine("A problem occurred while " _
        & "starting HelloWorldServer.")
      System.Console.WriteLine(Ex.Message)
    End Try
  End Sub
End Module
```

6. Now add to the project a new XML file called `HelloWorldRemotingServer.exe.config` and add the following XML content to the file.

```
<?xml version="1.0" encoding="utf-8" ?>
<configuration>
  <system.runtime.remoting>
    <application name="HelloWorld">
      <service>
        <wellknown mode="SingleCall"
          type="HelloWorldRemotingClass.HelloWorld,
          HelloWorldRemotingClass"
```

```
            objectUri="HelloWorldUri" />
        </service>
        <channels>
          <channel ref="tcp" port="9000" />
        </channels>
      </application>
    </system.runtime.remoting>
</configuration>
```

7. Compile this application and navigate (using Windows Explorer or via the command window) to the `HelloWorldRemotingServer` application in the directory where your Visual Studio projects are created. Launch the `HelloWorldRemotingServer.exe` application and you will get the following command window displayed. You will find the code in the `C:\BegVBXML\Chapter13\HelloWorldRemotingServer\bin` directory from the code download.

How It Works

The `HelloWorld` class is derived from the `MarshalByRefObject` class, which must be used for a remotable class that will pass data between application domains.

```
Public Class HelloWorld
   Inherits MarshalByRefObject
```

A single method called `SayHello()` that returns a string is then defined, which completes this class. When compiled, it creates an assembly with the name `HelloWorldRemotingClass`. We then have to actually set this class as a server and so a client application to host it is created.

This must reference the following namespaces; the first two being remoting namespaces that are required to use remoting and the last being the class we defined above, which is referenced in the config file so we must include a reference to it.

```
Imports System.Runtime.Remoting
Imports System.Runtime.Remoting.Channels
Imports HelloWorldRemotingClass
```

Within the `Main()` function of this class we try to create the remoting server using the `Configure()` method of the `RemotingConfiguration` class. The path to this method is our server configuration file, which will cause the remoting server object to be created according to the parameters specified in this file. Once this has been read and the object created, the application is left running so that clients can then connect to it.

The server configuration XML file specifies an application of the name `HelloWorld`, with a single service defined with an object instance created for each client request. Notice its `type` attribute:

```
type="HelloWorldRemotingClass.HelloWorld, HelloWorldRemotingClass"
```

The namespace and class name of the class library server we created is first specified and then the assembly is specified after a comma.

The `objectUri` attribute also specifies the URI that should be used to connect to this running instance.

```
objectUri="HelloWorldUri"
```

Finally, in the `<channels>` section, a single `tcp` channel has been created that will listen for request on port `9000`.

When the server is launched, it simply sits there and waits for any requests on this port for this application, and returns the result of the method(s) invoked.

Try It Out: Creating a Remoting Client

If we have created a server object, then it would be handy if we could demonstrate the end-to-end process by creating a client object that can call any available methods.

1. Create a new VB Windows Application project called HelloWorldRemotingClient. Add a `Label`, `Button`, and `TextBox` control to it. Set the label text to Who to say hello to? and the button text to Say Hello.

2. In the code for that form, add references to the remoting class and the class we created earlier. Add a reference to the `HelloWorldRemotingClass.dll` assembly using the Add Reference option in the context menu for that project.

```
Imports System.Runtime.Remoting
Imports HelloWorldRemotingClass
```

3. Double-click on the button and add the following code to the event handler:

```
Private Sub button1_Click(ByVal sender As System.Object, _
    ByVal e As System.EventArgs) Handles button1.Click
  Dim hw As HelloWorld = New HelloWorld()
  MessageBox.Show(hw.SayHello(textBox1.Text))
End Sub
```

4. Also add the following line to the Windows Form Designer-generated constructor:

```
Public Sub New()
  MyBase.New()
```

```
'This call is required by the Windows Form Designer.
InitializeComponent()
```

```
'Add any initialization after the InitializeComponent() call
RemotingConfiguration.Configure("..\HelloWorldRemotingClient.exe.config")
End Sub
```

5. In this project add a new XML file called `HelloWorldRemotingClient.exe.config` and enter the following code as the XML.

```xml
<?xml version="1.0" encoding="utf-8" ?>
<configuration>
  <system.runtime.remoting>
    <application name="HelloWorld">
      <client url="tcp://localhost:9000/HelloWorld">
        <wellknown type="HelloWorldRemotingClass.HelloWorld,
          HelloWorldRemotingClass"
          url="tcp://localhost:9000/HelloWorld/HelloWorldUri" />
      </client>
      <channels>
        <channel ref="tcp" />
      </channels>
    </application>
  </system.runtime.remoting>
</configuration>
```

6. Run this application (press *F5* or click the Start button) and the form will be displayed (ensure you have the HelloWorldRemotingServer application running). Enter some string into the text box and click the OK button. You will get a message saying hello, as shown below.

How It Works

Again the remoting namespace is required as the `RemotingConfiguration` class is used. Also, however, a reference to the `HelloWorldRemotingClass` assembly must be added; the object on the server is still called, but this local object acts as the proxy for your requests.

```
Imports System.Runtime.Remoting
Imports HelloWorldRemotingClass
```

The `Configure()` method is again used to create a client instance and refer to the server object that we want to invoke. After this has been created, an instance of the remote class can be directly created and calls to it, such as `SayHello()` are proxied across to the remote object and the value returned.

The client configuration file used has a `<wellknown>` element, which specifies the `type` attribute, and is the same as the server `type` attribute. Additionally it sets a `url` attribute, which specifies the URL specified by the server and appends the `objectUri` value to the end of this to directly reference the server instance. Similarly, a single `tcp` channel is defined for communication.

This is as far as we are going to go with remoting in this book. Clearly this is a potentially huge subject and we only touched on how XML is used within this technology. For further information see *Professional ASP.NET Web Services with VB.NET*, from Wrox Press (ISBN 1-86100-775-2).

Case Study and Web Services

All the sample code for this chapter is available for download from http://www.wrox.com. We will be storing the Case Study sample code for this chapter within the following folder:
`C:\BegVBXML\Chapter13\CS`.

In this final part of the case study, we are going to improve our service to allow it to take advantage of web services to allow the owner of the contacts database to be able to remotely add contacts to the database. This is just the start of the potential functionality that could be offered through web services, such as allowing searching and publishing of contact information.

Web Directory

If you wish to just use the downloaded code, then before you continue, you need to create a new application that will point to the web files required for this application. First open Internet Information Services (found in the **Administrative Tools**). Go to **Default Web Site** and right-click on this site and select **New | Virtual Directory...** and click **Next** when the dialog box pops up. Enter **CaseStudyWS** as the Alias and click **Next**. Click the **Browse** button and browse to the C:\BegVBXML\Chapter13\CS\CaseStudyWS directory (or wherever you unzipped the files for this chapter to) and click **OK**, and, click **Next**. Click **Next** again, leaving the settings as default, and finally click **Finish**.

Also ensure that anonymous access is allowed to the directory by right-clicking the **CaseStudyWS** virtual directory, selecting **Properties**, and then **Directory Security**, then clicking the **EDIT** button. Ensure the **Anonymous Access** checkbox is selected and click **OK**.

Security

When a web service is run, the execution is done under a user account specifically for ASP.NET; this is called the ASPNET account. Access to your file system is restricted by default for this account (for obvious security reasons), so any files that this account will be required to read or write to that are outside of the `wwwroot` hierarchy, will require this account to be explicitly set.

As you may have guessed, the reason we bring this up is because we need to make a slight modification to the privileges on the file system for our application. Go to the directory where you unzipped the download files, open the **CS** directory, and right-click on the **CaseStudy** folder, select **Properties** and choose the **Security** tab. Next, click the **Add** button and add the account called **ASPNET**. If you are using Windows XP/.NET Server you can just type this into the textbox, but you also have to click the **Advanced** button, ensure the **Replace Permission entries on all child objects with entries shown here that apply to child objects** checkbox is checked, and click **OK**.

Remember that in production you would want to tie down the privileges of the
ASPNET account to only allow read and write privileges when absolutely necessary.
We will allow read and write over the whole directory, but in reality only the XML
files that are updated need write access.

Ensure that this account has Read and Write privileges, as shown below, and click OK to close the window:

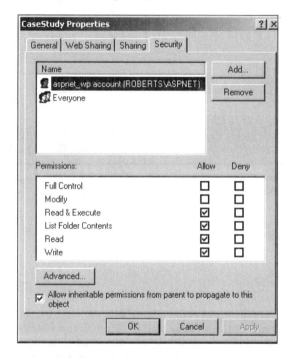

Modifying the Current Application

Currently the Case Study application we have been working with throughout the book runs only as a Windows Forms application, but to expose it as a web service we would have to have the functionality as a separate class in a DLL. In fact, in a typical application, you would have most of your functionality in classes, and just call the appropriate methods from the Windows Form or other environments.

We are going to remove the functionality from the Windows Form that allowed you to import other users contacts lists and put this functionality into a separate Class Library called
CaseStudyUtilities.

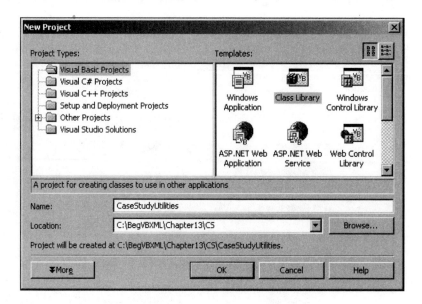

1. Create a new Class Library project called CaseStudyUtilities.

2. Delete the default .vb file and add a new one; calling it Import.vb, add the following code to the top of the file:

```
Imports System.Xml
Imports System.Xml.Schema
```

3. The vast majority of this file takes the methods by the same name from the Windows Form code (from the Chapter 11 case study) and inserts it almost exactly as it is into the new Import class. Therefore the code listing below highlights the differences between these two. **Remember that in order to run the application, you must change the** PathToFolder **variable to the location of your working folder.**

```
Public Class Import
  Public Shared _ValidationFailed As Boolean = False
  Private Shared PathToFolder As String = _
  "C:\BegVBXML\Chapter13\CS\CaseStudy\"

  'Validates a file against the XML instance
  Private Shared Sub ValidateDocument(ByVal strXMLDocName As String)

    Dim strXMLSchemaFile As String = PathToFolder + "Contacts.xsd"
    Dim strXMLfile As String = strXMLDocName
    ...
  End Sub

Private Shared Sub XMLDocumentValidationEvent(ByVal sender As Object, _
  ByVal args As ValidationEventArgs)
```

```
      If (args.Severity = XmlSeverityType.Error) Then
        _ValidationFailed = True
        Throw New Exception("The contacts could not be imported : " _
          & args.Exception.Message)
      End If
    End Sub


    'This method now has to be public !
    Public Sub ImportContacts(ByVal ImportFilePath As String)
      Dim FilePath As String = PathToFolder & "CaseStudy.xml"
      Dim FriendFilePath As String = ImportFilePath


      ...
    End Sub
End Class
```

The `ValidateDocument()` method was moved from the forms code and the `PathToFolder` appended to it to get the exact location of the document. Notice later in the code, in the `XMLDocumentValidationEvent` event handler for XML Schema validation that we also throw any exception that occurs to be handled by the web service.

```
      Throw New Exception("The contacts could not be imported : " _
        & args.Exception.Message)
```

Finally, the `ImportContacts()` method was also moved and now takes the file path or URL to the XML file that is to be imported. This class can then be compiled.

4. If we now return to the **CaseStudy** Windows Form Application, we have to modify this file so that it now uses the `Import` class rather than an internal method. Therefore, the methods discussed above are removed from the form's code and a reference to the `Import` is added to the top of the file:

```
Imports CaseStudyUtilities
```

5. A reference to the `Import` class also has to be made within the **CaseStudy** project by right-clicking on **References** and selecting **Add Reference**, browsing to the **CaseStudyUtilities** folder (one folder up), opening the **bin** folder and selecting **CaseStudyUtilities.dll**, then clicking **Open** and then **OK**.

6. Finally, the `ImportContacts()` method has to be modified in the form's code, so that it now calls the method in the `Import` class.

```
Shared _ValidationFailed As Boolean = False
Private Sub ImportContacts()
  Try
    Dim Import As Import = New Import()
    Import.ImportContacts("http://localhost/CaseStudyWS/MyContacts.xml")
```

627

```
      _ValidationFailed = Import._ValidationFailed
   Catch ex As Exception
      _ValidationFailed = Import._ValidationFailed
      MessageBox.Show(ex.Message)
   End Try
End Sub
```

7. Now we can compile the application and go on to create a web service that allows remote importing of contacts.

Creating the Web Service

1. Create a new Web Service project called **CaseStudyWS**.

2. Add a reference to the `CaseStudyUtilities` assembly by right-clicking on the project and selecting **Add Reference**. Browse to the **CaseStudyUtilities** folder and then the **bin** directory, select `CaseStudyUtilities.dll`, and press **Open**.

If this was done on a remote client, then you would create a proxy using the WSDL utility discussed earlier in the chapter, and the client would reference this locally (although the Web Service itself would be called).

3. Add a reference at the top of the `Service1.asmx` code file:

```
Imports CaseStudyUtilities
```

The single `ImportContacts()` method is defined using the `WebMethod` attribute to specify that it is available to web services. It takes as a parameter the URL of the file to import. Within the method a new `Import` class instance is created and the `ImportContacts()` method is called, which will import the contacts to the `CaseStudy.xml` file that our Windows Forms application uses.

4. Add the following code to the `Service1.asmx` code file:

```
<WebMethod()> Public Function ImportContacts(ByVal FileToImport As String) _
   As String
   Try
      Dim import As import = New import()
      import.ImportContacts(FileToImport)
      Return ("Contacts imported successfully")

   Catch ex As Exception
      Return (ex.Message)
   End Try
End Function
End Class
```

5. Add an XML file to the project, called `MyContacts.xml`, and enter the following code:

```
<?xml version="1.0" encoding="utf-8"?>
<ct:ContactDetails updateDate="2002-12-01T14:00:00"
xmlns:ct="http://www.deltabis.com/Contact">
  <!--This document contains contact information.-->
  <contact title="title:Mr." xmlns:title="http://www.deltabis.com/ns/titles/">
    <name>
      <first>Cochi</first>
      <middle />
      <last>Perez</last>
    </name>
    <ct:notes>Intelligent, young and dynamic genius.</ct:notes>
  </contact>
</ct:ContactDetails>
```

The full URL to this file is `http://localhost/CaseStudyWS/MyContacts.xml` (although your URL may be slightly different).

We can now compile this service and move on to testing it.

Testing the Web Service

To test the web service we can simply navigate to the URL where our service is defined. In our case this is `http://localhost/CaseStudyWS/Service1.asmx` and click on the ImportContacts link that appears. This will display the window below with a textbox to enter the parameter of the file to import. Enter the path to the `MyContacts.xml` file we looked at above and click the Invoke button.

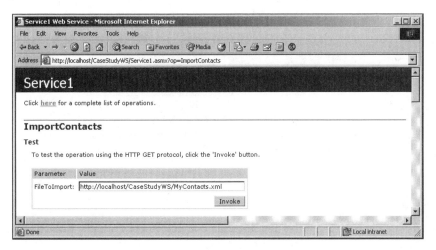

This will launch a new window and the `ImportContacts()` method of the web service will be called; you will returned an appropriate message in XML format. If it is successful, you will get the message below; if not, you will get some error details wrapped in XML – typically if you used the wrong path to the files.

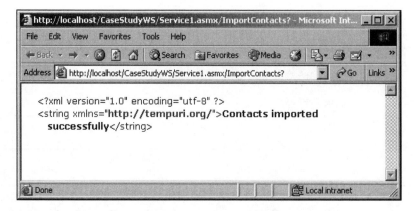

Finally, to validate that the contacts were in fact added, launch the Windows Forms application and you will see that Perez, Cochi has indeed been added to the Contacts list.

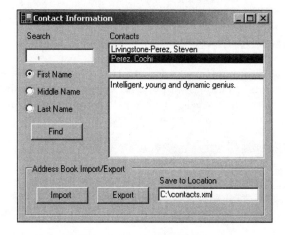

This example focused on providing a sample of how web services can be used to import contacts from theoretically any geographic location. You should look to build on these samples by providing a web interface to allow users to search on the contacts that are in your database.

Summary

This chapter focused on web services and distributed architectures, and how XML is employed within those architectures in the .NET Framework. Specifically we looked at:

❑ Web services

❑ The Global XML Architecture

❑ What the Simple Object Access Protocol is and how it uses XML

❑ The XML-based Web Service Description Language

❑ Microsoft's DISCO discovery XML document

❑ The Universal Description, Discovery and Integration Service

❑ Remoting and XML configuration files

❑ Using web services with the case study

Clearly the scope of these topics is huge, but you should see how essential XML is to the entire underlying framework of these technologies. As they become better defined and utilized more within enterprises, the use of XML is going to become more essential and an understanding of this usage will be very important.

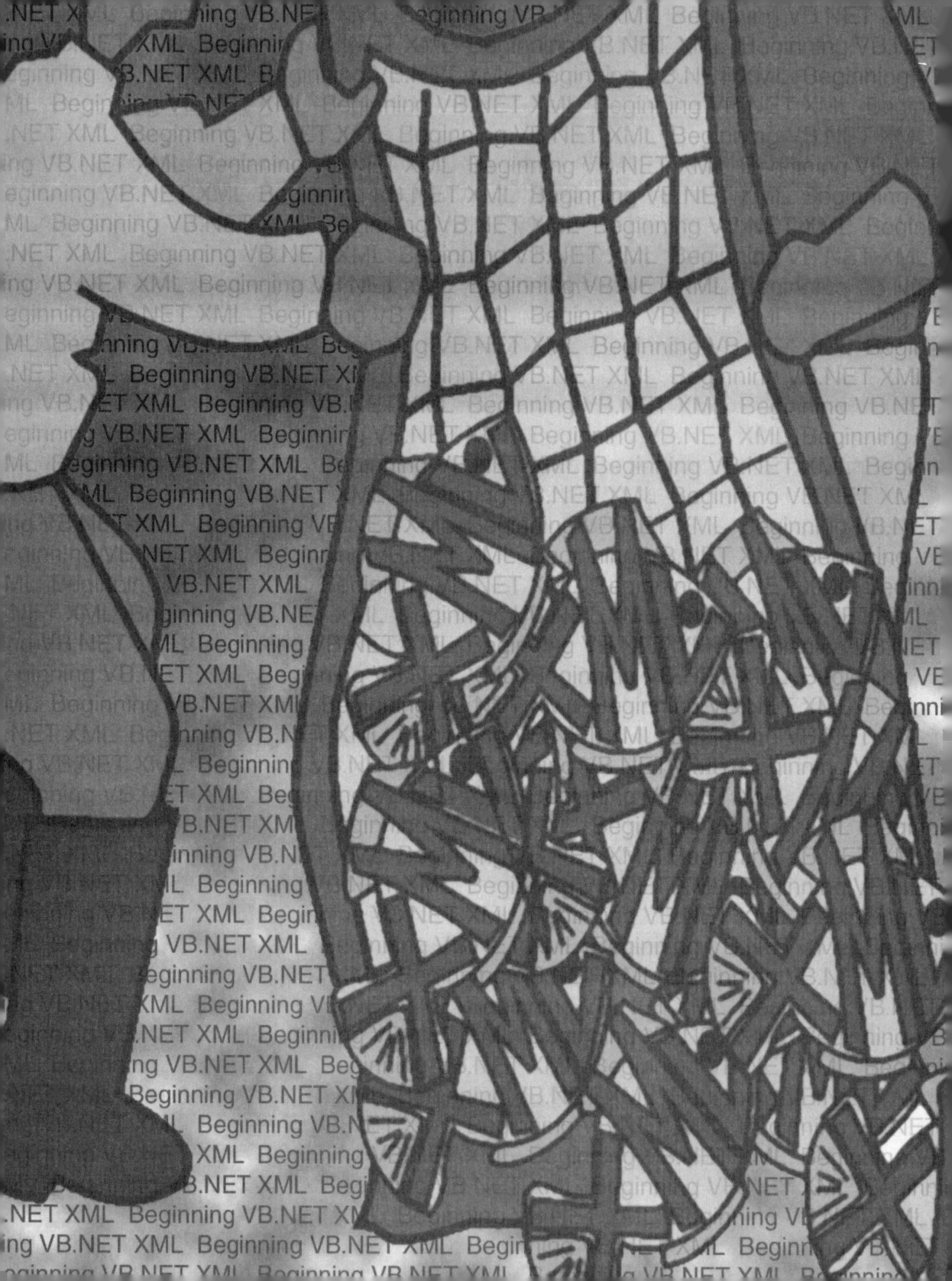
Beginning VB.NET XML

Case Study: A Simple News Portal

The goal of this case study is to demonstrate how we can exploit XML within a practical 3-tier web application written in VB.NET. The application takes the form of a news portal, the functionality of which can be divided into two main parts:

❑ Providing users with a browser-based view of categorized links to news items – the views are based on XSL transforms offering great flexibility in how the information is presented

❑ Allowing content providers to register and manage their content links in a secure area

The portal will demonstrate some useful functionality that can be achieved using VB.NET with XML in a simple ASP.NET application, and will specifically demonstrate the following:

❑ Using the `web.config` XML file to set up the application

❑ Three-tier ADO.NET data access using `SqlDataAdapters`, `SqlDataReaders` and stored procedures

❑ Forms Authentication using a SQL Server database for user names and passwords

❑ Returning XML from a SQL Server 2000 database using the `FOR XML` clause

❑ Generating HTML using server-side XSL Transforms (demonstrates several .NET XML classes including `XmlTextReader`, `XslTransform`, `XPathDocument`, `XPathNavigator`, `XsltArgumentList`, `XmlWriter`)

❑ Using the `XmlTextReader` and `XmlValidatingReader` classes in Schema Validation

❑ Manipulating data using `DataGrids`, `DataSets` and `XmlDataDocuments`

❑ Using SQL Server XML (SQLXML) Managed Classes

Let's start with a high-level overview of the application.

Application Overview

The application was designed to satisfy several key functional requirements:

❑ Must provide anonymous visitors to the site with categorized links to news items. The items can be held locally or remotely, but must be URL addressable.

❑ News items will be categorized into areas such as sport, business, and entertainment, and will be further categorized (or sub-categorized) within those categories. Typical examples within Sport, for instance, would be Football, Golf, and Tennis.

❑ Must provide the ability to easily modify how the content is presented both in terms of layout (grouped by category and sub-category or sub-categories only), and styling (colors, fonts, and so on.).

❑ Submitted news items can be in HTML or XML format.

❑ The application must provide users with a mechanism to change the color scheme of the main page for the duration of their session.

❑ Must allow content providers to register their details.

❑ Must provide a secure area for registered content providers to manage their content.

Application Architecture

Like many distributed web applications, the news portal has been designed around a 3-tier architecture. The 3 logical tiers (or layers) are shown below:

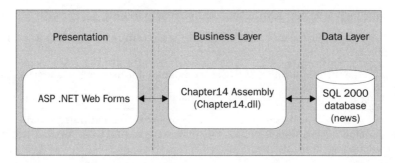

In this application, the Data layer refers to the database and the single stored procedure used for adding new content providers, the Business layer refers to the compiled assembly (which includes the code-behind classes for the ASP.NET pages), and the Presentation layer refers to the ASP.NET pages themselves.

Database Design

The first area we considered when designing the application was the database, so we'll look at the database design first. The database at the heart of the news portal application has four tables, as described below:

tbl_providers

This table holds logon information plus the Base URL (content root) for registered content providers, and has the following columns:

Column Name	Description
pk_providerID	The unique ID of the content provider.
provider	The name of the content provider. This is also the ID used by the content provider to log in to the secure content management area.
baseURL	This is the root URL of the content provider's content. All content they submit will be located relative to this URL.
password	The encrypted password as set by the user at registration.

tbl_metadata

This table holds information about each content item such as title, date created and categorization information, and contains the following columns:

Column Name	Description
pk_resourceID	The unique ID of the resource (news item).
fk_providerID	The provider who submitted the item.
Title	The title of the news item.
resDescription	The description of the news item.
dateCreated	The date the news item was created.
Identifier	The actual URL of the content item.
fk_categoryID	The category of the news item.
fk_subCategoryID	The sub-category of the news item.

tbl_lk_categories

This table stores news categories, and has the following columns:

Column Name	Description
pk_categoryID	The unique ID of the news category.
category	The category name.

tbl_lk_subCategories

This table stores news sub-categories, and contains the following columns:

Column Name	Description
subCategory	The sub-category name.
pk_subCategoryID	The unique ID of the news sub-category.

The database schema is very simple and is shown below.

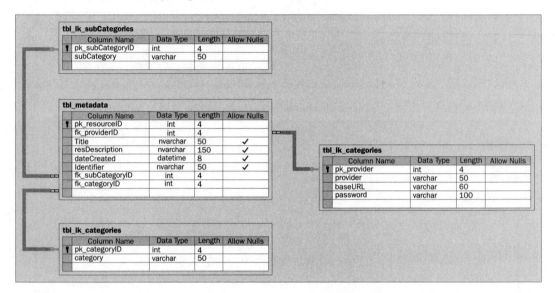

Stored Procedure

The news portal uses a single stored procedure called usp_AddResource to handle the addition of new content items to the metadata table.

```
CREATE Procedure usp_AddResource
(
    -- declare variables
    @fk_providerID      int,
    @Title              nvarchar(50),
    @resDescription     nvarchar(150),
    @DateCreated        datetime,
    @Identifier         nvarchar(50),
    @fk_subCategoryID   nvarchar(50),
    @fk_categoryID      nvarchar(50),
    @Identity           int  OUTPUT
)
AS

INSERT INTO tbl_metadata
(
    -- set columns
    fk_providerID,
    Title,
    resDescription,
    DateCreated,
```

```
        Identifier,
        fk_subCategoryID,
        fk_categoryID
    )

    VALUES
    (
        -- new value to insert
        @fk_providerID,
        @Title,
        @resDescription,
        @DateCreated,
        @Identifier,
        @fk_subCategoryID,
        @fk_categoryID
    )

    SELECT
        -- return Identity
        @Identity = @@Identity
    GO
```

The stored procedure takes several parameters as inputs, and returns the identity value of the newly inserted row (@@IDENTITY). We'll see later in the chapter how we call the stored procedure from our data access class.

Data Access Class

We've abstracted most of the methods that handle the addition, deletion and retrieval of data from our database into a single class called newsDB. The methods it provides are outlined in the following table:

Method	Description
`Public Function GetProviderID( ByVal Provider As String) As Integer`	Gets the provider ID for a given provider name
`Public Function GetBaseURL( ByVal Provider As String) As String`	Gets the base URL for a particular provider
`Public Function UpdateBaseURL( ByVal baseURL As String, ByVal Provider As String) As Integer`	Updates the base URL for a particular provider
`Public Function GetResources( ByVal Provider As String) As DataSet`	Returns all news items submitted by a particular provider
`Public Function deleteResource( ByVal resourceID As String) As Integer`	Deletes a news item with the given ID
`Public Function getConnectionString( ByVal connectionString As String) As String`	Reads the connection string from the web.config file

Method	Description
`Public Function GetCategory( ByVal CategoryID As Integer) As String`	Gets the category name with the given `categoryID`
`Public Function GetSubCategory( ByVal subCategoryID As Integer) As String`	Gets the sub-category name with the given `subCategoryID`
`Public Function GetCategories() As SqlDataReader`	Returns all categories
`Public Function GetSubCategories() As SqlDataReader`	Returns all sub-categories
`Public Sub addResource( ByVal ds As DataSet)`	Adds a new news item
`Public Sub updateResource( ByVal ds As DataSet)`	Updates news items

Business Layer

We've organized our functionality in various classes within a single assembly called Chapter 14. There are several classes that make up the assembly as shown:

Class Name	File Name	Purpose
`DisplayNews`	`default.aspx.vb`	Code-behind for `default.aspx`
`DisplayNewsSQLXML`	`default_SQLXML.aspx.vb`	Code-behind for `default.aspx`. This is the SQLXML implementation of `DisplayNews`, which we'll introduce towards the end of the chapter.
`LogIn`	`LogIn.aspx.vb`	Code-behind for `LogIn.aspx`
`Register`	`register.aspx.vb`	Code-behind for `register.aspx`
`GetPage`	`GetPage.aspx.vb`	Code-behind for `GetPage.aspx`
`ContentManagement`	`contentManager.aspx.vb`	Code-behind for `contentManager.aspx`
`newsDB`	`newsDB.vb`	Class providing all the methods used to get and send data

All of the middle-tier code is compiled into a single assembly (`Chapter14_VB.dll`), along with the code-behind logic of the ASP.NET pages in the presentation tier.

Presentation Layer

The presentation layer of the news portal was built using ASP.NET web forms. The ASP.NET pages implemented in the application are outlined below:

Page File Name	Description
default.aspx	Main page that displays the categorized links to content.
LogIn.aspx	Provider login page. This page is invoked if a user tries to access the secure content management section, and has no valid security ticket. Links to registration page for non-registered providers.
register.aspx	New provider registration page.
GetPage.aspx	Renders HTML and XML content items.
contentManager.aspx	Secure management of content items.

Before we take a closer look at the system design, you'll need to get the application deployed on your own system. The next section will lead you through the deployment process step by step.

Deployment

> The remainder of the chapter assumes you have Visual Studio .NET installed on your system. It also assumes you have access to a SQL Server 2000 database. You can use the Microsoft SQL Server Database Engine (MSDE) if need be. The MSDE installer program is copied to your system during the VS.NET install, but isn't installed by default. The default location of the installer is `C:\Program Files\Microsoft Visual Studio .NET\Setup\MSDE`.

1. The first thing you need to do is download and unzip the source code archive for this chapter. When you unzip the archive, a folder called `Chapter14_VB` will be created containing all the required files. If you're going to move the folder to another location, do so now, otherwise leave it in the default location.

2. You must ensure that the `IUSR_machinename` and `ASPNET` user accounts are granted access to this directory. The `IUSR_machinename` account is that used by IIS to control access to the files and folders by anonymous users. As we'll be allowing anonymous access to the main page in our application, we need to add it to the folder's Access Control List (ACL). The web application runs under the `ASPNET` account, so it too needs access to this folder. To grant the two user accounts access to the **Chapter14_VB** folder, locate and right-click the folder in Windows Explorer, select **Properties** from the menu, and select the **Security** tab. Click on the **Add** button, and select these two user accounts, then click **Add** again and **OK**. Grant the users only the default access permissions.

3. Next we're going to create a new Virtual Directory to point at the **Chapter14_VB** folder. We do this in the Internet Information Services (IIS) Manager Console, which can be launched by clicking **Start | Settings | Control Panel | Administrative Tools | Internet Services Manager**. Now expand the **Default Web Site** node in the left-hand pane and find the web-site you wish to add your virtual directory to. Right-click the website node and select **New | Virtual Directory** from the menu that appears. The **Virtual Directory Creation Wizard** will be launched. Click **Next**, then type **Chapter14_VB** in the **Alias** textbox, which will be the name of the virtual directory. Click **Next**, then browse to the location of the **Chapter14_VB** folder containing the application files, and click **Next**. Click **Next** again to select the default access permissions for the directory, then click **Finish** to close the wizard.

4. You should now see the new virtual directory in the left-hand pane. Right-click the new virtual directory and select **Properties** from the context sensitive menu. Under the **Application Settings** section on the **Directory** tab check if an application exists. If the **Application name** label and textbox are grayed out, no application exists, and you'll need to create one now by clicking the **Create** button – you'll have problems later if you don't. Next, select the **Directory Security** tab and click the **Edit** button. Ensure that both the **Anonymous Access** and **Integrated Windows Authentication** checkboxes are checked.

5. Next we'll create the news database. If you need to install the MSDE, do it now by double-clicking the `setup.exe` file in the MSDE folder and follow the wizard. A SQL script (`CreateNewsDB.sql`) has been included in the download to create and populate the database. The script assumes you have a folder on your `C:` drive called `BegVBXML\Chapter14`. If it doesn't already exist, create it. If you want the script to use a folder other than `C:\BegVBXML\Chapter14`, you'll have to open the `CreateNewsDB.sql` script in a text editor and change the paths of the `news.mdf` and `news_log.ldf` files to point at the folder of your choice. The script will fail if it cannot find the specified directories, so make sure they exist!

6. Run the `CreateNewsDB.sql` script to create and populate the database using the `osql` command line utility. The syntax of the command is shown below. (Note – Ensure the case of the switches are exactly as shown):

```
osql -S localhost -U sa -P -i c:\CreateNewsDB.sql
```

Where:

Switch	Description
S	The name of the server on which your instance of SQL Server is running (note – can also be *server name\instance name*)
U	User name
P	Password
i	Full path of the SQL script file you want to run

7. Now browse to the **Chapter14_VB** folder, locate the file `Chapter14_VB.sln` and double-click. The project should open in the VS.NET IDE. Open the `web.config` file and change the connection strings to suit your own installation. For example, you may not (and shouldn't for security reasons) have a blank password for your `sa` user, so you might need to change the password in the connection string.

The connection strings can be found in the `appSettings` configuration section of the `web.config` file, as shown below. By default, the connection strings are set up for connecting to the news database on a locally installed SQL Server instance using SQL Server Authentication:

```
<appSettings>
  <add key="newsDB1"
     value="data source=localhost;initial catalog=news;user id=sa;password="/>
  <add key="newsDB_SQLXML"
    value="Provider=SQLOLEDB;Server=localhost;database=news;user id=sa"/>
  ...
</appSettings>
```

You'll notice there are two connection strings defined here. The first, "newsDB1", will be used by the application by default. The second of the connection strings, "newsDB_SQLXML", will be used only by the SQLXML implementation of the `DisplayNews` class.

> `web.config` is an XML file used to store application specific configuration settings. The `web.config` file allows us to make changes to application configuration settings without having to recompile our component each time. We'll revisit the `web.config` file later when we introduce application security.

8. Set `default.aspx` to be the startup page by right-clicking the `default.aspx` file in the Solution Explorer pane and selecting **Set as start page** from the menu.

9. Compile and run the application.

Now we have the application installed, let's see it in action.

Using the News Portal Application

The main portal page (`default.aspx`) is the page the users see when they visit the site. On running the application for the first time, the main page will display no content (see the figure below), as there's no content in the database on installation.

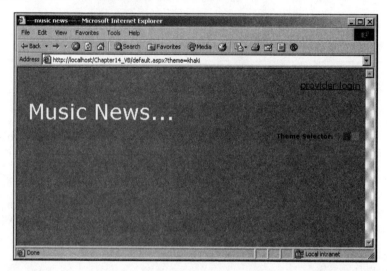

The "content" in the context of our portal is supplied by remote content providers, and can be any HTML (actually XHTML) or XML documents that conform to our schema (which we'll discuss later). The providers host their own pages, and all we hold locally is some metadata extracted from the document during the registration process, such as the document title, description, and published date.

To begin with we'll need to register some content providers. We'll register just two content providers which we'll call `provider1` and `provider2` for want of an imagination! The content provider sites have been set up as subdirectories of the portal's root directory for simplicity, but in practice the content providers would be more likely hosting their content on their own web servers at a remote location.

Security and Provider Registration

To begin the registration process we click the provider login link at the top left hand corner of the screen. When we click the provider login link, we attempt to access the Content Management page, which is a protected resource, and we invoke the application's security mechanism. The application uses **Forms Authentication**, which works as follows:

1. In the `web.config` file, which we looked at earlier, we configure our application to use Forms authentication by setting the `mode` attribute of the `authentication` element to `"Forms"`:

```
<configuration>
  <system.web>
    <authentication mode="Forms">
```

We then set the `forms` authentication attributes:

```
<forms name =".ASPXFORMSAUTH"
        loginUrl="http://localhost/Chapter14/LogIn.aspx"
        protection="All"
        timeout="10"/>
</authentication>
```

The attributes are described in the following table:

Attribute	Description
name	Sets the cookie's name suffix
loginUrl	Specifies the URL to which the request is redirected for logon if no valid authentication cookie is found
protection	When set to All, tells the application to use both data validation and encryption to protect the cookie
timeout	Specifies the amount of time, in integer minutes, after which the cookie expires

We then allow everyone access to the root directory of our application:

```
<authorization>
 <allow users = "*"/>
</authorization>
<system.web>
```

Next we deny access to all anonymous users on the `/secure` directory. This is where our content management page lives:

```
<!-- configuration settings for the secure directory-->
<location path="secure">
  <system.web>
    <authorization>
      <!--denies anonymous users-->
      <deny users="?"/>
    </authorization>
  </system.web>
</location>
</configuration>
```

2. The first time a user attempts to access a protected resource, they are redirected to the login page. This is where you should find yourself now, after clicking the provider login link on the main page.

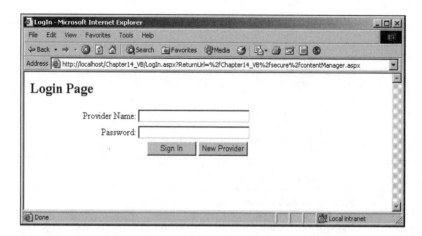

3. As our first content provider, provider1, has not yet been registered, click the New Provider button to register it.

4. Enter provider1 as the Provider Name and Password, and enter a Base URL of http://localhost/Chapter14_VB/remoteprovider1/, then click the Register button:

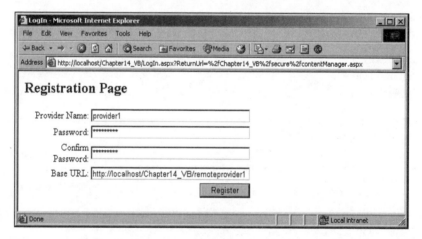

5. You'll be redirected back to the login page we saw a moment ago. Enter the Provider Name and Password we set up in the previous step, and click the Sign In button. If the Provider Name and Password are correct, an authentication ticket in the form of a cookie will be issued to you and you'll be redirected to the originally requested page – contentManager.aspx.

Content Management

Having just logged in as provider1, you should now see the content registration page as shown in the figure below. Ensure the base URL is http://localhost/Chapter14_VB/remoteprovider1/. If it isn't, for example, you may have included a typo – it happens to the best of us, change it and click the Update URL button.

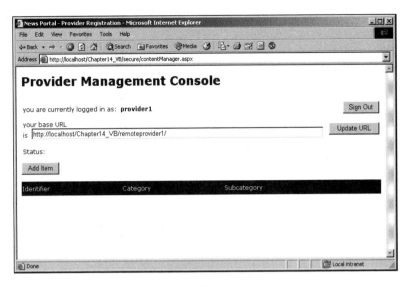

We'll be registering two pages for provider1 as follows:

Identifier	Category	Sub Category
sport.htm	Sport	Football
travel.htm	News	Travel

The travel.htm file, which we will be linking to for the content to display, is shown below. All other pages have the same structure:

```
<html>
  <head>
    <title>Motorway returns to normal after frog parade</title>
    <meta content="The M8 motorway is once... " name="description" />
    <meta content="http://localhost/chapter14..." name="identifier" />
    <meta content="04/06/2002 08:00" name="date" />
  </head>
  <body>
    <p>Rush hour traffic on the M8 motorway just east of Glasgow was brought
    to a standstill this morning due to a procession
    of frogs! The M8 crosses an ancient ceremonial processional route used
    for centuries by the frogs. A spokesperson for the frogs told reporters,
    "Our timing may not be the best, but we've marched over that motorway
    during rush hour on this day for centuries."
    </p>
  </body>
</html>
```

To register a page, click the Add Item button. The row will switch to edit mode, as you can see in the screenshot below:

645

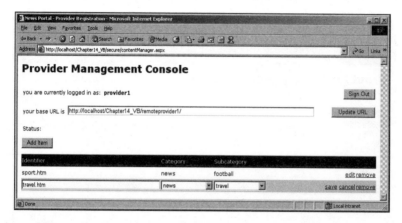

Enter the relative URL as given above in the Identifier column and select the relevant Category and Sub Categories from the drop-down lists. When you're happy with your choices, click the Save link. Repeat this for the second page. All going well, the pages will be submitted with no errors. If you have problems with the permissions, check that you've granted the IUSR_machinename and ASPNET accounts on your machine access to the project directory, as they need it to access the schema.

Click the Sign Out button to return to the main page. Next, we'll register provider2. Follow the same procedure as we did previously for provider1, but set the Base URL for provider2 to be http://localhost/Chapter14_VB/remoteprovider2/. We'll be registering four pages for provider2, as follows:

Identifier	Category	Sub Category
business.htm	Business	Economy
entertainment.xml	News	Music
entertainment1.htm	News	Music
entertainment2.htm	News	Music

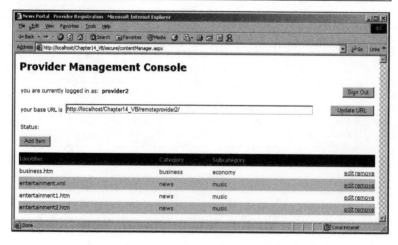

Content Management – How It Works

We've looked at the process behind registration and the management of content, so let's look now at what's going on behind the scenes. We'll start off by looking at the contentManager.aspx file.

contentManager.aspx

As we've already seen, the contentManager.aspx page displays all the content associated with a particular provider, and it allows us to enter, modify, add, and delete content items. We achieve this using a DataGrid control (resourcesGrid). The overall structure of the aspx page is shown below:

```
<%@ Page language="vb" Codebehind="contentManager.aspx.vb" AutoEventWireup="false"
Inherits="Chapter14_VB.contentManager" %>
<%@ Import Namespace="Chapter14_VB"%>
<!DOCTYPE HTML PUBLIC "-//W3C//DTD HTML 4.0 Transitional//EN" >
<html>
  <head>
    <title>News Portal - Provider Registration</title>
    <meta name="GENERATOR" content="Microsoft Visual Studio 7.0">
    <meta name="CODE_LANGUAGE" content="vb">
    <meta name="vs_defaultClientScript" content="JavaScript">
    <meta name="vs_targetSchema"
content="http://schemas.microsoft.com/intellisense/ie5">
  </head>
  <body style="FONT-SIZE: 9pt; FONT-FAMILY: Verdana, Arial">
    <form id="Form2" method="post" runat="server">

    <script language="vb" runat="server">
      dim oNews as NewsDB= new NewsDB()
    </script>

    <h2>Provider Management Console</h2>
    <table width="100%" style="FONT-SIZE: 9pt; FONT-FAMILY: Verdana, Arial">
      <tr height="40">
        <td>
          you are currently logged in as: 
          <b><label id="lblProvider" runat="server"></label></b>
        </td>
        <td align="right">
          <asp:button id="btnSignOut" runat="server" text="Sign Out"/>
        </td>
      </tr>
      <tr height="40">
        <td>
          your base URL is 
          <b><asp:TextBox id="txtBaseURL" runat="server" width="600px" /></b>
        </td>
        <td align="right">
          <asp:button id="changeBaseURL" runat="server" text="Update URL" />
        </td>
      </tr>
```

647

```
            <tr height="40">
              <td colspan="2">
              Status: 
              <asp:label id="errorLabel" forecolor="#ff0000" width="100%"
                  runat="server" />
              </td>
            </tr>
          </table>
          <asp:button id="btnAdd"
                      onclick="btnAdd_OnClick"
                      runat="server"
                      Text="Add Item" /><br>
          <br>
          <!--DataGrid goes here-->
          </form>
        </body>
      </html>
```

As can be seen from the listing above, the entire user interface is defined in the `aspx` page. As we'll be using the methods in our data access class, we've instantiated the class in a `<script>` block at the top of the `<body>` of our page:

```
<script language="vb" runat="server">
  dim oNews as NewsDB = new NewsDB()
</script>
```

The `DataGrid` server control is shown below:

```
<asp:datagrid id="resourcesGrid"
              Width="100%"
              Runat="server"
              OnDeleteCommand="resourcesGrid_DeleteCommand"
              OnUpdateCommand="resourcesGrid_UpdateCommand"
              OnCancelCommand="resourcesGrid_CancelCommand"
              OnEditCommand="resourcesGrid_EditCommand"
              AlternatingItemStyle-BackColor="#dcdcdc"
              HeaderStyle-Height="28px"
              headerstyle-font-size="9pt"
              ItemStyle-Height="28px"
              GridLines="None"
              HeaderStyle-ForeColor="#ffffff"
              HeaderStyle-BackColor="#000000"
              AutoGenerateColumns="False"
              DataKeyField="pk_resourceID"
              itemstyle-font-size="9pt">
  <columns>
    <asp:TemplateColumn HeaderText="Identifier" ItemStyle-Width="40%">
      <itemtemplate>
        <%# DataBinder.Eval(Container.DataItem, "identifier")%>
```

```
        </itemtemplate>
        <edititemtemplate>
          <asp:TextBox ID="IdentifierTextBox"
                       Width="100%"
                       Text='<%# DataBinder.Eval(Container.DataItem,
                             "identifier")%>'
                       runat="server">
          </asp:TextBox>
        </edititemtemplate>
      </asp:TemplateColumn>
      <asp:TemplateColumn HeaderText="Category" ItemStyle-Width="15%">
        <itemtemplate>
          <%# oNews.GetCategory(DataBinder.Eval(Container.DataItem,
          "fk_categoryID"))%>
        </itemtemplate>
        <edititemtemplate>
          <asp:dropdownlist ID="categoryList"
                            DataSource="<%#oNews.GetCategories()%>"
                            DataValueField = "pk_categoryID"
                            DataTextField = "category"
                            SelectedIndex ='<%# DataBinder.Eval(Container.DataItem,
                                             "fk_categoryID") -1%>'
                            runat="server"
                            Width="100%">
          </asp:dropdownlist>
        </edititemtemplate>
      </asp:TemplateColumn>
      <asp:TemplateColumn HeaderText="Subcategory" ItemStyle-Width="15%">
      <itemtemplate>
        <%# oNews.GetSubCategory(DataBinder.Eval(Container.DataItem,
        "fk_subCategoryID"))%>
      </itemtemplate>
      <edititemtemplate>
        <asp:dropdownlist ID="subCategoryList"
                          DataSource="<%#oNews.GetSubCategories()%>"
                          DataValueField = "pk_subCategoryID"
                          DataTextField = "subCategory"
                          SelectedIndex ='<%# DataBinder.Eval(Container.DataItem,
                                           "fk_SubCategoryID") -1%>'
                          runat="server"
                          Width="100%">
        </asp:dropdownlist>
      </edititemtemplate>
      </asp:TemplateColumn>
      <asp:EditCommandColumn EditText="edit"
                             UpdateText="save"
                             CancelText="cancel"
                             ItemStyle-Width="25%"
                             ItemStyle-HorizontalAlign="Right">
      </asp:EditCommandColumn>
      <asp:ButtonColumn CommandName="Delete"
                        Text="remove"
                        ButtonType="LinkButton"
```

```
                             ItemStyle-Width="5%"
                             ItemStyle-HorizontalAlign="Right">
        </asp:ButtonColumn>
      </columns>
    </asp:datagrid>
```

The first column is a `TemplateColumn` that displays the identifier (URI) of the content item. Using a `TemplateColumn` gives complete control over which controls are rendered in the column, and which data fields are bound to the controls. When the row is switched to edit mode, which we'll talk about in more depth later, the identifier is displayed in a textbox for editing. We use the `DataBinder.Eval()` method to bind the `Text` property of the `TextBox` to the `identifier` field:

```
<asp:TemplateColumn HeaderText="Identifier" ItemStyle-Width="40%">
  <itemtemplate>
    <%# DataBinder.Eval(Container.DataItem, "identifier")%>
  </itemtemplate>
  <edititemtemplate>
    <asp:TextBox ID="IdentifierTextBox"
                 Width="100%"
                 Text='<%# DataBinder.Eval(Container.DataItem, "identifier")%>'
                 runat="server">
    </asp:TextBox>
  </edititemtemplate>
</asp:TemplateColumn>
```

The second and third columns are again `TemplateColumns`, but this time we render drop-down lists in edit mode, so the user can select from the available categories and subcategories. This procedure is a little more complex than in the case of the textbox, as we have to first retrieve a `DataReader` using the `GetCategories` and `GetSubCategories` methods, which we bind to the drop-down list's `DataSource` property. We then set the `SelectedIndex` property of the drop-down list to the current category and subcategory IDs, decremented by one as list items are zero indexed. Note that because we only have access to the category and subcategory IDs, we need to perform a lookup on the category and subcategory tables so we can display the respective names in read mode. This is done by passing the category and subcategory IDs for each row to the `GetCategory` and `GetSubcategory` methods respectively:

```
<asp:TemplateColumn HeaderText="Category" ItemStyle-Width="15%">
  <itemtemplate>
    <%# oNews.GetCategory(DataBinder.Eval(Container.DataItem, "fk_categoryID"))%>
  </itemtemplate>
  <edititemtemplate>
    <asp:dropdownlist ID="categoryList"
                      DataSource="<%#oNews.GetCategories()%>"
                      DataValueField = "pk_categoryID"
                      DataTextField = "category"
                      SelectedIndex ='<%# DataBinder.Eval(Container.DataItem,
                                  "fk_categoryID") -1%>'
                      runat="server"
                      Width="100%">
    </asp:dropdownlist>
  </edititemtemplate>
</asp:TemplateColumn>
```

```
<asp:TemplateColumn HeaderText="Subcategory" ItemStyle-Width="15%">
  <itemtemplate>
    <%# oNews.GetSubCategory(DataBinder.Eval(Container.DataItem,
    "fk_subCategoryID"))%>
  </itemtemplate>
  <edititemtemplate>
    <asp:dropdownlist ID="subCategoryList"
                       DataSource="<%#oNews.GetSubCategories()%>"
                       DataValueField = "pk_subCategoryID"
                       DataTextField = "subCategory"
                       SelectedIndex ='<%# DataBinder.Eval(Container.DataItem,
                                          "fk_SubCategoryID") -1%>'
                       runat="server"
                       Width="100%">
    </asp:dropdownlist>
  </edititemtemplate>
</asp:TemplateColumn>
```

The last two columns are `EditCommandColumn` and `ButtonColumn`:

```
<asp:EditCommandColumn EditText="edit"
                        UpdateText="save"
                        CancelText="cancel"
                        ItemStyle-Width="25%"
                        ItemStyle-HorizontalAlign="Right">
</asp:EditCommandColumn>
<asp:ButtonColumn CommandName="Delete"
                   Text="remove"
                   ButtonType="LinkButton"
                   ItemStyle-Width="5%"
                   ItemStyle-HorizontalAlign="Right">
</asp:ButtonColumn>
  </columns>
</asp:datagrid>
```

Let's look now at the code-behind for this page.

contentManager.aspx.vb

The first thing we do in our code-behind is to declare all the required namespaces. The following are added automatically on the creation of the `aspx.vb` page:

```
imports System
imports System.Collections
imports System.ComponentModel
imports System.Data
imports System.Drawing
imports System.Web
imports System.Web.SessionState
imports System.Web.UI
imports System.Web.UI.WebControls
imports System.Web.UI.HtmlControls
```

We also need to make use of several classes in the following namespaces, so we need to add these in manually:

```
imports System.Data.SqlClient
imports System.Configuration
imports System.IO
imports System.Xml
imports System.Xml.Schema
imports System.Web.Security
```

The `Page_Load` event executes on every page request, so this is where we place our code to retrieve the data from the database and fill our `DataSet`. We don't want to do this every time a postback occurs in response to a server control click, due to the performance issues this would cause, so we make use of the `IsPostback` property, such that the `DataSet` is created and filled only when `IsPostback` is equal to `false`; that is, on the first page request. The filling of the `DataSet` is done by the `GetResources` method of the `newsDB` class.

Because Web Forms pages are stateless, meaning they don't automatically maintain state and page information over multiple page requests, we store several objects and variables in `Session` state, so they need only be initialized on the first page load or if they change. The use of `Session` state should be considered carefully, as the variables are held in memory for the lifetime of every application session, which could give rise to scalability issues on applications serving large numbers of users.

```
Private Sub Page_Load(ByVal sender As System.Object, ByVal e As _
    System.EventArgs) Handles MyBase.Load
    If Not Session("sessionds") Is Nothing Then
        ds = CType(Session("sessionds"), DataSet)
        xmlDoc = CType(Session("sessionXmlDataDoc"), XmlDataDocument)
    End If

    If Not IsPostBack Then

        'Create instance of NewsDB class
        oNews = New newsDB()
        Dim Provider As String = Request.ServerVariables("LOGON_USER")
        lblProvider.InnerText = Provider
        txtBaseURL.Text = oNews.GetBaseURL(Provider)

        Dim ds As DataSet = oNews.GetResources(Provider)
        Dim xmlDoc As XmlDataDocument = New XmlDataDocument(ds)

        'Set the DataSource property of the DataGrid
        resourcesGrid.DataSource = ds

        'Bind the control to the DataSet
        resourcesGrid.DataBind()
        Session("sessionds") = ds
        Session("sessionXmlDataDoc") = xmlDoc
    End If
End Sub
```

DataGrid Events

There are several handlers associated with DataGrid2, which are fired when editing, saving (updating), canceling, or removing rows. The UpdateCommand event handler is by far the most complex as it handles the two-stage process of validating the page, extracting the relevant metadata from the page, updating the DataGrid, and then finally updating the database. We'll look at this later, once we have examined the other event handlers.

Let's look at the EditCommand handler first.

```
Public Sub resourcesGrid_EditCommand(ByVal sender As Object, ByVal e As _
    DataGridCommandEventArgs) Handles resourcesGrid.EditCommand
  resourcesGrid.DataSource = ds
  resourcesGrid.EditItemIndex = e.Item.ItemIndex
  resourcesGrid.SelectedIndex = -1
  resourcesGrid.DataBind()
End Sub
```

The EditCommand handler sets the current row into edit mode when a user clicks the edit link. To control the edit mode, the DataGrid's EditItemIndex property is set to the index of the row to edit, which is determined from the DataGridCommandEventArgs class passed to the handler. After editing, the grid is rebound.

Next we'll look at the CancelCommand handler, which is shown below. The purpose of the CancelCommand handler is to switch the DataGrid from edit mode to display mode when a user clicks the cancel link. It does this by setting the EditItemIndex property to –1. What we also have to do here is check whether the current row was set into edit mode as a result of the user clicking the Add Item button. We can check the RowState property of the last row of the metadata data table; if it's state is Added, then we know the user has changed their mind about adding a new content item, so we need to delete the new row added to the data table before we rebind the DataGrid. We also clear the error display to remove any errors associated with the new content item.

```
Public Sub resourcesGrid_CancelCommand(ByVal sender As Object, ByVal e As
DataGridCommandEventArgs) Handles resourcesGrid.CancelCommand

  'Cancels the addition of a new row
  Dim dt As DataTable = ds.Tables("tbl_metadata")
  If (dt.Rows(dt.Rows.Count - 1).RowState = DataRowState.Added) Then
    dt.Rows(dt.Rows.Count - 1).Delete()
  End If
  resourcesGrid.EditItemIndex = e.Item.ItemIndex
  resourcesGrid.DataSource = ds
  resourcesGrid.EditItemIndex = -1
  resourcesGrid.DataBind()
  errorLabel.Text = ""
End Sub
```

Having mentioned how we cancel the addition of a new content item, let's look at how a new item is actually created. The code for the Add Item button's OnClick event handler is shown below:

653

```
Public Sub btnAdd_OnClick(ByVal sender As Object, ByVal e As EventArgs) Handles _
   btnAdd.Click
   Dim dt As DataTable = ds.Tables("tbl_metadata")
   Dim NewItemRow As DataRow = dt.NewRow()

   'set some default values (required for dropdown initialisation)
   NewItemRow("fk_categoryID") = 1
   NewItemRow("fk_subCategoryID") = 1
   dt.Rows.Add(NewItemRow)

   resourcesGrid.EditItemIndex = resourcesGrid.Items.Count
   resourcesGrid.SelectedIndex = -1
   resourcesGrid.DataSource = ds
   resourcesGrid.DataBind()
End Sub
```

When the **Add Item** button is clicked, a new row is added to the metadata data table. The category and subcategory IDs are defaulted to 1 to initialize the drop-down lists rendered when the new `DataGrid` row enters edit mode. The `EditItemIndex` is set to the `DataGrid`'s row (`Items`) count, and the grid rebound.

As well as adding new items, we can delete existing items. The `DeleteCommand` handler is shown below:

```
Public Sub resourcesGrid_DeleteCommand(ByVal source As Object, ByVal e As _
   DataGridCommandEventArgs) Handles resourcesGrid.DeleteCommand

   Dim dt As DataTable = ds.Tables("tbl_metadata")

   'Cancels the addition of a new row
   If (dt.Rows(dt.Rows.Count - 1).RowState = DataRowState.Added) Then
      dt.Rows(dt.Rows.Count - 1).Delete()
      resourcesGrid.EditItemIndex = -1
   Else
      Dim rowToDeleteDG As Integer = e.Item.ItemIndex
      Dim dataKey As String = resourcesGrid.DataKeys(rowToDeleteDG).ToString()

      'Find row to delete in dataset imports XPath query
      Dim XPathQuery As String = "/NewDataSet/tbl_metadata[pk_resourceID='" _
         + dataKey + "']"
      Dim xmlEl As XmlNode = xmlDoc.SelectSingleNode(XPathQuery)
      Dim row As DataRow = xmlDoc.GetRowFromElement(xmlEl)
      row.Delete()

      'create instance of NewsDB class
      oNews = New newsDB()
      oNews.updateResource(ds)
   End If
      resourcesGrid.DataSource = ds
      resourcesGrid.DataBind()
      errorLabel.Text = ""
End Sub
```

When deleting an item from the `DataGrid`, we identify the `DataGrid` row to be deleted as we have before, then we use the index value to get the corresponding value from the grid's `DataKeys` collection. As this will be the content item's unique ID, we can use it to locate the element in the `XmlDataDocument`, and because it is synchronized with the `DataSet`, we can use the `GetRowFromElement` method to return a reference to the row we want to delete in the `DataSet`. It's then a simple case of deleting the row in the `DataSet`, then propagating the update back to the database. This is handled by the `UpdateResource` method of the `newsDB` class.

The most complex of all the event handlers is that associated with the `UpdateCommand`. When the **update** button is clicked the `UpdateCommand` handler performs the following steps:

1. Establishes whether the row is new

2. Identifies the row in the `DataSet` to be updated

3. Finds the controls in the `DataGrid`

4. Validates the content

5. Populates the `DataSet`

6. Updates the database

7. Rebinds the `DataGrid`

We'll break the code down into these functional areas, describing each in turn.

1. Establishes Whether the Row is New

We first establish whether the row is new or not, as new and existing rows will have to be handled differently:

```
resourcesGrid.EditItemIndex = e.Item.ItemIndex
Dim dt As DataTable = ds.Tables("tbl_metadata")
Dim row As DataRow

'check for new row
If (dt.Rows(dt.Rows.Count - 1).RowState = DataRowState.Added) Then
  newRow = True
End If
```

2. Identifies the Row in the DataSet to be Updated

This code is very similar to that you've seen earlier. For existing records, use the index value of the current row to get the unique ID of the content item from the `DataKeys` collection. Use this to locate the element in the `XmlDataDocument`, and then use the `GetRowFromElement` method to return the row to be modified in the `DataSet`.

```
If Not newRow Then 'existing records
  Dim rowToModifyDG As Integer = e.Item.ItemIndex
  Dim dataKey As String = resourcesGrid.DataKeys(rowToModifyDG).ToString()
  Dim XPathQuery As String = "/NewDataSet/tbl_metadata[pk_resourceID='" + _
```

```
      dataKey + "']"
    Dim xmlEl As XmlNode = xmlDoc.SelectSingleNode(XPathQuery)
    row = xmlDoc.GetRowFromElement(xmlEl)
```

For new records, get a reference to the last row in the `DataSet` and set the provider ID:

```
Else 'new records
  'Get the last row in the dataset
  row = dt.Rows(dt.Rows.Count - 1)
  row("fk_providerID") = provID
End If
```

3. Finds the Controls in the DataGrid

As the `DataGrid` is still in edit mode, we need to find the controls displayed in each cell in the row so we can retrieve their values. To do this we pass the ID of the control to the `FindControl` method as shown below:

```
Dim identifierTextBox As TextBox = e.Item.FindControl("IdentifierTextBox")
Dim categoryList As DropDownList = e.Item.FindControl("categoryList")
Dim subCategoryList As DropDownList = e.Item.FindControl("subCategoryList")
```

4. Validates the Content

```
Dim bValidated As Boolean = ValidateSource(baseURL + identifierTextBox.Text)
```

The basic functionality of the `ValidateSource` method is to validate the content item against our schema (`content.xsd`), before they are submitted to the database. The schema is shown below:

```
<?xml version="1.0" encoding="UTF-8"?>
<xsd:schema
    xmlns:xsd="http://www.w3.org/2001/XMLSchema">

    <xsd:element name="body" type="xsd:string"/>

    <xsd:element name="head">
        <xsd:complexType>
            <xsd:sequence>
                <xsd:element ref="title"/>
                <xsd:element ref="meta" maxOccurs="unbounded"/>
            </xsd:sequence>
        </xsd:complexType>
    </xsd:element>

    <xsd:element name="html">
        <xsd:complexType>
            <xsd:sequence>
                <xsd:element ref="head"/>
                <xsd:element ref="body"/>
            </xsd:sequence>
```

```
            </xsd:complexType>
        </xsd:element>

        <xsd:element name="meta">
            <xsd:complexType>
                <xsd:attribute name="content" type="xsd:string" use="required"/>
                <xsd:attribute name="name" use="required">
                    <xsd:simpleType>
                        <xsd:restriction base="xsd:NMTOKEN">
                            <xsd:enumeration value="date"/>
                            <xsd:enumeration value="description"/>
                            <xsd:enumeration value="identifier"/>
                        </xsd:restriction>
                    </xsd:simpleType>
                </xsd:attribute>
            </xsd:complexType>
        </xsd:element>

        <xsd:element name="title" type="xsd:string"/>
    </xsd:schema>
```

The method takes the identifier of the content item, passes it into an `XmlTextReader`, and then passes the `XmlTextReader` object as the constructor of an `XmlValidatingReader`, which performs the validation against the schema. The `Try...Catch` block is there to handle any exceptions. We've cached our schema in the `XmlSchemaCollection`, which offers performance gains over accessing the schema via the file system or a URL.

```
Public Function ValidateSource(ByVal urlLocation As String) As Boolean

    Dim xRead As XmlTextReader = New XmlTextReader(urlLocation)
    Dim xVal As XmlValidatingReader = New XmlValidatingReader(xRead)

    xVal.ValidationType = ValidationType.Schema

    Dim Cache As XmlSchemaCollection = New XmlSchemaCollection()
    Cache.Add(String.Empty, "http://localhost/Chapter14_VB/content.xsd")
    xVal.Schemas.Add(Cache)

    Try
        ' Read XML data
        While xVal.Read()
        End While
    Catch e As Exception
        errorLabel.Text = "Error!! (" + e.Message + ")"
        Return (False)
    End Try
    Return (True)
End Function
```

Let's show a few examples to illustrate what happens if we attempt to add, firstly, a page that doesn't exist, and, secondly, a page with some missing metadata. If we try and add a page that doesn't exist, a (404) not found error is raised, as shown below:

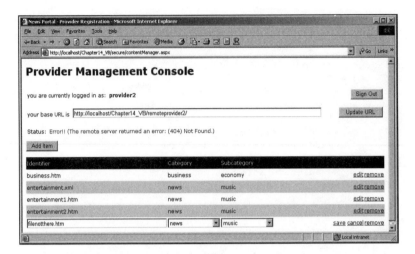

Next we'll try and add a page that exists, but doesn't conform to our schema. We'll attempt to register a page (`provider2invalid.htm`), which has its title missing (see below):

```html
<html>
  <head>
    <meta content="http://localhost/../invalid.htm" name="identifier" />
    <meta content="04/06/2002 19:00" name="date" />
    <meta content="Sales of Beer ...shares set to soar." name="description" />
  </head>
  <body>
    Sales of the new beer flavor chips have topped an all time high.
    Analysts predict the shares in LagerSnack Ltd, Britain's largest
    manufacturer of the snack to break the 3 pound mark for the first time by
    the end of the week.
  </body>
</html>
```

When we try to register this content item, a validation error is raised:

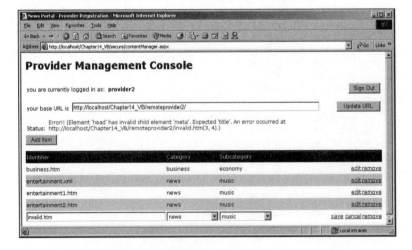

5. Populates the DataSet

The first thing we need to do before we populate the `DataSet` is to read the new content document into an `XmlTextReader`, which is then loaded into the DOM. We can then extract the relevant metadata to pass into the `DataSet` using simple XPath queries.

```
'load doc into DOM
Dim xReader As XmlTextReader = New XmlTextReader(baseURL + identifierTextBox.Text)
Dim xmlContent As XmlDocument = New XmlDocument()
xmlContent.Load(xReader)

'populate dataset
row("Title") = xmlContent.SelectSingleNode("/html/head/title").InnerText
row("resDescription") = xmlContent.SelectSingleNode("/html/head/meta[@name =
'description']/@content").InnerXml
row("dateCreated") = xmlContent.SelectSingleNode("/html/head/meta[@name =
'date']/@content").InnerXml
```

We also pass in the control values and provider ID we retrieved earlier:

```
row("identifier") = identifierTextBox.Text
row("fk_categoryID") = categoryList.SelectedItem.Value
row("fk_subCategoryID") = subCategoryList.SelectedItem.Value
row("fk_providerID") = provID
```

6. Updates the Database

For existing rows we call the `updateResource` method. If it's a new news item that we're adding, we call the `addResource` method. The two methods are shown below.

The `updateResource` method uses the `CommandBuilder` class to automatically generate the update command, and then calls the `Update` method of the data adapter to propagate changes back to the database.

```
Public Sub updateResource(ByVal ds As DataSet)

        'create new connection object
        Dim cnString As String = getConnectionString("newsDB1")

        Dim sqlCn As SqlConnection = New SqlConnection(cnString)

        Dim metadataDA As SqlDataAdapter = New SqlDataAdapter("SELECT * FROM
            tbl_metadata", sqlCn)
        'create CommandBuilder to auto generate SQL commands
        Dim myBuilder As SqlCommandBuilder = New SqlCommandBuilder(metadataDA)

        metadataDA.Update(ds, "tbl_metadata")
        sqlCn.Close()
End Sub
```

The `addResource` method executes a stored procedure that inserts a new row into the metadata table. It returns an auto-incremented identity value, which is then mapped back to the corresponding `Identity` column in the `DataSet`.

659

```
Public Sub addResource(ByVal ds As DataSet)

    'create new connection object
    Dim cnString As String = getConnectionString("newsDB1")

    Dim sqlCn As SqlConnection = New SqlConnection(cnString)
    Dim metadataDA As SqlDataAdapter = New SqlDataAdapter("SELECT * FROM
      tbl_metadata", sqlCn)

    'set the stored procedure
    metadataDA.InsertCommand = New SqlCommand("usp_AddResource", sqlCn)
    metadataDA.InsertCommand.CommandType = CommandType.StoredProcedure

    'add the input parameters
    metadataDA.InsertCommand.Parameters.Add("@fk_providerID", SqlDbType.Int,
      0, "fk_providerID")
    metadataDA.InsertCommand.Parameters.Add("@Title", SqlDbType.NVarChar, 50,
      "Title")
    metadataDA.InsertCommand.Parameters.Add("@resDescription",
      SqlDbType.NVarChar, 150, "resDescription")
    metadataDA.InsertCommand.Parameters.Add("@DateCreated",
      SqlDbType.DateTime, 0, "dateCreated")
    metadataDA.InsertCommand.Parameters.Add("@Identifier", SqlDbType.NVarChar,
      50, "Identifier")
    metadataDA.InsertCommand.Parameters.Add("@fk_subCategoryID",
      SqlDbType.NVarChar, 50, "fk_subCategoryID")
    metadataDA.InsertCommand.Parameters.Add("@fk_categoryID",
      SqlDbType.NVarChar, 50, "fk_categoryID")

    'add the output parameter
    Dim myParm As SqlParameter =
      metadataDA.InsertCommand.Parameters.Add("@Identity", SqlDbType.Int, 0,
      "pk_resourceID")
    myParm.Direction = ParameterDirection.Output
    sqlCn.Open()

    metadataDA.Update(ds, "tbl_metadata")
    sqlCn.Close()
End Sub
```

7. Rebinds the DataGrid

To complete the update sequence we rebind the DataGrid:

```
resourcesGrid.EditItemIndex = -1
resourcesGrid.DataSource = ds
resourcesGrid.DataBind()
errorLabel.Text = ""
```

The only functionality we haven't covered for this page yet is signing out. When the Sign Out button is clicked, the btnSignOut_Click handler is invoked:

```
Public Sub btnSignOut_Click(ByVal sender As Object, ByVal e As EventArgs)Handles _
    btnSignOut.Click
      FormsAuthentication.SignOut()
      Response.Redirect("../default.aspx")
End Sub
```

The handler calls the `SignOut` method of the `FormsAuthentication` class, which effectively kills the cookie and redirects the user to the main page.

We'll look at what happens behind the main page next.

Main Page

On re-entering the main page, some registered content items should now be visible as in the figure below:

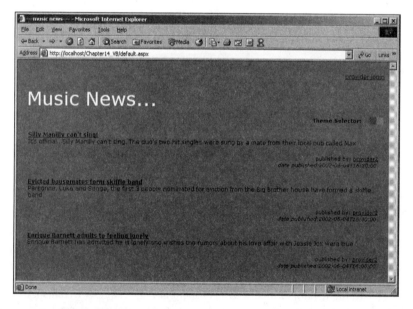

You may have noticed that only the news items sub-categorized as "music" are displayed. This is deliberate! What we aim to show here is that because we're using an XSL transform to generate our news page, we can write XSLs to display whatever type of news we like. In this case, we've demonstrated this with a specialist music news portal, but in theory we could have a portal offering news on any category or subcategory we like. It's also easy to implement, because all we need to do is change the reference to the XSLT in the `web.config` file. We'll look at this more later.

It is worth noting that if you don't like the color scheme I've picked, you have the choice of two additional schemes, Blue and Orange. To change the color scheme just click the colored boxes in the top right hand corner of the screen next to the **Theme Selector** label.

Main Page – How It Works

Lets take a closer look at what's going on with this main page.

Default.aspx

As we mentioned earlier, unlike the `contentManager.aspx` page, which used a web form containing several server controls for the presentation layer, the `default.aspx` page uses XSLT. As such, all it contains is the `@Page` script directive at the top of the page:

```
<%@ Page language="c#"
    Codebehind="default.aspx.cs"
    AutoEventWireup="false"
    Inherits="casestudy1._default"%>
```

Default.aspx.vb

The code-behind class file contains all the methods for retrieving the data as XML and transforming it to HTML for display in the browser.

Getting at the Data

First we declare the required namespaces:

```
imports System
imports System.Text
imports System.Data
imports System.Xml
imports System.Configuration
imports System.Xml.Xsl
imports System.Data.SqlClient
imports System.Xml.XPath
```

We mentioned earlier how we could change the color scheme or theme of our main page. We do this by passing the theme name in the query string, which is then passed into the transform to select the appropriate CSS file to apply. On the first page request, our query string is empty, so we have to initialize the theme to the default "khaki". On subsequent page requests we check if there's been a theme passed in the query string. If so, as would be the case if someone selected a different theme, we set the theme accordingly. We'll see how this is passed into the XSLT later.

```
dim theme as string

if Session("theme") = nothing then
  Session("theme") = "khaki"
elseif not Context.Request.QueryString("theme") = nothing then
  Session("theme") = Context.Request.QueryString("theme").ToString()
end if
```

Next we retrieve the connection string and transform path from the `web.config` file:

```
dim connectionString as string = ConfigurationSettings.AppSettings("newsDB1")
dim XSLTransformPath as string = ConfigurationSettings.AppSettings("XSLTransform")
```

Next we build the command text. We use the `StringBuilder` class to perform the string concatenation, as it's by far the most efficient way to build strings:

```
dim sb as StringBuilder = new StringBuilder()
sb.Append("SELECT tbl_providers.provider, tbl_providers.baseURL, ")
sb.Append("tbl_metadata.Title, tbl_lk_categories.category, ")
sb.Append("tbl_metadata.resDescription, tbl_metadata.Identifier, ")
sb.Append("tbl_metadata.dateCreated, ")
sb.Append("tbl_lk_subCategories.subCategory FROM tbl_lk_categories ")
sb.Append("INNER JOIN tbl_metadata ON tbl_lk_categories.pk_categoryID = ")
sb.Append("tbl_metadata.fk_CATEGORYID ")
sb.Append("INNER JOIN tbl_lk_subCategories ON tbl_metadata.fk_subCategoryID = ")
sb.Append("tbl_lk_subCategories.pk_subCategoryID ")
sb.Append("INNER JOIN tbl_providers ON tbl_providers.pk_providerID = ")
sb.Append("tbl_metadata.fk_providerID ")
sb.Append("ORDER BY tbl_lk_categories.category, tbl_lk_subCategories.subCategory ")
sb.Append("FOR XML RAW")
```

We've used the `FOR XML RAW` clause in our `SELECT` statement, which returns the result set in a flat XML structure as shown below (the results have been truncated for brevity):

```
<row provider="provider2"
    baseURL="http://localhost/chapter14/remoteprovider2/"
    Title="Evicted housemates form skiffle band"
    category="news"
    resDescription="Peregrine, Luke and Senga, the first 3 people nominated for
eviction from the Big Brother house have formed a skiffle band"
    Identifier="entertainment1.htm"
    dateCreated="2002-06-04T16:30:00"
    subCategory="music"/>
    ...
<row provider="provider2"
    baseURL="http://localhost/chapter14/remoteprovider2/"
    Title="Enrique Barnett admits to feeling lonely"
    category="news"
    resDescription="Enrique Barnett has admitted he is lonely and wishes the
rumors about his love affair with Jessie Jox were true"
    Identifier="entertainment2.htm"
    dateCreated="2002-06-04T14:00:00"
    subCategory="music"/>
```

Next we create the connection and command objects and assign the contents of the `StringBuilder` to the command class's `CommandText` property:

```
'Create new connection object
dim sqlCn as SqlConnection = new SqlConnection(connectionString)
```

663

```
'Create new command object and assign connection
dim cmd as SqlCommand = new SqlCommand(connectionString,sqlCn)

'Open connection
sqlCn.Open()

'Assign command text to command
cmd.CommandText = sb.ToString()
```

The `ExecuteXmlReader` method of the `SqlCommand` class returns an `XmlTextReader` object representing the XML returned above:

```
dim xmlRdr as XmlTextReader = cmd.ExecuteXmlReader()
```

Next we loop through the reader building an XML string as we go. Note that again we're using the `StringBuilder` to build the string:

```
sb.Remove(0,sb.Length)

xmlRdr.MoveToContent()

dim cur=xmlRdr.ReadOuterXml()
Do While (cur <> "")
    sb.Append(cur)
    cur=xmlRdr.ReadOuterXml()
Loop
xmlRdr.Close()
```

As our query has returned XML fragments, we create a new `XmlDocument` and add an element called news. This becomes the root node of our XML result set when we set its `InnerXml` to be the contents of the `StringBuilder`.

```
Dim xmlDoc As XmlDocument = New XmlDocument()
Dim newNode As XmlNode = xmlDoc.CreateNode(XmlNodeType.Element, "news", "")
newNode.InnerXml = sb.ToString()
xmlDoc.AppendChild(newNode)
```

The `XmlDocument` is used to create an `XmlNavigator`:

```
Dim xpNav As XPathNavigator = xmlDoc.CreateNavigator()
```

Next we create a new `Transform` object, and load the transform:

```
'Create a new XslTransform object.
Dim xt As XslTransform = New XslTransform()

'Load the stylesheet.
xt.Load(Server.MapPath(XSLTransformPath))
```

We pass our theme to the XSLT as a parameter using the `XsltArgumentList.AddPram()` method:

```
Dim al As XsltArgumentList = New XsltArgumentList()
al.AddParam("theme", "", theme)
```

Finally we create an `XmlWriter` object to output directly to the `Response`, which is passed along with the `XPathNavigator` object and `XsltArgumentList` as constructors to the `Transform` method of the `XslTransform` class:

```
'Create an XmlTextWriter which outputs to the response.
Dim writer As XmlWriter = New XmlTextWriter(Response.Output)

'Transform the data and send the output to the response
xt.Transform(xpNav, al, writer)
```

The XSL Transform

The XSL transform (`MusicNews.xsl`) used to generate our main page uses a combination of HTML and CSS to control the visual layout of the page. We'll talk through some of the highlights below.

```
<?xml version="1.0" encoding="UTF-8"?>
<xsl:stylesheet version="1.0" xmlns:xsl="http://www.w3.org/1999/XSL/Transform">
```

Here we declare our `theme` parameter:

```
<xsl:param name="theme"/>
<xsl:template match="/">
<html>
  <head>
    <title>---music news---</title>
```

The `theme` parameter declared earlier is used to build the filename of the CSS to be used:

```
<link rel="stylesheet" type="text/css" href="styles/{$theme}.css"/>
<script language="JavaScript"><![CDATA[

function openWindow(sURL)
{
  window.open(sURL,null,"height=400,width=600");
}

]]>
</script>
</head>
<body class="mainHeader">
  <table width="100%" cellspacing="0" cellpadding="0" border="0">
    <tr align="right" valign="middle" height="30px">
      <td colspan="2">
        <a href="secure/contentManager.aspx">provider login</a><br/>
      </td>
```

665

```
        </tr>
        <tr valign="middle" class="mainHeader">
          <td align="left" class="headerLogoText">Music News...</td>
          <td align="right" class="layout"/>
        </tr>
        <tr>
          <td colspan="2">
            <table valign="middle" border="0" width="100%">
              <tr>
                <td align="right" class="themeSelectorText">Theme Selector:</td>
                <td width="10px" class="theme1selector"
                    onclick="window.location='default.aspx?theme=khaki'"/>
                <td width="10px" class="theme2selector"
                    onclick="window.location='default.aspx?theme=blue'"/>
                <td width="10px" class="theme3selector"
                    onclick="window.location='default.aspx?theme=orange'"/>
              </tr>
            </table>
          </td>
        </tr>
        <tr>
          <td colspan="2">
            <table border="0" align="center" width="100%">
              <tr>
                <td/>
              </tr>
```

We match all nodes in the document with a subcategory attribute equal to `music`, building the links to the content items:

```
        <xsl:for-each select="//*[@subCategory = 'music']">
          <tr>
            <td class="categoryBorder">
              <a>
                <xsl:attribute name="href">
<xsl:text>javascript:openWindow('GetPage.aspx?URL=</xsl:text>
                  <xsl:value-of select="@baseURL"/>
                  <xsl:value-of
                    select="@Identifier"/><xsl:text>')</xsl:text>
                </xsl:attribute>
                <b>
                  <xsl:value-of select="@Title"/>
                </b>
              </a>
              <br/>
              <xsl:value-of select="@resDescription"/>
              <br/>
        <p align="right">
        <small>published by: </small>
                <a>
                <xsl:attribute name="href">
```

```
                        <xsl:text>javascript:openWindow('</xsl:text>
                        <xsl:value-of select="@baseURL"/><xsl:text>')</xsl:text>
                     </xsl:attribute>
                     <small><xsl:value-of select="@provider"/></small>
                       </a>
                       <br/>
                          <small>
                       <i>date published:<xsl:value-of select="@dateCreated"/></i>
                     </small>
                     </p>
                   </td>
                 </tr>
               </xsl:for-each>
             </table>
           </td>
         </tr>
       </table>
     </body>
   </html>
 </xsl:template>

</xsl:stylesheet>
```

Viewing the Content

When we click a link to a news item, the item is displayed in a pop-up window. This functionality is supplied by a simple javascript contained in our XSL transform:

```
function openWindow(sURL)
{
  window.open(sURL,null,"height=400,width=600");
}
```

Rendering the XHTML files is easy, but how do we handle the rendering of the XML documents? All we do is apply a transform. We've created a simple class called GetPage that we use to detect the content type and render it appropriately. GetPage is the code behind class for GetPage.aspx, so we pass a query string to the openWindow function (for example, GetPage.aspx?URL=entertainment.htm) and pull out the URL from the query string in the page's Page_Load event handler.

```
Option Explicit On

Imports System.Xml
Imports System.Xml.Xsl
Imports System.Xml.XPath

Public Class GetPage
  Inherits System.Web.UI.Page

  Private Sub Page_Load(ByVal sender As System.Object, ByVal e As _
    System.EventArgs) Handles MyBase.Load
    Dim sURL As String = Context.Request.QueryString("URL").ToString()
```

If an XML file is detected, we load an XSL transform and transform the XML file, sending the transformed output directly to the browser:

```
If (sURL.EndsWith("xml")) Then
  Dim xp As XPathDocument = New XPathDocument(sURL)
  Dim xpNav As XPathNavigator = xp.CreateNavigator()

  'Create a new XslTransform object.
  Dim xt As XslTransform = New XslTransform()

  'Load the stylesheet.
  xt.Load(Server.MapPath("content.xslt"))

  'Create an XmlTextWriter which outputs to the response.
  Dim writer As XmlWriter = New XmlTextWriter(Response.Output)

  'Transform the data and send the output to the response
  xt.Transform(xpNav, Nothing, writer)
```

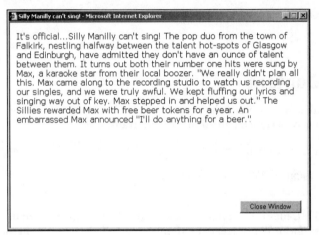

The XSL transform used (content.xslt) is listed below:

```
<?xml version="1.0" encoding="UTF-8"?>
<xsl:stylesheet version="1.0" xmlns:xsl="http://www.w3.org/1999/XSL/Transform">
  <xsl:output method="xml" version="1.0" encoding="UTF-8" indent="yes"/>
  <xsl:template match="/">
    <html>
      <head>
        <title><xsl:value-of select="//title"/></title>
      </head>
      <body style="font-size: 9pt; font-family: Verdana, Arial">
      <table width="100%" height="100%">
        <tr>
          <td valign="top" align="justify">
            <xsl:value-of select="//body"/>
          </td>
```

```
      </tr>
      <tr>
        <td align="right">
          <input type="button"
                 value="Close Window"
                 onclick="javascript:window.close();"/>
        </td>
      </tr>
    </table>
    </body>
    </html>
  </xsl:template>
</xsl:stylesheet>
```

If the document is XHTML we do a simple redirect to the content page:

```
    Else
       'Write out html doc as is
       Response.Redirect(sURL)
    End If
  End Sub
End Class
```

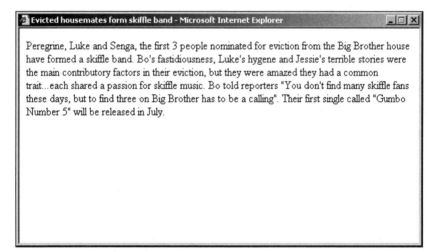

What Type of News shall we Deliver Today?

As mentioned earlier, we can easily swap out the XSLT we use in the application to provide a music news portal for any of the available categories or subcategories. We'll illustrate this with an example that groups all related categories of news below category headings. It's effectively displaying every news item submitted to our system, but in a very structured way. Let's see a screenshot:

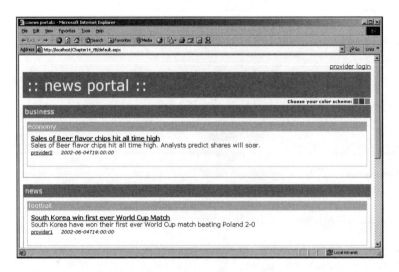

The XSL transform used to produce this view of the submitted news items is considerably more complex than that used in our music news portal, and is probably beyond the scope of this book. But if you're interested in having a look at it, you'll find it in the **Chapter14** folder. It's the file called `news.xsl`.

SQLXML Managed Classes

SQLXML (XML for SQL Server) is a downloadable and fully supported feature pack that extends the XML capabilities of SQL Server 2000. It enables you to:

- ❏ Query relational database with XPath: or query it with SQL and return XML results
- ❏ Update relational data just as if it were XML
- ❏ Load large XML files into existing SQL Server 2000 databases and convert them into relational data
- ❏ Query your SQL Server via URLs from the web browser or web application
- ❏ Access SQL Server XML functionality via OLEDB/ADO and .NET Managed Classes

The `Microsoft.Data.SqlXml` namespace contains the managed providers that allow .NET code to take advantage of these enhanced XML features. We've provided another version of our `DisplayNews` class (called `DisplayNewsSQLXML`) which functionally speaking does exactly the same as the `DisplayNews` class, but uses the SQLXML managed classes in place of the .NET data providers. Let's get started by setting our system up to use the SQLXML classes.

1. Before we do anything you need to download and install the latest version of SQLXML from http://msdn.microsoft.com/sqlxml.

2. Next, open the Chapter14_VB.sln file in the IDE.

3. To allow our VB.NET code to access the SQLXML Managed Classes, we need to add a reference to our solution. To do so, right-click on the **References** node in the Solution Explorer and select **Add Reference**. Find the **Microsoft.Data.SqlXml** component and click **Select**, then **OK** to finish. The class should appear under the **References** node as shown below:

4. Next we need to add the .vb file. Right-click the **Chapter14_VB** project node in the Solution Explorer and select **Add | Add Existing Item** from the menu. Browse to the **Chapter14_VB** folder and select the default_SQLXML.aspx.vb file.

5. Now open the default.aspx file in the IDE and switch to HTML view. Change the Codebehind attribute in the @ Page directive to be default_SQLXML.aspx.vb and Inherits to be Chapter14_VB.DisplayNewsSQLXML.

6. Compile and run the application. The main page should look as it did before. The code will look pretty similar too, as we'll see.

The complete code listing for the DisplayNewsSQLXML class is shown below. The main differences from the DisplayNews class have been highlighted.

```
Option Explicit On

Imports System
Imports System.Text
Imports System.Data
Imports System.Xml
Imports System.Configuration
Imports System.Xml.Xsl
Imports System.Data.SqlClient
Imports System.Xml.XPath
Imports Microsoft.Data.SqlXml
```

```
Public Class DisplayNewsSQLXML
  Inherits System.Web.UI.Page

  Private Sub Page_Load(ByVal sender As System.Object, ByVal e As _
    System.EventArgs) Handles MyBase.Load
    Dim theme As String

    If Session("theme") = Nothing Then
      Session("theme") = "khaki"
    ElseIf Not Context.Request.QueryString("theme") = Nothing Then
      Session("theme") = Context.Request.QueryString("theme").ToString()
    End If

    If Not IsPostBack Then
      theme = Session("theme")

    Dim connectionString As String = _
      ConfigurationSettings.AppSettings("newsDB_SQLXML")
    Dim XSLTransformPath As String = _
      ConfigurationSettings.AppSettings("XSLTransform")

    'Build query string
    Dim sb As StringBuilder = New StringBuilder()
    sb.Append("SELECT tbl_providers.provider, tbl_providers.baseURL, ")
    sb.Append("  tbl_metadata.Title, tbl_lk_categories.category, ")
    sb.Append("tbl_metadata.resDescription, tbl_metadata.Identifier, ")
    sb.Append("  tbl_metadata.dateCreated, ")
    sb.Append("tbl_lk_subCategories.subCategory FROM tbl_lk_categories ")
    sb.Append("INNER JOIN tbl_metadata ON tbl_lk_categories.pk_categoryID = ")
    sb.Append("  tbl_metadata.fk_CATEGORYID ")
    sb.Append("INNER JOIN tbl_lk_subCategories ON tbl_metadata.fk_subCategoryID = ")
    sb.Append("  tbl_lk_subCategories.pk_subCategoryID ")
    sb.Append("INNER JOIN tbl_providers ON tbl_providers.pk_providerID = ")
    sb.Append("  tbl_metadata.fk_providerID ")
    sb.Append("ORDER BY tbl_lk_categories.category, ")
    sb.Append("  tbl_lk_subCategories.subCategory ")
    sb.Append("FOR XML RAW")

    Dim cmd As SqlXmlCommand = New SqlXmlCommand(connectionString)
    cmd.RootTag = "news"
    cmd.CommandType = SqlXmlCommandType.Sql
    cmd.CommandText = sb.ToString()

    Dim xmlRdr As XmlTextReader = cmd.ExecuteXmlReader()

    Dim xp As XPathDocument = New XPathDocument(xmlRdr)
    Dim xpNav As XPathNavigator = xp.CreateNavigator()

    'Create a new XslTransform object.
    Dim xt As XslTransform = New XslTransform()

    'Load the stylesheet.
    xt.Load(Server.MapPath(XSLTransformPath))
```

```
          Dim al As XsltArgumentList = New XsltArgumentList()
          al.AddParam("theme", "", theme)

          'Create an XmlTextWriter which outputs to the response.
          Dim writer As XmlWriter = New XmlTextWriter(Response.Output)

          'Transform the data and send the output to the response
          xt.Transform(xpNav, al, writer)
      End If
      End Sub
  End Class
```

Suggestions for Improvement

We've made a couple of suggestions below, which would be worth considering if the scalability, usability and security of this application were to be enhanced:

❑   Implement a controlled vocabulary. For example, allow for better categorization of content through the application of controlled category/subcategory combinations (for example, restricting football to always be a sub-category of sport).

❑   Add the facility for providers to update their passwords.

❑   Automatically detect browser type and select appropriate XSLT for display.

❑   Improved error handling. The easiest way would be to use the `Application_Error()` method in the `Global.asax.vb` file.

❑   Order news items by date. Add a drop-down to the main page, so that only content submitted on a particular date is shown. You could then show only today's news items and auto-archive older submissions.

❑   Add personalization. Allow users to log in and allow them to store their own preferences of which type of news items they want to see when they visit the site.

Summary

The case study has demonstrated how many of the techniques shown throughout the book can be exploited to create a simple news portal. We used an editable `DataGrid` bound to a `DataSet` to facilitate the registration of content by remote content providers, and we showed how we could query the `DataSet` using XPath when synchronized with an `XmlDataDocument`.

We demonstrated how an XSD schema could be used to validate the content. This ensured that the submitted XML/HTML file was structured appropriately for use in our system. Finally, we showed how we could return XML directly from queries against a SQL Server 2000 database, which can be transformed directly to the browser using XSLT. This allows any browser type to be easily targeted, and the layout of the site easily changed.

This takes us to the end of the book. By reading this book you should now have a good understanding of how XML is used in .NET. Not only is it extremely popular for the developer, but it forms the foundation of many of the technologies used throughout the .NET Framework itself.

With the coming of the Global XML Architecture, the popularity of XML looks set to continue and even grow, with web services being built using .NET looking to be one of the biggest advances of component design in recent times. Combined with the ease and power of creating solutions with VB.NET and the .NET Framework, developers are going to use XML and VB.NET as the cornerstone of almost every development project.

There is still work to be done, but with .NET and the techniques you learned in this book we hope that you can start building .NET components with XML today. You should look to improve your knowledge of both subjects with *Professional XML 2nd Edition* from Wrox Press (ISBN 1-86100-505-9) and *Professional VB.NET 2nd Edition* also from Wrox Press (ISBN 1-86100-716-7).

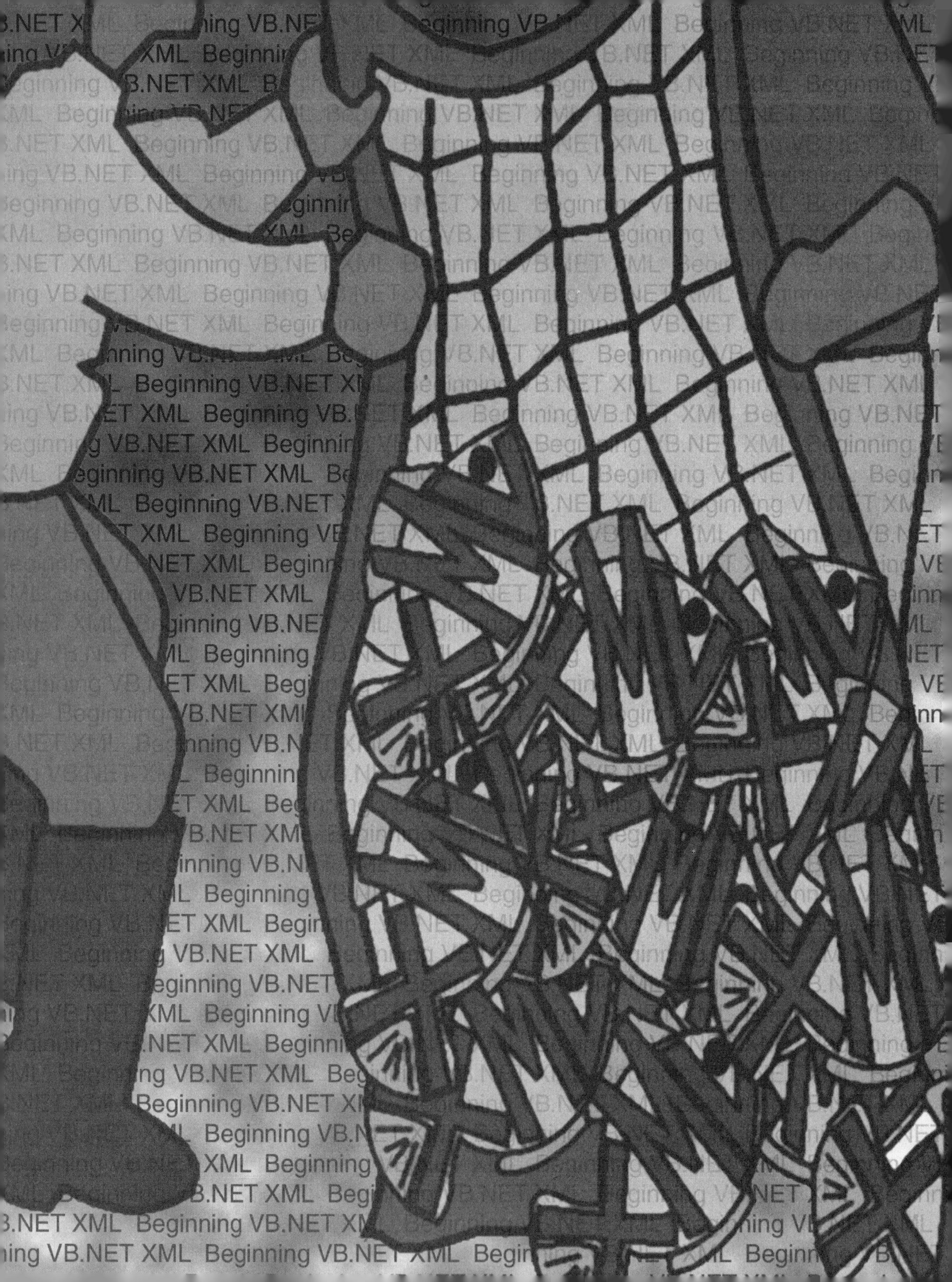
Beginning VB.NET XML

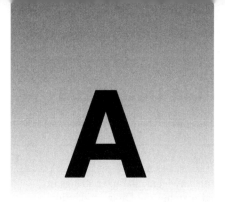

Schema Datatypes Reference

In this appendix, we will give a quick reference to the W3C Recommendation for XML Schema, Part 2: Datatypes. Datatypes were separated out into a specification in their own right, so that other XML-related technologies as well as XML Schema (for example, Relax NG) can use them.

XML Schema defines a number of **built-in** types that we can use to indicate the intended type of content, and indeed to validate it. We can further restrict these types using **facets** to create our own datatypes, known as **derived types**. The second part of the XML Schema Recommendation defines two sorts of datatype:

- ❑ **Built-in types**, which are available to all XML Schema authors, and should be implemented by a conforming processor.

- ❑ **User-derived types**, which are defined in individual schema instances, and are particular to that schema (although it is possible to import these definitions into other definitions.)

Remember, there are two sub-groups of built-in type:

- ❑ **Primitive types**, which are types in their own right. They are not defined in terms of other datatypes. Primitive types are also known as base types, because they are the basis from which all other types are built.

- ❑ **Derived types**, which are built from definitions of other datatypes.

In first part of this appendix, we will provide a quick overview of all the XML built-in datatypes, both primitive and derived. In the second part, we will give details of all of the constraining facets of these datatypes that can be used to restrict the allowed value space thereby deriving new types. Finally, we have tables that illustrate which of these constraining facets can be applied to which datatype.

XML Schema Built-in Datatypes

Here are the primitive types that XML Schema offers, from which we can derive other datatypes:

Primitive type	Description	Example
string	Represents any legal character strings in XML that matches the Char production in XML 1.0 Second Edition. (http://www.w3.org/TR/REC-xml)	Bob Watkins Note, if you need to use these characters in some text (in element content or an attribute value), you will need to escape them according to the XML rules: < or &#60 for < (an opening angled bracket) > or > for > (a closing angled bracket) & or &#30 for & (an ampersand) ' or ' for ' (an apostrophe) " or " for " (a quotation mark)
boolean	Represents binary logic, true or false.	true, false, 1, 0 (These are the only permitted values for this datatype.)
decimal	Represents arbitrary precision decimal numbers.	3.141 The ASCII plus (+) and minus (–) characters are used to represent positive or negative numbers, for example: -1.23, +00042.00.
float	Standard concept of real numbers corresponding to a single precision 32 bit floating point type.	-INF, -1E4, 4.5E-2, 37, INF, NaN NaN denotes not a number INF denotes infinity

Primitive type	Description	Example
double	Standard concept of real numbers corresponding to a double precision 64-bit floating-point type.	-INF, 765.4321234E11, 7E7, 1.0, INF, NaN NaN denotes not a number INF denotes infinity
duration	Represents a duration of time in the format PnYnMnDTnHnMnS, where: P is a designator that must always be present nY represents number of years nM represents number of months nD represents number of days T is the date/time separator nH is number of hours nM is number of minutes nS is number of seconds	P1Y0M1DT20H25M30S 1 year and a day, 20 hours, 25 minutes and 30 seconds Limited forms of this lexical production are also allowed. For example, P120D denotes 120 days.
dateTime	A specific instance in time in the format: CCYY-MM-DDThh:mm:ss where: CC represents the century YY represents the year MM represents the month DD represents the day T is the date/time separator hh represents hours mm represents minutes ss represents seconds (Fractional seconds can be added to arbitrary precision) There is also an optional time zone indicator.	2001-04-16T15:23:15 Represents the 16th of April 2001, at 3:23 and 15 seconds in the afternoon. (Note that the year 0000 is prohibited, and each of the fields CC, YY, MM and DD must be exactly 2 digits).

Table continued on following page

Primitive type	Description	Example
time	Represents an instance of time that occurs every day in the format `HH:MM:SS`.	`14:12:30`
	Fractional seconds can be added to arbitrary precision and there is also an optional time zone indicator.	Represents 12 minutes and thirty seconds past two in the afternoon.
date	Represents a calendar date from the Gregorian calendar (the whole day) in the format `CCYY-MM-DD`. There is also an optional time zone indicator.	`2001-04-16` Represents the 16th of April 2001.
	This complies with the ISO Standard 8601.	
gYearMonth	Represents a month in a year in the Gregorian calendar, in the format `CCYY-MM`.	`1999-02` Represents February 1999.
gYear	Represents a year in the Gregorian calendar in the format `CCYY`.	`1986`
	There is also an optional time zone indicator and optional leading minus sign.	Represents 1986.
gMonthDay	Represents a recurring day of a recurring month in the Gregorian calendar in the format `--MM-DD`.	`--04-16`
	There is also an optional time zone indicator.	Represents the 16th of April, ideal for birthdays, holidays, and recurring events.
gDay	Represents a recurring day in the Gregorian calendar in the format `--DD`.	`--16`
		Represents the sixteenth day of a month. Ideal for monthly occurrences, such as pay day.
gMonth	Represents a recurring month in the Gregorian calendar in the format `--MM--`.	`--12--`
	There is also an optional time zone indicator.	Represents December.

Primitive type	Description	Example
hexBinary	Represents hex-encoded arbitrary binary data.	0FB7
base64Binary	Represents Base64-encoded arbitrary binary data.	GpM7
anyURI	Represents a URI. The value can be absolute or relative, and may have an optional fragment identifier, so it can be a URI Reference.	http://www.example.com mailto://info@example.com mySchemafile.xsd
QName	Represents any XML element together with a prefix bound to a namespace, both separated by a colon. *The XML Namespace Recommendation can be found at:* http://www.w3.org/TR/REC-xml-names/. Namespaces were discussed in Chapter 3.	xs:element
NOTATION	Represents the NOTATION type from XML 1.0 Second Edition. Only datatypes derived from a NOTATION base type (by specifying a value for enumeration) are allowed to be used in a schema. Should only be used for attribute values.	

In order to create new simple datatypes – known as **derived types** – you place further restrictions on an existing built-in type (or another simple type that has been defined). The type that you place the restrictions upon is known as the new type's **base-type**. Here is a list of the **built-in derived types**:

Derived type	Description	Base type	Example
normalizedString	Represents white space normalized strings. Whitespace normalized strings do not contain carriage return (#xD), line feed (#xA) or tab (#x9) characters.	string	Like this

Table continued on following page

681

Derived type	Description	Base type	Example
token	Represents tokenized strings, they do not contain line feed or tab characters and contain no leading or trailing spaces, and no internal sequences of more than two spaces.	normalizedString	One Two Three
language	Natural language identifiers, as defined in RFC 1766, and valid values for xml:lang as defined in XML 1.0 Second Edition.	token	en-GB, en-US, fr
NMTOKEN	XML 1.0 Second Edition NMTOKEN.	token	small
Name	Represents XML Names.	token	for:example
NCName	Represents XML "non-colonized" Names, without the prefix and colon.	Name	Address
ID	Represents the ID attribute type from XML 1.0 Second Edition.	NCName	
IDREF	Represents the IDREF attribute type from XML 1.0 Second Edition.	NCName	
IDREFS	IDREFS attribute type from XML 1.0 Second Edition. (An aggregation with one and only one member type: ENTITY.)	A list with itemType IDREF	
ENTITY	Represents the ENTITY attribute type from XML 1.0 Second Edition.	NCName	Note that the ENTITY has to be declared externally to the schema in a DTD.
ENTITIES	Represents the ENTITIES attribute type from XML 1.0 Second Edition. ENTITIES is a set of ENTITY elements separated by an XML whitespace character.	A list with itemType ENTITY *All elements of an ENTITIES instance are of type ENTITY, which also forms some kind of base type*	Note that the ENTITIES list has to be declared externally to the schema in a DTD.

Derived type	Description	Base type	Example
integer	Standard mathematical concept of integer numbers.	decimal	-4, 0, 2, 7
nonPositiveInteger	Standard mathematical concept of a non-positive integer (includes 0).	integer	-4, -1, 0
negativeInteger	Standard mathematical concept of negative integers (does not include 0).	nonPositiveInteger	-4, -1
long	An integer between -9223372036854775808 and 9223372036854775807.	integer	-23568323, 52883773203895
int	An integer between -2147483648 and 2147483647.	long	-24781982, 24781924
short	An integer between -32768 and 32767.	int	-31353, -43, 345, 31347
byte	An integer between −128 and 127.	short	-127, -42, 0, 54, 125
nonNegativeInteger	A positive integer including zero.	integer	0, 1, 42
unsignedLong	A nonNegativeInteger between 0 and 18446744073709551615.	nonNegativeInteger	0, 356, 38753829383
unsignedInt	An unsignedLong between 0 and 4294967295.	unsignedLong	46, 4255774, 2342823723
unsignedShort	An unsignedInt between 0 and 65535.	unsignedInt	78, 64328

Table continued on following page

Derived type	Description	Base type	Example
unsignedByte	An unsignedShort between 0 and 255.	unsignedShort	0, 46, 247
positiveInteger	An integer of 1 or higher.	nonNegativeInteger	1, 24, 345343

Constraining Facets

The constraining facets defined in the XML Schema Datatypes specification are:

❑ length

❑ minLength

❑ maxLength

❑ pattern

❑ enumeration

❑ whitespace

❑ maxInclusive

❑ minInclusive

❑ maxExclusive

❑ minExclusive

❑ totalDigits

❑ fractionDigits

length

This allows us to specify the exact length of a datatype. If the datatype is a string, then it specifies the number of characters in it. If it's a list, then it specifies the number of items in the list. It is always used inside a restriction element, and can in turn contain an annotation element.

Example

```
<xs:simpleType name="USA_SSN">
   <xs:restriction base="xs:string">
      <xs:length value="11" />
   </xs:restriction>
</xs:simpleType>
```

Attributes

Attribute	Value Space	Description
fixed	boolean	If a simple type has its `length` facet's fixed attribute set to `true`, then it cannot be used to derive another simple type with a different length facet. Default is `false`.
id	ID	Gives a unique identifier to the type.
value	nonNegativeInteger	The actual length of the datatype.

For more information: see §4.3.1 of the Datatypes Recommendation.

minLength

This sets the minimum length of a datatype. If the base type is `string`, then it sets the minimum number of characters. If it is a list, it sets the minimum number of members. It is always used inside a `restriction` element to do this. It can contain an `annotation` element.

Example

```
<xs:simpleType name="USA_LicensePlate">
    <xs:restriction base="xs:string">
        <xs:minLength value="1" />
        <xs:maxLength value="9" />
    </xs:restriction>
</xs:simpleType>
```

Attributes

Attribute	Value Space	Description
fixed	boolean	If `true`, then any datatypes derived from the one in which this is set cannot alter the value of `minLength`. The default is `false`.
id	ID	Gives a unique identifier to the type.
value	nonNegativeInteger	Sets the minimum length of the datatype, if applicable; must be a non-negative integer.

For more information: see §4.3.2 of the Datatypes Recommendation.

maxLength

This sets the maximum length of a datatype. If the base type is `string`, then it sets the maximum number of characters. If it is a list, it sets the maximum number of members. It is always used inside a `restriction` element to do this. It can contain an `annotation` element.

Example

```
<xs:simpleType name="USA_LicensePlate">
    <xs:restriction base="xs:string">
        <xs:minLength value="1" />
        <xs:maxLength value="9" />
    </xs:restriction>
</xs:simpleType>
```

Attributes

Attribute	Value Space	Description
fixed	boolean	If fixed is true, then any datatypes derived from the one in which this is set cannot alter the value of maxLength. The default is false.
id	ID	Gives a unique identifier to the type.
value	nonNegativeInteger	Sets the maximum length of the datatype, if applicable; must be a non-negative integer.

For more information: see §4.3.3 of the Datatypes Recommendation.

pattern

This allows us to restrict any simple datatype by specifying a regular expression. It acts on the lexical representation of the type, rather than the value itself. It is always used inside a restriction element to do this. It can contain an annotation element.

Example

```
<xs:simpleType name="USA_SSN">
    <xs:restriction base="xs:string">
        <xs:pattern value="[0-9]{3}-[0-9]{2}-[0-9]{4}" />
    </xs:restriction>
</xs:simpleType>
```

Attributes

Attribute	Value Space	Description
id	ID	Gives a unique identifier to the type.
value	anySimpleType	The value contained within this attribute is any valid regular expression.

For more information: see §4.3.4 of the Datatypes Recommendation.

enumeration

The enumeration element is used to restrict the values allowed within a datatype to a set of specified values. It is always used inside a restriction element to do this. It can contain an annotation element.

Example

```
<xs:simpleType name="Sizes">
    <xs:restriction base="xs:string">
        <xs:enumeration value="S" />
        <xs:enumeration value="M" />
        <xs:enumeration value="L" />
        <xs:enumeration value="XL" />
    </xs:restriction>
</xs:simpleType>
```

Attributes

Attribute	Value Space	Description
id	ID	Gives a unique identifier to the element.
value	anySimpleType	One of the values of an enumerated datatype. Multiple enumeration elements are used for the different choices of value.

For more information: see §4.3.5 of the Datatypes Recommendation.

whiteSpace

This dictates what (if any) whitespace transformation is performed upon the XML instances data, before validation constraints are tested. It is always used inside a restriction element to do this. It can contain an annotation element.

Example

```
<xs:simpleType name="token">
    <xs:restriction base="xs:normalizedString">
        <xs:whiteSpace value="collapse" />
    </xs:restriction>
</xs:simpleType>
```

Attributes

Attribute	Value Space	Description
fixed	boolean	If fixed is true, then any type derived from this one cannot set whiteSpace to a value other than the one specified. The default is false.
id	ID	Gives a unique identifier to the type.

Table continued on following page

Attribute	Value Space	Description
`value`	`collapse` | `preserve` | `replace`	`preserve` means that all whitespace is preserved as it is declared in the element. If `replace` is used, then all whitespace characters such as carriage return and tab and so on are replaced by single whitespace characters. `collapse` means that any series of whitespace characters are collapsed into a single whitespace character. Note that a type with its `whiteSpace` attribute set to `preserve` cannot be derived from one where with a value of `replace` or `collapse`, and similarly, one with a value of `replace` cannot be derived from one with a value of `collapse`.

For more information: see §4.3.6 of the Datatypes Recommendation.

maxInclusive

This sets the *inclusive* upper limit of an ordered datatype (number, date type or ordered list). So, the value stated here is therefore the highest value that can be used in this datatype. `maxInclusive` must be equal to or greater than any value of `minInclusive` and greater than the value of `minExclusive`. It is always used inside a `restriction` element to do this. It can contain an `annotation` element.

Example

```
<xs:simpleType name="TheAnswer">
    <xs:restriction base="xs:integer">
        <xs:minInclusive value="42" />
        <xs:maxInclusive value="42" />
    </xs:restriction>
</xs:simpleType>
```

Attributes

Attribute	Value Space	Description
`fixed`	`boolean`	If `true`, then any datatypes derived from this one cannot alter the value of `maxInclusive`; the default is `false`.
`id`	`ID`	Gives a unique identifier to the type.
`value`	`anySimpleType`	If the base datatype is numerical, this would be a number; if a date, then this would be a date.

For more information: see §4.3.7 of the Datatypes Recommendation.

maxExclusive

This sets the *exclusive* upper limit of an ordered datatype (number, date type, or ordered list). The maxExclusive value is therefore one higher than the maximum value that can be used. maxExclusive must be greater than or equal to the value of minExclusive and greater than the value of minInclusive. It is always used inside a restriction element to do this. It can contain an annotation element.

Example

```
<xs:simpleType name="TheAnswer">
    <xs:restriction base="xs:integer">
        <xs:minExclusive value="42" />
        <xs:maxExclusive value="42" />
    </xs:restriction>
</xs:simpleType>
```

Attributes

Attribute	Value Space	Description
fixed	boolean	If true, then any datatypes derived from this one cannot alter the value of maxExclusive; the default is false.
id	ID	Gives a unique identifier to the type.
value	anySimpleType	If the base datatype is numerical, this is a number; if a date, then it is a date.

For more information: see §4.3.8 of the Datatypes Recommendation.

minExclusive

This sets the *exclusive* lower limit of an ordered datatype (number, date type or ordered list). The minExclusive value is therefore one lower than the lowest value the data can take. minExclusive must be less than the value of maxInclusive, and less than or equal to the value of maxExclusive. It is always used inside a restriction element to do this. It can contain an annotation element.

Example

```
<xs:simpleType name="TheAnswer">
    <xs:restriction base="xs:integer">
        <xs:minExclusive value="42" />
        <xs:maxExclusive value="42" />
    </xs:restriction>
</xs:simpleType>
```

Attributes

Attribute	Value Space	Description
fixed	boolean	If true, then any datatypes derived from this one cannot alter the value of minExclusive; the default is false.
id	ID	Gives a unique identifier to the type.
value	anySimpleType	If the base datatype is numerical, this would be a number; if a date, then a date.

For more information: see §4.3.9 of the Datatypes Recommendation.

minInclusive

This sets the *inclusive* lower limit of an ordered datatype (number, date type, or ordered list). The value stated here is therefore the lowest value that can be used in this datatype. minInclusive must be equal to or less than any value of maxInclusive and must be less than the value of maxExclusive. It is always used inside a restriction element to do this. It can contain an annotation element.

Example

```
<xs:simpleType name="TheAnswer">
   <xs:restriction base="xs:integer">
      <xs:minInclusive value="42" />
      <xs:maxInclusive value="42" />
   </xs:restriction>
</xs:simpleType>
```

Attributes

Attribute	Value Space	Description
fixed	boolean	If true, then any datatypes derived from this one cannot alter the value of minInclusive; the default is false.
id	ID	Gives a unique identifier to the type.
value	anySimpleType	If the base datatype is numerical, this would be a number; if a date, then a date.

For more information: see Chapter 4 and §4.3.10 of the Datatypes Recommendation.

totalDigits

This facet applies to all datatypes derived from the decimal type. The value stated is the *maximum* number of decimal digits allowed for the entire number (which must always be a positive integer).

Example

```
<xs:simpleType name="Datapoint">
   <xs:restriction base="xs:decimal">
      <xs:totalDigits value="9" />
      <xs:fractionDigits value="3" />
   </xs:restriction>
</xs:simpleType>
```

Attributes

Attribute	Value Space	Description
fixed	boolean	If true, then any datatypes derived from this one cannot alter the value of totalDigits; the default is false.
id	ID	Gives a unique identifier to the type.
value	positiveInteger	The actual value of the totalDigits attribute.

For more information: see §4.3.11 of the Datatypes Recommendation.

fractionDigits

This facet applies to all datatypes derived from the decimal type. The value stated is the *maximum* number of digits in the fractional portion of the number (always a *non-negative* integer that is less than or equal to the value of totalDigits).

Example

```
<xs:simpleType name="Datapoint">
   <xs:restriction base="xs:decimal">
      <xs:totalDigits value="9" />
      <xs:fractionDigits value="3" />
   </xs:restriction>
</xs:simpleType>
```

Attributes

Attribute	Value Space	Description
fixed	boolean	If true, then any datatypes derived from this one cannot alter the value of totalDigits; the default is false.
id	ID	Gives a unique identifier to the type.
value	nonNegativeInteger	The actual value of the value fractionDigits attribute. This cannot be any larger than the totalDigits value.

For more information: see §4.3.12 of the Datatypes Recommendation.

The two tables below indicate which of these constraining facets may be applied to which datatypes, in order to derive new types. First, for the primitive built-in types:

Datatypes	length	minLength	maxLength	whiteSpace	pattern	enumeration	minExclusive	maxExclusive	minInclusive	maxInclusive	totalDigits	fractionDigits
String Types												
string	X	X	X	preserve	X	X						
anyURI	X	X	X	collapse	X	X						
NOTATION	X	X	X	collapse	X	X						
QName	X	X	X	collapse	X	X						
Binary Encoding Types												
boolean				collapse	X							
hexBinary	X	X	X	collapse	X	X						
base64Binary	X	X	X	collapse	X	X						
Numeric Types												
decimal				collapse	X	X	X	X	X	X	X	X
float				collapse	X	X	X	X	X	X		
double				collapse	X	X	X	X	X	X		
Date/Time Types												
duration				collapse	X	X	X	X	X	X		
dateTime				collapse	X	X	X	X	X	X		
date				collapse	X	X	X	X	X	X		
time				collapse	X	X	X	X	X	X		
gYear				collapse	X	X	X	X	X	X		
gYearMonth				collapse	X	X	X	X	X	X		
gMonth				collapse	X	X	X	X	X	X		
gMonthDay				collapse	X	X	X	X	X	X		
gDay				collapse	X	X	X	X	X	X		

Second, and for the derived built-in types:

Datatypes	length	minLength	maxLength	whiteSpace	pattern	enumeration	minExclusive	maxExclusive	minInclusive	maxInclusive	totalDigits	fractionDigits
Types Derived from string												
normalizedString	X	X	X	replace	X	X						
token	X	X	X	collapse	X	X						
language	X	X	X	collapse	X	X						
Name	X	X	X	collapse	X	X						
NCName	X	X	X	collapse	X	X						
ID	X	X	X	collapse	X	X						
IDREF	X	X	X	collapse	X	X						
IDREFS	X	X	X	collapse		X						
NMTOKEN	X	X	X	collapse	X	X						
NMTOKENS	X	X	X	collapse		X						
ENTITY	X	X	X	collapse	X	X						
ENTITIES	X	X	X	collapse		X						
Types Derived from decimal												
integer				collapse	X	X	X	X	X	X	X	0
negativeInteger				collapse	X	X	X	X	X	X	X	0
positiveInteger				collapse	X	X	X	X	X	X	X	0
nonNegativeInteger				collapse	X	X	X	X	X	X	X	0
nonPositiveInteger				collapse	X	X	X	X	X	X	X	0

Table continued on following page

Datatypes	length	minLength	maxLength	whiteSpace	pattern	enumeration	minExclusive	maxExclusive	minInclusive	maxInclusive	totalDigits	fractionDigits
byte				collapse	X	X	X	X	X	X	X	0
short				collapse	X	X	X	X	X	X	X	0
int				collapse	X	X	X	X	X	X	X	0
long				collapse	X	X	X	X	X	X	X	0
unsignedByte				collapse	X	X	X	X	X	X	X	0
unsignedShort				collapse	X	X	X	X	X	X	X	0
unsignedInt				collapse	X	X	X	X	X	X	X	0
unsignedLong				collapse	X	X	X	X	X	X	X	0

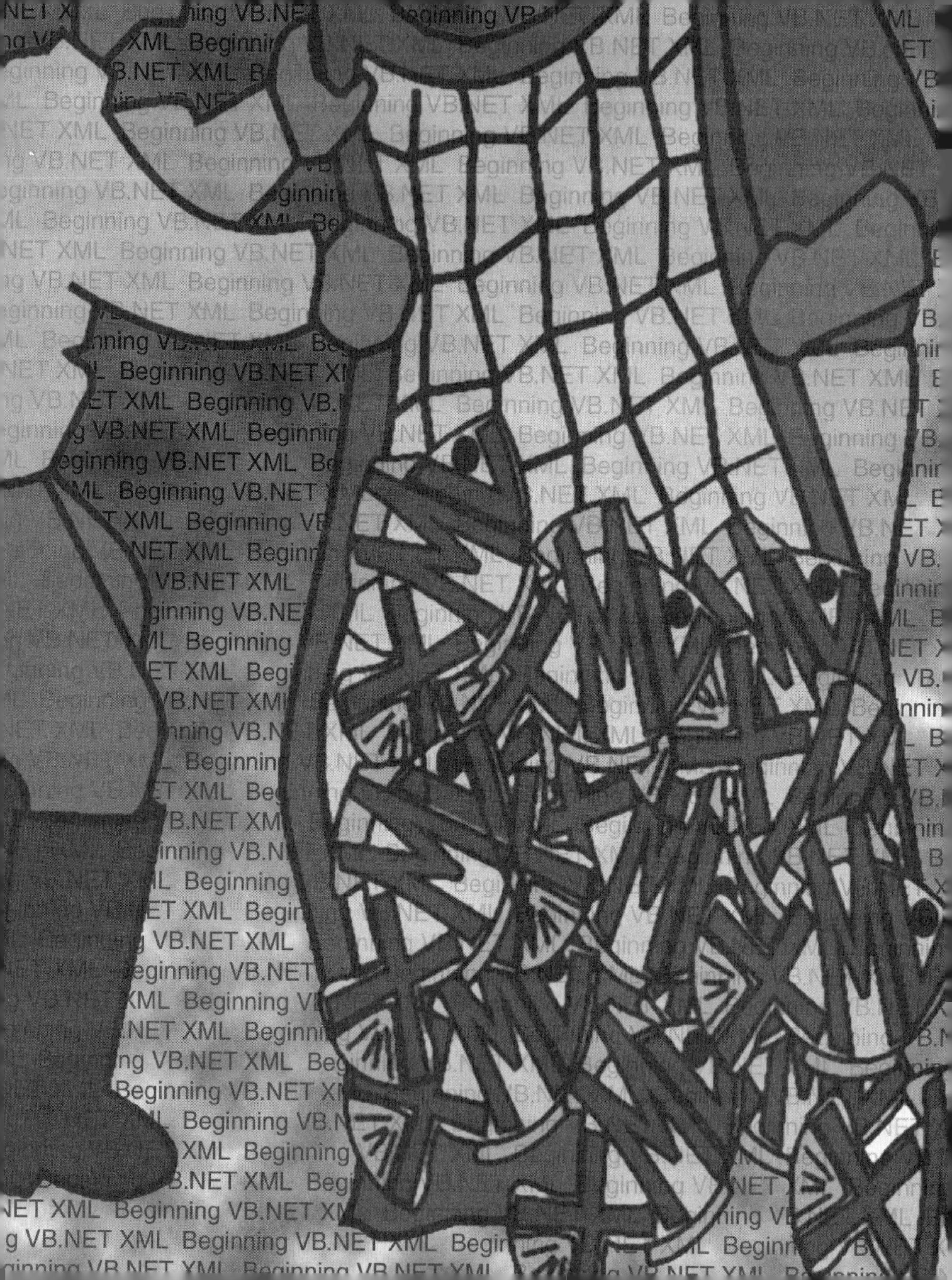
Beginning VB.NET XML

Support of XSL

Internet Explorer 5.0 was released with MSXML 2.0 and Internet Explorer 5.5 was released with MSXML 2.5. MSXML 2.5 supports the pre-standard Microsoft XSL implementation defined by the namespace http://www.w3.org/TR/WD-xsl. Internet Explorer 4.0 never directly supported browsing of XML documents and hence of XSL transforms, and so IE 5.0 was the first opportunity to gain widespread use of XSL.

MSXML 2.6, MSXML 3.0, and MSXML 4.0 (available as separate downloads and installations) support both the pre-standard implementation and the W3C standard implementation http://www.w3.org/1999/XSL/Transform. Remember that namespaces can be used to associate elements of the XSL document with a particular implementation in the XML parser – these two namespaces had very different parsers to process the elements that were qualified in their namespaces and so you should ensure you check any older XSL documents to see what namespace it uses.

As of Internet Explorer 6.0 and Windows XP, MSXML 3.0 is now part of the browser download and so you can write W3C-compliant stylesheets that can be correctly interpreted by the browser. Note also, that the MSXML 4.0 parser no longer supports the older Microsoft XSL implementation, instead providing full support only for the official XSL standard.

The parsers as of version MSXML 3.0 were available as separate downloads and this vastly improved the potential of working with XML technologies on the Microsoft platform. No matter what client is accessing your XML documents, because we can use the latest XML parser on the server, we can transform the output to some format suitable for the client. This has perhaps been the greatest success story of XSL, and indeed will continue to be during the adoption of .NET.

The move to .NET will not result in many changes to how your XSL stylesheets (that you may have inherited from some other application) have been defined, but will greatly improve the control and ability you have when working with stylesheets on the server.

We looked at how transformations on the server can be used to general output for any device via programmatic transforms. The .NET Framework also allows you to programmatically interact with XML and XSL documents to perform transforms on the server via a set of classes in the System.Xml.Xsl namespace conform to the XSL 1.0 standard. Furthermore you can use procedural code (such as VB.NET, C#, or JavaScript) within these stylesheets to perform some logic that XSLT may not provide (for example, executing some algorithm that your data uses). This indicates that there will likely be a further gradual movement for stylesheets created specifically for working on the server and those that are designed to work on the client for specific end devices (particularly with the latest version of Netscape Navigator 6.x, Mozilla 5.x providing support for the XSL W3C 1.0 standard).

The following table summarizes support for the **W3C 1.0** XSL standard among the major browsers and on the various platforms.

Platform	Supported	Not Supported
Windows	IE 5.0 with MSXML3	< IE 5.0
	IE 5.5 with MSXML3	IE 5.0 (draft XSL implementation)
	IE 6	IE 5.5 (draft XSL implementation)
	Netscape 6.1	< Netscape Navigator 6.0
	Netscape 7.0	Amaya
	Mozilla 0.9.4	Opera
	Mozilla 0.9.5	Lynx
Macintosh	Netscape 6.1	IE 5.0 (draft XSL implementation)
	Mozilla	< Netscape Navigator 6.0
		Opera
		Lynx
Linux / Unix	Netscape 6.1	< Netscape Navigator 6.0
	Netscape 7.0	Amaya
	Mozilla 0.9.4	Opera
	Mozilla 0.9.5	Lynx

Details on XSLT support for Netscape Navigator can be found
http://devedge.netscape.com/library/manuals/2001/xslt/1.0/.

Details on XSLT support for Mozilla can be found at
http://www.mozilla.org/projects/xslt/.

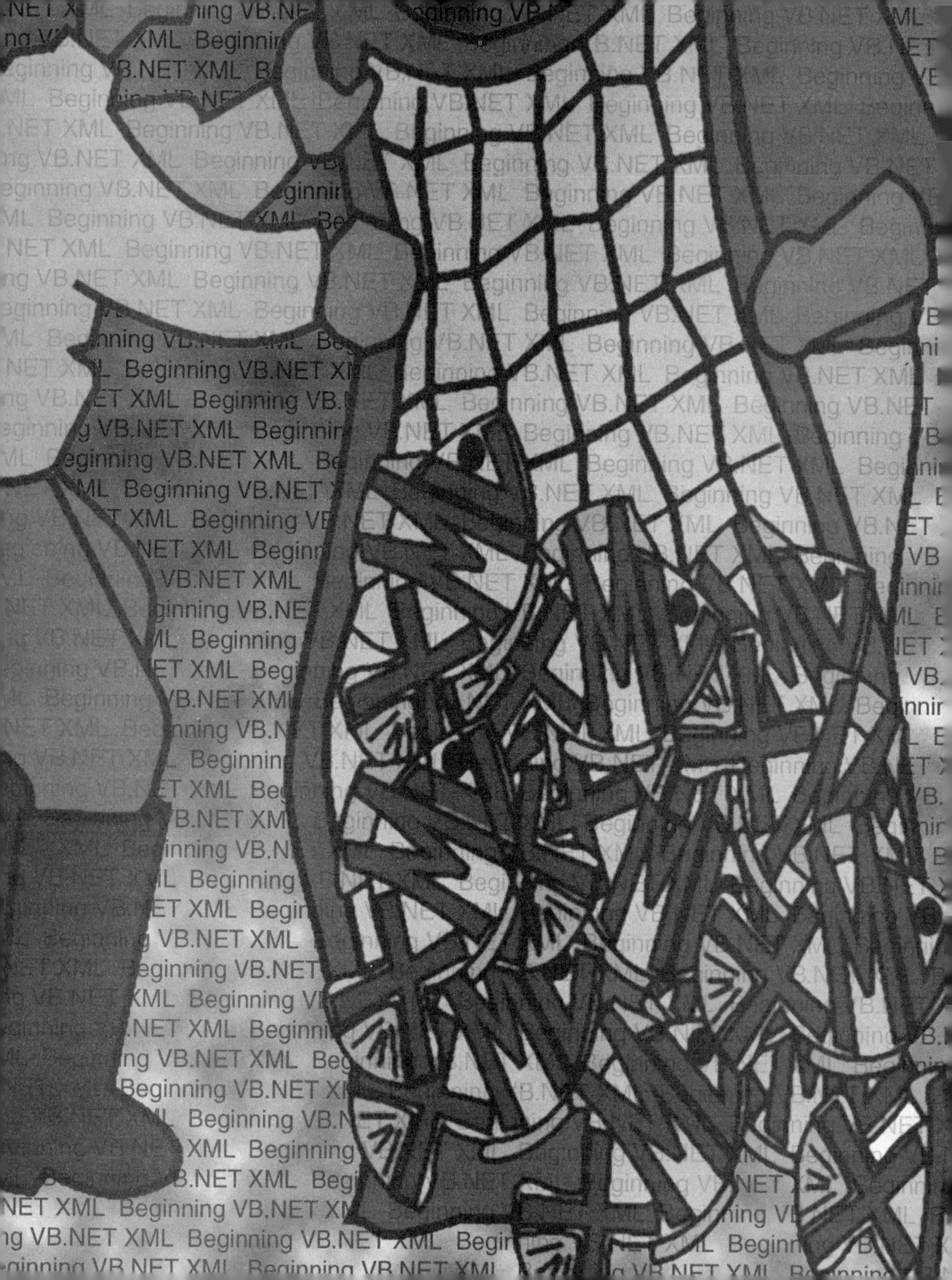
Beginning VB.NET XML

Index

A Guide to the Index

The ~ character is used to reduce the need to duplicate almost identical entries, For example, Business*Entities*/ ~ *Services* properties refers to both the BusinessEntities property and the BusinessServices property. The part which is replaced by the ~ is shown in normal (not italic) type.

The use of Xyz is to indicate that numerous options exist, as is the case for NodeXyz events.

M

N

R

Read method
DataReader classes, 535
XmlTextReader class, 136
ReadBase64 method
XmlTextReader class, 156, 208
XmlTextWriter class, 202
ReadBinHex method, XmlTextReader class, 156
ReadChars method, XmlTextReader class, 153
ReadDocument method, 182, 206
reading data
forward only, 534
ReadOuterXml method, XmlTextReader class
adding an attribute, 182
performing a simple transform, example, 399
ReadSchema, XmlReadMode enumeration, 559
ReadState property, XmlTextReader class, 141
ReadToEnd method, StreamReader class
optimizing transforms to memory, example, 403
ReadXml method, DataSet class, 550, 559, 562
ReadXmlSchema method, DataSet class, 550, 563
Recurse class, 248, 252
recursion
finding elements with recursion, example, 247
ref attribute
dynamic DISCO files, 599
ref attribute, xsd:element, 442
complex data types, example, 459
referencing elements, XSD, 439
schema positioning, 444
references to web sites
Amazon web service information, 578
common data types, XML, 446
CSS (Cascading Stylesheets), 337
DOM (Document Object Model), 22
DTDs, 23
Google web service information, 578
IE XML/XSL Viewer Tools, 62
namespaces, XML related technology, 22
Netscape support for XML, 39
ODBC .NET Data Provider, 531
open source implementation of .NET, 13
Oracle .NET Data Provider, 531
SAX (Simple API for XML), 22, 131
SAX parser using XmlTextReader class, 132
SQL Server, 539
SQLXML .NET Data Provider, 531
Tamino, 20
TextML, 20
UDDI, 604
W3C, 21
W3C DOM Level 2 specification, 89, 211
web services, 23
well-formed XML documents, 40
WSDL specification, 590
XHTML, 16
XHTML (Extensible HTML), 22
XInclude, 22
XLink, 22
XML 1.0 Recommendation, 22
XML Documentation Tool, 123
XML-DEV mailing list, 131

XPath, 22, 95
XPath data model, 103
XPointer, 22
XQuery, 20
XQuery demo, 20
XSL-FO (XSL-Formatting Objects), 332
XSLT, 23
XSLT support for Mozilla, 698
XSLT support for Netscape Navigator, 698
referencing, xsd:element, 438
relationships, 547
populating DataSet from multiple tables, 547
relative location path, XPath expressions, 107
Remote Procedure Calls
see RPC.
remoting, 28, 125, 309, 616–24
<channel> element, 618
<channels> element, 618
<client> element, 618
<service> element, 618
<system.runtime.remoting> element, 618
architecture, 617
channel, 617
configuration, 617
creating remoting client, example, 622
creating remoting server, example, 619
formatter, 617
proxy, 617
RemotingConfiguration class,
System.Runtime.Remoting
creating remoting client, example, 623
creating remoting server, example, 621
RemoveAll method, XmlNode class, 234
RemoveChild method, XmlNode class, 234
removing nodes with XPath queries, 262
RemoveExtensionObject method, XsltArgumentList
class, 418
RemoveNamedItem method, XmlNamedNodeMap
class, 217
RemoveParam method, XsltArgumentList class, 418
replace value, whiteSpace data type facet, 449
ReplaceChild method, XmlNode class, 231
replacing existing nodes, example, 259
#REQUIRED
DTD attribute value declaration, 60
restriction element, XSD
applying data type facets, 449
include element, XML schemas, 475
simpleContent element, 461
simpleType element restriction, example, 455
ReturnType property, XPathExpression class, 303
reverse axis, XPath, 96
root element, XML document, 40
example, 138
reading and writing out values, 287
well-formed XML documents, 41
root element, XSD, 434
root element, XSL stylesheet, 348
root node, XML documents, 104
rows
returning from data source, 534
Rows collection, DataTable class, 537
RPC (Remote Procedure Calls), 18

S

Got more Wrox books than you can carry around?

Wroxbase is the new online service from Wrox Press. Dedicated to providing online access to books published by Wrox Press, helping you and your team find solutions and guidance for all your programming needs.

The key features of this service will be:

- Different libraries based on technologies that you use everyday (ASP 3.0, XML, SQL 2000, etc.). The initial set of libraries will be focused on Microsoft-related technologies.
- You can subscribe to as few or as many libraries as you require, and access all books within those libraries as and when you need to.
- You can add notes (either just for yourself or for anyone to view) and your own bookmarks that will all be stored within your account online, and so will be accessible from any computer.
- You can download the code of any book in your library directly from Wroxbase

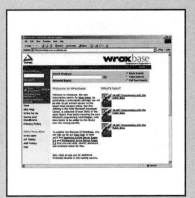

Visit the site at: www.wroxbase.com

wrox
Programmer to Programmer™

p2p.wrox.com
The programmer's resource centre

A unique free service from Wrox Press
With the aim of helping programmers to help each other

Wrox Press aims to provide timely and practical information to today's programmer. P2P is a list server offering a host of targeted mailing lists where you can share knowledge with four fellow programmers and find solutions to your problems. Whatever the level of your programming knowledge, and whatever technology you use P2P can provide you with the information you need.

ASP — Support for beginners and professionals, including a resource page with hundreds of links, and a popular ASP.NET mailing list.

DATABASES — For database programmers, offering support on SQL Server, mySQL, and Oracle.

MOBILE — Software development for the mobile market is growing rapidly. We provide lists for the several current standards, including WAP, Windows CE, and Symbian.

JAVA — A complete set of Java lists, covering beginners, professionals, and server-side programmers (including JSP, servlets and EJBs)

.NET — Microsoft's new OS platform, covering topics such as ASP.NET, C#, and general .NET discussion.

VISUAL BASIC — Covers all aspects of VB programming, from programming Office macros to creating components for the .NET platform.

WEB DESIGN — As web page requirements become more complex, programmer's are taking a more important role in creating web sites. For these programmers, we offer lists covering technologies such as Flash, Coldfusion, and JavaScript.

XML — Covering all aspects of XML, including XSLT and schemas.

OPEN SOURCE — Many Open Source topics covered including PHP, Apache, Perl, Linux, Python and more.

FOREIGN LANGUAGE — Several lists dedicated to Spanish and German speaking programmers, categories include. NET, Java, XML, PHP and XML

How to subscribe
Simply visit the P2P site, at http://p2p.wrox.com/

wrox

Programmer to Programmer™

Registration Code : 77873C3J3D1K7RJ01

Wrox writes books for you. Any suggestions, or ideas about how you want
information given in your ideal book will be studied by our team.
Your comments are always valued at Wrox.

Free phone in USA 800-USE-WROX
Fax (312) 893 8001

UK Tel.: (0121) 687 4100   Fax: (0121) 687 4101

Beginning VB .NET XML – Registration Card

Name _____

Address _____

_____

_____

City _____ State/Region _____

Country _____ Postcode/Zip _____

E-Mail _____

Occupation _____

How did you hear about this book?

☐ Book review (name) _____

☐ Advertisement (name) _____

☐ Recommendation _____

☐ Catalog _____

☐ Other _____

Where did you buy this book?

☐ Bookstore (name) _____ City_____

☐ Computer store (name) _____

☐ Mail order_____

☐ Other _____

What influenced you in the purchase of this book?

☐ Cover Design   ☐ Contents   ☐ Other (please specify):

_____

How did you rate the overall content of this book?

☐ Excellent   ☐ Good   ☐ Average   ☐ Poor

What did you find most useful about this book? _____

_____

What did you find least useful about this book? _____

_____

_____

Please add any additional comments. _____

_____

What other subjects will you buy a computer book on soon?

_____

What is the best computer book you have used this year?

_____

Note: This information will only be used to keep you updated
about new Wrox Press titles and will not be used for
any other purpose or passed to any other third party.

7787   Check here if you DO NOT want to receive support for this book ■   7787

wrox

Programmer to Programmer™

Note: If you post the bounce back card below in the UK, please send it to:

Wrox Press Limited, Arden House, 1102 Warwick Road,
Acocks Green, Birmingham B27 6HB. UK.

Computer Book Publishers